Financial Modelling with Dynamic Arrays

Dr. Liam Bastick

Published in 2024 by SumProduct Pty Limited. Ground Floor, 470 St Kilda Road, Melbourne, Vic 3004, Australia.

Author: Dr. Liam Bastick

Editors: Kathryn Newitt and Oscar Hagan

Indexer: Cheryl Lenser

Compositor: Bronkella Publishing

Cover Design: Shannon Travise

Distributed by Independent Publishers Group, Chicago, IL

ISBN 978-1-61547-087-7 Print, 978-1-61547-173-7 Digital

Library of Congress Control Number: 2024939407

Version 20240704a

For Brenda & Patrick, together again.

About the Author

Dr. Liam Bastick FCA FCMA CGMA MVP

Starting off as a university lecturer, Liam has over 30 years' experience in financial model development / auditing, and liaised with Microsoft when they were first considering dynamic arrays, both their behaviour and prospective features / functions.

He has considerable experience in many different sectors (*e.g.* banking, energy, media, mining, oil and gas, private equity, retail, transport and utilities) and has worked in many countries (including Australia, Belgium, Denmark, France, Germany, Hong Kong, Indonesia, Malaysia, Netherlands, New Zealand, Philippines, Singapore, Switzerland, United Kingdom, United States and Vietnam). He has worked with internationally recognised clients, constructing and reviewing strategic, operational, planning and valuation models for many high profile assignments.

With over 2,000 articles written for the accounting profession, he is a regular contributor to the American Institute of Certified Public Accountants (AICPA), Chartered Accountants Australia and New Zealand (CAANZ), Certified Practising Accountants Australia (CPAA), the Chartered Institute of Management Accountants (CIMA), the Institute of Chartered Accountants in England and Wales (ICAEW), Microsoft's Excel Blog and various LinkedIn specialist discussion groups.

Liam is a Fellow of the Institute of Chartered Accountants (FCA), a Fellow of the Institute of Chartered Management Accountants (FCMA), a Chartered Global Management Accountant (CGMA), and is also a professional mathematician, specialising in probability and number theory.

A frequent public speaker, Liam attends Excel and Power BI conferences around the globe and has been a central organiser for the Excel Summit South, Unlock Excel and Excel Virtually Global. He has also authored and edited several books including the sister volumes *Introduction to Financial Modelling*, *Continuing Financial Modelling, Financial Modelling in Power BI* and *Financial Modelling for Project Finance,* as well as the *Power BI MVP Book* and *Excel Insights*.

Since 2012, he has been recognised by Crimewatch and Microsoft, the latter as a Most Valuable Professional (MVP) in Excel, one of *c.*130 such awardees worldwide (as at the time of writing). In 2021, Liam was the recipient of the inaugural Lifetime Achievement Award for Financial Modelling by the Financial Modeling Institute (the inconsistent spelling of "Modelling" is as intended!).

He still follows Derby County, the England cricket team and trails of breadcrumbs.

Preface

Wow, Book 5! At this rate, I might get syndicated. I will probably be 173 by then.

This book revisits the topics of the first book in a new light. It looks to create and think about financial modelling purely using dynamic arrays. Of course, there are tips and tricks from the past books, but this one is all about array modelling – and it does require a different mindset.

I continue to be lucky enough to be appointed a Most Valuable Professional (MVP) by Microsoft for services to Excel – one of over one hundred "experts" as at the time of writing. I have used this fabulous network to create simpler solutions to some of the problems I was faced with in developing this book. In fact, a lot of concepts are similar here to *Financial Modelling in Power BI*, which helped a lot.

I'd like to thank those that helped contribute to this book. There are quite a few: Oscar Hagan and Talia Cao helped devise cunning alternatives to some of my original formulae used to build the model, and the ever-vigilant Kathryn Newitt edited it technically with the help of Oscar, as they endeavoured to spot all my clangers. I am pretty confident there are now no errors whatsojggjgrjlwg.

I'd also like to thank Bill Jelen for continuing to publish these books, and most importantly my immediate family, Nancy and Layla, who continue to support me, especially when I tend to do so much writing during the Christmas break. As always, I allow my daughter, Layla Bastick, to have the usual final word:

"If you're getting an advance, will you buy me a guitar please? Love you daddy xxx"

Liam Bastick, April 2024

Editor's Notes

When Liam said that creating a financial model with dynamic arrays would be less of a drag, I was hoping for a much shorter book! Of course, he meant that the clicking and dragging across that is required for "CRaFT"ily consistent standard excel formulae is redundant when using dynamic arrays.

What *is* needed, is a thorough explanation of what dynamic arrays are, and how they open up a world of possibilities for financial modellers. Which is why this is the longest book so far, needing not just one, but two editors this time around.

In order to appreciate some of the more complex formulae needed to model financial statements with dynamic arrays, I encourage you to build the model as you read. If you take the time to get to grips with the concepts in this book, you will soon have some clever new tricks to add to your repertoire, and some very old jokes!

Kathryn Newitt

www.sumproduct.com

Helping put together the case study for this book and the book itself was an exciting process (though I might be the only person in the world that thinks so), once I got past how intimidating some of the formulae are.

I've found that this process has helped me really start thinking with dynamic arrays and opened my eyes up to the possibilities they create in Excel. Hopefully this book will leave you feeling the same way.

As Kathryn has already said, for the best experience do consider building the model as you read through the book. I've found no better way to wrap my head around the more complex formulae derived by Liam and Talia than to build them up step by step within the model. If you can make it through Liam's terrible jokes (we tried to remove them, he won't let us!) then you really will learn a lot about what's now possible in Excel using dynamic arrays.

Oscar Hagan

www.sumproduct.com

Downloadable Resources

Throughout the book, we have included relevant images to help follow the process. However to really get to grips with the build, and check your own results, nothing beats being able to read through the actual model. We have also provided useful supporting Excel examples for the concepts discussed in this book. All of the milestones of the case study as well as a selection of other examples can be accessed by using the link:

https://www.sumproduct.com/fm-with-da-book-resources

Contents

CHAPTER 0: INTRODUCTION

I said I wanted *a raise* for writing this book and I guess the publishing company misheard me. Instead, I sit here and write a book on *arrays*. Good job I am not a cosmologist writing about Uranus.

I sit here pondering over this latest book's introduction reading an email from one "verified reader" who is annoyed that *Financial Modelling in Power BI* did not explain how to create the calculations in Tableau and wanting to know why it did not discuss programming languages in detail. Therefore, I realise I need to be very clear here about the following.

This book continues the series on financial modelling, but this time looks to take on Excel's latest weaponry. Since I wrote *Introduction to Financial Modelling*, Microsoft's spreadsheeting behemoth has become Turing-complete. Whilst it always had array formulae, it now has dynamic arrays, a **LET** function, a **LAMBDA** function, lambda helper functions and eta lambdas. And few seem to know what all this means and how it can make building financial models more versatile.

So, you are presented with a choice, dear reader. You can continue to keep building financial models using all the traditional, "legacy" tools of Excel (I wouldn't hold your breath waiting for artificial intelligence or chatbots to do it for you) or you can dip your proverbial toe in the new dynamic array waters.

The water is reasonably warm and not too murky. Some calculations have to become more complex with good reason, but the benefits are immense. With practice, experience and increasing expertise, you can build models that will grow with your projects and businesses, just by changing an input rather than rebuilding sections.

Some have told me that I am not the first to build a model using dynamic arrays. I am aware others have tried and built models that use dynamic array formulae. I think the example model here is different though: it uses dynamic array formulae for pretty much every calculation. I am not aware of any other model out there mirroring this. We are going to build a model that uses dynamic array formulae *throughout / completely*.

When some calculations get too hard, I note my peers have reverted to traditional formulae. Instead, I have spent countless hours with a wet towel over my head in a darkened room refusing to give in. This model has dynamic array formulae for inventory, depreciation and tax losses – can you honestly say you've seen these calculations elsewhere?

As always, I have my usual dilemma. Not everyone reading this book is going to be aware of the other books in this series, let alone have read them. Do I repeat myself or do I assume everyone has read everything else in the series? It's obvious: I need to make each book stand alone. If you are a loyal reader of the series, you will see there is necessary repetition, but if you're a loyal reader, you keep returning, you understand my reasoning and you have accepted this. I have to make this book self-contained. Don't let it dissuade you from considering the sibling books: they address different topics.

The plan is therefore as follows:

- **Key Excel functions:** to kick off, I have put together a refresher on key *traditional* functions previously used in financial modelling, many of which will still be needed. Don't be put off by the attendees. If you are reading the guest list and noting appearances from **IF**, **SUM** and **VLOOKUP**, and you're thinking, "this book is very basic", I can assure you there are some scary surprises in store as I show typical mistakes made every day with these functions and other popular ones too. Don't become a casualty.

- **Key Excel functionalities:** There's other attributes that we need to exploit. In this section, I will discuss key functionalities such as absolute referencing, number formatting, conditional formatting, Data Tables, data validation, range names, hyperlinks and the like.

- **Other Excel pointers:** There are other points / settings to note that make for an easier life when modelling. I detail them in this section.

- **Remembering arrays:** now we start to veer off into the wide blue yonder. If we are going to utilise dynamic arrays, it might be an idea to understand why they are so radical and what Excel used to have before – and why the calculation engine had to change.

- **Introducing dynamic arrays:** this section introduces dynamic array modelling and the key functions Microsoft introduced to exploit the new world. I explain the concepts in detail and provide comprehensive examples of how the spreadsheet world is moving on.

- **LET, LAMBDA et al:** the brave new world doesn't stop there, with new functions to help you create your own modelling vision. **LET** invites complexity but reduces memory requirements, whilst **LAMBDA** quite literally allows you to build *anything*. It needs help though with lambda helper functions and the latest eta lambdas, but hey, Excel has become "Turing-complete" – if only I knew what that meant! Well, be prepared to find out here.

- **"Best Practice" methodology:** Now that the new tools have been introduced, I need to provide a reminder of "Best Practice". I discuss a conceptual framework and I propose something very simple – something our company calls **CRaFT**.

- **Layout tips:** No matter whether you use traditional functions or the new breed, everyone can benefit from useful tips and insights on how best to layout a spreadsheet – and a financial model.

- **Time series analysis:** If we are going to build a model, we will have to work with dates – and that's perhaps not quite as straightforward as you might think. In this section, I will explain how dates ought to be constructed and why – including periodicity issues – and how to ensure they work in the realm of dynamic arrays.

- **Checks**: Talking of issues, checks remain part of any modelling ecosystem. Unfortunately, they are often added as an afterthought. They shouldn't be. In this section, I will explain why they should be at the forefront of your model development, explaining the three types you need to consider.

- **Base template:** Whilst all models are different, they do share common attributes. It's this foundation which I can translate into a base template to use at the outset of developing a financial model, be it for legacy modelling or financial modelling with dynamic arrays.

- **Financial statement theory:** Here, I consider just what is an Income Statement, a Balance Sheet and a Cash Flow Statement. Yes, you may know what they are – but

I want to do it from the perspective of understanding the purpose of each statement so that it guides you in determining the order of building a financial model.

- **Control accounts**: Debits and credits may be the accountants' way of keeping the mystery alive in finance, but the whole transactional nature of accounting and finance is often understood better by the majority of end users if we adopt control accounts. I explain what they are here, why they are useful, and most importantly, if you choose to use control accounts, Balance Sheet errors and similar mistakes will become a thing of the past.

- **Example of a model build using dynamic arrays**: It might be a small paragraph here, but it's a big part of this book as we reinvent financial models using completely new formulae drawn from the world of **LET**, **LAMBDA** and dynamic arrays.

As always, this is intended to be a practical book. There are many supporting Excel examples to review and use, grouped by chapter / section, to visualise the important concepts discussed here. Don't be a wallflower and just "review" the examples. Recreate them for yourself. The mistakes you make will prove invaluable in learning key elements of this exciting new topic.

Let's go!

CHAPTER 0.1: FILE LOCATION

There is little point in me creating useful supporting Excel examples for the concepts discussed in this book without being very specific about where you can find them! All of the milestones of the case study as well as a selection of other examples can be accessed by using the link:

https://www.sumproduct.com/dynamic-arrays-book-resources

CHAPTER 1: KEY EXCEL FUNCTIONS

This chapter is dedicated entirely to going over the key functions most commonly used when developing <u>any</u> sort of financial model in Excel. And you might be surprised regarding what's on my shopping list:

- **SUM**
- **IF**
- **IFERROR**
- **SUMIF**
- **SUMIFS**
- **SUMPRODUCT**
- **VLOOKUP / HLOOKUP**
- **LOOKUP**
- **INDEX** and **MATCH**
- **XLOOKUP** and **XMATCH**
- **CHOOSE**
- **OFFSET**
- **MOD**
- **EOMONTH** and **EDATE**
- **MAX** and **MIN**

There is a very simple, basic rule I iterate time and time again:

KEEP IT SIMPLE STUPID

That's it. A colleague of mine once talked about the **Rule of Thumb**: Excel formulae in your Formula bar should be no longer than your thumb:

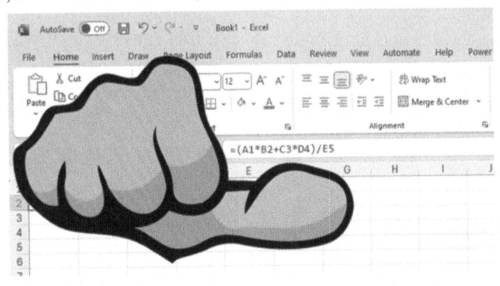

I love this idea. It means the modeller – *i.e.* you – is forced into stepping out the logic making it easier for others to follow and more difficult for you to stuff up. I used to run a large Financial Model Audit team and I trained my staff to always be on the look-out for overly complex formulae: the chances are the logic would contain errors and it may be that the model user might be trying to hide something too. Try not to fall into that trap.

OK, so with no further ado, let's take a look at our function list in more detail.

CHAPTER 1.1: SUM

Is there really anyone out there that hasn't encountered the **SUM** function? Given this book is intended to be about financial modelling rather than an introduction to Excel functions, is there anything new for me to tell you about **SUM**..?

Well, let me try.

SUM adds things up. It may include cells, numbers or ranges. In the context of financial modelling, summations are usually of numbers either directly above or to the left of the cell in question:

G5				fx ✓	=SUM(C5:F5)	
	A	B	C	D	E	F	G
1	**Summary**						
2							
3			Product A	Product B	Product C	Product D	
4	Business Unit 1		54	46	78	31	209
5	Business Unit 2		40	72	25	47	184
6	Business Unit 3		91	82	76	80	329
7	Business Unit 4		79	12	28	92	211
8			264	212	207	250	

There is a great keyboard shortcut available on most PC's *(PC = proper computer)*. If you select the cell to the right or directly below the values to be aggregated and then use the shortcut **ALT** + **=** you will see that the range is summed automatically. If you find this doesn't work for you, make sure you keep the **ALT** button held down on your keyboard.

I use this all of the time in modelling. It's a fast shortcut, it ensures you don't miss cells within the range, it requires the range to be contiguous and you can't leave blank cells. This shortcut actually forces you to build in a manner that will reduce the number of errors you might make. This reinforces one of my on-going themes:

A lazy modeller is to be encouraged; lazy modelling isn't.

Let me be clear what I mean by a **"lazy modeller"**: this is someone who finds a way to keep formulae and constructs simple, so that their models are highly efficient and can be reproduced in seconds. It encourages flexibility, transparency and robustness – three key qualities of a "Best Practice" model *(more on that later)*.

Lazy modelling may include typing in hard code, changing a formula on a cell-by-cell basis when it doesn't quite work and refusing to add error checks to ensure model integrity. Lazy modelling always comes back to bite you. It may take longer initially to develop your model, but it will pay off many times over as the model continues to be used.

Be careful with **SUM**. Consider the following example:

| E9 | ⌄ ⋮ ✕ ✓ *fx* ⌄ | =E3+E4+E5+E6+E7 |

	A	B	C	D	E	F	G
1							
2					Values		
3					1		
4					2		
5					3		
6					4		
7					5		
8			Using SUM		15	=SUM(E3:E7)	
9			Using +		15	=E3+E4+E5+E6+E7	
10							

In this example, I have totalled the values in cells **E3:E7** in two distinct ways: the first uses the aforementioned **SUM** function with **ALT** + **=**, the other has added each cell individually using the '**+**' operator. Are you thinking you'd be mad to use the alternative (second) approach – especially if there were many more rows?

Well, take another look:

| E9 | ⌄ ⋮ ✕ ✓ *fx* ⌄ | =E3+E4+E5+E6+E7 |

	A	B	C	D	E	F	G
1							
2					Values		
3					1		
4					2		
5					3		
6					4		
7					5		
8			Using SUM		12	=SUM(E3:E7)	
9			Using +		15	=E3+E4+E5+E6+E7	
10							

In this example, cell **E5** has been modified. It has been stored as text, even though it looks like the number 3. **SUM** treats this as having zero value whereas the more convoluted addition carries on regardless. Simplest may not always be bestest.

In an example like the previous one, this may be easy to spot, but would you stake your life that the **SUM**

B23 ✕ ✓ *fx* ✓ =SUM(B2:M21)

	A	B	C	D	E	F	G	H	I	J	K	L	M
1													
2		49	88	67	21	29	93	77	82	71	24	46	5
3		20	81	56	36	86	26	74	57	11	52	18	28
4		37	9	63	7	11	83	82	12	95	90	81	91
5		60	14	99	29	81	73	55	42	64	84	25	58
6		33	45	38	49	56	99	76	31	89	77	86	8
7		60	65	22	19	42	42	33	41	93	91	57	21
8		57	94	79	43	68	65	83	37	63	75	67	70
9		52	30	45	57	23	13	26	67	77	2	17	83
10		54	78	78	76	45	34	47	30	63	37	78	59
11		52	90	59	80	76	38	4	97	52	17	39	48
12		41	21	92	77	68	4	96	37	97	23	52	47
13		28	78	15	79	17	67	3	52	77	77	13	77
14		17	34	6	7	95	42	44	70	79	60	34	62
15		71	63	39	94	58	54	57	75	44	30	29	41
16		38	50	9	43	58	45	20	99	31	13	88	20
17		100	30	83	6	47	87	52	97	37	71	39	4
18		90	26	1	21	93	10	87	18	49	51	90	63
19		43	45	12	55	19	59	87	63	9	13	97	40
20		21	98	47	88	85	17	55	20	92	77	44	90
21		21	57	91	97	59	16	43	49	76	21	12	100
22													
23		12,566											
24													

is correct?

There is a simple way to check using the **COUNT** function. **COUNT** counts the number of <u>numbers</u> in a range, so we can use it to spot numbers that aren't numbers:

G5 ✕ ✓ *fx* ✓ =1-COUNT(E5)

	A	B	C	D	E	F	G	H	I
1									
2					Values				
3					1		-		=1-COUNT(E3)
4					2		-		=1-COUNT(E4)
5					3		1		=1-COUNT(E5)
6					4		-		=1-COUNT(E6)
7					5		-		=1-COUNT(E7)
8			Using SUM		12				=SUM(E3:E7)
9			Using +		15				=E3+E4+E5+E6+E7
10									

Here, the formula in column **I** highlights when a number is not a number. Note how it reports by exception: if the cell in question contains a number then **COUNT(Cell_Reference)** equals 1 and **=1-COUNT(Cell_Reference)** equals zero. Only non-numbers will be highlighted – it's better to know I have two errors rather than 14,367 values working correctly.

If you don't think this applies to you, have you ever worked with PivotTables? This book isn't about PivotTables, but as an aside, for those of you who have ever worked with this Excel feature, have you ever been frustrated when the following has happened?

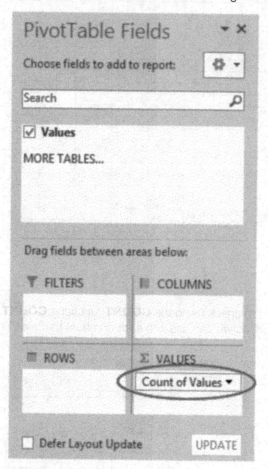

You want your aggregation of values to default to **SUM** but instead they display as **COUNT**. This could be highlighting that some of your data is non-numerical and / or blank. Just a thought.

CHAPTER 1.2: IF

So, what's the most Important Function in Excel? Any takers for **IF**? The syntax for **IF** demonstrates just how useful this function is for financial modelling:

> **=IF(logical_test, [value_if_TRUE], [value_if_FALSE])**

This function has three arguments:

- **logical_test**: this is the "decider", *i.e.* a test that results in a value of either TRUE or FALSE. Strictly speaking, the **logical_test** tests whether something is TRUE; if not, it is FALSE

- **value_if_TRUE**: what to do if the **logical_test** is TRUE. Note that you do not put square brackets around this argument! This is just the Excel syntax for saying sometimes this argument is optional. If this argument is indeed omitted, this argument will have a default value of TRUE

- **value_if_FALSE**: what to do if the **logical_test** is FALSE (strictly speaking, not TRUE). If this argument is left blank, this argument will have a default value of FALSE.

This function is actually more efficient than it may look at first glance. Whilst the **logical_test** is always evaluated, only one of the remaining two arguments is computed, depending upon whether the **logical_test** is TRUE or FALSE. For example:

In this example, the intention is to evaluate the quotient **Numerator / Denominator**. However, if the **Denominator** is either blank or zero, this will result in an *#DIV/0!* error. Excel has several errors that it cannot evaluate, *e.g.* *#REF!*, *#NULL!*, *#N/A*, *#Brown*, *#Pipe*. OK, so one or two of these I may have made up, but **prima facie** errors should be avoided in Excel as they detract from the key results and cause the user to doubt the overall model integrity. Worse, in some instances these errors may contribute to Excel crashing and / or corrupting. Note to self: prevent these errors from occurring.

This is where **IF** comes in. In my example above, **=IF(Denominator=0,,Numerator/ Denominator)** tests whether the **Denominator** is zero, If so, the value is unspecified (blank) and will consequently return a value of zero in Excel. Otherwise, the quotient is calculated as intended.

This is known as creating an **error trap**. Errors are "trapped" and the 'harmless' value of zero is returned instead. You could put "n.a" or "This is an error" as the **value_if_TRUE**, but you get the picture.

It is my preference not to put a zero [0] in for the **value_if_TRUE**: personally, I think a formula looks clearer this way, but inexperienced end users may not understand the formula and you should consider your audience when deciding to put what may appear to be an unnecessary zero in a formula. The aim is to keep it simple **for the end user**.

An **IF** statement is often used to make a decision in the model, *i.e.*

> **=IF(Decision_Criterion=TRUE, Do_it, Don't_Do_It)**

This automates a model and aids management in decision making and what-if analysis. **IF** is clearly a very powerful tool when used correctly. However, sometimes it is used when another function might be preferable. For example, if you find yourself writing a formula that begins

> **=IF(IF(IF(IF...**

then I humbly suggest you are using the wrong function. **IF** should never be used to look up data: there are plenty of functions out there to help with that problem, but we will come to that in time. However, sometimes your **logical_test** might consist of multiple criteria, *e.g.*

> **=IF(Condition1=TRUE,IF(Condition2=TRUE,IF(Condition3=TRUE,1,),),)**

Here, this formula only gives a value of 1 if all three conditions are true. This nested **IF** statement may be avoided using the logical function **AND(Condition1,Condition2,...)** which is TRUE if and only if all dependent arguments are TRUE, *i.e.*

> **=IF(AND(Condition1,Condition2,Condition3),1,)**

This is actually easier to read. There are two other useful logic functions sometimes used with **IF**:

- **OR(Condition1,Condition2,...)** is TRUE when at least one of the arguments is TRUE

- **NOT(Condition)** gives the opposite logic value, so that if the **Condition** is TRUE it will be FALSE and vice versa.

Even using these logic functions, formulae may look complex quite quickly. There is an alternative: **flags**. In its most common form, flags are evaluated as

> **=(Condition=TRUE)*1**

Condition=TRUE will give rise to a value of either TRUE or FALSE; the brackets will ensure this is evaluated first; multiplying by 1 will provide an end result of zero (if FALSE, as FALSE*1 = 0) or one (if TRUE, TRUE*1 = 1). I know some modellers prefer TRUEs and FALSEs everywhere, but I think 1's and 0's are easier to read (when there are lots of them) and more importantly, easier to sum when you need to know how many issues there are, *etc*.

Flags make it easier to follow the tested conditions. Consider the following:

		1	2	3	4	5	6	7	8	9	10	
Counter		1	2	3	4	5	6	7	8	9	10	
Divisible by 3		-	-	1	-	-	1	-	-	1	-	=(MOD(@Counter,3)=0)*1
Greater than 4		-	-	-	-	1	1	1	1	1	1	=(@Counter>4)*1
Less than or equal to 9		1	1	1	1	1	1	1	1	1	-	=(@Counter<=9)*1
Is not 6		1	1	1	1	1	-	1	1	1	1	=(@Counter<>6)*1
Product		-	-	-	-	-	-	-	-	1	-	=PRODUCT(D4:D7)

In this illustration, you might not yet understand what the **MOD** function does (more on that later), but hopefully, you can follow each of the flags in rows 4 to 7 without being an Excel guru. Row 9, the product, simply multiplies all of the flags together. This produces an **AND** flag.

I might wish to use **MIN** instead (more on that later):

		1	2	3	4	5	6	7	8	9	10	
Counter		1	2	3	4	5	6	7	8	9	10	
Divisible by 3		-	-	1	-	-	1	-	-	1	-	=(MOD(@Counter,3)=0)*1
Greater than 4		-	-	-	-	1	1	1	1	1	1	=(@Counter>4)*1
Less than or equal to 9		1	1	1	1	1	1	1	1	1	-	=(@Counter<=9)*1
Is not 6		1	1	1	1	1	-	1	1	1	1	=(@Counter<>6)*1
Product		-	-	-	-	-	-	-	-	1	-	=MIN(D4:D7)

This has the same effect and is perhaps easier to remember when considering the following counterpart. If I wanted the flag to be a one [1] as long as one of the above conditions is TRUE (*i.e.* represent an **OR**), that is easy too:

		1	2	3	4	5	6	7	8	9	10	
Counter		1	2	3	4	5	6	7	8	9	10	
Divisible by 3		-	-	1	-	-	1	-	-	1	-	=(MOD(@Counter,3)=0)*1
Greater than 4		-	-	-	-	1	1	1	1	1	1	=(@Counter>4)*1
Less than or equal to 9		1	1	1	1	1	1	1	1	1	-	=(@Counter<=9)*1
Is not 6		1	1	1	1	1	-	1	1	1	1	=(@Counter<>6)*1
MAX		1	1	1	1	1	1	1	1	1	1	=MAX(D4:D7)

Flags frequently make models more transparent, and this example provides a great learning point. Often, we mistakenly believe that condensing a model into fewer cells makes it more efficient and easier to follow. On the contrary, it is usually better to step out a calculation. If it can be followed on a piece of paper (without access to the Formula bar), then more people will follow it. If more can follow the model logic, errors will be more easily spotted. When this occurs, a model becomes trusted and therefore is of more value in decision-making.

I'd like to finish on a word of caution. Sometimes you just <u>can't</u> use flags. Let me go back to my first example in this section – but this time using the flag approach:

fx ✓	=(Numerator/Denominator)*(Denominator<>0)					
D	**E**	**F**	**G**	**H**	**I**	**J**
	Numerator	3				
	Denominator	-				
	Decimal	#DIV/0!				

Here, the flag does not trap the division by zero error. This is because this formula evaluates to

=#DIV/0! x 0

which equals *#DIV/0!* If you need to trap an error, you <u>must</u> use an **IF** function.

CHAPTER 1.3: IFERROR

IFERROR first came into being back in Excel 2007. It was something users had asked Microsoft for, for a very long time. But let me go back in time first and explain why.

At the time of writing, there are 12 **IS** functions, *i.e.* functions that give rise to a TRUE or FALSE value depending upon whether a certain condition is met:

1. **ISBLANK(reference):** checks whether the **reference** is to an empty cell

2. **ISERR(value):** checks whether the **value** is an error (*e.g. #REF!, #DIV/0!, #NULL!*). This check specifically excludes *#N/A*

3. **ISERROR(value):** checks whether the **value** is an error (*e.g. #N/A, #REF!, #DIV/0!, #NULL!*). This is probably the most commonly used of these functions in financial modelling

4. **ISEVEN(number):** checks to see if the **number** is even

5. **ISFORMULA(reference):** checks to see whether the **reference** is to a cell containing a formula

6. **ISLOGICAL(value):** checks to see whether the **value** is a logical (TRUE or FALSE) value

7. **ISNA(value):** checks to see whether the **value** is *#N/A*. This gives us the rather crude identity **ISERR + ISNA = ISERROR**

8. **ISNONTEXT(value):** checks whether the **value** is not text (*N.B.* blank cells are not text)

9. **ISNUMBER(value):** checks whether the **value** is a number

10. **ISODD(number):** checks to see if the **number** is odd. Personally, I find the number 46 very odd, but Excel doesn't

11. **ISREF(value):** checks whether the **value** is a reference

12. **ISTEXT(value):** checks whether the **value** is text.

You get the idea. As mentioned previously, sometimes you need to trap errors that may originate from a formula that is correct most of the time. Where possible, you should be specific with regard to what you are checking, *e.g.*

> **=IF(Denominator=0, Error_Trap, Numerator/Denominator)**

In this example, I am checking to see whether the **Denominator** is zero. I could use this formula instead:

> **=IF(ISERROR(Numerator/Denominator), Error_Trap, Numerator/Denominator)**

The difference here is that this will check for anything that may give rise to an error:

f_x ∨	=IF(ISERROR(Numerator/Denominator),"Kebab",Numerator/Denominator)								
D	E	F	G	H	I	J	K	L	M
	Numerator	Dog							
	Denominator	4							
	Decimal	Kebab							

Do you see the problem here? I have to put the same formula in *twice*. If that is a long formula, then the calculation becomes doubly long. This is where **IFERROR** comes in; it halves the length of the calculation but still achieves the same effect

=IFERROR(calculation, error_trap)

Essentially, this formula is the illegitimate lovechild of **IF** and **ISERROR**. It checks to see whether the **calculation** will give rise to a *prima facie* error. If it does, it will return **error_trap**; otherwise, it will perform the said **calculation**, *e.g.*

f_x ˅	=IFERROR(Numerator/Denominator,"Kebab")

D	E	F	G	H	I
	Numerator	Dog			
	Denominator	4			
	Decimal	Kebab			

You shouldn't just sprinkle **IFERROR** throughout your models like your formulae are confetti. Used unwisely, **IFERROR** can disguise the fact that your formula isn't working correctly and that modifications to the logic may be required. Try to use it sparingly.

Sometimes you have to use **IF** and **ISERROR** in combination anyway:

=IF(ISERROR(calculation), error_trap, different_calculation)

In this example, the formula is checking to see whether a particular **calculation** gives rise to an error. If it does, the **error_trap** will be referenced in the usual way, but if not a **different_calculation** (not the **calculation** used for the test) will be computed.

These two methodologies should be mastered. You will create more robust and flexible models once your errors become a thing of the past. Not just the model – but your own expertise – will become more trusted in your organisation if users never encounter *prima facie* errors in your model.

CHAPTER 1.4: SUMIF

If you are unfamiliar with this function, you can still probably guess what **SUMIF** does: it combines **SUM** with **IF** to provide conditional summing, *i.e.* where you wish to add numerical values provided they meet a certain condition (criterion). For example, imagine you were reviewing the following data summary:

H26	⌄	:	✕ ✓ *fx* ⌄	=SUMIF(F12:F21,G26,H12:H21)

	A	B	C	D	E	F	G	H	I
8									
9			Dummy Database						
10									
11						Business Unit	Product Type	Sales	
12						1	X	$100	
13						1	Y	$200	
14						1	Z	$300	
15						1	Z	$400	
16						2	X	$500	
17						2	X	$600	
18						2	Z	$700	
19						3	Y	$800	
20						3	Z	$900	
21						4	Y	$1,000	
22									
23									
24			SUMIF Illustration						
25									
26			Business Unit				1	$1,000	
27									

The function **SUMIF(range, criterion, sum_range)** is ideal for summing data based on one requirement:

- **range** is the array that you wanted evaluated by the criterion (in this instance, cells **F12:F21**)

- **criterion** is the criterion in the form of a number, expression, or text that defines which cell(s) will be added, e.g. "X", 1, **G26** or **"<>"&G27** (this last one means "not equal to the value in cell **G27**")

- **sum_range** are the actual cells to be added if their corresponding cells in **range** match the **criterion**.

So, to find the sales for Business Unit 1 in the above example, you can use the formula **=SUMIF(F12:F21,1,H12:H21)** (which is $1,000), or to find the total sales of Product X, the formula could be modified to **=SUMIF(G12:G21,"X",H12:H21)** (which is $1,200) (note that any text must be in inverted commas).

SUMIF is fine when there is only one condition. However, how would you find the total sales of Product Z in Business Unit 1 using this function? That's two criteria and **SUMIF**

does not work with multiple conditions. There are various alternatives using other functions, but it is possible to solve this problem simply using **SUMIF**.

It is often possible to cheat with **SUMIF** by making a 'mega-criterion' out of multiple criteria. This works on joining criteria together usually by using the ampersand ('**&**') operator.

Let's consider our example, slightly revised, from above.

G29		⌄	⋮	✕	✓	*fx* ⌄	=SUMIF(H12:H21,G26&G27,I12:I21)

	A	B	C	D	E	F	G	H	I
8									
9		Dummy Database							
10									
11						Business Unit	Product Type	'Mega-Criterion'	Sales
12						1	X	1X	$100
13						1	Y	1Y	$200
14						1	Z	1Z	$300
15						1	Z	1Z	$400
16						2	X	2X	$500
17						2	X	2X	$600
18						2	Z	2Z	$700
19						3	Y	3Y	$800
20						3	Z	3Z	$900
21						4	Y	4Y	$1,000
22									
23									
24		SUMIF Illustration							
25									
26			Business Unit				1		
27			Product Type				Z		
28									
29			Solution				$700		
30									

A new column has been inserted (column **H**), with a formula combining the contents of columns **F** and **G** (*e.g.* the formula in cell **H12** is =F12&G12). Provided that all possible combinations are unique (*i.e.* no duplicates can be generated), a simple **SUMIF** can then be applied, *e.g.*

=SUMIF(H12:H21,"1Z",I12:I21).

This is by far and away the simplest solution – *if it works*. It can fall down though (in another example, the concatenation "111" might refer to Product 1 in Business Unit 11 or Product 11 in Business Unit 1).

As I say, there are other ways to solve this issue...

CHAPTER 1.5: SUMIFS

SUMIFS is similar to the **SUMIF** function. The syntax might not look similar when you first inspect it:

=SUMIFS(sum_range, criterion_range1, criterion1,...)

If you think about it, the syntax is consistent with **SUMIF**. This function allows various ranges (**criterion_range1**, **criterion_range2**, ...) to be assessed against multiple criteria (**criterion1**, **criterion2**, ...). The key difference is that the range to be conditionally summed, **sum_range**, is the first argument of the function rather than the last. This is so there is never any confusion regarding what is to be totalled.

G29			f_x	=SUMIFS(I12:I21,F12:F21,G26,G12:G21,G27)

	A B C D E	F	G	H	I	J
8						
9	Dummy Database					
10						
11		Business Unit	Product Type	'Mega-Criterion'	Sales	
12		1	X	1X	$100	
13		1	Y	1Y	$200	
14		1	Z	1Z	$300	
15		1	Z	1Z	$400	
16		2	X	2X	$500	
17		2	X	2X	$600	
18		2	Z	2Z	$700	
19		3	Y	3Y	$800	
20		3	Z	3Z	$900	
21		4	Y	4Y	$1,000	
22						
23						
24	SUMIFS Illustration					
25						
26	Business Unit		1			
27	Product Type		Z			
28						
29	Solution		$700			
30						

Unlike the solution proffered in the **SUMIF** section, the helper column (column **H**) is no longer required. However, **SUM**, **SUMIF** and **SUMIFS** have an Achilles' Heel: numbers that look like numbers but are considered text (a common problem with data imported from management information systems) are treated as zero. This can lead to right formula wrong result:

| G29 | ⌄ | ⋮ | ✕ ✓ ƒx ⌄ | =SUMIFS(I12:I21,F12:F21,G26,G12:G21,G27) |

	A	B	C	D	E	F	G	H	I	J
8										
9				Dummy Database						
10										
11						Business Unit	Product Type	'Mega-Criterion'	Sales	
12						1	X	1X	$100	
13						1	Y	1Y	$200	
14						1	Z	1Z	$300	
15						1	Z	1Z	$400	
16						2	X	2X	$500	
17						2	X	2X	$600	
18						2	Z	2Z	$700	
19						3	Y	3Y	$800	
20						3	Z	3Z	$900	
21						4	Y	4Y	$1,000	
22										
23										
24				SUMIFS Illustration						
25										
26				Business Unit			1			
27				Product Type			Z			
28										
29				Solution			$300			
30										

There is only one difference between this example and the previous one: cell **I15** has now been entered as text. Therefore, the $400 is not recognised as a value and the summation has been reduced by this amount accordingly.

Care needs to be taken with these functions if conditional summations are to be relied upon in a financial model (the same may be said for PivotTables too).

But there's a more robust alternative…

CHAPTER 1.6: SUMPRODUCT

I must admit this is one of my favourite functions in Excel – so much so our company was named after it (time for a shameless plug)!

At first glance,

SUMPRODUCT(vector1, vector2,...)

appears quite humble. Before showing an example, though, let's look at the syntax carefully:

- A **vector** for Excel purposes is a collection of cells either one column wide or one row deep. For example, **A1:A5** is a column vector, **A1:E1** is a row vector, cell **A1** is a unit vector and the range **A1:E5** is <u>not</u> a vector (it is actually an array, but more on that later). The ranges must be contiguous; *and*

- This basic functionality uses the comma delimiter (,) to separate the arguments (vectors). Unlike most Excel functions, it is possible to use other delimiters, but this will be revisited shortly below.

So, before I continue, I think it's time to have a moan and reminisce about how I have been ripped off in the past. Back when I was a student, I supported my studies by working at a petrol station. The hours were long (12 hours per day), and my boss would not buy an electronic till (yes, electricity had been invented back then), so all sales were recorded manually. Consequently, all sales had to be kept in a tally chart, *i.e.* the pricing points were listed in the first column and the sales were then noted in the second column. At the end of the day, I would have to calculate the total revenue and reconcile it with the payments received:

H23			fx	=SUM(H12:H21)

	Pricing Point	# of Sales	Total Sales
	1	14	14
	2	7	14
	5	9	45
	10	5	50
	25	3	75
	50	4	200
	100	8	800
	250	2	500
	500	1	500
	1000	1	1,000
			3,198

Basic Example

Dummy Database

The sales in column **H** are simply the product of columns **F** and **G**, *e.g.* the formula in cell **H12** is simply **=F12*G12**. Then, to calculate the entire amount cell **H23** sums column **H**. This could all be performed much quicker using the following formula:

=SUMPRODUCT(F12:F21,G12:G21)

i.e. **SUMPRODUCT** does exactly what it says on the tin: it <u>sums</u> the individual <u>products</u>.

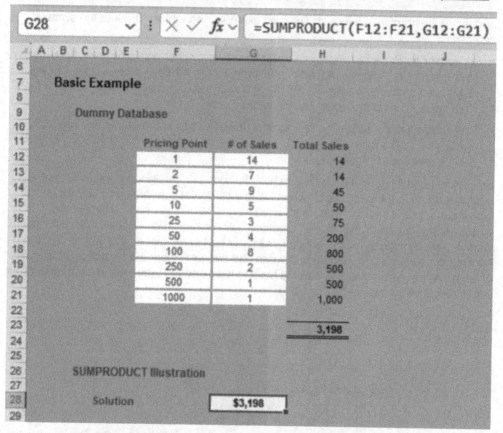

I mentioned the comma delimiter earlier. You can multiply the vectors together instead.

=SUMPRODUCT(F12:F21*G12:G21)

will produce the same result. However, there is an important difference. If you think back to our earlier example

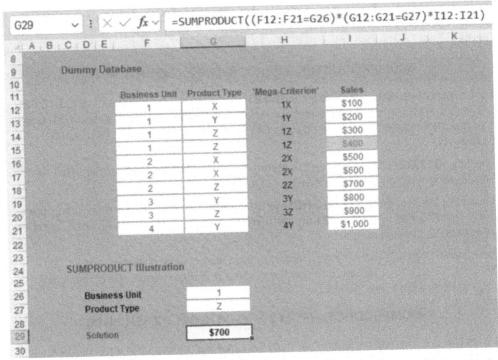

SUMPRODUCT will work with numbers that aren't really numbers. However, if you look at the formula in the example, you can be forgiven for not understanding the formula. Let me explain.

Where **SUMPRODUCT** comes into its own is when dealing with multiple criteria. This is done by considering the properties of TRUE and FALSE in Excel, namely:

- TRUE*number = number (*e.g.* TRUE*7 = 7); *and*

- FALSE*number = 0 (*e.g.* FALSE*7=0).

Consider the following example:

Business Unit	Product Type	Sales
1	X	$100
1	Y	$200
1	Z	$300
1	Z	$400
2	X	$500
2	X	$600
2	Z	$700
3	Y	$800
3	Z	$900
4	Y	$1,000

we can test columns **F** and **G** to check whether they equal our required values.
SUMPRODUCT could be used as follows to sum only sales made by Business Unit 1 for Product Z, *viz.*

=SUMPRODUCT((F12:F21=1)*(G12:G21="Z")*H12:H21).

For the purposes of this calculation, (**F12:F21=1**) replaces the contents of cells **F12:F21** with either TRUE or FALSE depending on whether the value contained in each cell equals 1 or not. The brackets are required to force Excel to compute this first before cross-multiplying.

Similarly, (**G12:G21="Z"**) replaces the contents of cells **G12:G21** with either TRUE or FALSE depending on whether the value "Z" is contained in each cell.

Therefore, the only time cells **H12:H21** will be summed is when the corresponding cell in the arrays **F12:F21** and **G12:G21** are both TRUE, then you will get TRUE*TRUE*number, which equals the said number.

Note also that this uses the ***** delimiter rather than the comma, analogous to TRUE*number, *etc*. If you were to use the comma delimiter instead, the syntax would have to be modified thus:

=SUMPRODUCT(--(F12:F21=1),--(G12:G21="Z"),H12:H21)

Minus minus? The first negation in front of the brackets converts the array of TRUEs and FALSEs to numbers, albeit substituting -1 for TRUE and 0 for FALSE. The second minus sign negates these numbers so that TRUE is effectively 1, rather than -1, whilst FALSE remains equals to zero. This variant often confuses end users which is why I recommend the first version described above.

You can get more sophisticated:

G26	⌄ : ✕ ✓ *fx* ⌄	=SUMPRODUCT((F12:F21=G12:G21)*H12:H21)

	A B C D E	F	G	H	I	J	K
8							
9	Dummy Database						
10							
11		Invoice No.	Checked No.	Amt			
12		017358	017358	$100			
13		041456	041456	$200			
14		092675	092666	$300			
15		111258	111258	$400			
16		157792	157792	$500			
17		256148	256148	$600			
18		336691	336691	$700			
19		479020	479019	$800			
20		500838	500838	$900			
21		771496	771496	$1,000			
22							
23							
24	SUMPRODUCT Illustration						
25							
26	Authorised to Pay		$4,400				
27							

In this scenario, the end user pays invoices only where the invoice number matches the number "checked" on an authorised list. In the illustration above, two invoices (highlighted in red) do not match. **SUMPRODUCT** can be used to sum the authorised amounts only as follows:

=SUMPRODUCT((F12:F21=G12:G21)*H12:H21)

The argument in brackets only gives a value of TRUE for each row when the values in columns **F** and **G** are identical.

SUMPRODUCT and **SUMIFS** truly part company in the following comprehensive example. Consider the following:

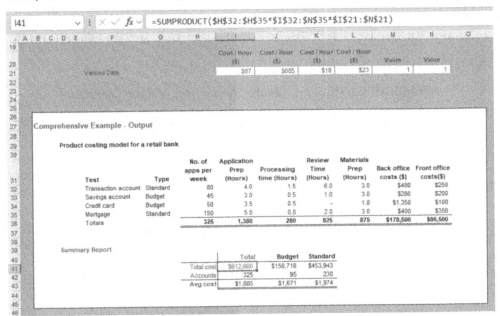

So far, I have only considered **SUMPRODUCT** with vector ranges. Using the multiplication delimiter (*****), it is possible to use **SUMPRODUCT** with arrays (an array is a range of cells consisting of both more than one row and more than one column).

In the above example, **SUMPRODUCT** has been used in its elementary form in cells **I36:N36**. For example, the formula in cell **I36** is:

=SUMPRODUCT($H$32:$H$35,I$32:I$35)

and this has then been copied across to the rest of the cells.

To calculate the total costs of this retail bank example, this could be calculated as:

=SUMPRODUCT($I$36:$N$36,$I$21:$N$21)

However, the formula in cell **I41** appears more – and unnecessarily – complicated:

=SUMPRODUCT($H$32:$H$35*$I$32:$N$35*$I$21:$N$21)

The use of the multiplication delimiter is deliberate (the formula will not work if the delimiters were to become commas instead). It should be noted that this last formula is essentially

=SUMPRODUCT(Column_Vector*Array*Row_Vector)

where the number of rows in the **Column_Vector** must equal the number of rows in the **Array**, and also the number of columns in the **Array** must equal the number of columns in the **Row_Vector**.

The reason for this extended version of the formula is in order to divide the costs between Budget and Standard costs in my example. For example, the formula in cell **J41** becomes:

=SUMPRODUCT($H$32:$H$35*$I$32:$N$35*$I$21:$N$21*($G$32:$G$35=J$40))

i.e. the formula is now of the form

=SUMPRODUCT(Column_Vector*Array*Row_Vector*Condition)

where **Condition** uses similar logic to the TRUE / FALSE examples detailed earlier. This is a powerful concept that can be used to replace PivotTables for instance.

There are valid / more efficient alternatives to **SUMPRODUCT** in some instances. For example, dealing with multiple criteria for vector ranges, the **SUMIFS** function is up to six times faster, but will only work with Excel 2007 and later versions. Further, it cannot work with arrays where the dimensions differ such as in the example above.

Over-use of **SUMPRODUCT** can slow the calculation time down of even the smallest of Excel files, but it is a good all-rounder. Used sparingly it can be a highly versatile addition to the modeller's repertoire. It is a sophisticated function, but once you understand how it works, you can start to use **SUMPRODUCT** for a whole array of problems (pun intended!).

CHAPTER 1.7: VLOOKUP / HLOOKUP

Often you will need to look up data in a table – and two functions most modellers are very familiar with are **VLOOKUP** and **HLOOKUP**. But do you realise it's very easy to make a mistake with these functions? For those unsure of these functions, let me first start with a refresher.

> **VLOOKUP(lookup_value, table_array, col_index_num, [range_lookup])**

has the following syntax:

- **lookup_value:** What value do you want to look up?

- **table_array:** Where is the lookup table?

- **col_index_num:** Which column has the value you want returned?

- **[range_lookup]:** Do you want an exact or an approximate match? This is optional and to begin with, I am going to ignore this argument exists.

HLOOKUP is similar but works on a row rather than a column basis (**h**orizontal rather than **v**ertical).

I am going to use **VLOOKUP** throughout to keep things simple. **VLOOKUP** always looks for the **lookup_value** in the first column of a table (the **table_array**) and then returns a corresponding value so many columns to the right, determined by the **col_index_num** column index number.

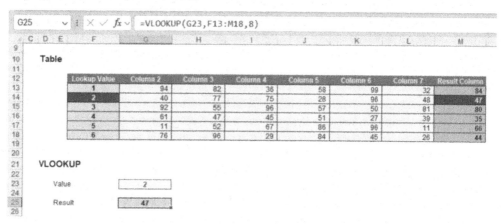

In this above example, the formula in cell **G25** seeks the value 2 in the first column of the table **F13:M18** and returns the corresponding value from the eighth column of the table (returning 47). Pretty easy to understand – so far so good. So, what goes wrong? Well, what happens if you add or remove a column from the table range?

Adding gives us the wrong value:

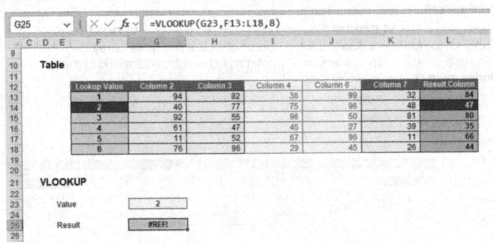

With a column inserted, the formula contains hard code (8) and therefore, the eighth column (**M**) is still referenced, giving rise to the wrong value. Deleting a column instead is even worse:

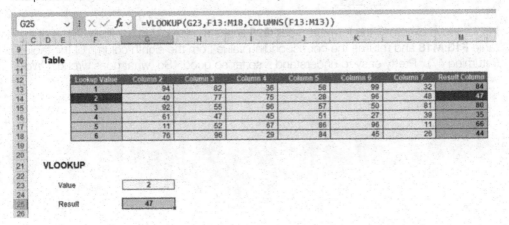

Now there are only seven columns so the formula returns #*REF!* Oops.

It is possible to make the column index number dynamic using the **COLUMNS** function:

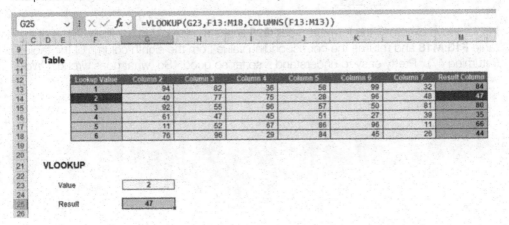

COLUMNS(reference) counts the number of columns in the **reference**. Using the range **F13:M13**, this formula will now keep track of how many columns there are between the lookup column (**F**) and the result column (**M**). This will prevent the problems illustrated above.

But there are more issues. Consider duplicate values in the lookup column. With one duplicate, the following happens:

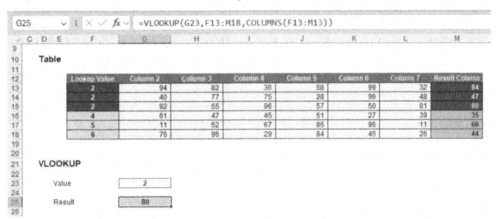

Here, the second value is returned, which might not be what is wanted. With two duplicates:

Ah, it looks like it might take the last occurrence. Testing this hypothesis with three duplicates:

29

Yes, there seems to be a pattern: **VLOOKUP** takes the last occurrence. I had better make sure:

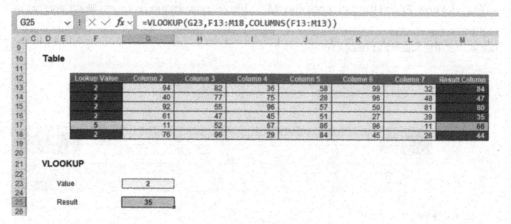

Oh dear. In this example, the value returned is the fourth of five. The problem is, there's no consistent logic and the formula and its result cannot be relied upon. It gets worse if we exclude duplicates but mix up the lookup column a little:

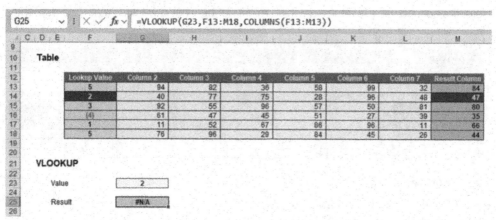

In this instance, **VLOOKUP** cannot even find the value 2!

So what's going on? The problem – and common modelling mistake – is that the fourth argument has been ignored:

> **VLOOKUP(lookup_value, table_array, col_index_num, [range_lookup])**

[range_lookup] appears in square brackets, which means it is optional. It has two values:

- **TRUE**: this is the <u>default</u> setting if the argument is not specified. Here, **VLOOKUP** will seek an approximate match, looking for the largest value less than or equal to the value sought. There is a price to be paid though: the values in the first column (or row for **HLOOKUP**) must be in <u>strict ascending</u> order – this means that each value must be larger than the value before, so no duplicates.

- This is useful when looking up postage rates for example where prices are given in categories of kilograms, and you have 2.7kg to post (say). It's worth noting though that this isn't the most common lookup when modelling.

- **FALSE**: this has to be specified. In this case, data can be any which way – including duplicates – and the result will be based upon the first occurrence of the value sought. If an exact match cannot be found, **VLOOKUP** will return the value #N/A.

And this is the problem highlighted by the above examples. The final argument was never specified so the lookup column data has to be in strict ascending order – and this premiss was continually breached.

The robust formula needs both **COLUMNS** and a fourth argument of **FALSE** to work as expected:

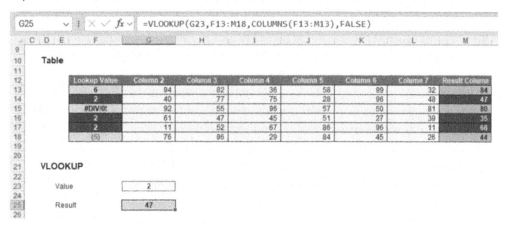

Using a fourth argument of **FALSE**, **VLOOKUP** will return the corresponding result for the first occurrence of the **lookup_value**, regardless of number of duplicates, errors or series order. If an approximate match is required, the data must be in strict ascending order.

VLOOKUP (and consequently **HLOOKUP**) are not the simple, easy to use functions modellers think they are. In fact, they can never be used to return data for columns to the left (**VLOOKUP**) or rows above (**HLOOKUP**). So what should modellers use instead...?

CHAPTER 1.8: LOOKUP

Now that I have taken **VLOOKUP** and **HLOOKUP** to task, some of you may have considered **LOOKUP** is conspicuous by its absence. It may seem a less versatile function upon first glance, but it is quite useful for modelling. Allow me to explain.

LOOKUP has two forms: an array form and a vector form. As a reminder:

- An **array** is a collection of cells consisting of at least two rows and at least two columns

- A **vector** is a collection of cells across just one row (row vector) or down just one column (column vector).

The diagram should be self-explanatory:

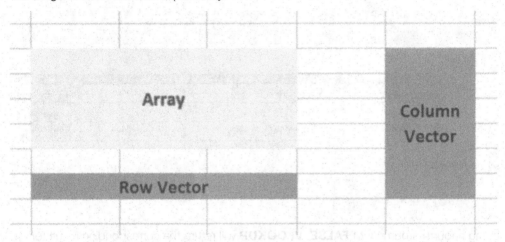

The array form of **LOOKUP** looks in the first row or column of an array for the specified value and returns a value from the same position in the last row or column of the same array:

LOOKUP(lookup_value, array)

where:

- **lookup_value** is the value that **LOOKUP** searches for in an array. The **lookup_value** argument can be a number, text, a logical value or a name or reference that refers to a value

- **array** is the range of cells that contains text, numbers or logical values that you want to compare with **lookup_value**.

The array form of **LOOKUP** is very similar to the **HLOOKUP** and **VLOOKUP** functions. The difference is that **HLOOKUP** searches for the value of **lookup_value** in the first row, **VLOOKUP** searches in the first column, and **LOOKUP** searches according to the dimensions of **array**.

If **array** covers an area that is wider than it is tall (*i.e.* it has more columns than rows), **LOOKUP** searches for the value of **lookup_value** in the first row and returns the result from the last row. Otherwise, **LOOKUP** searches for the value of **lookup_value** in the first column and returns the result from the last column instead.

The alternative form is the vector form:

> ## LOOKUP(lookup_value, lookup_vector, [result_vector])

The **LOOKUP** function vector form syntax has the following arguments:

- **lookup_value** is the value that **LOOKUP** searches for in the first vector
- **lookup_vector** is the range that contains only one row or one column
- **[result_vector]** is optional – if ignored, **lookup_vector** is used – this is the where the result will come from and must contain the same number of cells as the **lookup_vector**.

Like the default versions of **HLOOKUP** and **VLOOKUP**, **lookup_value** must be located in a range of strictly ascending values, *i.e.* where each value is larger than the one before and there are no duplicates.

So why do I advocate for **LOOKUP** when I said don't use the other functions just recently? Well, it's because it is simpler to use, doesn't rely on row or index column numbers and allows modellers to create inputs that do not need to be specified for all periods modelled. Let me demonstrate with the following example:

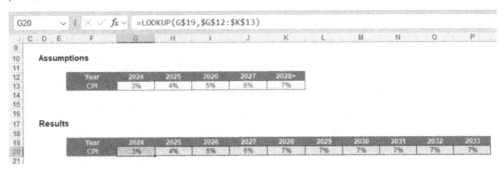

Imagine you have an annual model forecasting for many years into the future. Creating inputs will be time consuming if data has to be entered on a period-by-period basis. But there is a shortcut.

Do you see the data table in cells **F12:K13** above? The value in the final cell of the first row is actually "2028" not "2028+". It appears that way due to custom number formatting (**CTRL + 1**):

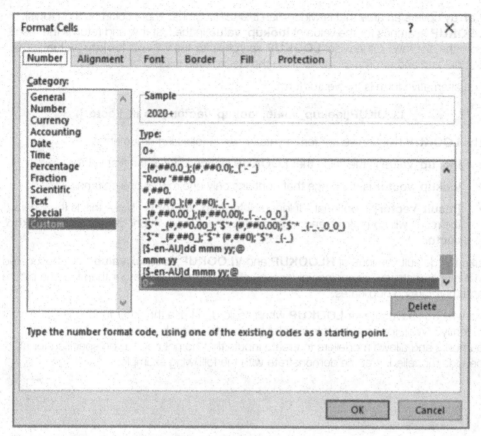

The syntax "0+" adds a plus sign to the number although Excel still reads the value as 2020. Number formatting is discussed in more detail later on.

The formula uses the array version of **LOOKUP**, looking up the year in the first row of the data table and returning the corresponding value from the final row. When a year is selected which is greater than 2020, the 2020 value is used, as **LOOKUP** seeks out the largest value less than or equal to the value sought. Therefore, we don't need to have lengthy data tables – once we assume inputs will be constant thereafter, we can just curtail the input section.

Using the array form of **LOOKUP** is dangerous though. What if someone accidentally inserts rows? The lookup will "flip" to look at the first and last columns instead, which is not what is required. Using the vector form is safer:

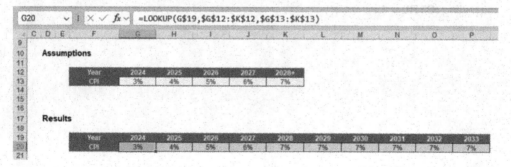

Whilst the formula contains one more argument, the formula is more stable. Further, the **lookup_vector** and the **result_vector** do not need to be in the same worksheet or even the same workbook. In fact, as long as there are the same number of elements in each, one can be a row vector and the other a column vector.

LOOKUP is very useful when the **lookup_vector** contains data in strict ascending order. Where do we find this? Dates in time series – **LOOKUP** is very useful for financial modelling / forecasting. Just be careful though; consider the following scenario:

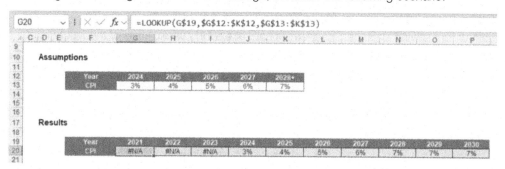

Here, the same formula generates an #N/A error. This is because the date is smaller than the smallest value in the data range. **LOOKUP** is not quite clever enough to use the first value unprompted, but a simple tweak of the formula will suffice:

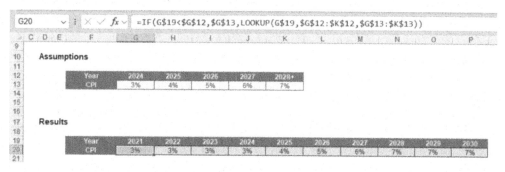

Here, the formula has been modified to:

=IF(G$19<$G$12,$G$13,**LOOKUP(G$19,$G$12:$K$12,$G$13:$K$13))**

The added **IF** statement checks to see if the year is smaller than the first year in the data table and if so, returns the first result. Simple. It is with this final modification – in its vector form – that I usually use **LOOKUP** to return values for certain time periods where I do not want to have an input for each period modelled. Very useful!

CHAPTER 1.9: INDEX and MATCH

INDEX and **MATCH** – as a combination – are two of the most useful functions at a modeller's disposal. They provide a versatile lookup in a way that **LOOKUP**, **HLOOKUP** and **VLOOKUP** simply cannot. The best way to illustrate this point is by means of an example.

Here is a common problem. Imagine you have built a financial model and your Balance Sheet – ahem! – contains misbalances. You need to fix it. Now I am sure you have never had this mistake yourself, but you have "close friends" that have encountered this feast of fun: solving Balance Sheet errors can take a *long* while. One of the first things modellers will do is locate the first period (in ascending order) that has such an error, as identifying the issue in this period may often solve the problem for all periods. Consider the following example:

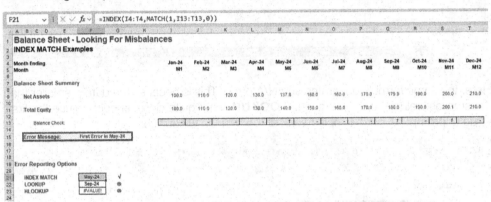

This is a common modelling query. The usual suspects, **LOOKUP** and **HLOOKUP** / **VLOOKUP** do not work here:

- **LOOKUP(lookup_value, lookup_vector, [result_vector])** gives the wrong date as the balance checks are not in <u>strict</u> ascending order (*i.e.* ascending alphanumerically with no duplicates); *whilst*

- **HLOOKUP(lookup_value, table_array, row_index_num, [range_lookup])** gives *#VALUE!* since the first row must contain the data to be 'looked up', but the Balance Check is in row 13 in our example above, whereas the dates we need to return are in row 4 – hence we get a syntax error.

There is a solution, however: **INDEX MATCH**. They form a highly versatile tag team but are worth introducing individually.

INDEX

Essentially, **INDEX(array, row_num, [column_num])** returns a value or the reference to a value from within a table or range (list). For example, **INDEX({7,8,9,10,11,12},3)** returns the third item in the list {7,8,9,10,11,12}, *i.e.* 9. This could have been a range: **INDEX(A1:A10,5)** gives the value in cell **A5**, *etc*.

INDEX can work in two dimensions as well (hence the **column_num** reference). Consider the following example:

		1	2	3	4	5	6	7
		F	G	H	I	J	K	L
1	11	1	2	3	4	5	6	7
2	12	8	9	10	11	12	13	14
3	13	15	16	17	18	19	20	21
4	14	22	23	24	25	26	27	28
5	15	29	30	31	32	33	34	35
6	16	36	37	38	39	40	41	42
7	17	43	44	45	46	47	48	49
8	18	50	51	52	53	54	55	56
9	19	57	58	59	60	61	62	63
10	20	64	65	66	67	68	69	70
11	21	71	72	73	74	75	76	77

INDEX(F11:L21,4,5) returns the value in the fourth row, fifth column of the table array **F11:L21** (clearly 26 in the above illustration).

MATCH

MATCH(lookup_value, lookup_vector, [match_type]) returns the relative position of an item in an array that (approximately) matches a specified value. It is <u>not</u> case sensitive.

The third argument, **match_type**, does not have to be entered, but for many situations, I strongly recommend that it is specified. It allows one of three values:

- **match_type 1** [default if omitted]**:** finds the largest value less than or equal to the **lookup_value** – but the **lookup_vector** must be in strict ascending order, limiting flexibility;

- **match_type 0:** probably the most useful setting, **MATCH** will find the position of the first value that matches **lookup_value** exactly. The **lookup_array** can have data in any order and even allows duplicates; *and*

- **match type -1:** finds the smallest value greater than or equal to the **lookup_value** – but the **lookup_array** must be in strict descending order, again limiting flexibility.

When using **MATCH**, if there is no (approximate) match, *#N/A* is returned (this may also occur if data is not correctly sorted depending upon **match_type**).

MATCH is fairly straightforward to use:

	E	F
12	1	a
13	2	b
14	3	a
15	4	c
16	5	b
17	6	d
18	7	d
19	8	e
20	9	f
21	10	a
22	11	c

In the figure above, **MATCH("d",F12:F22,0)** gives a value of 6, being the relative position of the first 'd' in the range. Note that having **match_type** 0 here is important. The data contains duplicates and is not sorted alphanumerically. Consequently, using **match_type** 1 and -1 would give the wrong answer: 7 and #N/A respectively.

INDEX MATCH

Whilst useful functions in their own right, combined they form a highly versatile partnership. Consider the original problem:

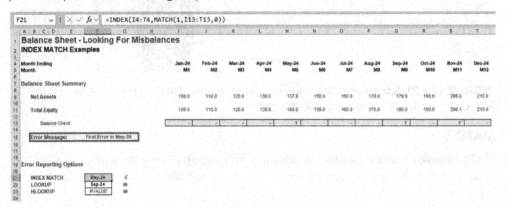

MATCH(1,I13:T13,0) equals 5, *i.e.* the first period the Balance Sheet does not balance in is Period 5. But we can do better than that. **INDEX(I4:T4,5)** equals May-24, so combining the two functions:

INDEX(I4:T4,MATCH(1,I13:T13,0))

equals May-24 in one step. This process of stepping out two calculations and then inserting one into another is often referred to as "staggered development". No, this is not how you construct a financial model late in the evening after having the odd drink or two!

Do note how flexible this combination really is. We do not need to specify an order for the lookup range, we can have duplicates and the value to be returned does not have to be in a row / column below / to the right of the lookup range (indeed, it can be in another workbook never mind another worksheet!). With a little practice, the above technique can be extended to match items on a case sensitive basis, use multiple criteria and even 'grade'.

CHAPTER 1.10: XLOOKUP and XMATCH

I have just explained why **INDEX MATCH** was a more powerful LOOKUP combination than **VLOOKUP**, which to this day still remains the third most used Excel function (behind **SUM** and **AVERAGE**).

XLOOKUP

However, in many versions of Excel, there are new functions to be **ex**plored:

> **XLOOKUP(lookup_value, lookup_array, return_array, [if_not_found], [match_mode], [search_mode])**

This function seeks out a **lookup_value** in the **lookup_array** and returns the corresponding value in the **return_array**. Similar to **RANDARRAY**, Microsoft decided to make a change before they pulled the pin and made both of these functions Generally Available. They decided to include an error trap for when a value cannot be found. Having said that, most of the time you will only require the first three arguments:

- **lookup_value:** this is required and defines what value you want to look up

- **lookup_array:** this reference is required and is the row or column of data you are referencing to look up **lookup_value**

- **return_array:** this is where the corresponding item you wish to return is located and is also required (even if it is the same as **lookup_array**). This does not have to be a vector (*i.e.* one row or one column of cells): it may be an array (with at least two rows and at least two columns of cells). The only stipulation is that the number of rows / columns must equal the number of rows / columns in the column / row vector – but more on that later

- **if_not_found:** this optional argument allows you to replace the usual return of #N/A with something more informative like an alternative formula, text or a value

- **match_mode:** this argument is optional. There are four choices:
  - **0:** exact match (default)
  - **-1:** exact match or else the largest value less than or equal to **lookup_value**
  - **1:** exact match or else smallest value greater than or equal to **lookup_value**
  - **2:** wildcard match. You should use the special character **?** to match any character and ***** to match any run of characters.

What's impressive, though, is that for certain selections of the final argument (**search_mode**), you don't need to put your data in alphanumerical order! As far as I am aware, this is a first for Excel

- **search_mode:** this argument is also optional. There are again four choices:
  - **1:** search first to last (default)

- **-1:** search last to first

- **2:** what is known as a binary search, first to last (requires **lookup_array** to be sorted). Just so you know, a binary search is a search algorithm that finds the position of a target value within a sorted array. A binary search compares the target value to the middle element of the array. If they are not equal, the half in which the target cannot lie is eliminated and the search continues on the remaining half, again taking the middle element to compare to the target value, and repeating this until the target value is found

- **-2:** another binary search, this time last to first (and again, this requires **lookup_array** to be sorted).

Let's have a look at **XLOOKUP** versus **VLOOKUP**:

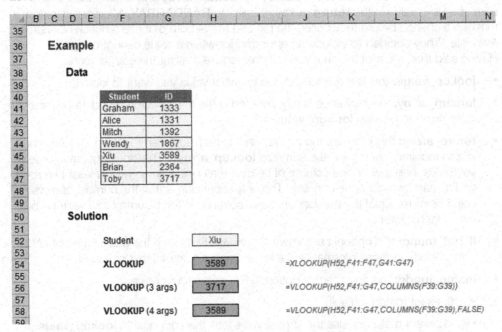

You can clearly see the **XLOOKUP** function is shorter:

=XLOOKUP(H52,F41:F47,G41:G47)

Only the first three arguments are needed, whereas **VLOOKUP** requires both a fourth argument, and, for full flexibility, the **COLUMNS** function as well. **XLOOKUP** will automatically update if rows / columns are inserted or deleted. It's just *simpler*.

HLOOKUP has similar issues:

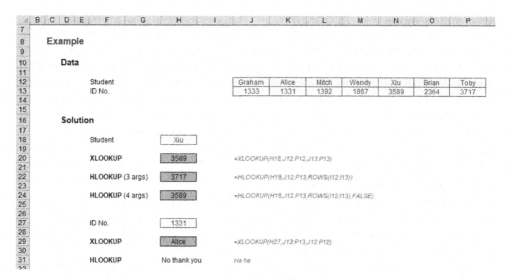

Here, this highlights what happens if I try to deduce the student's name from the Student ID. **HLOOKUP** cannot refer to earlier rows, just as **VLOOKUP** cannot consider columns to the left. Given any unused elements of the table are ignored also, it's just good news all round. Goodbye limitations, hello **XLOOKUP**.

Indeed, things get even more interesting when you start considering **XLOOKUP**'s final two arguments, namely **match_mode** and **search_mode**, *viz.*

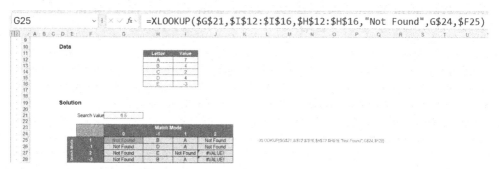

Notice that I am searching the 'Value' column, which is neither sorted nor contains unique items. Do you see how the results have changed once more, depending upon **match_mode** and **search_mode**?

	Match Mode			
	0	**-1**	**1**	**2**
1	Not Found	B	A	Not Found
-1	Not Found	D	A	Not Found
2	Not Found	E	Not Found	#VALUE!
-2	Not Found	B	A	#VALUE!

The **match_mode** zero [0] returns "Not Found" now instead of #*N/A* because there is no exact match, and the formula has now stipulated what to do in such an instance.

When **match_mode** is -1, **XLOOKUP** seeks an exact match or else the largest value less than or equal to **lookup_value** (6.5). That would be 4 – but this occurs more than once (B and D both have a value of 4). **XLOOKUP** chooses depending upon whether it is searching top down (**search_mode** 1, where B will be identified first) or bottom up (**search_mode** -1, where D will be identified first). Note that with binary searches (with a **search_mode** of 2 or -2), the data needs to be sorted. It isn't – hence we have garbage answers that cannot be relied upon.

With **match_mode** 1, the result is clearer cut. Only one value is the smallest value greater than or equal to 6.5. That is 7, and is related to A. Again, binary search results should be ignored, although it is worth noting "Not Found" occurs when Excel identifies the lookup value has not been found.

The **match_mode** 2 results are spurious. This is seeking wildcard matches, but there are no matches, hence "Not Found" instead of *N/A* for the only **search_modes** that may be seen as creditable (1 and -1). It's interesting to note a binary search causes errors which are not trapped by the new argument.

Clearly binary searches are higher maintenance. In the past, it was worth investing in them as they did return results more quickly. However, according to Microsoft, this is no longer the case: apparently, there is "…no significant benefit to using *(sic)* the binary search options…". If this is indeed the case, then I would strongly recommend not using them going forward with **XLOOKUP**.

Comparisons with LOOKUP

Whilst **XLOOKUP** wins hands down against **HLOOKUP** and **VLOOKUP**, the same cannot necessarily be said for **LOOKUP**. You may recall **LOOKUP** has two forms: an array form and a vector form. As a reminder:

- an **array** is a collection of cells consisting of at least two rows and at least two columns

- a **vector** is a collection of cells across just one row (row vector) or down just one column (column vector).

The diagram should be self-explanatory:

The array form of **LOOKUP** looks in the first row or column of an array for the specified value and returns a value from the same position in the last row or column of the same array:

LOOKUP(lookup_value, array)

where:

- **lookup_value** is the value that **LOOKUP** searches for in an array. The **lookup_value** argument can be a number, text, a logical value, or a name or reference that refers to a value

- **array** is the range of cells that contains text, numbers, or logical values that you want to compare with **lookup_value**.

The array form of **LOOKUP** is very similar to the **HLOOKUP** and **VLOOKUP** functions. The difference is that **HLOOKUP** searches for the value of **lookup_value** in the first row, **VLOOKUP** searches in the first column, and **LOOKUP** searches according to the dimensions of array.

If **array** covers an area that is wider than it is tall (*i.e.* it has more columns than rows), **LOOKUP** searches for the value of **lookup_value** in the first row and returns the result from the last row. Otherwise, **LOOKUP** searches for the value of **lookup_value** in the first column and returns the result from the last column instead.

The alternative form is the vector form:

LOOKUP(lookup_value, lookup_vector, [result_vector])

The **LOOKUP** function vector form syntax has the following arguments:

- **lookup_value** is the value that **LOOKUP** searches for in the first vector

- **lookup_vector** is the range that contains only one row or one column

- **[result_vector]** is optional – if ignored, **lookup_vector** is used – this is where the result will come from and must contain the same number of cells as the **lookup_vector**.

Like the default versions of **HLOOKUP** and **VLOOKUP**, **lookup_value** must be located in a range of ascending values.

Let me demonstrate with an example:

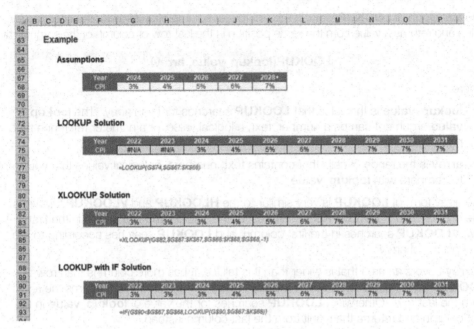

LOOKUP is a great function to use with time series analysis / forecasting. Dates are in ascending order and the **LOOKUP** syntax is remarkably simple. As a modeller, I use it regularly when I am modelling many more forecast periods than I want assumption periods.

Here, you can see I carry assumptions only for 2024 until 2028 (the final value is 2028, just with a "+" in number formatting). The formula

=LOOKUP(G$74,$G$67:$K$68)

returns the corresponding value for the period that is either an exact match or else the largest value less than or equal to the **lookup_value**. **LOOKUP** uses the top row of the table for looking up its data and the final row for returning the corresponding value. Simple. As for **XLOOKUP**:

= XLOOKUP(G$82,$G$67:$K$67,$G$68:$K$68,$G$68,-1)

This formula is longer and requires three additional arguments (the **if_not_found** argument must be populated such that earlier periods do not return an error and **match_mode** -1 is required to mirror the behaviour of **LOOKUP**). Although an **IF** statement is required to ensure no errors for earlier periods when using **LOOKUP**, *e.g.*

=IF(G$90<$G$67,$G$68,LOOKUP(G$90,$G$67:$K$68))

it may be argued that **LOOKUP** is a simpler function to use here than its counterpart.

This isn't the only time **LOOKUP** outperforms **XLOOKUP**:

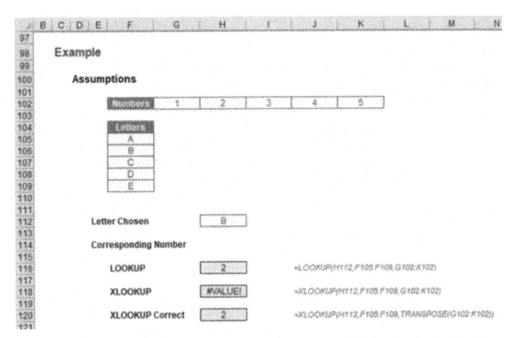

Here, we do see a limitation of **XLOOKUP**. Whilst the third argument of **XLOOKUP**, **return_array**, does not need to be a vector, it cannot be the transposition of the **lookup_array**. You would have to transpose it using the **TRANSPOSE** function, for example. This makes **LOOKUP** much easier to use – compare:

> **=LOOKUP(H112,F105:F109,G102:K102)**

with

> **=XLOOKUP(H112,F105:F109,TRANSPOSE(G102:K102))**

In this instance, **LOOKUP** wins.

Useful Features of XLOOKUP

XLOOKUP can be used to perform a two-way match, similar to **INDEX MATCH MATCH**:

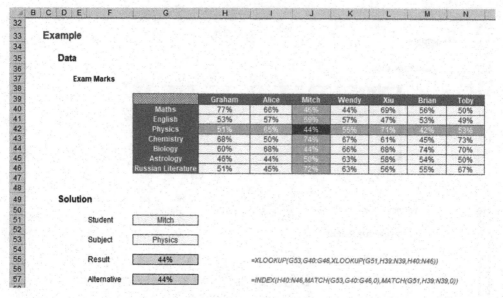

Many advanced users might use the formula

=INDEX(H40:N46,MATCH(G53,G40:G46,0),MATCH(G51,H39:N39,0))

where:

- **INDEX(array, row_number, [column_number])** returns a value or the reference to a value from within a table or range (list) citing the **row_number** and the **column_number**

- **MATCH(lookup_value, lookup_vector, [match_type])** returns the relative position of an item in an array that (approximately) matches a specified value. It's most commonly used with **match_type** zero [0], which requires an exact match.

Therefore, this formula finds the position in the row for the student and the position in the column of the subject. The intersection of these two provides the required result.

XLOOKUP does it differently:

=XLOOKUP(G53,G40:G46,XLOOKUP(G51,H39:N39,H40:N46))

Welcome to the wonderful world of the *nested* **XLOOKUP** function! Here, the internal formula

=XLOOKUP(G51,H39:N39,H40:N46)

demonstrates a key difference between this and your typical lookup function – the first argument is a cell, the second argument is a column vector and the third is an array – with, most importantly, the same number of rows as the **lookup_array**. This means it returns a column vector of data, not a single value. This is great news in the brave new world of dynamic arrays.

In essence, this means the formula resolves to

=XLOOKUP(G53,G40:G46,J40:J46)

as **J40:J46** is the resultant vector of **=XLOOKUP(G51,H39:N39,H40:N46)**. This is a really powerful – and virtually new – concept to get your head around, that admittedly **SUMPRODUCT** exploits too. Once you understand this, it's clear how this formula works and opens your eyes to the power of nested **XLOOKUP** functions.

I can't believe I am talking about the virtues of nested functions here! Let me change the subject quickly…

I will cover dynamic arrays in detail later, but here, I will whet your appetite! To show you how dynamic arrays can make the most of being able to create resultant vectors, consider the following example:

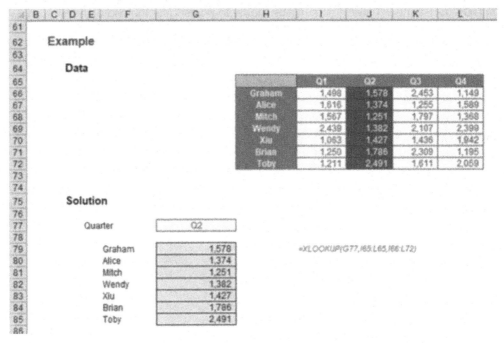

The formula

=XLOOKUP(G77,I65:L65,I66:L72)

again, resolves to a vector – but this time is allowed to spill as a dynamic array.

Once you start playing with the dynamic range side, you can start to get imaginative. For example:

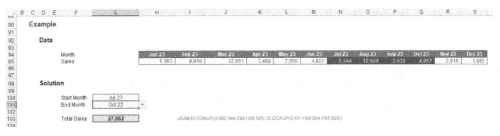

In this illustration, I want to calculate the sales between two periods:

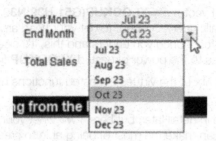

This might seem like a simple drop-down list using data validation (**ALT + D + L**), but **XLOOKUP** has been used in determining the list to be used for the end months.

Let me explain. I have hidden the range of relevant dates in cell **H101** spilled across

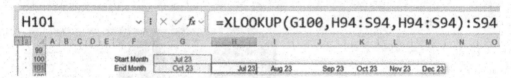

XLOOKUP can return a reference, so the formula

=XLOOKUP(G100,H94:S94,H94:S94):S94

evaluates to the row vector **N94:S94** (since the start month is July). This spilled dynamic array formula is then referenced in the data validation:

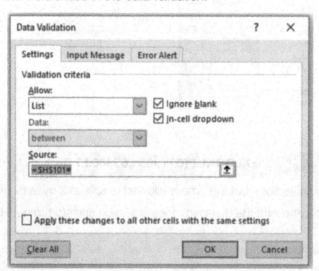

(**$H$101#** means the spilled range starting in cell **H101** – we will look in detail at how to reference dynamic arrays later.) It should be noted that the formula **=XLOOKUP(G100,H94:S94,H94:S94):S94** may not be used directly in the 'Data Validation' dialog, but this is a neat trick to ensure you cannot select an end month before the start month (assuming you are a rational human being that selects the start before the end!).

The formula to sum the sales then is

=SUM(XLOOKUP(G100,H94:S94,H95:S95):XLOOKUP(G101,H94:S94,H95:S95))

Again, this uses the fact **XLOOKUP** can return a reference, so this formula equates to

=SUM(N95:Q95)

Easy! Now I am combining two **XLOOKUP** formulae with a colon (:) to form a range. This joins other illustrious functions used this way such as **CHOOSE**, **IF**, **IFS**, **INDEX**, **INDIRECT**, **OFFSET, SINGLE (@)**, **SWITCH** and **TEXT**. First nesting, now joining – what's next?

Partial and Exact Matching

Seeking partial matches (sounds like an unfussy dating agency!) suddenly became a lot easier too. You can use wildcards if you want to – just set the **match_mode** to 2:

	B	C	D	E	F	G	H	I	J	K	L
168											
169		**Example**									
170											
171			**Data**								
172											
173							Item	Amount			
174							John	1			
175							Jon	2			
176							Jonathan	4			
177							Jonathon	8			
178							Johnny	16			
179							Jonny	32			
180											
181											
182			**Solution**								
183											
184					Selection	J?n*n*					
185											
186					First Result	4		=XLOOKUP(G184,H174:H179,I174:I179,,2)			
187											
188					Last Result	32		=XLOOKUP(G184,H174:H179,I174:I179,,2,-1)			
189											

Here, I am searching for **J?n*n*** - which is fine as long as you know what the wildcard characters mean:

- **?** means "any character", but just one character. If you wanted to make space for two and only two characters you would use **??**

- ***** means "any number of characters" – including zero.

For example, **M?n*m*** would identify "Manmade", "minimum" and "Manikum" but would not accept "millennium". Here, our formulae

=XLOOKUP(G184,H174:H179,I174:I179,,2)
=XLOOKUP(G184,H174:H179,I174:I179,,2,-1)

would locate the first and last items that satisfied the condition **J?n*n*** (*i.e.* "Jonathan" and "Jonny" respectively).

But what if you wanted an exact match with case sensitivity? You just have to think a little bit outside of the proverbial box:

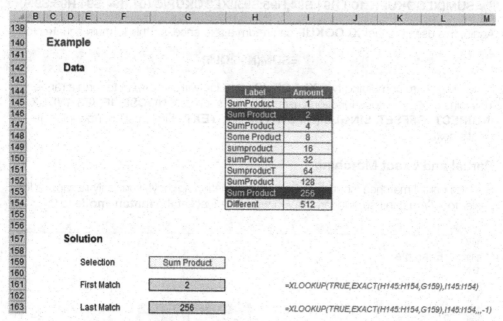

Here, we use another feature of **XLOOKUP** – its ability to search a virtual vector, *i.e.* one that has been constructed in memory, rather than physically within the spreadsheet cells. Consider the formula

=XLOOKUP(TRUE,EXACT(H145:H154,G159),I145:I154)

Here, the interim calculation **=EXACT(H145:H154,G159)**, looks at the range **H145:H154** and deduces whether the cells are an exact match for the selection 'Sum Product' in cell **G159**. The **EXACT** function would evaluate as

{FALSE; TRUE; FALSE; FALSE; FALSE; FALSE; FALSE; FALSE; TRUE; FALSE}

Therefore, the formula coerces to

=XLOOKUP(TRUE,{FALSE; TRUE; FALSE; FALSE; FALSE; FALSE; FALSE; FALSE; TRUE; FALSE},I145:I154)

and then the formula becomes simple to understand.

XMATCH

However, **XLOOKUP** did not land in isolation. In addition to **XLOOKUP**, **XMATCH** has arrived with a similar signature to **XLOOKUP**, but instead it returns the index (position) of the matching item. **XMATCH** is both easier to use and more capable than its predecessor **MATCH**.

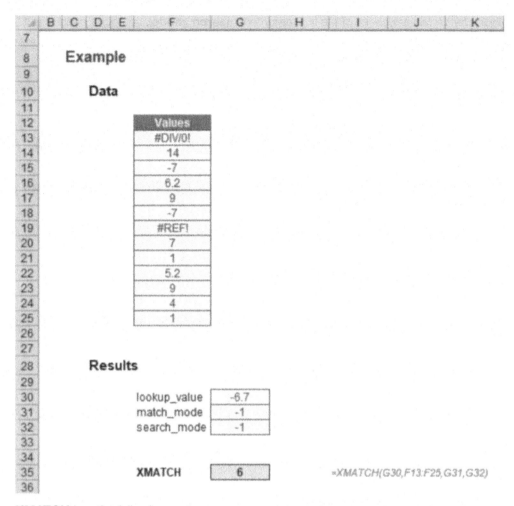

XMATCH has the following syntax:

> **XMATCH(lookup_value, lookup_array, [match_mode], [search_mode])**

where:

- **lookup_value:** this is required and defines what value you want to look up

- **lookup_array:** this reference is required and is the array (or vector) you are referencing to look up **lookup_value**

- **match_mode:** this argument is optional. There are four choices:

    - **0:** exact match (default)

    - **-1:** exact match or else the largest value less than or equal to **lookup_value**

    - **1:** exact match or else smallest value greater than or equal to **lookup_value**

    - **2:** wildcard match. You should use the special character **?** to match any character and ***** to match any run of characters.

Again, for certain selections of the final argument (**search_mode**), you <u>don't</u> need to put your data in alphanumerical order

- **search_mode:** this argument is also optional. There are again four choices:
    - **1:** search first to last (default)
    - **-1:** search last to first
    - **2:** this is a binary search, first to last (requires **lookup_array** to be sorted)
    - **-2:** another binary search, this time last to first (and again, this requires **lookup_array** to be sorted).

As you can see, it's a fairly straightforward addition to the **MATCH** family. It acts similarly to **MATCH** – just with heaps more functionality.

CHAPTER 1.11: CHOOSE

Do you choose to use **CHOOSE**? Certainly, it is a function used in modelling, but perhaps it is not used as regularly as some of the others discussed. This is useful for non-contiguous references:

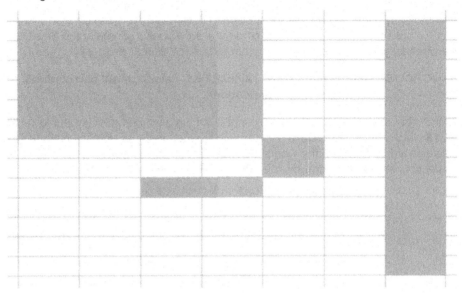

Just so that we are clear on jargon: a **non-contiguous** range (with reference to Excel) means a range that cannot be highlighted with the mouse alone. In the image above, to highlight the cells coloured you would have to press down the **CTRL** key as well.

INDEX, **LOOKUP**, **VLOOKUP** and **HLOOKUP** all require contiguous references. They refer to lists, row vectors, column vectors and / or arrays. **CHOOSE** is different:

=CHOOSE(index_num, value1, [value2]…)

This function requires an index number, **index_num**, to make a selection out of the ensuing list **value1**, **value2**, … and so on. The values may be numbers, cell references, defined names, formulae, functions or text. There is a restriction on the number of items in the list though: 254 (Excel 2007 onwards) or 29 (Excel 2003 and earlier). The **index_num** argument has to be a number between one [1] and one less than the total number of arguments, otherwise you can expect an #*VALUE!* error. It should be noted that **index_num** rounds down if it is not an integer.

This function allows references to different calculations, workbook / worksheet references, *etc*. Try to use the function appropriately. For instance, a well-known Excel website proposes the following formula for calculating the US Thanksgiving date. Assuming cell **A1** has the year:

=DATE(A1,11,CHOOSE(WEEKDAY(DATE(A1,11,1)),26,25,24,23,22,28,27))

To understand this formula, note that **DATE(year, month, day)** returns a date and **WEEKDAY(date)** returns a number 1 (Sunday) through 7 (Saturday). But doesn't this formula look horrible? It is full of hard code, and it contains an unnecessary number of arguments. The formula could exclude **CHOOSE** *viz.*

> **=DATE(A1,11,28-MOD(WEEKDAY(DATE(A1,11,1))+1,7))**

Now let me be clear here. I am not saying this is a simple, transparent formula (I am going to discuss **MOD** shortly). Test it. They both provide the same answer. **CHOOSE** – and plenty of additional hard code – has been used unnecessarily.

That's not to say there isn't a time and a place for **CHOOSE**. It is useful when you need to refer to cells on different worksheets or in other workbooks. Some argue that it is useful when a calculation needs to be computed using different methods, *e.g.*

> **=CHOOSE(selection_number, calculation1, calculation2, calculation3, calculation4, ...)**

I disagree. Let me explain. In the example below, I have created a lookup table in cells **E10:E13** which I have called **Data** (I will explain how to create range names later). The calculations are all visible on the worksheet, rather than hidden away in the Formula bar. The selection, **selection_number**, is input in cell **E2**. The result?

| E4 | ⌄ | ⋮ | ✕ ✓ *fx* ⌄ | =INDEX(Data,Selection_Number) |

◢	A	B	C	D	E	F
1						
2				**Selection**	3	
3						
4				**Result**	88	
5						
6						
7				*Calculations*		
8						
9					Data	
10				**Calculation 1**	17	
11				**Calculation 2**	94	
12				**Calculation 3**	88	
13				**Calculation 4**	53	
14						
15						

It's identical, but easier to follow

> **=INDEX(Data,Selection_Number)**

I have taught financial modelling to many gifted analysts over the years and a common mistake made by many is that they build models that are easy to build rather than *models that are easy to understand*. The end user is the customer. It should be simple to use: taking shortcuts invariably only helps the modeller – and even then, more often than not, shortcuts will backfire.

CHOOSE can lead to opaque models that need to be rebuilt and are often less flexible to use. You have been warned!

CHAPTER 1.12: OFFSET

The older I get, the more invaluable **OFFSET** becomes. The syntax for **OFFSET** is as follows:

OFFSET(reference, rows, columns, [height], [width]).

The arguments in square brackets (**height** and **width**) can be omitted from the formula (they both have a default value of 1 which is explained further below).

In its most basic form, **OFFSET(ref, x, y)** will select a reference **x** rows down (**-x** would be **x** rows up) and **y** columns to the right (**-y** would be **y** columns to the left) of the reference **ref**. For example, consider the following grid:

	A	B	C	D	E	F
1	1	2	3	4	5	6
2	7	8	9	10	11	12
3	13	14	15	16	17	18
4	19	20	21	22	23	24
5	25	26	27	28	29	30
6	31	32	33	34	35	36

OFFSET(A1,2,3) would take us two rows down and three columns across to cell **D3**. Therefore, **OFFSET(A1,2,3)** = 16, *viz.*

	A	B	C	D	E	F
1	1	2	3	4	5	6
2	7	8	9	10	11	12
3	13	14	15	16	17	18
4	19	20	21	22	23	24
5	25	26	27	28	29	30
6	31	32	33	34	35	36

OFFSET(D4,-1,-2) would take us one row up and two columns to the left, returning cell **B3**. Therefore, **OFFSET(D4,-1,-2)** = 14, *viz.*

	A	B	C	D	E	F
1	1	2	3	4	5	6
2	7	8	9	10	11	12
3	13	14	15	16	17	18
4	19	20	21	22	23	24
5	25	26	27	28	29	30
6	31	32	33	34	35	36

We can use these mechanics to construct a very simple scenario table:

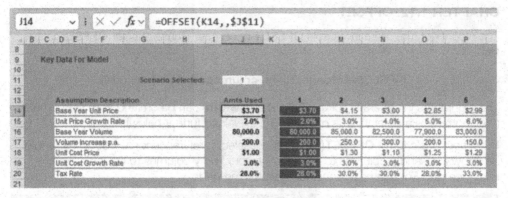

Essentially, the assumptions used in this illustration are linked from cells **J14:J20** (in yellow). These values are drawn from the scenario table to the right of the highlighted yellow range (*e.g.* cells **L14:L20** constitute Scenario 1, cells **M14:M20** constitute Scenario 2).

The Scenario Selector is located in cell **J11**. Using **OFFSET** scenarios may be selected at will. For example, the formula in cell **J14** is simply **OFFSET(K14,,$J$11)**, that is, start at cell **K14** and displace zero rows down and the value in **J11** columns across. In the image above, the formula locates the cell one column to the right, which is Scenario 1.

The advantage of **OFFSET** over other functions such as **INDEX**, **CHOOSE** and **LOOKUP** is that the range of data can be added to. Whilst the other functions require a specified range, with **OFFSET** we can keep adding scenarios without changing the formula / making the model inefficient.

Furthermore, **OFFSET** has other practical uses in Excel, taking advantage of the **height** and **width** arguments. Consider the **OFFSET** example from earlier. If we extend the formula to **OFFSET(D4,-1,-2,-2,3)**, it would again take us to cell **B3** but then we would select a range based on the **height** and **width** parameters. The **height** would be two rows going up the sheet, with row 14 as the base (*i.e.* rows 13 and 14), and the **width** would be three columns going from left to right, with column **B** as the base (*i.e.* columns **B**, **C** and **D**).

Hence **OFFSET(D4,-1,-2,-2,3)** would select the range **B2:D3**, *viz.*

	A	B	C	D	E	F
1	1	2	3	4	5	6
2	7	8	9	10	11	12
3	13	(14)	15	16	17	18
4	19	20	21	(22)	23	24
5	25	26	27	28	29	30
6	31	32	33	34	35	36

Note that **OFFSET(D4,-1,-2,-2,3)** equals *#VALUE!* in legacy Excel as it cannot display a matrix in one cell, but it does recognise it, as evidenced in Excel 365 where it will spill as a dynamic array. Dynamic arrays are something of a prerequisite for this book, but if you do find yourself using **OFFSET** in earlier versions of Excel, help is at hand. If it does not display, after typing in **OFFSET(D4,-1,-2,-2,3)** we press **CTRL + SHIFT + ENTER**, we turn the formula into an array formula: **{OFFSET(D4,-1,-2,-2,3)}** (do not type the braces in, they will appear automatically as part of the Excel syntax). This gives a value of 8, which is the value in the top left-hand corner of the matrix, *but even the earlier versions of Excel are storing more than that*. This can be seen as follows:

- **SUM(OFFSET(D4,-1,-2,-2,3))** = 72 (*i.e.* **SUM(B2:D3)**)

- **AVERAGE(OFFSET(D4,-1,-2,-2,3))** = 12 (*i.e.* **AVERAGE(B2:D3)**).

Indeed, you may construct a simple depreciation calculation or transpose references using **OFFSET**'s **height** and **width** functionalities. But more on that later…

There are a couple of problems with **OFFSET**:

- Values returned by an **OFFSET** function confuse Excel. Only the original **reference** is recognised as a precedent reference to the formula by Excel's auditing tools.

- The result returned is most likely to come from another cell which will not be highlighted by this technique. If you think about it, this actually makes sense as potentially all of the cells on a worksheet are potential precedents.

- To take account of this, I suggest you give the **reference** a **range name**. Range names are discussed in detail later in this book, but for now to name a cell, click on the cell and then type the desired name in the 'Name box' in Excel:

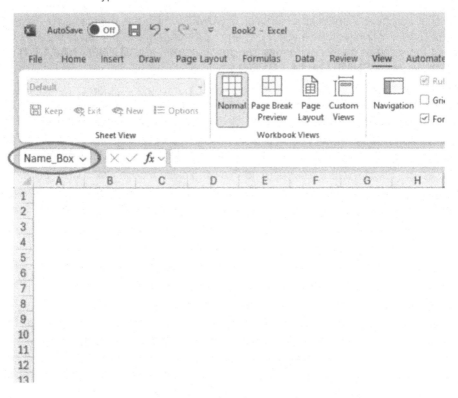

- This range name should start with **BC_**. This prefix stands for "Base Cell" and makes it easier to sort / locate range names later. When users or model auditors alike inspect a formula with a **Reference** starting with **BC_** for **B**ase **C**ell (*e.g.* **BC_ Example_Reference**), this can alert them to the fact that the model may be using cells in the region of this **Reference** that do not appear to have any dependents.

- The other issue is that **OFFSET** is what is known as a **volatile** function. A volatile function is one that causes recalculation of the formula in the cell where it resides every time Excel recalculates. This can really slow down your model if there are too many **OFFSET** functions, for example.

Aside: Volatile Functions

As stated above, a **volatile function** is one that causes recalculation of the formula in the cell where it resides every time Excel recalculates. This occurs regardless of whether precedent cells / calculations have changed, or whether the formula also contains non-volatile functions. One test to check whether your workbook is volatile is to close a file after saving and see if Excel prompts you to save it a second time (this is an indicative test only). This can really slow down your model.

Just because a function is volatile in one version of Excel does not mean it is volatile in all versions. Perhaps the best example of this is **INDEX**, which was volatile prior to Excel 97. Microsoft still states this function is volatile, but this does not appear to be the case except when used as the second part of a range reference, for example **$A$1:INDEX($A$2:A$10,4)**, will also cause the reference to be flagged as "dirty" (*i.e.* needs to be recalculated) when the workbook is opened only.

Another common 'semi-volatile' function is **SUMIF**, which has been so since Excel 2002. This function becomes volatile whenever the size of the first range argument is not the same as the second (**sum_range**) argument, *e.g.* **SUMIF(A1:A4,1,B1)** is volatile whereas **SUMIF(A1:A4,1,B1:B4)** is not.

IF and **CHOOSE** do not calculate all arguments, but if any of the arguments are volatile – regardless of whether they are used – the formula is deemed to be volatile. Therefore, **IF(1>0,1,RAND())** is always volatile, even though the **value_if_false** argument will never be calculated. It is not quite as simple as this though. If the formula in cell **A1** is **=NOW()** then this cell will be volatile, but **IF(1>0,1,A1)** will not be.

In essence, direct references or dependents of volatile functions will always be recalculated, whereas indirect ones will only recalculate when activated or in certain other functions that always calculate all arguments such as **AND** and **OR**.

CHAPTER 1.13: MOD

Does **MOD** cause division amongst the financial modelling community? Well, the [bad] jokes keep coming I'm afraid. The **MOD** function, **MOD(number, divisor)**, returns the remainder after the **number** (first argument) is divided by the **divisor** (second argument). The result has the same sign as the **divisor**.

For example, 9 / 4 = 2.25, or 2 remainder 1. **MOD(9,4)** is an alternative way of expressing this, and hence equals 1 also. Note that the 1 may be obtained from the first calculation by (2.25 - 2) x 4 = 1, i.e. in general:

$$\textbf{MOD(n,d) = n - d*INT(n/d),}$$

where **INT()** is the integer function in Excel.

This function has various uses and I provide three common examples below:

1. **Obtaining "residuals":** In some instances in modelling, you need the integer part of a number, *e.g.* how many payments fall between two dates may calculate as 9.94 – but that's nonsense. In this instance, you would have only made nine payments, *i.e.* **INT(9.94)**.

   Similarly, you might want to accrue the fee for payments not yet made. Using **MOD(9.94,1)** = 0.94, *i.e.* the number after the decimal place. Note that **9.94 - INT(9.94)** gives the same result here; the **MOD** approach is simply shorter.

2. **Calculations at regular time intervals:** Consider tax payments as an example. Many companies make tax payments quarterly (*i.e.* once every three months). If we assume these payments are made in March, June, September and December then we can formulate the payment as **IF(MOD(Month_Number,3)=0,Make_ Payment,0)**, *etc.*

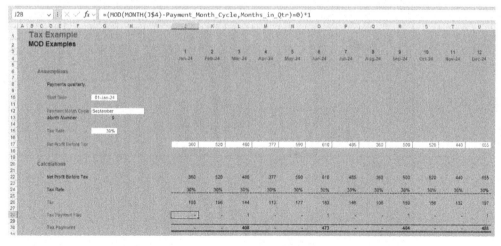

3. **Summing every nth row:** It is not uncommon for users to want to sum every **n**th cell (*e.g.* second, third, fourth,...) in a spreadsheet. Excel has no standard function which will do this, but **MOD** can come to the rescue. For example, the array formula (working in all versions of Excel)

$$\textbf{\{=SUM(IF(MOD(\$E\$19:\$E\$48,\$G\$13)=0,\$F\$19:\$F\$48,0))\}}$$

was used in cell **H53** in the following example:

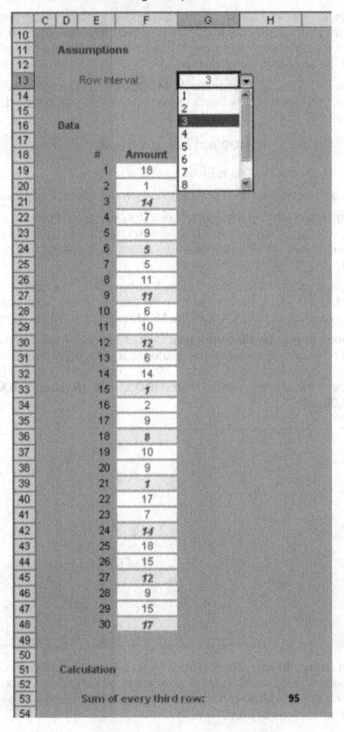

Arrays using large ranges can cause calculations to slow down considerably. This is why I used a counter rather than the volatile **ROW()** function (as a reminder, volatile functions calculate each time you press **ENTER** or **F9**).

If accuracy is vital, be careful with **MOD** as it may give very slightly erroneous results:

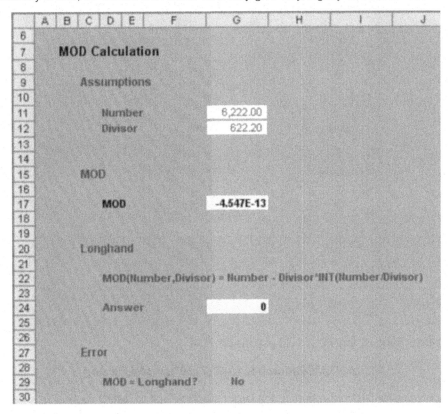

The result for **MOD** in cell **G17** might seem inconsequential, but imagine you were making calculations based on **MOD(number, divisor)=0**. In this case **MOD** would not equal zero and the calculation would not work.

This issue tends to occur more commonly when working with non-integers.

The problem here isn't really **MOD**. Calculations are performed in binary [1,0] format and most floating-point numbers have no exact binary representation (just as 1/3 has no exact decimal representation). In this instance, 10 times the binary approximation to 622.2 is

6222.0000000000004547....

i.e. you may need to use the **ROUND(number, num_digits)** as part of your formula too in order to round your **number** to **num_digits** number of digits (after the decimal point).

Another weird anomaly is if the number is 134,217,728 (2²⁷) times greater or more than the divisor this gives rise to an *#NUM!* error *viz.*

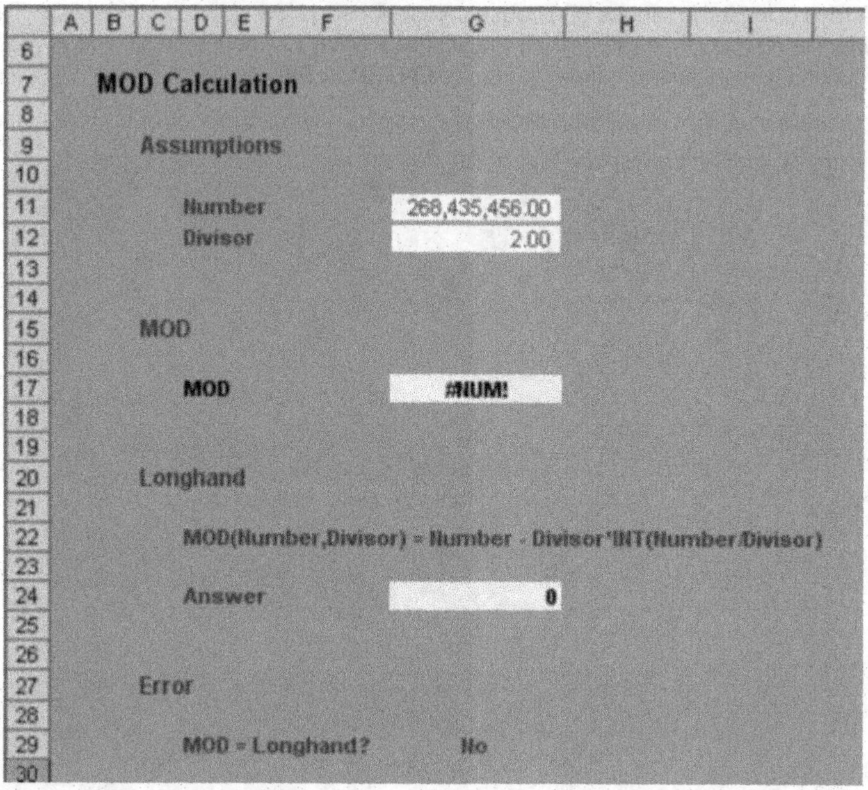

	A	B	C	D	E	F	G	H	I
6									
7	**MOD Calculation**								
8									
9			Assumptions						
10									
11			Number				268,435,456.00		
12			Divisor				2.00		
13									
14									
15		MOD							
16									
17			**MOD**				#NUM!		
18									
19									
20		Longhand							
21									
22			MOD(Number,Divisor) = Number - Divisor*INT(Number/Divisor)						
23									
24			Answer				0		
25									
26									
27		Error							
28									
29			MOD = Longhand?				No		
30									

Some texts suggest that you could use the formula

=MOD(MOD(number,134217728*divisor),divisor)

This will solve for larger numbers much larger than the limit for **MOD**, but theoretically will hit the same problem when the number being evaluated reaches 134,217,728*134,217,728***divisor**. For most uses, this limit is large enough that it will never be reached, but I suggest sticking with Microsoft's recommended solution which is calculating the "long handed" result as illustrated above (cell **G24**).

Also, when using the **MOD** function with one negative number and the expected result is the numerator, **MOD(9,-10)** actually returns -1, whereas you could argue the correct result should be 9:

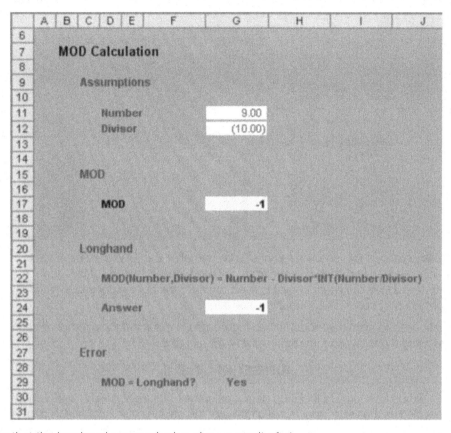

Note that the longhand approach also gives a result of -1.

Microsoft explains that this approach has been taken deliberately in order to be consistent with the dBase MOD function. If you always need **MOD** to deliver a value of **x** where $0 \leq$ **x** < divisor, then use the adjusted formula:

=IF(MOD(number, divisor)<0,ABS(divisor)+MOD(number, divisor)).

Common Example with MOD and OFFSET

Now that I have explained **MOD**, I can show you a really good use of this function for a situation which causes many working in finance plenty of consternation. The solution works in conjunction with **OFFSET**, which I have just explained but reiterate below. For those that skipped that section, the syntax of **OFFSET** is as follows:

OFFSET(reference, rows, columns, [height], [width]).

The arguments in square brackets (**height** and **width**) can be omitted from the formula in this instance. In its most basic form, **OFFSET(reference, x, y)** will select a **reference x** rows down (**-x** would be **x** rows up) and **y** columns to the right (**-y** would be **y** columns to the left).

Imagine you have set up a scenario table in Excel to determine which inputs should be used in your model (*i.e.* "what-if? Analysis"):

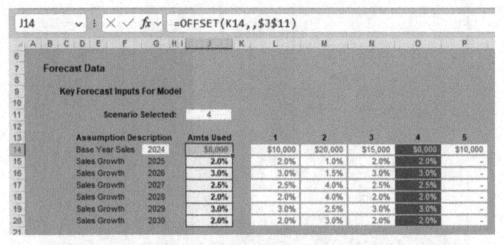

This method allows for various scenarios to be modelled easily with a different set of input data inserted into each column (from column **L** onwards in this illustration). A selector (cell **J11** in the figure above) is used to select the active scenario, which may be highlighted using conditional formatting (see later).

The data used to drive the model is then highlighted in column **J** (here, emphasised in yellow) using the following formula in cell **J14** for example:

=OFFSET(K14,,$J$11)

In other words, this formula looks up data **x** columns to the right of column **K**, where **x** is specified as the value input in cell **J11** (here, this value is 4 so column **O**'s data is selected).

Clearly, using a columnar approach here makes it very straightforward to set the various scenarios out. However, most financial models are displayed with dates going from left to right across columns rather than down the page using rows. This requires us to transpose the data, and again we may use **OFFSET** to 'flip' the data:

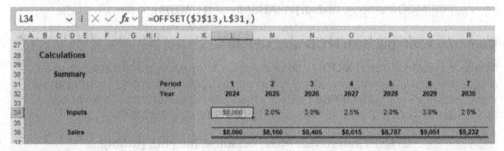

Here, the period numbers specified in row 31 make it easy for us to transpose the data. For example, the formula in cell **L34** would be:

=OFFSET($J$13,L$31,)

i.e. insert the data **x** rows down from cell **J13** in the first graphic, where **x** is again specified as the value input in cell **J11**.

64

Take care, however, if using an amount followed by growth rates approach for forecast / budget data. The amounts using these examples should be as follows:

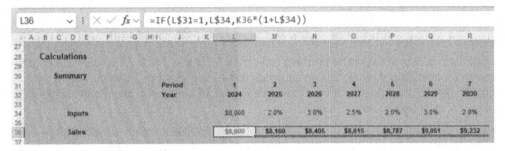

The correct formula here is:

$$\text{=IF(L\$31=1,L\$34,K36*(1+L\$34))}$$

for cell **L36** (say), *i.e.* if it is the first period take the amount, otherwise take the amount calculated in the preceding period and multiply it by (1 + growth rate specified in the current period, <u>not</u> the next period).

When actual data is input into a model, frequently it replaces the original information, and therefore management loses the ability to see how accurate forecasts were originally and how budgeting may be improved. One way round this would be to simply have "Actuals" as one of the scenarios so that all forecasts are retained. This is often all that is required, and if so, simply do that – Keep It Simple Stupid (KISS).

However, often we may wish to undertake variance analysis by comparing actual data with the original budgeted information. In this case, I would suggest the following approach.

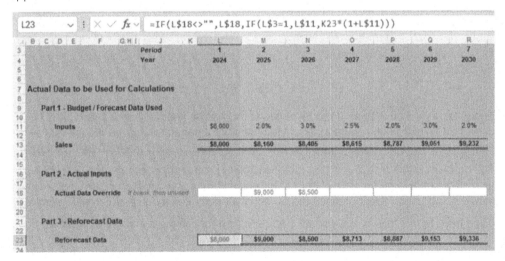

Rows 9 to 13 of this illustration simply reiterate the calculations already detailed above regarding the original forecasting. Note row 18 however: this is where actual data is added instead. In my example, I simply use hard coded inputs for my data, but it only requires a simple variation to this methodology to revise growth rates, *etc.*

Using my logic, we simply use actual data where it is available; otherwise, we fall back on the original data and calculations. This is achieved by the formula in row 23 in my example, which is (for cell **L23**):

> **=IF(L$18<>"",L$18,IF(L$3=1,L$11,K23*(1+L$11)))**,

i.e. if there is data in the corresponding cell in row 18 use it; if not, if it is the first period take the original input value, otherwise simply inflate the prior period amount by (1 + growth rate for that period). It may include a nested **IF** statement, but it is still a relatively simple and straightforward calculation.

Performing the calculations is only half of the battle. Modellers often have difficulty comparing the original outputs with the reforecast counterparts in an effective and efficient manner. If sufficient, the following would be relatively straight forward:

				Counter	1	2	3	4	5	6	7
Simple Outputs Example				Year	2024	2025	2026	2027	2028	2029	2030
					$	$	$	$	$	$	$
Simple Outputs Example											
Sales											
Budget					$8,000	$8,160	$8,405	$8,615	$8,787	$9,051	$9,232
Act. / Refcast					$8,000	$9,000	$8,500	$8,713	$8,887	$9,153	$9,336
Variance	Favourable / (Unfavourable)				-	$840	$95	$98	$100	$103	$105

This is very easy to put together, but alas, more often than not, the following presentation is required by senior management instead:

			Counter	1	2	3	4	5	6	7	8	9	10
Bad Outputs Example			Year	2024	2024	2024	2025	2025	2025	2026	2026	2026	2027
			Description	Budget	Act / Refcast	Variance	Budget	Act / Refcast	Variance	Budget	Act / Refcast	Variance	Budget
Bad Outputs Example													
Sales				$8,000	$8,000	-	$8,160	$9,000	$840	$8,405	$8,500	$95	$8,615

Seem familiar? I have been a model reviewer for many a year and seen this type of output on an extremely regular basis. Many senior management teams like it this way and it is not my role to challenge the status quo – it doesn't stop me from trying though!

The problem with this layout is that it lends itself to promoting poor practice. Modellers tend to create a large number of unique formulae across a row, which in turn slows down model construction and increases the potential for mistakes, such as referencing errors.

If you have to use this layout, consider first creating the simple summary elsewhere:

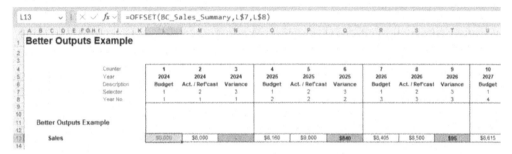

Part 4 - Summary									
	Year No.		1	2	3	4	5	6	7
	Budget		$8,000	$8,160	$8,405	$8,615	$8,787	$9,051	$9,232
	Act. / Ref'cast		$8,000	$9,000	$8,500	$8,713	$8,837	$9,153	$9,336
	Variance		-	$840	$95	$98	$100	$103	$105

Look carefully at this graphic. The shading in cell **K28** above may appear innocuous, but it is the most important cell on the worksheet and has been named **BC_Sales_Summary** accordingly (**BC** means "Base Cell" for an **OFFSET** function). Consider:

- For every column moved to the right, the cursor is in a different year. One column across is Year 1, two columns across is Year 2 and so on

- For every row moved down, the cursor reports a different figure. One row down is the Budget data, two rows down is the Actual / Reforecast data, and three rows down is the Variance. The depth of this table (three rows) has been defined as **List_Depth** so that it may be used in formulae.

Now, if we return to the outputs worksheet and modify it slightly by inserting two additional lines. Using the **OFFSET** function once more may make your potential troubles a thing of the past, *viz.*

L13   =OFFSET(BC_Sales_Summary,L$7,L$8)

Better Outputs Example

	Counter	1	2	3	4	5	6	7	8	9	10
	Year	2024	2024	2024	2025	2025	2025	2026	2026	2026	2027
	Description	Budget	Act. / Ref'cast	Variance	Budget	Act. / Ref'cast	Variance	Budget	Act. / Ref'cast	Variance	Budget
	Selector	1	2	3	1	2	3	1	2	3	1
	Year No.	1	1	1	2	2	2	3	3	3	4
Better Outputs Example											
Sales		$8,000	$8,000		$8,160	$9,000	$840	$8,405	$8,500	$95	$8,615

You will see that each row of the revised output example contains only one unique formula copied across, making it easy to edit, extend and review. This is achieved by adding two rows:

- **Selector (row 7):** identifies whether the column should be reporting the budget information, the actual data or the variance. The equation used makes use of the **MOD** function:

$$=MOD(L\$4-1,List\_Depth)+1$$

As stated above, **List_Depth** is the number of selections (Budget, Act / Ref'cast, Variance) permissible – in this case three. **=MOD(L$4,List_Depth)** takes the counter and converts each one to 1, 2 and zero (i.e. the remainder upon dividing the counter by three). By subtracting one inside the **MOD** function and adding it once more outside, this simply forces a zero to a three instead, so that the Selector reports the values 1, 2 and 3 alternately.

- **Year No. (row 8):** simply notes which year the column is reporting using the formula:

=IF(L$7=1,K8+1,K8),

i.e. the year increases in the column that the counter in row 7 equals 1 (in this example).

Therefore, in my example, row 13 requires a very simple formula to generate the required outputs:

=OFFSET(BC_Sales_Summary,L$7,L$8).

For example, cell **Q13** equals **OFFSET(BC_Sales_Summary,3,2)**, which would refer to the Year 2 Variance figure of $840.

Easy!

CHAPTER 1.14: EOMONTH and EDATE

Dates are commonplace in models and usually run across one of the top rows in an Excel worksheet as part of a time series analysis:

In this example, a monthly model has been constructed starting in July 2024. The dates in cells **J5** onwards are formatted to show only the month and year. This can be performed easily by selecting the date (here, 31 July 2024) and then formatting the cell (**CTRL + 1**).

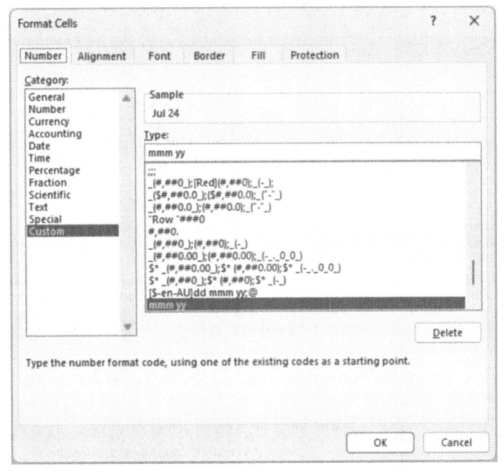

More interestingly, if the General category were to be selected instead, we note that the Sample (circled in red) would be displayed as follows.

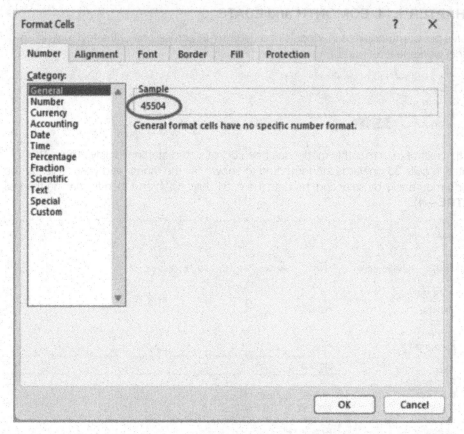

In other words, 31 July 2024 is no more than a number: 45,504. Microsoft Excel for Windows supports what is called the 1900 date system. This means that 1 January 1900 is considered to be day 1 by Excel, 2 January 1900 is day 2 and so on.

Extrapolating, 31 July 2024 would be day 45,503 (not 45,504). The reason that the 1900 date system views it as one day later is because this system considers 1900 to be a leap year – which it wasn't! Years ending in '00' have to be divisible by 400 to be a leap year, so 1 March 1900 in this system was day 61 rather than day 60.

Most modellers are not concerned about how the days are numbered as long as Excel calculates correctly. However, early Macintosh computers used a different start date to prevent issues with the 1900 leap year and used 1 January 1904 as the start date. This is known as the 1904 date system and the date values can be calculated as:

=1900 date system value - 1,462

Care has to be taken with Excel files opened on both PCs and Macs, as the date systems may vary. You can force Excel to use a particular date system as follows:

- Go to Excel Options (**ALT** + **T** + **O** is the keyboard shortcut)
- Select 'Advanced' from the left-hand column
- Scroll down to the 'When calculating this workbook' section
- Check / uncheck 'Use 1904 date system' as desired

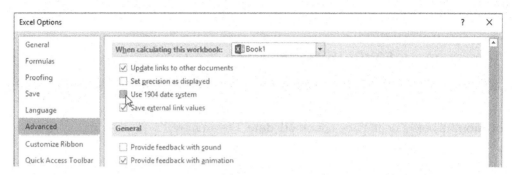

Clearly, dates are not as easy to manipulate as you might think. Extracting the day, month or even the year from any given date is not straightforward because the date is really a number known as a serial number. (If I were to delete a date, would this make me a serial killer?)

To extract the day, month or year requires making use of the following three functions:

- **DAY(serial_number)** gives the day in the date (for example, **DAY(31-Jul-24)** = 31)

- **MONTH(serial_number)** gives the month in the date (for example, **MONTH(31-Jul-24)** = 7)

- **YEAR(serial_number)** gives the year in the date (for example, **YEAR(31-Jul-24)** = 2024).

It is just as awkward the other way round. If the day, month and year are already known, the date can be calculated using the following function:

DATE(year, month, day) (for example, DATE(2024,7,32) = 1 August 2024, *etc.*).

Since dates are nothing more than serial numbers, they behave just like formatted numbers in Excel, for example, 31-Jul-24 + 128 = 6-Dec-2024.

This is all great, but time series still cause us problems. If we want to have the month end date in each column, we cannot simply take the previous month's date and add a constant to it, since the numbers of days in months vary. Fortunately, there is a function in Excel that will perform this calculation for us:

EOMONTH(specified_date, number_of_months)

The "End of month" function therefore calculates the end of the month as the **number_of_months** after the **specified_date**. For example:

- **EOMONTH(31-Jul-24,0)** = 31-Jul-24

- **EOMONTH(3-Apr-05,2)** = 30-Jun-05

- **EOMONTH(29-Feb-08,-12)** = 28-Feb-07

Although the examples use typed in dates, for it to work in Excel, it is best to have the **specified_date** either as a cell reference to a date or else use the **DATE** function to ensure that Excel understands it is a date (otherwise the formula may calculate as *#VALUE!*).

In some instances (for example, appraisal of large-scale capital infrastructure projects), the dates may need to be for the same day of the month (for example, the 15th) rather than for the month end. The **DATE** function can often be used to calculate these dates

71

– unless it is near the end of the month as problems may arise with February, April, June, September and November.

A function similar to **EOMONTH**, **EDATE** can be used instead:

EDATE(specified_date, number_of_months).

The 'Equivalent day' function therefore calculates the date that is the indicated **number_of_months** before or after the **specified_date**. For example:

- **EDATE(15-Jul-24,2)** = 15-Sep-24
- **EDATE(3-Apr-05,-2)** = 3-Feb-05
- **EDATE(29-Feb-28,-12)** = 28-Feb-27

If an equivalent date cannot be found (as in the last example), month end is used instead.

Similar to **EOMONTH**, it should be noted that although these examples also use typed-in dates, for it to work in Excel, it is best to have the **specified_date** either as a cell reference to a date or else use the **DATE** function to ensure that Excel understands it is a date (otherwise the formula may calculate as #*VALUE!*).

Certain functions are not in the 'main library' of Excel functions and will give rise to #*NAME?* errors in Excel if not recognised. Unfortunately, **EOMONTH** and **EDATE** were two such functions in Excel 2003 and earlier versions. Since you are reading a book about dynamic arrays, you can't be using one of those versions!

For those who are still using older versions of Excel, to ensure they work / are recognised correctly, the Analysis ToolPak had to be added in. To ensure it is, in all versions, use the keyboard shortcut **ALT** + **T** + **I** to load up the Add-Ins dialog box:

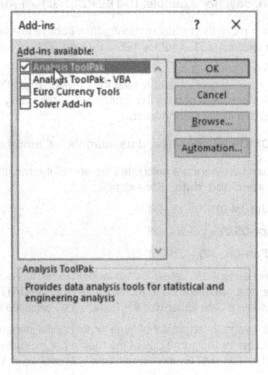

It is important that model developers and end users alike have this ToolPak added in for all versions of Excel up to and including Excel 2003, otherwise these functions will not work.

Since Excel 2007, **EOMONTH** and **EDATE** have been added to the 'standard' functions database in Excel, so it is not necessary to ensure that the Analysis ToolPak has been added in. This avoids our first common problem, but unfortunately, it sometimes causes a bigger one due to an apparent compatibility issue between Excel 2007 and earlier versions of Excel.

If Excel 2003 Analysis ToolPak functions such as **EOMONTH** or **EDATE** are used in a file created in Excel 2003 (or earlier) that is then opened in Excel 2007 (or later), the formulae that incorporate these functions may be replaced by **=#N/A** or simply *#N/A*. Some experienced users believe that if you ensure the Analysis ToolPak is switched on in Excel 2007 before you open the file (albeit in compatibility mode), the problem will be avoided, but the modelling community as a whole is not sure this is the case necessarily.

The only sure-fire way I have found to avoid this problem is to not use these functions if the file will be opened in Excel 2007 or later and earlier versions of Excel. This means that you need to find equivalent formulae that do not use Analysis ToolPak formulae.

For developers and users in this predicament you might wish to consider the following alternative formulae. For **EOMONTH(specified_date, number_of_months)** use:

=DATE(YEAR(specified_date), MONTH(specified_date)+IF(number_of_months, ROUNDDOWN(number_of_months,0),)+1,)

For **EDATE(specified_date, number_of_months)** use:

=MIN(DATE(YEAR(specified_date), MONTH(specified_ date)+ROUNDDOWN(number_of_months, 0), DAY(specified_date)), DATE(YEAR(specified_date), MONTH(specified_date)+ROUNDDOWN(number_ of_months, 0)+1, 0))

CHAPTER 1.15: MAX, MIN, LARGE and SMALL

MAX does exactly what it says on the tin – it calculates the maximum <u>value</u> in a range:

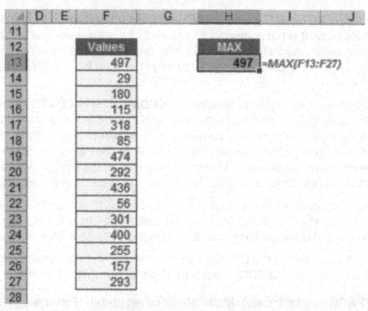

MIN works very similarly but calculates the minimum <u>value</u>. I have underlined <u>value</u> for both of these functions: in fact, all four functions only work on numerical data, so bear this in mind when trying to calculate relative ranking / sizing. Even so, modellers frequently make mistakes with **MAX** (and similar ones with **MIN**):

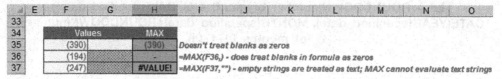

These examples highlight that you should be careful with using blanks both in the ranges and in the formulae themselves. You might notice I often omit zeros in my formulae but with **MAX** and **MIN** I will often take care to explicitly use zeros.

Later versions of Excel, such as the one you are using, have extended **MAX** and **MIN** with new functions **MAXIFS** and **MINIFS**. However, end users may see #*NAME?* errors in their spreadsheets if they are opened in earlier versions of Excel. That's not exactly ideal.

However, if you do need to create models for users of earlier versions of Excel, you can achieve a similar result combining **MAX** (or **MIN**) with **IF** in an array formula (where the curly braces are not typed but entered using **CTRL** + **SHIFT** + **ENTER** rather than **ENTER**):

{=MAX(IF(range_condition, range))}

The **range_condition** is a logical test on the **range**: it could be to test for positives, negatives, even numbers, odd numbers, *etc.*

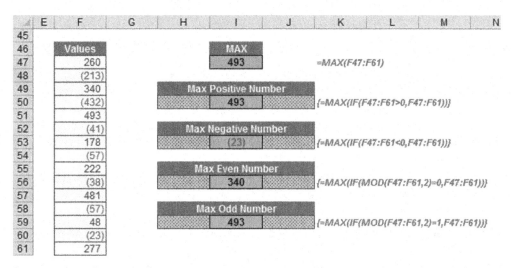

Once you get the hang of them, they are very easy to construct.

There is a highly relevant finance example combining **MAX** and **MIN** functions, namely calculating the maximum dividend allowable for a particular period. Dividends may only be paid out of what are known as distributable reserves (this is a bit of an oxymoron as dividends are also known as **distributions**). Revaluation reserves, share premium accounts, capital redemption reserves are all non-distributable. Essentially, dividends may only be paid out of the current year's Net Profit After Tax (NPAT) and the aggregation of all previous years' profits after past distributions, Retained Earnings. Dividends may not make the Balance Sheet's Total Equity become negative. This shows insolvency and this sort of distribution is illegal in most territories. Given non-distributable reserves may not become negative allow me to concentrate simply on NPAT and Retained Earnings here.

To derive the maximum dividend allowable, let me consider some scenarios. Let's imagine the following scenario:

Retained Earnings	100
NPAT	40
Maximum Dividend	**140**

It isn't rocket science that if Retained Earnings and NPAT are both positive, then the maximum dividend allowed is the sum of the two.

Retained Earnings	100
NPAT	(40)
Maximum Dividend	**60**

If NPAT is negative, but Retained Earnings are positive and exceed the NPAT figure, then the maximum dividend allowed is the net of the two figures. Should the net be negative, no dividend is allowed.

Retained Earnings	(100)
NPAT	40
Maximum Dividend	**40**

Here is the one that often surprises people. If Retained Earnings is negative but NPAT is positive, regardless of whether the net is positive or negative, the maximum dividend allowed is the NPAT amount. This may seem incomprehensible upon first thought, but it is typically dependent upon two conditions:

- The company's auditors must sign off on it. This is to ensure the company is still seen to be a going concern (*i.e.* it can still continue to operate and trade its way out of any short-term difficulties).

- The shareholders must vote for it. Almost as hilarious as when Members of Parliament solemnly vote for their 50% pay rise each year.

If you think about it some more, this makes sense. Remember, dividends cannot be paid if the company is insolvent. The auditors check to see whether the company can "afford" it for other reasons. But if you don't allow this scenario how would anyone ever attract share capital for a start-up company? A new company may have to provide for certain factors which may never come to fruition. A large non-current asset may have to be written off as not fit for purpose if a company's strategy changes without any cash consequence. Is it acceptable that shareholders have to wait 10 years for the Retained Earnings losses to be covered even if the business is hugely profitable in the meantime? No, and this is precisely why this is the rule in many territories.

The next scenario is more obvious:

Retained Earnings	(100)
NPAT	(40)
Maximum Dividend	**-**

With both a negative NPAT and Retained Earnings, there is no leeway now. These scenarios seem to suggest the following formula:

=MAX(NPAT + Retained Earnings, NPAT, 0)

This allows for the above scenarios. The check to ensure that the value is non-negative (*i.e.* the inclusion of zero in the **MAX** formula) is so that shareholders do not get asked to pay a dividend to the company. I can't imagine that would go down too well.

We are not done yet though. Let's go back to the penultimate scenario but now consider the cash position as well:

Retained Earnings	(100)
NPAT	40
Cash Available	30
Maximum Dividend	**30**

76

Here, the Cash Available is the total amount of cash available to pay the dividend. Technically, this includes any cash reserves built up over time, but many companies only consider the cash position for the period the dividend relates to (this is the scenario I shall be modelling in the case study shortly). This seems to suggest the formula:

=MIN(MAX(NPAT + Retained Earnings, NPAT, 0), Cash Available)

Let me just check with slightly revised numbers:

Retained Earnings	(100)
NPAT	40
Cash Available	(30)
Maximum Dividend	(30)

In this scenario, the company is overdrawn. Oops. Here, this company is going to be asking for money again from its shareholders. Not a good idea. This leads to the slightly revised – and finally correct – formula:

Maximum Dividend = MAX(MIN(MAX(NPAT + Retained Earnings, NPAT), Cash Available), 0)

⊿	E	F	G	H	I	J	K	L	M
69									
70		Retained Earnings			(100)				
71		NPAT			40				
72									
73		Cash Available			(30)				
74									
75		**Maximum Dividend**			-		=MAX(MIN(MAX(I70+I71,I71),I73),)		
76									

Ah yes, the wonderful **MAX(MIN(MAX))** formula. It may not be the prettiest formula in the world, but the point is, it gives the right number.

Now let's consider **LARGE** and **SMALL**. These are similar functions, but require two arguments:

=LARGE(range, n)
=SMALL(range, n)

These two functions return the **n**th largest and smallest values in a given **range**. **n** must be a positive integer less than or equal to the number of non-blank items in the **range**. For example,

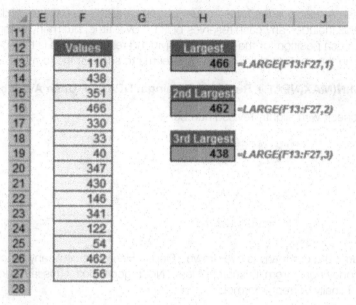

SMALL acts very similarly. As with **MAX** and **MIN**, there are opportunities to create errors using these reasonably straightforward functions:

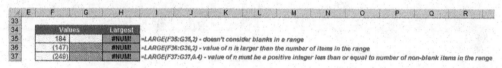

Again, other than choosing an inappropriate **n** (*e.g.* choosing a negative value, too large a value or a non-integer), blank cells may again cause problems. Please ensure you do not include blank cells in your given **range**.

LARGE may be used to rank numerical data in descending order using the **ROWS** function:

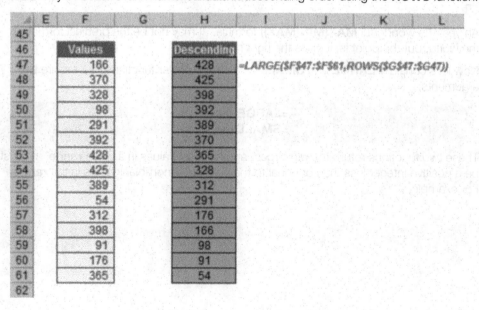

A similar formula using **SMALL** will create the reverse ordered list (*i.e.* in ascending order). In both instances, **ROWS** is used to create a counter which will increase **n** by one as the formula is copied down column **H** in my example above.

LARGE and **SMALL** may also be used to derive statistical data from a range, sometimes requiring an array formula and sometimes not (this is often a case of trial and error for the inexperienced). For example, here's two ways to calculate the sum of the top three (largest) values in the following range:

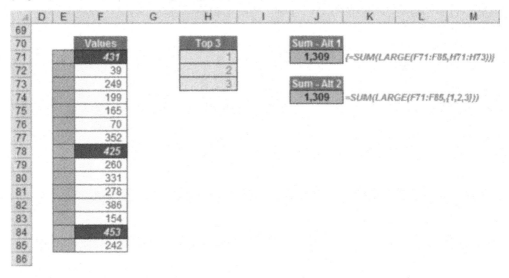

The formulae

> **{=SUM(LARGE(F71:F85,H71:H73))} and**
> **=SUM(LARGE(F71:F85,{1,2,3}))**

will both sum the top three items in the list. You should note that an array formula is avoided in the second formula as **n** is specified as **{1,2,3}** – effectively creating an array of data without pressing **CTRL** + **SHIFT** + **ENTER**.

Similar formulae may be created for the sum of the bottom five, the average of the fourth, eighth and 12th largest items and so on. Try doing that with **MAX** or **MIN**!

CHAPTER 2: KEY EXCEL FUNCTIONALITIES

Congratulations, you made it! Hopefully you learned something as we detailed many of the common functions used in financial modelling.

Apart from functions, you should also familiarise yourself with various key functionalities of Excel often required for developing financial models. Just as with functions, I am going to discuss some aspects that you may consider you understand fully already. Again, I'd like to encourage you to stick with the programme, as whether you are a novice or an expert, hopefully, there may be some useful tips for all.

In this section, I plan to explain the merits (or otherwise) of each of the following:

- Absolute referencing
- Number formatting
- Styles
- Conditional formatting
- Range names
- Data validation
- Data Tables
- Goal Seek and Solver
- Hyperlinks.

If nothing else, this should provide useful reference material as we make sure we have the complete toolkit for putting together a "Best Practice" financial model.

CHAPTER 2.1: ABSOLUTE REFERENCING

Some people say that financial modelling may be all about the dollar signs – well, they may be right in more ways than one.

Consider the following situation:

C14		✕ ✓ *fx*	=C4				

⊿	A	B	C	D	E	F	G	H
1								
2		*Data*						
3								
4			1	2	3	4	5	6
5			7	8	9	10	11	12
6			13	14	15	16	17	18
7			19	20	21	22	23	24
8			25	26	27	28	29	30
9			31	32	33	34	35	36
10								
11								
12		*Formula*						
13								
14			1					
15								

In this example, I have created data in cells **C4:H9** inclusive and then written a formula in cell **C14** linking to cell **C4** (a bit of an incendiary reference, I know). If I were to copy this formula down and across over a similarly dimensioned range, I would get the following result:

H19		✕ ✓ *fx*	=H9				

⊿	A	B	C	D	E	F	G	H
1								
2		*Data*						
3								
4			1	2	3	4	5	6
5			7	8	9	10	11	12
6			13	14	15	16	17	18
7			19	20	21	22	23	24
8			25	26	27	28	29	30
9			31	32	33	34	35	36
10								
11								
12		*Formula*						
13								
14			1	2	3	4	5	6
15			7	8	9	10	11	12
16			13	14	15	16	17	18
17			19	20	21	22	23	24
18			25	26	27	28	29	30
19			31	32	33	34	35	36
20								

81

As the formula is copied down and / or across, so the reference moves in a corresponding fashion. This is known as **relative referencing** and forms the cornerstone of formula construction whenever a modeller refers to another location in the same workbook.

This is not what happens when you refer to another workbook:

C14		fx	=[Book2]Sheet1!$A$1				
	A	B	C	D	E	F	G	H
1								
2		Data						
3								
4			1	2	3	4	5	6
5			7	8	9	10	11	12
6			13	14	15	16	17	18
7			19	20	21	22	23	24
8			25	26	27	28	29	30
9			31	32	33	34	35	36
10								
11								
12		Formula						
13								
14			99					
15								

becomes

H19		fx	=[Book2]Sheet1!$A$1				
	A	B	C	D	E	F	G	H
1								
2		Data						
3								
4			1	2	3	4	5	6
5			7	8	9	10	11	12
6			13	14	15	16	17	18
7			19	20	21	22	23	24
8			25	26	27	28	29	30
9			31	32	33	34	35	36
10								
11								
12		Formula						
13								
14			99	99	99	99	99	99
15			99	99	99	99	99	99
16			99	99	99	99	99	99
17			99	99	99	99	99	99
18			99	99	99	99	99	99
19			99	99	99	99	99	99
20								

once copied down and across as before. The default for external references is this **absolute** referencing.

It is the dollar (**$**) signs that do the damage. These can be added or removed by directly typing them into the cell reference or else clicking in the Formula bar (alternatively, use the **F2** function key) to enable Edit mode and highlight the relevant references and press the **F4** function key repeatedly

Toggling with F4 Function Key
=A1
=$A$1
=A$1
=$A1
=A1

The dollar sign makes the reference to the right of the sign constant, *viz.*

=A1	Relative referencing
=$A$1	Column and row static, *i.e.* absolute referencing
=A$1	Row constant (column will change), *i.e.* semi-absolute referencing
=$A1	Column constant (row will change), *i.e.* semi-absolute referencing
=A1	Relative referencing

It is important that all would-be modellers master this referencing. It is an essential skill as you need to be able to copy formulae down and across ranges with little effort. If you are unsure, try the following exercise. Create the following spreadsheet:

In this example (assuming you have set up the spreadsheet identically to the one illustrated), the aim is to create a "times table" in cells **E7:I11** inclusive. The numbers should be equal to

Column Header Number x Row Header Number x Multiplier

So that the formula in the first cell is **=D7*E6*C3**. All you need to do is add dollar signs to these cell references so that the formula may be copied across and down the range correctly. Have a go now without peeking.

Have you had a go? Here's my solution below:

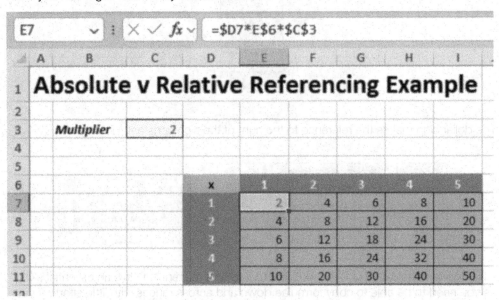

The formula I constructed was:

=$D7*E$6*$C$3

i.e. the first reference has the column anchored (so that it always references the correct Column Header), the second reference has the row anchored (so that it always references the appropriate Row Header) and the final reference is fully anchored (that is, it is an absolute reference).

Let's get a little more sophisticated and deal with more of a real-world problem. Imagine you had the following sample business data:

	A	B	C	D	E	F	G

Business Data

Business Unit 1

Revenue	1,000
Costs Of Goods Sold	(270)
Gross Profit	730
Operating Expenditure	(150)
EBITDA	580
Depreciation	(60)
EBIT	520
Interest	(30)
Net Profit Before Tax	490
Tax	(175)
Net Profit After Tax	315

Business Unit 2

Revenue	2,770
Costs Of Goods Sold	(1,144)
Gross Profit	1,626
Operating Expenditure	(490)
EBITDA	1,136
Depreciation	(55)
EBIT	1,081
Interest	(80)
Net Profit Before Tax	1,001
Tax	(350)
Net Profit After Tax	651

Business Unit 3

Revenue	3,970
Costs Of Goods Sold	(1,250)
Gross Profit	2,720
Operating Expenditure	(880)
EBITDA	1,840
Depreciation	(175)
EBIT	1,665
Interest	(80)
Net Profit Before Tax	1,585
Tax	(590)
Net Profit After Tax	995

You might wish to create an output which summarises the revenue by business unit. You will need to construct formulae such as

> ='Business Data'!G10
> ='Business Data'!G25
> ='Business Data'!G40, ... *etc.*

If you had, say, 500 of these business units you would have a busy but boring morning ahead of you. Surely there is a simpler way that does not require the implementation of macros?

Actually, I can think of two ways of dealing with this common query and I present both solutions below.

Method 1: Text Little Time

This approach requires the first two formulae to be entered into the output sheet as usual, *viz.*

B3	⌄ : ✕ ✓ *fx* ⌄	='Business Data'!G25

	A	B	C	D	E
1					
2		1000			
3		2770			

In our example, cell **B2** contains the formula **='Business Data'!G10** and cell **B3** contains the formula **='Business Data'!G25** (displayed). Next, edit both formula by typing an apostrophe (') before the equals sign in each formula:

B3	⌄ : ✕ ✓ *fx* ⌄	'='Business Data'!G25

	A	B	C	D
1				
2		='Business Data'!G10		
3		='Business Data'!G25		

Now these formulae are treated as text and are displayed in the two cells. If you then highlight cells **B2:B3** together and copy the formulae down, Excel's AutoFill feature will copy the cells similar to below:

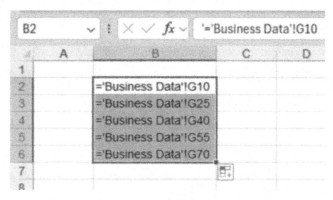

Now, all we need to do is remove the apostrophes. The first idea that comes to mind is to use 'Replace…' (**CTRL** + **H**) and replace **'=** with **=**. Unfortunately, this does not work in all versions of Excel as 'Replace…' does not seem to recognise apostrophes in certain instances.

There is a very simple trick to circumvent this problem. With this data still selected, click on the 'Text to Columns' button in the 'Data Tools' group of the 'Data' tab on the Ribbon (**ALT** + **D** + **E** for all versions of Excel or **ALT** + **A** + **E** in Excel 2007 onwards):

This launches the 'Text to Columns Wizard' dialog box. In the first step, ensure that the '…file type that best describes your data…' is set to 'Delimited':

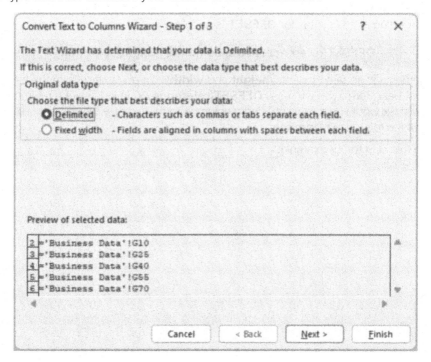

Then, simply depress the 'Finish' button. The spreadsheet will then reinstate the formulae, *viz.*

B2		✕ ✓ *fx* ⌄	='Business Data'!G10	
	A	B	C	D
1				
2		1000		
3		2770		
4		3970		
5		660		
6		8400		
7				

Simple!

Now this approach is fairly simple, but has two major drawbacks:

1. This method only works with rows. Using **R1C1** formula notation it is possible to create a similar approach for columns, but this technique can be confusing.

2. Once the formulae have been reinstated it is not simple to extend the formulae if necessary. This can be cumbersome where the output summaries may differ period to period for example.

The **OFFSET** approach counters these issues.

Method 2: OFFSET from the Outset

For all those similar to me with the memories of a goldfish (I had to look that up, because I keep forgetting it), the syntax for **OFFSET** is as follows:

OFFSET(reference, rows, columns, [height], [width]).

The arguments in square brackets (**height** and **width**) can be omitted from the formula. In its most basic form, you will recall **OFFSET(reference, x, y)** will select a reference **x** rows down (**-x** would be **x** rows up) and **y** columns to the right (**-y** would be **y** columns to the left) of the reference **reference**.

Applying this idea to our example:

Business Data

Business Unit 1

Revenue	1,000
Costs Of Goods Sold	(270)
Gross Profit	730
Operating Expenditure	(150)
EBITDA	580
Depreciation	(60)
EBIT	520
Interest	(30)
Net Profit Before Tax	490
Tax	(175)
Net Profit After Tax	315

Business Unit 2

Revenue	2,770
Costs Of Goods Sold	(1,144)
Gross Profit	1,626
Operating Expenditure	(490)
EBITDA	1,136
Depreciation	(55)
EBIT	1,081
Interest	(80)
Net Profit Before Tax	1,001
Tax	(350)
Net Profit After Tax	651

Business Unit 3

Revenue	3,970
Costs Of Goods Sold	(1,250)
Gross Profit	2,720
Operating Expenditure	(880)
EBITDA	1,840
Depreciation	(175)
EBIT	1,665
Interest	(80)
Net Profit Before Tax	1,585
Tax	(590)
Net Profit After Tax	995

Note that the Business Unit data is 15 rows apart (*e.g.* the first block begins in row 8 and ends in row 22, taking the blank rows into account). Therefore, I can create one formula I may copy down:

B2		× ✓ *fx*	=OFFSET('Business Data'!$G$10,ROWS('Business Data'!$C$8:$C$22)*(ROWS($A$2:$A2)-1),)								
	A	B	C	D	E	F	G	H	I	J	K	L
1												
2		1000										
3		2770										
4		3970										
5		660										
6		8400										
7												

In this example, we have started the formula in cell **B2** and copied it down to cell **B6**. The formula in cell **B2** is:

> **=OFFSET('Business Data'!$G$10,ROWS('Business Data'!$C$8:$C$22)*(ROWS($A$2:$A2)-1),)**

The first reference is the Revenue for Business Unit 1. The **Rows** reference takes the depth of each block (defined here by **ROWS('Business Data'!$C$8:$C$22)**) multiplied by **ROWS($A$2:$A2)-1**, *e.g.* in row 2 this factor will be zero, in row 3 it will be 1, in row 4 it will be 2, *etc.* This ensures that the next Revenue item is referred to in the next row down.

This may seem complex to begin with, but with practice this idea can be adapted for columns to be skipped as well and to allow for other line items (*e.g.* Gross Profit, Tax) to be selected instead.

CHAPTER 2.2: NUMBER FORMATTING

Given that one of the primary purposes of financial modelling is to present numerical data, it is important how numerical data is presented. Cells may be individually formatted using **CTRL** + **1** or **ALT** + **O** + **E** in all versions of Excel:

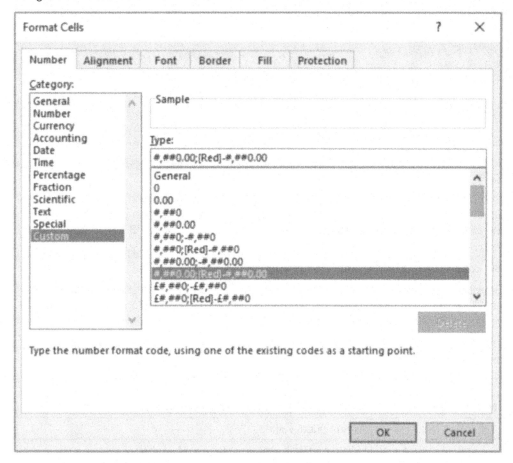

Formatting only changes the appearance, not the underlying value, of a cell. For example, if cells **A1** and **B1** had the number '1.4' typed in but were formatted to zero decimal places, then if cell **C1 = A1 + B1**, you would truly have 1 + 1 = 3 (well, 1.4 + 1.4 = 2.8 anyway).

This should not be confused with 'Set precision as displayed' (from the Ribbon, **File -> Excel Options -> Advanced -> When calculating this workbook -> Set precision as displayed**).

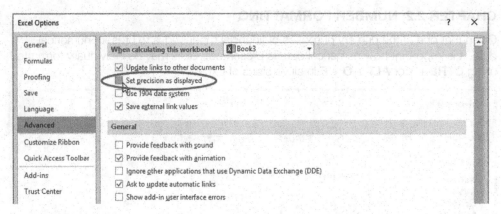

Selecting this option and clicking 'OK' will <u>permanently</u> change stored values in cells to whatever format has been selected, including the number of decimal places (*e.g.* 15.75 formatted to one decimal place would become precisely 15.8).

Excel has many built-in number formats that are fairly easy to understand, *e.g.* Currency, Date, Percentage. The default format is 'General' where Excel will endeavour to provide the most appropriate format for the contents. For example, typing '3 3/4' into a cell will result in Excel selecting a mixed format.

But what do you do if you can't find an appropriate format?

Selecting the 'Custom' category activates the 'Type' input box and allows between 200 and 250 custom number formats in a particular workbook, depending upon the language version of Excel that has been installed.

The 'Type' input box allows up to four aspects of formatting to be specified in a cell. These aspects are referred to as sections and are separated by a semi-colon (;). To ascertain what is contained in each section depends on the total number of sections used, *viz.*

No. of Sections	Section Details (assuming no conditions)
1 (min)	All numerical values
2	Non-negative Numbers; Negative Numbers
3	Positive Numbers; Negative Numbers; Zero Values
4 (max)	Positive Numbers; Negative Numbers; Zero Values; Text

To the uninitiated, coding custom number formats may appear incomprehensible. However, understanding the following tables from Microsoft soon puts things into perspective.

Number Code	Description
General	General number format
0	Digit placeholder (if no number, a '0' will be used to 'pad')
#	Digit placeholder (does not display extra zeros)
?	Digit placeholder (leaves space for extra zeros, but does not display them)
. (decimal point / full stop)	Decimal point!

Number Code	Description
%	Percentage displayed
, (comma)	Thousands separator
/	Used to delineate numerator from denominator in Fraction category
E+ e+ E- e-	Scientific notation

Text Code	Description
$ - + / ( ) : space	These characters are displayed in the number.
"text"	For other characters, in order to ensure Excel does not misinterpret them, it is best to use enclose the character(s) in quotation marks…
\character	…or precede it with a backslash
*	Repeats the next character in the format to fill the column width. Only one asterisk per section of a format is allowed
_character	Skips the width of the next character. In particular, this syntax is often used with the closing parenthesis, _) , in a positive number format (when the negative format includes brackets). This allows the values to line up at the decimal point
@	Text placeholder

Date Code	Description
m	Month as a number without leading zeros (1 to 12)
mm	Month as a number with leading zeros (01 to 12)
mmm	Month as an abbreviation (Jan - Dec)
mmmm	Unabbreviated month (January - December)
mmmmm	First letter of month (J, F, M, A, M, J, J, A, S, O, N, D)
d	Day without leading zeros (1 to 31)
dd	Day with leading zeros (01 to 31)
ddd	Week day as an abbreviation (Sun - Sat)
dddd	Unabbreviated week day (Sunday - Saturday)
y or yy	Year as a two digit number (e.g. 09, 97)
yyy or yyyy	Year as a four digit number (e.g. 2009, 1997)

Time Code	Description
h	Hours as a number without leading zero (0 to 23)
hh	Hours as a number with leading zero (00 to 23)

Time Code	Description
m	Minutes as a number without leading zero (0 to 59)
mm	Minutes as a number with leading zero (00 to 59)
s	Seconds as a number without leading zero (0 to 59)
ss	Seconds as a number with leading zero (00 to 59)
[h]	With times only, will increment hours to 24 and beyond
[m]	With times only, will increment minutes to 60 and beyond
[s]	With times only, will increment seconds to 60 and beyond
AM/PM am/pm	Time based on the 12-hour clock [24-hour clock is the default]

Miscellaneous Code	Description
[Black], [Blue], [Cyan], [Green], [Magenta], [Red], [White], [Yellow]	Displays the characters in the specified colours
[Color n]	Displays the characters in a specified colour, where n is a value from 1 to 56, and refers to the nth colour in the color palette
;	Delineates a section
[Condition Value]	Condition may be any one of the comparison operators, <, >, =, <=, >=, <> and Value may be any number. A number format may contain up to two conditions

Allow me to go through several examples.

Example 1: Comprehensive

[Blue]$* _(#,##0.0,_0_);[Red]$* (#,##0.00,);[Color 7]\-_._0_0_);[Cyan]@*."is text"

Comprehensive Example

Distinguishing between positive numbers, negative numbers, zero values and text.

Format	[Blue]$* _(#,##0.0,_0_);[Red]$* (#,##0.00,);[Color 7]\-_._0_0_);[Cyan]@*."is text"

Cell Value		Appearance
123456789	$	123,456.8
-123456789	$	(123,456.79)
0		-
This is text	This is text	is text

This format has all four sections, so the first section, **[Blue]$* _(#,##0.0,_0_)**, specifies the formatting for positive numbers. In this case, positive numbers will be formatted blue and be preceded with a $ sign. Note the use of the asterisk followed by a space: this means that the cell width will be 'padded out' with spaces so that the dollar sign will be pushed to the very left of the cell and the number formatting will be to the very right. _(is not necessary, strictly speaking, but ensures there is space made for an open bracket, even though there is no such character shown. **#,##0.0,** ensures positive numbers contain thousand separators (where needed) and displays the number to the nearest 0.1 of a thousand. Two commas at the end would have the number displayed to the nearest 0.1 of a million, and so on. Finally, the **_0_)** requires Excel to maintain enough space at the right end of a cell for a digit (not necessarily zero) and a close bracket. It should be noted that a separate underscore is required for each character that is to be allowed for.

The second section, **[Red]$* (#,##0.00,)**, specifies the formatting for negative numbers. It is similar to the first section, but colours the number red, reports numbers to 0.01 of a thousand and encloses it in brackets.

The third section, **[Color 7]\-_._0_0_)**, specifies the formatting for zero values. This colours zero values "Color 7" which is a delightful pink in Excel's standard color palette. I am a great believer in using a dash, generated by using **\-** here, to denote zero as it distinguishes a zero value from something that is approximately zero, which can be useful for error checking, etc. The final four underscored characters, **_._0_0_)**, ensure that the dash will line up with the units value of a positive or negative value.

Finally, the fourth section, **[Cyan]@*."is text"**, defines how text is to be formatted. If omitted, text is simply formatted as 'General', but here it will be coloured cyan. The **@** symbol specifies the relative location of the text within the cell (left-hand side of the cell), the ***.** will 'fill' the cell with period characters and **"is text"** will add these words to the end of the text, right-aligned (note no '&' concatenation is required since these words appear in the formatting only).

Example 2: Hiding the Contents of a Cell

;;;

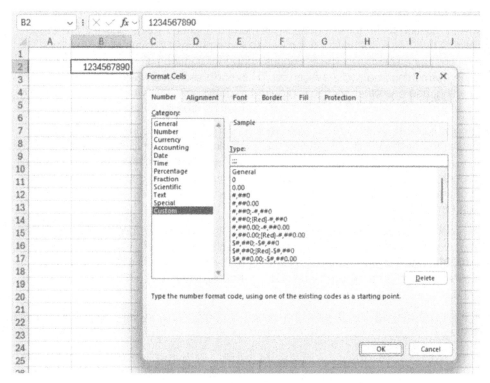

Colouring the font and the background the same may hide a cell's contents on screen, but it will often reappear when printed out (especially if 'black and white printing' is selected). By choosing the above formatting (three semi-colons), numbers and text are simply 'blanked out' and will only appear in Excel's Formula bar instead.

Example 3: Formatting Based on Conditions

`[>=1000000]#,##0,,"M";[>=1000]#,##0,"K";0`

Thousands Etc. Format Examples

Various ways of representing larger numbers.

Format		[>=1000000]#,##0,,"M";[>=1000]#,##0,"K";0
	Number	Appearance
	0.1	0
	1	1
	10	10
	100	100
	1,000	1K
	10,000	10K
	100,000	100K
	1,000,000	1M
	10,000,000	10M
	100,000,000	100M
	1,000,000,000	1,000M

Above, I mentioned what the four sections mean most commonly. This third example highlights that this is not always the case. Custom number formats allow up to two conditions to be specified. This is because only four sections are allowed for custom number formatting and two are reserved. The fourth section always specifies text formatting, and one other section is required to detail how 'everything else' (numerically) will be formatted. It is a bit like conditional formatting (see later) just for numbers.

The conditions are included in square brackets such that if the condition is true, the following formatting will be applied. In this example, there are only three sections, so text will be formatted as 'General'. The first section, **[>=1000000]#,##0,,"M"**, will format all numbers greater than or equal to a million to the nearest million and add an "M" to the end of the number. Note that the commas effectively make it look like each has been divided by 1,000.

The second section will only be considered if the first condition is not true, so the order of the two 'conditional formats' needs to be thought through. Here, the second section, **[>=1000]#,##0,"K"**, will format all numbers greater than or equal to a thousand (but necessarily less than a million) to the nearest thousand and add a "K" to the end of the number.

The third and final section, **0**, will format all other numbers (every value less than 1,000) to the nearest integer without thousands separator(s).

Use with Caution

Using lots of custom number formats in a single workbook uses considerable memory and can slow down the calculation time of an Excel file unnecessarily. Many of these formats are created accidentally. Each time a custom number format is edited, it will generate an additional listing for Custom Category Types. Any custom formats created inadvertently in this manner (that are not being used in the file) should be deleted; good housekeeping is essential.

CHAPTER 2.3: STYLES

Do you know the difference between formats and styles, other than formatting is what you do in Excel and style is what I lack? Take the illustration below. How easy is it to find the key data, or see which cells should be changed to facilitate updated information? Have you ever noticed that spreadsheets built by colleagues do not look similar to your own? How easy are these things in your own spreadsheets? Have I asked enough questions in this paragraph? No?

⏴	A	B	C	D	E
1	Sample Data				
2		Q1	Q2	Q3	Q4
3	Revenue	3700	4142	4099	5008
4	Costs Of Goods Sold	-1577	-1746	-1680	-1931
5	Gross Profit	2123	2396	2419	3077
6	Rent	-440	-440	-440	-440
7	Electricity	-212	-240	-242	-308
8	Other Operating Expenditure	-770	-790	-745	-977
9	Total Operating Expenditure	-1422	-1470	-1427	-1725
10	EBITDA	701	926	992	1352
11					

Later on, I will discuss the four key qualities of a "Best Practice" model, but as a taster, two of these key qualities are consistency and transparency.

Examples of consistency:

- formulae are copied without amendment across rows
- cells with a common purpose (for example, inputs that are assumptions, such as inflation rates) are formatted similarly
- titles are positioned in the same cells in different worksheets
- assumption cells (cells containing data that can be changed by the user to affect model outputs) are unlocked, where all other cells are locked, so that only these cells can be changed

Examples of transparency:

- assumptions are formatted to be instantly recognisable
- key outputs (for example, totals) can be identified immediately, with their derivation made obvious.

Excel's 'Styles' features can assist with both transparency and consistency. Frequently, the words 'formats' and 'styles' are used interchangeably, but they are not the same thing. To see this, select any cell in Excel and apply the shortcut keystroke **CTRL + 1**. As mentioned previously, this shortcut brings up the 'Format Cells' dialog box:

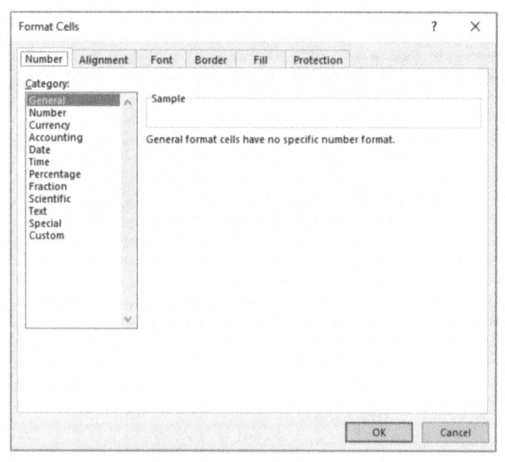

Excel has six format properties: Number, Alignment, Font, Border, Patterns and Protection. A style is simply a pre-defined set of these various formats. With a little forethought, these styles can be set up and applied to a worksheet cell or range very easily.

Creating your own styles is straightforward with Excel's Style dialog box. Simply go to the Home tab, click the arrow in the bottom right corner at the very right-hand corner of the 'Styles' section:

This expands the section:

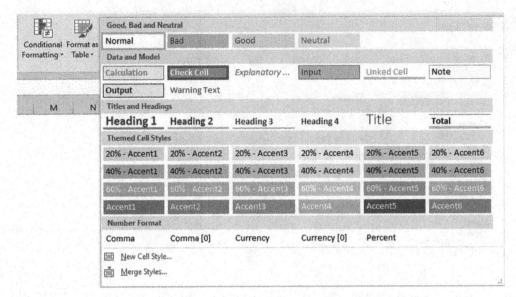

You can then select a New Cell Style (see the list at the bottom of the pop-up or **ALT** + **H** + **J** + **N**), use an existing style or modify an existing style (right-click with the mouse). If you decide to create a new style or edit an existing one, the following dialog box will appear:

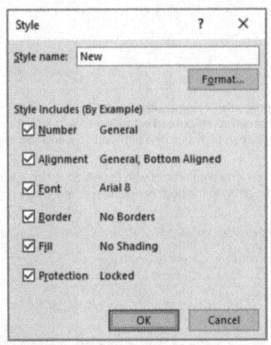

Let's create an assumption format for entering data in dollars. First, select a cell or range of cells. Then, call up the above dialog box. The dropdown box (highlighted above) can be edited. We'll change the name to "Dollar Assumptions" and click the 'Modify' or 'Format' button (depending upon the version of Excel you have).

The 'Format Cells' dialog box reappears:

- **Number:** select the Currency category, with zero decimal places and apply the '$' symbol

- **Alignment:** Horizontal – Right (Indent) with zero indent

- **Fill:** select an 'easy-on-the-eye' colour such as pale green

- **Protection:** uncheck the Locked check box (allows the cell to be changed in a protected worksheet)

- Click 'OK' to return to the Style dialog box.

Note that no formats have been ascribed for Font or Border in this example. We don't want the style to control (that is, overwrite) these properties, so the 'Style includes' check boxes for these two format properties should be unchecked:

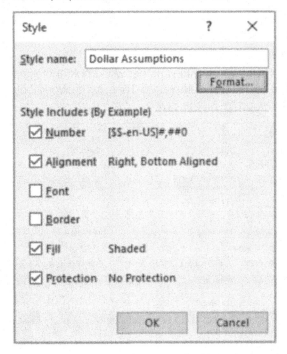

This allows you to combine multiple styles in one cell, although there is no point having more than six as you will be overwriting an earlier style otherwise. Returning to the graphic, by clicking 'OK' or 'Add', the cell or range has now been formatted with the 'Dollar Assumptions' style. Now that this style has been added, you simply select the range and then click on the style in the Styles gallery on the Home tab.

The main difference between Formats and Styles becomes obvious when you realise you want to change (update) a style. Just select one of the cells that the style is attached to and call up the Style dialog box in the usual way, modifying the style as required. Click 'OK' when finished. Note that every cell in the open workbook that uses this style has automatically updated. Once you start using styles, you will never look back!

You will only want to set up styles once. When you're finished, simply save the file as a template using **File-->Save As** (you may wish to delete or remove formatted cells first so that you have a blank workbook). Using **File-->New** will call up your saved styles.

With very little practice, you will find yourself being able to style worksheets faster than you can say "floccinaucinihilipilification" (I am impressed my spell checker recognises this word!). Returning to our original example, which do you prefer?

Before Styles						After Styles				

Before Styles

	A	B	C	D	E
1	Sample Data				
2		Q1	Q2	Q3	Q4
3	Revenue	3700	4142	4099	5008
4	Costs Of Goods Sold	-1577	-1746	-1680	-1931
5	Gross Profit	2123	2396	2419	3077
6	Rent	-440	-440	-440	-440
7	Electricity	-212	-240	-242	-308
8	Other Operating Expenditure	-770	-790	-745	-977
9	Total Operating Expenditure	-1422	-1470	-1427	-1725
10	EBITDA	701	926	992	1352

After Styles

	A	B	C	D	E
1	Sample Data				
2		Q1	Q2	Q3	Q4
3	Revenue	3,700	4,142	4,099	5,008
4	Costs Of Goods Sold	(1,577)	(1,746)	(1,680)	(1,931)
5	Gross Profit	2,123	2,396	2,419	3,077
6	Rent	(440)	(440)	(440)	(440)
7	Electricity	(212)	(240)	(242)	(308)
8	Other Operating Expenditure	(770)	(790)	(745)	(977)
9	Total Operating Expenditure	(1,422)	(1,470)	(1,427)	(1,725)
10	EBITDA	701	926	992	1,352

By clicking 'OK' or 'Add', the cell or range has now been formatted with the 'Dollar Assumptions' style. Now that this style has been added, you simply select the range and then click on the style in the Styles gallery on the 'Home' tab.

Should you have the Styles you want in another workbook, there is a quick way to copy them in. Simply have both workbooks open. Then, in the workbook in which you would like to import the Styles, go to 'Merge Styles...' *viz.*

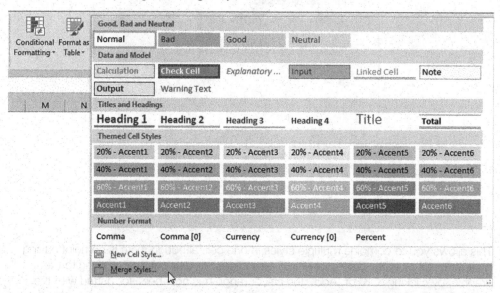

A dialog box will pop up from which you may select the workbook with the Styles you require.

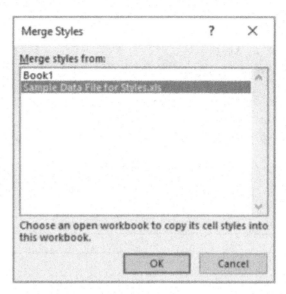

Click on the correct workbook and then on 'OK' and all of the Styles from that workbook will be imported (including any duplicates).

This leads me on to mentioning one issue with Styles. If worksheets or ranges are copied from other workbooks, the Styles from that workbook may be copied across too, leading to hundreds – if not thousands – of Styles you don't want, artificially bloating the size of your financial model. To delete Styles, you right-click on the Style of your choice and select 'Delete' – but this has to be performed *one at a time*. Yuck!

There are two workarounds to this issue:

- When copying from another workbook, copy the range to be imported (**CTRL + C**) and then paste special twice. First, in the destination workbook, select where you want the data to go and Paste Special as Formulas (**ALT + E + S + F + ENTER**) and then Paste Special as Formats (**ALT + E + S + T + ENTER**).

- Use a macro to delete Styles.

I provide an example of such a macro below. This one allows you to choose which custom (*i.e.* not those that are built in) Styles should be deleted in the workbook:

```
Sub RemoveStyles()
    Dim StyleCustom As Style
    Dim ReturnedInteger As Integer

    For Each StyleCustom In ActiveWorkbook.Styles
        If Not StyleCustom.BuiltIn Then
            ReturnedInteger = MsgBox("Delete style '" & StyleCustom.Name &
"'?", vbYesNo)
            If ReturnedInteger = vbYes Then StyleCustom.Delete
        End If
    Next StyleCustom
End Sub
```

Macros

This book is not about macros, so forgive me if I only mention them in passing here and there. Essentially, a **macro** is a coded procedure using the language Visual Basic for Applications (**VBA**) often used to automate actions. Since Excel 2007, files must not be saved as *.xlsx files (these Excel workbooks will not allow macros). Your best bet is probably a macro-enable workbook - *.xlsm.

Even then, because macros may execute all sorts of undesirable code, Excel's default setting is set so that macros will not run automatically. To ensure the macro below will work, you will first need to check / amend Excel's security settings:

- On the File tab, go to 'Excel Options' (**ALT** + **T** + **O** is the equivalent of these first two steps)

- Select 'Trust Center' from the left-hand columnar list

- In the 'Microsoft Office Excel Trust Center' section, click on the 'Trust Center Settings...' button

- Select 'Macro Settings' from the left-hand columnar list (if the 'Developer' tab is displayed on the Ribbon, **ALT** + **L** + **AS** will get you to this point immediately)

- In the 'Macro Settings' section, select 'Enable all macros'.

To enter a typed (rather than recorded) macro, open the Visual Basic Editor (**ALT** + **F11**), select the file (if more than one open) from the Project Explorer (top left-hand window) and then from the menu, click **Insert->Module** and type your code into the right-hand pane.

To run the macro may be trickier if you don't have the 'Developer' tab open (although you can choose **Run->Macro** (or **F5**) from the Visual Basic Editor).

In Excel 2010 and later, go to 'Customize Ribbon':

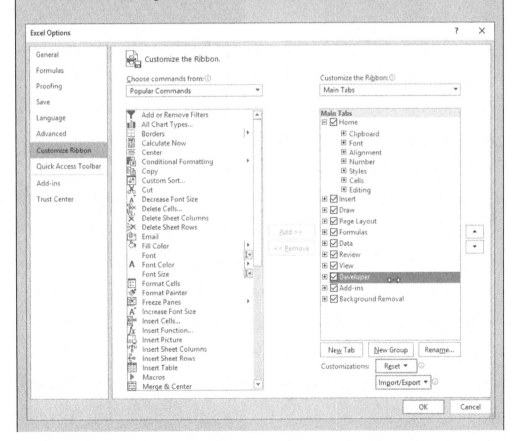

Macros may then be run from the 'Developer' tab by clicking on the 'Macro' button:

You can also avoid all of this with the keyboard shortcut **ALT** + **F8**!!

CHAPTER 2.4: CONDITIONAL FORMATTING

With Excel's **IF** function, the contents of a cell can be modified depending upon (a) certain condition(s) being met (*i.e.* held to be TRUE). However, the formatting or style of the cell cannot be changed in this manner.

Macros are not needed.

First introduced in Excel 97, conditional Formatting is an Excel feature that indeed allows you to apply formats to a cell or range of cells and have that formatting change depending on the value of the cell or the value of a corresponding formula. This was one of the features that was given a major overhaul in Excel 2007.

Accessed from the 'Home' tab (or **ALT** + **O** + **D**), conditional formatting formats the cell(s) selected depending upon whether a condition is TRUE. In Excel 2003 and earlier versions, conditional formatting would work as follows:

```
If Condition1 = True Then
    Apply Format1
Else
    If Condition2 = True Then
        Apply Format2
    Else
        If Condition3 = True Then
            Apply Format3
        Else
            Apply DefaultFormat
        End If
    End If
End If
```

Essentially, as soon as Excel finds a condition that is held it formats accordingly and stops. If none of the three conditions is met, the underlying format (*i.e.* the fourth format) is retained.

As explained above, conditional formatting was completely revamped and reinvented in Excel 2007. Located in the 'Styles' group of the 'Home' tab, the conditional formatting feature has had a raft of new features added:

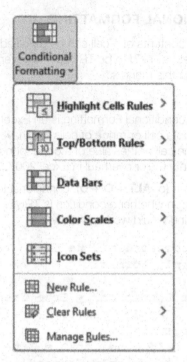

For instance, inspecting 'Highlight Cells Rules' is akin to many of the "Cell Value Is" functionalities of its predecessor, such as Greater Than, Less Than, Between, Equal To, or even More Rules:

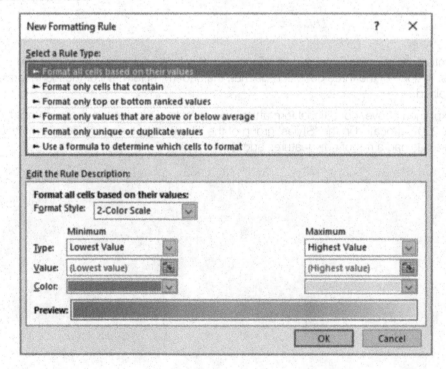

Other options are also available: Date Occurring and Duplicate Values. All you have to do is highlight the list, select the option and colour scheme required. Simple (no need to concoct hideous formulae such as **=IF(COUNTIF($A:$A,$A1)>1,COUNTIF($A$1:$A1,$A1)>1)** for locating duplicates, for example).

Users should not be fooled by the easy-to-use Top / Bottom Rules either. Top 10 Items, Top 10%, Bottom 10 Items and Bottom 10% all highlight items that conform to these labels. However, the '10' can be changed to a number of the user's choice. Who could possibly live without the Bottom 37% Debtors Report for instance?

Above average and below average data can be highlighted also in one or two clicks and even graded shading of a cell as well. For example, if cells **A1:A10** had the values 10, 20, 30, ..., 100 respectively, the cells could be filled in as follows:

Using Data Bars	Using Color Scales

Clearly, looking at the Color Scales example, conditional formatting lends itself neatly to traffic light reporting. This is compounded by Icon Sets that will stratify data into between three and five sections using various icons (such as the red, amber and green traffic lights). Given that conditional formatting now permits cells to be sorted dependent upon their background colour (**ALT** + **D** + **S**, then choose 'Cell Color' in 'Sort On' field), you can make monthly reporting a colourful adventure!

Conditional formatting in Excel 2007 does differ logically from its predecessor.

With Excel 2003 and earlier, as soon as Excel finds a condition that is held, it formats accordingly and stops. This can be performed for up to three conditions. These days, there is 'no limit' and testing does not have to stop (more than one format can be applied in a cell at a time), *i.e.*

```
If Condition1 = True Then
     Apply Format1
End If
If Condition2 = True Then
     Apply Format2
End If
If Condition3 = True Then
     Apply Format3
End If
```

To highlight this, consider the following data set before and after multiple conditional formatting:

Before Multiple Conditional Formatting	After Multiple Conditional Formatting
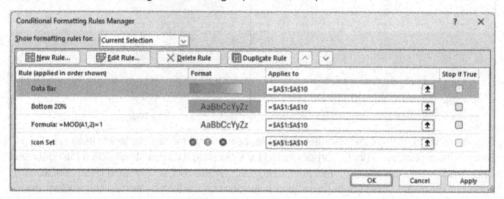	

No less than four conditional formats have been applied, as can be seen by opening up the Conditional Formatting Rules Manager (**ALT + O + D**):

Rule (applied in order shown)	Format	Applies to	Stop If True
Data Bar		=$A$1:$A$10	☐
Bottom 20%	AaBbCcYyZz	=$A$1:$A$10	☐
Formula: =MOD(A1,2)=1	AaBbCcYyZz	=$A$1:$A$10	☐
Icon Set	⊘ ⊘ ⊘	=$A$1:$A$10	☐

Using the blue up and down arrows can reorder the sequence and the sequence can be stopped if certain conditions are true (simply check the box in the fourth column). This gives conditional formatting significantly greater flexibility these days.

One tip though: always try to add conditional formatting after completing all of the calculations in your model. This is because conditional formatting sometimes misbehaves when rows or columns are deleted and / or inserted. Trust me, it's less work to add it at the end!

CHAPTER 2.5: RANGE NAMES

If you were to ask modelling professionals about the merits of using range names you will find that opinion is strongly divided. In spreadsheets, used appropriately and sparingly, great value can be obtained from using range names, as it can make formulae easier to read. In macros (not discussed here), they are vital. Overuse, on the other hand, can lead to end user confusion.

There are various ways range names may be created in Excel. One way is to use the **Name Box**:

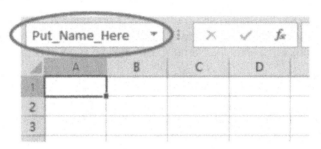

Note that range names must start with a letter or an underscore character (_) and cannot be mistaken for a cell reference (can you imagine the fun you would have calling cell **A1 D3** *etc*?). Spaces are not allowed either.

Space: the Final Frontier?

There is a very good reason that spaces are not allowed in range names. Not many modellers – even advanced ones – seem to appreciate the following functionality. Consider the following extract:

C11   ✕ ✓ *fx*   =F2:F7 B5:G5

	A	B	C	D	E	F	G
1							
2		1	2	3	4	5	6
3		7	8	9	10	11	12
4		13	14	15	16	17	18
5		19	20	21	22	23	24
6		25	26	27	28	29	30
7		31	32	33	34	35	36
8		37	38	39	40	41	42
9							
10							
11		Formula:	23				
12							

Space (" ") is actually the **intersect** operator in Excel. This is why you should never put spaces in formulae in Excel – the software may inadvertently try to intersect your ranges. If you do need to break out a formula, use **ALT + ENTER**: this will put line breaks in instead.

Regarding range names, if you need to make a name readable, I suggest using the underscore (_) character, *e.g.* **Range_name**. This will avoid Excel believing that you are trying to intersect one undefined range name with another.

Remaining characters in the name can be letters, numbers, periods, and underscore characters. Spaces are not allowed but two words can be joined with an underscore (_) or period (.), for example, to enter the Name 'Cash Flow' you should enter 'Cash_Flow' or 'Cash.Flow.'.

There is no limit on the number of names you can define, but a name may only contain up to 255 characters (why on earth you would want something this long is beyond me). Names can contain uppercase and / or lowercase letters. Excel does not distinguish between uppercase and lowercase characters in names. For example, if you have created the global name 'Profit' and then create another global name called 'PROFIT' in the same workbook, the second name will replace the first one.

It is not a syntax issue, but I strongly recommend thought is given to adding prefixes to range names. When I discussed **OFFSET** earlier, I recommended using the prefix '**BC_**' (**B**ase **C**ell). Similarly, I use '**LU_**' for **L**ook **U**p lists and so on. Using these prefixes means that not only do I understand the purpose of the range name, but also ensures that names with a common purpose are grouped together in a list. This is not to say all range names should contain a prefix. 'Tax_Rate', for instance, makes sense on its own and adding a prefix would only detract from the name given, potentially confusing the end user.

Once you have decided upon a name for your range, perhaps the quickest way of all to add a range name such that it is easy to edit it is using the Name Manager (**CTRL + F3**):

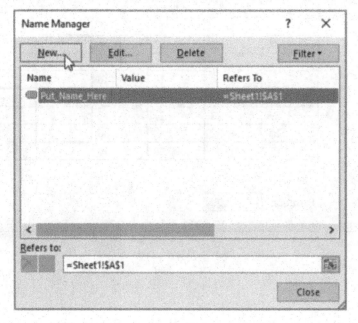

This is where you go to delete range names – one of the most common questions I am asked in financial modelling!! I'll cover exactly how to do so in more detail shortly.

In Excel 2007 and later versions, if you click on 'New…' (above), the following dialog box appears:

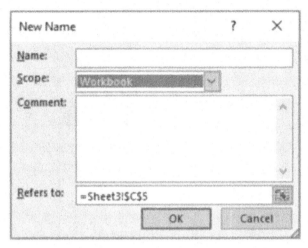

Note the highlighted section (Scope). All names have a scope, either to a specific worksheet (also called the local worksheet level) or to the entire workbook (also called the global workbook level). The scope of a name is the location within which the name is recognised without qualification.

For example, if you have defined a range name as 'Profit' with its scope as 'Sheet1' (say) rather than 'Workbook', then it will only be recognised in 'Sheet1' as 'Profit' (*i.e.* without qualification). To use this local name in another worksheet, you must qualify it by preceding it with the localised worksheet name:

=Sheet1!Profit

If you have defined a name, such as 'Cashflow', and its scope is the workbook, that name is recognised for all worksheets in that workbook (but not for any other workbook).

A name must always be unique within its scope. Excel prevents you from defining a name that is not unique within its scope. However, you can use the same name in different scopes. For example, you can define a name, such as 'Profit' that is scoped to Sheet1, Sheet2, and Sheet3 in the same workbook. Although each name is the same, each name is unique within its scope. You might do this to ensure that a formula that uses the name 'Gross_Profit' (say) is always referencing the same cells at the local worksheet level.

You can even define the same name, 'Profit' for the global workbook level, but again this scope is unique. In this case, there may be a name conflict. To resolve this conflict, Excel uses the name that is defined for the worksheet by default. The local worksheet level takes precedence over the global workbook level. This can be circumvented by adding the following prefix to the name, *e.g.* rename it 'WorkbookFile!Profit' instead.

It is possible to override the local worksheet level for all worksheets in the workbook, except for the first worksheet. This will always use the local name if there is a name conflict and cannot be overridden.

From experience, I strongly recommend that you never duplicate a range name within a workbook. It can cause formulaic errors. For similar reasons, I also suggest that you try never to have range names on a worksheet that may be copied.

There is a nifty shortcut for creating range names using existing names. Consider the following list:

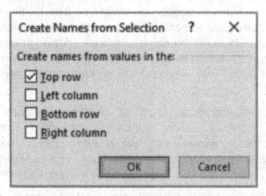

Imagine you were to highlight cells **N12:N27** in the above example and then use the shortcut **CTRL + SHIFT + F3**:

With the first check box ('Top row') checked, by clicking on 'OK' the range **N13:N27** (not **N12:N27**) will be named 'Phonetic_Alphabet' (*i.e.* the underscore will be added automatically). Ranges across rows can be named in seconds similarly using 'Left column' similarly.

The reason this dialog box uses check boxes (rather than option buttons) is to allow users to select more than one at a time. For example, consider the following data:

	M	N	O	P	Q	R
30						
31			Jan	Feb	Mar	Apr
32		Sales	7,000	8,000	9,000	10,000
33		Costs	(2,270)	(3,817)	(4,522)	(5,712)
34		Gross Margin	4,730	4,183	4,478	4,288
35						

Highlighting cells **N31:R34** and then employing the keyboard shortcut **CTRL + SHIFT + F3** would generate the following dialog box:

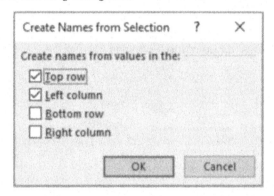

Highlighting **N31:R34** and using the keyboard shortcut **CTRL + SHIFT + F3** once more should generate the 'Create Names…' dialog box as above with both 'Top row' and 'Left column' checked. This means that **O32:O34** will be called 'Jan', **O33:R33** will be called 'Costs' and so on. This would take considerably longer to perform manually.

This example also reinforces why spaces are illegal characters in range names (and for that matter, should not be added to formulae either). As I said earlier, space is the *intersect operator* in Excel. If you were to type the following formula:

=Gross_Margin Feb,

Excel would return the value in cell **P34** (the intersection of the two ranges, above), *i.e.* $4,183. This can be a powerful yet quick and simple analytical tool for key outputs.

One of the reasons I like using the **CTRL + F3** shortcut is that it is part of the **F3** 'Names family of shortcuts'. We have just seen how **CTRL + SHIFT + F3** can be useful – and so can **F3** on its own. Perhaps superseded by the fact that in Excel 2007 and later versions of Excel will now prompt as you type formulae, **F3** has been very useful in the past as the 'Paste Names' shortcut. For example, as you type a formula, you can refer to a range name by simply typing **F3** to get the Paste Names dialog box, *viz.*

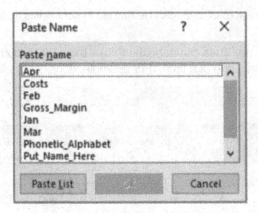

Selecting one of the names and clicking 'OK' inserts the range name. However, look closer at the dialog box. The 'Paste List' button in the bottom left-hand corner, if depressed, will paste the list and their definitions into a pre-selected range of cells in an Excel worksheet, which can be invaluable for model auditing purposes.

Sometimes, formulae have been written before the range name was created. In some circumstances, it is possible to apply these names retrospectively using 'Apply Names' within the 'Defined Names' group of the 'Formulas' tab, *viz.*

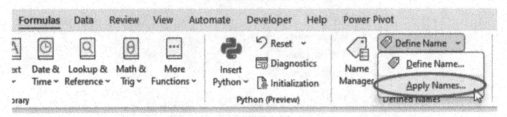

Note that the keyboard shortcut **ALT** + **I** + **N** + **A** will work in all versions of Excel. Selecting the required range names in the resulting dialog box

will see formulae on the active worksheet(s) updated accordingly.

Deleting Range Names

If I got paid just $1 for every time I have been asked how to delete range names I would probably have nearly $10 by now. This was chiefly attributable to the counter-intuitive menu in Excel 2003 and earlier versions:

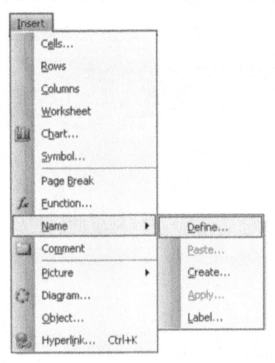

From the resulting dialog box, you would then select the range name (unfortunately, only one at a time could be selected) and hit 'Delete', *viz.*

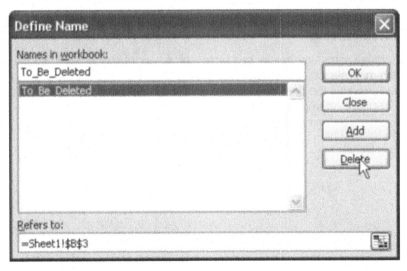

Excel 2007 onwards makes this much simpler. In this case, users are more likely to go to the Name Manager rather than the confusing 'Insert' drop down menu:

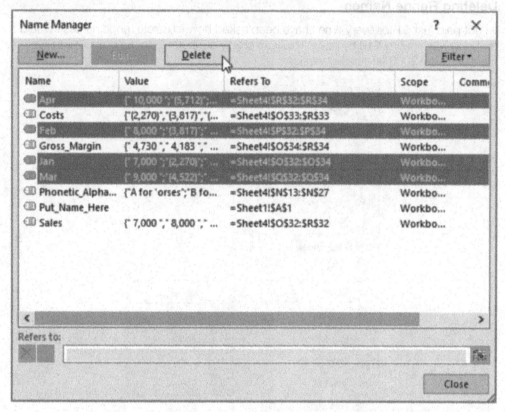

The other marked improvement is that multiple names may be deleted simultaneously by using the **CTRL** or **SHIFT** buttons to make multiple selections before hitting the 'Delete' button. In fact, range names may even be filtered to find names with errors, scoped to the workbook, scoped to the worksheet *etc*.

Relative Referencing

By default, range names are referenced absolutely (i.e. contain the **$** sign so that references remain static). However, imagine a scenario where you are modelling revenue and you wish to grow the prior period value by inflation (already given a range name, say cell **C3** on 'Sheet1'). Simply click on any cell (for example, I will use **D17** arbitrarily), then define the new range name as follows:

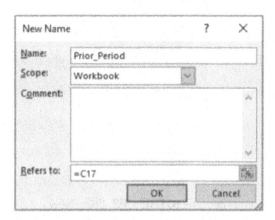

Note the 'Refers to:' entry. Cell **C17** (the cell to the left of **D17**) has been chosen without the dollar signs. This is a relative reference. Once we click on 'OK', the range name '**Prior_Period**' will be defined as the cell immediately to the left of the active cell. We can then inflate values easily by copying the formula

=Prior_Period*(1+Inflation)

across the row.

Other Types of Names

Most of us use the terms 'names' and 'range names' synonymously. However, this is not strictly true. We can create names simply using hard-coded values, *e.g.*

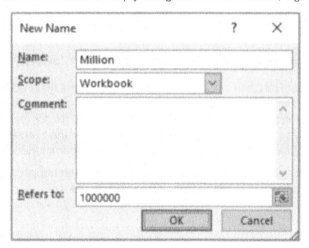

Names may also refer to functions, dates and constants in order to avoid inserting hard code into a formula.

Another useful type is what are called **dynamic ranges**. These ranges vary in size depending upon how they are defined. Consider the following range:

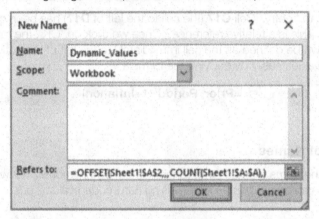

Let's define the following range name (**CTRL** + **F3**, then 'New'):

Here, the range name has been defined by an **OFFSET** formula:

=OFFSET(Sheet1!$A$2,,,COUNT(Sheet1!$A:$A),)

This formula creates a range in cell **A2** with a depth of how many numbers there are in column **A**. In our example, there are six numbers so the range extends to **$A$2:$A$7**. This can be useful for creating versatile ranges for lists or charts, for example. It should be noted that these type of range names will not be visible in the Name Box and will not work with all Excel functions – trial and error is very much recommended!

One interesting quirk of names relating to range names is what happens if you actually reduce the scale of Zoom View (**ALT** + **W** + **Q**) to 39% or below:

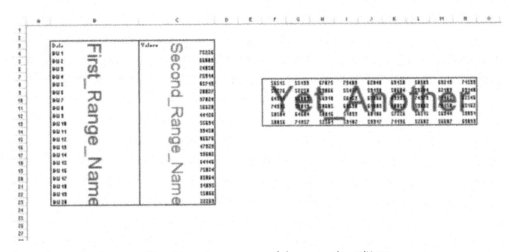

It can be a simple way of tracking down some of those pesky critters.

This section discusses just the tip of the Names iceberg. Experimenting can pay dividends. The aim is not to go overboard however, as a preponderance of names in a workbook may actually make formulae – and hence your model – more difficult to follow.

Further, be careful if you name ranges that are then deleted. The range names will not be deleted (even though they will no longer appear in the Name Box). They will need to be deleted as described above in order to avoid causing potential errors going forward. These types of errors (known as **redundant range name errors**) can cause significant issues and have been known to crash and / or corrupt Excel files on occasion.

CHAPTER 2.6: DATA VALIDATION

Another useful Excel functionality is data validation. This feature restricts what end users may type into a cell. I must admit that this is one of Excel's functionalities I am guilty of assuming everyone knows. However, it's like Styles: many aren't aware of this in Excel, but once you use this functionality and understand what it can do for you, you never go back to whatever it was you were doing before.

To access data validation, from any cell in Excel:

- On the Data tab of the Ribbon, go to the Data Tools group and click the Data Validation icon (**ALT** + **A** + **V** + **V**)

- **ALT** + **D** + **L** still works from earlier versions of Excel.

This brings up the following dialog box:

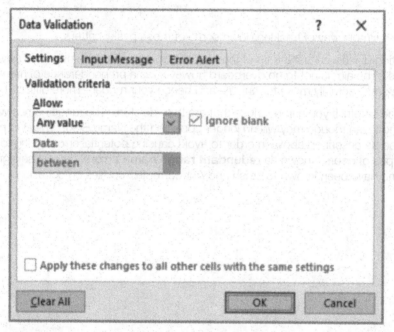

The default setting for all cells in Excel is to allow any value (pictured). This can be changed by changing the selection in the 'Allow' drop down box. It may be modified to any of the following:

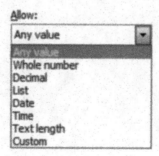

Most of these criteria do exactly what they say on the tin: by choosing 'Decimal', the input must be a number, whereas 'Whole Number' allows for integers only. However, making a selection from the 'Allow' drop down box is only the first part of the data validation process.

Once a selection has been made (for example, I will use 'Whole Number'), the dialog box will change appearance, *viz.*

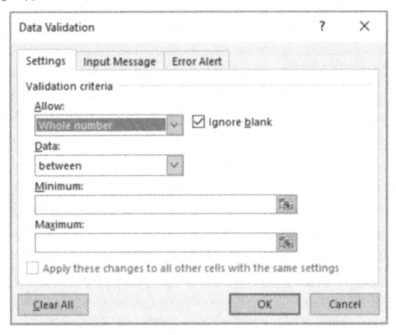

The 'Ignore blank' check box is no longer greyed out. This allows blank cells to be 'valid' regardless of the criteria selected. The remainder of the dialog box is governed by the 'Data' drop down box. There are various selections that may be made:

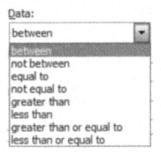

Depending upon the choice made, the box will prompt for values (*e.g.* Minimum and Maximum in the illustration above) which can be typed in, or else the values can refer to cell references directly or indirectly via range names.

Once the choices have been made, you might wish to utilise the other two tabs of the Data Validation dialog box.

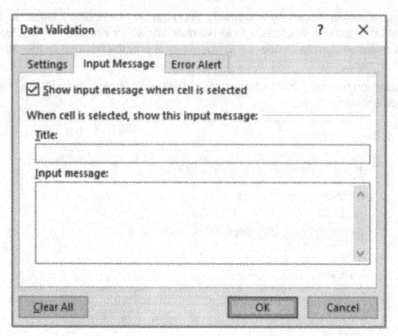

With the 'Show input message when cell is selected' option checked, if the end user selects the data-validated cell, the message typed in here will appear. This can make data inputs in a model much simpler as end users are 'spoon fed' with a pop-up box detailing what to do. In the example below, the 'Input Restrictions' comment only appears when the cell is selected:

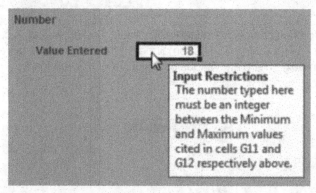

The third tab selects what to do if invalid data is entered in the cell:

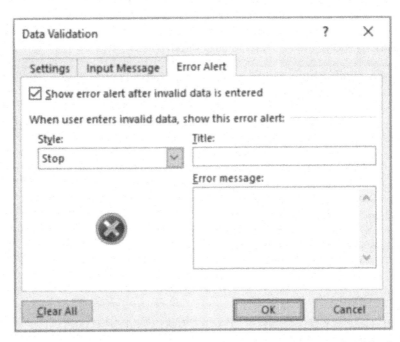

This alerts the end user when an invalid entry has been made (*e.g.* typing "dog" when a number is expected) – as long as the 'Show error alert after invalid data is entered' check box is ticked.

There are three styles available (latest dialogs displayed):

Stop	Warning	Information
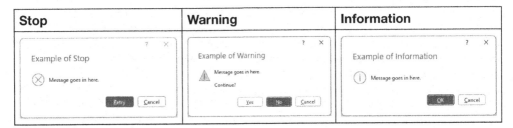		

The three styles provide differing treatment of invalid data:

- **Stop** – the value will not be accepted, and the end user will be prompted to retry;

- **Warning** – the end user will be warned that the data is invalid, but be asked whether it is OK to continue; *and*

- **Information** – the end user will be advised that the data is invalid but that the data has been accepted.

If the 'Show error alert after invalid data is entered' check box is not ticked, no prompt will occur, and invalid data will be accepted in the cell without any warning.

Other Types of Data Validation

Whole Number, Decimal, Date, Time and Text Length are all relatively straightforward, albeit very similar in nature. This leaves just two remaining categories to consider.

List

This functionality allows the end user to select from a list.

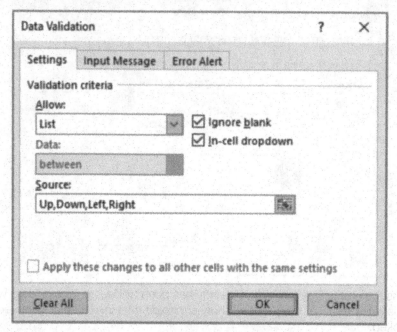

With 'List' selected, the dialog box prompts for a source for the list. In the illustration above, the entries have been typed in, separated by a comma (the delimiter). However, the source can reference cells which are in a column – or a row – as long as the cells are on the same worksheet in versions of Excel up to and including Excel 2003. This can be limiting, and a viable workaround is to name a row or column of data (using the prefix '**LU_**' for **L**ook **U**p) and then use the range name here (which may be pasted in, using the **F3** function key).

For lists, I strongly recommend using the 'In-cell dropdown' which provides a dropdown list of valid entries once the cell has been selected.

Custom

As you become more experienced, you may find the functionality limiting. This is where the final 'Allow' category comes in useful, as you design your own data validation. My recommendation is to experiment with the other types first and then graduate to this classification if you realise the required validation may not be created using the built-in options.

Data Validation is Reactive Not Proactive

Data validation will not solve all of your data entry problems. If data has already been entered into a cell and data validation is applied retrospectively such that the contents of the cell would be deemed invalid, no warning will ensue. Similarly, if the contents of a list are altered, any cells that selected the changed value will not update automatically.

To counter these issues, invalid data may be identified on a worksheet as follows:

- On the Data tab of the Ribbon, go to the Data Tools group and click the drop-down menu next to the Data Validation icon

- Select 'Circle Invalid Data' (**ALT** + **A** + **V** + **I**)

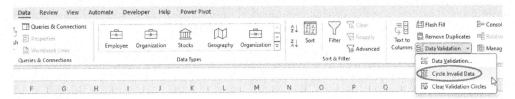

This will circle all invalid data on the worksheet.

One other issue is locating cells that have been data-validated in the first place (i.e. no longer allow 'any value'). The simplest way to do this is through the 'Go to' dialog box (**F5**), click on the 'Special…' button and then select 'Data Validation' (either all data validated cells on the worksheet or else those validated similarly to the cell(s) presently selected):

Select 'Special…' on the Go To Dialog Box	Choose Data Validation
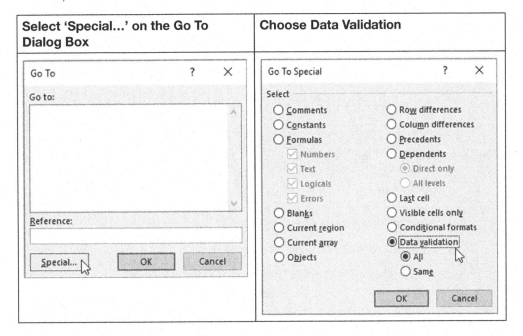	

Best Excel Tip Ever…?

Our company produces a monthly newsletter (feel free to subscribe). A short while ago, we polled our readers for their Best Excel Tip ever – and I think it revealed more about the psyche of our average reader than it ever did about improving efficiencies and effectiveness in the workplace…

As discussed above, data validation is a useful way to control what end users can type into a worksheet cell. You can use this functionality to play a trick. Please use this at your own risk: if you get fired, you will get no sympathy here.

If someone is unfortunate enough to leave a spreadsheet unprotected, simply highlight the whole worksheet and then activate Data Validation (**ALT** + **D** + **L**). In the 'Settings' tab, select settings similar to the following (the aim is to pick a number the user won't use):

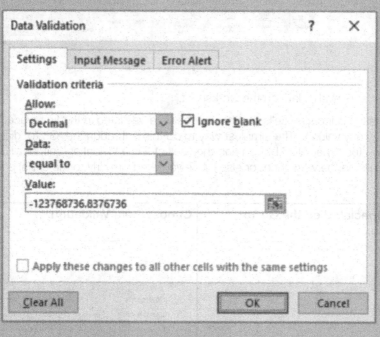

Then, select the 'Error Alert' tab:

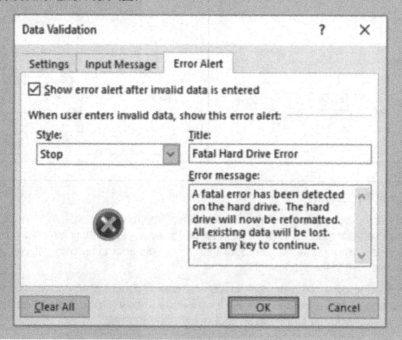

Now, de-select the range and wait for your victim to use the worksheet. As soon as they type an invalid entry, they will be greeted with the following error alert:

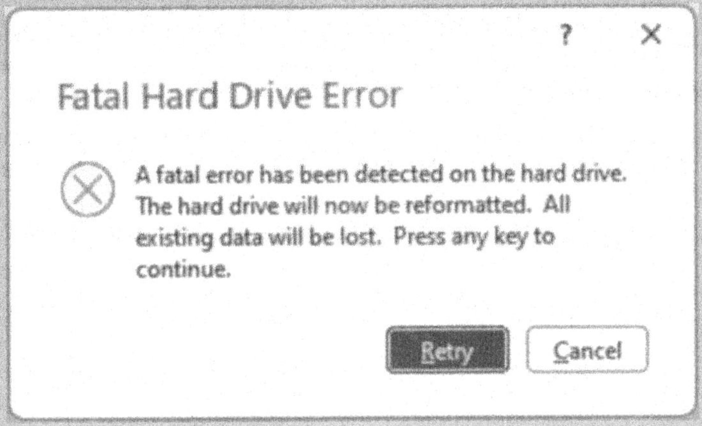

?   X

Fatal Hard Drive Error

A fatal error has been detected on the hard drive. The hard drive will now be reformatted. All existing data will be lost. Press any key to continue.

Retry   Cancel

Who says spreadsheets can't be fun..?

CHAPTER 2.7: DATA TABLES

The next built-in feature I'd like to address, assists with what-if analysis and is an alternative to copy and paste macros. Just to be clear, when I refer to "sensitivity analysis" here, I mean the flexing of one or at most two variables to see how these changes in input affect key outputs. Excel has various built-in features that assist with this type of analysis, but here we will focus on **Data Tables**.

Data Tables are ideal for executive summaries where you wish to show how changes in a particular input affect a key output. However, as always with modelling, Keep It Simple Stupid (KISS). If you can achieve the same functionality without using Data Tables in a simple, straightforward fashion, then do it that way. Consider the following example:

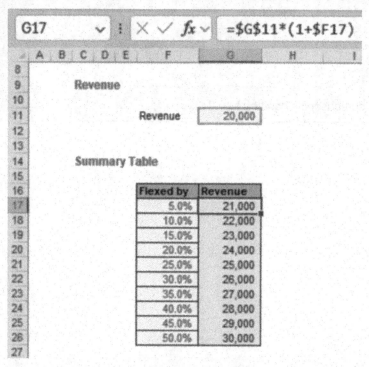

In this illustration, the key output revenue has been given in cell **G11**. We want to summarise what happens if we increase ("flex") this figure by a given percentage, with the inputs specified in cells **F17:F26**. This can be simply computed by using the formula

=$G$11*(1+$F17)

in cell **G17** and simply copying this calculation down.

Data Tables should really be used when such simple calculations are not possible, and you want to flex one variable (known as a "one-variable" or "one-dimensional (**1-D**)" Data Table) or two (known as a "two-variable" or "two-dimensional (**2-D**)" Data Table).

I will now consider each in turn.

1-D Data Tables

This is best illustrated using the following example.

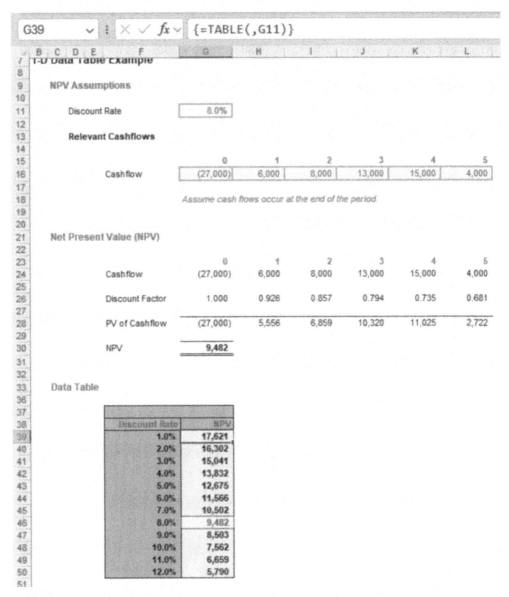

Now I do appreciate this example could be constructed using a similar technique to our revenue example using the **NPV** function: I just wanted to construct a slightly more complex alternative that could still be followed!

Here, a simple Net Present Value calculation is calculated for a total of six periods (0 to 5 inclusive). If you don't understand what this is, don't worry, the point is we are building a calculation. The output for a discount rate of 8.0% (cell **G11**) is +$9,482 (cell **G30**). But what if I wanted to know how the NPV would change if I varied the discount rate?

It is very easy to construct a table (a Data Table) similar to the one displayed in cells **F38:G50** above. The required discount rates are simply typed into cells **F39:F50**, but the headings in cells **F38:G38** are not what they seem.

For a 1-D Data Table to work using a columnar table similar to the one illustrated, the top row has to contain the reference to the input cell in the left-hand cell (**F38** must be **=G11**) and to the output cell in the right-hand cell (**G38** must be **=G30**). Many modellers will do this, putting the headings in the row above instead and then they may or may not hide row 38 in order to compensate.

There is a crafty alternative (employed above).

Using **CTRL** + **1** or **ALT** + **O** + **E** to Format Cells, if we go to the 'Number' tab we can still type the formulae in but change the outward appearance of the cell. For example, cell **F38** is formatted as follows:

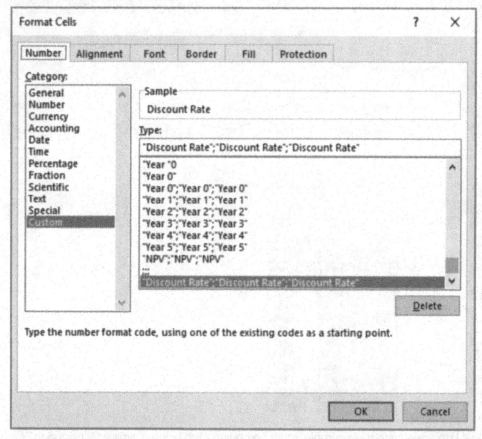

Here, I have typed in "Discount Rate";"Discount Rate";"Discount Rate". Custom number formatting was explained in detail earlier, but essentially this syntax forces Excel to display any numerical output as "Discount Rate". Note that simply typing "Discount Rate" here once would be insufficient: e.g. if the output were negative, the cell would be displayed as "-Discount Rate". **G38** is formatted similarly.

Once row 38 has been finalised, highlight cells **F38:G50** and then create the Data Table as follows:

- Click on the 'Data' tab on the Ribbon

- In the 'Data Tools' group, click on the 'What-If Analysis' icon and select 'Data Table...' (**ALT** + **D** + **T** or **ALT** + **A** + **W** + **T**).

This gives rise to the following dialog box:

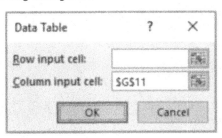

In a 1-D Data Table only one of these two input cells should be populated. When the table is of a columnar format, 'Column input cell:' should be populated, referring to the input cell, as above.

If the table had been across a row instead, ensure that the input values are in the top row, and that the 'headings' are in the first column (i.e. transpose the example table above). Then, you would populate the 'Row input cell:' box above instead.

Once 'OK' has been clicked, the Data Table will populate showing what the NPV would be for alternative discount rates. The formula should be noted: **{=TABLE(,G11)}** shows this is an array function with **G11** as the column input cell. The use of array functions here means that once constructed, the Data Table may not be modified partially.

1-D Data Tables do not need to be simply two columns or two rows. It is entirely possible to display the effects on more than one output at the same time provided you wish to use the same inputs throughout the sensitivity analysis, *viz.*

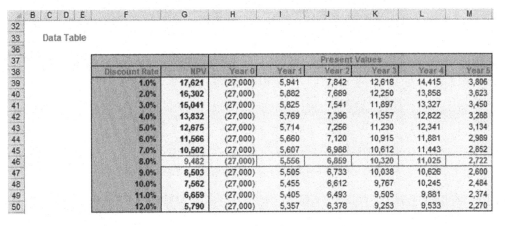

Discount Rate	NPV	Year 0	Year 1	Year 2	Year 3	Year 4	Year 5
				Present Values			
1.0%	17,621	(27,000)	5,941	7,842	12,618	14,415	3,806
2.0%	16,302	(27,000)	5,882	7,689	12,250	13,858	3,623
3.0%	15,041	(27,000)	5,825	7,541	11,897	13,327	3,450
4.0%	13,832	(27,000)	5,769	7,396	11,557	12,822	3,288
5.0%	12,675	(27,000)	5,714	7,256	11,230	12,341	3,134
6.0%	11,566	(27,000)	5,660	7,120	10,915	11,881	2,989
7.0%	10,502	(27,000)	5,607	6,988	10,612	11,443	2,852
8.0%	9,482	(27,000)	5,556	6,859	10,320	11,025	2,722
9.0%	8,503	(27,000)	5,505	6,733	10,038	10,626	2,600
10.0%	7,562	(27,000)	5,455	6,612	9,767	10,245	2,484
11.0%	6,659	(27,000)	5,405	6,493	9,505	9,881	2,374
12.0%	5,790	(27,000)	5,357	6,378	9,253	9,533	2,270

2-D Data Tables

These Data Tables are similar in idea: they simply allow for two inputs to be varied at the same time. Let's extend the 1-D example as follows:

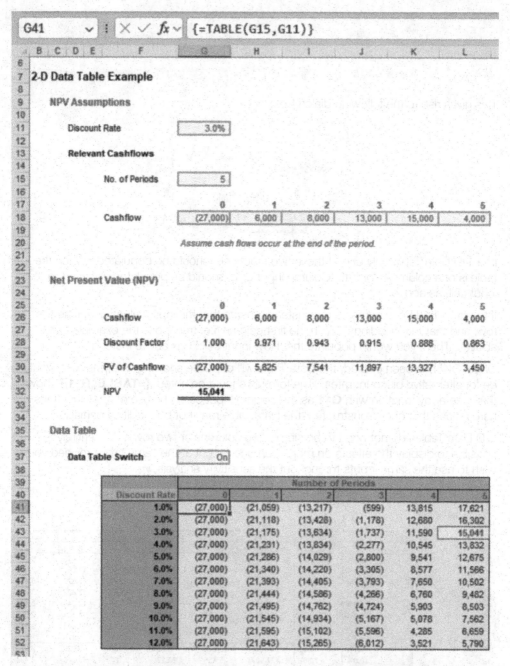

| G41 | ⌄ | : | ✕ ✓ *fx* ⌄ | {=TABLE(G15,G11)} |

	B C D E	F	G	H	I	J	K	L
6								
7	**2-D Data Table Example**							
8								
9	NPV Assumptions							
10								
11	Discount Rate		3.0%					
12								
13	Relevant Cashflows							
14								
15	No. of Periods		5					
16								
17			0	1	2	3	4	5
18	Cashflow		(27,000)	6,000	8,000	13,000	15,000	4,000
19								
20		*Assume cash flows occur at the end of the period.*						
21								
22								
23	Net Present Value (NPV)							
24								
25			0	1	2	3	4	5
26	Cashflow		(27,000)	6,000	8,000	13,000	15,000	4,000
27								
28	Discount Factor		1.000	0.971	0.943	0.915	0.888	0.863
29								
30	PV of Cashflow		(27,000)	5,825	7,541	11,897	13,327	3,450
31								
32	NPV		15,041					
33								
34								
35	Data Table							
36								
37	Data Table Switch		On					
38								
39					Number of Periods			
40		Discount Rate	0	1	2	3	4	5
41		1.0%	(27,000)	(21,059)	(13,217)	(599)	13,815	17,621
42		2.0%	(27,000)	(21,118)	(13,428)	(1,178)	12,680	16,302
43		3.0%	(27,000)	(21,175)	(13,634)	(1,737)	11,590	15,041
44		4.0%	(27,000)	(21,231)	(13,834)	(2,277)	10,545	13,832
45		5.0%	(27,000)	(21,286)	(14,029)	(2,800)	9,541	12,675
46		6.0%	(27,000)	(21,340)	(14,220)	(3,305)	8,577	11,566
47		7.0%	(27,000)	(21,393)	(14,405)	(3,793)	7,650	10,502
48		8.0%	(27,000)	(21,444)	(14,586)	(4,266)	6,760	9,482
49		9.0%	(27,000)	(21,495)	(14,762)	(4,724)	5,903	8,503
50		10.0%	(27,000)	(21,545)	(14,934)	(5,167)	5,078	7,562
51		11.0%	(27,000)	(21,595)	(15,102)	(5,596)	4,285	6,659
52		12.0%	(27,000)	(21,643)	(15,265)	(6,012)	3,521	5,790
53								

This example is similar, but only calculates the NPV for a certain number of periods – specified in cell G15. Our 2-D Data Table (which is cells **F40:L52**, not **F39:L52**) can answer the question, "What is the NPV of our project over **x** periods with a discount rate of **y**%?". It also displays the current value in blue using conditional formatting. Again, if you don't follow, it doesn't matter – the point is, there's a sophisticated calculation here dependent upon two inputs and the output may be summarised easily.

If anything, a 2-D Data Table is simpler than its 1-D counterpart since there is little confusion over row and column input cells. The formula for analysis is always positioned in the top left-hand corner of the Data Table (in this example, this is cell **F40**). Again, the output needs to be in the table, this time it must be in the top left-hand corner of the array. In our example, it is disguised as "Discount Rate" using similar number formatting to that described earlier.

The inputs required now form the remainder of the top row and the first column of the Data Table. With cells **F40:L52** highlighted, the Data Table dialog box is opened as before:

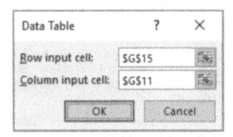

Since the top row are the inputs for the Number of Periods, the 'Row input cell:' should reference **$G$15**, whilst the discount rate inputs ('Column input cell:') should link to **$G$11** once more.

Once 'OK' is depressed, the Data Table will populate as required – simple!

Important Considerations

Data Tables can be really useful for executive summaries, but there are drawbacks to consider:

- The variable inputs to be flexed should always be hard coded since formulae may not work as envisaged with this feature. This is due to the fact that these calculations may be dependent upon other calculations that may vary for differing inputs, which may change as the Data Table calculates. This can prove cumbersome if you wish to change the Data Tables regularly;

- Data Tables can slow down the file calculation time dramatically. For example, if you have just three 2-D Data Tables, each with ten inputs on each axis, the model calculation time could increase by a factor of up to 300 (= 3 x 10 x 10).

  Microsoft has recognised this issue and allows you to change Excel's Calculation option (found in ALT + T + O, under 'Calculation') to 'Automatic except for data tables':

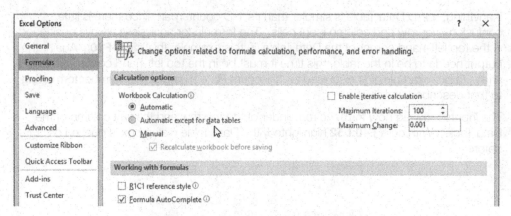

I strongly recommend you do not implement this option. End users tend to assume Excel is always calculating everything automatically and some do not know how to check / modify this functionality.

Instead, I would build in 'On / Off' switches next to the Data Tables themselves. These are transparent and intuitive and have the same effect. All that is required is that the output formula is revised to be

=IF(Switch="On",Calculation,)

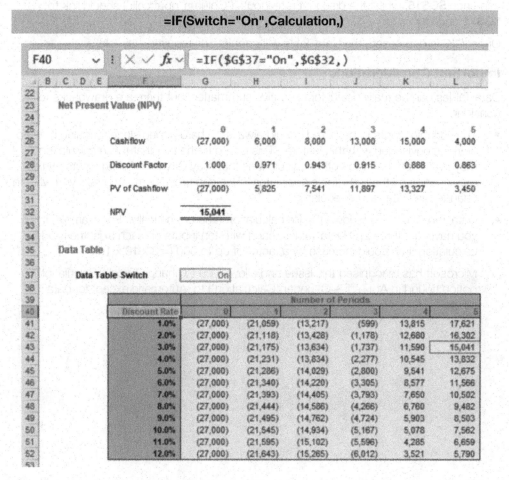

- Data Tables will only flex one or two variables at a time. If more variations are changed, consider using Excel's **Scenario Manager** or the **Solver add-in** (depending upon your requirements, discussed in the next chapter).

One other point to note is that although there are workarounds, in general the inputs and outputs should be on the same worksheet as the Data Table. This is not always ideal, but this Excel restriction may be circumvented as follows.

Data Table on Other Sheets

I have a saying that anything is possible in Excel. Maybe one day I may come unstuck, but today is not that day. The issue is that Excel restricts where the referred inputs must be located, *i.e.* they must be positioned on the same page. If you try and reference cells on another worksheet, or become cunning and use range names which refer to cells on another worksheet (a useful workaround on many occasions), you will encounter the following error message:

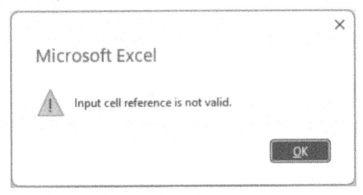

Most financial modellers will recall the mantra of keeping inputs separate from calculations separate from outputs. Data Tables force you to put outputs on the same worksheet as the inputs which can confuse end users and make it difficult to put all key outputs together.

So how can you get round this? My solution assumes you do not wish to hide Data Tables on the input sheet and then link them to another worksheet (this is cumbersome and can make the model less efficient).

To make things more "difficult", I will assume that you have already built your financial model and the Data Tables are to be incorporated as an afterthought. There could be two inputs to incorporate. I will explain how to create one of them (you then just have to follow this process twice).

Firstly, create a "dummy" input cell on the same worksheet as the Data Table. This needs to be protected such that data cannot be entered into this cell. I will assume that this cell is **W44** (say) on the Sheet2 worksheet, *i.e.* the same sheet as the Data Table.

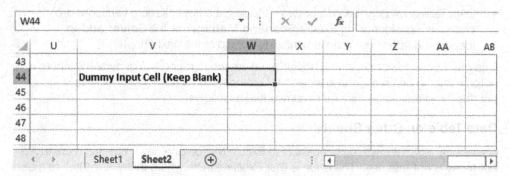

Secondly, link the Data Table (**ALT** + **D** + **T**) to this dummy input (in the illustration here, I assume that the Data Table is a 1-dimensional Data Table):

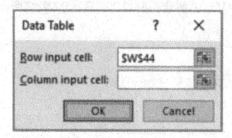

Thirdly, let us assume you actually want the Data Table to link to "Input 1" (cell **D4**) on 'Sheet1':

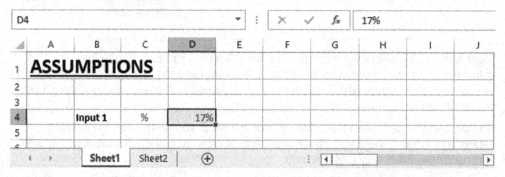

Fourthly, since we have already built the model, this input will already be linked throughout the model. Since I do not wish to change all the dependent formulae, I first cut (NOT copy) the input into an adjacent cell:

Fifthly, a <u>copy</u> is pasted back into the original cell (here, this was cell **D4**):

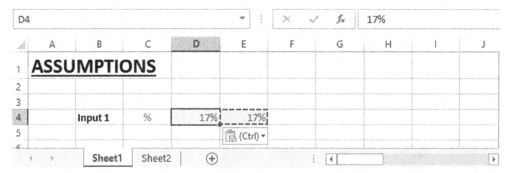

Finally, the value in cell **E4** is replaced with the following formula

=IF(Sheet2!W44="",D4,Sheet2!W44)

and then formatted / protected to ensure end users do not actually type into this cell:

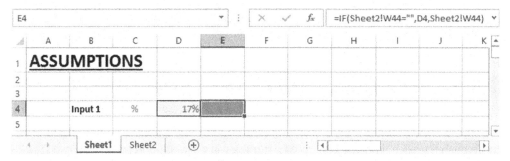

The Data Table will now work. This is because:

- The Data Table links directly to a cell on the same sheet as the Data Table, but indirectly to the input on the other worksheet;

- Cell **E4** on 'Sheet1' is now the cell that drives all calculations throughout the model, even though it appears to have been added;

- Cell **D4** on 'Sheet1' still appears to be – and acts like – the original input it replaces.

CHAPTER 2.8: GOAL SEEK and SOLVER

Three accountants go for a job interview. The first one goes in and is handed a glass of water, precisely half-filled. The interviewer asks him to describe the contents, to which he replies, "It's half empty". "Thank you," replies the interviewer, "We will let you know". The accountant walks out and shrugs his shoulders as he walks past the remaining two candidates.

The second accountant walks in and is asked the same question. She thinks for a second and then responds, "It's half full". "Thank you," replies the interviewer, "We will let you know". The second accountant walks out. She scratches her head quizzically as she walks away from the final interviewee.

The third accountant – who is also a financial modeller – walks in and is asked the very same question. "What would you like it to be?" the modeller enquires. "When can you start?" asks the interviewer.

Ever since spreadsheets and calculators were invented there have been two types of forecasting task: those that seek accurate forecasting and those that, well, seek the number first thought of. It is commonplace in modelling for users to ascertain what value an input must have in order to achieve a desired outcome. Modellers need to possess the skills to facilitate this even with the most complex spreadsheets. Luckily, there are tools available.

Consider the following example:

1 Jan 24	18 Mar 24	24 Aug 24	24 Aug 25	18 Oct 25	19 Oct 27	17 Apr 28	18 Apr 30
-	($50,000.00)	$18,750.00	$12,412.00	$57.16	$1,655.22	$19,450.66	-

Here, let's imagine we have been asked to calculate the internal rate of return (**IRR**) on these cash flows (*i.e.* imagine you could put money in the bank and either invest or pay interest at the same compounding rate. IRR would be the rate which would make the totals including all interest add up to zero).

NPV and IRR

The **Present Value** (**PV**) of a cashflow is defined as "what it is worth today". Some describe it as compound interest in reverse. If you were to deposit $100 in the bank today at an interest rate of 10% p.a., then in one year's time it would be worth $110, in two years' time it would be worth $121 and in three years' time it would be worth $133.10, *etc.*

With a **discount factor** of 10%, the present value of $110 in one year's time would be $100 today; the present value of $121 in two years' time would be $100 now; the present value of $133.10 in three years' time would also be $100 today.

The sum of all present values, both positive and negative is known as the **Net Present Value** (**NPV**). Theoretically, if you invest in a project with a particular discount rate – also known as the cost of capital – you should only proceed with the project (from a financial perspective) if the NPV is greater than zero. This is known as **value accreting**.

The **Internal Rate of Return** (**IRR**) is the discount rate which makes the NPV precisely zero.

It will probably not surprise you that I have deliberately chosen a set of values which cause problems for Excel. Excel has two functions which calculate the IRR: **IRR** (when cashflows occur on a regular / periodic basis) and **XIRR** (when cashflows do not occur on a regular basis). Neither will work on the above:

- **IRR** will not work as the periods are not equidistant;

- **XIRR** gives an incorrect answer (0.00%). If this were correct, then the sum of the cash flows excluding any interest effects (known as the **undiscounted cashflows**) must equal zero. They do not:

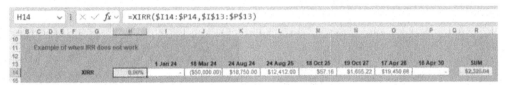

You may have noted that the valuation functions **IRR**, **XIRR**, **NPV** and **XNPV** have neither been demonstrated nor explained fully anywhere in this book. This is because they do not always calculate correctly. I am a keen advocate of taking these computations back to first principles instead so that everyone may understand how the results have been derived.

So, allow me to take this example back to first principles. Here, I have created an elementary Net Present Value calculation:

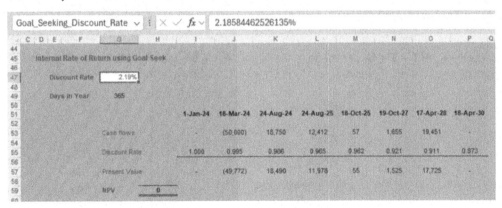

To generate the value in cell **G47**, I have manually kept changing it to try to get a zero NPV in cell **H59**. I did this as follows:

- Typed in a rate of 0%: NPV was $2,325 (positive)

- Tried a higher rate of 10%; NPV was negative, ($6,650)

- Tried a rate of 5% (mid-point between the two rates): NPV was ($2,666) (still negative)

- Tried a rate of 2.5% (mid-point between 0% and 5%): NPV was ($315) (negative, but getting smaller)

- Tried a rate of 1.25% (mid-point of 0% and 2.5%): NPV was $966 (positive)

  etc.

After a gazillion attempts (look it up, it's a technical term), I will get very close if I keep bisecting the two rates that provide the smallest positive and smallest negative NPVs. You can imagine this will become heavily time-consuming and I will have less time to do the things I would rather do than this – like pulling out my toenails...

The general rule with financial modelling is whenever you catch yourself doing the same thing over and over again, it's very likely you haven't realised there is an easier way to do whatever it is you are doing. Like here. I can use Excel's Goal Seek functionality to derive the discount rate that will make the NPV zero:

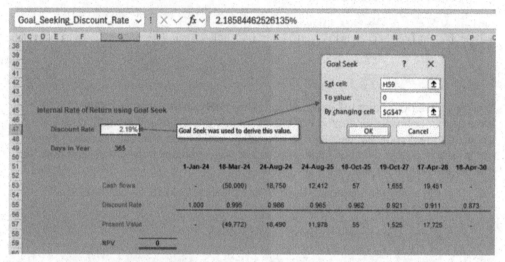

Goal Seek (**ALT** + **T** + **G**, or else go to the 'Data' tab on the Ribbon, then in the 'Data Tools' group, select 'What-If Analysis' and then choose 'Goal Seek...') requires three inputs:

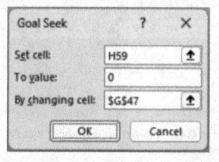

The 'Set cell:' value is the NPV output here, 'To value' is the desired outcome (e.g. zero) and 'By changing cell:' defines the variable input (e.g. discount rate). So, what happens if you want to set the 'To value:' to refer to a cell value rather than a typed-in number?

I have a very simple response: you can't.

So, what can you do instead..?

Introducing Solver

Excel includes a (hidden) tool called **Solver** that uses techniques from operations research to find optimal solutions for all kind of decision problems. It is not situated in the standard load set: it has to be loaded from Excel's add-ins.

In any version of Excel, a simple way to access add-ins is to use the keystroke shortcut **ALT + T + I**:

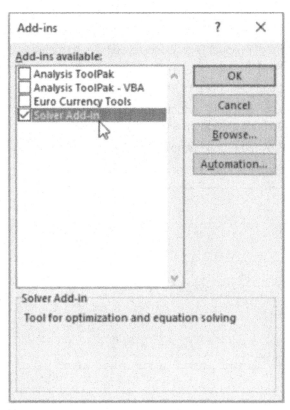

Checking the Solver add-in will add Solver to the 'Data' tab of the Ribbon:

Solver is often used to optimise / minimise outputs. Consider the following example:

	kg	Profit / kg ($)	Profit ($)
Maximising Product			
Product A	100	$ 9.00	$ 900.00
Product B	50	$ 10.00	$ 500.00
Product C	475	$ 11.00	$ 5,225.00
Product D	375	$ 12.00	$ 4,500.00
	1,000		**$ 11,125.00**

Imagine you run a company with four products: A, B, C and D. Your intention is to maximise company profits, but you only have 1,000kg of the raw material necessary for these four products. If this is all there is to the problem, then it would be simple – only produce Product D. However, imagine you had the following operational constraints:

- For every kilogram of Product B produced, you have to manufacture at least two kilograms of Product A;

- You must produce at least 50kg of Product B;

- Product C is a by-product of Products A and D: the total weight of Products A and D must equal the number of kilograms of Product C produced.

The above graphic shows the optimal solution; the question is, how did I derive it?

To recreate the solution, open the Solver dialog box:

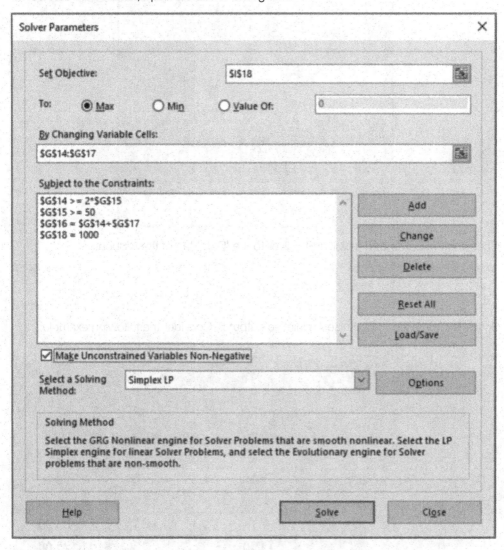

The "objective" here would be the output, i.e. total profit (cell **I18** in the example) and the aim is to maximise it (note the other two alternatives of minimisation or trying to generate a particular output value). This is achieved by selecting which cells may be varied (here the kg produced), subject to the constraints specified. Constraints are simple to include – merely click the 'Add' button:

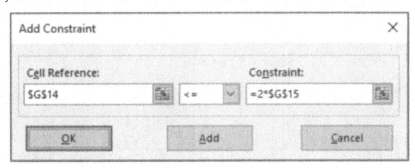

In Excel 2010 and later versions, Solver explicitly allows one of three Solving methods:

- **Simplex Method:** this method is used for solving linear problems (i.e. where the relationship between variables could be charted using a straight line). Our example above is one such instance;

- **GRG Nonlinear:** this is used for solving smooth nonlinear problems;

- **Evolutionary Solver:** this approach uses genetic algorithms to find its solutions. While the Simplex and GRG solvers are used for linear and smooth nonlinear problems, the Evolutionary Solver can be used for any Excel formulas or functions, even when they are not linear or smooth nonlinear. Spreadsheet functions such as **IF** and **VLOOKUP** fall into this category.

In summary, Solver is a more powerful variant of Goal Seek, allowing forecasters to derive inputs to achieve specific goals and objectives. However, upon first inspection, Solver still does not appear to allow the value to be set to be a cell reference.

Therefore, you need to employ a simple trick.

Using Solver with a Reference

I will return to the NPV example:

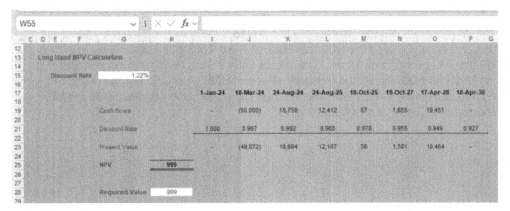

In this instance, I could have used Goal Seek as before, but instead I got out the heavy artillery:

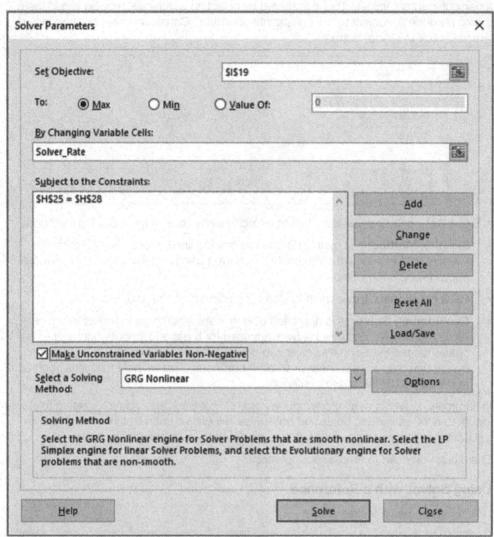

The discount rate (**Solver_Rate**) here is cell **G15**. You should notice two little tricks though: I have not used the NPV (cell **H25**) as the output, but a dummy value of cell **I19** (the first period's cash flow). This allows us to select a very useful constraint: that the NPV (cell **H25**) equals the required value (cell **H28**). It should also be noted that compounding discount rates is clearly a non-linear calculation technique so Simplex should not be used as a Solving Method.

This has allowed me to show you a neat trick, but I am not entirely convinced of this solution. I cannot help feeling we are cracking a walnut with a thermonuclear warhead and besides, you still have to activate the Solver – this method will not update values automatically as inputs change.

So, is there another way..?

VBA Approach

Well, yes there is, although it involves VBA, which regular readers will note is a method I try to fall back on only when all else fails. This could be argued (perhaps!) as one such instance.

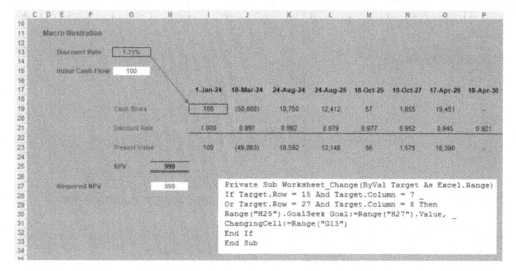

In this example, there are two inputs, initial cash flow and required NPV (cells **G15** and **H27** respectively). Typing a value in either cell will change the discount rate in cell **G13** so that the NPV (cell **H25**) equals the required value.

This was achieved using a macro.

I have included the macro code by right-clicking on the relevant worksheet tab and selecting 'View Code', *viz.*

This will launch the Visual Basic Editor:

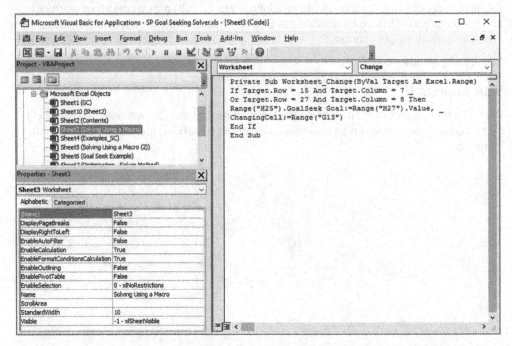

Not all of the above panes may be visible, but in the right-hand pane, paste in the following code (as shown in the graphic above):

```
Private Sub Worksheet_Change(ByVal Target As Excel.Range)
If Target.Row = 15 And Target.Column = 7 _
Or Target.Row = 27 And Target.Column = 8 Then
Range("H25").GoalSeek Goal:=Range("H27").Value, _
ChangingCell:=Range("G13")
End If
End Sub
```

It is very straightforward: if cell **G15** (row 15, column 7) or **H27** (row 27, column 8) is edited the macro is invoked and changes the discount rate in cell **G13** such that the NPV in cell **H25** equals the required output specified in cell **H27**.

Assuming macros are enabled (see earlier), this will change the discount rate without calling either Goal Seek or Solver. If you choose to use the macro solution, do remember to save the Excel file as a macro enabled workbook!

CHAPTER 2.9: HYPERLINKS

I commonly use hyperlinks in my Excel files as they are a great way to move around a file. If you create a central worksheet with hyperlinks to all of the other worksheets, you are only ever two clicks away from anywhere else in the workbook. They make life very easy for end users and once you know how to construct them, they take mere seconds to insert.

The 'Insert Hyperlink' dialog box is fairly straightforward to use and readily accessed via one of two keyboard shortcuts, either **ALT** + **I** + **I** or **CTRL** + **K**. Alternatively, from the Ribbon, select the 'Insert' tab, click on 'Link' in the 'Links' group (this may say 'Hyperlink' in some versions of Excel):

Hyperlinks can be used to link to a variety of places, but in this instance, I will focus on linking to elsewhere within the same workbook.

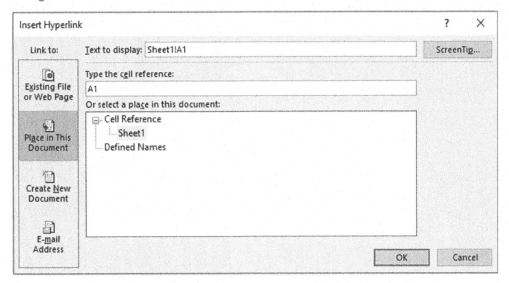

To create a hyperlink, first select the cell or range of cells that you wish to act as the hyperlink (*i.e.* clicking on any of these cells will activate the hyperlink). Then, open the 'Insert Hyperlink' dialog box (above) and select 'Place in This Document' as the 'Link to:', which will change the appearance of the rest of the dialog box.

Insert the text for the hyperlink in the 'Text to display:' input box (clicking on the 'ScreenTip…' button will allow you to create an informative message in a message box when you hover over the hyperlink).

The next two input boxes, 'Type the cell reference:' and 'Or select a place in this document:', work in tandem – sort of:

- If you type a cell reference in the first input box without making a selection in the second input box, the hyperlink will link to the cell reference on the current (active) worksheet;

149

- If you type a cell reference in the first input box and select a worksheet reference in the second box, the hyperlink will link to the specified cell in the given worksheet. In my example above, this hyperlink will jump to 'Sheet1' cell **A1**; *or*

- If you select a 'Defined Name' (*i.e.* a pre-defined range name) in the second input box, this will link to the cell(s) specified. This is the recommended option, where available, if you wish to link to cell(s) on another worksheet within the same workbook. This is because if the destination worksheet's sheet name were to be changed, the link would still work. I recommend that the range name should start with **HL_** for **H**yper **L**ink, to make it easier to sort through range names if necessary.

It should be noted that there is an Excel function, **HYPERLINK(link_location,[friendly_name])**. I tend not to use this as it is not so user-friendly.

CHAPTER 3: OTHER EXCEL POINTERS

Now that we have reviewed key functions and features, before I start developing a work-sheet, let me discuss setting up Excel in the first instance. There are ways to make your life a little easier when setting up a spreadsheet – so allow me to set up some of the founda-tions…

Quick Analysis

One useful addition initially came out in Excel 2013: **Quick Analysis**.

To ensure it is enabled, go to Excel Options (**ALT** + **T** + **O**) and select 'General' from the left-hand column. Then, ensure 'Show Quick Analysis options on selection' from 'User Interface options' is ticked:

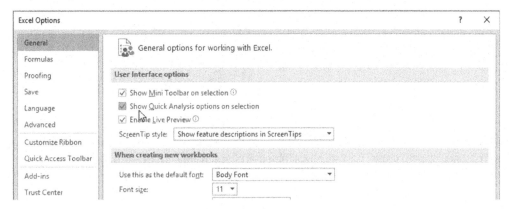

This feature is clearly aimed at those still feeling their way round some of the more sophisticated analytical tools in Excel. All you need to do is highlight the entire data set to be analysed (including headings) and click on the Quick Analysis icon in the bottom right-hand corner, *viz.*

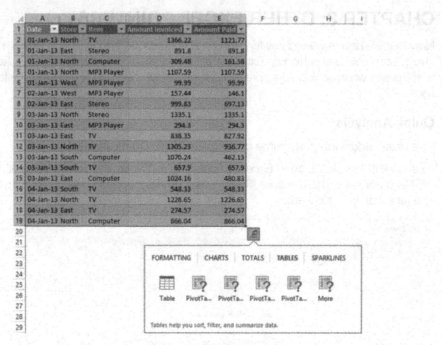

This generates a pop-up menu where the user can make simple selections regarding formatting, charts, totals, Tables, PivotTables and sparklines (charts in a cell). For example:

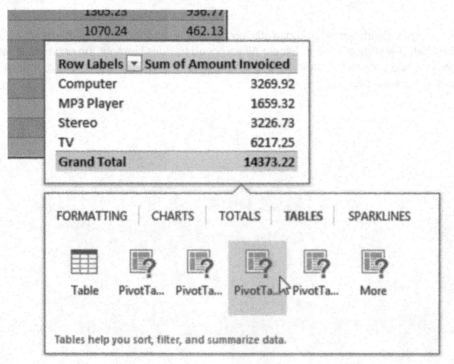

I recall when Excel 2013 first came out that I ought to be on commission for Microsoft. I used to demonstrate why this tool was so useful by creating a reasonably sophisticated chart with just a couple of clicks of the mouse. In seconds, I used to transform the example:

Business Unit	Sales	Gross Margin
A	$ 100	22%
B	$ 80	18%
C	$ 65	34%
D	$ 125	25%
E	$ 45	17%
F	$ 140	30%
G	$ 90	20%
H	$ 105	22%

by clicking on the Quick Analysis tool and converting the data into the following chart:

Now yes, I appreciate it isn't *that* difficult to construct that chart. The point I make here is that Excel can create it *immediately*.

New Workbook Defaults

I hate to admit it, but I find as I get older my eyesight has deteriorated. Therefore, consider the options in 'When creating new workbooks':

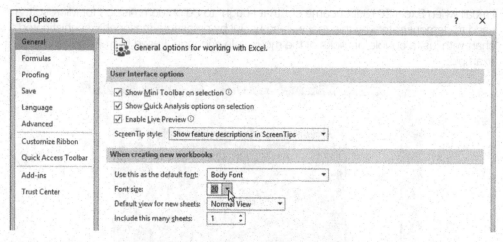

Changing the font size scales up the workbook fonts including – most importantly – the Formula toolbar. This is particularly useful for tired eyes, presentations, and training.

The final option in this section, 'Include this many sheets' is also useful if you find yourself copying / deleting worksheets in a newly created workbook on a regular basis.

Formulas Options

The options in Excel Options (**ALT** + **T** + **O**) -> **'Formulas'** are useful too.

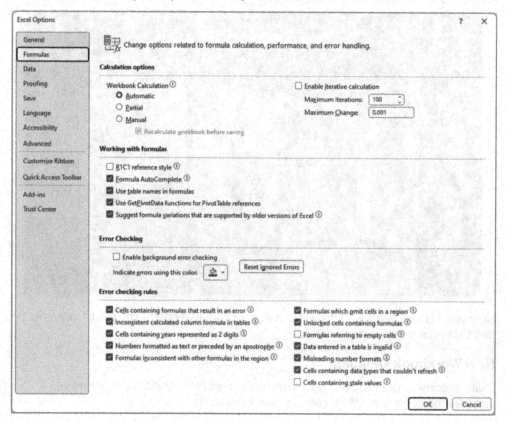

The Workbook Calculation in 'Calculation options' should <u>always</u> be set to 'Automatic'. No exception. Why? Well, how many times have you opened another's workbook, changed inputs, and relied upon the outputs? On those occasions, how often did you check the model calculations were set to 'Automatic'? Exactly.

There are some professional modelling firms out there that advise you should set calculations to 'Automatic except for data tables' (earlier versions of Excel) or 'Partial' (later versions of Excel). I disagree. Yes, Data Tables may slow a model down, but if you want a Data Table to cease calculating, it should be done *transparently*. Whilst this is not about Data Tables, just to reiterate, data validation could be employed to do this on the face of a worksheet, rather than hidden away in Excel Options.

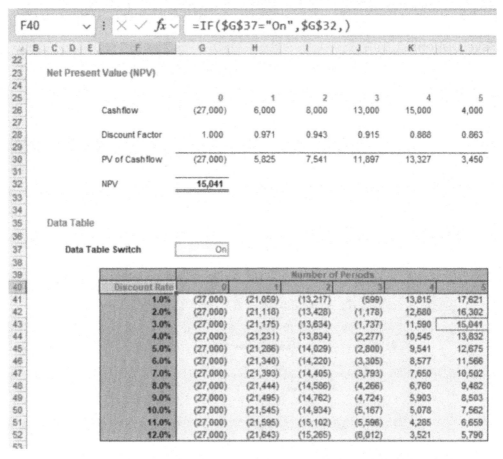

There are other functionalities to consider on this page of Excel Options as well. 'Formula AutoComplete' provides the prompt that has made entering calculations simpler since the advent of Excel 2007.

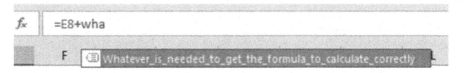

I would recommend keeping that option checked. 'Use table names in formulas' and 'Use GetPivotData functions for PivotTable references' do similar things. Given Tables and PivotTables may both change structure depending upon filters and the data added, linking to a structured reference such as

> **=GETPIVOTDATA("Amount Paid",$A$1,"Item","Stereo")**

can ensure the correct reference is always applied no matter how the structure of the underlying Table or PivotTable may vary.

The last section in 'Formulas' concerns error checking. I strongly recommend that 'Enable background error checking' is selected. This allows Excel to identify and highlight common errors that modellers make, and essentially protects you from yourself.

Save Options

The options in Excel Options (**ALT** + **T** + **O**) -> **'Save'** is another area to review.

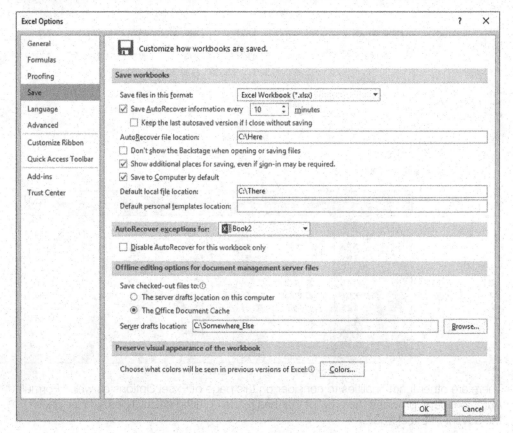

Note the default save format: it is as an Excel Workbook (***.xlsx**) file. This type of file does not permit macros. I can understand that Microsoft wants to err on the side of caution and therefore does not allow macros by default, but there are hidden dangers with selecting this option. If you receive an Excel file from a third party and open it, say, from Microsoft Outlook, when you try to save it, Excel will save it as an **xlsx** file. If there are macros contained within the workbook, these may be removed if the warning message when saving is not read properly. Therefore, it is arguably safer to modify the 'Save files in this format:' option to 'Excel Macro-Enabled Workbook (*.xlsm)' instead.

The next option down can also be troublesome. For years, scientists have been spending millions on developing AI (Artificial Intelligence). I really do not know why they have bothered. Microsoft perfected this nearly 30 years ago. Ever made a clanger in Excel and you were just about to undo when Excel automatically saved your file?

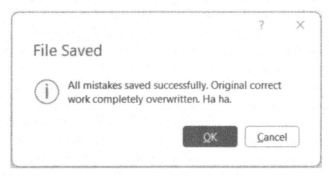

Microsoft has long since learned when it's the most inopportune time to save. In the middle of a long, complex formula? Presenting the results to the board? Trying to get work out in a rush? No problem, Excel will autosave now, thank you very much. This can be very frustrating – but there is a remedy: either extend the duration or switch it off completely.

Now be careful here. I once recommended this to a group of accountants who the next time they bumped into me had brought along a tree, gallows, and a noose. If you switch AutoSave off, *make sure you save regularly* or you may lose your work. Professional modellers tend to switch AutoSave off but train themselves to save every two to five minutes. Seriously. This way, you can save a file on your own terms.

Saving Files

It is a good idea to have a good nomenclature set up for file saving. I tend to use the format:

'Meaningful Filename vLB1.01'.xlsm

Meaningful Filename is not 'INT RND OMG FG ex Crs' or 'Project Wildebeast'. I am a professional consultant and I have liaised on many confidential projects in my time. Not only have some of the codenames been a mite questionable over the years, but 12 - 24 months later you cannot remember which project goes with which codename. It is better to keep your files in a secure location and call it 'Chess Pieces Sales Five Year Forecasts' so you can find it quickly when you need to.

LB simply represents my initials. Don't use mine, use yours. It's good to know who the author was, as so few modellers bother to update this in File Properties. It gives the end user a fighting chance as to who they ought to approach should they have any queries.

v..1.01 is the version number. Rather than using dates, I use numbering. The date information is stored in the metafile in any case. I tend to add 0.01 to the numbering every two hours. This means that if a file were to corrupt, I never have to do too much re-work. It also helps in the consulting industry as I know vLB1.15 represents approximately 30 hours work.

I add one [1] to the version number when something significant has happened. This may be to signify that the model has been presented to senior management, or that sales calculations were totally re-worked or that a particular subsidiary's data has been completely added / removed. These are "landmarks", and it is these changes that should be documented in a File Changes document (I am optimistic that you might be creating one of these!).

Another major source of irritation is trying to save a file for the first time, only to watch Excel spend six weeks thinking about it whilst it endeavours to connect to the Cloud. Checking 'Save to Computer by default' will save you tearing out all of your hair.

One last item on this page is 'Disable AutoRecover for this workbook only'. This should not be confused with AutoSave. This is the option whereby Excel will make a valiant attempt to save something of your file should Excel crash, so that when you re-open, the 'recovered' file will be available. It will not overwrite your existing work, but instead create a temporary recovery file for you to inspect and decide whether you wish to retain it.

Now it might seem like switching this option off is like buying a new car without brakes, but if your PC is struggling with memory issues, this may be a reason for considering disabling the option. I vehemently suggest you don't though: closing other applications down is immensely preferable. It may be better to live without iTunes for an hour or two, rather than your friends or family for the weekend...

Advanced Options

The largest selection of options in Excel Options (**ALT** + **T** + **O**) is contained in the **'Advanced'** section. I could probably write a book just going through these options, but I think it might be even more boring than this one.

It is worth perusing this section and changing options deciding upon personal preferences. Some of the multitude of options include:

- In 'Editing options', un-check 'Allow editing directly in cells'. This will mean all formulae when typed will appear in the Formula bar rather than in the worksheet making it easier to read and easier to select nearby cells with the mouse. Further, with this option unchecked double-clicking on a formula reveals precedent cells (the **F5** key will take you back afterwards). This is always the first thing I do in Excel after installing a new edition.

- Checking 'Enable automatic percent entry' in the 'Editing options' section allows you to type percentages into Excel faster as you do not always have to hunt out the pesky % symbol.

- For those in other regions of the world where the decimal point is replaced by the comma and the comma replaced by the semi-colon for example, it's possible to change these settings without changing the regional settings on your computer. Simply uncheck 'Use system separators' in 'Editing options' and make your own choice.

- If you want to access the last few files in the Backstage area of your workbook, check 'Quickly access this number of Recent Workbooks' in the 'Display' section and specify the number of workbooks you wish to view.

- Sometimes, graphics go missing in Excel. No one is quite sure why, but it does happen. To make these objects reappear, go to 'Display options for this workbook' and ensure 'For objects, show:' is set to 'All'.

- Don't want zeros to be displayed? This can be achieved with number formatting or else you can un-check 'Show a zero in cells that have zero value' in the 'Display options for this workbook' section.

- If you have a more powerful computer and / or you are using 64-bit Excel, you may require a bit more grunt for some of your formulae. In the 'Formulas' section, consider checking 'Enable multi-threaded calculation' to ensure you are availing yourself of all of your hardware's capabilities.

- Ever typed in 'Jan' in one cell, 'Feb' in the next cell and then completed the rest of the months by highlighting both cells and using Excel's AutoFill feature? You are exploiting one of the built-in lists in Excel. If you want to add other lists, it's easy – simply click on the 'Edit Custom Lists…' button in the 'General' section and either type the list in manually or link to a pre-existing list in your spreadsheet.

Quick Access Toolbar

Everyone has favourite features / functions in Excel, some of which are buried away deep in the software. Let me give you an example. Ever closed that final file in Excel 2013 or later version only for the application to close down as well? There is a workaround.

In Excel 2013, simply right-click on the Quick Access Toolbar and select 'Customize Quick Access Toolbar…' *viz.*

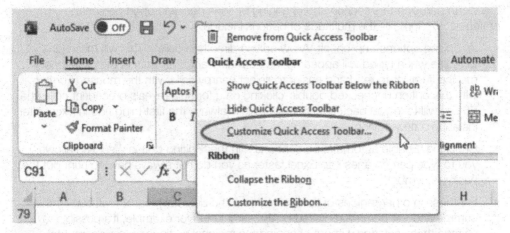

In the subsequent dialog box, select 'All Commands' in the 'Choose commands from' drop down box and then select 'Close' (with the folder icon, please see the illustration below). Next, click on the 'Add > >' button to add it to the Quick Access Toolbar and finally click on 'OK' to exit the dialog box.

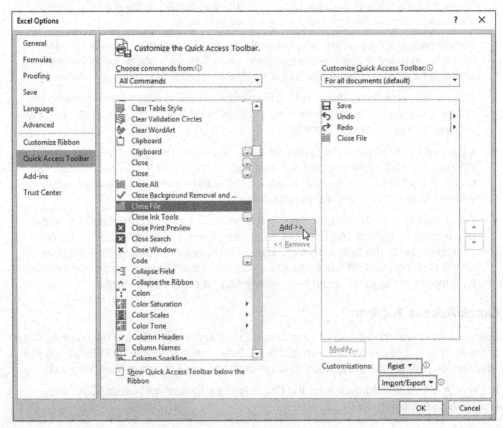

From now on, simply click on this 'Close' icon (Excel 2013 and earlier) / 'Close File' icon (Excel 2016 and later) in the Quick Access Toolbar and you will never have to say goodbye to Excel again. In fact, you will see it has its very own keyboard shortcut too: press the **ALT** button in Excel and it will reveal the number (in the illustration below, it is **ALT** + **4**):

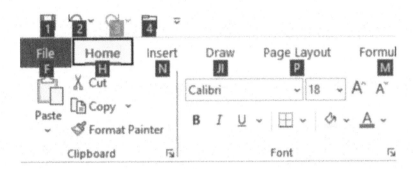

CHAPTER 4: INTRODUCING ARRAYS

When my daughter was very young (about five or six), at the weekend we'd often share daddy and daughter time watching some age-appropriate movie or other. To introduce this chapter, I'd like to make a quote from one of her favourite movies of that time, *Saw*:

"I want to play a game."

Consider the following four highlighted ranges in an Excel spreadsheet:

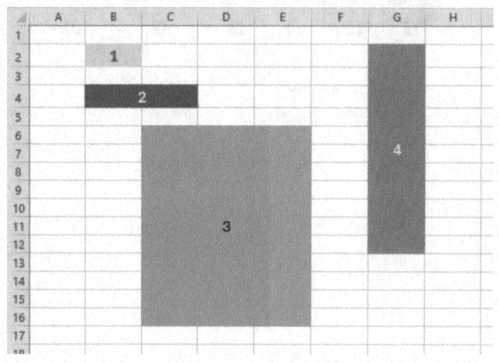

Which of the above regions, 1, 2, 3 and 4 represents an **array**? If you said, "all of them" – well done:

- Region 1 (cell **B2**) is a **cell** in Excel, but is also an array consisting of one row by one column ("1x1 array")

- Region 2 (cells **B4:C4**) is an example of a **row vector** in Excel. A **vector** is a collection of contiguous cells either being one row deep (high) or one column wide (this is a "1x**n** array")

- Region 3 (cells **C6:E16**) is an example of an **array**, constituting a collection of contiguous cells with more than one row and more than one column (this is an "**m**x**n** array")

- Region 4 (cells **G2:G12**) is an example of a **column vector** in Excel (this is a "**m**x1 array").

So how many arrays in total? If you said four, you'd be *wrong*. I could consider all four shaded areas as one non-contiguous array, or merely some combination of the four. I might also consider the intersection of some and the union of others, *etc.* You can have an array of arrays. Yes, this is a problem: the collective noun for all of the above is also an **array**.

There are <u>different</u> types of arrays. When I talk about cells, vectors and arrays in this book, I am referring to the following pseudo-definitions:

- **cell:** this is simply a range in Excel consisting of one row and one column

- **vector:** this is a contiguous range in Excel consisting of no more than one column or no more than one row

- **array:** this is a contiguous range in Excel consisting of at least two rows and at least two columns.

The reason I am making this important distinction in this book, is because some functions only work with certain types. For example, some only work with cells (*e.g.* **SIGN**), some with vectors (*e.g.* **MATCH**) and some with arrays (*e.g.* **MMULT**). Some will work with all sorts of combinations (*e.g.* **MAX**, **SUM**, **SUMPRODUCT**). We need to be clear what we are referencing.

And more to the point, we need to know what version of Excel we're in – as the last paragraph isn't necessarily true anymore, if you are working in the latest and greatest versions of Excel. But more on that anon.

Let's consider the following example:

	A	B	C	D	E	F	G
1							
2			Given this "target cell" and the array of dates and corresponding data, I need a formula that				
3			returns the "most recent date at which the data is equal to or less than the target cell.				
4							
5				Formula:	16 Aug 24		
6							
7				Target Cell:	20.00		
8							
9							
10				Dates	Data		
11				16 Aug 24	14.50		
12				2 Jul 24	44.21		
13				11 Aug 24	62.59		
14				30 Jul 24	74.54		
15				20 Jul 24	55.01		
16				24 Aug 24	21.11		
17				19 Jul 24	37.61		
18				31 Jul 24	72.68		
19				21 Jul 24	46.76		
20				14 Jul 24	66.91		
21				30 Jul 24	96.60		
22				20 Aug 24	68.97		
23				11 Aug 24	36.36		
24				8 Aug 24	20.67		
25				27 Jul 24	99.51		
26				2 Jul 24	67.43		
27				5 Aug 24	40.91		
28				31 Jul 24	15.72		
29				29 Jul 24	14.91		
30				22 Aug 24	28.21		
31				20 Aug 24	94.59		
32				7 Jul 24	55.60		
33				21 Jul 24	80.79		
34							

The challenge here is to create a simple formula to put in cell **E5** (the grey cell) which will return the most recent date at which the corresponding data was less than or equal to the value in the 'Target' cell (cell **E7**). The dates may not necessarily be in ascending order, as is the case here, but you can assume there will be at most one value per date.

Let's consider some possible solutions, assuming the calculation must be formulated all in one cell.

=MAX(INDEX(($D$11:$D$33)*($E$11:$E$33<=$E$7),))

E5			✕ ✓ *fx*	=MAX(INDEX(($D$11:$D$33)*($E$11:$E$33<=$E$7),))				
	A	B	C	D	E	F	G	H	I
1								
2		Given this "target cell" and the array of dates and corresponding data, I need a formula that						
3		returns the "most recent date at which the data is equal to or less than the target cell.						
4								
5				Formula:	16 Aug 24		=MAX(INDEX(($D$11:$D$33)*($E$11:$E$33<=$E$7),))	
6								
7				Target Cell:	20.00			
8								
9								
10				Dates	Data			
11				16 Aug 24	14.50			
12				2 Jul 24	44.21			
13				11 Aug 24	62.59			
14				30 Jul 24	74.54			

Here, this solution considers the flag approach to evaluating which data points are less than or equal to the target using **($E$11:$E$33<=$E$7)**. This will give values of TRUE and FALSE down a column vector stored in memory. Cross-multiplying by the dates

($D$11:$D$33)*($E$11:$E$33<=$E$7)

then provides another column vector in memory consisting of the dates if the flag is TRUE and zero [0] otherwise. At this point, you wish to apply the **MAX** function, but in old legacy Excel this will not work as **MAX** needs to see the results "written down". We have to wrap the expression in an **INDEX** first:

=MAX(INDEX(($D$11:$D$33)*($E$11:$E$33<=$E$7),))

Note the second argument of **INDEX** is a blank which is treated as zero. This "forces" the vector to be returned, which allows **MAX** to recognise the vector and hence return the correct result. The **INDEX** function has been applied here to force an array (here used as the overall collective noun) so that the vector type of array may be recognised.

Let's look at a second solution:

=SUMPRODUCT(MAX($D$11:$D$33*($E$11:$E$33<=$E$7)))

164

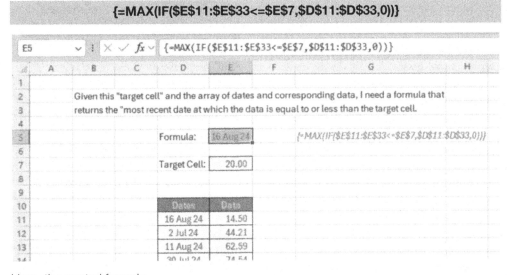

You should be able to see similarities between this alternative and the previous formula. Again, I start with a flag to identify those dates that meet the target criterion, **($E$11:$E$33<=$E$7)**. I then cross-multiply as before:

($D$11:$D$33)*($E$11:$E$33<=$E$7)

MAX still cannot return the result on its own, but due to how **SUMPRODUCT** operates, it will when contained within the pseudo-array formula:

=SUMPRODUCT(MAX($D$11:$D$33*($E$11:$E$33<=$E$7)))

I say "pseudo-array" as in old legacy Excel, array formulae must be entered using the keyboard command **CTRL** + **SHIFT** + **ENTER** rather than just **ENTER**. To demonstrate this, consider the next suggested solution:

{=MAX(IF($E$11:$E$33<=$E$7,$D$11:$D$33,0))}

Here, the central formula,

IF($E$11:$E$33<=$E$7,$D$11:$D$33,0)

checks to see which data is less than or equal to the target value (**$E$7**) and returns the corresponding dates (otherwise it provides a default value of FALSE since the **value_if_false** in the **IF(logical_test, [value_if_true], [value_if_false])** syntax is not defined).

Hence we get an array in the form {Date_1, FALSE, FALSE, FALSE,...}. **MAX** simply takes the largest value, *i.e.* the most recent date.

Since we have already learned that **MAX** will not support assessing a virtual vector in legacy Excel, I have had to advise the calculation engine this should be treated as an array formula by entering it using the keystroke combination **CTRL + SHIFT + ENTER**, which results in the braces (curly brackets) surrounding the resulting formula.

Array Functions

As I have already explained above, in Excel, an **array** is a contiguous set of items in a single row (called a one-dimensional horizontal array or vector) or in a single column (a one-dimensional vertical vector), or in a table consisting of at least two rows and two columns (a two-dimensional array). If you need more dimensions, you are better served with relational databases such as MS Access.

Array formulae perform multiple calculations on one or more of the items in an array. Array formulae can return either multiple outputs or a single result. There are two types:

- Formulae that work with an array or series of data and aggregate it, typically using **SUM**, **AVERAGE**, **MIN**, **MAX** or **COUNT**, to return a single value to a single cell. Microsoft calls these **single cell array formulae**

- Formulae that return a result in to two or more cells (there are various formulae that will do this including **MINVERSE**, **LINEST** and **TRANSPOSE**). These types of array formulae return an array of values as their result and are referred to as **multi-cell array formulae**.

  Multi-cell formulae can cause problems as the range of cells to hold your results must be selected before you enter the formula. Once entered, the contents of an individual cell in a multi-cell array formula cannot be edited and / or deleted. Only Chuck Norris may change part of an array.

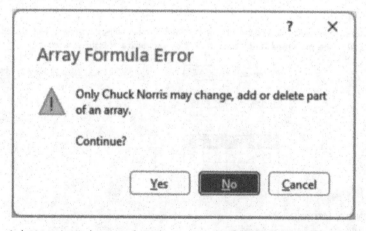

As I have just demonstrated, some functions such as **SUMPRODUCT**, **INDEX** and **OFFSET** will allow you to work with an array in a single cell by just pressing **ENTER**.

However, Excel often needs to know you are working with an array formula, and this is performed by entering the formula using **CTRL** + **SHIFT** + **ENTER**. This will result in the formula appearing in braces (**{}**). These braces cannot be typed in.

The Future

Clearly, array formulae are highly versatile and allow you to perform tasks that would require multiple cells otherwise. There is a possible price to pay. End users may not understand your array formulae. How many basic Excel users would understand the **{MAX(IF)}** array explained above? Advanced users will all too often use an array function when there are simpler, easier to understand alternatives. Further, large array formulae can slow down calculations significantly. Worse still, they can simply stop calculating with no error message provided.

However, since 2018, a formula can result in an array which appears in the worksheet. These are dynamic arrays, and they will transform the way Excel works. Let's look at one more suggested solution to end this section.

=MAX(IF($E$11:$E$33<=$E$7,$D$11:$D$33,0))

	E5		⌄ ⋮ ✕ ✓ f_x ⌄		=MAX(IF($E$11:$E$33=$E$7,$D$11:$D$33,0))			
	A	B	C	D	E	F	G	H
1								
2		Given this "target cell" and the array of dates and corresponding data, I need a formula that						
3		returns the "most recent date at which the data is equal to or less than the target cell.						
4								
5				Formula:	16 Aug 24		=MAX(IF($E$11:$E$33<=$E$7,$D$11:$D$33,0))	
6								
7				Target Cell:	20.00			
8								
9								
10				Dates	Data			
11				16 Aug 24	14.50			
12				2 Jul 24	44.21			
13				11 Aug 24	62.59			
14				30 Jul 24	74.54			

Pardon? No braces..?

CHAPTER 5: DYNAMIC ARRAYS

September 24, 2018, is the day Excel moved on – although I'm not quite sure how many noticed it. Yes, we've had Power Pivot, Power Query / Get & Transform and Power BI, but Microsoft's "Calc" team has been busy behind the scenes rearranging the furniture.

By "furniture" I mean the "calculation engine": it's had a complete re-write, and there are benefits general Excel users will reap for years to come. The first wave sees a new array calculation ("Dynamic Array"), seven new functions and two new error messages. And that's just the start. There's going to be plenty more coming in the next few years.

This feature is available to Office 365 users, having been included in Excel on the Web from November 2019. However, it is not clear what "perpetual licences" will have dynamic arrays (*e.g.* Office 2019 does not have it). Microsoft is attempting to make users move to its subscription model.

So, what's the big deal?

Spilling the Beans

Let me begin by just looking at what a Dynamic Array is. Consider the following data:

	Shape	Colour	Sides
	Original Data		
	Shape	Colour	Sides
	Triangle	Red	3
	Rectangle	Amber	4
	Circle	Green	1
	Triangle	Red	3
	Square	Blue	4
	Rectangle	Blue	4
	Rectangle	Amber	4
	Circle	Amber	1
	Triangle	Red	3
	Square	Green	4
	Circle	Blue	1
	Square	Amber	4
	Triangle	Blue	3
	Circle	Green	1
	Rectangle	Blue	4

If I were to type **=F12:H27** into another cell, Excel in the past would have thought I had gone mad. I'd need to wrap it in an aggregation function such as **SUM**, **COUNT** or **MAX**, to name but a few. Otherwise, I would have to wrap it in braces using **CTRL** + **SHIFT** + **ENTER** and use it as an array formula.

But as we have just seen, if you are in the right version of Excel, this keystroke combination is required no more.

Look at what happens when I type **=F12:H27** into cell **F33**:

| F33 | ⌄ | : | ✕ ✓ *fx* ⌄ | =F12:H27 |

◢	C	D	E	F	G	H

Dynamic Array Result

Shape	Colour	Sides
Triangle	Red	3
Rectangle	Amber	4
Circle	Green	1
Triangle	Red	3
Square	Blue	4
Rectangle	Blue	4
Rectangle	Amber	4
Circle	Amber	1
Triangle	Red	3
Square	Green	4
Circle	Blue	1
Square	Amber	4
Triangle	Blue	3
Circle	Green	1
Rectangle	Blue	4

The formula *automatically extends* to three columns by 16 rows! It has *spilled*. Get used to the vernacular. There's a reason this section got the name it did!

Any formula that has the potential to return multiple results can be referred to as a **Dynamic Array** formula. Formulae that are currently returning multiple results, and are successfully spilling, can be referred to as **Spilled Array Formulae**.

Notice I did not have to highlight all of the cells **F33:H48**. As I said, it has spilled. Also take note I formatted cell **F33** – er, that didn't spill, because presently formatting isn't propagated.

And don't let this basic example put you off either. If you feel a general sense of underwhelm coming over you, it's because I haven't yet communicated how powerful this all is as my example was too basic.

However, before I carry on there is a question I do need to cover with my far too simple example: what happens if something gets in the way?

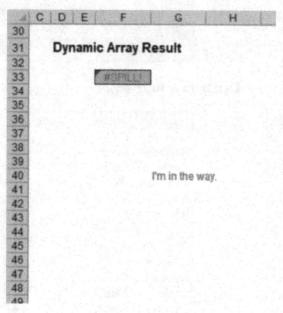

In this example, in cell **G40**, I have typed in the obtrusive text, "I'm in the way". And it quite literally is. Consequently, I have generated the *#SPILL!* error. The formula cannot spill, so the error message is generated accordingly.

#SPILL! Errors

#SPILL! errors are returned when a formula returns multiple results, and Excel cannot return the results to the spreadsheet. There are various reasons a *#SPILL!* error could occur:

- **spill range is not blank:** as in my example *(above)*, this error occurs when one or more cells in the designated spill range are not blank and thus may not be populated.

    When the formula is selected, a dashed border will indicate the intended spill range. You may select the error "floatie" (believe it or not, this is what Microsoft call these things!),

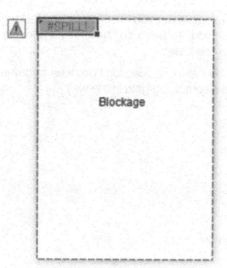

and choose the 'Select Obstructing Cells' option to immediately go the obstructing cell.

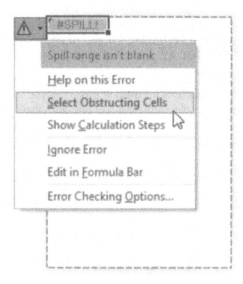

You can then clear the error by either deleting or moving the obstructing cell's entry. As soon as the obstruction is cleared, the array formula will spill as intended

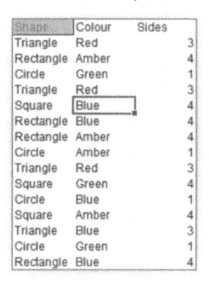

- **the range is volatile in size:** this means the size is not "set" and can vary. Excel was unable to determine the size of the spilled array because it's volatile and resizes between calculation passes. For example, the new function **SEQUENCE(x)** *(explained in detail below)* generates a list of **x** numbers increasing by 1 from 1 to **x** (in its simplest form). That's fine, but the following formula will trigger this #*SPILL!* error:

=SEQUENCE(RANDBETWEEN(1,1000)).

171

Dynamic array resizes may trigger additional calculation passes to ensure the spreadsheet is fully calculated. If the size of the array continues to change during these additional passes and does not stabilise, Excel will resolve the dynamic array as *#SPILL!*. This error type is generally associated with the use of **RAND**, **RANDARRAY** and **RANDBETWEEN** functions. Other volatile functions such as **OFFSET**, **INDIRECT** and **TODAY** do not return different values on every calculation pass so tend not to generate this error

- **extends beyond the worksheet's edge:** in this situation, the spilled array formula you are attempting to enter will extend beyond the worksheet's range. You should try again with a smaller range or array. For example, moving the following formula to cell **A1** will resolve the error, and the formula will spill correctly

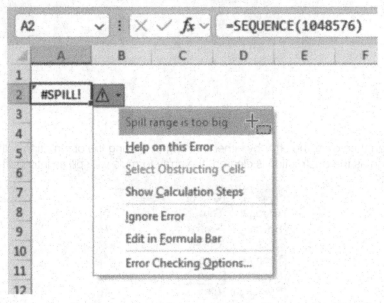

- **Table formula:** as I will explain shortly, Tables and dynamic arrays are not yet best friends. Spilled array formulae aren't supported in Excel Tables (generated by **CTRL + T**). Try moving your formula out of the Table, or go to **Table Tools -> Convert to range**

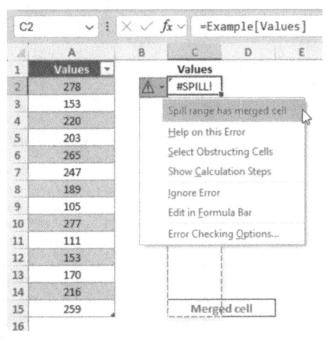

- **out of memory:** I have forgotten what this one means. Sorry, I couldn't resist that. The spilled array formula you are attempting to enter has caused Excel to run out of memory. You should try referencing a smaller array or range

- **spill into merged cells:** spilled array formulae cannot spill into merged cells. You will need to un-merge the cells in question or else move the formula to another range that doesn't intersect with merged cells.

When the formula is selected, a dashed border will indicate the intended spill range. You can again select that wonderfully named error floatie and choose the 'Select Obstructing Cell' option to immediately go to the obstructing cell. As soon as the merged cells are cleared, the array formula will spill as intended

- **unrecognised / fallback error:** the "catch all" variant. Excel doesn't recognise, or cannot reconcile, the cause of this error. Here, you should make sure your formula contains all of the required arguments for your scenario.

Returning to Dynamic Arrays

Now that we have considered what happens if you block a Dynamic Array, let me now turn my attention to what happens if you *don't*. You get the following:

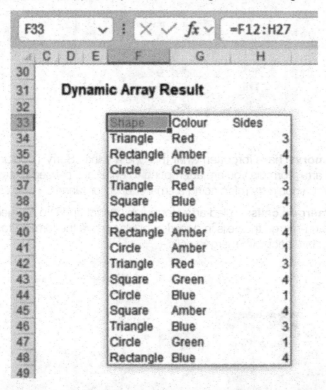

Do you see I am not having to anchor cells (*i.e.* use dollar [$] signs)? The formula just *spills*. Let me be clear. If I select cell **F34**, I get the following:

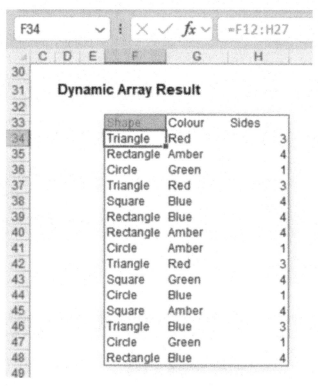

Here's a first. Check out the formula in the Formula bar. It's *greyed out*. Effectively, cell **F34** contains the value 'Triangle' but it does not actually contain an "Excel" formula in the usual sense. To demonstrate this, let me show you the VBA Immediate Window, which can be demonstrated in some versions of Excel:

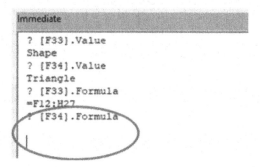

But, to quote Bill Jelen, similar to Schrodinger's Cat, if you select cells **F33:H48** and use 'Go To Special' (**F5 -> Special**), and then select 'Formulas', cells **F33:H48** are shown as formula cells. You can even copy and paste them as values. Ladies and gentlemen, welcome to The Twilight Zone (cue eerie music).

I mentioned in the #*SPILL!* errors section that you cannot use dynamic arrays in a Table, but dynamic arrays may refer to a Table, *viz.*

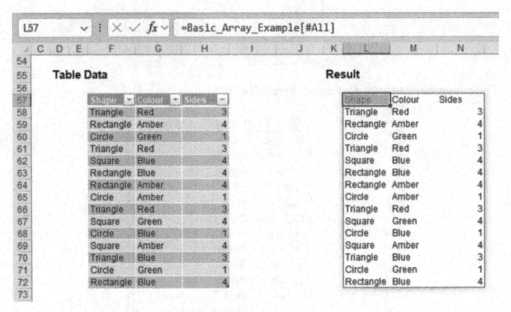

In this above illustration, cells **F57:H72** have been converted into a Table (**CTRL + T**), with the Table named **Basic_Array_Example**. In cell **L57**, I have simply typed '=' and then highlighted the entire Table. It was all replicated.

The advantage of linking a Dynamic Array to a Table is clear:

I can add rows and / or columns and the Dynamic Array will update automatically. Do note that this does not breach the #*SPILL!* range is volatile in size error. This is because the range size will not vary on every calculation pass.

Talking of varying sizes, it's clear to see one potential issue with dynamic arrays. If we are not referring to a Table, what happens if the source data changes dimensions? This may be why you should refer to a Table for safety.

However, once you have a Dynamic Array, referring to it is simple using what is known as the **Spilled Range Operator**. For example, if I want to refer to the Dynamic Array in the previous examples, it initially had a range of **L57:N72**. However, once I had added a row and column to the Table, this resized to **L57:O73**. I can easily refer to this array, whatever its size as follows. In its initial state:

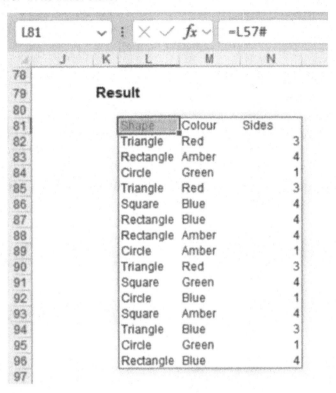

The formula **=L57#** allows for variations – you simply type in the top left-hand cell reference (*i.e.* the cell with the non-greyed out formula) and add '**#**', known as the Spilled Range Operator. Simple!

Implicit Intersection Implications

It may be an alliteration and sound like something you can get arrested for, but dynamic arrays do come at a price. There aren't many users out there who used them, but there are some – and hence there will be some legacy calculations affected.

In the past, if you entered **=A$1:A$10** anywhere in rows 1 through 10, the formula would return only the value from that row. In fact, a spreadsheet our company is presently auditing relies on this behaviour. However, in the brave new world of Office 365, typing this formula would create a Spilled Array Formula. To protect existing formulae, we need a new – if not instantly breathtaking – function…

SINGLE Function / @ Operator

Don't judge the remaining functions on this feature, originally a function, now an operator. This one is essential to keep Excel running smoothly, but it's probably safe to say it won't set the world alight. It's like toilet roll – imagine your situation without it…

When dynamic arrays first came out, the **SINGLE** function returned a single value using logic known as implicit intersection. **SINGLE** could return a value, single cell range or an error.

The function had the following syntax:

=SINGLE(value).

The function has just one argument:

- **value:** this argument is required and represents the array to be selected.

When the supplied argument is a range, **SINGLE** would return the cell at the intersection of the row or column of the formula cell. Where there is no intersection, or more than one cell falls in the intersection, then **SINGLE** would return a #*VALUE!* error. When the supplied argument is an array, **SINGLE** would return the first item (Row 1, Column 1).

In the example below, the two **SINGLE** formulae are supplied a range, **H13:H27**, and return the values in cells **H17** and **H22** respectively.

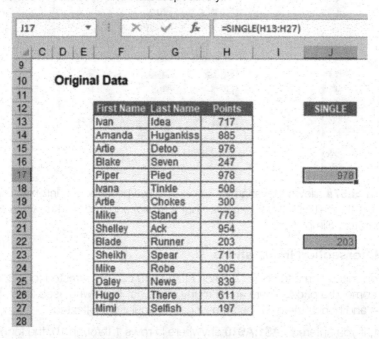

However, more recently, **SINGLE** was replaced with the @ operator as follows:

| J17 | | ✕ ✓ fx ⌄ | =@H13:H27 | | | | |

	C	D	E	F	G	H	I	J
9								
10		**Original Data**						
11								
12				First Name	Last Name	Points		@
13				Ivan	Idea	717		
14				Amanda	Hugankiss	885		
15				Artie	Detoo	976		
16				Blake	Seven	247		
17				Piper	Pied	978		978
18				Ivana	Tinkle	508		
19				Artie	Chokes	300		
20				Mike	Stand	778		
21				Shelley	Ack	954		
22				Blade	Runner	203		203
23				Sheikh	Spear	711		
24				Mike	Robe	305		
25				Daley	News	839		
26				Hugo	There	611		
27				Mimi	Selfish	197		
28								

Now, I mention this history with good reason. Excel will only remove **@** from a formula where previous Excel versions would have used implicit intersection *(as described above)* to return a single value from a range, a named range or function parameter.

On the positive side, if you attempt to enter such a formula, Excel will warn you and do its utmost to stop you. It is still possible to cause an issue though. For example, in Office 365, you could create the following formula:

| C2 | | ✕ ✓ fx | =@A2 | | |

	A	B	C	D	E
1	Value		DA Formula		
2	1		1		=@A2
3	2		2		
4	3		3		
5	4		4		
6	5		5		

In older versions of Excel, this would appear as:

| C2 | ▾ | ⋮ | ✕ ✓ *fx* | =_xlfn.SINGLE(A2) | | |

	A	B	C	D	E	F
1	Value		DA Formula			
2	1		1		=_xlfn.SINGLE(A2)	
3	2		2			
4	3		3			
5	4		4			
6	5		5			

Notice the formula is **=_xlfn.SINGLE(A2)**, not **=_xlfn.@(A2)**. This is confusing if you don't know the history of the @ operator. Worse comes if you try to evaluate this formula:

| C2 | ▾ | ⋮ | ✕ ✓ *fx* | =_xlfn.SINGLE(A2) | | |

	A	B	C	D	E	F
1	Value		DA Formula			
2	1		#NAME?		=_xlfn.SINGLE(A2)	
3	2		#NAME?			
4	3		#NAME?			
5	4		#NAME?			
6	5		#NAME?			

It generates an *#NAME?* error, which is far from ideal.

Dynamic Arrays vs. Legacy Array Formulae

Prior to dynamic arrays, if you wanted to work with ranges in Excel, you used to have to build array formulae, where references would refer to ranges and be entered as **CTRL + SHIFT + ENTER** formulae. The main differences are as follows:

- Dynamic Array formulae may spill outside the cell bounds where the formula is entered. The Dynamic Array formula technically only exists in the cell in the top left-hand corner of the spilled range *(as shown earlier)*, whereas with a legacy **CTRL + SHIFT + ENTER** formula, the formula would need to be entered in the entire range

- Dynamic arrays will automatically resize as data is added or removed from the source range. **CTRL + SHIFT + ENTER** array formulae will truncate the return area if it's too small, or return *#N/A* errors if too large

- Dynamic array formulae will calculate in a 1 x 1 context

- Any new formulae that return more than one result will automatically spill. There's simply no need to press **CTRL + SHIFT + ENTER**

- According to Microsoft, **CTRL** + **SHIFT** + **ENTER** array formulae are only retained for backwards compatibility reasons. Going forward, you should use Dynamic Array formulae instead

- Dynamic Array formulae may be easily modified by changing the source cell, whereas **CTRL** + **SHIFT** + **ENTER** array formulae require that the entire range be edited simultaneously

- Column and row insertion / deletion is prohibited in an active **CRL** + **SHIFT** + **ENTER** array formula range. You first need to delete any existing array formulae that are in the way.

Everybody clear? I think we are finally good to start introducing the other functions…

SORT Function

I am not going to do these alphabetically – let me show the new functions then in an order that makes sense (well, to me, anyway).

The **SORT** function sorts the contents of a range or array:

> **=SORT(array, [sort_index], [sort_order], [by_column]).**

It has four arguments:

- **array:** this is required and represents the range that is required to be sorted

- **sort_index:** this is optional and refers to the position of the row or the column in the selected **array** (*e.g.* second row, third column). 99 times out of 98 you will be defining the column, but to select a row you will need to use this argument in conjunction with the fourth argument, **by_column**. And be careful, it's a little counter-intuitive! The default value is 1

- **sort_order:** this is also optional. The choices for **sort_order** are 1 for ascending order (default) or -1 for descending. It should be noted that you might not want to hold your breath waiting for 'Sort by Color' *(sic)*, 'Sort by Formula' or 'Sort by Custom List' using this function

- **by_column:** this final argument is also optional. Most people want to sort rows of data, so they will want the value to be FALSE (which is the default value if not specified). Should you be booking your mental health check, you may wish to use TRUE to sort by column in certain instances.

This is a function people had been crying out for, for *years*. Enterprising spreadsheets gurus developed array formulae and user-defined functions that have replicated this functionality, but you don't need it anymore!

To show you how devilishly simple it is, consider the following data:

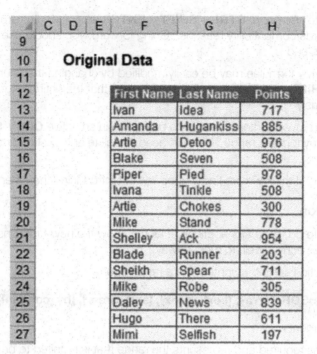

Original Data

First Name	Last Name	Points
Ivan	Idea	717
Amanda	Hugankiss	885
Artie	Detoo	976
Blake	Seven	508
Piper	Pied	978
Ivana	Tinkle	508
Artie	Chokes	300
Mike	Stand	778
Shelley	Ack	954
Blade	Runner	203
Sheikh	Spear	711
Mike	Robe	305
Daley	News	839
Hugo	There	611
Mimi	Selfish	197

Sorting the 'Points' column in order is as easy as this:

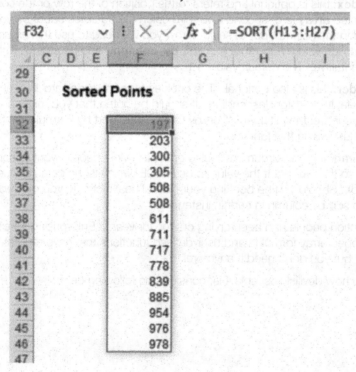

`=SORT(H13:H27)`

Sorted Points

197
203
300
305
508
508
611
711
717
778
839
885
954
976
978

All you have to do is type **=SORT(H13:H27)** into cell **F32**. That's it! Note that the duplicates are repeated; there is no cull. If you want it in descending order, simply specify the requirement in the formula:

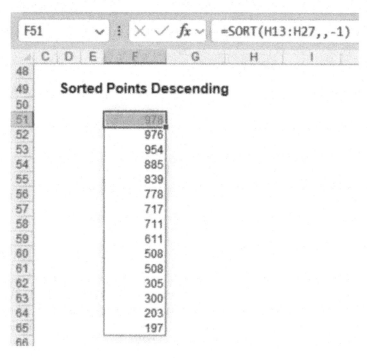

This formula is only slightly more sophisticated, in that the **sort_order** (third argument) needs to be specified as -1 to switch the sort to descending order:

=SORT(H13:H27,,-1).

You probably won't want the points displayed on their own:

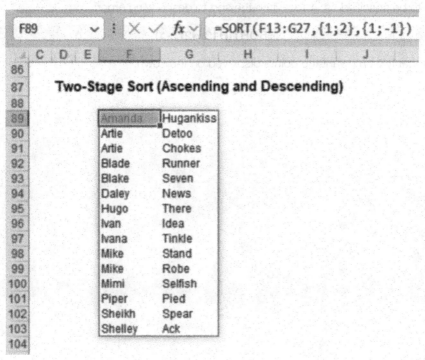

Sorted Points Descending Full Table

Piper	Pied	978
Artie	Detoo	976
Shelley	Ack	954
Amanda	Hugankiss	885
Daley	News	839
Mike	Stand	778
Ivan	Idea	717
Sheikh	Spear	711
Hugo	There	611
Blake	Seven	508
Ivana	Tinkle	508
Mike	Robe	305
Artie	Chokes	300
Blade	Runner	203
Mimi	Selfish	197

Now all of these arguments start to make more sense. **SORT(F13:H27,3,-1)** produces the whole array (**array** is **F13:H27**), sorts it on the third (**sort_index** is 3) column in descending (**sort_order** is -1) order. Blake and Ivana tie on 508 points, but Blake appears first as he was first in the original (source) table.

So far, I have only performed the one **SORT**. You can have more than one though:

Two-Stage Sort (Ascending and Descending)

Amanda	Hugankiss
Artie	Detoo
Artie	Chokes
Blade	Runner
Blake	Seven
Daley	News
Hugo	There
Ivan	Idea
Ivana	Tinkle
Mike	Stand
Mike	Robe
Mimi	Selfish
Piper	Pied
Sheikh	Spear
Shelley	Ack

184

Here, I have created a second (two-level) **SORT**. Here, you need to create what is known as an array constant for the second and third arguments (you just type the braces in – don't use **CTRL** + **SHIFT** + **ENTER**):

=SORT(F13:G27,{1;2},{1;-1}).

This will sort on column 1 ('First Name') first, then sort on column 2 ('Last Name') next. This will be in ascending order (1) for the first column and descending order (-1) for the latter. It's not as straightforward a formula entry as most Excel modellers are used to, but it's relatively painless once you have committed it to erm, um, what do you call it, memory.

My final example of **SORT** is not something that is limited to this function, but it does show how things fit together. From all that has been written above, it appears you can only get one value (using **@**) or all of them (using dynamic arrays). That's not true as this illustration clearly demonstrates:

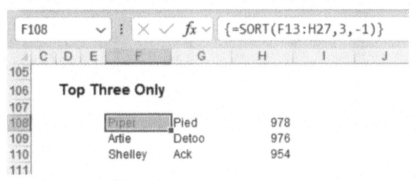

Only the top three have spilled in this example. How? Well, I cheated. I highlighted cells **F108:H110** first, then typed in the formula

=SORT(F13:H27,3,-1)

and then pressed **CTRL** + **SHIFT** + **ENTER** (thus generating the **{** and **}** braces). This restricted the spill to the range stipulated. Cool. Other than making sure no one can delete or insert any rows by creating an array formula such as **{=1}** across the restricted area, these appear to be the only two uses of **CTRL** + **SHIFT** + **ENTER** now.

SORT is really useful then, but what if you want to sort on a field you don't want displayed in the results..?

SORTBY Function

The **SORTBY** function sorts the contents of a range or array based on the values in a corresponding range or array, which does not need to be displayed. The syntax is as follows:

=SORTBY(array, by_array1, [sort_order1], [by_array2], [sort_order2], ...).

It has several arguments:

- **array:** this is required and represents the range that is required to be sorted
- **by_array1:** this is the first range that **array** will be sorted on and is required

- **sort_order1**, **sort_order2**, …: these are optional. The choices for each **sort_order** are 1 for ascending (default) or -1 for descending

- **by_array2**, …: these arguments are also optional. These represent the second and subsequent ranges that **array** will be sorted on.

There are some important considerations to note:

- the **by_array** arguments must either be one row high or one column wide

- all of the **by_array** arguments must be the same size and contain the same number of rows as **array** if sorting on rows, or the same number of columns as **array** if sorting on columns

- if the sort order argument is not 1 or -1, the formula will result in a *#VALUE!* error.

It's pretty simple to use. Consider the following source data once more:

	C	D	E	F	G	H	

Original Data

First Name	Last Name	Points
Ivan	Idea	717
Amanda	Hugankiss	885
Artie	Detoo	976
Blake	Seven	508
Piper	Pied	978
Ivana	Tinkle	508
Artie	Chokes	300
Mike	Stand	778
Shelley	Ack	954
Blade	Runner	203
Sheikh	Spear	711
Mike	Robe	305
Daley	News	839
Hugo	There	611
Mimi	Selfish	197

I can use **SORTBY** as follows:

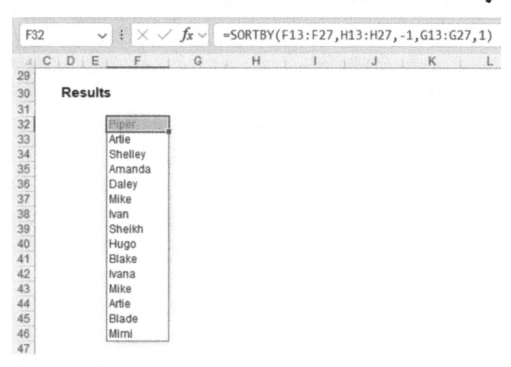

Here, using the formula

=SORTBY(F13:F27,H13:H27,-1,G13:G27,1)

I have sorted the 'First Name' field (**F13:F27**) on the 'Points' column (**H13:H27**) in descending (-1) order and then used the second sort on 'Last Name' (**G13:G27**) in ascending (1) order. No need for those pesky array references in multiple sorts with the **SORT** function *(as detailed above)*.

FILTER Function

The **FILTER** function will accept an array, allow you to filter a range of data based upon criteria you define and return the results to a spill range.

The syntax of **FILTER** is as follows:

=FILTER(array, include, [if_empty]).

It has three arguments:

- **array:** this is required and represents the range that is to be filtered

- **include:** this is also required. This specifies the condition(s) that must be met

- **if_empty:** this argument is optional. This is what will be returned if no data meets the criterion / criteria specified in the **include** argument. It's generally a good idea to at least use "" here.

For example, consider the following source data:

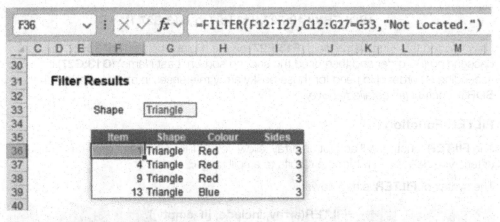

	C	D	E	F	G	H	I
9							
10	**Original Data**						
11							
12				Item	Shape	Colour	Sides
13				1	Triangle	Red	3
14				2	Rectangle	Amber	4
15				3	Circle	Green	1
16				4	Triangle	Red	3
17				5	Square	Blue	4
18				6	Rectangle	Blue	4
19				7	Rectangle	Amber	4
20				8	Circle	Amber	1
21				9	Triangle	Red	3
22				10	Square	Green	4
23				11	Circle	Blue	1
24				12	Square	Amber	4
25				13	Triangle	Blue	3
26				14	Circle	Green	1
27				15	Rectangle	Blue	4
28							

To begin with, I will perform a simple **FILTER**:

F36	⌄	:	✕ ✓ *fx* ⌄	=FILTER(F12:I27,G12:G27=G33,"Not Located.")

	C	D	E	F	G	H	I	J	K	L	M
30											
31	**Filter Results**										
32											
33		Shape		Triangle							
34											
35				Item	Shape	Colour	Sides				
36				1	Triangle	Red	3				
37				4	Triangle	Red	3				
38				9	Triangle	Red	3				
39				13	Triangle	Blue	3				
40											

Here, in cell **F36**, I have created the formula

=FILTER(F12:I27,G12:G27=G33,"Not Located.")

F12:I27 is my source **array** and I wish only to **include** shapes (**G12:G27**) that are 'Triangles' (specified by cell **G33**). If there are no such shapes, then **"Not Located."** is returned instead. To show this, I will change the shape as follows:

188

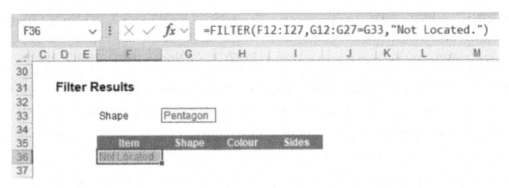

That is about as basic as it gets. I can get cleverer. Consider the following example:

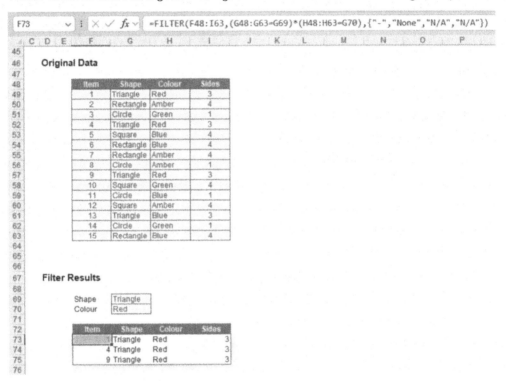

I have repeated the source **array** (cells **F48:I63**) for clarity. The formula

=FILTER(F48:I63,(G48:G63=G69)*(H48:H63=G70),{"-","None","N/A","N/A"})

looks horrible to begin with, but it's not quite as bad as it appears upon further scrutiny. The **include** argument,

(G48:G63=G69)*(H48:H63=G70)

contains two conditions. Firstly, **G48:G63=G69** means that the 'Shape' (**G48:G63**) has to be a 'Triangle' (cell **G69**) and that the 'Colour' (**H48:H63**) has to be 'Red' (cell **G70**). The multiplication operator (*) is used to denote **AND**. The Excel function **AND** cannot be used with arrays – this is nothing special to dynamic arrays; **AND** does not work with

CTRL + **SHIFT** + **ENTER** formulae either. This syntax is similar to how you would create **AND** criteria with the **SUMPRODUCT** function, for example.

The final argument is similar to the syntax in **SORT**: **{"-","None","N/A","N/A"}**. Braces (typed in!) are used to create an array argument that specifies what should be written in each column should there be no record that meets both criteria, *e.g.*

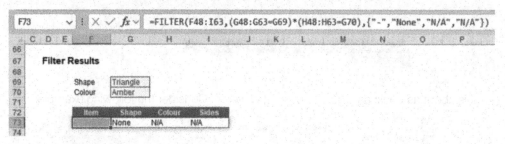

See? Not as bad as you might first think.

My final example is *very* similar:

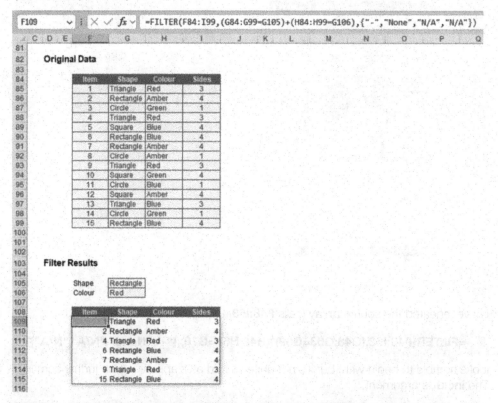

Once you realise I have simply repeated referencing for clarity, the formula

=FILTER(F84:I99,(G84:G99=G105)+(H84:H99=G106),{"-","None","N/A","N/A"})

is nothing more than the **OR** equivalent of the previous example, with '**+**' replacing '*****' to switch from ensuring both conditions are met to only one condition being met. As at the time of writing, **XOR** is not catered for, but I am sure some clever person will create an equivalent in due course (if Microsoft doesn't beat them to it), necessity being the mother of invention and all that jazz.

Interlude: the #CALC! Error

I mentioned there were two error messages associated with dynamic arrays. There are others (*e.g. #FIELD!*), but that's another story for another section. I have only referred to *#SPILL!* so far. There is another, lurking in the background: *#CALC!* To add to the myriad of error messages such *#REF!*, *#DIV/0!*, *#VALUE!*, *#BROWN* and *#PIPE*, let's introduce *#CALC!* properly.

A *#CALC!* error occurs when Excel's calculation engine encounters a scenario that is not supported. Currently, these scenarios are:

- **nested array:** Excel can't calculate an array within an array.

- **array of ranges:** arrays may only contain numbers, strings, errors, Boolean values (*e.g.* 1 or 0, TRUE or FALSE) or linked data types. Range references are not supported

- **empty array:** Excel cannot return an empty set

- **too many cells:** custom functions that refer to more than 10,000 cells cannot be calculated in Excel for the web and will produce this *#CALC!* error instead (this is easily remedied by opening the file in a desktop version of Excel)

- **other:** this error occurs when Excel's calculation engine encounters an unspecified calculation error with an array, and represents Microsoft's *Get out of Jail Free* card.

I just want to delve a little further into one of these above situations, as both an illustration and a discussion point.

An **empty array** error occurs when an array formula returns an empty (sometimes referred to as *null*) set. According to Microsoft, *#CALC!* is returned when a formula returns an empty array. That's not always true though. Consider the " " (space) operator in Excel, which represents the intersect function:

B9		×	✓	*fx*	=B2:F3 C1:D5	
▲	A	B	C	D	E	F
1	1	2	3	4	5	6
2	7	8	9	10	11	12
3	13	14	15	16	17	18
4	19	20	21	22	23	24
5	25	26	27	28	29	30
6	31	32	33	34	35	36
7						
8						
9			9	10	=B2:F3 C1:D5	
10			15	16		
11						

If I change the references to two non-intersecting ranges, I get *#NULL!* not *#CALC!*

191

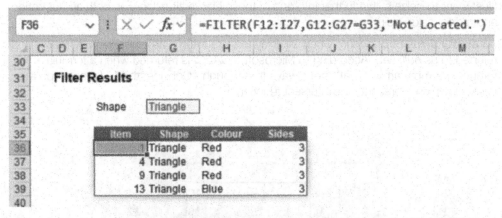

B9		▾	⋮	✕	✓	*fx*	=A1:C1 D3:F6	

◢	A	B	C	D	E	F
1	1	2	3	4	5	6
2	7	8	9	10	11	12
3	13	14	15	16	17	18
4	19	20	21	22	23	24
5	25	26	27	28	29	30
6	31	32	33	34	35	36
7						
8						
9	⊕	#NULL!			=A1:C1 D3:F6	
10						

I think this is partially to keep old functions behaving as old functions did, but it may also be the distinction between an empty subset (*#CALC!*) and an invalid range (*#NULL!*). The latter error is displayed when you use an incorrect range operator in a formula (valid operators include a colon or a comma), or when you use an intersection operator (space character) between range references to specify an intersection of two ranges that do not intersect, as above. It's best to remember that what you perceive as empty arrays might not always be represented by this new error message.

To illustrate a genuine occurrence of *#CALC!*, allow me to revisit the first **FILTER** example:

F36	▾	⋮	✕	✓	*fx* ▾	=FILTER(F12:I27,G12:G27=G33,"Not Located.")

◢	C	D	E	F	G	H	I	J	K	L	M
30											
31	**Filter Results**										
32											
33		Shape			Triangle						
34											
35			Item	Shape	Colour	Sides					
36			1	Triangle	Red	3					
37			4	Triangle	Red	3					
38			9	Triangle	Red	3					
39			13	Triangle	Blue	3					
40											

I am going to remove the third (**if_empty**) argument and switch the shape in cell **F36** to 'Pentagon':

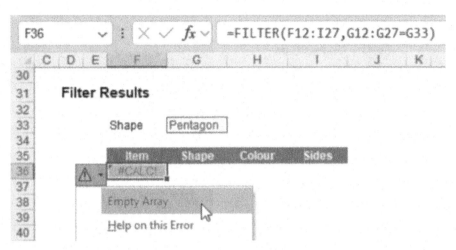

This produces the *#CALC!* error in cell **F36** as the result returns an empty array. To resolve this error, simply change the criterion, the formula, or add the **if_empty** argument to the **FILTER** function. This is why I had "Not Located." as the third argument previously.

Let's move on.

UNIQUE Function

The hilarious thing about **UNIQUE** is that it does two things (!). It details distinct items (*i.e.* provides each value that occurs with no repetition) and also it can return values which occur once and only once in a referred range. I understand that Excel users may welcome the former use with open arms and that database developers may be very interested in the latter. I still think there should have been two functions though. Otherwise, let's just extend the **AGGREGATE** function to do just *everything* (it almost does now) and be done with it!

The **UNIQUE** function has the following syntax:

=UNIQUE(array, [by_column], [occurs_once]).

It has three arguments:

- **array:** this is required and represents the range or array from which to return unique values

- **by_column:** this argument is optional. This is a logical value (TRUE / FALSE) indicating how to compare. If you wish to compare by row, the argument should be FALSE or omitted (since this is the default). To compare by column, you will need to select TRUE

- **occurs_once:** this argument is also optional. This requires a logical value too:

  - **TRUE:** only return unique values that occur once

  - **FALSE:** include all distinct values (default if omitted).

It's probably clearer with some examples. Let's give it a go. As always, I need source data:

Original Data

Store	Salesperson	Section	Manager
North	Alice	White Goods	Zack
North	Barbara	Groceries	Zack
North	Charlie	White Goods	Zack
North	Dion	Computers	Yvonne
North	Echo	Insurance	Xander
North	Fred	Bedding	Winnie
North	George	Audio Video	Yvonne
North	Helen	Furniture	Winnie
North	Iris	White Goods	Zack
North	Jack	Furniture	Winnie
North	Karla	Groceries	Zack
East	Lindsay	Insurance	Xander
East	Barbara	Groceries	Zack
East	Iris	White Goods	Zack
East	Michael	Computers	Yvonne
East	Fred	Bedding	Winnie
East	Dion	Computers	Yvonne
South	Nancy	Audio Video	Yvonne
South	Oprah	Furniture	Winnie
South	Helen	Furniture	Winnie
South	Alice	White Goods	Zack
South	Pete	Groceries	Zack
West	Karla	Groceries	Zack
West	Pete	Groceries	Zack
West	Charlie	White Goods	Zack
West	Dion	Computers	Yvonne
West	George	Audio Video	Yvonne
West	Nancy	Audio Video	Yvonne
West	Michael	Computers	Yvonne

Time for the most basic illustration:

| L13 | | ⌄ | : | ✕ ✓ _fx_ ⌄ | =UNIQUE(F13:F41) |

⊿	J	K	L	M	N	O
9						
10		**Results**				
11						
12			Store	Salesperson	Section	Manager
13			North	Alice	White Goods	Zack
14			East	Barbara	Groceries	Yvonne
15			South	Charlie	Computers	Xander
16			West	Dion	Insurance	Winnie
17				Echo	Bedding	
18				Fred	Audio Video	
19				George	Furniture	
20				Helen		
21				Iris		
22				Jack		
23				Karla		
24				Lindsay		
25				Michael		
26				Nancy		
27				Oprah		
28				Pete		
29						

In cell **L13**, I have simply typed

=UNIQUE(F13:F41).

No optional arguments; everything in default. If I have made an error, it's going to be my default. This has simply listed each store that appears; if "North" and "North " (extra space) were there, then both would appear. **UNIQUE** is not case sensitive though and each entry would appear as it first occurs reading down the range **F13:F41**. The other columns contain similar formulae and **UNIQUE** looks like it takes seconds to learn. Presently, there's an in-joke going around the Excel Most Valuable Professionals (MVPs) that array expert Mike Girvin is going to be choked as he dedicated *an entire chapter* in one of his books to creating that list with an array formula! Sorry Mike. Excel i̲s fun!

It's just as simple if you want to see unique records for two (or more) columns, *viz.*

| L13 | | ⌄ | : | ✕ ✓ _fx_ ⌄ | =UNIQUE(F13:F41) |

⊿	K	L	M	N	O
38					
39		Section	Manager		
40		White Goods	Zack		
41		Groceries	Zack		
42		Computers	Yvonne		
43		Insurance	Xander		
44		Bedding	Winnie		
45		Audio Video	Yvonne		
46		Furniture	Winnie		
47					

You can see **UNIQUE** is sort of crying out for **SORT**, but we'll get to that shortly.

As mentioned earlier, it's not the only way of using **UNIQUE** (no, having a unique use would be just what "they" were expecting, whoever "they" are…). You can use it to determine values that only occur once:

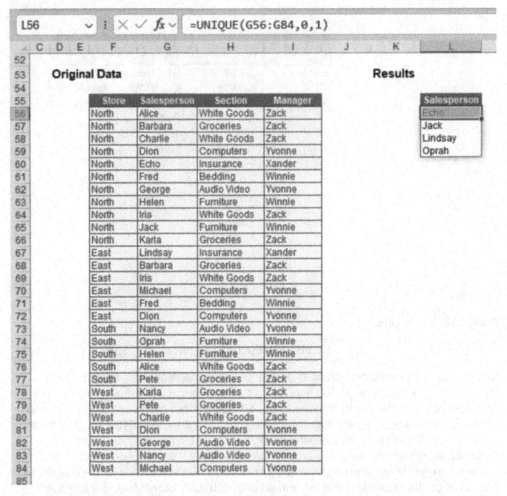

Here, the formula in cell **L56**,

=UNIQUE(G56:G84,0,1)

uses the non-default value of 1 for the optional **occurs_once** (third) argument. This means it identifies the salespeople who only occur once in cells **G56:G84**. Brilliant; I can die content knowing now.

The real power starts coming when you start playing with Excel's existing functions and features, together with these new functions. Take this comprehensive example:

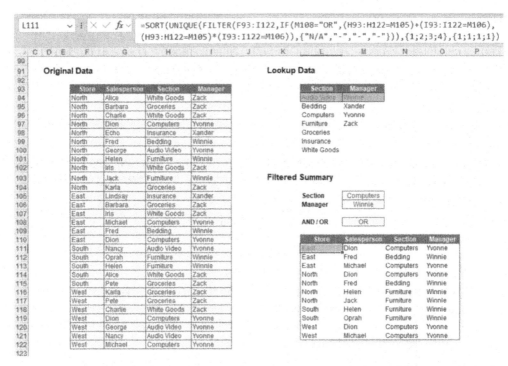

L111 `=SORT(UNIQUE(FILTER(F93:I122,IF(M108="OR",(H93:H122=M105)+(I93:I122=M106),(H93:H122=M105)*(I93:I122=M106)),{"N/A","-","-","-"})),{1;2;3;4},{1;1;1;1})`

Original Data

Store	Salesperson	Section	Manager
North	Alice	White Goods	Zack
North	Barbara	Groceries	Zack
North	Charlie	White Goods	Zack
North	Dion	Computers	Yvonne
North	Echo	Insurance	Xander
North	Fred	Bedding	Winnie
North	George	Audio Video	Yvonne
North	Helen	Furniture	Winnie
North	Iris	White Goods	Zack
North	Jack	Furniture	Winnie
North	Karla	Groceries	Zack
East	Lindsay	Insurance	Xander
East	Barbara	Groceries	Zack
East	Iris	White Goods	Zack
East	Michael	Computers	Yvonne
East	Fred	Bedding	Winnie
East	Dion	Computers	Yvonne
South	Nancy	Audio Video	Yvonne
South	Oprah	Furniture	Winnie
South	Helen	Furniture	Winnie
South	Alice	White Goods	Zack
South	Pete	Groceries	Zack
West	Karla	Groceries	Zack
West	Pete	Groceries	Zack
West	Charlie	White Goods	Zack
West	Dion	Computers	Yvonne
West	George	Audio Video	Yvonne
West	Nancy	Audio Video	Yvonne
West	Michael	Computers	Yvonne

Lookup Data

Section	Manager
Audio Video	Winnie
Bedding	Xander
Computers	Yvonne
Furniture	Zack
Groceries	
Insurance	
White Goods	

Filtered Summary

Section	Computers
Manager	Winnie

AND / OR	OR

Store	Salesperson	Section	Manager
East	Dion	Computers	Yvonne
East	Fred	Bedding	Winnie
East	Michael	Computers	Yvonne
North	Dion	Computers	Yvonne
North	Fred	Bedding	Winnie
North	Helen	Furniture	Winnie
North	Jack	Furniture	Winnie
South	Helen	Furniture	Winnie
South	Oprah	Furniture	Winnie
West	Dion	Computers	Yvonne
West	Michael	Computers	Yvonne

Let me step you through *some* of this. The formulae in cells **L94** and **M94** use **UNIQUE** in a similar manner to my first example, to generate the list of distinct values in the 'Section' and 'Manager' fields. However, did you notice they have been sorted? That's because I used the formula

=SORT(UNIQUE(H94:H122))

in cell **L94**, for example. Honestly, I think **UNIQUE** should have another argument for sorting (ascending / descending / none [default]). Watch Microsoft ignore that suggestion.

But then I did something really cool. Cells **M105** and **M106** use data validation (**ALT** + **D** + **L**) to generate a list from the 'Lookup Data' section. That requires taking a closer look:

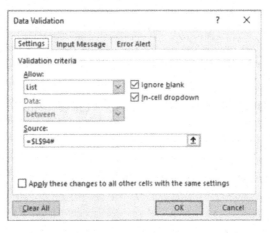

Do you see the source for the data validation in cell **M105**? **=$L$84#** - so elegant! This takes the 'Section' list and automatically makes the drop-down list the required length! People create all sorts of tricks using **OFFSET**, dynamic range names and the like to achieve a similar effect. No more. **=$L$84#** (with the '**#**', the Spilled Range Operator) is all that is needed. That's my favourite thing in all of these functions and features. I'm impressed – and I'm easily impressed.

The 'AND / OR' dropdown is a bit of an anti-climax after that, but the final formula that generates the final table, namely

> **=SORT(UNIQUE(FILTER(F93:I122,IF(M108="OR",(H93:H122=M105)+(I93:I122=M106), (H93:H122=M105)*(I93:I122=M106)),{"N/A","-","-","-"})),{1;2;3;4},{1;1;1;1})**

is rather fun. I am not going to go through it though – as every aspect of this formula is simply a re-hash of an earlier point (assuming you know the **IF** function!). See if you can work your way through it for yourself.

SEQUENCE Function

I mentioned **SEQUENCE** in passing earlier, but let's take a more in-depth look. This function allows you to generate a list of sequential numbers in an array, such as 1, 2, 3, 4. It doesn't sound particularly exciting, but again, it really ramps up when combined with other functions and features. Our model is going to make great use of this function to build our timing sheet and dates. The syntax is given by:

> **=SEQUENCE(rows, [columns], [start], [step]).**

It has four arguments:

- **rows:** this argument is required and specifies how many **rows** the results should spill over

- **columns:** this argument is optional and specifies how many **columns** (surprise, surprise) the results should spill over. If omitted, the default value is 1

- **start:** this argument is also optional. This specifies what number the **SEQUENCE** function should start from. If omitted, the default value is 1

- **step:** this final argument is also optional. This specifies the amount each number in the **SEQUENCE** should increase by (the "**step**"). It may be positive, negative or zero. If omitted, the default value is 937,444. Wait, I'm kidding; it's 1. They're very unimaginative down in Redmond.

Therefore, **SEQUENCE** can be as simple as **SEQUENCE(x)**, which will generate a list of numbers in a column: 1, 2, 3, …, **x**. Therefore, be mindful not to create a formula where **x** may be volatile and generate alternative values each time it is calculated, *e.g.* **=SEQUENCE(RANDBETWEEN(10,99))** as this will generate the #*SPILL!* error as the range is volatile in size.

A vanilla example is rather bland:

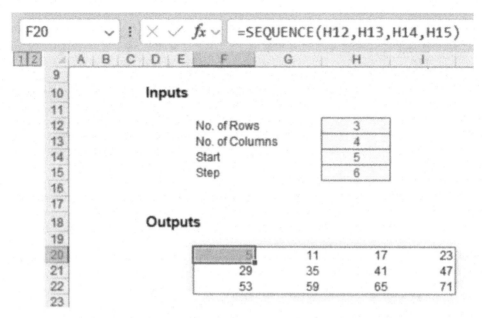

Do you see how **SEQUENCE** propagates across the row first and then down to the next row, just like reading a book? I wonder how that might work in alternative languages of Excel where users read right to left (it has to be the same or there would be chaos when workbooks were shared!).

Some of my peers had fun combining it with the **ROMAN** function:

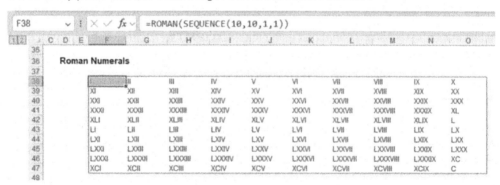

To my mind though, my favourite simple illustration is creating a monthly calendar. A little magic with the **DATE** and **WEEKDAY** functions combined with some conditional formatting and suddenly you have:

Dates

Month	Sep					
Year	2018					

Sun	Mon	Tue	Wed	Thu	Fri	Sat
						1 Sep 18
2 Sep 18	3 Sep 18	4 Sep 18	5 Sep 18	6 Sep 18	7 Sep 18	8 Sep 18
9 Sep 18	10 Sep 18	11 Sep 18	12 Sep 18	13 Sep 18	14 Sep 18	15 Sep 18
16 Sep 18	17 Sep 18	18 Sep 18	19 Sep 18	20 Sep 18	21 Sep 18	22 Sep 18
23 Sep 18	24 Sep 18	25 Sep 18	26 Sep 18	27 Sep 18	28 Sep 18	29 Sep 18
30 Sep 18						

As I mentioned above, **SEQUENCE** is arguably more powerful when included in a more complex formula. For example:

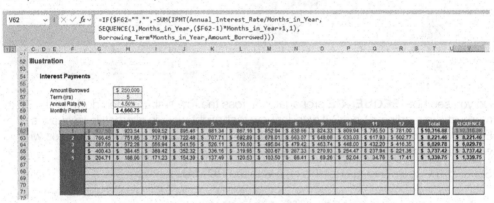

In this instance, I have created a grid using the Excel **IPMT** function to determine the amount of interest to be paid in each monthly instalment. Cells **G62:R71** calculate each monthly amount and column **T** sums these amounts to calculate the annual interest payment, a figure which is non-trivial to compute. The whole table may be replaced by the formula in cell **V62**:

> **=IF($F62="","",-SUM(IPMT(Annual_Interest_Rate/Months_in_Year,**
> **SEQUENCE(1,Months_in_Year,($F62-1)*Months_in_Year+1,1),**
> **Borrowing_Term*Months_in_Year,Amount_Borrowed))).**

I am not going to explain this and let me tell you why. Our company, SumProduct builds and reviews financial models for a living. We see terrible modelling practices established day-in, day-out. We proactively try to discourage these traits by emphasising that complex formulae should be stepped out and made transparent. Here, that can be done using the original table. I don't *want* people using **SEQUENCE**, dynamic arrays or other spilled formulae to wrap up complicated calculations into an opaque Pandora's Box. Yes, calculation times may be slower. Live with it. Sometimes you need to see the scenery to appreciate the beauty. I'm just a little fearful that people will embrace these functions a little too readily and the Road to Excel Hell beckons shortly. Sorry to be a miserable git.

On an upbeat note, I put a formula in cell **G61** which is simple:

> **=TRANSPOSE(SEQUENCE(Months_in_Year)).**

200

This calls for a (very) quick aside.

TRANSPOSE Function

Yes, I am using **TRANSPOSE** without **CTRL** + **SHIFT** + **ENTER**. We are in different territory here…

The **TRANSPOSE** function is pretty straightforward. It just takes a vertical range of cells and returns it as a horizontal range and vice versa. The syntax is very simple

=TRANSPOSE(array)

The leftmost column will always turn into the top row and the top row will turn into the leftmost column.

Back to the SEQUENCE Function

I find the **SEQUENCE** function very useful in financial modelling. It makes it easy to extend calculations such as

Example

		Jul 24	Aug 24	Sep 24
Date	Date			
Start Date	Date	1 Jul 24	1 Aug 24	1 Sep 24
End Date	Date	31 Jul 24	31 Aug 24	30 Sep 24
Counter	#	1	2	3
Number of Days	#	31	31	30
Not Revenue	Date	136	136	136
Revenue	Date	174	110	171
COGS	Date	(38)	(27)	(62)
Profit	Date	**136**	**83**	**109**
Not Profit	$'000	328	328	328

into

Example

		Jul 24	Aug 24	Sep 24	Oct 24	Nov 24
Date	Date					
Start Date	Date	1 Jul 24	1 Aug 24	1 Sep 24	1 Oct 24	1 Nov 24
End Date	Date	31 Jul 24	31 Aug 24	30 Sep 24	31 Oct 24	30 Nov 24
Counter	#	1	2	3	4	5
Number of Days	#	31	31	30	31	30
Not Revenue	Date	145	145	145	145	145
Revenue	Date	135	189	145	196	151
COGS	Date	(84)	(99)	(142)	(132)	(51)
Profit	Date	51	90	3	64	100
Not Profit	$'000	307	307	307	307	307

simply by changing the number of periods (as an input) and incorporating **SEQUENCE** into many of the usual financial modelling formulae. Don't worry about the numbers being different (I used a randomiser), but if you are thinking I want to know how to do that, then great, you have the right book!

Changing depreciation grids also becomes trivial. A change of input converts

Summary

Year	Year		2024	2025	2026	2027	2028
Total	$'000		874	1,806	2,537	3,256	3,616
1 Depn - 2024	$'000	4,371	874	874	874	874	874
2 Depn - 2025	$'000	4,659		932	932	932	932
3 Depn - 2026	$'000	3,653			731	731	731
4 Depn - 2027	$'000	3,599				720	720
5 Depn - 2028	$'000	1,800					360

into

Summary

Year	Year		2024	2025	2026	2027	2028	2029	2030	2031	2032	2033
Total	$'000		367	766	1,686	2,432	2,750	2,701	2,872	2,777	2,958	3,559
1 Depn - 2024	$'000	1,833	367	367	367	367	367	-	-	-	-	-
2 Depn - 2025	$'000	1,999		400	400	400	400	400	-	-	-	-
3 Depn - 2026	$'000	4,596			919	919	919	919	919	-	-	-
4 Depn - 2027	$'000	3,730				746	746	746	746	746	-	-
5 Depn - 2028	$'000	1,590					318	318	318	318	318	-
6 Depn - 2029	$'000	1,588						318	318	318	318	318
7 Depn - 2030	$'000	2,858							572	572	572	572
8 Depn - 2031	$'000	4,119								824	824	824
9 Depn - 2032	$'000	4,635									927	927
10 Depn - 2033	$'000	4,597										919

momentarily. In the past, this would have required much more sophisticated formulae.

RANDARRAY Function

Onto the next function: **RANDARRAY**. Back in March 2019, as it was not yet Generally Available, this function became the first function *ever* to change its syntax once released. This is something that is possible to do before a function or feature becomes Generally Available – "Preview" means Microsoft reserves the right to change something as they see fit. That's a *good* thing here.

Originally, the **RANDARRAY** function returned an array of random numbers between 0 and 1. However, there was a general sense of underwhelm with this function and the new and improved version was released. It now allows you to set your own maximum and minimum *and* decide whether you want the values returned to be decimals (*e.g.* 17.4381672…) or integers (whole numbers).

The improved syntax for the function is as follows:

=RANDARRAY([rows], [columns],[min],[max],[integer]).

The function has five arguments, all supposedly optional (having used the function, we aren't quite convinced):

- **rows:** this specifies how many **rows** the results should spill over. If omitted, the default value is 1

- **columns:** this specifies how many **columns** the results should spill over. If omitted, the default value is also 1

- **min:** this is the minimum value that may be selected randomly. If this is not specified, it is assumed to be zero [0]

- **max:** this is the maximum value that may be selected randomly. If this is not specified, it is assumed to be one [1]

- **integer:** if this is set to TRUE, only integer outputs are allowed; the default value (FALSE) provides non-integer (decimal) results.

Other points to note:

- if **rows** or **columns** refers to a blank cell reference, this will generate the new *#CALC!* error

- if **rows** or **columns** are entered as decimals, the values used will be truncated to the number before the decimal point (*e.g.* 3.999999 will be treated as 3)

- if **rows** or **columns** is a value less than 1, *#CALC!* will be returned

- if **integer** is set to TRUE and either **min** or **max** is not an integer, this will generate an *#VALUE!* error

- **max** must be greater than or equal to **min**, else the error *#VALUE!* is returned.

When demonstrating the original syntax of the **RANDARRAY** function, we often used this rather comprehensive example to create a list of random integers between two values:

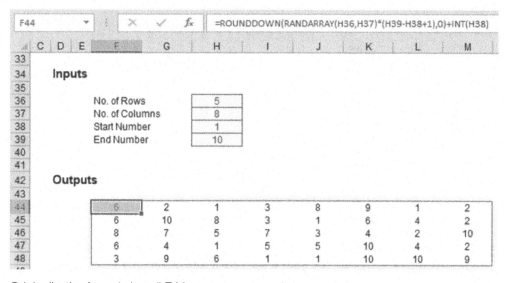

Originally, the formula in cell **F44** was

=ROUNDDOWN(RANDARRAY(H36,H37)*(H39-H38+1),0)+INT(H38)

Now, it's much easier:

203

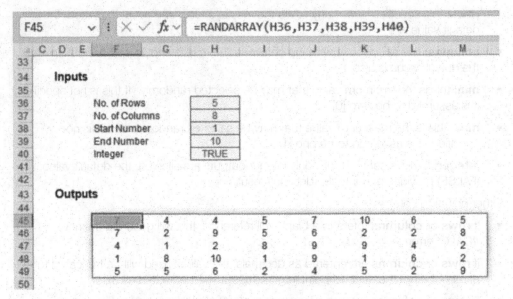

The "new improved" formula in cell **F45** (it's moved down a row due to the additional argument required in cell **H40**) is simply:

=RANDARRAY(H36,H37,H38,H39,H40).

This is much simpler – and pretty cool.

For a final example, imagine you are a schoolteacher, and you have 10 five-year-old children:

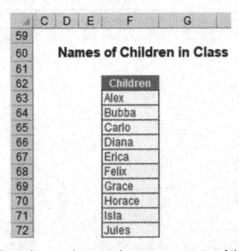

For each of the next 10 weeks, you have topics you want one of them to present on:

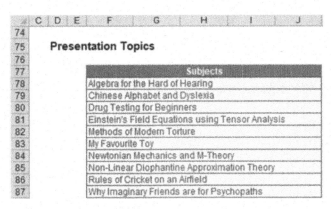

I can use **RANDARRAY** in tandem with **SORTBY** to determine a presentation order for the term:

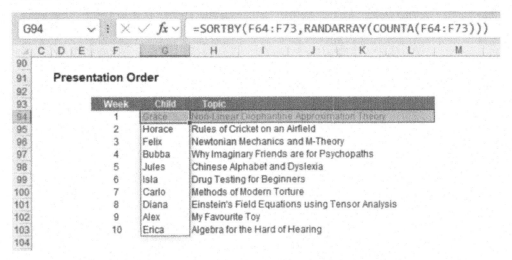

Oh dear. I do hope Grace has prepared well or it could all end in tears. She could try swapping with Horace, I suppose. On a serious note, the formula

=SORTBY(F63:F72,RANDARRAY(COUNTA(F63:F72)))

sorts the 'Child' order randomly (and a similar formula is used for 'Topic' too). In a past life, as an independent expert, I once had to attest that drug testing was being performed entirely randomly, *i.e.* free from any material bias. **SORTBY(RANDARRAY)** dries up that well for me once and for all.

Death of Data Tables and PivotTables?

I near the end of this rather long section on an interesting note or two. There are some significant ramifications for Excel, let me explain.

I begin with a two-dimensional Data Table (**ALT + D + T**) with an old favourite for this sort of thing, calculating monthly payments on various loan amounts over various durations.

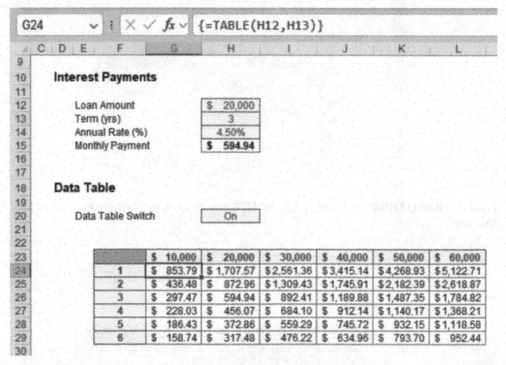

I have no plans to go through Data Tables again here, suffice to say they are a great tool for "what-if?" analysis, albeit they can consume vast quantities of memory. This summary table shows how the monthly instalments would vary for different terms (in years) and different amounts borrowed.

Now, take a look at using three Dynamic Array formulae:

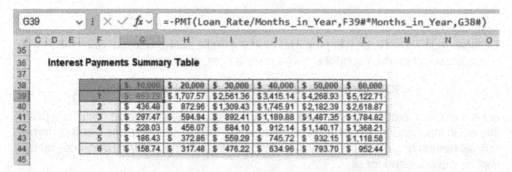

Can you spot the difference? In the second table, I have highlighted three cells:

- **G38** contains the formula **=SEQUENCE(1,6,10000,10000)**
- **F39** contains the formula **=SEQUENCE(6)**
- **G39** has the formula **=-PMT(Loan_Rate/Months_in_Year,F39#*Months_in_Year,G38#)**.

See how using the Spilled Range Operator ('#') makes all the difference?

That's it! Now I am not saying that all Data Tables may be replaced by Dynamic Array formulae, but can you see the future? And guess what, it doesn't stop there. Let me replicate one feature in Excel many of us are familiar with: the PivotTable…

In this illustration, I have created a 1,200-record Table (**CTRL + T**):

Football Club	Month	Month No	Pts Achieved
Data			
Nottingham Forest	January	6	3
Sheffield Wednesday	January	6	3
Ipswich Town	December	5	0
Millwall	March	8	1
Nottingham Forest	September	2	3
Bristol City	February	7	1
Bristol City	March	8	3
Queens Park Rangers	August	1	3
Leeds United	March	8	1
Preston North End	A…	9	1
… City			0

Bre…	September	2	
Aston Villa	March	8	0
Sheffield Wednesday	September	2	3
Brentford	November	4	3
Ipswich Town	March	8	1
Ipswich Town	August	1	3
Birmingham City	November	4	1

It's all made up randomly generated data, and you will just have to guess who I support. The important thing to note is I have created a Table, called **Football_Data**, so I may add records and the Table will extend automatically.

Next, I created a "Pseudo PivotTable":

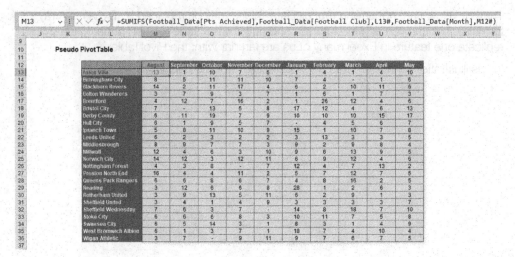

M13   =SUMIFS(Football_Data[Pts Achieved],Football_Data[Football Club],L13#,Football_Data[Month],M12#)

Pseudo PivotTable

	August	September	October	November	December	January	February	March	April	May
Aston Villa	13	1	10	7	5	1	4	1	4	10
Birmingham City	8	5	11	11	10	7	4	-	1	6
Blackburn Rovers	14	2	11	17	4	6	2	10	11	6
Bolton Wanderers	3	7	9	3	7	1	6	1	7	3
Brentford	4	12	7	16	2	1	26	12	4	6
Bristol City	7	-	13	5	8	17	12	4	6	13
Derby County	6	11	19	7	9	10	10	10	15	17
Hull City	6	1	9	5	7	-	4	5	6	7
Ipswich Town	5	8	11	10	9	15	1	10	7	8
Leeds United	6	2	3	2	2	3	13	3	3	5
Middlesbrough	8	9	7	7	3	9	2	9	8	4
Millwall	12	4	6	3	10	9	6	13	9	5
Norwich City	14	12	3	12	11	6	9	12	4	6
Nottingham Forest	4	3	8	-	7	12	4	7	13	2
Preston North End	16	4	4	11	2	5	7	12	7	5
Queens Park Rangers	6	6	8	6	7	4	8	16	2	5
Reading	3	12	6	6	8	28	1	2	6	3
Rotherham United	3	9	13	5	11	6	2	9	1	3
Sheffield United	3	4	1	4	9	3	3	3	3	7
Sheffield Wednesday	7	6	3	7	-	14	8	18	7	10
Stoke City	6	6	6	8	3	10	11	7	5	8
Swansea City	6	5	14	3	1	8	3	1	4	9
West Bromwich Albion	6	1	3	7	1	18	7	4	10	4
Wigan Athletic	3	7	-	9	11	9	7	6	7	5

This was created using three Dynamic Array formulae (again, highlighted):

- **M12** contains the formula **=TRANSPOSE(UNIQUE(SORTBY(Football_Data[Month],Football_Data[Month No])))**, which sorts the months into the required order

- **L13** contains the formula **=SORT(UNIQUE(Football_Data[Football Club]))**, which simply sorts the clubs into alphabetical order

- **M13** contains the formula **=SUMIFS(Football_Data[Pts Achieved],Football_Data[Football Club],L13#,Football_Data[Month],M12#)**, which spills out the points earned each month using a standard **SUMIFS** formula and the Spilled Range Operator ('**#**').

Think about it. I have created a formulaic PivotTable which calculates no discernibly slower than the real thing. However, the source data may be extended, values may change, *and I don't need to hit 'Refresh'*. Is this the end for PivotTables?

It's easy to get carried away. Dynamic Array formulae make league tables a breeze:

League Table

	P	W	D	L	Pts
Derby County	48	33	15	-	114
Brentford	67	22	24	21	90
Norwich City	56	27	8	21	89
Bristol City	56	21	22	13	85
Ipswich Town	68	18	30	20	84
Blackburn Rovers	56	22	17	17	83
Sheffield Wednesday	56	19	23	14	80
Millwall	54	22	11	21	77
Reading	49	21	12	16	75
Preston North End	57	18	19	20	73
Stoke City	52	19	13	20	70
Queens Park Rangers	40	18	14	8	68
Middlesbrough	47	17	15	15	66
Wigan Athletic	50	16	16	18	64
Birmingham City	52	16	15	21	63
Rotherham United	49	14	20	15	62
West Bromwich Albion	44	17	10	17	61
Nottingham Forest	54	14	18	22	60
Aston Villa	41	15	11	15	56
Swansea City	44	15	9	20	54
Hull City	39	13	11	15	50
Bolton Wanderers	37	12	11	14	47
Leeds United	43	8	18	17	42
Sheffield United	41	10	10	21	40

However, rather than get side tracked, I'd rather stay "on track" with PivotTables and finish this section unpivoting the PivotTable we have just created (the references have changed as they are on a different worksheet in my example):

Data

	1	2	3	4	5	6	7	8	9	10
	August	September	October	November	December	January	February	March	April	May
Aston Villa	13	1	10	7	5	1	4	1	4	10
Birmingham City	8	5	11	11	10	7	4	-	1	6
Blackburn Rovers	14	2	11	17	4	6	2	10	11	6
Bolton Wanderers	3	7	9	3	7	1	6	1	7	3
Brentford	4	12	7	16	2	1	26	12	4	6
Bristol City	7	-	13	5	8	17	12	4	6	13
Derby County	6	11	19	7	9	10	10	10	15	17
Hull City	6	1	9	5	7	-	4	5	6	7
Ipswich Town	5	8	11	10	9	15	1	10	7	8
Leeds United	6	2	3	2	2	3	13	3	3	5
Middlesbrough	8	9	7	7	3	9	2	9	8	4
Millwall	12	4	6	3	10	9	6	13	9	5
Norwich City	14	12	3	12	11	6	9	12	4	6
Nottingham Forest	4	3	8	-	7	12	4	7	13	2
Preston North End	16	4	4	11	2	5	7	12	7	5
Queens Park Rangers	6	6	8	6	7	4	8	16	2	5
Reading	3	12	6	6	8	28	1	2	6	3
Rotherham United	3	9	13	5	11	6	2	9	1	3
Sheffield United	3	4	1	4	9	3	3	3	3	7
Sheffield Wednesday	7	6	3	7	-	14	8	18	7	10
Stoke City	6	6	6	8	3	10	11	7	5	8
Swansea City	6	5	14	3	1	8	3	1	4	9
West Bromwich Albion	6	1	3	7	1	18	7	4	10	4
Wigan Athletic	3	7	-	9	11	9	7	6	7	5

Unpivoting can be a nightmare, but it is possible. You don't need to use dynamic arrays to do it, but I will to showcase them:

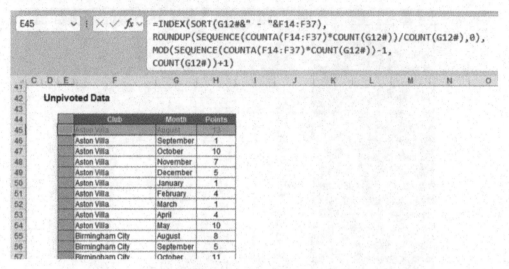

There is a hidden formula in cell **E45**. You can see why it is hidden – for those of you with a nervous disposition, please look away now:

=INDEX(SORT(G12#&" - "&F14:F37),ROUNDUP(SEQUENCE(COUNTA(F14:F37)*COUNT(G12#))/ COUNT(G12#),0),MOD(SEQUENCE(COUNTA(F14:F37)*COUNT(G12#))-1, COUNT(G12#))+1)

Oh dear. That's a horror. Rather than write 1,000 words trying to explain this, let me detail the concept instead. **SORT(G12#&" - "&F14:F37)** provides every combination of **Month Number** concatenated with a **Football Club**, separated by a " - " delimiter, *e.g.*

1 - Aston Villa, 2 - Aston Villa, …, 10 - Aston Villa, 1 - Birmingham City, 2 - Birmingham City, …

The problem is **SORT(G12#&" - "&F14:F37)** spills this into a 10-column by 24-row array. I want it as a list, so the entire rest of the formula simply forces the array down a column of 240 rows instead. **INDEX** is used to locate the next record in the array, with contrived formulae to determine the row and column numbers of the virtual grid.

SUMIFS is used to create the points total for each row, and to be honest, simpler formulae could have been used elsewhere too. But that's my point. As I have written this section, it's hard not to get carried away with all this and try and do everything in dynamic arrays. I have worked for years with Excel and been a keen advocate for keeping everything simple. Dynamic arrays scare me that we may not help ourselves and write monsters like the formula above. Some mad fool will probably try and create linked financial statements using just dynamic arrays…

Maybe Excel's simpler functions and features will live on after all.

Dynamic Charts

Until late 2022, if you wanted to create a chart where the range might vary, you were compelled to either use an Excel Table (**CTRL + T**) or else write convoluted formulae using **INDEX** or **OFFSET**, say. Not anymore!

You can now create a chart with a data source range aligned to the result of an array formula. The chart will now update to capture all data whenever the array recalculates, rather than being fixed to a specific number of data points.

For example, consider the following:

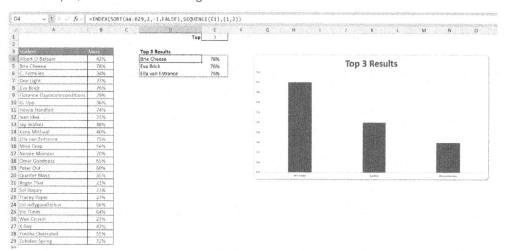

In cells **A4:B29** (purposely not placed in an Excel Table), I have entered the results of the Home Cookery & Poisoning (Joint Honours) vocational course. Cell **E1** contains an input number that specifies the top "**X**" students to chart, and the formula

=INDEX(SORT(A4:B29,2,-1,FALSE),SEQUENCE(E1),{1,2})

has been entered into cell **D4** as a Dynamic Array formula to summarise the said top **X** students and their respective marks.

Finally, a chart has been inserted linking to the dynamic range (cells **D4:E6** in the above illustration) in the usual way (*e.g.* **Insert -> Recommended Charts**). Nothing that exciting so far, but then, let's change the value in cell **E1** to 10 *(say)*:

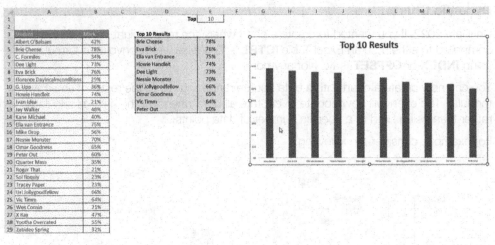

or even 20:

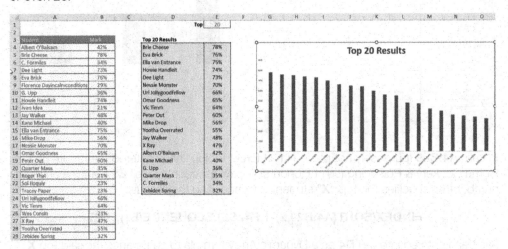

How cool is that!? Goodbye opaque formulae using **OFFSET** and / or **INDEX**!

Calculation Order Concern

If it feels like you have aged a year since you started reading this section, you probably have. There's a lot to get excited about and I have highlighted some of the issues too. However, I am not sure the following concern will be going away any time soon.

When I calculate something in Excel, if I use the same formula, I must get the same answer, right? Well – not necessarily. Consider the following:

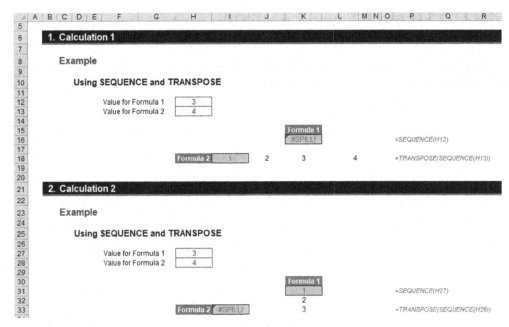

In the example above, Calculations 1 and 2 are identical but deliver different results (*i.e.* different *#SPILL!* errors). Why?

- In Calculations 1 and 2, both values for Formula 1 and Formula 2 were originally set to 1. This causes no *#SPILL! errors*

- In Calculation 1, the value for Formula 2 (cell **H13**) was then changed to 4 with no error

- Then, in Calculation 1, the value for Formula 1 (cell **H12**) was changed to 3. This caused the resultant *#SPILL!* error in cell **K16**

- Next, in Calculation 2, the value for Formula 1 (cell **H27**) was changed to 3 with no error

- Then, in Calculation 2, the value for Formula 2 (cell **H28**) was changed to 4. This caused the resultant *#SPILL!* error in cell **I33**.

I am not sure what the solution is for this problem. Technically, *#SPILL!* is working correctly, but it doesn't seem right that two results may be generated in this instance depending upon what input I change first. The jury is out on this one.

CHAPTER 6: LET and LAMBDA

This book is not all about dynamic arrays. There are quite a few other functions that spill that, well, quite frankly need *help*. Let me show you with a quick illustration. Consider **SEQUENCE** and **OFFSET** endeavouring to work together:

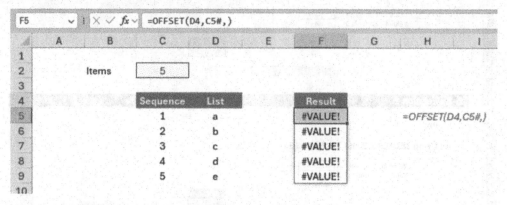

With cells **C5:C9** containing the result of the formula,

> ### =SEQUENCE(C2)

I have a list in cells **D5:D9**: "a", "b", "c", "d" and "e". For some reason, let's imagine I want to create the list in cells **F5:F9** using the **OFFSET** function. Let's ignore the fact I could just write the formula

> ### =D5:D9

This might be because this formula forms part of a much larger calculation, for example. The formula

> ### =OFFSET(D4,C5#,)

does not work, whereas using **INDEX** it does:

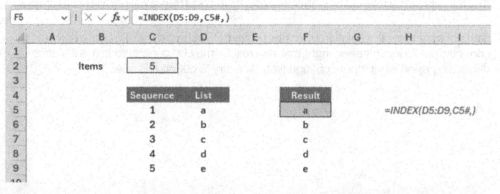

Some functions will not spill: they will just report in one cell (*e.g.* **SUM**). Others just don't seem to want to work at all, like **OFFSET**. I wouldn't recommend spending too much time figuring out why this is the case. I have tried since September 2018. Rather than head for a logical reason, my best guess (and although I am an MVP I have absolutely

214

no inside information here) is that it is to do with how the functions were originally coded "back in the day".

Great. So, what do I do if I want **OFFSET** to work as envisaged? You implement something like the following:

F5		× ✓ *fx*	=MAP(C5#,LAMBDA(x,OFFSET(D4,x,)))						
	A	B	C	D	E	F	G	H	I	J
1									
2		Items	5						
3									
4			Sequence	List		Result			
5			1	a		a		=MAP(C5#,LAMBDA(x,OFFSET(D4,x,)))	
6			2	b		b			
7			3	c		c			
8			4	d		d			
9			5	e		e			

That's right. For success, you use the highly intuitive formula

> **=MAP(C5#,LAMBDA(x,OFFSET(D4,x,)))**

Huh? What is **MAP**? What is **LAMBDA**? What is **x**? Stick with me. All will be revealed during this chapter. However, before I address either of these functions, **LET** me introduce another one…

Introducing LET

Originally released back in March 2020 (see? I have hindsight with 2020 vision), Microsoft "let" loose a new Excel function, **LET**, for Office 365. **LET** allows you to stop writing the same expressions time and time again in a formula or allows portability of segments of a computation for different formulae. As Microsoft puts it, it's "…names on a formula level".

In essence, this function assigns values or expressions to defined names and then passes these to calculation results. It can store intermediate calculations, values or defining names inside a formula. The defined names only apply within the scope of the **LET** function in a similar way to variables in general programming scenarios.

If you reuse the same expression multiple times in a formula, Excel calculates that expression multiple times. That's *not* a good thing. **LET** allows you to name the expression and refer to it using that name, similar to **VAR** in a **DAX** expression, for those that know the language. Any named expression is calculated only once, even though it may be referred to many times in the formula. This can significantly improve performance and speed up your spreadsheets.

To use the **LET** function, we must define pairs of names and associated values, and a calculation that uses them all, as the final argument. At least one name / value pair must be defined.

It has the following syntax to operate:

> **LET(name1, value1, [name2…], [value2…], calculation)**

where:

- **name1**: the name for the first value
- **value1**: the value to associate with the first name
- **name2** (optional): additional names for second and subsequent values
- **value2** (optional): additional values for the second and subsequent values
- **calculation**: this is the calculation to perform. This is always the final argument, and it can refer to any of the defined names in the **LET** formula.

The main benefits of using the **LET** function include:

- **readability**: the **LET** function tracks the changes in defined cells or expression in a dynamic way, so there is no need to remember what a specific range / cell reference referred to. With the ability to define variables, it can provide more meaningful context to end users

- **performance: LET** enables the use of a named expression which is calculated only once, even if it is referred to many times in the formula. This can significantly improve performance for complex expressions.

Let's look at an example. If I am considering **LET**, how about we use the property rental market! Suppose we run a company where salespeople make commission based upon 1% of the average of the square of the weekly rent, *e.g.* if Annie makes two sales of $400 and $300, then the average of the amounts squared would be (300² + 400²) / 2 = 125,000 and 1% of that would be $1,250. Not much incentive to make lots of sales, is there? It's not my fault she negotiated her contract badly…

Anyway, it's convoluted, I know, but I am trying to construct an example which I cannot simply solve using a standard Excel formula like **AVERAGEIFS**!

	A	B	C	D	E	F
1						
2		Business Unit	Salesperson	Sales Amount		
3		A	Annie	374		
4		A	Brad	347		
5		A	Charlie	159		
6		A	Dee	393		
7		B	Brad	478		
8		B	Charlie	354		
9		B	Charlie	159		
10		C	Dee	203		
11		C	Brad	371		
12		C	Annie	300		
13		C	Annie	400		
14		D	Dee	187		
15		D	Brad	140		
16						
17		Business Unit	C			
18		Salesperson	Annie			
19		Comm. Rate	1.00%			
20						
21		Commission	$1,250.00	=LET(BusinessUnit,B3:B15=C17, SalesPerson,C3:C15=C18, Selection,BusinessUnit*SalesPerson, Commission,C19, SalesAmt,D3:D15, SUMPRODUCT(Selection*SalesAmt^2)*Commission/SUMPRODUCT(Selection))		

The formula in cell **C21** is given by

> **=LET(BusinessUnit, B3:B15=C17,**
> **SalesPerson, C3:C15=C18,**
> **Selection, BusinessUnit*SalesPerson,**
> **Commission, C19,**
> **SalesAmt, D3:D15,**
> **SUMPRODUCT(Selection*SalesAmt^2)*Commission/SUMPRODUCT(Selection))**

The final argument is the formula – but more on that shortly. Before that, there are pairs of expressions where the first element is the name and the second is an expression for a value. Let's go through all of these arguments (mainly in pairs):

- **BusinessUnit, B3:B15=C17** define the array **BusinessUnit**, which is an array of TRUE and FALSE values depending on whether the Business Unit is equal to the value in cell **C17** (which is 'C' in the illustration). Therefore, we have {FALSE, FALSE, FALSE, FALSE, FALSE, FALSE, FALSE, TRUE, TRUE, TRUE, TRUE, FALSE, FALSE}

- **SalesPerson, C3:C15=C18** generate a similar array (named **SalesPerson**), which provides TRUE and FALSE values depending on whether the salesperson was 'Annie'. Therefore, we have {TRUE, FALSE, FALSE, FALSE, FALSE, FALSE, FALSE, FALSE, FALSE, TRUE, TRUE, FALSE, FALSE}

- **Selection, BusinessUnit*SalesPerson** now shows the value of **LET**. This names the value of the product of the first two parameters **Selection** without having to write out the formula again and, more importantly, *without having to calculate them a second time unnecessarily*. This results in TRUE/FALSE expressions multiplied by other TRUE/FALSE expressions, which results in a one if both are TRUE, and zero [0] otherwise. Therefore, we have {0, 0, 0, 0, 0, 0, 0, 0, 0, 0, 1, 1, 0, 0}

- **Commission, C19** simply name the value in cell **C19** (1%) **Commission**

- Similarly, **SalesAmt, D3:D15** apply the name **SalesAmt** to the range **D3:D15** *for the purposes of this formula*. Therefore, we have {374, 347, 159, 393, 478, 354, 159, 203, 371, 300, 400, 187, 140}

- Finally, the formula
  SUMPRODUCT(Selection*SalesAmt^2)*Commission/
  SUMPRODUCT(Selection) calculates the commission similarly to the approach explained above. However, **Selection**, **SalesAmt** and **Commission** are merely referenced and neither need to be recalculated nor written out in full.

This may seem verbose, but it speeds up calculation time considerably, and makes formulae easier to read (once you get your head around this new approach). Further, **LET** only defines the range name *within* the formula. These are not general range names in the spreadsheet – Excel will not recognise them outside of this **LET** formula.

To be crystal clear, I see two key differences between defined range names and this new **LET** function:

1. **LET** allows you to see the definition of the name there and then, without jumping to the definition elsewhere. Yes, the formula may be longer in the cell, but the user can hopefully follow it without audit tools

2. When Excel sees a defined name in a formula, it pauses the current formula, evaluates the defined name's formula to get a result, and returns to the original formula. A variable defined using **LET** is only ever evaluated once.

    An example that shows the difference is **=LET(x, RANDBETWEEN(1, 1000000), x - x)**. This formula will always return zero, since **RANDBETWEEN(1, 1000000)** gets evaluated and then assigned to **x**, which never changes, so **x - x** = 0.

    If you instead use the Name Manager to define the name **x** as **=RANDBETWEEN(1, 1000000)**, then entering **=x - x** is almost never going to be zero, since each **x** in the formula causes **RANDBETWEEN** to be evaluated.

It should also be noted that you must be careful with your order of arguments and defining reference names. Name definitions can only make use of prior and not subsequent names. In the example above, **Selection** could only be defined once **BusinessUnit** and **SalesAmt** had both been defined.

LAMBDA Function

Just nine months after **LET** was unleashed, its sibling **LAMBDA** came out to play too. Simply put, **LAMBDA** "completes" Excel and allows you to define your own custom functions using Excel's formula language. Moreover, one function can call another (including itself!), so there is no limit to the power you can deploy with a single function call. Additionally, you can use other functions (which we'll get to shortly) to apply these functions in more versatile ways. This will be essential to building up our financial model later in the book.

One of the more challenging parts of working with formulae in Excel is that you often get fairly complex formulae that are re-used numerous times through the sheet (often by just copying / pasting). This can make it hard for others to read and understand what's going on, put you more at risk of errors, and make it harder to find and fix the errors. With **LAMBDA**, you have reusability and composability. You can create libraries for any pieces of logic you plan to use multiple times, which offers convenience and reduces the risk of errors.

Some people are put off by **LAMBDA** and "lambda". A lambda function (sometimes referred to as a "Small Anonymous Function") is IT parlance for a self-contained block of functionality that is transferrable / portable throughout your code.

Think of Excel formulae as your "code". You can create a user-defined function (a lambda function) using the Excel function **LAMBDA** to define it. Clear as mud, yes?

So how does it work?

The syntax of **LAMBDA** is perhaps not the most informative:

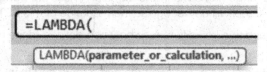

That's, er, great. Its syntax suffers because it is so flexible. Perhaps a run-through might be best. There are three key pieces of **LAMBDA** to understand:

1. **LAMBDA** function components

2. Naming a lambda

3. Calling a lambda function.

LAMBDA function components

Let's take a simple example. Consider the following formula:

=LAMBDA(x, x+1)

where we have **x** as the argument, which you may pass in when calling the **LAMBDA**, and **x+1** is the logic / operation to be performed. For example, if you were to call this lambda function and define **x** as equal to five [5], then Excel would calculate

$$5 + 1 = 6$$

Except it wouldn't. If you tried this you would get #*CALC!*

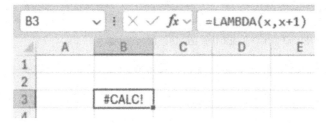

Oops. That's because it's not *quite* as simple as that. There are two [2] ways to fix this. The first is to name your **LAMBDA**.

Naming a LAMBDA

To give your **LAMBDA** a name so it can be re-used, you have to use the Name Manager (**CTRL** + **F3** / go to the Ribbon and then go to **Formulas -> Name Manager**):

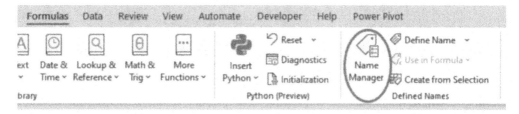

Once you open the Name Manager you will see the following dialog:

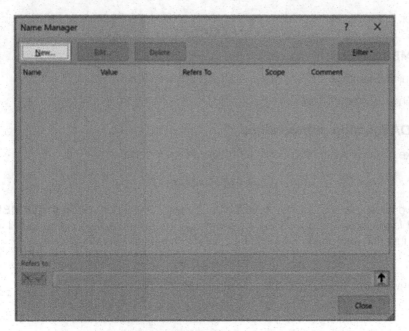

You then click on 'New' and fill out the related fields, *viz.*

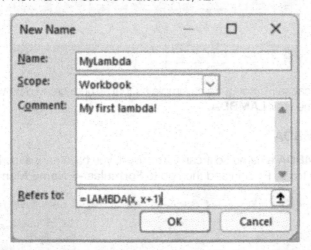

It's no harder than clicking 'OK' at this point.

Calling LAMBDA

Now that you have done this, your first new lambda function may be called in just the same way as every other Excel function is cited, *e.g.*

$$=MYLAMBDA(5)$$

which would equal six [6] and not *#CALC!* as before.

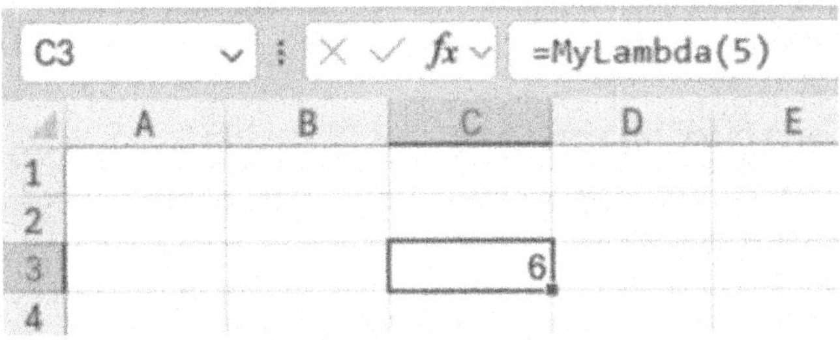

You DON'T have to do it this way though if you don't want to. You may call a lambda without naming it, and this is the second way to fix the *#VALUE!* error we had earlier. If we hadn't named this marvellous calculation, and simply authored it in the grid as we had first attempted, we could call it by simply typing:

=LAMBDA(x, x+1)(5)

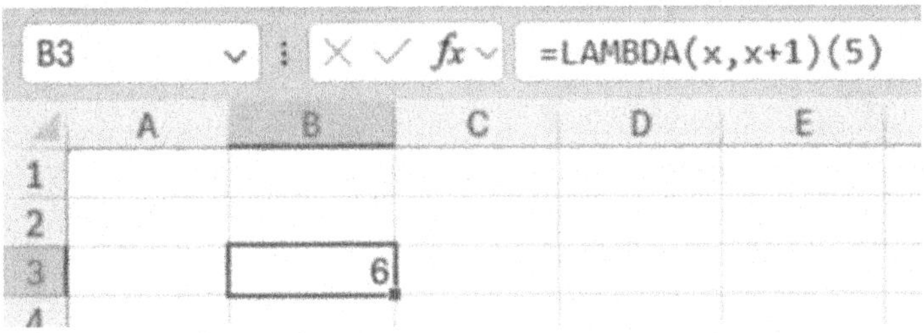

This trick won't always work though: something called **recursion** might catch this idea out...

LAMBDA Has No Aversion to Recursion

To be clear, **LAMBDA** has no aversion; in fact, it enables it. But it makes for a great sub-heading. The "aversion" is that when you use recursion in a **LAMBDA**,

LAMBDA(*appropriate syntax*)(*variable or reference*)

may not give the expected result. Instead, it will most likely generate an error, making you think you have written your expression incorrectly. Let me illustrate with a simple example. Consider the following:

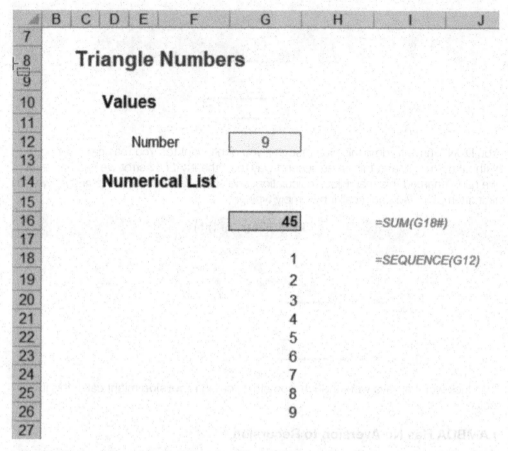

Triangle Numbers

Values

Number 9

Numerical List

45   =SUM(G18#)

1   =SEQUENCE(G12)
2
3
4
5
6
7
8
9

In cell **G12**, I have typed the number nine [9], which generates the list of numbers one [1] through nine [9] from cell **G18** downwards, using the **SEQUENCE** function, *viz.*

=SEQUENCE(G12)

Cell **G16** simply sums this list:

=SUM(G18#)

Therefore, inputting the numbers one [1] through [9] in cell **G12** would generate the results

1, 3, 6, 10, 15, 21, 28, 36, 45, …

In cell **G16**. These numbers are known as the **triangle numbers:**

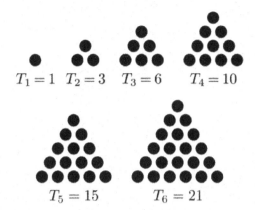

$$T_1 = 1 \quad T_2 = 3 \quad T_3 = 6 \quad T_4 = 10$$

$$T_5 = 15 \quad T_6 = 21$$

in mathematics, for very obvious reasons.

I want to show you how you can generate this sequence using a **LAMBDA**. Now, yes, I know the formula above works and you can even use the algebraic solution

=G12*(G12+1)/2

too, but the point is here, I want to show you how to create a recursive **LAMBDA** function that is simple to follow.

On the Ribbon, go to the Formulas tab and click on Name Manager *(as above)* (**CTRL + F3**) and click on the 'New…' button.

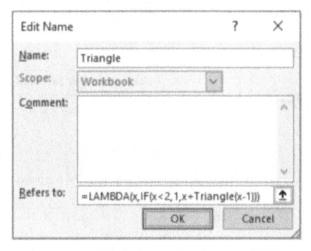

I have named my lambda function **Triangle**, and the reference ('Refers to:') is given by

=LAMBDA(x, IF(x<2, 1, x+Triangle(x-1)))

Here, the lambda function takes a parameter **x** and defines it as one [1] if it is less than two [2], else it takes the value **x** and adds the lambda value for **x-1** – hence the recursion. This lambda function has been named **Triangle** (in the 'Name:' box) and is referred to in the formula too.

223

Therefore, for **x** equals nine [9]:

```
Triangle(9)   = 9 + Triangle(8)
              = 9 + 8 + Triangle (7)
              = 9 + 8 + 7 + Triangle (6)
              = 9 + 8 + 7 + 6 + Triangle(5)
              = 9 + 8 + 7 + 6 + 5 + Triangle(4)
              = 9 + 8 + 7 + 6 + 5 + 4 + Triangle(3)
              = 9 + 8 + 7 + 6 + 5 + 4 + 3 + Triangle(2)
              = 9 + 8 + 7 + 6 + 5 + 4 + 3 + 2 + Triangle(1)
              = 9 + 8 + 7 + 6 + 5 + 4 + 3 + 2 + 1
              = 45
```

Drawn out long-hand, the recursion is clear. With the addition of custom functions that can call each other and recursively call themselves, Excel's formula language has now become what is known as Turing-complete, effectively meaning that Excel users can compute anything without resorting to another programming language.

Back to our example, the above presupposes that **x** is an integer, and I have ensured this by incorporating data validation (**Data -> Data Validation** or **ALT** + **D** + **L**) into my input cell (keep it simple!):

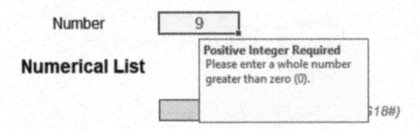

Triangle Numbers

Values

Number   9

Numerical List

Positive Integer Required
Please enter a whole number
greater than zero (0).

G18#)

Now that the lambda function **Triangle** has been defined, the formula in Excel is easy:

45   =Triangle(G12)

I have purposely created a simple recursive formula to demonstrate how such a calculation might work. In reality, recursive formulae are likely to be much more sophisticated and / or complex.

Let's assume that wasn't the case though, and you wanted to check whether your formula was working. Not everyone (anyone?) can type a formula and have it work first time, every time. Many of us would want to try the formula in a cell first:

#CALC!   =LAMBDA(x,IF(x<2,1,x+Triangle1(x-1)))

Oh dear. That didn't work. Of course it doesn't. As explained above, it needs the parameter (**x**) to be defined:

#NAME?   *=LAMBDA(x, IF(x<2, 1, x+Triangle1(x-1)))($G$12)*

Rats. This is the problem I alluded to earlier. My definition of the function refers to itself (*i.e.* recursion is exhibited). The name has not yet been defined.

Now *watch out* here. Note the function here is **Triangle1**, not **Triangle**. There is a very important distinction. If I use **Triangle**, a similar formula *will* work:

          45   *=LAMBDA(x, IF(x<2, 1, x+Triangle(x-1)))($G$12)*

This is very easy to explain. I have already defined **Triangle** in the Name Manager! This is why I am using **Triangle1** to avoid this classic *gotcha*.

OK, let's define **Triangle1** then. That will mean wrapping the expression in a **LET** function.

#NAME?   *=LET(Triangle1, LAMBDA(x, IF(x<2, 1, x+Triangle1(x-1))), Triangle1($G$12))*

This has not worked either, even though **Triangle1** has supposedly been cited by **LET**. The problem is, **Triangle1** has not been defined when we are creating the lambda. This is where we can use a trick which is all about *ME*. Let's add a parameter (**ME**) to **Triangle1**, and replace the recursive call to **Triangle1** with **ME** (ensuring you pass in **ME** as the first parameter):

#VALUE!   *=LET(Triangle1, LAMBDA(ME, x, IF(x<2, 1, x+ME(ME, x-1))), Triangle1($G$12))*

Believe it or not, we are getting somewhere now. Even though #*NAME?* has been replaced with #*VALUE!*, the formula has evolved. Assuming you have background error checking enabled (**File -> Options -> Formulas -> Enable background error checking**), you can click on the error to see the issue:

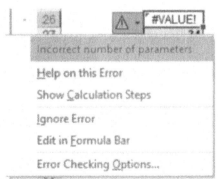

We have an incorrect number of parameters. We have added a parameter to **Triangle1** (namely, **ME**), so the final argument of **LET** (**Triangle1($G$12)**) should also have two parameters. We do this by getting **Triangle1** to refer to itself, *viz.*

          45   *=LET(Triangle1, LAMBDA(ME, x, IF(x<2, 1, x+ME(ME, x-1))), Triangle1(Triangle1, $G$12))*

It works! We have checked / debugged our **LAMBDA** in Excel. We started by calling **Triangle1(Triangle1,$G$12)**, and when we evaluate that lambda, we end up calling **Triangle1(Triangle1,$G$12-1)**, *etc.*

This technique has employed the **ME** parameter: by passing **Triangle1** as a parameter to itself, it can then use that parameter to call itself.

Once you've got your head around this, proved for yourself Einstein's Theory of General Relativity and demonstrated Schwarzschild's solution to Einstein's field equations using tensor analysis, you have probably got your lambda working properly! Now, simply remove all references to **ME**. Exclude **ME** as the first parameter and replace the **ME** calls with the defined name you want to use (here, **Triangle1**). Therefore, in this instance,

> **=LET(Triangle1, LAMBDA(ME, x, IF(x<2, 1, x + ME(ME, x - 1))), Triangle1(Triangle1, $G$12))**

becomes

> **=LAMBDA(x, IF(x<2, 1, x + Triangle1(x - 1)))**

i.e. we have proved our expression is correct. We can now add this to the Name Manager.

Taking it Further: Pascal's Triangle

Sorry to bring back childhood recollections of mathematics, but triangle (or triangular) numbers feature in Pascal's Triangle:

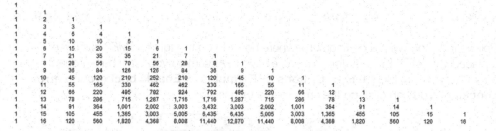

Starting with a 1 in what is conventionally known as the "zeroth" row (!), each subsequent row's value is calculated as the sum of the cell directly above it and the cell to the left of the cell above the cell you are in. Notice the triangle numbers occur in both the third column and the third diagonal from the top.

This is an almost "ultimate" recursion, as you can trace any number on any row back through its constituent elements higher up the Triangle. Note that this beast is useful in mathematics as this array displays the binomial coefficients of $(x + 1)n$. For example:

- $(x + 1)^0 = 1$ – which is the coefficient on the zeroth [0th] row

- $(x + 1)^1 = x + 1 = 1x + 1$ – the coefficients 1 and 1 are on row 1 of Pascal's Triangle

- $(x + 1)^2 = x^2 + 2x + 1 = 1x^2 + 2x + 1$ – the coefficients 1, 2 and 1 are on row 2 of Pascal's Triangle

- $(x + 1)^3 = x^3 + 3x^2 + 3x + 1 = 1x^3 + 3x^2 + 3x + 1$ – the coefficients **1**, **3**, **3** and **1** are on row **3** of Pascal's Triangle, *etc.*

Now, yes, I know, Excel has a function that calculates these coefficients – and hence any element of Pascal's Triangle. If you are often **COMBIN** the Excel functions to see how many subsets you can make, then **COMBIN** is for you. This function returns the number of combinations for a given number of items (*i.e.* the number of distinct subsets of items where order is unimportant). You should use **COMBIN** to determine the total possible number of groups for a given number of items.

The **COMBIN** function employs the following syntax to operate:

COMBIN(number, number_chosen)

The **COMBIN** function has the following arguments:

- **number:** this is required and represents the number of items

- **number_chosen:** this is also required. This denotes the number of items in each combination.

However, in the context of Pascal's Triangle, it may be seen to be

COMBIN(row_number, column_number)

where both **row_number** and **column_number** start at zero, rather than one for the reasons demonstrated above.

The technique for calculating this using a recursive lambda function is very similar to the **Triangle** example *(above)*. You can define **Pascal** in the Name Manager (**CTRL + F3**) as

=LAMBDA(row_num, col_num, IF(OR(row_num < 0, col_num < 0), 0, IF(row_num = 0, IF(col_num = 0, 1, 0), Pascal(row_num - 1, col_num - 1) + Pascal(row_num - 1, col_num))))

This may be checked in a cell using the **ME** technique *(as above)*:

=LET(Pascal1, LAMBDA(ME, row_num, col_num, IF(OR(row_num < 0, col_num < 0), 0, IF(row_num = 0, IF(col_num = 0, 1, 0), ME(ME, row_num - 1, col_num - 1) + ME(ME, row_num -1, col_num)))), Pascal1(Pascal1, $I$12, $I$13))

I don't plan to go through this here: the point is you can write more sophisticated formulae – and trust me, we will have a few during our case study model build!

This **Pascal** lambda function is a more complex example of recursion that highlights an important design consideration. On my reasonably powerful computer, when I tried to select an element from row 30 of Pascal's Triangle, Excel took *c.*55 seconds to calculate, due to all the interim recursive calculations.

Be careful. Lambda calculations in Excel are very fast, but if you adopt an excessive recursive approach as I have done here, any powerful PC will be slowed down to a "crawling speed". The problem here is that the calculation speed in this instance is proportional to $4^n / \sqrt{n}$, where **n** is the row number.

A better lambda might be **Pascal_Row**, where the time taken is proportional to n^2:

```
=LAMBDA(a, b, LET(Pascal_Row,
   LAMBDA(ME, x,
      IF(x=0, 1, IF(x=1, {1, 1},
         LET(seq, SEQUENCE(, x + 1), previous_row, ME(ME, x - 1), shifted,
IF(seq=1, 0, INDEX(previous_row, 1, seq - 1)),
            IFERROR(previous_row + shifted, 1)
)))), INDEX(Pascal_Row(Pascal_Row, a), 1, b + 1)))
```

This is achieved by calculating on a row, rather than an element, basis.

But even this may be improved upon. Consider **Pascal_Fast**:

```
=LAMBDA(n, k,
   IF(k * 2 > n, Pascal_Fast(n, n - k),
   IF(k = 0, 1,
   LET(gcd_cutoff, 2 ^ 53 / n,
         previous, Pascal_Fast(n, k - 1) * (n + 1 - k) / k,
      IF(n <= gcd_cutoff, previous,
         LET(gcd, GCD(previous, k),
            remainder, k / gcd,
            previous / gcd * ((n + 1 - k) / remainder)))
   ))))
```

This is very quick compared to both of the previous alternatives, as the time here is proportional to just **n**, the row number. The problem as you may have noticed here, is that as you maximise the iterative approach, the transparency of the calculation – for the average user – tends to become more and more opaque. PhDs in Computer Science are available upon request.

As a compromise, perhaps

=LAMBDA(n, k, IF(k=0, 1, Pascal_Almost_As_Fast(n, k - 1) * (n + 1 - k) / k))

{**Pascal_Almost_As_Fast**) might work best, which takes approximately twice as long as the above monster (*i.e.* "almost" instantly).

Care with IFS and SWITCH

Given how calculations may "blow out" quickly when creating iterative functions, it's best to avoid another classic *gotcha*. Let me illustrate with one of the best-known iterative sequences, the Fibonacci sequence:

1, 1, 2, 3, 5, 8, 13, 21, 34, 55, 89, 144, 233, 377, …

This sequence is calculated as $F_n = F_{n-1} + F_{n-2}$.

You might choose to define a lambda function using **IFS** as follows:

=LAMBDA(x, IFS(x=1, 1, x = 2, 1, TRUE, Fibonacci(x - 1) + Fibonacci(x - 2)))

If you are starting to follow lambdas, you should see this appears to make sense (the final argument of **IFS**, given the corresponding **logical_test** is simply TRUE, defines what to do when **x** is neither equal to one [1] nor two [2]). There is a problem though. This function will run forever, since each parameter in this **IFS** statement must be evaluated before **IFS** gets evaluated. Therefore, when evaluating **Fibonacci(1)**, it will try to evaluate **Fibonacci(0) + Fibonacci(-1)**, and so on. Not good!

Therefore, you should use **IF** instead:

=LAMBDA(x, IF(x = 1, 1,IF(x = 2, 1, Fibonacci(x - 1) + Fibonacci(x - 2))))

as **IF** does not evaluate a parameter it does not return.

Be advised, **SWITCH** exhibits a similar such property, and you should choose to use **CHOOSE** instead.

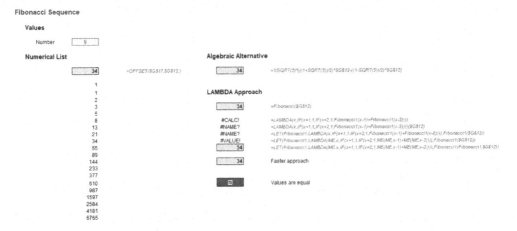

229

Just to highlight the point earlier about optimisation, the **Fibonacci** lambda function may be improved upon too – again, at the risk of mathematical / formulaic comprehension:

=LAMBDA(n, LET(Fibonacci_Faster, LAMBDA(ME, x, F_1, F, current, IF(x <= 2, 1,
IF(x = current, F,
ME(ME, x, F, F_1 + F, current + 1)
))),
Fibonacci_Faster(Fibonacci_Faster, n, 1, 1, 2)))

Now you have something to study the next time you are stranded on a desert island.

In Summary

Playing with newly discovered functions is highly addictive and can lead you to using them when they are **not** needed. No matter how optimised recursive calculations are, I strongly advise that if you don't need them, don't use them. Formulaic alternatives, such as **COMBIN** for Pascal's Triangle are instant and simple, to the naked eye.

Furthermore, do note that the current operand stack limit in Excel is 1,024. This should be borne in mind together with calculation times, as the current recursion limit is set as 1,024 divided by (number of lambda parameters + 1).

Finally, some common problems faced in financial modelling are **not** recursive in nature, so try not to confuse the issue unnecessarily. For example, the most common financial modelling illustration is the calculation of interest on an average cash balance. This is actually an instance of solving two simultaneous equations. Applying recursive logic would be inappropriate.

CHAPTER 7: LAMBDA HELPER FUNCTIONS

Whilst **LET** allows you to create formula-specific range names to ensure long, complex expressions do not have to be calculated repeatedly (thus reducing computing time and memory requirements), **LAMBDA** is going to take that further, allowing you to create your own user-defined functions using more memory-efficient expressions. There will be times **LET** and **LAMBDA** go hand in hand.

As you become more experienced and your expertise grows, you will realise that some transformations may be cumbersome using the functions you already know from "legacy Excel". For instance, you might find the following awkward:

- combining arrays
- shaping arrays
- resizing arrays.

This is where a set of "lambda helper functions" come into play. These allow you to write lambdas more easily. Let me take a look at some of them. As Excel develops, this list will grow and the following is not intended to be an exhaustive list, just highlights of those I have found more useful for financial modelling with dynamic arrays.

BYCOL and BYROW

BYCOL is not a region of the Philippines, but rather a function that takes an array or range and calls a lambda, with all the data grouped by each row or column and then returns an array of single values. Its syntax is as follows:

BYCOL(array, [lambda])

It has the following arguments:

- **array:** this is required and represents an array to be separated by column
- **lambda:** an optional argument, this is a **LAMBDA** that takes a column as a single parameter and calculates just one result.

As an example, imagine I have decided to make small talk and discuss the weather – in particular, whether we use Celsius or Fahrenheit as our temperature scale. You might use Fahrenheit if you are based in the United States whereas I use Celsius because I am right.

I have made up some average monthly temperatures for Melbourne (Australia), not that it matters much since I don't get out much (not since the restraining orders all came into place):

A	B	C	D	E	F	G	H	I	J	K	L
1	**Average Temperatures**										
2											
3	Month	2015	2016	2017	2018	2019	2020	2021	2022	2023	2024
4	January	25.0	17.5	18.0	21.0	18.4	14.6	24.6	20.6	16.2	25.3
5	February	14.7	18.3	23.3	20.7	17.3	24.2	24.5	23.8	17.0	14.7
6	March	21.2	15.4	14.4	19.7	15.9	21.9	14.4	18.2	14.2	22.1
7	April	13.1	13.0	19.8	13.9	17.2	18.5	12.2	11.4	16.9	11.4
8	May	11.6	11.5	13.6	15.6	10.0	10.5	14.8	15.3	14.0	12.4
9	June	7.6	10.4	6.9	10.0	9.3	13.3	13.5	11.1	7.8	10.7
10	July	9.0	11.2	6.8	12.5	12.0	12.5	12.1	9.4	11.1	6.7
11	August	8.2	7.5	11.5	11.8	10.7	9.3	10.7	14.4	6.7	13.2
12	September	14.2	10.3	14.7	17.3	9.4	14.9	8.1	10.2	15.8	14.4
13	October	15.7	15.4	14.0	13.9	16.9	13.3	18.2	11.2	17.8	18.8
14	November	22.0	11.6	21.6	21.4	16.9	11.5	18.6	11.2	11.8	15.0
15	December	13.2	20.0	20.1	14.0	14.0	20.5	13.8	15.4	20.2	18.8

I have called this Excel Table (**CTRL** + **T**) Temps, but it is a permanent name…

For the years 2015 to 2024 inclusive, I want to provide a detailed monthly breakdown of temperatures where the average temperature for the year was above 15 degrees Celsius. At this point, you would normally calculate the average temperature for each column using a formula such as

=AVERAGE(Temps[2017])

for column **C** of this example spreadsheet. This would be a "helper row", *e.g.*

A	B	C	D	E	F	G	H	I	J	K	L
1	**Average Temperatures**										
2											
3	Month	2015	2016	2017	2018	2019	2020	2021	2022	2023	2024
4	January	25.0	17.5	18.0	21.0	18.4	14.6	24.6	20.6	16.2	25.3
5	February	14.7	18.3	23.3	20.7	17.3	24.2	24.5	23.8	17.0	14.7
6	March	21.2	15.4	14.4	19.7	15.9	21.9	14.4	18.2	14.2	22.1
7	April	13.1	13.0	19.8	13.9	17.2	18.5	12.2	11.4	16.9	11.4
8	May	11.6	11.5	13.6	15.6	10.0	10.5	14.8	15.3	14.0	12.4
9	June	7.6	10.4	6.9	10.0	9.3	13.3	13.5	11.1	7.8	10.7
10	July	9.0	11.2	6.8	12.5	12.0	12.5	12.1	9.4	11.1	6.7
11	August	8.2	7.5	11.5	11.8	10.7	9.3	10.7	14.4	6.7	13.2
12	September	14.2	10.3	14.7	17.3	9.4	14.9	8.1	10.2	15.8	14.4
13	October	15.7	15.4	14.0	13.9	16.9	13.3	18.2	11.2	17.8	18.8
14	November	22.0	11.6	21.6	21.4	16.9	11.5	18.6	11.2	11.8	15.0
15	December	13.2	20.0	20.1	14.0	14.0	20.5	13.8	15.4	20.2	18.8
16											
17	Average	14.6	13.5	15.4	16.0	14.0	15.4	15.5	14.4	14.1	15.3
18											
19		=AVERAGE(Temps[2015])										

But I am not going to do it that way. Instead, let's use **BYCOL**. First of all, let's see how it works. Consider the calculation that sums each column (rather than calculates the average – I am not looking to complicate this with *#DIV/0!* errors):

=BYCOL(Temps, LAMBDA(column, SUM(column)))

Note I have used **Temps** as my array, which is cells **B4:L15**, *i.e.* it omits the header row of the table (cells **B3:L3**). I have to ignore the headers because the years would be included in the column totals being numbers – a classic gotcha!

This would produce the following result:

▲	A	B	C	D	E	F	G	H	I	J	K	L
1	**Average Temperatures**											
2												
3		Month	2015	2016	2017	2018	2019	2020	2021	2022	2023	2024
4		January	25.0	17.5	18.0	21.0	18.4	14.6	24.6	20.6	16.2	25.3
5		February	14.7	18.3	23.3	20.7	17.3	24.2	24.5	23.8	17.0	14.7
6		March	21.2	15.4	14.4	19.7	15.9	21.9	14.4	18.2	14.2	22.1
7		April	13.1	13.0	19.8	13.9	17.2	18.5	12.2	11.4	16.9	11.4
8		May	11.6	11.5	13.6	15.6	10.0	10.5	14.8	15.3	14.0	12.4
9		June	7.6	10.4	6.9	10.0	9.3	13.3	13.5	11.1	7.8	10.7
10		July	9.0	11.2	6.8	12.5	12.0	12.5	12.1	9.4	11.1	6.7
11		August	8.2	7.5	11.5	11.8	10.7	9.3	10.7	14.4	6.7	13.2
12		September	14.2	10.3	14.7	17.3	9.4	14.9	8.1	10.2	15.8	14.4
13		October	15.7	15.4	14.0	13.9	16.9	13.3	18.2	11.2	17.8	18.8
14		November	22.0	11.6	21.6	21.4	16.9	11.5	18.6	11.2	11.8	15.0
15		December	13.2	20.0	20.1	14.0	14.0	20.5	13.8	15.4	20.2	18.8
16												
17		-	175.5	162.1	184.7	191.8	168.0	185.0	185.5	172.2	169.5	183.5
18												
19		=BYCOL(Temps, LAMBDA(column, SUM(column)))										

BYCOL produces a row vector, summing up each column of the table **Temps**, excluding the header row. The formula spills, using dynamic array logic, and matches the width of the underlying array (*i.e.* the Table **Temps**). It only produces one row of data, as we have created a summation (just one value to report for each column).

Now, let's define Temperature as cells **C4:L15** (*i.e.* excluding the text in the **Month** column). Consider the following formula:

=FILTER(Temperature, BYCOL(Temperature, LAMBDA(year, AVERAGE(year) > 15)))

Here, **BYCOL** produces a row of TRUE or FALSE values, depending upon whether the average for each column exceeds 15 degrees Celsius. The dynamic array function **FILTER**, one of the dynamic array functions we introduced earlier, then filters each column in Temps based upon whether the corresponding **LAMBDA** equates to TRUE or FALSE, *viz.*

18.0	21.0	14.6	24.6	25.3
23.3	20.7	24.2	24.5	14.7
14.4	19.7	21.9	14.4	22.1
19.8	13.9	18.5	12.2	11.4
13.6	15.6	10.5	14.8	12.4
6.9	10.0	13.3	13.5	10.7
6.8	12.5	12.5	12.1	6.7
11.5	11.8	9.3	10.7	13.2
14.7	17.3	14.9	8.1	14.4
14.0	13.9	13.3	18.2	18.8
21.6	21.4	11.5	18.6	15.0
20.1	18.7	20.5	13.8	18.8

This returns the columnar data for the years 2017, 2018, 2020, 2021 and 2024 respectively – not that you would know from the above numerical dataset. I really wanted the headings, but having numerical values in the Table header did not help my cause (it would have caused my averages to calculate incorrectly). It is usually not a good idea to have numerical values in Table headers, and perhaps now you can understand why.

If I modify the Table's headers as follows, I can now use the revised **Temperature** range which has extended to the column headers too, but not the first column):

Month	Yr 2015	Yr 2016	Yr 2017	Yr 2018	Yr 2019	Yr 2020	Yr 2021	Yr 2022	Yr 2023	Yr 2024
January	25.0	17.5	18.0	21.0	18.4	14.6	24.6	20.6	16.2	25.3
February	14.7	18.3	23.3	20.7	17.3	24.2	24.5	23.8	17.0	14.7
March	21.2	15.4	14.4	19.7	15.9	21.9	14.4	18.2	14.2	22.1
April	13.1	13.0	19.8	13.9	17.2	18.5	12.2	11.4	16.9	11.4
May	11.6	11.5	13.6	15.6	10.0	10.5	14.8	15.3	14.0	12.4
June	7.6	10.4	6.9	10.0	9.3	13.3	13.5	11.1	7.8	10.7
July	9.0	11.2	6.8	12.5	12.0	12.5	12.1	9.4	11.1	6.7
August	8.2	7.5	11.5	11.8	10.7	9.3	10.7	14.4	6.7	13.2
September	14.2	10.3	14.7	17.3	9.4	14.9	8.1	10.2	15.8	14.4
October	15.7	15.4	14.0	13.9	16.9	13.3	18.2	11.2	17.8	18.8
November	22.0	11.6	21.6	21.4	16.9	11.5	18.6	11.2	11.8	15.0
December	13.2	20.0	20.1	14.0	14.0	20.5	13.8	15.4	20.2	18.8

The formula remains

=FILTER(Temperature, BYCOL(Temperature, LAMBDA(year, AVERAGE(year) > 15)))

which will produce a more informative spilled array:

Yr 2017	Yr 2018	Yr 2020	Yr 2021	Yr 2024
18	21	14.6	24.6	25.3
23.3	20.7	24.2	24.5	14.7
14.4	19.7	21.9	14.4	22.1
19.8	13.9	18.5	12.2	11.4
13.6	15.6	10.5	14.8	12.4
6.9	10	13.3	13.5	10.7
6.8	12.5	12.5	12.1	6.7
11.5	11.8	9.3	10.7	13.2
14.7	17.3	14.9	8.1	14.4
14	13.9	13.3	18.2	18.8
21.6	21.4	11.5	18.6	15
20.1	14	20.5	13.8	18.8

BYROW works very similarly to **BYCOL** (it is analogous to the relationship between **HLOOKUP** and **VLOOKUP**). This function applies a **LAMBDA** to each row and returns an array of the results. Its syntax is as follows:

BYROW(array, [lambda])

It has the following arguments:

- **array:** this is required and represents an array to be separated by row

- **lambda:** an optional argument, this is a **LAMBDA** that takes a row as a single parameter and calculates just one result.

Let's return to my above example:

Month	Yr 2015	Yr 2016	Yr 2017	Yr 2018	Yr 2019	Yr 2020	Yr 2021	Yr 2022	Yr 2023	Yr 2024
January	25.0	17.5	18.0	21.0	18.4	14.6	24.6	20.6	16.2	25.3
February	14.7	18.3	23.3	20.7	17.3	24.2	24.5	23.8	17.0	14.7
March	21.2	15.4	14.4	19.7	15.9	21.9	14.4	18.2	14.2	22.1
April	13.1	13.0	19.8	13.9	17.2	18.5	12.2	11.4	16.9	11.4
May	11.6	11.5	13.6	15.6	10.0	10.5	14.8	15.3	14.0	12.4
June	7.6	10.4	6.9	10.0	9.3	13.3	13.5	11.1	7.8	10.7
July	9.0	11.2	6.8	12.5	12.0	12.5	12.1	9.4	11.1	6.7
August	8.2	7.5	11.5	11.8	10.7	9.3	10.7	14.4	6.7	13.2
September	14.2	10.3	14.7	17.3	9.4	14.9	8.1	10.2	15.8	14.4
October	15.7	15.4	14.0	13.9	16.9	13.3	18.2	11.2	17.8	18.8
November	22.0	11.6	21.6	21.4	16.9	11.5	18.6	11.2	11.8	15.0
December	13.2	20.0	20.1	14.0	14.0	20.5	13.8	15.4	20.2	18.8

BYROW effectively produces a column vector, summing up each row of the table **Temps**.

If I want the year-on-year comparisons for each month where the average temperature is above 15 degrees Celsius, I can again avoid using a "helper column" and instead use the formula

=FILTER(Temps, BYROW(Temps, LAMBDA(year, AVERAGE(year) > 15)))

This time, I can ignore the header row. This will return the array

January	25.0	17.5	18.0	21.0	18.4	14.6	24.6	20.6	16.2	25.3
February	14.7	18.3	23.3	20.7	17.3	24.2	24.5	23.8	17.0	14.7
March	21.2	15.4	14.4	19.7	15.9	21.9	14.4	18.2	14.2	22.1
October	15.7	15.4	14.0	13.9	16.9	13.3	18.2	11.2	17.8	18.8
November	22.0	11.6	21.6	21.4	16.9	11.5	18.6	11.2	11.8	15.0
December	13.2	20.0	20.1	14.0	14.0	20.5	13.8	15.4	20.2	18.8

CHOOSECOLS and CHOOSEROWS

The **CHOOSECOLS** function returns the specified columns from an array. It has the following syntax:

CHOOSECOLS(array, column number 1, [column number 2, ...])

The **CHOOSECOLS** function has the following arguments:

- **array:** this is required and represents the selected array

- **column number 1:** this is also required and denotes the column number of the first column to be returned

- **column number 2:** this and subsequent arguments are optional. This / these represent(s) the second and subsequent column numbers to be returned.

It should be noted that Excel will return an *#VALUE!* error if the absolute value of any of the **column number** arguments is zero or exceeds the number of columns in the **array**.

Some examples:

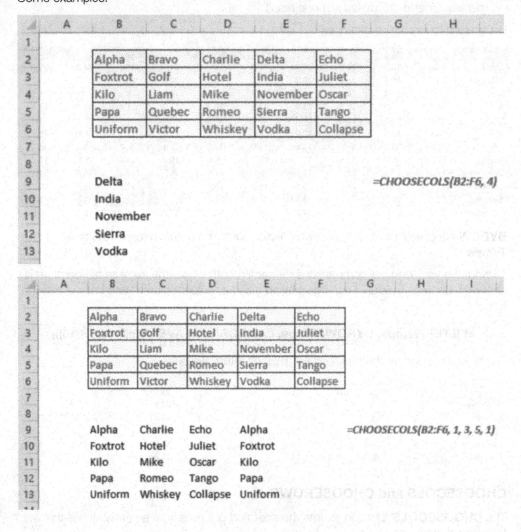

▲	A	B	C	D	E	F	G	H
1								
2		Alpha	Bravo	Charlie	Delta	Echo		
3		Foxtrot	Golf	Hotel	India	Juliet		
4		Kilo	Liam	Mike	November	Oscar		
5		Papa	Quebec	Romeo	Sierra	Tango		
6		Uniform	Victor	Whiskey	Vodka	Collapse		
7								
8								
9		#VALUE!						=CHOOSECOLS(B2:F6,)

▲	A	B	C	D	E	F	G	H	I
1									
2		Alpha	Bravo	Charlie	Delta	Echo			
3		Foxtrot	Golf	Hotel	India	Juliet			
4		Kilo	Liam	Mike	November	Oscar			
5		Papa	Quebec	Romeo	Sierra	Tango			
6		Uniform	Victor	Whiskey	Vodka	Collapse			
7									
8									
9		#VALUE!						=CHOOSECOLS(B2:F6, 2, 4, 6)	

The **CHOOSEROWS** function returns the specified rows from an array. Similar to **CHOOSECOLS**, it has the following syntax:

CHOOSEROWS(array, row number 1, [row number 2, ...])

The **CHOOSEROWS** function has the following arguments:

- **array:** this is required and represents the selected array

- **row number 1:** this is also required and denotes the row number of the first row to be returned

- **row number 2:** this and subsequent arguments are optional. This / these represent(s) the second and subsequent row numbers to be returned.

It should be noted that Excel will return an *#VALUE!* error if the absolute value of any of the **row number** arguments is zero or exceeds the number of rows in the **array**.

Illustrations:

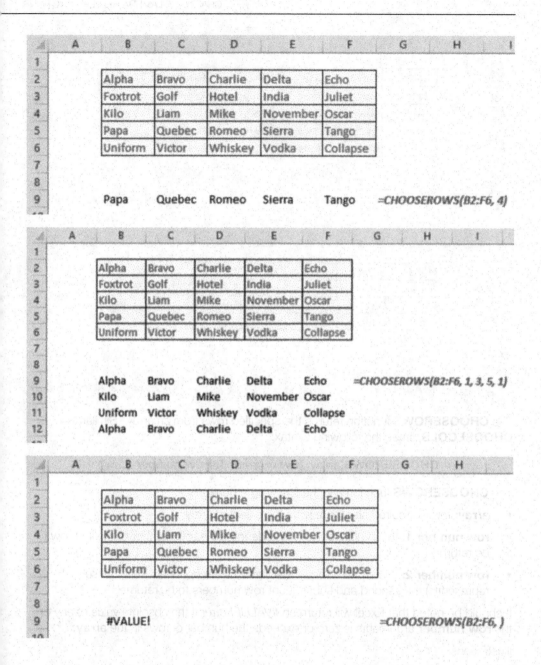

	A	B	C	D	E	F	G	H	I
1									
2		Alpha	Bravo	Charlie	Delta	Echo			
3		Foxtrot	Golf	Hotel	India	Juliet			
4		Kilo	Liam	Mike	November	Oscar			
5		Papa	Quebec	Romeo	Sierra	Tango			
6		Uniform	Victor	Whiskey	Vodka	Collapse			
7									
8									
9		Papa	Quebec	Romeo	Sierra	Tango	=CHOOSEROWS(B2:F6, 4)		

	A	B	C	D	E	F	G	H	I
1									
2		Alpha	Bravo	Charlie	Delta	Echo			
3		Foxtrot	Golf	Hotel	India	Juliet			
4		Kilo	Liam	Mike	November	Oscar			
5		Papa	Quebec	Romeo	Sierra	Tango			
6		Uniform	Victor	Whiskey	Vodka	Collapse			
7									
8									
9		Alpha	Bravo	Charlie	Delta	Echo	=CHOOSEROWS(B2:F6, 1, 3, 5, 1)		
10		Kilo	Liam	Mike	November	Oscar			
11		Uniform	Victor	Whiskey	Vodka	Collapse			
12		Alpha	Bravo	Charlie	Delta	Echo			

	A	B	C	D	E	F	G	H
1								
2		Alpha	Bravo	Charlie	Delta	Echo		
3		Foxtrot	Golf	Hotel	India	Juliet		
4		Kilo	Liam	Mike	November	Oscar		
5		Papa	Quebec	Romeo	Sierra	Tango		
6		Uniform	Victor	Whiskey	Vodka	Collapse		
7								
8								
9		#VALUE!					=CHOOSEROWS(B2:F6,)	

238

	A	B	C	D	E	F	G	H	I
1									
2		Alpha	Bravo	Charlie	Delta	Echo			
3		Foxtrot	Golf	Hotel	India	Juliet			
4		Kilo	Liam	Mike	November	Oscar			
5		Papa	Quebec	Romeo	Sierra	Tango			
6		Uniform	Victor	Whiskey	Vodka	Collapse			
7									
8									
9		#VALUE!					=CHOOSEROWS(B2:F6, 2, 4, 6)		

DROP

The **DROP** function excludes a specified number of contiguous rows or columns from either the start or the end of an array. It has the following syntax:

DROP(array, rows, [columns])

The **DROP** function has the following arguments:

- **array:** this is required and represents the selected array from which to drop the rows or columns

- **rows:** this is also required and denotes the number of rows to drop (exclude) from the top. If this number is negative, the values drop from the bottom of the **array**

- **columns:** this is optional and denotes the number of columns to drop (exclude). If this number is negative, the values drop from the end of the **array**.

It should be noted that:

- when **rows** or **columns** are not provided or missing, all rows and columns are returned

- if the absolute value of **rows** or **columns** is greater than the number of rows or columns in the **array**, then all rows or columns are supposed to be returned, but presently #*VALUE!* appears to be the favoured treatment

- Excel returns an #*CALC!* error to indicate an empty **array** when **rows** or **columns** is zero [0]

- Excel returns an #*NUM!* when **array** is too large.

Some examples:

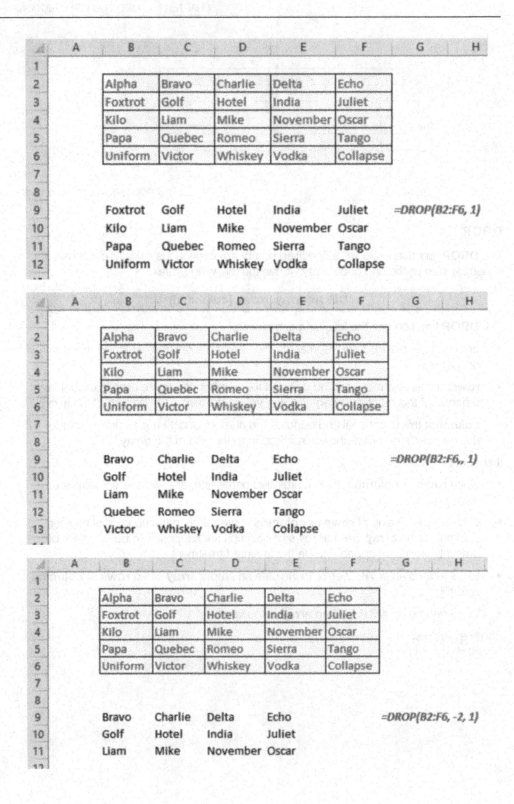

⁄4	A	B	C	D	E	F	G	H
1								
2		Alpha	Bravo	Charlie	Delta	Echo		
3		Foxtrot	Golf	Hotel	India	Juliet		
4		Kilo	Liam	Mike	November	Oscar		
5		Papa	Quebec	Romeo	Sierra	Tango		
6		Uniform	Victor	Whiskey	Vodka	Collapse		
7								
8								
9	#VALUE!					=DROP(B2:F6,, 6)		

EXPAND

The **EXPAND** function expands (or pads) an array to specified row and column dimensions. It has the following syntax:

> **EXPAND(array, rows, [columns], [pad with])**

The **EXPAND** function has the following arguments:

- **array:** this is required and represents the selected array to be expanded

- **rows:** this is also required and denotes the number of rows in the expanded **array**. If this argument is missing (not bad for a required argument!), **rows** will not be expanded

- **columns:** this is optional and denotes the number of columns in the expanded **array**. Again, should **columns** not be specified, this dimension will not be expanded

- **pad with:** this is an optional value with which to pad. The default is *N/A*.

It should be noted that:

- if **rows** isn't provided or is empty, the default value is the number of rows in the **array** argument (as aforementioned)

- if **columns** isn't provided or is empty, the default value is the number of columns in the **array** argument

- if **pad with** is not provided and array has one value for that dimension, then that value is used. This operation is commonly referred to as array "broadcasting"; however, this does not appear to work presently

- Excel returns an #*VALUE!* error when the rows or columns argument is less than the **rows** or **columns** in the **array** argument

- Excel returns an #*N/A* error when **pad with** is greater than a single column or row

- Excel returns an #*NUM!* when **array** is too large.

More illustrations:

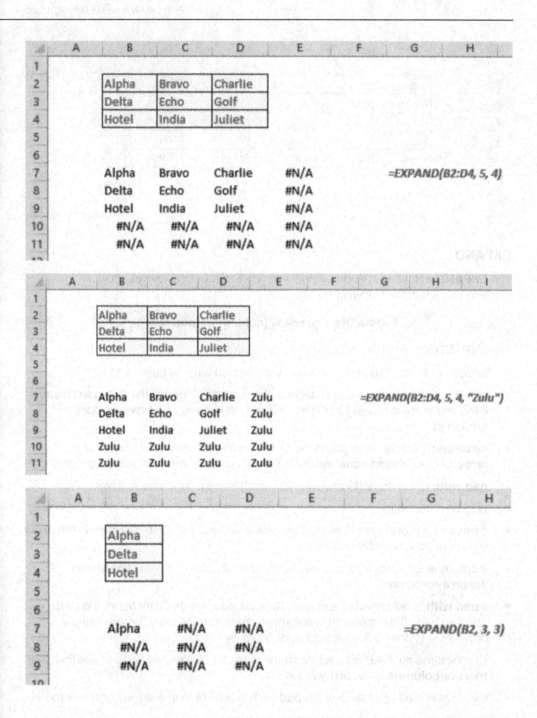

	A	B	C	D	E	F	G	H
1								
2		Alpha	Bravo	Charlie				
3		Delta	Echo	Golf				
4		Hotel	India	Juliet				
5								
6								
7		#VALUE!					=EXPAND(B2:D4,, 2)	

HSTACK and VSTACK

The **HSTACK** function returns the array formed by appending each of the array arguments in a column-wise fashion (Microsoft's jargon, not ours). It has the following syntax:

> **HSTACK(array1, [array2, ...])**

The **HSTACK** function has the following argument(s):

- **array:** the first argument is required (others are optional) and represents the **array**(s) to append.

It should be noted that:

- **HSTACK** returns the array formed by appending each of the array arguments in a column-wise fashion. The resulting **array** will be the following dimensions:
  - columns: the combined count of all the columns from each of the array arguments
  - rows: the maximum of the row count from each of the array arguments
- Excel returns an #N/A error if an array has fewer rows or columns than the maximum in any selected array. To remove the errors, you should use the **IFERROR** function.

More examples:

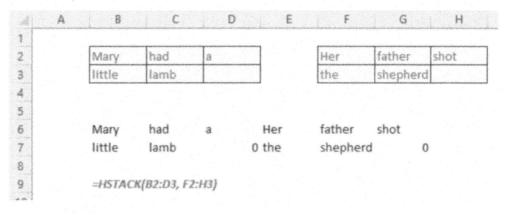

	A	B	C	D	E	F	G	H
1								
2		Mary	had	a		Her	father	shot
3		little	lamb			the	shepherd	
4								
5								
6		Mary	had	a	Her	father	shot	
7		little	lamb		0 the	shepherd	0	
8								
9		=HSTACK(B2:D3, F2:H3)						

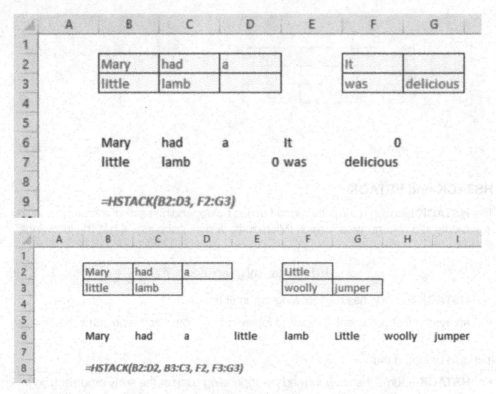

The **VSTACK** function returns the array formed by appending each of the array arguments in a row-wise fashion. It has the following syntax:

VSTACK(array1, [array2, ...])

The **VSTACK** function has the following argument(s):

- **array:** the first argument is required (others are optional) and represents the **array**(s) to append.

It should be noted that:

- **VSTACK** returns the array formed by appending each of the array arguments in a row-wise fashion. The resulting **array** will be the following dimensions:

  - rows: the combined count of all the rows from each of the array arguments

  - columns: the maximum of the column count from each of the array arguments

- Excel returns an #N/A error if an array has fewer rows or columns than the maximum in any selected array. To remove the errors, you should use the **IFERROR** function.

Some illustrations:

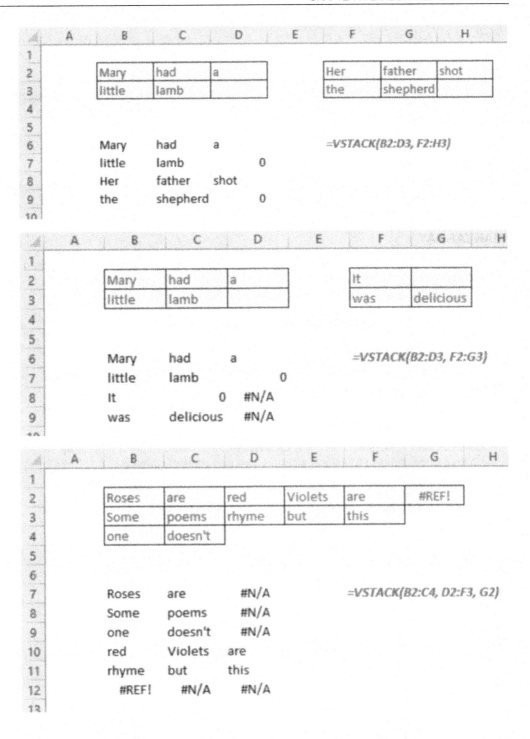

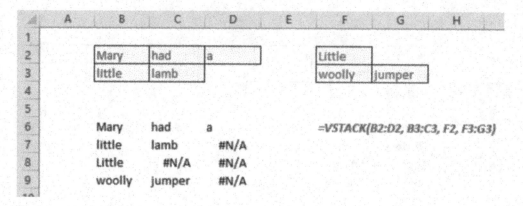

MAKEARRAY

MAKEARRAY returns a calculated array of a specified row and column size, by applying a **LAMBDA** function. This function is useful for situations where you wish to combine or transform arrays, as well as being useful for generating data. The syntax is as follows:

MAKEARRAY(rows, columns, lambda)

It has the following arguments:

- **rows:** this argument is required and represents the number of rows in the array (which must be greater than zero)

- **columns:** this argument is also required and represents the number of columns in the array (which again must be greater than zero)

- **lambda:** also necessary, this is the **LAMBDA** that is called to create the array. In particular, this lambda function must take two parameters, namely:

  - **row_index:** the index of the row (row number)

  - **column_index:** the index of the column (column number).

As an example, consider the following:

	A	B	C	D	E	F	G
1							
2		Number of rows		5			
3		Number of columns		3			
4							
5		Colours of Rainbow					
6		Red			Red	Orange	Violent
7		Orange			Orange	Red	Blue
8		Yellow			Red	Violent	Indigo
9		Green			Blue	Indigo	Violent
10		Blue			Green	Blue	Red
11		Indigo					
12		Violent					

246

Imagine, for reasons best known to myself, I wanted to generate an array of colours of the rainbow (albeit with the final colour, ahem, slightly amended). In the image above, I have specified the number of rows (cell **D2**) and the number of columns (cell **D3**) in my array and listed the colours in cells **B6:B12** inclusive.

The formula in cell **E6** is given by:

> **=MAKEARRAY(D2, D3, LAMBDA(row, column, INDEX(B6:B12, RANDBETWEEN(1,7))))**

The first two arguments in this formula are **D2** and **D3**, which refer to the number of rows and columns for the array to be generated respectively. The final argument of **MAKEARRAY** is the **LAMBDA**, which must take two parameters, corresponding to the value generated by **LAMBDA**, namely:

- **row:** the index of the row

- **column:** the index of the column.

The calculation thus uses the non-dynamic array function **RANDBETWEEN** to generate an integer between one [1] and seven [7] to select from the list of colours of the rainbow, stipulated in cells **B6:B12**. For example, if Excel generates the number 5, the value "Blue" will be chosen, *etc.*

Now it is true that existing functions could be used to achieve the same result, *e.g.*

> **=INDEX(B6:B12, RANDARRAY(D2, D3, 1, 7, TRUE))**

This formula seems shorter and simpler, and indeed, may be the better option for this above illustration. But that is exactly what this is – a simple example. As more complex arrays need to be created, existing function counterparts may prove difficult, convoluted or impossible to construct – and this is precisely where **MAKEARRAY** and **LAMBDA** come in.

MAP

The **MAP** function returns an array formed by mapping each value in the array(s) to a new value and applying a **LAMBDA** to create a new value accordingly. It has the following syntax:

> **MAP(array1, lambda or array2, [lambda or array3, ...])**

where:

- **array1:** this is a required argument and represents the (first) array to be mapped

- **array2 and subsequent arrays:** these are optional arguments and represent additional arrays to be mapped

- **lambda:** this is a required argument which represents a **LAMBDA** which must be the final argument and must have a parameter for each array passed or another array to be mapped.

In short, **MAP** transforms values. Let's return to my Melbourne temperatures data:

Month	Yr 2015	Yr 2016	Yr 2017	Yr 2018	Yr 2019	Yr 2020	Yr 2021	Yr 2022	Yr 2023	Yr 2024
January	25.0	17.5	18.0	21.0	18.4	14.6	24.6	20.6	16.2	25.3
February	14.7	18.3	23.3	20.7	17.3	24.2	24.5	23.8	17.0	14.7
March	21.2	15.4	14.4	19.7	15.9	21.9	14.4	18.2	14.2	22.1
April	13.1	13.0	19.8	13.9	17.2	18.5	12.2	11.4	16.9	11.4
May	11.6	11.5	13.6	15.6	10.0	10.5	14.8	15.3	14.0	12.4
June	7.6	10.4	6.9	10.0	9.3	13.3	13.5	11.1	7.8	10.7
July	9.0	11.2	6.8	12.5	12.0	12.5	12.1	9.4	11.1	6.7
August	8.2	7.5	11.5	11.8	10.7	9.3	10.7	14.4	6.7	13.2
September	14.2	10.3	14.7	17.3	9.4	14.9	8.1	10.2	15.8	14.4
October	15.7	15.4	14.0	13.9	16.9	13.3	18.2	11.2	17.8	18.8
November	22.0	11.6	21.6	21.4	16.9	11.5	18.6	11.2	11.8	15.0
December	13.2	20.0	20.1	14.0	14.0	20.5	13.8	15.4	20.2	18.8

We used the formula

=FILTER(Temps, BYROW(Temps, LAMBDA(year, AVERAGE(year) > 15)))

which returned the array:

January	25.0	17.5	18.0	21.0	18.4	14.6	24.6	20.6	16.2	25.3
February	14.7	18.4	23.3	20.7	17.3	24.2	24.5	23.8	17.0	14.7
March	21.2	15.4	14.4	19.7	15.9	21.9	14.4	18.2	14.2	22.1
October	15.7	15.4	14.0	13.9	16.9	13.3	18.2	11.2	17.8	18.8
November	22.0	11.6	21.6	21.4	16.9	11.5	18.6	11.2	11.8	15.0
December	13.2	20.0	20.1	18.7	14.0	20.5	13.8	15.4	20.2	18.8

The problem is, these temperatures have all been provided in Celsius, which those situated in the United States don't understand. In the US, if there is a temperature of 25 degrees, they will be breaking out the gloves, bobble hat and duffle coat, whereas us Aussies will be heading for the beach.

We need to convert – transform – this data to Fahrenheit, so our US colleagues may better understand. All I need to do is wrap the above formula in a **MAP** function:

=MAP(FILTER(Temps, BYROW(Temps, LAMBDA(year, AVERAGE(year) > 15))), LAMBDA(temperature, IF(ISNUMBER(temperature), CONVERT(temperature, "C", "F"), temperature)))

January	77.0	63.5	64.4	69.8	65.1	58.3	76.3	69.1	61.2	77.5
February	58.5	64.9	73.9	69.3	63.1	75.6	76.1	74.8	62.6	58.5
March	70.2	59.7	57.9	67.5	60.6	71.4	57.9	64.8	57.6	71.8
October	60.3	59.7	57.2	57.0	62.4	55.9	64.8	52.2	64.0	65.8
November	71.6	52.9	70.9	70.5	62.4	52.7	65.5	52.2	53.2	59.0
December	55.8	68.0	68.2	57.2	57.2	68.9	56.8	59.7	68.4	65.8

CONVERT(temperature, "C", "F") simply converts the variable temperature from degrees Celsius to degrees Fahrenheit. This is wrapped in an **IF(ISNUMBER())** check to ensure that we don't try to convert text values (as this would cause an error): the **IF** statement leaves the value of temperature "as is" in this instance, and **LAMBDA** just wraps around all of this in order to declare the variable temperature, so that **MAP** may do its work.

It's true you could generate this result in stages, but the whole idea of these **LAMBDA** helper functions is to be able to create dynamic arrays in one fell swoop. **MAP LAMBDA** is one of the key combinations we will use in our financial model.

REDUCE

The **REDUCE** function reduces an array to an accumulated value by applying a **LAMBDA** function to each value and returning the total value in what is known as the accumulator. Its syntax is as follows:

> **REDUCE([initial_value], array, lambda)**

where:

- **initial_value:** this is an optional argument and represents the starting value for the accumulator, *i.e.* the "running total" prompted by the lambda expression

- **array:** this is a required value and represents the array to be reduced

- **lambda:** this is also a required value and represents a **LAMBDA** function called to reduce the array, that consists of two parameters:

    - **accumulator:** the returned (aggregated) value from **LAMBDA**

    - **value: a** value from array.

Returning to our temperature example given by the Excel Table **Temps**:

Month	Yr 2015	Yr 2016	Yr 2017	Yr 2018	Yr 2019	Yr 2020	Yr 2021	Yr 2022	Yr 2023	Yr 2024
January	25.0	17.5	18.0	21.0	18.4	14.6	24.6	20.6	16.2	25.3
February	14.7	18.3	23.3	20.7	17.3	24.2	24.5	23.8	17.0	14.7
March	21.2	15.4	14.4	19.7	15.9	21.9	14.4	18.2	14.2	22.1
April	13.1	13.0	19.8	13.9	17.2	18.5	12.2	11.4	16.9	11.4
May	11.6	11.5	13.6	15.6	10.0	10.5	14.8	15.3	14.0	12.4
June	7.6	10.4	6.9	10.0	9.3	13.3	13.5	11.1	7.8	10.7
July	9.0	11.2	6.8	12.5	12.0	12.5	12.1	9.4	11.1	6.7
August	8.2	7.5	11.5	11.8	10.7	9.3	10.7	14.4	6.7	13.2
September	14.2	10.3	14.7	17.3	9.4	14.9	8.1	10.2	15.8	14.4
October	15.7	15.4	14.0	13.9	16.9	13.3	18.2	11.2	17.8	18.8
November	22.0	11.6	21.6	21.4	16.9	11.5	18.6	11.2	11.8	15.0
December	13.2	20.0	20.1	14.0	14.0	20.5	13.8	15.4	20.2	18.8

we could count how many months in the 10-year period had an average temperature between 15 and 20 degrees Celsius as follows:

> **=REDUCE(0, Temps, LAMBDA(accumulator, value,**
> **IF(AND(value >= 15, value <= 20), 1 + accumulator, accumulator)))**

For each element of the **Temps** Table, defined by the **LAMBDA** function as value, the **IF** statement tests whether the temperature is between 15 and 20 degrees Celsius:

> **AND(value >= 15, value <= 20)**

If this is true, one gets added to the running total (**accumulator**), so that a count is maintained. The first argument of **REDUCE** – zero [0], the optional argument – simply specifies the starting value (**initial_value**) for the **accumulator**, which must be zero in order for the count to make sense.

Again, we could create a second array which performs a corresponding check for each cell and count the TRUE values, but this formula reduces the workload (*i.e.* it reduces the array of values to just one value by making use of the specified **LAMBDA**), allowing the computation to be performed once again without any helper stages.

SCAN

This function scans an array by applying a **LAMBDA** to each value and returns an array made up of each intermediate value. The syntax is as follows:

SCAN([initial_value], array, lambda)

where:

- **initial_value:** this is an optional argument and represents the starting value for the accumulator, *i.e.* the "running total" prompted by the lambda expression

- **array:** this is a required value and represents the array to be scanned

- **lambda:** this is also a required value and represents a **LAMBDA** function called to scan the array, that consists of two parameters:

  - **accumulator:** the returned (aggregated) value from **LAMBDA**

  - **value:** a value from array.

As a simple example, let's consider a common problem when working with structured references, *i.e.* Excel Tables (**CTRL + T**). Imagine I have the following sales for the first six [6] months of the year:

	A	B
1	Month	Sales
2	January	971
3	February	559
4	March	784
5	April	635
6	May	858
7	June	917

I might wish to create a running total of these sales. One way I have seen people do this is as follows:

	A	B	C	D	E
1	Month	Sales	Cumulative		
2	January	971	971		=N(C1)+[@Sales]
3	February	559	1,530		
4	March	784	2,314		
5	April	635	2,949		
6	May	858	3,807		
7	June	917	4,724		

This is a horrible formula, consisting partly of Excel references and partly of Excel Table's Structured References:

=N(C1) + [@Sales]

It mixes Excel cell referencing (cell **C1**, because you cannot refer to a value for a different record simply in an Excel Table), structured referencing (**[@Sales]**) and the **N** function, in order to treat the numerical value of text as zero [0] and therefore avoid *#VALUE!* errors when adding amounts together.

It seems to work if values are added:

	A	B	C	D	E
1	Month	Sales	Cumulative		
2	January	971	971		=N(C1)+[@Sales]
3	February	559	1,530		
4	March	784	2,314		
5	April	635	2,949		
6	May	858	3,807		
7	June	917	4,724		
8	July	1,000	5,724		
9	August	2,000	7,724		

However, it all goes awry when values are inserted:

	A	B	C	D	E
1	Month	Sales	Cumulative		
2	January	971	971		=N(C1)+[@Sales]
3	February	559	1,530		
4	March	784	2,314		
5	April	635	2,949		
6	Additional	1,000,000	1,002,949		
7	May	858	3,807		
8	June	917	4,724		
9	July	1,000	5,724		
10	August	2,000	7,724		

This is where **SCAN** comes to the rescue. Assuming the Table is also called **Sales** (not just the field in column **B**), we can create the formula

=SCAN(0, Sales[Sales], LAMBDA(accumulator, value, accumulator + value))

SCAN "scans" the array (*i.e.* the Excel Table **Sales**) by applying a **LAMBDA** to each value. It then returns an array of results corresponding to the accumulator value returned by the **LAMBDA**. As stated above, **SCAN** takes two parameters:

- **accumulator:** the initial value returned by **SCAN** and each **LAMBDA** call

- **value:** a value from the supplied array.

As above, the **initial_value** is zero [0] so that the running total calculates correctly.

	A	B	C	D
1	Month	Sales		Cumulative
2	January	971		971
3	February	559		1,530
4	March	784		2,314
5	April	635		2,949
6	Additional	1,000,000		1,002,949
7	May	858		1,003,807
8	June	917		1,004,724
9	July	1,000		1,005,724
10	August	2,000		1,007,724

SCAN LAMBDA is another of the key combinations we will use in our financial model.

TAKE

The **TAKE** function returns a specified number of contiguous rows or columns from either the start or the end of an array. It has the following syntax:

TAKE(array, rows, [columns])

The **TAKE** function has the following arguments:

- **array:** this is required and represents the selected array from which to take (extract) the rows or columns

- **rows:** this is also required and denotes the number of rows to take from the top. If this number is negative, the values are taken from the bottom of the **array**

- **columns:** this is optional and denotes the number of columns to take. If this number is negative, the values are taken from the end of the **array**.

It should be noted that:

- when **rows** or **columns** are not provided or missing, all rows and columns are returned

- if the absolute value of **rows** or **columns** is greater than the number of rows or columns in the **array**, then all rows or columns are supposed to be returned, but presently #*VALUE!* appears to be the favoured treatment

- Excel returns an #*CALC!* error to indicate an empty **array** when **rows** or **columns** is zero [0]

- Excel returns an #*NUM!* when **array** is too large.

Here are some examples:

◢	A	B	C	D	E	F	G	H
1								
2		Alpha	Bravo	Charlie	Delta	Echo		
3		Foxtrot	Golf	Hotel	India	Juliet		
4		Kilo	Liam	Mike	November	Oscar		
5		Papa	Quebec	Romeo	Sierra	Tango		
6		Uniform	Victor	Whiskey	Vodka	Collapse		
7								
8								
9		Alpha	Bravo	Charlie	Delta	Echo	=TAKE(B2:F6, 1)	

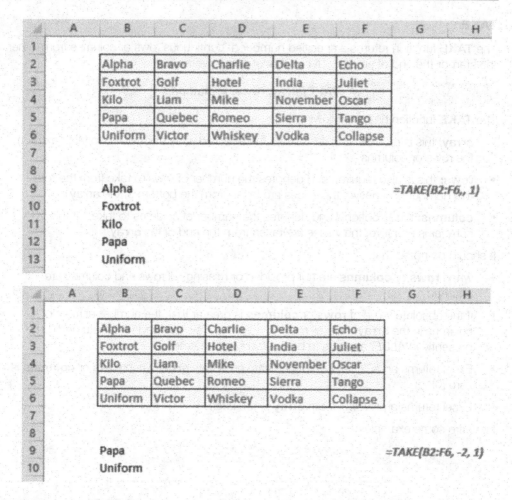

TOCOL and TOROW

The **TOCOL** function returns a column vector containing all of the items in the source array. It has the following syntax:

> **TOCOL(array, [ignore], [scan by column])**

The **TOCOL** function has the following arguments:

- **array:** this is required and denotes the array or reference to return as a column

- **ignore:** this is optional and identifies whether to ignore certain types of values; by default, no values are ignored. The omissions are governed as follows:

Value	Meaning
0	Keep all values (default)
1	Ignore blanks
2	Ignore errors
3	Ignore blanks and errors

- **scan by column:** this is optional and sets the scan of the array by column. However, by default, the **array** is scanned by row.

It should be noted that:

- if **scan by column** is omitted or FALSE, the **array** is scanned by row; if TRUE, the **array** is scanned by column

- Excel returns an #*VALUE!* error when an **array** constant contains one or more numbers that is not a whole number

- Excel returns an #*NUM!* error when **array** becomes too large.

Just for a change, some examples:

◢	A	B	C	D	E
1					
2		One	Two	Three	Four
3		Five	Six	Seven	Eight
4		Nine	Ten	Eleven	Twelve
5					
6					
7		One		=TOCOL(B2:E4)	
8		Two			
9		Three			
10		Four			
11		Five			
12		Six			
13		Seven			
14		Eight			
15		Nine			
16		Ten			
17		Eleven			
18		Twelve			

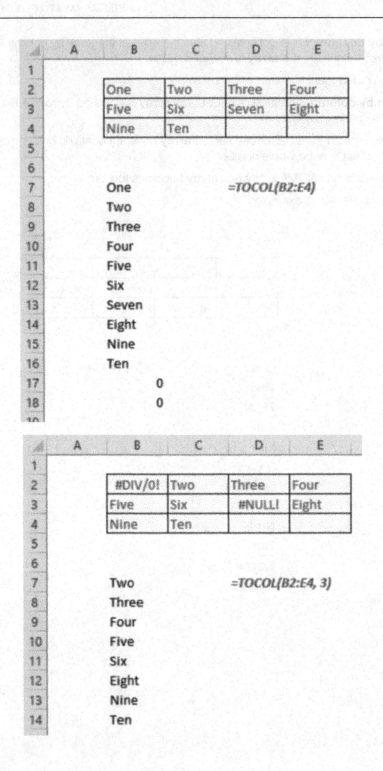

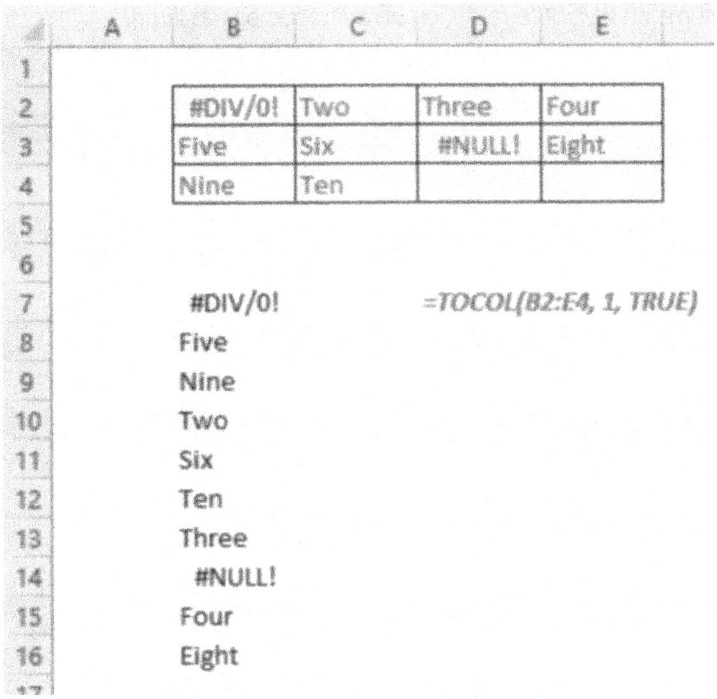

▲	A	B	C	D	E
1					
2		#DIV/0!	Two	Three	Four
3		Five	Six	#NULL!	Eight
4		Nine	Ten		
5					
6					
7		#DIV/0!		=TOCOL(B2:E4, 1, TRUE)	
8		Five			
9		Nine			
10		Two			
11		Six			
12		Ten			
13		Three			
14		#NULL!			
15		Four			
16		Eight			

The **TOROW** function returns a row vector containing all of the items in the source array. It has the following syntax:

TOROW(array, [ignore], [scan by column])

The **TOROW** function has the following arguments:

- **array:** this is required and denotes the array or reference to return as a row

- **ignore:** this is optional and identifies whether to ignore certain types of values; by default, no values are ignored. The omissions are governed as follows:

Value	Meaning
0	Keep all values (default)
1	Ignore blanks
2	Ignore errors
3	Ignore blanks and errors

- **scan by column:** this is optional and sets the scan of the array by column. However, by default, the **array** is scanned by row.

It should be noted that:

- if **scan by column** is omitted or FALSE, the **array** is scanned by row; if TRUE, the **array** is scanned by column

- Excel returns an *#VALUE!* error when an **array** constant contains one or more numbers that are not a whole number

- Excel returns an #*NUM!* error when **array** becomes too large.

Some illustrations:

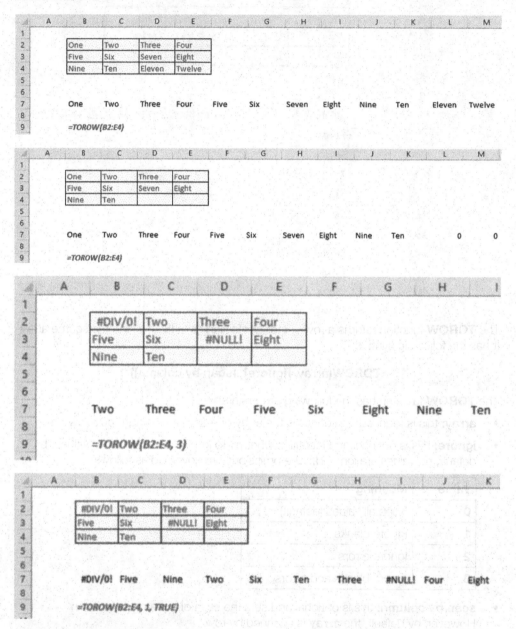

WRAPCOLS and WRAPROWS

The **WRAPCOLS** function wraps the provided vector by columns after a specified number of elements. It has the following syntax:

> **WRAPCOLS(vector, wrap count, [pad with])**

The **WRAPCOLS** function has the following arguments:

- **vector:** this is required and denotes the row or column vector / reference to wrap

- **wrap count:** this is also required and represents the maximum number of values (depth / height) for each column

- **pad with:** this is optional and defines the value with which to pad. The default is *N/A*.

It should be noted that:

- the elements of the **vector** are placed into a two-dimensional array by column

- each column has **wrap count** elements

- the column is padded with **pad with** if there are insufficient elements to fill it

- if **wrap count** is greater or equal to the number of elements in **vector**, then the **vector** is simply returned as the column vector result of the function

- Excel returns an *#VALUE!* error when **vector** is not a one-dimensional array

- Excel returns an *#VALUE!* error when **wrap count** is less than one [1] or is not an integer.

Please see the following examples:

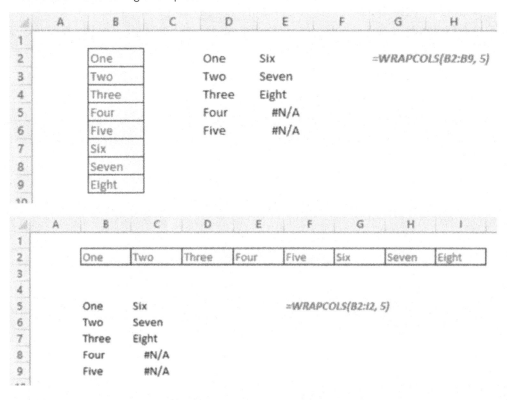

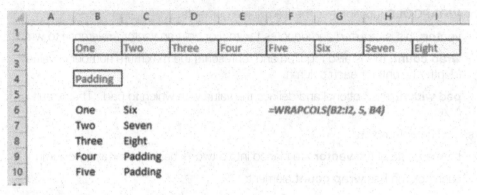

The **WRAPROWS** function wraps the provided vector by rows after a specified number of elements. It has the following syntax:

WRAPROWS(vector, wrap count, [pad with])

The **WRAPROWS** function has the following arguments:

- **vector:** this is required and denotes the row or column vector / reference to wrap

- **wrap count:** this is also required and represents the maximum number of values (width) for each row

- **pad with:** this is optional and defines the value with which to pad. The default is *N/A*.

It should be noted that:

- the elements of the vector are placed into a two-dimensional array by row

- each row has **wrap count** elements

- the row is padded with **pad with** if there are insufficient elements to fill it

- if **wrap count** is greater or equal to the number of elements in **vector**, then the **vector** is simply returned as the row vector result of the function

- Excel returns an *#VALUE!* error when **vector** is not a one-dimensional array

- Excel returns an *#VALUE!* error when **wrap count** is less than one [1] or is not an integer.

My final examples for this chapter:

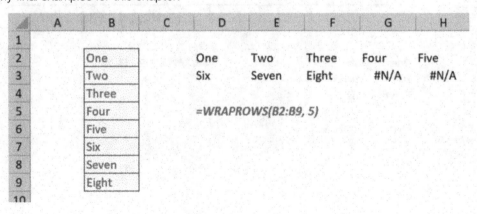

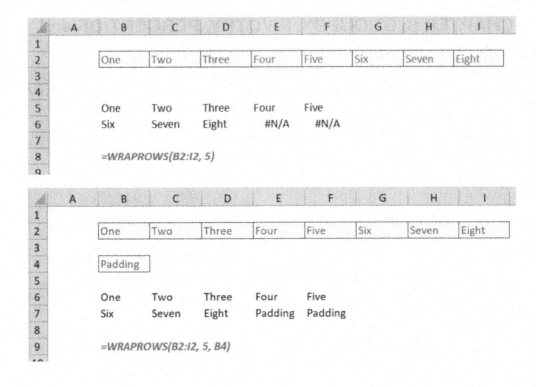

CHAPTER 8: GROUPBY, PIVOTBY, PERCENT OF and ETA LAMBDAS

I have decided to add this section as its own chapter. In late 2023, Microsoft announced three new functions and "eta reduced lambda" functions (known as "eta lambdas") into the Excel family. This introduced a new concept that will help with building financial models *eventually*. Presently, they make automating data analysis really simple – as long as you have access to all of these functions! They are rolling out on the beta channel for Excel for Windows and Excel for Mac as we write.

eta Lambdas

These "eta reduced lambda" functions may sound scary, but they make the world of dynamic arrays more accessible to the inexperienced. They help make the other three functions simpler to use. Dynamic array calculations using basic aggregation functions often require syntax such as

LAMBDA(x, SUM(x))
LAMBDA(y, AVERAGE(y))

etc.

However, given **x** and **y** *(above)* are merely substitute variables, an "eta lambda" function simply replaces the need for this structure with the so-easy-anyone-can-understand-it syntax of

SUM
AVERAGE

etc.

Even I can do it. For example, consider the following formula in cell **G17** below:

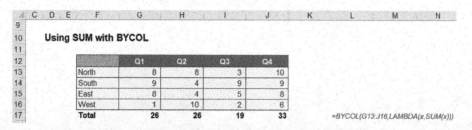

	Q1	Q2	Q3	Q4
North	8	8	3	10
South	9	4	9	9
East	8	4	5	8
West	1	10	2	6
Total	**26**	**26**	**19**	**33**

=BYCOL(G13:J16,LAMBDA(x,SUM(x)))

=BYCOL(G13:J16,LAMBDA(x,SUM(x)))

This sums the range **G13:J16** by column using that **LAMBDA(x, SUM(x))** trick. But there is no need for this anymore, *viz.*

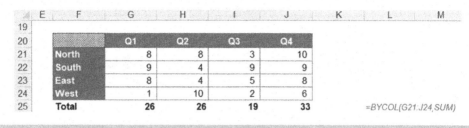

	Q1	Q2	Q3	Q4
North	8	8	3	10
South	9	4	9	9
East	8	4	5	8
West	1	10	2	6
Total	26	26	19	33

=BYCOL(G21:J24,SUM)

=BYCOL(G21:J24,SUM)

That's much simpler!

Presently, the following built-in functions are available to Excel users lucky enough to get all these functions and functionalities:

- **ARRAYTOTEXT**
- **AVERAGE**
- **CONCAT**
- **COUNT**
- **COUNTA**
- **MAX**
- **MEDIAN**
- **MIN**
- **MODE.SNGL**
- **PERCENTOF**
- **PRODUCT**
- **STDEV.P**
- **STDEV.S**
- **SUM**
- **VAR.P**
- **VAR.S**

These will pop up when they may be used, but they don't appear in alphabetical order. It's more a ranking of what Microsoft perceives to be the most common aggregation operations:

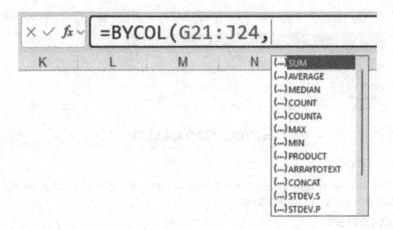

INDEX and **OFFSET** are notable absentees, but I imagine this is because they need several arguments to operate unlike the functions listed above.

GROUPBY

The new **GROUPBY** function allows you to create a summary of your data formulaically. It supports grouping along one axis and aggregating the associated values. For instance, if you had a table of sales data, you might generate a summary of sales by year, or by salesperson, or by category, or by…

In essence, it allows you to group, aggregate, sort and filter data based upon the fields you specify.

The syntax of the **GROUPBY** function is given by:

> **GROUPBY(row_fields, values, function, [field_headers], [total_depth], [sort_ order], [filter_array], [field_relationship])**

It has the following arguments:

- **row_fields:** this is required and represents a column-oriented array or range that contains the values which are used to group rows and generate row headers. The array or range may contain multiple columns. If so, the output will have multiple row group levels

- **values:** this is also required and denotes a column-oriented array or range of the data to aggregate. The array or range may contain multiple columns. If so, the output will have multiple aggregations

- **function:** also required, this is an explicit or eta reduced lambda (*e.g.* **SUM, PERCENTOF, AVERAGE, COUNT**) that is used to aggregate **values**. A vector of lambdas may be provided. If so, the output will have multiple aggregations. The orientation of the vector will determine whether they are laid out row- or column-wise

- **field_headers:** this and the remaining arguments are all optional. This represents a number that specifies whether the **row_fields** and **values** have headers and whether field headers should be returned in the results. The possible values are:

- **Missing:** Automatic
- **0:** No
- **1:** Yes and don't show
- **2:** No but generate
- **3:** Yes and show

It should be noted that "Automatic" assumes the data contains headers based upon the **values** argument. If the first value is text and the second value is a number, then the data is assumed to have headers. Fields headers are shown if there are multiple row or column group levels

- **total_depth:** this optional argument determines whether the row headers should contain totals. The possible values are:

  - **Missing**: Automatic, with grand totals and, where possible, subtotals
  - **0:** No Totals
  - **1:** Grand Totals
  - **2:** Grand and Subtotals
  - **-1:** Grand Totals at Top
  - **-2:** Grand and Subtotals at Top

  It should be noted that for subtotals, fields must have at least two [2] columns. Numbers greater than two [2] are supported provided there are sufficient columns

- **sort_order:** again optional, this argument denotes a number indicating how rows should be sorted. Numbers correspond with the columns in **row_fields** followed by the columns in **values**. If the number is negative, the rows are sorted in descending / reverse order. A vector of numbers may be provided when sorting based upon only **row_fields**

- **filter_array:** the penultimate optional argument, this represents a column-oriented one-dimensional array of Boolean values [1, 0] that indicate whether the corresponding row of data should be considered. It should be noted that the length of the array must match the length of **row_fields**

- **field_relationship:** the final optional argument, this is the relationship between fields when multiple columns are supplied to the **row_fields** argument. There are two options:

  - **0 (default):** hierarchy
  - **1:** flat.

At the time of writing, these values do not come in the ToolTips.

You should use the value one [1] when you have multiple columns to group by and you want to sort by a column other than the first column returned in the formula. But be careful: when subtotals are included (see **total_depth**) you cannot use the value one [1] for this **field_relationship**, *i.e.* the relationship cannot be flat.

To show how GROUPBY works, we took inspiration from Microsoft's data table:

Example Data

Table Used for Formulae

Year	Category	Item	Sales	Rating
2020	Components	Wheels	4,000	10%
2022	Components	Pedals	3,200	50%
2020	Components	Brakes	3,300	45%
2020	Clothing	Jerseys	1,100	10%
2020	Components	Saddles	500	85%
2020	Clothing	Jerseys	1,500	30%
2021	Accessories	Bike Racks	2,600	85%
2020	Bikes	Touring Bikes	1,100	30%
2022	Clothing	Tights	800	65%
2021	Clothing	Bib-Shorts	1,000	45%
2021	Accessories	Helmets	2,700	45%
2020	Clothing	Gloves	800	20%
2022	Clothing	Vests	1,100	30%
2021	Components	Brakes	1,100	100%
2022	Components	Handlebars	3,200	25%
2022	Accessories	Locks	400	55%
2021	Accessories	Tyres and Tubes	500	70%
2020	Components	Pedals	1,000	45%
2021	Accessories	Helmets	3,600	60%
2020	Bikes	Touring Bikes	200	55%
2021	Clothing	Gloves	4,000	100%
2020	Accessories	Locks	1,500	75%
2022	Bikes	Road Bikes	600	75%
2022	Clothing	Gloves	900	65%
2022	Components	Chains	100	10%
2022	Components	Chains	1,600	45%
2021	Bikes	Touring Bikes	2,400	70%

I have converted this data table into an Excel Table by selecting all the data and using **Insert -> Table** (**CTRL + T**) and calling the resultant Table **tbl**. Look, it's late as I write this and I have no imagination, OK!?

I can summarise my Table very simply using the formula

=GROUPBY(tbl[Category],tbl[Sales],SUM)

Description	Amount
Accessories	485,500
Bikes	495,800
Clothing	509,700
Components	493,200
Total	1,984,200

=GROUPBY(tbl[Category],tbl[Sales],SUM)

How easy is that!? Essentially, I am summing the sales (using the eta lambda **SUM**) by the **Category** field.

If you want to aggregate by more than one **row_field**, as stated above, this is possible. One way is to use **HSTACK**:

=GROUPBY(HSTACK(tbl[Year],tbl[Category]),tbl[Sales],SUM)

Year	Category	Sales
2020	Accessories	193,500
2020	Bikes	144,300
2020	Clothing	182,900
2020	Components	175,600
2021	Accessories	145,400
2021	Bikes	161,800
2021	Clothing	173,600
2021	Components	142,400
2022	Accessories	146,600
2022	Bikes	189,700
2022	Clothing	153,200
2022	Components	175,200
Total		1,984,200

=GROUPBY(HSTACK(tbl[Year],tbl[Category]),tbl[Sales],SUM)

This simply combines the **Year** and **Category** fields in the **tbl** Table, and then sums **Sales** across them. However, I think I prefer the **CHOOSECOLS** approach:

=GROUPBY(CHOOSECOLS(tbl,1,2),tbl[Sales],SUM)

Year	Category	Sales
2020	Accessories	193,500
2020	Bikes	144,300
2020	Clothing	182,900
2020	Components	175,600
2021	Accessories	145,400
2021	Bikes	161,800
2021	Clothing	173,600
2021	Components	142,400
2022	Accessories	146,600
2022	Bikes	189,700
2022	Clothing	153,200
2022	Components	175,200
Total		1,984,200

=GROUPBY(CHOOSECOLS(tbl,1,2),tbl[Sales],SUM)

Here, the idea is that I shall **SUM Sales** by columns 1 (**Year**) and 2 (**Category**) of the **tbl** Table. This might not seem as clear as the **HSTACK** alternative at first glance as you have to refer to the Table to identify what the columns are. However, stick with me. Let me make the formula more complex:

=GROUPBY(CHOOSECOLS(tbl,MATCH(F$12,tbl[#Headers],0),
MATCH(G$12,tbl[#Headers],0)),tbl[Sales],SUM)

Year	Category	Sales
2020	Accessories	193,500
2020	Bikes	144,300
2020	Clothing	182,900
2020	Components	175,600
2021	Accessories	145,400
2021	Bikes	161,800
2021	Clothing	173,600
2021	Components	142,400
2022	Accessories	146,600
2022	Bikes	189,700
2022	Clothing	153,200
2022	Components	175,200
Total		1,984,200

`=GROUPBY(CHOOSECOLS(tbl,MATCH(F$12,tbl[#Headers],0),MATCH(G$12,tbl[#Headers],0)),tbl[Sales],SUM)`

Looks horrible, yes? I have replaced the values 1 and 2 in the previous formula with

MATCH(F$12,tbl[#Headers],0)

and

MATCH(G$12,tbl[#Headers],0)

which return the positions in the **Headers** row of the Table **tbl**. Now, this may seem overkill but consider the following image:

Year	Category	Sales
2020	Accessories	193,500
2020	Bikes	144,300
2020	Clothing	182,900
2020	Components	175,600
2021	Accessories	145,400
2021	Bikes	161,800
2021	Clothing	173,600
2021	Components	142,400
2022	Accessories	146,600
2022	Bikes	189,700
2022	Clothing	153,200
2022	Components	175,200
Total		1,984,200

Brilliant. I have changed the background colour of the first two headers to yellow. Well, no, it's a little more than that. I have used data validation dropdown lists (**ALT** + **D** + **L**) to create input headers!!

Year	▼ Category	Sales
Year	Accessories	193,500
Category	Bikes	144,300
Item	Clothing	182,900
Sales	Components	175,600
Rating	Accessories	145,400
2021	Bikes	161,800
2021	Clothing	173,600
2021	Components	142,400
2022	Accessories	146,600
2022	Bikes	189,700
2022	Clothing	153,200
2022	Components	175,200
Total		**1,984,200**

Thus, if I change the selections, I have dynamic summarisations, such as

Category	Item	Sales
Accessories	Bike Racks	82,700
Accessories	Helmets	115,700
Accessories	Lights	64,900
Accessories	Locks	72,000
Accessories	Pumps	72,900
Accessories	Tyres and Tube	77,300
Bikes	Cargo Bikes	149,300
Bikes	Mountain Bikes	122,500
Bikes	Road Bikes	108,100
Bikes	Touring Bikes	115,900
Clothing	Bib-Shorts	52,300
Clothing	Caps	53,300
Clothing	Gloves	72,400
Clothing	Jerseys	79,000
Clothing	Shorts	67,000
Clothing	Socks	58,700
Clothing	Tights	64,700
Clothing	Vests	62,300
Components	Bottom Bracket	60,000
Components	Brakes	53,100
Components	Chains	65,000
Components	Handlebars	85,600
Components	Pedals	87,900
Components	Saddles	64,700
Components	Wheels	76,900
Total		**1,984,200**

or

Rating	Category	Sales
0.05	Accessories	20,800
0.05	Bikes	32,200
0.05	Clothing	25,800
0.05	Components	24,800
0.1	Accessories	25,800
0.1	Bikes	30,800
0.1	Clothing	28,200
0.1	Components	32,000
0.15	Accessories	32,000
0.15	Bikes	15,600
0.15	Clothing	26,500
0.15	Components	18,400
0.2	Accessories	26,600
0.2	Bikes	19,800
0.2	Clothing	17,900
0.2	Components	27,600
0.25	Accessories	22,100
0.25	Bikes	31,000
0.25	Clothing	19,500
0.25	Components	23,300
0.3	Accessories	25,000
0.3	Bikes	36,000
0.3	Clothing	24,700
0.3	Components	30,300
0.35	Accessories	26,800
0.35	Bikes	18,600
0.35	Clothing	16,200

Multiple summary statistics may be created similarly, or else you can simply connect them if the reporting fields are contiguous, *e.g.*

=GROUPBY(CHOOSECOLS(tbl,1,2),tbl[[Sales]:[Rating]],AVERAGE)

Year	Category	Sales	Rating
2020	Accessories	2,059	48%
2020	Bikes	1,659	51%
2020	Clothing	2,204	49%
2020	Components	2,116	52%
2021	Accessories	1,795	48%
2021	Bikes	1,926	49%
2021	Clothing	2,019	51%
2021	Components	2,064	54%
2022	Accessories	2,065	53%
2022	Bikes	2,062	54%
2022	Clothing	1,990	55%
2022	Components	1,947	50%
Total		1,990	51%

=GROUPBY(CHOOSECOLS(tbl,1,2),tbl[[Sales]:[Rating]],AVERAGE)

Here, **tbl[[Sales]:[Rating]]** may be used to specify the **values** as they are side by side.

Obviously, there are many more arguments to play with, but hopefully, you get the general idea, such as ranking the **Item** field in descending order by **Sales** using the formula

=GROUPBY(tbl[Item],tbl[Sales],SUM,,,-2)

Item	Sales
Cargo Bikes	149,300
Mountain Bikes	122,500
Touring Bikes	115,900
Helmets	115,700
Road Bikes	108,100
Pedals	87,900
Handlebars	85,600
Bike Racks	82,700
Jerseys	79,000
Tyres and Tubes	77,300
Wheels	76,900
Pumps	72,900
Gloves	72,400
Locks	72,000
Shorts	67,000
Chains	65,000
Lights	64,900
Tights	64,700
Saddles	64,700
Vests	62,300
Bottom Brackets	60,000
Socks	58,700
Caps	53,300
Brakes	53,100
Bib-Shorts	52,300
Total	1,984,200

=GROUPBY(tbl[Item],tbl[Sales],SUM,,,-2)

Indeed, the outputs summarised don't have to be numerical. A more comprehensive example summarising the **Items** field might look like this:

=GROUPBY(tbl[Category],tbl[Item],LAMBDA (x,ARRAYTOTEXT(SORT(UNIQUE(x)))))

PIVOTBY

The **PIVOTBY** function allows you to create a summary of your data via a formula too, akin to a formulaic PivotTable. It supports grouping along two axes and aggregating the associated values. For instance, if you had a table of sales data, you might generate a summary of sales by state and year.

It should be noted that **PIVOTBY** is a function that returns an array of values that can spill to the grid. Furthermore, at this stage, not all features of a PivotTable appear to be replicable by this function.

The syntax of the **PIVOTBY** function is:

> **PIVOTBY(row_fields, col_fields, values, function, [field_headers], [row_total_depth], [row_sort_order], [col_total_depth], [col_sort_order], [filter_array],[relative_to])**

It has the following arguments:

- **row_fields:** this is required and represents a column-oriented array or range that contains the values which are used to group rows and generate row headers. The array or range may contain multiple columns. If so, the output will have multiple row group levels

- **col_fields:** also required and represents a column-oriented array or range that contains the values which are used to group columns and generate column headers. The array or range may contain multiple columns. If so, the output will have multiple column group levels

- **values:** this is also required and denotes a column-oriented array or range of the data to aggregate. The array or range may contain multiple columns. If so, the output will have multiple aggregations

- **function:** also required, this is an explicit or eta reduced lambda (*e.g.* **SUM**, **PERCENTOF**, **AVERAGE**, **COUNT**) that is used to aggregate **values**. A vector of lambdas may be provided. If so, the output will have multiple aggregations. The orientation of the vector will determine whether they are laid out row- or column-wise

- **field_headers:** this, and the remaining arguments are all optional. This represents a number that specifies whether the **row_fields**, **col_fields** and **values** have headers and whether field headers should be returned in the results. The possible values are:

  - **Missing:** Automatic

  - **0:** No

  - **1:** Yes and don't show

  - **2:** No but generate

  - **3:** Yes and show

  It should be noted that "Automatic" assumes the data contains headers based upon the **values** argument. If the first value is text and the second value is a number, then the data is assumed to have headers. Fields headers are shown if there are multiple row or column group levels

- **row_total_depth:** this optional argument determines whether the row headers should contain totals. The possible values are:

  - **Missing**: Automatic, with grand totals and, where possible, subtotals

  - **0:** No Totals

  - **1:** Grand Totals

  - **2:** Grand and Subtotals

  - **-1:** Grand Totals at Top

  - **-2:** Grand and Subtotals at Top

It should be noted that for subtotals, **row_fields** must have at least two [2] columns. Numbers greater than two [2] are supported provided **row_field** has sufficient columns

- **row_sort_order:** again optional, this argument denotes a number indicating how rows should be sorted. Numbers correspond with the columns in **row_fields** followed by the columns in **values**. If the number is negative, the rows are sorted in descending / reverse order. A vector of numbers may be provided when sorting based upon only **row_fields**

- **col_total_depth:** this optional argument determines whether the column headers should contain totals. The possible values are:

  - **Missing**: Automatic, with grand totals and, where possible, subtotals

  - **0:** No Totals

  - **1:** Grand Totals

  - **2:** Grand and Subtotals

  - **-1:** Grand Totals at Top

  - **-2:** Grand and Subtotals at Top

  It should be noted that for subtotals, **col_fields** must have at least two [2] columns. Numbers greater than two [2] are supported provided **col_field** has sufficient columns

- **col_sort_order:** again optional, this argument denotes a number indicating how they should be sorted. Numbers correspond with the columns in **col_fields** followed by the columns in **values**. If the number is negative, these are sorted in descending / reverse order. A vector of numbers may be provided when sorting based upon only **col_fields**

- **filter_array:** this optional argument represents a column-oriented one-dimensional array of Boolean values [1, 0] that indicate whether the corresponding row of data should be considered. It should be noted that the length of the array must match the length of **row_fields** and **col_fields**.

- **relative_to:** the final optional argument allows you to summarise functions relative to row and column totals or the grand total. Five alternatives are possible:

  - **0:** Column Totals (default) *(Screentip: Calculation performed relative to all values in column)*

  - **1:** Row Totals *(Calculation performed relative to all values in row)*

  - **2:** Grand Total *(Calculation performed relative to all values)*

  - **3:** Parent Column Total *(Calculation performed relative to all values in column parent)*

  - **4:** Parent Row Total *(Calculation performed relative to all values in row parent)*.

Similar in many ways to **GROUPBY**, **PIVOTBY** is fairly straightforward to use:

```
=PIVOTBY(tbl[Category],tbl[Year],tbl[Sales],AVERAGE)
```

	2020	2021	2022	Total
Accessories	2,059	1,795	2,065	1,974
Bikes	1,659	1,926	2,062	1,885
Clothing	2,204	2,019	1,990	2,072
Components	2,116	2,064	1,947	2,038
Total	2,007	1,948	2,014	1,990

You can get more imaginative and sort in descending order by the **AVERAGE** of **Rating**, viz.

=PIVOTBY(tbl[Item],tbl[Year],tbl[Rating],AVERAGE,,,-2)

	2020	2021	2022	Total
Brakes	46%	61%	65%	59%
Locks	50%	58%	71%	56%
Pumps	70%	41%	56%	56%
Shorts	52%	52%	64%	55%
Vests	54%	51%	60%	55%
Touring Bikes	54%	51%	59%	55%
Pedals	58%	57%	50%	54%
Bib-Shorts	43%	48%	69%	54%
Gloves	49%	64%	52%	53%
Road Bikes	46%	54%	58%	53%
Cargo Bikes	56%	51%	51%	53%
Saddles	63%	43%	47%	52%
Tights	56%	53%	46%	51%
Handlebars	53%	52%	47%	51%
Caps	60%	39%	51%	51%
Chains	52%	49%	51%	51%
Socks	50%	45%	56%	50%
Wheels	41%	67%	45%	50%
Tyres and Tubes	46%	54%	46%	50%
Lights	47%	46%	49%	47%
Mountain Bikes	48%	42%	48%	46%
Bottom Brackets	48%	42%	45%	46%
Helmets	47%	43%	47%	45%
Bike Racks	31%	51%	54%	44%
Jerseys	27%	53%	45%	44%
Total	50%	50%	53%	51%

The final optional parameter **relative_to** may be used to change the frame of reference of the totals. If we consider the following Table, called **Data** (*truncated*):

Source Table

Year	Quarter	Category	Item	Sales	Rating
2022	Q1	Components	Wheels	$ 4,000	10%
2024	Q1	Components	Pedals	$ 3,200	50%
2022	Q4	Components	Brakes	$ 3,300	45%
2022	Q4	Clothing	Jerseys	$ 1,100	10%
2022	Q2	Components	Saddles	$ 500	85%
2022	Q1	Clothing	Jerseys	$ 1,500	30%
2023	Q2	Accessories	Bike Racks	$ 2,600	85%
2022	Q1	Bikes	Touring Bikes	$ 1,100	30%
2024	Q4	Clothing	Tights	$ 800	65%
2023	Q1	Clothing	Bib-Shorts	$ 1,000	45%
2023	Q1	Accessories	Helmets	$ 2,700	45%
2022	Q4	Clothing	Gloves	$ 800	20%
2024	Q3	Clothing	Vests	$ 1,100	30%
2023	Q4	Components	Brakes	$ 1,100	100%
2024	Q2	Components	Handlebars	$ 3,200	25%
2024	Q3	Accessories	Locks	$ 400	55%
2023	Q3	Accessories	Tyres and Tubes	$ 500	70%
2022	Q4	Components	Pedals	$ 1,000	45%
2023	Q4	Accessories	Helmets	$ 3,600	60%
2022	Q4	Bikes	Touring Bikes	$ 200	55%
2023	Q4	Clothing	Gloves	$ 4,000	100%
2022	Q4	Accessories	Locks	$ 1,500	75%
2024	Q1	Bikes	Road Bikes	$ 600	75%
2024	Q3	Clothing	Gloves	$ 900	65%
2024	Q1	Components	Chains	$ 100	10%
2024	Q1	Components	Chains	$ 1,600	45%
2023	Q4	Bikes	Touring Bikes	$ 2,400	70%

Here, we have two parent / child relationships:

1. **Year** and **Quarter**

2. **Category** and **Item**.

To demonstrate the impact of changing the value of **reference_to,** the following examples combine **PIVOTBY** with **PERCENTOF**. We will explore **PERCENTOF** in more detail below. In summary, it is used to return the percentage that a subset makes up of a given dataset.

Sales as a Percentage, Displayed by Category and Item vs. Year and Quarter

Default

		2022 Q1	2022 Q2	2022 Q3	2022 Q4	2023 Q1	2023 Q2	2023 Q3	2023 Q4	2024 Q1	2024 Q2	2024 Q3	2024 Q4	Total
Accessories	Bike Racks	10.7%	4.8%	2.8%	0.3%	1.6%	3.1%		5.2%	1.2%	5.0%	2.0%	11.2%	4.2%
Accessories	Helmets	4.4%	2.0%	4.4%	11.1%	2.8%	10.3%	10.9%	4.0%	1.8%	4.5%	4.7%	10.2%	5.8%
Accessories	Lights	6.4%	2.7%	6.4%	3.3%	5.1%	1.1%	4.2%	1.9%	2.1%	3.9%	1.4%	0.7%	3.3%
Accessories	Locks	5.1%	4.0%	2.9%	12.3%	3.1%	3.9%	1.0%	0.8%	3.2%	3.6%	1.5%	1.1%	3.6%
Accessories	Pumps	1.7%	3.7%	9.3%	0.8%	11.8%	0.1%		0.6%	7.0%	3.6%	2.2%	3.9%	3.7%
Accessories	Tyres and Tubes	5.4%	1.8%	3.9%	1.2%	5.0%	2.7%	7.5%	7.1%	3.3%	3.2%	5.9%	0.4%	3.9%
Bikes	Cargo Bikes	5.6%	2.5%	8.7%	6.4%	9.2%	6.3%	5.8%	10.4%	4.6%	8.7%	14.2%	9.0%	7.5%
Bikes	Mountain Bikes	3.4%	6.5%	3.7%	7.2%	5.6%	6.6%	4.6%	9.1%	7.3%	5.3%	8.7%	5.8%	6.2%
Bikes	Road Bikes	3.3%	2.9%	3.7%	10.7%	0.7%	8.7%	6.9%	3.7%	8.0%	4.3%	5.6%	7.1%	5.4%
Bikes	Touring Bikes	4.5%	3.7%	5.4%	5.3%	5.6%	5.4%	6.9%	7.5%	6.9%	6.2%	8.3%	4.9%	5.8%
Clothing	Bib-Shorts	2.0%	2.0%	4.6%	5.2%	2.2%	1.6%	0.4%	1.9%	1.8%	2.7%	4.9%	2.2%	2.6%
Clothing	Caps	2.1%	5.2%	3.1%	1.1%	4.4%	4.9%		0.7%	1.3%	6.3%	2.5%	0.5%	2.7%
Clothing	Gloves	4.3%	10.7%	3.9%	2.6%		2.6%	1.4%	6.0%	2.9%		2.9%	4.8%	3.6%
Clothing	Jerseys	0.8%	2.6%		7.5%	6.3%	6.8%	6.4%	4.1%	5.9%	0.1%	3.5%	4.6%	4.0%
Clothing	Shorts	3.1%	6.2%	0.7%	0.7%	2.0%	4.7%	3.7%	8.7%	2.3%	3.7%	1.2%	2.6%	3.4%
Clothing	Socks	4.6%	2.2%	6.7%	3.1%	1.7%	1.6%	1.8%	2.8%	7.0%	2.6%	0.3%	0.8%	3.0%
Clothing	Tights	1.1%		7.8%	2.6%	3.8%	4.5%	1.9%	6.2%	5.9%	1.8%	2.3%	2.2%	3.3%
Clothing	Vests	3.3%	3.0%	0.3%	2.1%	7.2%	2.8%	4.8%	2.2%	0.5%	2.7%	3.9%	5.4%	3.1%
Components	Bottom Brackets	6.1%	2.9%	3.0%		2.5%		3.9%	4.0%		3.6%	2.5%	4.2%	3.0%
Components	Brakes	2.6%	3.3%		1.9%	7.5%		7.0%	0.6%	2.7%	0.8%	3.5%	2.9%	2.7%
Components	Chains	1.8%	3.8%	0.4%	3.1%	1.3%	2.0%	5.0%	3.5%	5.6%	3.3%	5.2%	4.1%	3.3%
Components	Handlebars	6.8%	8.5%	5.2%	2.5%	2.8%	7.8%	5.8%	1.8%	1.4%	2.7%	4.2%	2.4%	4.3%
Components	Pedals	0.1%	5.5%	2.2%	4.8%	4.7%	3.9%	1.8%	2.1%	7.8%	11.1%	2.9%	5.8%	4.4%
Components	Saddles	2.7%	5.8%	2.9%	0.9%	2.8%	3.0%	2.7%	3.2%	5.0%	6.5%		2.9%	3.3%
Components	Wheels	8.1%	3.7%	8.1%		0.1%	5.4%	5.6%	1.9%	4.5%	3.8%	5.6%	0.3%	3.9%
Total		100.0%	100.0%	100.0%	100.0%	100.0%	100.0%	100.0%	100.0%	100.0%	100.0%	100.0%	100.0%	100.0%

Note that each column of sales is represented as a percentage of that column (including the Total column).

The behaviour of **relative_to**, is the same in scenario **0**: Column Totals. This is the default view:

```
=PIVOTBY(Data[[Category]:[Item]],Data[[Year]:[Quarter]],Data[Sales],
PERCENTOF,,,,,,,0)
```

Sales as a Percentage, Displayed by Category and Item vs. Year and Quarter

Column Totals (Relative Value 0)

		2022 Q1	2022 Q2	2022 Q3	2022 Q4	2023 Q1	2023 Q2	2023 Q3	2023 Q4	2024 Q1	2024 Q2	2024 Q3	2024 Q4	Total
Accessories	Bike Racks	10.7%	4.8%	2.8%	0.3%	1.6%	3.1%		5.2%	1.2%	5.0%	2.0%	11.2%	4.2%
Accessories	Helmets	4.4%	2.0%	4.4%	11.1%	2.8%	10.3%	10.9%	4.0%	1.8%	4.5%	4.7%	10.2%	5.8%
Accessories	Lights	6.4%	2.7%	6.4%	3.3%	5.1%	1.1%	4.2%	1.9%	2.1%	3.9%	1.4%	0.7%	3.3%
Accessories	Locks	5.1%	4.0%	2.9%	12.3%	3.1%	3.9%	1.0%	0.8%	3.2%	3.6%	1.5%	1.1%	3.6%
Accessories	Pumps	1.7%	3.7%	9.3%	0.8%	11.8%	0.1%		0.6%	7.0%	3.6%	2.2%	3.9%	3.7%
Accessories	Tyres and Tubes	5.4%	1.8%	3.9%	1.2%	5.0%	2.7%	7.5%	7.1%	3.3%	3.2%	5.9%	0.4%	3.9%
Bikes	Cargo Bikes	5.6%	2.5%	8.7%	6.4%	9.2%	6.3%	5.8%	10.4%	4.6%	8.7%	14.2%	9.0%	7.5%
Bikes	Mountain Bikes	3.4%	6.5%	3.7%	7.2%	5.6%	6.6%	4.6%	9.1%	7.3%	5.3%	8.7%	5.8%	6.2%
Bikes	Road Bikes	3.3%	2.9%	3.7%	10.7%	0.7%	8.7%	6.9%	3.7%	8.0%	4.3%	5.6%	7.1%	5.4%
Bikes	Touring Bikes	4.5%	3.7%	5.4%	5.3%	5.6%	5.4%	6.9%	7.5%	6.9%	6.2%	8.3%	4.9%	5.8%
Clothing	Bib-Shorts	2.0%	2.0%	4.6%	5.2%	2.2%	1.6%	0.4%	1.9%	1.8%	2.7%	4.9%	2.2%	2.6%
Clothing	Caps	2.1%	5.2%	3.1%	1.1%	4.4%	4.9%		0.7%	1.3%	6.3%	2.5%	0.5%	2.7%
Clothing	Gloves	4.3%	10.7%	3.9%	2.6%		2.6%	1.4%	6.0%	2.9%		2.9%	4.8%	3.6%
Clothing	Jerseys	0.8%	2.6%		7.5%	6.3%	6.8%	6.4%	4.1%	5.9%	0.1%	3.5%	4.6%	4.0%
Clothing	Shorts	3.1%	6.2%	0.7%	0.7%	2.0%	4.7%	3.7%	8.7%	2.3%	3.7%	1.2%	2.6%	3.4%
Clothing	Socks	4.6%	2.2%	6.7%	3.1%	1.7%	1.6%	1.8%	2.8%	7.0%	2.6%	0.3%	0.8%	3.0%
Clothing	Tights	1.1%		7.8%	2.6%	3.8%	4.5%	1.9%	6.2%	5.9%	1.8%	2.3%	2.2%	3.3%
Clothing	Vests	3.3%	3.0%	0.3%	2.1%	7.2%	2.8%	4.8%	2.2%	0.5%	2.7%	3.9%	5.4%	3.1%
Components	Bottom Brackets	6.1%	2.9%	3.0%		2.5%		3.9%	4.0%		3.6%	2.5%	4.2%	3.0%
Components	Brakes	2.6%	3.3%		1.9%	7.5%		7.0%	0.6%	2.7%	0.8%	3.5%	2.9%	2.7%
Components	Chains	1.8%	3.8%	0.4%	3.1%	1.3%	2.0%	5.0%	3.5%	5.6%	3.3%	5.2%	4.1%	3.3%
Components	Handlebars	6.8%	8.5%	5.2%	2.5%	2.8%	7.8%	5.8%	1.8%	1.4%	2.7%	4.2%	2.4%	4.3%
Components	Pedals	0.1%	5.5%	2.2%	4.8%	4.7%	3.9%	1.8%	2.1%	7.8%	11.1%	2.9%	5.8%	4.4%
Components	Saddles	2.7%	5.8%	2.9%	0.9%	2.8%	3.0%	2.7%	3.2%	5.0%	6.5%		2.9%	3.3%
Components	Wheels	8.1%	3.7%	8.1%		0.1%	5.4%	5.6%	1.9%	4.5%	3.8%	5.6%	0.3%	3.9%
Total		100.0%	100.0%	100.0%	100.0%	100.0%	100.0%	100.0%	100.0%	100.0%	100.0%	100.0%	100.0%	100.0%

It is clear to see that this is identical to the first output. But let's see what happens when we start playing with the final argument. Let's change this value to **1:** Row Totals.

```
=PIVOTBY(Data[[Category]:[Item]],Data[[Year]:[Quarter]],Data[Sales],
PERCENTOF,,,,,,,1)
```

Now, each row of sales is represented as a percentage of that row (including the Total row), *viz.*

3. Row Totals (Relative Value 1)

Sales as a Percentage, Displayed by Category and Item vs. Year and Quarter

Row Totals (Relative Value 1)

		2022 Q1	2022 Q2	2022 Q3	2022 Q4	2023 Q1	2023 Q2	2023 Q3	2023 Q4	2024 Q1	2024 Q2	2024 Q3	2024 Q4	Total
Accessories	Bike Racks	24.1%	10.9%	5.1%	0.7%	2.9%	5.6%		11.2%	2.5%	10.3%	3.7%	23.0%	100.0%
Accessories	Helmets	7.1%	3.3%	5.7%	16.9%	3.7%	13.1%	13.6%	6.1%	2.6%	6.7%	6.2%	15.0%	100.0%
Accessories	Lights	18.5%	7.9%	14.6%	8.8%	12.0%	2.5%	9.4%	5.4%	5.4%	10.3%	3.4%	1.8%	100.0%
Accessories	Locks	13.2%	10.3%	6.0%	29.9%	6.5%	8.1%	2.1%	2.1%	7.6%	8.6%	3.2%	2.5%	100.0%
Accessories	Pumps	4.4%	9.5%	19.1%	1.9%	24.6%	0.3%		1.5%	16.5%	8.5%	4.7%	9.2%	100.0%
Accessories	Tyres and Tubes	12.9%	4.3%	7.6%	2.7%	9.8%	5.2%	14.0%	16.4%	7.4%	7.1%	11.6%	0.9%	100.0%
Bikes	Cargo Bikes	7.0%	3.1%	8.7%	7.5%	9.3%	6.2%	5.6%	12.5%	5.2%	9.9%	14.6%	10.2%	100.0%
Bikes	Mountain Bikes	5.2%	9.8%	4.5%	10.3%	6.9%	7.9%	5.4%	13.4%	10.2%	7.4%	10.9%	8.0%	100.0%
Bikes	Road Bikes	5.6%	5.0%	5.2%	17.4%	1.0%	11.9%	9.3%	6.1%	12.7%	6.8%	8.0%	11.1%	100.0%
Bikes	Touring Bikes	7.2%	5.9%	5.9%	8.0%	7.3%	6.8%	8.6%	11.6%	10.2%	9.1%	11.0%	7.2%	100.0%
Clothing	Bib-Shorts	7.1%	7.3%	13.0%	17.4%	6.5%	4.6%	1.1%	6.7%	5.9%	8.8%	14.5%	7.1%	100.0%
Clothing	Caps	7.5%	18.2%	8.6%	3.6%	12.6%	13.7%		2.4%	4.3%	20.1%	7.3%	1.7%	100.0%
Clothing	Gloves	11.0%	27.3%	8.0%	6.4%		5.4%	2.8%	14.8%	6.8%		6.2%	11.3%	100.0%
Clothing	Jerseys	1.9%	6.2%		16.6%	12.0%	12.8%	11.6%	9.4%	12.7%	0.1%	6.9%	9.9%	100.0%
Clothing	Shorts	8.7%	17.2%	1.6%	1.8%	4.5%	10.3%	8.1%	23.3%	5.8%	9.4%	2.7%	6.7%	100.0%
Clothing	Socks	14.5%	6.8%	17.0%	9.4%	4.4%	3.9%	4.4%	8.7%	20.3%	7.7%	0.7%	2.2%	100.0%
Clothing	Tights	3.1%		17.9%	7.1%	9.0%	10.2%	4.2%	17.2%	15.5%	4.6%	5.4%	5.9%	100.0%
Clothing	Vests	9.8%	9.0%	0.6%	5.9%	17.5%	6.6%	11.1%	6.4%	1.4%	7.4%	9.6%	14.6%	100.0%
Components	Bottom Brackets	18.8%	8.8%	7.5%	8.8%	6.3%		9.5%	11.8%		10.2%	6.3%	11.8%	100.0%
Components	Brakes	9.2%	11.5%		6.2%	21.3%		19.0%	2.1%	8.7%	2.4%	10.2%	9.4%	100.0%
Components	Chains	5.2%	10.8%	0.9%	8.5%	2.9%	4.6%	11.1%	9.7%	14.8%	8.6%	12.3%	10.6%	100.0%
Components	Handlebars	14.7%	18.5%	9.1%	5.1%	5.0%	13.4%	9.8%	3.7%	2.8%	5.4%	7.6%	4.8%	100.0%
Components	Pedals	0.2%	11.6%	3.8%	9.6%	8.1%	5.6%	3.0%	4.3%	15.1%	21.5%	5.1%	11.1%	100.0%
Components	Saddles	7.9%	16.7%	6.6%	2.5%	6.6%	7.0%	6.0%	8.8%	13.1%	17.2%		7.6%	100.0%
Components	Wheels	19.5%	8.8%	15.7%		0.3%	10.4%	10.5%	4.6%	10.0%	8.3%	11.2%	0.7%	100.0%
Total		9.4%	9.4%	7.5%	8.8%	7.6%	7.4%	7.3%	9.1%	8.6%	8.6%	7.7%	8.6%	100.0%

If you wish, you can show the sales as a percentage of the Grand Total, using **2:** Grand Total:

=PIVOTBY(Data[[Category]:[Item]],Data[[Year]:[Quarter]],Data[Sales], PERCENTOF,,,,,,,2)

4. Grand Total (Relative Value 2)

Sales as a Percentage, Displayed by Category and Item vs. Year and Quarter

Grand Total (Relative Value 2)

		2022 Q1	2022 Q2	2022 Q3	2022 Q4	2023 Q1	2023 Q2	2023 Q3	2023 Q4	2024 Q1	2024 Q2	2024 Q3	2024 Q4	Total
Accessories	Bike Racks	1.0%	0.5%	0.2%	0.0%	0.1%	0.2%		0.5%	0.1%	0.4%	0.2%	1.0%	4.2%
Accessories	Helmets	0.4%	0.2%	0.3%	1.0%	0.2%	0.8%	0.8%	0.4%	0.2%	0.4%	0.4%	0.9%	5.8%
Accessories	Lights	0.6%	0.3%	0.5%	0.3%	0.4%	0.1%	0.3%	0.2%	0.2%	0.3%	0.1%	0.1%	3.3%
Accessories	Locks	0.5%	0.4%	0.2%	1.1%	0.2%	0.3%	0.1%	0.1%	0.3%	0.3%	0.1%	0.1%	3.6%
Accessories	Pumps	0.2%	0.3%	0.7%	0.1%	0.9%	0.0%		0.1%	0.6%	0.3%	0.2%	0.3%	3.7%
Accessories	Tyres and Tubes	0.5%	0.2%	0.3%	0.1%	0.4%	0.2%	0.5%	0.6%	0.3%	0.3%	0.5%	0.0%	3.9%
Bikes	Cargo Bikes	0.5%	0.2%	0.7%	0.6%	0.7%	0.5%	0.4%	0.9%	0.4%	0.7%	1.1%	0.8%	7.5%
Bikes	Mountain Bikes	0.3%	0.6%	0.3%	0.6%	0.4%	0.5%	0.3%	0.8%	0.6%	0.5%	0.7%	0.5%	6.2%
Bikes	Road Bikes	0.3%	0.3%	0.3%	0.9%	0.1%	0.7%	0.5%	0.3%	0.7%	0.4%	0.4%	0.6%	5.4%
Bikes	Touring Bikes	0.4%	0.3%	0.4%	0.5%	0.4%	0.4%	0.5%	0.7%	0.6%	0.5%	0.6%	0.4%	5.8%
Clothing	Bib-Shorts	0.2%	0.2%	0.3%	0.5%	0.2%	0.1%	0.0%	0.2%	0.2%	0.2%	0.4%	0.2%	2.6%
Clothing	Caps	0.2%	0.5%	0.2%	0.1%	0.3%	0.4%		0.1%	0.1%	0.5%	0.2%	0.0%	2.7%
Clothing	Gloves	0.4%	1.0%	0.3%	0.2%		0.2%	0.1%	0.5%	0.2%		0.2%	0.4%	3.6%
Clothing	Jerseys	0.1%	0.2%		0.7%	0.5%	0.5%	0.5%	0.4%	0.5%	0.0%	0.3%	0.4%	4.0%
Clothing	Shorts	0.3%	0.6%	0.1%	0.1%	0.2%	0.3%	0.3%	0.8%	0.2%	0.3%	0.1%	0.2%	3.4%
Clothing	Socks	0.4%	0.2%	0.5%	0.3%	0.1%	0.1%	0.1%	0.3%	0.6%	0.2%	0.0%	0.1%	3.0%
Clothing	Tights	0.1%		0.6%	0.2%	0.3%	0.3%	0.1%	0.6%	0.5%	0.2%	0.2%	0.2%	3.3%
Clothing	Vests	0.3%	0.3%	0.0%	0.2%	0.5%	0.2%	0.3%	0.2%	0.0%	0.2%	0.3%	0.5%	3.1%
Components	Bottom Brackets	0.6%	0.3%	0.2%	0.3%	0.2%		0.3%	0.4%		0.3%	0.2%	0.4%	3.0%
Components	Brakes	0.2%	0.3%		0.2%	0.6%		0.5%	0.1%	0.2%	0.1%	0.3%	0.3%	2.7%
Components	Chains	0.2%	0.4%	0.0%	0.3%	0.1%	0.2%	0.4%	0.3%	0.5%	0.3%	0.4%	0.3%	3.3%
Components	Handlebars	0.6%	0.8%	0.4%	0.2%	0.2%	0.6%	0.4%	0.2%	0.1%	0.2%	0.3%	0.2%	4.3%
Components	Pedals	0.0%	0.5%	0.2%	0.4%	0.4%	0.3%	0.1%	0.2%	0.7%	1.0%	0.2%	0.5%	4.4%
Components	Saddles	0.3%	0.5%	0.2%	0.1%	0.2%	0.2%	0.2%	0.3%	0.4%	0.6%		0.2%	3.3%
Components	Wheels	0.8%	0.3%	0.6%		0.0%	0.4%	0.4%	0.2%	0.4%	0.3%	0.4%	0.0%	3.9%
Total		9.4%	9.4%	7.5%	8.8%	7.6%	7.4%	7.3%	9.1%	8.6%	8.6%	7.7%	8.6%	100.0%

There are still two further scenarios – and this is why our example contained two parent / child relationships. The first is **3:** Parent Column Total:

=PIVOTBY(Data[[Category]:[Item]],Data[[Year]:[Quarter]],Data[Sales], PERCENTOF,,,,,,,3)

Sales as a Percentage, Displayed by Category and Item vs. Year and Quarter

Parent Column Totals (Relative Value 3)

		2022 Q1	2022 Q2	2022 Q3	2022 Q4	2023 Q1	2023 Q2	2023 Q3	2023 Q4	2024 Q1	2024 Q2	2024 Q3	2024 Q4	Total
Accessories	Bike Racks	59.1%	26.7%	12.5%	1.8%	14.7%	28.2%		57.1%	6.4%	26.0%	9.5%	58.1%	100.0%
Accessories	Helmets	21.5%	10.0%	17.3%	51.2%	10.2%	35.9%	37.1%	16.8%	8.5%	21.8%	20.4%	49.3%	100.0%
Accessories	Lights	37.2%	15.8%	29.4%	17.6%	41.1%	8.4%	32.1%	18.4%	25.7%	49.3%	16.2%	8.8%	100.0%
Accessories	Locks	22.2%	17.3%	10.1%	50.4%	34.8%	43.0%	11.1%	11.1%	34.8%	39.2%	14.6%	11.4%	100.0%
Accessories	Pumps	12.6%	27.2%	54.7%	5.5%	93.2%	1.0%		5.7%	42.4%	21.9%	12.0%	23.7%	100.0%
Accessories	Tyres and Tubes	46.9%	15.5%	27.7%	9.9%	21.7%	11.4%	30.8%	36.2%	27.3%	26.3%	43.1%	3.3%	100.0%
Bikes	Cargo Bikes	26.6%	11.9%	33.0%	28.4%	27.7%	18.5%	16.7%	37.1%	13.1%	24.8%	36.5%	25.6%	100.0%
Bikes	Mountain Bikes	17.5%	32.9%	15.1%	34.5%	20.6%	23.5%	16.0%	39.8%	27.9%	20.3%	29.9%	21.9%	100.0%
Bikes	Road Bikes	17.0%	15.0%	15.6%	52.4%	3.6%	42.2%	32.7%	21.6%	32.9%	17.5%	20.7%	28.8%	100.0%
Bikes	Touring Bikes	25.8%	20.9%	24.6%	29.6%	21.4%	19.8%	25.1%	33.7%	27.1%	24.3%	29.4%	19.3%	100.0%
Clothing	Bib-Shorts	15.8%	16.2%	29.1%	38.9%	34.3%	24.2%	6.1%	35.4%	16.3%	24.2%	40.0%	19.5%	100.0%
Clothing	Caps	19.8%	48.0%	22.8%	9.4%	43.8%	47.7%		8.5%	12.9%	60.1%	21.9%	5.1%	100.0%
Clothing	Gloves	20.9%	51.8%	15.2%	12.0%		23.5%	12.0%	64.5%	27.8%		25.6%	46.6%	100.0%
Clothing	Jerseys	7.7%	25.1%		67.2%	26.2%	27.9%	25.4%	20.4%	42.9%	0.4%	23.2%	33.5%	100.0%
Clothing	Shorts	29.6%	58.7%	5.6%	6.1%	9.7%	22.3%	17.5%	50.5%	23.6%	38.2%	10.9%	27.3%	100.0%
Clothing	Socks	30.4%	14.3%	35.7%	19.6%	20.6%	18.3%	20.6%	40.5%	65.7%	24.9%	2.2%	7.2%	100.0%
Clothing	Tights	11.0%		63.7%	25.3%	22.1%	25.2%	10.3%	42.4%	49.3%	14.8%	17.2%	18.7%	100.0%
Clothing	Vests	38.6%	35.4%	2.5%	23.4%	42.1%	15.8%	26.6%	15.4%	4.4%	22.3%	29.1%	44.2%	100.0%
Components	Bottom Brackets	42.8%	20.1%	17.0%	20.1%	22.9%		34.3%	42.8%		35.9%	22.4%	41.8%	100.0%
Components	Brakes	34.3%	42.7%		23.1%	50.2%		44.9%	4.9%	28.2%	8.0%	33.1%	30.7%	100.0%
Components	Chains	20.6%	42.4%	3.6%	33.3%	10.3%	16.3%	39.1%	34.2%	31.9%	18.6%	26.6%	22.9%	100.0%
Components	Handlebars	31.0%	38.9%	19.2%	10.8%	15.7%	42.0%	30.7%	11.7%	13.6%	26.1%	36.9%	23.3%	100.0%
Components	Pedals	0.9%	46.2%	14.9%	38.0%	36.8%	30.1%	13.5%	19.7%	28.6%	40.6%	9.7%	21.1%	100.0%
Components	Saddles	23.4%	49.5%	19.7%	7.3%	23.4%	24.5%	21.2%	31.0%	34.7%	45.3%		20.0%	100.0%
Components	Wheels	44.2%	20.1%	35.7%		1.0%	40.4%	40.9%	17.7%	33.2%	27.6%	37.1%	2.2%	100.0%
Total		26.8%	26.7%	21.5%	25.1%	24.3%	23.7%	23.2%	28.8%	25.7%	25.6%	23.1%	25.6%	100.0%

Here, the Total column is 100% throughout. It is a little confusing as, if anything, it looks a little like Scenario **1:** Row Totals. This is because the column here refers to the headings in each column, *i.e.* **Year** and **Quarter**. You can see that for any row, the sum of the four quarters for any given year totals 100% (including the Total row).

Finally, Scenario **4:** Parent Row Total considers the other parent / child relationship:

=PIVOTBY(Data[[Category]:[Item]],Data[[Year]:[Quarter]],Data[Sales],
PERCENTOF,,,,,,,4)

Sales as a Percentage, Displayed by Category and Item vs. Year and Quarter

Parent Row Totals (Relative Value 4)

		2022 Q1	2022 Q2	2022 Q3	2022 Q4	2023 Q1	2023 Q2	2023 Q3	2023 Q4	2024 Q1	2024 Q2	2024 Q3	2024 Q4	Total
Accessories	Bike Racks	31.7%	25.4%	9.5%	1.2%	5.4%	14.6%		26.4%	6.6%	20.8%	11.4%	40.6%	17.8%
Accessories	Helmets	13.1%	10.7%	14.9%	38.4%	9.6%	48.4%	46.0%	20.2%	9.4%	18.9%	26.5%	37.2%	23.8%
Accessories	Lights	19.1%	14.4%	21.4%	11.2%	17.4%	5.1%	17.9%	9.9%	11.0%	16.4%	8.1%	2.6%	13.4%
Accessories	Locks	15.1%	20.8%	9.7%	42.3%	10.5%	18.5%	4.4%	4.3%	17.3%	15.2%	8.5%	3.8%	14.8%
Accessories	Pumps	5.1%	19.4%	31.3%	2.8%	40.0%	0.6%		3.1%	37.7%	15.2%	12.5%	14.3%	15.0%
Accessories	Tyres and Tubes	15.9%	9.3%	13.3%	4.1%	17.0%	12.7%	31.7%	36.1%	17.9%	13.5%	33.1%	1.5%	15.9%
Bikes	Cargo Bikes	33.4%	16.3%	40.5%	21.6%	43.4%	23.4%	24.0%	33.8%	17.0%	35.4%	38.5%	33.6%	30.1%
Bikes	Mountain Bikes	20.4%	41.5%	17.1%	24.3%	26.6%	24.4%	18.9%	29.8%	27.3%	21.8%	23.7%	21.5%	24.7%
Bikes	Road Bikes	19.4%	18.7%	17.4%	36.2%	3.4%	32.4%	28.6%	12.0%	29.9%	17.5%	15.2%	26.4%	21.8%
Bikes	Touring Bikes	26.8%	23.5%	24.9%	17.9%	26.6%	19.8%	28.6%	24.4%	25.8%	25.4%	22.6%	18.5%	23.4%
Clothing	Bib-Shorts	9.3%	6.4%	16.9%	20.8%	8.1%	5.5%	2.0%	6.0%	6.6%	13.6%	23.0%	9.4%	10.3%
Clothing	Caps	10.1%	16.4%	11.4%	4.3%	16.0%	15.7%		2.2%	4.9%	31.7%	11.8%	2.3%	10.5%
Clothing	Gloves	20.2%	33.4%	14.4%	10.5%		8.9%	6.8%	18.2%	10.4%		13.6%	20.9%	14.2%
Clothing	Jerseys	3.8%	8.3%		30.0%	22.7%	23.2%	31.3%	12.6%	21.3%	0.3%	16.3%	19.8%	15.5%
Clothing	Shorts	14.6%	19.4%	2.7%	2.7%	7.2%	15.8%	18.4%	26.6%	8.3%	18.6%	5.4%	11.5%	13.1%
Clothing	Socks	21.5%	6.7%	24.8%	12.6%	6.2%	5.3%	8.8%	8.7%	25.3%	13.3%	1.2%	3.3%	11.5%
Clothing	Tights	5.1%		28.8%	10.5%	13.8%	15.1%	9.2%	18.9%	21.3%	8.9%	10.6%	9.7%	12.7%
Clothing	Vests	15.4%	9.4%	1.0%	8.5%	26.0%	9.4%	23.5%	6.8%	1.9%	13.6%	18.1%	23.2%	12.2%
Components	Bottom Brackets	21.5%	8.5%	13.8%	18.6%	11.6%		12.4%	23.1%		11.3%	10.3%	18.5%	12.2%
Components	Brakes	9.3%	9.8%		11.6%	34.3%		22.0%	3.6%	10.0%	2.4%	14.7%	13.1%	10.8%
Components	Chains	6.5%	11.3%	1.8%	19.3%	5.8%	9.1%	15.7%	20.5%	20.8%	10.4%	21.7%	18.0%	13.2%
Components	Handlebars	24.0%	25.5%	23.9%	15.4%	13.1%	35.1%	18.3%	10.4%	5.2%	8.5%	17.7%	10.7%	17.4%
Components	Pedals	0.4%	16.5%	10.1%	29.5%	21.8%	17.7%	5.7%	12.4%	28.9%	35.0%	12.2%	25.6%	17.8%
Components	Saddles	9.7%	17.4%	13.2%	5.6%	13.1%	13.7%	8.5%	18.6%	18.4%	20.6%		12.8%	13.1%
Components	Wheels	28.6%	11.0%	37.1%		0.6%	24.4%	17.6%	11.4%	16.7%	11.9%	23.4%	1.3%	15.6%
Total		100.0%	100.0%	100.0%	100.0%	100.0%	100.0%	100.0%	100.0%	100.0%	100.0%	100.0%	100.0%	100.0%

In this final illustration, the Total row is 100% throughout. This looks similar to the default Scenario **0:** Column Totals. This is because the row here refers to the headings in each row, *i.e.* **Category** and **Item**. You can see that for any row the sum of any category for any given **Quarter** and **Year** totals 100% (including the Total column).

PERCENT OF

This final function can be used in conjunction with **GROUPBY** and **PIVOTBY**, or else on its own. This is used to return the percentage that a subset makes up of a given dataset. It is logically equivalent to

SUM(subset) / SUM(everything)

It sums the values in the subset of the dataset and divides it by the sum of all the values. It has the following syntax:

=PERCENTOF(data_subset, data_all)

The arguments are as follows:

- **data_subset:** this is required and represents the values that are in the data subset

- **data_all:** this too is required and denotes the values that make up the entire set.

You can use it, for example, with **GROUPBY**:

=GROUPBY(tbl[Category],tbl[Sales],PERCENTOF)

Description	Percentage
Accessories	24.47%
Bikes	24.99%
Clothing	25.69%
Components	24.86%
Total	100.00%

=GROUPBY(tbl[Category],tbl[Sales],PERCENTOF)

Alternatively, it may be used on its own:

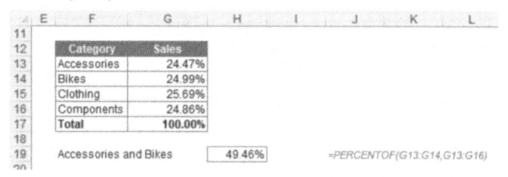

	Category	Sales
12		
13	Accessories	24.47%
14	Bikes	24.99%
15	Clothing	25.69%
16	Components	24.86%
17	Total	100.00%
19	Accessories and Bikes	49.46%

=PERCENTOF(G13:G14,G13:G16)

Still in beta

Be careful. At the time of writing, these functions have just come out. They are rolling out to users enrolled in the beta channel for Windows Excel and Mac Excel. Don't be upset if you don't get them straight away – they are coming!

It is possible the syntax for these functions might change (this happened with **RANDARRAY** for instance), so do be careful. There may be bugs too. Indeed, I have noted the following so far:

- there is nothing to prohibit creating a named range with the same name as an eta lambda, *e.g.* **SUM**. This can cause the formula to produce an *#VALUE!* error. To distinguish between an eta lambda and a range name with the same moniker, use _ **xleta.** as a prefix which might update automatically, *e.g.***=GROUPBY(tbl[Category], tbl[Sales], _xleta.SUM)**

- it has been noted already within the Excel community that titles do not always seem to fully appear:

=GROUPBY(F12:G20,H12:H20,SUM,3,0)

	E	F	G	H	I	J	K	L
11								
12		Division	Product	Cost		Division	Product	
13		A	Alfred	100		A	Alfred	100
14		A	Beater	200		A	Beater	200
15		A	Gammon	300		A	Gammon	300
16		B	Goodrem	400		B	Echo Echo	500
17		B	Echo Echo	500		B	Goodrem	400
18		C	Charleston	600		C	Charleston	600
19		C	GTI	700		C	GTI	700
20		C	Motel	800		C	Motel	800
21								
22								

=GROUPBY(F12:G20,H12:H20,SUM,3,0)

These functions are still fledgling, and hopefully such issues shall be rectified soon.

Don't let these minor gremlins (and others you may find) deter you!

CHAPTER 9: BEST PRACTICE METHODOLOGY

Spreadsheeting is often seen as a core skill for accountants. Many analysts might already be reasonably conversant with Excel, but dynamic arrays, **LET** and **LAMBDA** are just going to take everything to a whole new level.

This might be the first book you've read on the subject, or you might just be seeking a refresher; if not, feel free to skip the momentary meanderings of a modeller. But "Best Practice" is important.

Many of us that build spreadsheets frequently forget that the key end users of a model (*i.e.* the decision makers) are not necessarily sophisticated Excel users and often only see the final output on a printed page, *e.g.* as an appendix to a Word document or as part of a set of PowerPoint slides.

With this borne in mind, it becomes easier to understand why there have been numerous high-profile examples of material spreadsheet errors. I am not saying that well-structured models will ensure no mistakes, but in theory it should *reduce* both the number and the magnitude of these errors. If you're looking to pay off what you borrow and / or invest, surely this becomes doubly important?

Modellers should strive to build "Best Practice" models. Here, I want to avoid the semantics of what constitutes 'best' in "Best Practice". "B" and "P" are in capitals deliberately as I see this as a proper noun insofar no method is truly "best" for all eventualities. There's plenty of texts out there that include copious amounts on what thou shalt and shalt not do regarding building a spreadsheet.

I would rather we consider the term as a proper noun to reflect the idea that a good model has four key attributes:

- **C**onsistency;
- **R**obustness;
- **F**lexibility; *and*
- **T**ransparency.

Our company calls this **CRaFT**. We try to keep it simple. Looking at these four attributes in turn can help model developers decide how best to design financial models.

Consistency

Models constructed consistently are easier to understand as users become familiar with both their purpose and content. This will in turn give users more comfort about model integrity and make it easier to add / remove business units, categories, numbers of periods, scenarios *etc.*

Consistent formatting and use of styles cannot be over-emphasised. Humans take in much information on a non-verbal basis. Consider the following old 'Print' dialog box from *c.* Excel 2003:

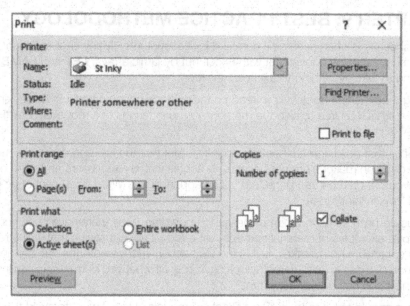

True, this interface has long since been replaced, but the point is still clear. Review the dialog box. It has a dropdown box, check boxes, option buttons, scroll bars – all manner of data validation. You may have never seen this dialog box before in your life, but you just *know* where you need to input data. We may not realise it, but we have all been indoctrinated by Microsoft. Whilst the above dialog box appears quite flexible, we know the only things we are able to change are the objects in white (for example, I know I cannot print out a list from the above dialog box since the selection has been greyed out).

Those of you familiar with our models may now realise I exploit this mindset: the worksheets in my workbooks containing objects or cells that may be modified by the user are readily identifiable without the reading of any instructions.

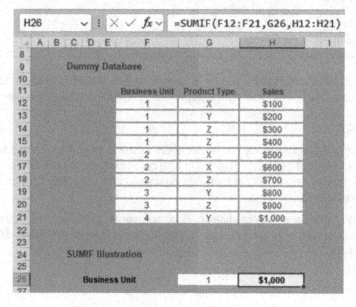

There are other key elements of a workbook that should be consistent. These include:

- formulae should be copied uniformly across ranges, to make it easy to add / remove periods or categories as necessary;

- sheet titles and hyperlinks should be consistently positioned to aid navigation and provide details about the content and purpose of the particular worksheet;

- for forecast spreadsheets incorporating dates, the dates should be consistently positioned (*i.e.* first period should always be in one particular column), the number of periods should be consistent where possible and the periodicity should be uniform (the model should endeavour to show all sheets monthly or quarterly, *etc.*). If periodicities must change, they should be in clearly delineated sections of the model. If you do have a model where you want the first 12 months (say) to be monthly, then annually thereafter, always model everything at the lowest level of granularity (here, monthly) and then use **SUMIF** to aggregate months into years on output sheets later – it makes formulae so much easier to create and manipulate.

This should reduce referencing errors, increase model integrity, and enhance workbook structure.

Robustness

Models should be materially free from error, mathematically accurate and readily auditable. Key output sheets should ensure that error messages such as *#DIV/0!*, *#VALUE!*, *#REF! etc.* cannot occur (ideally, these error messages should not occur anywhere).

My old boss used to promote the idea of "cockroach theory": once you saw one of these errors in a model, you would believe the model was infested and never trust it after that. Removing these *prima facie* errors is straightforward and often highlights that the modeller has not undertaken a basic review of their work after completing the task (see later).

When building, it is often worth keeping in mind hidden assumptions in formulae. For example, a simple gross margin calculation may calculate profit divided by sales. However, if sales are non-existent or missing, this calculation would give *#DIV/0!* The user therefore has two options:

- Use an **IF** statement to check that sales are not zero (proactive test); or

- Construct an error check to flag if sales are zero (reactive test, not recommended in this instance).

However, checks are useful in many situations, and essentially each will fit into one of three categories:

1. **Error checks** – the model contains flawed logic or prima facie errors, *e.g.* the Balance Sheet does not balance, cash in the Cash Flow Statement does not reconcile with the Balance Sheet, or the model contains *#DIV/0!* errors *etc*;

2. **Sensitivity checks** – the model's outputs are being derived from inputs that are not deemed to be part of the base case. This can prevent erroneous decisions being made using the "Best Case"; *and*

3. **Alert checks** – everything else! This flags points of interest to users and / or developers' issues that may need to be reviewed: *e.g.* revenues are negative, debt covenants have been breached, *etc.*

Incorporating dedicated worksheets into the model that summarise these checks will enhance robustness and give users more confidence that the model is working / calculating as intended.

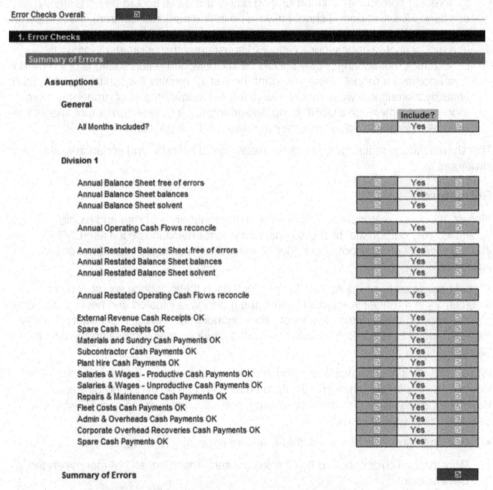

The above is a sanitised screenshot from a real financial model. It is an extract from a worksheet with no fewer than 800 checks with the overall total included at the bottom (this links to the overall check at the top of the sheet, displayed in all worksheets throughout the model). Each check may be switched off if necessary and each check hyperlinks back to where the check is in the model. If you were the recipient of such a model, assuming the checks have been calculated correctly (!), would you feel more comfortable with this model compared to the usual fare received?

Flexibility

One benefit of modelling in a spreadsheet package such as Excel is to be able to change assumptions and see how these adjustments affect various outputs. Therefore, when building a model, the user should consider what inputs should be variable and *how* they should be able to vary. This may force the model builder to consider how assumptions should be entered.

The most common method of data entry in practice is simply typing data into worksheet cells, but this may allow a model's inputs to vary outside of scoped parameters. For example, if I have a cell seeking 'Volumes', without using data validation I could enter '3', '-22.8' or 'dog' in that cell. Negative volumes are nonsensical and being able to enter text may cause formula errors throughout the model. Therefore, the user may wish to consider other methods of entry including using drop down boxes, option buttons, check boxes and so on.

I strongly recommend that all inputs are entered as positive numbers, wherever possible, just change the descriptions accordingly. If I were to tell you that last year costs were $10,000 but they have increased 10% this year. You would understand me. But what would you make of me telling you costs were minus $10,000 and had increased by -10%!?

The aim is to have a model provide sufficient flexibility without going overboard.

Transparency

As stated above, many modellers often forget that key decision makers base their choices on printed materials: consequently, models must be clear, concise, and fit for the purpose intended. I always say if you can follow it on a piece of paper (*i.e.* no Formula bar), it's transparent.

Most Excel users are familiar with keeping inputs / assumptions away from calculations away from outputs. However, this concept can be extended: it can make sense to keep different areas of a model separate, *e.g.* revenue assumptions on a different worksheet from cost(s) of goods sold assumptions, and capital expenditure assumptions on a third sheet, and so on. This makes it easier to re-use worksheets and ringfence data. Keeping base case data away from sensitivity data is also important, as many modelling mistakes have been made from users changing the wrong, yet similar, inputs.

Aside from trying to keep formulae as simple as possible, it makes sense to consider the logical flow of a model at the outset too. Indeed, including a simple flowchart within an Excel workbook can be invaluable: as the saying goes, a picture is worth a thousand words, and can actually help to plan the structure and order of the spreadsheet build.

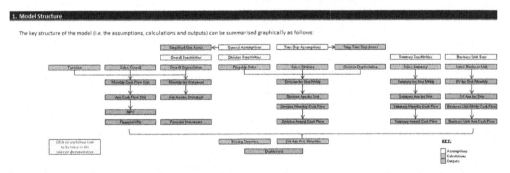

Again, this graphic comes from a genuine model, albeit modified. It should be noted that not only does this graphic show how the model flows, but each box within the graphic is also actually a hyperlink that takes you to the relevant section of the model, complete with documentation.

Similarly, a Table of Contents constructed with hyperlinks helps users and developers alike navigate through larger Excel models:

Navigator

Error Checks:

Documentation / Instructions
Frequently Asked Questions
Style Guide

General Assumptions
Time Dependent Assumptions and Calculations

Simplified General Assumptions
Simplified Time Dependent Assumptions

Dashboard Summary
Pricing Structure
Standard Annual Pricing Structure

Financial Key Performance Indicators
Overall Financial Statements
Overall Annual Income Statement
Overall Annual Cash Flow Statement
Overall NPV Calculation
Overall Sensitivities

Division Annual Income Statement
Division Sensitivities

Summary Annual Income Statement
Summary Sensitivities

Business Unit Annual Income Statement
Business Unit Sensitivities

In summary, it's all about design and scoping. The problem is, we are all time poor in today's business environment with perpetual pressure on producing results more and more quickly. Consequently, we dust off old templates, fit square pegs in round holes and produce mistake-laden spreadsheets time and time again resulting in costly management decisions. The whole process is simply a false economy. Time spent on better scoping out the model and designing the layout will lead to fewer mistakes and greater efficiencies in the long term.

Hey, that leads me nicely into the next section...

CHAPTER 10: LAYOUT TIPS

In light of the discussion on "Best Practice", I want to provide some tips on laying out a typical worksheet in a financial model. I want to be clear: no one is holding a gun to your head and saying you *must* do it this way. I have been modelling for a long time and was even fortunate enough to win the inaugural Lifetime Achievement Award[1] and I'd like to pass on some of the things I have learned – more often than not, the hard way.

To begin with then, here's something I *didn't* prepare earlier:

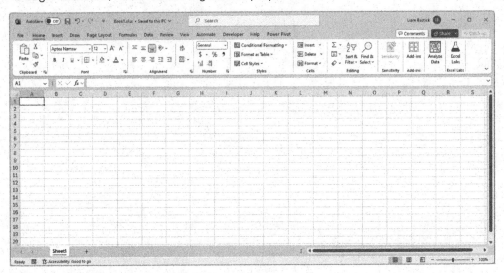

To reiterate, it's all about design and scoping. We are all time-poor in today's business environment having to produce results more and more quickly. Getting a layout structure won't solve all of your problems but it's a start.

Let me show you how I develop this basic worksheet. Assuming this isn't a dashboard output page where column widths may be more critical, I tend to narrow the first few columns (highlight columns, then right-click):

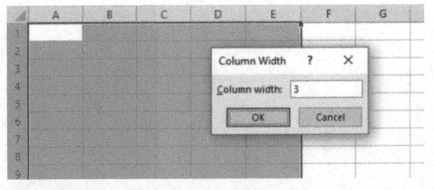

I choose a width of 3, as this effectively makes the cells in these columns square.

---

1   Financial Modeling Institute, 2021

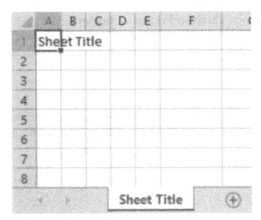

You can elect to highlight more or less columns and you can modify the width too. There are two key points to this:

- Keep column **A** blank other than for the sheet headings (I will explain later)

- Be consistent, both with the widths of the columns narrowed here and with other worksheets within the same workbook (again, I will explain soon).

Next, let's put the Sheet Title in cell **A1**. This should be the same as the description in the sheet tab:

There are three reasons for this:

- Given sheet tab names cannot be infinitely long, sheet titles become more succinct and easier for the end user to understand

- Given the sheet title appears on the worksheet, the name has to be written formally and cannot be an incomprehensible abbreviation, similar to many sheet tab names out there

- This approach promotes consistency, one of the four key concepts of Best Practice modelling.

In cell **A2**, I will put the model name. This may surprise some of you as this is possible to put in the header or footer of each worksheet instead:

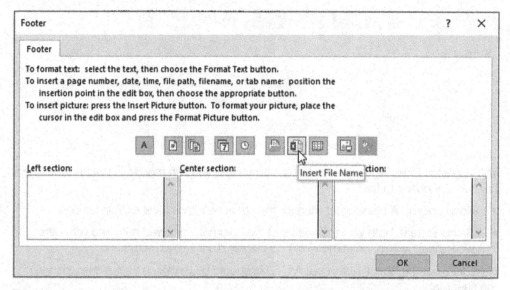

For a start, how many of you know how to locate this dialog box (**ALT** + **P** + **SP** -> **'Header / Footer' tab** -> **'Custom Footer...' button**)? This filename will only display when the worksheet is printed. What if it is an image on a PowerPoint slide or, say, as Appendix 4 in a Word document? This is why I keep the model name front and centre on my worksheets.

There's a formula too:

=IFERROR(MID(CELL("filename",A1),FIND("[",CELL("filename",A1))+1,FIND("]",CELL("filename",A1))-FIND("[",CELL("filename",A1))-1),"")

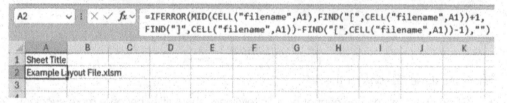

The formula is obvious, yes? I suspect I may need to explain it a little more. It revolves around the **CELL** function in Excel.

CELL

This function returns information about the formatting, location, or contents of the upper-left cell in a reference (in our example, we will be using cell **A1** as our reference in the active worksheet, but this selection is entirely arbitrary). The syntax is:

CELL(Information_type, [Reference])

and works as follows:

Information_type	Returns
"address"	Reference of the first cell in reference, as text.
"col"	Column number of the cell in reference.
"color"	1 if the cell is formatted in colour for negative values; otherwise returns 0 [zero].
"contents"	Value of the upper-left cell in reference; not a formula.
"filename"	Filename (including full path) of the file that contains reference, as text. Returns empty text ("") if the worksheet that contains reference has not yet been saved.
"format"	Text value corresponding to the number format of the cell. Returns "-" at the end of the text value if the cell is formatted in colour for negative values. Returns "()" at the end of the text value if the cell is formatted with parentheses for positive or all values.
"parentheses"	1 if the cell is formatted with parentheses for positive or all values; otherwise returns 0.
"prefix"	Text value corresponding to the "label prefix" of the cell. Returns single quotation mark (') if the cell contains left-aligned text, double quotation mark (") if the cell contains right-aligned text, caret (^) if the cell contains centred text, backslash (\) if the cell contains fill-aligned text, and empty text ("") if the cell contains anything else.
"protect"	0 if the cell is not locked, and 1 if the cell is locked.
"row"	Row number of the cell in reference.
"type"	Text value corresponding to the type of data in the cell. Returns "b" for blank if the cell is empty, "l" for label if the cell contains a text constant, and "v" for value if the cell contains anything else.
"width"	Column width of the cell rounded off to an integer. Each unit of column width is equal to the width of one character in the default font size.

I therefore use the syntax **=CELL("filename",A1)**. An example of a returned filename might be:

C:\Documents and Settings\Liam\My Documents\Wretched Book\Layout Chapter\ [Example Layout File.xlsm]Sheet1

This is not what is required, there's 'padding'. All I want is the actual filename, in this case 'Example Layout File.xlsm'. Therefore, I need to extract the filename from this worksheet directory path.

This will be a three-step process.

Step 1: FINDing the Beginning and the End

The directory path will vary for each file, so I need to spot a foolproof method of finding the beginning and the end of the workbook name. Fortunately, Excel assists us here. '**[**' and '**]**' are reserved characters in Excel's syntax and denote the beginning and the end of the workbook name.

The example returned filename above is 105 characters long. If I can find the position of the '[' and ']' I will be on my way.

FIND(find_text, within_text, [start_num]) is the function I need, where:

- **find_text** is the text you want to find;

- **within_text** is the text containing the text you want to find; and

- **start_num** (which is optional) specifies the character at which to start the search. The first character in **within_text** is character number 1. If you omit **start_num**, it is assumed to be 1.

So, in our example, **=FIND("[",CELL("filename",A1))** returns the value 74 and the formula **=FIND("]",CELL("filename",A1))** returns the value 99. In other words, for our illustration, if I can get Excel to return the character string in positions 75 to 99 inclusive (*i.e.* between the square brackets) I will have the workbook name.

Step 2: LEFT a bit, RIGHT a bit, Aim for the MID Section

There are various functions in Excel that will return part of a character string:

- **LEFT(text, num_characters)** returns the first few characters of a string depending upon the number specified (**num_characters**). This is not useful here as I do not want the first few characters of the text string;

- **RIGHT(text, num_characters)** returns the last few characters of a string depending upon the number specified (**num_characters**). This is not useful here either as I do not want the last few characters of the text string; and

- **MID(text, start_num, num_characters)** returns a specific number of characters from a text string, starting at the position specified, based on the number of characters chosen.

Therefore, I should use the **MID** function here. In hard-code form, the formula would be:

=MID(CELL("filename",A1),75,24)

where:

- 75 = position one character to the right of '**[**' (74 + 1); and

- 24 which is the length of the filename string, being the position of '**]**' less the position of '**[**' less 1, i.e. 99 - 74 - 1 = 24.

This gives us the filename 'Example Layout File.xlsm'.

The problem is I don't want hard code: a flexible formula is required. Using the concepts explained above, I derive:

=MID(CELL("filename",A1),FIND("[",CELL("filename",A1))+1,FIND("]",CELL("filename",A1))-FIND("[",CELL("filename",A1))-1)

And so, we are done. Except we aren't.

Step 3: Error Trapping

A good modeller will always ensure that a formula will work in all foreseeable circumstances. The above formula will only work if the file has been named and saved. Otherwise, **CELL("filename",A1)** will return empty text (""), which will cause the embedded **FIND** formulae to return #*VALUE!* errors, and hence the overall formula will also return the #*VALUE!* error.

I therefore need an error trap, *i.e.* a check that ensures if the file has not yet been saved, I just get empty text ("") returned. To do this, I can use the following formula:

> **=IFERROR(MID(CELL("filename",A1),FIND("[",CELL("filename",A1))+1,FIND("]",C ELL("filename",A1))-FIND("[",CELL("filename",A1))-1),"")**

IFERROR(Formula, Error_trap) prevents the #*VALUE!* error. It isn't pretty, it's not short, it's not transparent, but it's flexible and robust.

The formula above is intended to be copied – as is – straight into an Excel worksheet by pasting it directly into the Excel Formula bar and pressing **ENTER**. In certain situations, it will not work due to the exact method of copying employed, fonts used or the setup of the ASCII characters.

Sheet Title Revision

You have to admit that is quite a comprehensive example. Assuming you are still awake, we can employ a very similar formula to the Sheet Title in cell **A1:**

> **=IFERROR(RIGHT(CELL("filename",A1),LEN(CELL("filename",A1))-FIND("]",CELL ("filename",A1))),"")**

A1		$\times \checkmark f_x$	=IFERROR(RIGHT(CELL("filename",A1),LEN(CELL("filename",A1))- FIND("]",CELL("filename",A1))),"")

	A	B	C	D	E	F	G	H	I	J	K
1	Sheet Title										
2	Example Layout File.xlsm										
3											
4											
5											
6											
7											
8											
9											
10											
11											
12											
13											
14											
15											
16											
17											
18											
19											

Sheet Title　+

The aim is to automate as much as possible. It may not adhere to the "Rule of Thumb" (the rule that no formula should be longer than your thumb), but sometimes, you have to balance transparency against flexibility and robustness.

Back to Layout Tips

20,000 pages into this discussion and I am about to consider what to put on row 3.

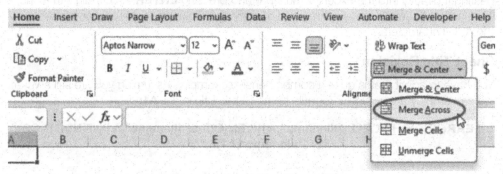

It looks like I have added a hyperlink in cell **A3**, right? Not quite. I am a little craftier than that. Actually, I have highlighted cells **A3:F3** and then merged the cells using Excel's 'Merge Across' functionality (**ALT + H + M + A**):

You may create hyperlinks using the keyboard shortcut **CTRL + K**. The intention is to set up a central Table of Contents on a dedicated worksheet where all of the hyperlinks to the other worksheets reside:

1. Table of Contents

Cover
Style Guide
Model Parameters
Timing
Error Checks
Change Log

The hyperlink should link to cell **A1** of that worksheet and that cell should have a range name such as **HL_TOC** for reasons explained previously. The reason cells **A3:F3** are merged is so that if the end user clicks anywhere in that range the hyperlink will activate; otherwise, the user will have to click on cell **A3** only for the hyperlink to work.

This brings us on nicely to cell **A4**:

◢	A	B	C	D	E	F	G	H
1	Sheet Title							
2	Example Layout File.xlsm							
3	Go to Table of Contents							
4	Error Checks:							
5								

Not much to say about typing text into cell **A4**, but there is more to do on this row:

◢	A	B	C	D	E	F	G	H	I	J	K	L	M	N
1	Sheet Title													
2	Example Layout File.xlsm													
3	Go to Table of Contents													
4	Error Checks:					OK	Units			Date 1	Date 2	Date 3	Date 4	Date 5
5														
6														

Cell **F4** is not just the word "OK"; it actually links back to an 'Error Checks' worksheet. I am going to talk about constructing error checks in a subsequent chapter, so imagine for the moment that cell **F4** is a formula to another worksheet. In reality, it will also be a hyperlink, but as I said, more anon.

In my layout, I have made column **G** my **Units** column: down this column I shall put in all of my units so end users may distinguish between numerical fields. How often have you seen an output and not known if it is in $, $'000, $m, kg, or MWh? This will make this issue a thing of the past. It should be noted that this column is not always required. For instance, on an outputs worksheet, you may simply state near the top of the sheet, "All outputs are displayed in $m unless stated otherwise".

Cells **J4:N4** contain the date headings. Later, I will explain that you actually need more than one row of details for the dates, but that can keep for now. The dates should be periodic (*e.g.* monthly, quarterly, annually) and should always start and end in the same columns (and rows) on each forecast worksheet. That is not always possible: sometimes, you require some of your model to be annually forecast and other aspects monthly. Where this occurs, this should be in clearly delineated areas of the workbook.

Certainly, under no circumstances should the periodicity be inconsistent across any row of an input or calculations worksheet. It is foreseeable that an output sheet may summarise differently, but this should use a methodology such as **SUMIF** or **SUMIFS** (*see earlier*) to summarise data from other worksheets where the periodicity was consistent throughout, *e.g.*

D17		× ✓ *fx*	=SUMIF($D$8:$AA$8,D$15,$D$10:$AA$10)													
◢	A	B	C	D	E	F	G	H	I	J	K	L	M	N	O	P	Q
1																	
2		*Input*															
3																	
4		Month No.		1	2	3	4	5	6	7	8	9	10	11	12	13	14
5		Month		M1	M2	M3	M4	M5	M6	M7	M8	M9	M10	M11	M12	M1	M2
6		Quarter		Q1	Q1	Q1	Q2	Q2	Q2	Q3	Q3	Q3	Q4	Q4	Q4	Q1	Q1
7		Year		Y1	Y1	Y1	Y1	Y1	Y1	Y1	Y1	Y1	Y1	Y1	Y1	Y2	Y2
8		SUMIF Ctr	=IF(D$7="Y1",IF(D$4<=6,D$5,D$6),D$7)	M1	M2	M3	M4	M5	M6	Q3	Q3	Q3	Q4	Q4	Q4	Y2	Y2
9																	
10		Sales		100	200	300	400	500	600	700	800	900	1,000	1,100	1,200	1,300	1,400
11																	
12																	
13		*Output*															
14																	
15		Period		M1	M2	M3	M4	M5	M6	Q3	Q4	Y2					
16																	
17		Sales	=SUMIF($D$8:$AA$8,D$15,$D$10:$AA$10)	100	200	300	400	500	600	2,400	3,300	22,200					
18																	

You may have noticed as well that there is a line inserted in between rows 4 and 5 of the image:

◢	A	B	C	D	E	F	G	H	I	J	K	L	M	N
1	Sheet Title													
2	Example Layout File.xlsm													
3	Go to Table of Contents													
4	Error Checks:					OK	Units			Date 1	Date 2	Date 3	Date 4	Date 5
5														

This is not a drawn line. This is a frozen pane. Frozen panes break up the worksheet in to as many as four pieces. Located in the 'Window' grouping of the 'View' tab of the Ribbon, there are three ways to create a frozen pane:

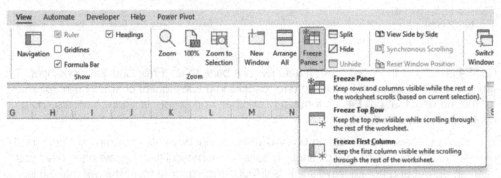

- **Freeze top row:** Keeps the top row visible no matter how far down the spreadsheet you scroll

- **Freeze first column:** Keeps the first column visible no matter how far to the right you scroll the spreadsheet

- **Custom (Freeze Panes):** Creates a frozen locus at the intersection of the top row and the first column of the cell(s) selected.

That final option is a little confusing. Essentially, the frozen panes are created as follows:

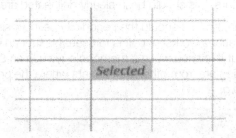

Frozen panes are created for the region the selection is in, the region directly above, the region to the immediate left and diagonally opposite the top left-hand corner of the selection. If the selection were in column **A**, there would only be two frozen panes: the rows immediately above and the remainder. If the selection were in row 1, again, there would only be two frozen panes: the columns to the left and the remainder.

Splits

Splits are similar to frozen panes. They are created like Freeze Panes (keyboard shortcut: **ALT** + **W** + **S**) but create scrollbars in all quadrants, which means no section is truly fixed.

In our example, cell **A5** has been made the basis of the frozen pane, so that rows 1 to 4 will always be visible. This cell should be given a range name, *e.g.* **HL_Home**, as this is the cell to which hyperlinks to this sheet should link. This cell 'resets' the sheet and makes the model easier to navigate as a consequence.

Hyperlink Home Cell

The cell that effectively resets the worksheet can be readily identified. If there is a split or frozen pane on the worksheet, then the chances are cell **A1** is not the correct cell. The cell can be identified by the keyboard shortcut **CTRL** + **HOME**. It is always the top left-hand corner of the bottom right-hand quadrant of any frozen panes. It is the top left-hand corner cell of the range selected to freeze panes in the first place.

Back to our example, headings should start in column **B**, not **A**, and then move out a column or two for subheadings and sub subheadings respectively. I then put data labels directly beneath sub subheadings:

	A	B	C	D	E	F	G	H	I	J	K	L	M	N
1	Sheet Title													
2	Example Layout File.xlsm													
3	Go to Table of Contents													
4	Error Checks:					OK	Units			Date 1	Date 2	Date 3	Date 4	Date 5
5														
6		Main Heading												
7														
8			Sub Heading											
9														
10				Sub Sub Heading										
11				Label										
12				Label										
13				Label										
14				Label										
15				Label										
16														

I have called them "Headings" and "Sub Headings" *etc.* to make it clear, but if I develop a stutter I might be in column **Q** before you know it! Renaming the headings "Heading 1" and so on may be clearer. This also makes them consistent with pre-existing Style names *(hint, hint)*:

	A	B	C	D	E	F	G	H	I	J	K	L	M	N
1	Sheet Title													
2	Example Layout File.xlsm													
3	Go to Table of Contents													
4	Error Checks:					OK	Units			Date 1	Date 2	Date 3	Date 4	Date 5
5														
6		Heading 1												
7														
8			Heading 2											
9														
10				Heading 3										
11				Label										
12				Label										
13				Label										
14				Label										
15				Label										
16														
17														
18		Heading 1												
19														
20			Heading 2											
21														
22				Heading 3										
23				Label										
24				Label										
25				Label										
26				Label										
27				Label										
28														

Aside from keeping column **A** clear, do you now see why I have narrowed columns **B, C** and **D** (I am keeping column **E** "just in case")? The narrowing of the columns effectively indents the headings and makes worksheets easier to read and navigate (especially if the gridlines, **ALT + W + VG**, are toggled off).

Take special note of the spacing: one blank row between headings; two lines between sections. That's my preference. You choose your own if you would prefer – just be consistent. This treatment will reap dividends as our financial model case study later will demonstrate.

Blank columns **H** and **I** are in existence in case I have any calculations, inputs or referred values that do not refer to a particular time period. If they are not required, I tend to narrow the columns to a width of 1 (say), so that they are still there in case they are needed later.

Adding labels, data, and formulae:

	A	B	C	D	E	F	G	H	I	J	K	L	M	N
1	Sheet Title													
2	Example Layout File.xlsm													
3	Go to Table of Contents													
4	Error Checks:					OK	Units			Date 1	Date 2	Date 3	Date 4	Date 5
5														
6		Heading 1												
7														
8			Heading 2											
9														
10				Heading 3										
11				Label			Number			7481	2962	19411	8388	7157
12				Label			$/unit			3.8	3.81	3.82	3.83	3.84
13				Label			$/unit			2.95	2.94	2.93	2.92	2.91
14				Label			$/unit			4.5	4.5	4.5	4.5	4.5
15				Label			$/unit			3.75	3.7	4.1	3.9	4.22
16														
17														
18		Heading 1												
19														
20			Heading 2											
21														
22				Heading 3										
23				Label			Number			7481	2962	19411	8388	7157
24				Label			$'000			28427.8	11285.22	74150.02	32126.04	27482.88
25				Label			$'000			22068.95	8708.28	56874.23	24492.96	20826.87
26				Label			$'000			33664.5	13329	87349.5	37746	32206.5
27				Label			$'000			28053.75	10959.4	79585.1	32713.2	30202.54
28														

It's starting to look more like a spreadsheet now. If I start adding / taking into account Styles (**ALT** + **H** + **J**),

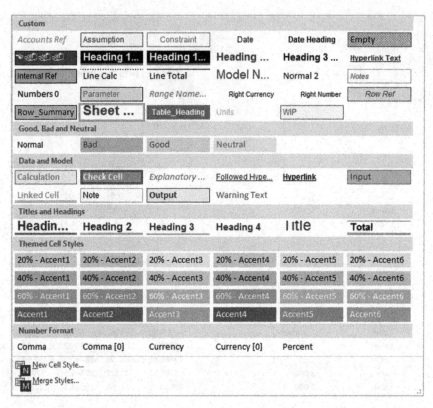

these may be applied:

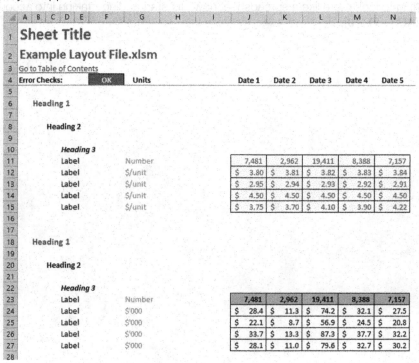

Do you see? It's starting to look more like a spreadsheet already. I switch off gridlines on my spreadsheets so that the majority of my files appear to have a white background. There is more to this point than merely aesthetics. Adding a colour to the background of a spreadsheet can make a file significantly larger – unnecessarily.

The spacing is deliberate too. Not only does it look neater (remember, Excel 2007 onwards has 1,048,576 rows and 16,384 columns, *i.e.* it is 1,024 times larger than an Excel 2003 worksheet so there is plenty of room), but the space is functional too.

Want to navigate between the main headings in column **B**? Click on cell **B6**, go **CTRL + Down Arrow** and you will arrive at cell **B18**. Repeat this action and the next cell you will hit is cell **B1048576**, *i.e.* the very bottom of the spreadsheet because there is nothing else in this column.

Click on cell **D10** (**Heading 3**) and press **CTRL + Down Arrow** to be taken to cell **D15**, the final cell in the contiguous range. **CTRL + Up Arrow**, **CTRL + Right Arrow** and **CTRL + Left Arrow** will all perform similar actions. Need to highlight a range? Click on any cell within the range and **CTRL + A** will select the whole contiguous range. This makes the model easier for developer and user alike to navigate and manipulate.

So why have I kept column **A** blank? The reason is to take into account work in progress. How often have you started creating a spreadsheet only to be interrupted, have to go to a meeting, take a telephone call, go home, or go to sleep? The point is, when we are interrupted, we need to remember how far along we were. If you design a spreadsheet similar to the one discussed here, imagine you are interrupted without notice. Before you turn your attention to the disruption, whichever row you are working on, pressing the **HOME** key which will take you to column **A** of that row. Type anything in that cell, *e.g.* "w" for "work in progress" or "check" and so on. That's it.

How does that help you? Before you hand the model to anyone else, we need to undertake some checks before saving and distributing. One of those checks will be to ensure there is nothing in column **A** of any worksheet after the frozen pane.

Summary

That's all I wanted to say about layout. Keep it consistent, make it transparent, ensure there are checks to protect the robustness and that inputs are clearly marked to aid flexibility. See? I have developed a simple layout adhering to the **CRaFT** methodology.

CHAPTER 11: TIME SERIES ANALYSIS

There comes a time in most people's lives that they realise it's time to confront the world head-on, go out there and ask for a date. You can imagine asking a model for a date can be even more stressful. Well, puns completed, it's not that difficult, but it does deserve its own chapter.

Most forecast models project key outputs over multiple periods. Typically, these periods are not headed "Date 1", "Date 2", *etc.* like in our example from the last chapter, but display end dates to assist users to understand payback periods, seasonality, trends, and so on.

An example time series could contain some or all of the following:

Month Ending	Jan-24	Feb-24	Mar-24	Apr-24	May-24	Jun-24
Month	M1	M2	M3	M4	M5	M6
Period End Year	2024	2024	2024	2024	2024	2024
Financial Year	2024	2024	2024	2024	2024	2024
Days in Period End Year	366	366	366	366	366	366
Days in Financial Year	366	366	366	366	366	366
Financial Year Period	M1	M2	M3	M4	M5	M6
Period Start Date (From Start of Day...)	1/1/24	1/2/24	1/3/24	1/4/24	1/5/24	1/6/24
Period End Date (Until End of Day...)	31/1/24	29/2/24	31/3/24	30/4/24	31/5/24	30/6/24
Months in Month	1	1	1	1	1	1
Days in Period	31	29	31	30	31	30
Days in Month	31	29	31	30	31	30
Counter	1	2	3	4	5	6

The above is an example of time series data in a real-life financial model. My question is this though: are all of these rows absolutely necessary?

I would suggest not.

Essentially, three lines are necessarily needed when modelling (the rest may be derived as necessary):

- **Start date:** This will allow for models where the first period is not a "full" period (often called a 'stub' period), *e.g.* a business may wish to project its profits from now until the end of the calendar year for the first year;

- **End date:** This will define the end of the period and will often coincide with reporting dates, *e.g.* end of financial year or quarter ends. By having both the start date and end date defined, a modeller can determine the number of days / weeks / months in the period, which financial year the period pertains to, and so forth;

- **Counter:** Start and end dates are insufficient. Constructing calculations based on consideration of a date is fraught with potential issues in Excel. This is because dates are really serial numbers in Excel, which may differ depending upon the underlying operating system (I discuss this in detail in Chapter 1.14). Further, if you are building a monthly model you may wish to divide an annual figure evenly instead of based on the number of days. This is also the easiest way to identify the first and last periods in a robust manner.

So, bearing this in mind, how do you build up the necessary formulae for these three line items allowing for the more common eventualities? Well, to begin with, there's only really one troublesome formula. This is because:

- The Counter is simply the last period's number plus one. I tend to use the formula **=N(Previous_Cell)+1**, where the **N()** function takes the numerical value in the previous cell, and more importantly, text is ignored so that #*VALUE!* errors will not arise;

- The Start Date is simply the Model Start Date for the first period and the day following the last period's end date otherwise. This can simply be written as **=IF(Counter=1,Model_Start_Date,Previous_Period_End_Date+1)**.

Therefore, I need only consider the formula for the Period End Date. Consider the following simple example:

1. Timing Assumptions

Data (do not change once modelling has commenced)

Model Start Date	01 Jan 24
Number of Months in a Full Period	3
Example Reporting Month	12 *e.g. 31-Dec-24*
Reporting Month Factor	3

I have selected an arbitrary start date (**Model_Start_Date**) of 1 January 2024, and assumed that the number of months in a full period (**Periodicity**) is three [3]. The third line item is a little more subtle: this specifies which periods are period ends by specifying one month that will be a period end month. For example, tax may be paid quarterly in the months of March, June, September, and December. By entering a **Periodicity** of 3 and specifying an **Example_Reporting_Month** of any of 3, 6, 9 or 12, this will provide sufficient information to work out the quarter ends, i.e. 31-Mar, 30-Jun, 30-Sep and 31-Dec. The **Reporting_Month_Factor** is simply the minimum of these acceptable alternative values and is calculated automatically here. The approach I will use here requires that the periodicity is a divisor of the number of months in a year (**Months_in_Year**) – which is why my example only allows the **Periodicity** to be 1, 2, 3, 4, 6 or 12.

In the example above, we are building a quarterly model where December is one of the quarter ends. Therefore, the possible quarter end months are:

End Date Month
3
6
9
12

This example table allows for up to 12 month ends (*i.e.* for a monthly model).

So how do I derive the necessary formula? I will give you some insight into my simplistic view of the world. First, I would construct the following table:

Model Start Date Month	End Date Month	Addition Reqd
1	3	2
2	3	1
3	3	0
4	6	2
5	6	1
6	6	0
7	9	2
8	9	1
9	9	0
10	12	2
11	12	1
12	12	0

This simple table considers all 12 months of the year for the **Model_Start_Date** (first column). The middle column displays which month would be the first quarter, given the assumption regarding the month of the **Model_Start_Date**. Therefore, a start date in January, February or March will give rise to a March quarter end, etc.

I can use an array formula to calculate this month number dynamically. This is not necessary, and the values could just be typed in – remember, this table is simply a tool to ascertain how to construct the formula required.

The final column is then the difference between the end date month and the **Model_Start_Date** month. It is slightly more complicated than this as I need to consider what happens if the **Model_Start_Date** month exceeds the final end date month. For example, considering a tax example, tax arising in November (month 11) could be after the final payment period of the year (month 10). This would be paid in month 1 of the following year instead.

The point is the final column highlights the pattern of how many months after the **Model_Start_Date** the first reporting period will occur. I can now use two of the functions I covered earlier in tandem to derive this first period end date:

- **EOMONTH(date, months)** returns the last day of the month so many months from the date specified. For example, **=EOMONTH(11-Dec-20,14)** would be 28-Feb-22, *i.e.* the end date 14 months after the end of December 2020.

- **MOD(number, divisor)** returns the remainder when **Number** is divided by the **Divisor**. For example, **=MOD(17,6)** is 5, since 17/6 = 2 remainder 5.

With trial and error, the number of months I need to add on can be calculated as follows:

=MOD(Perodicity+Reporting_Month_Factor-MONTH(Model_Start_Date),Perodicity)

and therefore, if I call this equation the **Additive_Factor**, then the reporting end date will be:

=EOMONTH(Model_Start_Date,Additive_Factor)

In the example file, I have checked my workings, *viz.*

Model Start Date Month	End Date Month	Addition Reqd	Dates Calc	Verification
1	3	2	2	3
2	3	1	1	3
3	3	0	0	3
4	6	2	2	6
5	6	1	1	6
6	6	0	0	6
7	9	2	2	9
8	9	1	1	9
9	9	0	0	9
10	12	2	2	12
11	12	1	1	12
12	12	0	0	12

Furthermore, a robust yet flexible time series can be constructed:

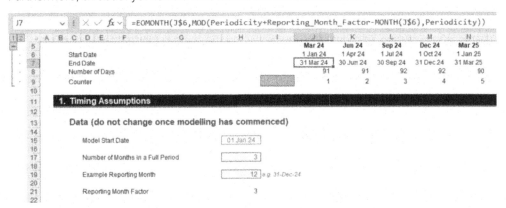

Even allowing for flexible start dates and "Reporting Month Factors", the above will not work in all circumstances. Other periodicities may be sought, whilst some businesses require weekly reporting or 5-4-4-week period regimes. Nonetheless, the above approach can be modified and extrapolated to consider most complications.

In our case study, we will need to return to this logic, as we will need to modify the formulae to incorporate dynamic arrays. However, at this stage the aim is merely to understand the concepts.

CHAPTER 12: ERROR CHECKS

You may recall during our discussion on robustness, one of the four key qualities of a "Best Practice" model, I sang the praises of including as many checks as possible. I use the generic "error check" descriptor to cover three types of check:

1. **Error checks** – the model contains flawed logic or *prima facie* errors, e.g. Balance Sheet does not balance, cash in Cash Flow Statement does not reconcile with the Balance Sheet, or the model contains #DIV/0! errors *etc*;

2. **Sensitivity checks** – the model's outputs are being derived from inputs that are not deemed to be part of the base case. This can prevent erroneous decisions being made using the "Best Case"; *and*

3. **Alert checks** – everything else! This flags points of interest to users and / or developers' issues that may need to be reviewed: *e.g.* revenues are negative, debt covenants have been breached, *etc.*

Many modellers add checks as an afterthought. Basically, it is too late to create them then. While building a model, a developer knows what situation might break a formula. *That is when you should create the check.* When the issue is foremost in your mind, create the check there and then.

Let me give you an example. I am going to create the world's simplest Balance Sheet:

	A	B	C	D	E
1	**Simple Balance Sheet Example**				
2					
3			$m		
4		Total Assets	100		
5		Total Liabilities	30		
6		**Net Assets**	**70**		
7					
8		Shareholders' Equity	50		
9		Retained Profits	20		
10		**Total Equity**	**70**		
11					
12					

You may be a Fellow of one of the accounting institutes or you may know very little on financial reporting. In either case, one thing everybody knows: *Balance Sheets have to balance*.

So let me put a check in to ensure it balances:

C13		✕ ✓ fx ∨	=C6=C10		

◢	A	B	C	D	E
1	**Simple Balance Sheet Example**				
2					
3			$m		
4		Total Assets	100		
5		Total Liabilities	30		
6		**Net Assets**	70		
7					
8		Shareholders' Equity	50		
9		Retained Profits	20		
10		**Total Equity**	70		
11					
12					
13		Balance Check:	TRUE		
14					

The formula **=C6=C10** is pretty straightforward, but I don't recommend it. Any financial model I build will have many time periods and I will need a check for each period. Further, that's just one check out of many. How do you feel about reading through all of your error checks and making sure they all equal TRUE?

It is true you could use a **SUMIF** formula to count all of the TRUE responses, but surely there is an easier way? Of course there is; let me walk you through it. First thing is to put the formula in brackets and multiply the bracketed expression by one [1]:

C13		✕ ✓ fx ∨	=(C6=C10)*1		

◢	A	B	C	D	E
1	**Simple Balance Sheet Example**				
2					
3			$m		
4		Total Assets	100		
5		Total Liabilities	30		
6		**Net Assets**	70		
7					
8		Shareholders' Equity	50		
9		Retained Profits	20		
10		**Total Equity**	70		
11					
12					
13		Balance Check:	1		
14					

The requirement for brackets is due to the order of operations in a calculation using the **BODMAS** principle:

B rackets

p O wers

D ivision

M ultiplication

A ddition

S ubtraction

i.e. calculations in brackets are performed before raising numbers to powers (computing exponentials), before division, and so on.

The problem with this formula is that this will count all the times the Balance Sheet balances. Is it really that informative knowing that your Balance Sheet balances in 17,212 instances? Would it be preferable to learn that you have two errors? Of course it would. This is known as **reporting by exception**. To revise the formula:

C13		:	X ✓ *fx* ✓	=(C6<>C10)*1		
	A		B	C	D	E
1	**Simple Balance Sheet Example**					
2						
3				$m		
4			Total Assets	100		
5			Total Liabilities	30		
6			**Net Assets**	70		
7						
8			Shareholders' Equity	50		
9			Retained Profits	20		
10			**Total Equity**	70		
11						
12						
13			Balance Check:			

The "<>" symbol means "is not equal to" so **=(C6<>C10)*1** flags (*i.e.* displays a '1') when Net Assets does not equal Total Equity. That sounds good, but this is not quite sufficient either. In additions and other calculations within Excel, sometimes Excel produces minor rounding errors simply due to the way the software has been programmed. This error may occur at the eighth or ninth decimal place and is not caused by the modeller's formula *per se*, it is more of an anomaly in the coding of Excel itself. To circumvent this, I use the **ROUND** function:

ROUND(number, number_of_digits)

This rounds **number** to **number_of_digits** decimal places, *e.g.* **ROUND(2.928,2)** equals 2.93.

C13	⌄	:	✕ ✓ *fx* ⌄	=(ROUND(C6-C10,5)<>0)*1		

◢	A	B	C	D	E
1	**Simple Balance Sheet Example**				
2					
3			$m		
4		Total Assets	100		
5		Total Liabilities	30		
6		**Net Assets**	**70**		
7					
8		Shareholders' Equity	50		
9		Retained Profits	20		
10		**Total Equity**	**70**		
11					
12					
13		Balance Check:	-		

In this illustration, **=(ROUND(C6-C10,5)<>0)*1** alerts when **C6** (Net Assets) does not equal **C10** (Total Equity) to five decimal places.

Just before I continue, I am going to be pedantic here – with good reason. There are three hard-coded values in that last formula, 5, 0 and 1. Some hard code (*i.e.* typed in numbers) is acceptable and some is not:

- '5' is essentially a variable. In this example, I am rounding to five decimal places, but this could be argued as an arbitrary choice. It is better to have this as an input value and to make its reference clearer, provide it with a range name, *e.g.* **Rounding_ Factor**.

- '0' is not a variable. This is a **constant**. I am testing to see whether the difference between two values (given a **Rounding_Factor** tolerance) is zero. I am unlikely to want to change this so I may determine whether the difference between the two values is 44.8 *(say)*. Therefore, this value is acceptable in a formula.

- '1' is also a constant. This converts TRUE or FALSE values to 1's and 0's respectively so that they may be added together to determine the number of errors. For this reason, the use of the number 1 in this formula is also deemed acceptable.

In this example, I will leave hard code in the above formula alone, but perhaps a "better practice" version of the calculation might be **=(ROUND(C6-C10,Rounding_Factor)<>0)*1**. However, there is still a large issue. What if someone deletes a key reference?

C13		$\times \checkmark fx$	=(ROUND(C6-C10,5)<>0)*1		
	A	B	C	D	E
1	**Simple Balance Sheet Example**				
2					
3			$m		
4		Total Assets	100		
5		Total Liabilities	#REF!		
6		**Net Assets**	#REF!		
7					
8		Shareholders' Equity	50		
9		Retained Profits	20		
10		**Total Equity**	70		
11					
12					
13		Balance Check:	#REF!		

In the example, the reference in cell **C5** no longer exists giving rise to an *#REF!* error. Unfortunately, this does happen in models. Even if you protect a worksheet (**ALT** + **T** + **P** + **P**), the end user may still delete the sheet! (Protecting the workbook – **ALT** + **T** + **P** + **W** – will prevent this, but the workbook can still be deleted.)

Therefore, if someone does manage to accidentally delete a key reference, I would want the error check to alert me accordingly. The problem is, in our example above, while our check may alert us, *#REF!* is not necessarily the ideal way to display this. I would prefer to be alerted using our 1 / 0 system already utilised:

	A	B	C	D	E
1		**Simple Balance Sheet Example**			
2					
3			$m		
4		Total Assets	100		
5		Total Liabilities	#REF!		
6		**Net Assets**	**#REF!**		
7					
8		Shareholders' Equity	50		
9		Retained Profits	20		
10		**Total Equity**	**70**		
11					
12		Prima Facie Check:	1		*=IF(ISERROR(C6-C10),1,)*
13		Balance Check:	-		*=IF(C12,,(ROUND(C6-C10,5)<>0)*1)*
14					

Now the checks are becoming more sophisticated. In cell **C12** *(above)*, I have added a check and modified the existing one. The first check, **=IF(ISERROR(C6-C10),1,)**, provides the value 1 if Net Assets less Total Equity may not be evaluated. This is <u>not</u> the same as the formula:

> **=IFERROR(C6-C10,1)**

Whilst this formula will provide a value of 1 if the subtraction cannot be evaluated, the alternative is not necessarily zero. This formula is not intended to be my balance check, merely a check to ensure that my balance check will work. If I were to use **IFERROR** rather than **IF(ISERROR)** the values could be *anything*. I want values of zero and one only.

Turning our attention to the second formula in cell **C13**, did you check out that this check contains a check to check the check can be checked? Did you just check out with that last sentence? I really should have been a poet – then even fewer would read my drivel…

Consider the following variant of the formula in cell **C13**:

> **=IF(C12<>0,0,(ROUND(C6-C10,5)<>0)*1)**

To be honest, this is the formula I would probably use in a model as it is easier for users to understand. This check verifies that the error check in cell **C12** (the "prima facie check") has not been triggered before checking whether Net Assets equals Total

Equity. I wrote the formula a different way above, *i.e.* **=IF(C12,,...)**, to demonstrate two "shortcuts":

- Putting a cell reference or value in as the first argument in an **IF** statement is the same as checking whether the value is non-zero. All numerical values other than zero are treated as if they were TRUE by Excel, whereas a value of precisely zero is FALSE.

- Omitting a value (just putting two commas) in this instance is the same as assuming a **Value_if_TRUE** value of zero [0].

I don't have to stop there:

	A	B	C	D	E
1	**Simple Balance Sheet Example**				
2					
3			$m		
4		Total Assets	100		
5		Total Liabilities	130		
6		Net Assets	(30)		
7					
8		Shareholders' Equity	50		
9		Retained Profits	(80)		
10		Total Equity	(30)		
11					
12		Prima Facie Check:	-	=IF(ISERROR(C6-C10),1,)	
13		Balance Check:	-	=IF(C12,,(ROUND(C6-C10,5)<>0)*1)	
14		Insolvency Check:	1	=IF(AND(C12=0,C13=0),(C6<0)*1,)	
15					

With this third check, it may be getting easier to see why order of checks is so important.

=IF(AND(C12=0,C13=0),(C6<0)*1,)

checks to see if Net Assets are negative, but only if there are no *prima facie* errors in the output *and* the Balance Sheet balances. In fact, this last check is a different type of check. The first two are error checks, *i.e.* these highlight issues that <u>must</u> be resolved before the model may be relied upon. Materiality is not relevant. Until these issues are fixed, the model is not calculating correctly.

The insolvency check, on the other hand, is an example of an alert check. The model is calculating correctly and there appear to be no *prima facie* errors. However, if actuality coincides with the forecast, your business will become insolvent with more owing than owed. Warning!

This whole idea may be extrapolated further:

	A	B	C	D	E	F	G	H	I
1	**Simple Balance Sheet Example**								
2									
3					2024	2025	2026	2027	2028
4					$m	$m	$m	$m	$m
5		Total Assets			100	100	100	140	185
6		Total Liabilities			30	130	90	100	130
7		Net Assets			70	(30)	10	40	55
8									
9		Shareholders' Equity			50	70	(30)	10	40
10		Retained Profits			20	(100)	40	30	15
11		Total Equity			70	(30)	10	40	55
12									
13		Prima Facie Check:	-	=MAX(E13:I13)	-	-	-	-	-
14		Balance Check:	-	=MAX(E14:I14)	-	-	-	-	-
15		Insolvency Check:	1	=MAX(E15:I15)	-	1	-	-	-

In this illustration I have demonstrated how checks may be incorporated across periods of time. The checks in cells **E13:I15** are similar to those described above already, but the checks in column **C** are new. These are aggregator checks, summarising issues across their respective rows. The formula used in cell **C13** could be,

=MIN(SUM(E13:I13),1)

but it is simpler to use

=MAX(E13:I13)

These checks could be linked to an overall 'Error Checks' worksheet at this stage or else there may be one additional step to take:

	A	B	C	D	E	F	G	H	I
1	**Simple Balance Sheet Example**								
2									
3					2024	2025	2026	2027	2028
4					$m	$m	$m	$m	$m
5		Total Assets			100	100	100	140	185
6		Total Liabilities			30	130	90	100	130
7		Net Assets			70	(30)	10	40	55
8									
9		Shareholders' Equity			50	70	(30)	10	40
10		Retained Profits			20	(100)	40	30	15
11		Total Equity			70	(30)	10	40	55
12									
13		Prima Facie Check:	-	=MAX(E13:I13)	-	-	-	-	-
14		Balance Check:	-	=MAX(E14:I14)	-	-	-	-	-
15		Insolvency Check:	1	=MAX(E15:I15)	-	1	-	-	-
16			1	=MAX(C13:C15)					

Here, I have created an overall check for this section. The check in cell **C16** summarises the checks in column **C** above it, using a similar construct of the **MAX** function to create a check that may only ever be one or zero.

Adding conditional formatting, number formatting and wingdings font whilst removing gridlines arguably makes for a more aesthetic look:

	A	B	C	D	E	F	G	H	I
1	**Simple Balance Sheet Example**								
2									
3					2024	2025	2026	2027	2028
4					$m	$m	$m	$m	$m
5		Total Assets			100	100	100	140	185
6		Total Liabilities			30	130	90	100	130
7		Net Assets			70	(30)	10	40	55
8									
9		Shareholders' Equity			50	70	(30)	10	40
10		Retained Profits			20	(100)	40	30	15
11		Total Equity			70	(30)	10	40	55
12									
13		Prima Facie Check:	☑	=MAX(E13:I13)	☑	☑	☑	☑	☑
14		Balance Check:	☑	=MAX(E14:I14)	☑	☑	☑	☑	☑
15		Insolvency Check:	☑	=MAX(E15:I15)	☑	☑	☑	☑	☑
16			☑	=MAX(C13:C15)					

It will be a preference call, whether to include checks on a row-by-row basis, or on an overall section basis (just be consistent), but these checks may then be summarised on an overall 'Error Checks' worksheet *viz*.

Error Checks Overall: ☑

1. Error Checks

Summary of Errors

Assumptions

General

		Include?	
All Months included?	☑	Yes	☑

Division 1

Annual Balance Sheet free of errors	☑	Yes	☑
Annual Balance Sheet balances	☑	Yes	☑
Annual Balance Sheet solvent	☑	Yes	☑
Annual Operating Cash Flows reconcile	☑	Yes	☑
Annual Restated Balance Sheet free of errors	☑	Yes	☑
Annual Restated Balance Sheet balances	☑	Yes	☑
Annual Restated Balance Sheet solvent	☑	Yes	☑
Annual Restated Operating Cash Flows reconcile	☑	Yes	☑
External Revenue Cash Receipts OK	☑	Yes	☑
Spare Cash Receipts OK	☑	Yes	☑
Materials and Sundry Cash Payments OK	☑	Yes	☑
Subcontractor Cash Payments OK	☑	Yes	☑
Plant Hire Cash Payments OK	☑	Yes	☑
Salaries & Wages - Productive Cash Payments OK	☑	Yes	☑
Salaries & Wages - Unproductive Cash Payments OK	☑	Yes	☑
Repairs & Maintenance Cash Payments OK	☑	Yes	☑
Fleet Costs Cash Payments OK	☑	Yes	☑
Admin & Overheads Cash Payments OK	☑	Yes	☑
Corporate Overhead Recoveries Cash Payments OK	☑	Yes	☑
Spare Cash Payments OK	☑	Yes	☑

Summary of Errors ☑

As mentioned previously, this screenshot is from a sanitised version of a real-life financial model. The first column of checks are merely links from checks built throughout the model – but hyperlinked, so that if the end user clicks on either this column or the second column of checks they will be taken back to the source. Do remember that the destination cell of a hyperlink should be given a range name, *e.g.* **HL_Check01**, in case the destination worksheet is renamed.

A Yes / No data validation list separates the two columns of checks, with a "No" making the check OK in all situations. This is fine during model development as construction can generate interim model errors (*e.g.* Balance Sheet does not balance), but all <u>error</u> checks should be switched on prior to a model being used operationally.

Finally, the summary check at the foot of the image is the overall check for the model. It is this one which is linked to the overall check at the top of each worksheet, just as I described when discussing the model layout. This should also be a hyperlink, so not only do you have a hyperlink to the Table of Contents for each worksheet, but you also have immediate access to the 'Error Checks' worksheet too.

To conclude this chapter, I have concentrated just on one section, suggesting just *some* of the checks to consider for the Balance Sheet. This is not intended to be an exhaustive list. As you build a model, you will realise which checks you need to incorporate. If you forget one or two, it is likely they will come back to haunt you later when you are trying to diagnose an issue in your model!

Again, in our case study, we will need to return to this logic, as we will need to modify the formulae to incorporate dynamic arrays. However, at this stage the aim is merely to understand the concepts.

CHAPTER 13: MODEL TEMPLATE EXAMPLE

This template is a **suggestion**. It will <u>not</u> work for everybody and that was never the intention in any case. Hopefully, it will give you several ideas whilst developing your own. And when I mean "your own", be careful: models should never be personalised. They are for business use (generally). "Template" means precisely that. Models built by colleagues should have a similar look and feel. If you think of models circulating in your office, are they all similar? Chances are, that will not be the case. Using styles, spacing and hyperlinks should therefore be consistent. Opening a template will assist.

Difference Between a Template and a Reusable File

A **template file** is a file that has been created specifically to be a template (*i.e.* it is a base for building upon) and whilst the file is created in the usual way, it is saved as either a template or macro-enabled template, which makes it (slightly) more difficult than a standard Excel file to overwrite.

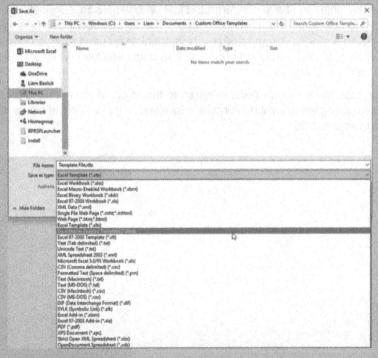

Reusable files can be more problematic, even if this is what many modellers often opt to use. A reusable file is akin to dusting off an "old favourite" and attempting to fit square pegs in round holes. Why? Because this is based on an existing model, not a foundation. The danger here is not only does the model not fit the purpose it is intended for, but irrelevant aspects are not fully deleted leading to potential errors in the model.

Unless scenario modelling where different versions of files need to be kept, always try to start with a template model whereby nothing needs to be deleted.

Let's take a guided tour of a suggested template for financial modelling. Where to start? How about on the front page? Imagine you had just opened up the file:

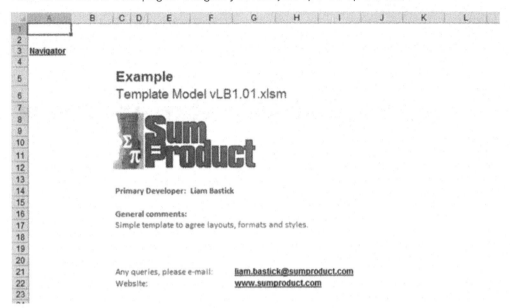

Do you see where the file opens up? I am situated in cell **A1** on the Cover sheet. Now you might be thinking, "wow, big deal", but reflect some more. Whenever you open up a Word or PowerPoint document it always opens in a similar location: the top of page 1. But what about Excel? Excel remains wherever it was saved last.

The problem with Excel is that people are not always good at tidying up after themselves. As mentioned when discussing how to construct a model layout, saving a workbook so that all sheets are repositioned back to cell **A1** and restoring the model back to the front worksheet are just examples of good manners.

This sheet does more than this though. It actually tells me who built it. No need to go to **File->Properties** (wherever that is this week) and finding out the model has been attributed to someone who left in 1997. Moreover, this model actually provides contact details so that end users can get in touch with the author to ask questions where necessary. If you are a model developer, does that scare you? Well, perhaps it should. If we were all a little more accountable for a poor spreadsheet that is often referred to as a "financial model" then maybe we would take more pride in our Excel doodling and meanderings.

Aside from the shameless plug on the sheet (logo), did you notice the other key element on this worksheet? Cell **A3** contains a hyperlink that leads us on to our Table of Contents:

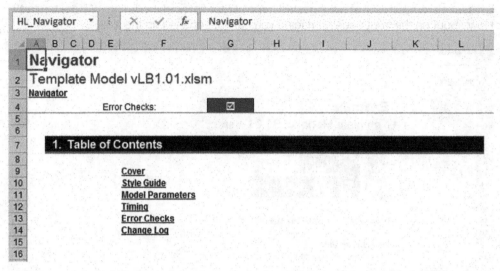

Clicking on the aforementioned hyperlink takes us to the top of the worksheet that contains the Table of Contents, our dedicated navigation page. Do note that the destination cell chosen has been given a range name (**HL_Navigator**). See? I have been following my own advice.

With the overall error check (another hyperlink) clearly visible in cell **G4**, the sheet title and workbook name clearly visible in accordance with my layout suggestions earlier, it is clear to an end user with no guidance whatsoever how to access other worksheets.

There are two other points to note on this worksheet. Firstly, the section heading, "Table of Contents" in row 7, has been given a section number. You may think this is unnecessary on this worksheet as it is the only section. That is true, but on other worksheets, there may be more sections. I want the worksheets all to have a similar look and feel. Other sheets may have more sections. In that case, section numbers would be useful (*e.g.* to make it easier to discuss a printout of the model with a third party over the telephone). Cell **B7** has not been hard-coded. The number has been deduced by formula:

$$=MAX(\$B\$6:\$B6)+1$$

This will add one to the largest value located in column **B** prior to the row the formula is on. This way, if sections are reordered later, the numbering will update automatically (depending upon how you cut or copy the sections).

The second point concerns generating the Table of Contents itself. Contrary to many recipients' beliefs, this has not been created manually. Remember that I discussed macros earlier? Macros are ideal for menial, repetitive tasks and this is one such example.

In this template, I have added a macro that creates the Table of Contents: it generates the worksheets in order and their associated hyperlinks. This is a macro that I would retain only whilst developing the model. Once all sheets have been constructed and the order has been finalised, there would no longer be a reason for this macro.

This macro was created as follows. On the Table of Contents worksheet, called 'Navigator' in the graphic *(below)*, right click on the sheet tab and select 'View code'.

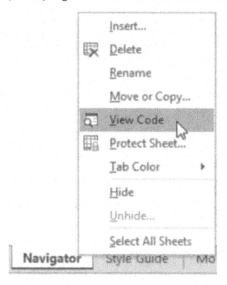

This launches the Visual Basic Editor. Ensuring the right-hand pane is the code for 'Worksheet' and 'Activate', code may then be added to the right-hand pane which will run each time the worksheet is selected:

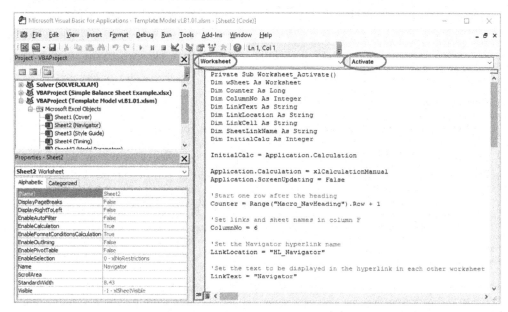

The actual code to use is reproduced below, including comments that explain how it works:

```
Private Sub Worksheet_Activate()
Dim wSheet As Worksheet
Dim Counter As Long
Dim ColumnNo As Integer
Dim LinkText As String
Dim LinkLocation As String
Dim LinkCell As String
Dim SheetLinkName As String
Dim InitialCalc As Integer

InitialCalc = Application.Calculation

Application.Calculation = xlCalculationManual
Application.ScreenUpdating = False

'Start one row after the heading
Counter = Range("Macro_NavHeading").Row + 1

'Set links and sheet names in column F
ColumnNo = 6

'Set the Navigator hyperlink name
LinkLocation = "HL_Navigator"

'Set the text to be displayed in the hyperlink in each other worksheet
LinkText = "Navigator"

'Set which cell in each other worksheet will contain the hyperlink
LinkCell = "A3"

'The following code clears column 6 (column F), types "Table of Contents" in
a pre-designated cell
'(named Macro_NavHeading) and adds a range name for cell A1 (1st row, 1st
column)
'The destination of all hyperlinks are given range names (starting with HL_)
'Range names allow the worksheet name to change without breaking the hyper-
link
'Me refers to the worksheet where this code is (currently the Navigator
worksheet)


With Me
    .Columns(ColumnNo).ClearContents
    .Range("Macro_NavHeading") = "Table of Contents"
    .Range("A1").Name = LinkLocation
End With
```

```vba
'The code looks for all other worksheets and adds a hyperlink in the cell
specified ("A3")
'The hyperlink is called "Navigator" (TextToDisplay), but this may be
changed (variable LinkText)
'Typically cell references are not entered in this way in VBA (reduced flexi-
bility)
'However, putting it in here anchors the hyperlink always to cell A3 and al-
lows for transparency
'Changing the initial Counter value (above) and the column number (6, above
and in Me.Cells())
'moves the location of the Table of Contents list

For Each wSheet In Worksheets

    If wSheet.Name <> Me.Name Then

        'Increment the counter to shift to the next line in the Navigator
sheet
        Counter = Counter + 1

        SheetLinkName = "HL_" & wSheet.Index

        'Make changes to the target worksheet
        With wSheet
            .Range(LinkCell).Name = SheetLinkName
            .Hyperlinks.Add Anchor:=.Range(LinkCell), Address:="", _
            SubAddress:=LinkLocation, TextToDisplay:=LinkText
        End With

        'Add the hyperlink to the Navigator page
        Me.Hyperlinks.Add Anchor:=Me.Cells(Counter, ColumnNo), Address:="",
_
        SubAddress:=SheetLinkName, TextToDisplay:=wSheet.Name

    End If

Next wSheet

Application.Calculation = InitialCalc
Application.ScreenUpdating = True

End Sub
```

This book is not about Visual Basic for Applications, so if you wish to understand it more, feel free to read through the comments and experiment. No doubt some of you may just copy the code, set it, and forget it (works for me)!

The next sheet in the template may surprise you. Many modellers will spend time setting up fancy colour schemes, complete with shading, conditional formatting and so on – and not explain their system of formatting anywhere. As a model auditor, I salute you. All that effort for nought. Together with an element of luck, a successful business thrives on three key components:

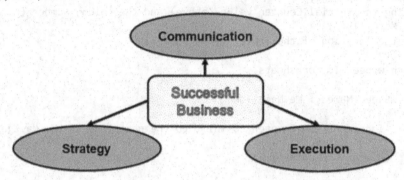

From a modeller's perspective, the key component here is **communication**. The aim of a financial model – aside from quantifying potential business critical decisions – is to communicate the business plan and understand variances so that remedial actions may be taken in a timely manner. If instead you have wonder formulae such as

=IF(ISERROR(IF(INDEX('TI''S & LC''s'!$K$31:$BN$31,MATCH('XYZ (BS)'!R$8,'TI''S & LC''s'!$K$8:$BN$8))<0,0,INDEX('TI''S & LC''s'!$K$31:$BN$31,MATCH('XYZ (BS)'!R$8,'TI''S & LC''s'!$K$8:$BN$8)))=TRUE),0,IF(INDEX('TI''S & LC''s'!$K$31:$BN$31,MATCH('XYZ (BS)'!R$8,'TI''S & LC''s'!$K$8:$BN$8))<0,0,INDEX('TI''S & LC''s'!$K$31:$BN$31,MATCH('XYZ (BS)'!R$8,'TI''S & LC''s'!$K$8:$BN$8))))

you pretty much deserve all you get – and the same can be said for excluding a Styles Key:

Style Guide
Template Model vLB1.01.xlsm
Navigator

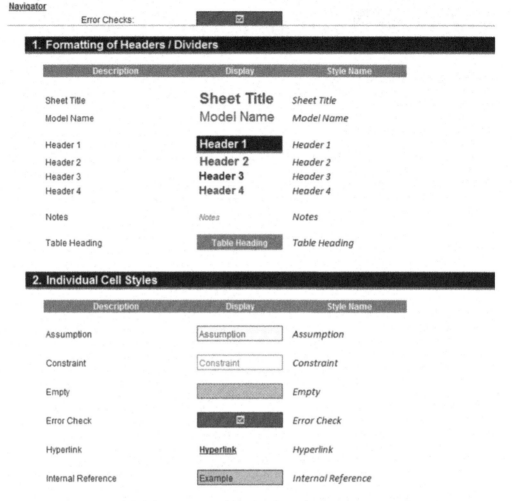

The above is an extract from the template model. There are actually more styles set up in this workbook than displayed above. I would imagine most people and / or organisations would probably not want our colour scheme. That is no problem. Changing an existing style is simple. Within the 'Styles' group of the 'Home' tab (**ALT** + **H** + **J**), right click on the style you wish to modify and click, er, 'Modify…':

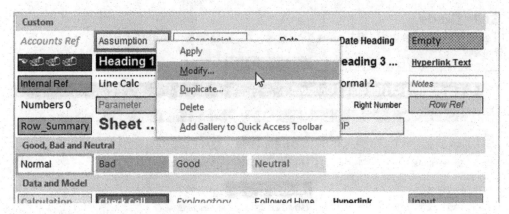

This gives rise to the 'Style' dialog box:

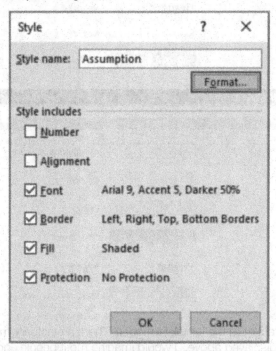

Clicking on the 'Format' button (in some versions of Excel this may be 'Modify') then allows you to revise the Style as discussed previously. Given the 'Style Guide' worksheet has all styles displayed using their respective styles, as you change a style, the style displayed on the worksheet will change accordingly.

Before a template goes "live", developers should agree on spacing, check methodologies and colour schemes. This makes it easier for one modeller to take over another's work and it also promotes brand identity / consistency.

The next sheet, 'Model Parameters', also explains to the end user key constants:

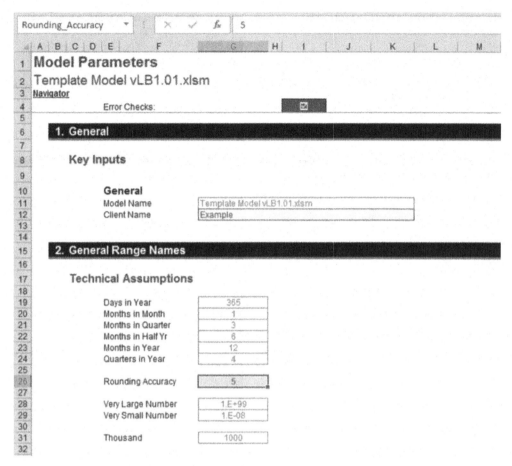

I have talked previously about the distinction between a variable and a constant (constants are sometimes referred to as constraints or parameters). Variables are just the standard inputs of a model, whereas constants are values that are entered to ensure *transparency* so that end users may understand certain constraints that the model is operating under. In this template, as previously suggested, these constants are not only labelled but are also assigned range names (note that the Name Box in the image above contains the range name **Rounding_Accuracy**).

Other types of parameters may be entered here. Our firm works in the professional services industry, so I include a 'Client Name' input (row 12). That may not be relevant to you, but you might wish to include project name, team leader, category, *etc*.

The model name is just that wonderful name formula explained previously:

=IFERROR(MID(CELL("filename",A1),FIND("[",CELL("filename",A1))+1,FIND("]", CELL("filename",A1))-FIND("[",CELL("filename",A1))-1),"")

PhD's available upon request.

The next worksheet is critical for any financial model: you need to get the time series correct. Too often in models, developers hard-code the dates but this leads to a lack of flexibility in the model going forward. I have already explained the mechanics of a Timing worksheet:

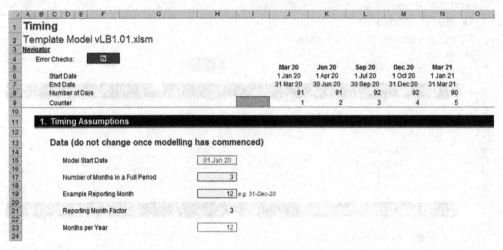

Relax, I am not planning to walk through all of this again. My intention here is simply to show you its application, but I will point out one interesting observation. Have you noticed the shaded cell in cell **I9** in the image above?

This is a "deliberately blank" cell. In an exam, you may have encountered a page such as

THIS PAGE HAS BEEN
LEFT BLANK INTENTIONALLY.

Actually, that has always irked me. By stating that, "This page has been left blank intentionally" the page *isn't* blank. Anyway, I digress. The shaded cell in **I9** *(above)* is analogous to this notion: the cell is <u>required</u> to be blank.

This is because the cells immediately to the right (cells **J9:N9**) are counters and add one to the value in the cell to its immediate left. If a number were to be entered in cell **I9** the counter values would be wrong.

By styling the cell as an **empty cell**, cell protection can prevent the cell being typed in and at the same time convey to the end user that this cell must remain blank. This point does not really have anything to do with time series modelling, but it is salient nonetheless.

The penultimate sheet in this template is the 'Error Checks' summary sheet:

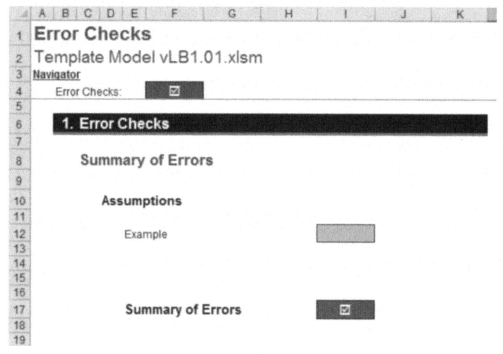

I discussed error checks and the importance of using a summary sheet in the last chapter. Cell **I17** sums the error checks above it in column **I**, with a dummy check set up in cell **I12** for illustrative purposes. Each reportable check should be linked to this sheet via a hyperlink. Then, the check in cell **F4** is simply equal to the summary check (cell **I17**), which it also hyperlinks to. Simple!

The final sheet in the template keeps the auditors happy:

Change Log

Template Model vLB1.01.xlsm

<u>Navigator</u>

Error Checks:

1. Change Log

Summary

Date	Model Version	Details of change	Worksheet Reference	Row, column, cell reference	Author
1 Jan 20	v1.01	I changed it	Change Log	F11	Albert
2 Jan 20	v1.01	So did I.	Timing	A4	Betty
5 Jan 20	v1.01	And me.	Navigator	B9	Charlie

This is simply a worksheet that keeps track of *significant* changes. As a model auditor myself, it would be ludicrous to track *every* change. Can you imagine? You would have to note that you had noted a change and then note that you had noted that you had noted a change…

My general rule for detailing changes is when:

- there is a material change (say, 10% change in one of the key outputs);
- a milestone has been achieved; *or*
- the model is saved with a non-incremental new filename (*e.g.* to draw upon earlier discussions, upon saving when the filename changes from vLB1.19 to vLB2.01 rather than vLB1.20).

These are the main worksheets I would include in a template model. You and your colleagues may decide to add others, such as:

- blank time series sheet (for inputs, calculations, and outputs)
- documentation worksheets
- depreciation schedules
- dashboard summary
- working capital adjustment worksheets
- taxation schedules.

That is all fine; create what works for you and try to never delete a worksheet from an existing template – it's better to add than subtract. If necessary, create more than one template (but this may cause version control issues).

CHAPTER 14: FINANCIAL STATEMENT THEORY

Are you all sleeping comfortably? Then I shall begin. If you have read about my recommended methods for creating financial statements in previous works of mine, you may skip this chapter. If you'd like a refresher, or need a good sleep aid, then stay and enjoy. I need to talk through the financial statements. Yes, I appreciate you may work in finance, be accountants or experienced analysts, but I need to ensure we are all on the same page. The reason is simple. I wish to propose a method of building up a financial model. I have discussed key Excel functions and functionalities, "Best Practice" methodology, layout tips, time series, error checks and even an example template. I want to put it all together to explain why you should build the model in a particular order, but I appreciate no one likes to learn by rote. I need to explain *why*. That is why I need to summarise the layout and purpose of each financial statement.

This summary is simply intended to provide a "jump start" into the world of financial modelling. I am not going to talk about Accounting Standards (such as the International Financial Reporting Standards, IFRS, or the US Generally Accepted Accounting Principles, US GAAP), but rather just explain generic principles. I appreciate things work differently in different parts of the world so I intend to be as general as I can be.

Nevertheless, most accounting regimens recognise the same three primary financial statements, so let's start by reviewing all of them.

Income Statement

Also known as the profit and loss account, revenue statement, statement of financial performance, earnings statement, operating statement, or the statement of operations, this is the financial statement that shows the net operating profit of an entity for a given period of time. It works on an accruals basis, which whether you are an accountant or not, is probably how you think. Allow me to explain.

Most of you will be employees, presumably paid on a monthly basis. If you are such a reader, do you find you have too much month at the end of the money? Most try not to get into that situation; we **accrue**. The Income Statement is essentially the Net Operating Profit (accrued income less accrued expenditure) for a period of time after tax.

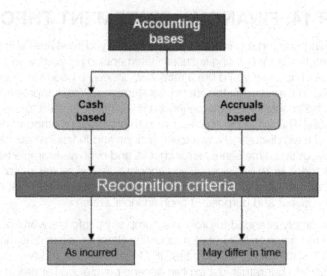

Income is recognised when products are delivered or services are provided, not when payment is received. Similarly, costs are attributed to the period they are incurred, which is not necessarily the period when they are paid. If our company sells one million widgets within the financial year at $1 each and incurs direct cost of 75c per widget, I would expect a gross profit of $250,000, *viz.*

Number of Widgets:	1,000,000
Unit Price:	$ 1.00
Unit Cost:	$ 0.75

	$
Sales	1,000,000
Cost of Goods Sold	(750,000)
Gross Profit	250,000

The cash position could be radically different. We may have had to pay all of the costs and not yet received any monies. However, this is not how we think. We all attribute on an accruals basis, *i.e.* what pertains to the period in question.

And there's more. If I asked, what would you model first, then second, then third, who here was thinking, revenue, costs of goods sold and then operating expenditure? Like it or not, we are walking talking income statements:

Revenue	X
COGS	(X)
Gross Profit	X
Operating Expenditure	(X)
EBITDA	X
Depreciation	(X)
EBIT	X
Interest Expense	(X)
Net Profit Before Tax (NPBT)	X
Tax Expense	(X)
Net Profit After Tax (NPAT)	XX

I love that accountants always put 'X' everywhere. I very much feel loved. Although I can't help feeling that if the Revenue is X and the Costs of Goods Sold is X and the Gross Profit is X, solving for X, X is zero and therefore I have proved all accounting examples are based on not-for-profit organisations... Maybe I need to get out more.

Now most of us are familiar with this income statement, but do you fully appreciate the majesty of its order? The order shouldn't just be learned by rote; it should be understood. For example, Revenue being first makes perfect sense for any company endeavouring to turn a profit. But why is Costs of Goods Sold (COGS) above Operating Expenditure?

Who here was thinking COGS is a variable cost whilst Operating Expenditure is a (stepped) fixed cost? That may be true up to a point, but that explains little. The point is that Costs of Goods Sold is defined as costs **directly** attributable to the sale. Direct costs may include raw material and some labour costs. Indirect costs, on the other hand, are legitimate costs of the business too, just not directly attributable to the sale. Typical examples include rent and utilities. Some could be argued either way (*e.g.* freight); the aim is to be consistent. Therefore, it makes sense that the direct costs are attributed first so that the gross profit (often referred to as **contribution**) can be assessed before the allocation of other costs, which in some instances may be rather arbitrary.

Clearly, Tax Expense is the final expense as it encapsulates all of the other incomes and expenses, but why does Depreciation Expense come before Interest Expense? This is perhaps not so clear cut and I offer two reasons, both of which can be argued with:

1. **Funding:** If you consider the income statement to contain the period's "fair share" of income and expenditure, one significant cost is Capital Expenditure. I am going to talk about this large cost in detail later, but essentially this is ascribed to the purchase of significant business assets to generate future profits for more than one year. It would be wrong to apportion all of this expenditure to one period if the benefit will extend over several / many years and depreciation is the allocation of that cost to

the period in question. If financing, you often want to compare the funding – and its associated costs – against this allocated amount. Therefore, Depreciation Expense should be stated ahead of Interest Expense in the Profit and Loss account.

2. **Valuation:** It is hard to believe that Discounted Cash Flow (DCF) valuations and Net Present Value (NPV) analysis are still fairly recent valuation tools. Prior to the popularity of these approaches, the main method of choice was based on earnings multiples. For example, if companies A and B were similar in operation and profit margins, but B were twice the size of A, shouldn't B have a valuation approximately double A? It's difficult to argue with this logic. Capital structures (*i.e.* the mix of debt to equity) are irrelevant as if a company is purchased, the chances are the capital structure will be revised by the purchaser. Since depreciation is a relevant expense in the earnings multiple calculation, it should appear ahead of the debt expense (*i.e.* interest) so that the earnings figure to be used is readily visible.

Why have I made such a big deal of the order? Go and ask a non-accountant the order they would build a model in: the vast majority would build the income calculations first, the direct costs second and so on. The reason the Income Statement is always so popular is this is how people think. I am a great believer in "if it ain't broke, don't fix it" and this ideology very much applies here.

Balance Sheet

How would you explain the Balance Sheet to a layperson? For those going, "it's the comparison for a moment in time of an entity's assets, liabilities and equity", please explain "assets", "liabilities" and "equity".

The Balance Sheet used to be known as the Net Worth statement; the Income Statement reports on financial performance, the Balance Sheet summarises the corresponding financial position. For a particular moment in time (the date stated) it displayed what a business was worth. It is a cumulative statement aggregating all of the factors that contribute to the value:

Non-Current Assets	
Property, plant and equipment	X
Other non-current assets	X
Total Non-Current Assets	***X***
Current Assets	
Cash	X
Account receivable	X
Other current assets	X
Total Current Assets	***X***
Total Assets	**X**
Current Liabilities	
Accounts payable	X
Other current liabilities	X
Total Current Liabilities	***X***
Non-Current Liabilities	
Debt	X
Other Non-Current Liabilities	X
Total Non-Current Liabilities	***X***
Total Liabilities	**X**
Net Assets	**X**
Equity	
Ordinary Equity	X
Net Profit After Tax (NPAT)	X
Retained Earnings	X
Total Equity	**X**

There are various ways of presenting the Balance Sheet. I am quite fond of this approach as it places Current Assets (items worth something to the business that will be held for less than or equal to one year) next to Current Liabilities (amounts owed that need to be paid within the next year). The ratio Current Assets divided by Current Liabilities assesses a business' ability to pay its bills and Current Assets less Current Liabilities shows the working capital of a business on the face of a primary financial statement.

The line items down to Net Assets are often colloquially known as the "top half" of the Balance Sheet (even if it is nearer 90% of all line items!) and the Total Equity section is known as the "bottom half". What is good about this presentation is the top half summarises what is controlled by a business, whereas the bottom half communicates ownership.

This is why debt is not in the bottom half of the Balance Sheet. In the past, the Equity section was often headed "Financed by" and that always confused me as I did not understand why debt was not there. The reason it is not, is because the shareholders of the business (the Equity) control the debt repayments and servicing. Yes, banks and other financial institutions may put contracts in place, but that is so they may go to court to force companies to pay if payment is not made voluntarily. Consequently, debt is "controlled", it usually is for a period of greater than one year and hence it is not in the bottom half but rather in the Long Term Liabilities section instead.

It may be clearer with another example. Ever bought a house? Did you buy it outright for cash? Chances are if you are lucky enough to be climbing the real estate ladder, in your first purchase you were not the principal stakeholder. So, what about the risks and rewards? If the house goes up significantly in price, will you be splitting the profits in proportion to the amount financed? Of course you wouldn't.

Similarly, imagine the house were to be damaged in a storm. Would you be on the phone the next day to get them to arrange someone to fix it? Good luck with that.

The house would be a non-current (fixed) asset. The mortgage would be the linked non-current liability and – assuming the debt is less than the value of the house – the difference between them would be your equity stake. You control the house and the debt (top half), the equity goes in the bottom half. Easy.

Modellers tend to create Balance Sheets as a bit of an afterthought, but they are more important than that. Values may not be stated in the dollars of the day when purchased (this is known as **historical cost accounting**), which makes any summary meaningless as you are comparing apples with pears, but it is still better than nothing.

In fact, modellers *hate* Balance Sheets. They never seem to balance, reconcile, or be understood. But this can all be circumvented with **control accounts** which I shall discuss in the next chapter. Balance Sheets are essential.

There is one other issue. Balance Sheets by their very nature are cumulative. They are stated at a point in time. They have to balance. So, what if the Balance Sheet did not balance at the model start date? As a modeller, there is nothing you can do about this: this is an opening assumption (the Opening Balance Sheet). If this were to happen to you, reject the Opening Balance Sheet and wait until someone who knows what they are doing gives you a proper one.

All a modeller may ever be held accountable for is that the change in Net Assets equals the change in Total Equity.

Cash Flow Statement

Originally, this was the reconciliatory note that demonstrated how the cash stated on the Balance Sheet had been derived. Changes in Balance Sheet and Income Statement numbers are often known as a "revision of accounting policies" and as long as the auditors and shareholders agree to the changes everyone nods sagely and does not even bat an eyelid. If you start messing around with the Cash Flow Statement that's called fraud and you can go to jail.

There are three sections to the Cash Flow Statement:

1. Operating

2. Investing

3. Financing.

Can you think of an example of an Operating Cash Flow? Who said Revenue? That *isn't* one. Cash Receipts is the cash flow equivalent of Revenue. Be careful: it's making mistakes like this in modelling that cause Balance Sheets not to balance. Similarly, an example of Investing Activities might be Purchases of Non-Current Assets rather than "Capital Expenditure". Debt drawdowns and repayments would be two examples of Financing Activities.

Now, what about the other way around? Where does Interest Paid go? (You didn't realise you were taking a multiple-choice exam?) The "proper" answer is Operating Activities, although I imagine you might be thinking Financing Activities. Three points:

1. As a company expands, sometimes its working capital (essentially cash and cash equivalents readily available after setting aside current bills) is insufficient to facilitate the growth required. Business owners may put more cash into their business (equity) or alternatively take out financing (debt). Should they choose the latter option, the mandatory servicing of that debt is an operational cost of the business – so Interest Paid should go in Operating Activities.

2. A simpler – although not quite correct – explanation is as follows. As detailed above, the Income Statement is essentially the Net Operating Profit after tax. Interest Expense is clearly an expense in the Profit and Loss Account. Therefore, it makes sense that the cash equivalent of Interest Expense – Interest Paid – is in the cash proxy for the P&L, namely the Cash Flows from Operating Activities section.

3. Some companies do indeed place Interest Paid in the Financing section of the Cash Flow Statement. This has been due to past practices (consistency) and case law precedent. So it can reside here, although it probably makes more sense to be in Operating Activities as explained above.

Hopefully, that makes sense. So what about Interest Received? Where should that be placed? Operating? Investing? Financing? In essence:

- Banks and other financial institutions may place Interest Received in Operating Activities. This is because Interest Received may be their main source of income, *e.g.* from mortgages and unsecured loans.

- Other companies may place Interest Received in Investing Income. In this instance, interest has been earned and received from surplus cash on deposit.

Do you see in either scenario it would be incorrect to net off this amount with Interest Paid? The only time the two line items are in the same section (Operating Activities) is when Interest Received is essentially Cash Receipts and why would you want to combine this with debt servicing? This clearly highlights the accounting point of **no net off**. It is better if line items are shown gross so that end users may better understand their financials / forecasts.

One last one: let's consider Dividends Paid. This line item goes in Financing Activities. Some people do not understand why Interest Paid and Dividends Paid are (usually) placed in different sections of the Cash Flow Statement. Interest Paid is the *mandatory* servicing of debt; Dividends Paid is the *voluntary* servicing of equity. Hence it is a financing decision and therefore placed in the Financing Activities section.

I have concentrated on these elements as this is where many modellers make mistakes. Hopefully, this discussion makes things clearer and will prevent you from falling for some of the same traps your peers have repeated time and time again.

This all leads us nicely into the example Cash Flow Statement:

Operating Cash Flows

Cash Receipts	X
Cash Payments	X
Interest Paid	X
Tax Paid	X
Net Operating Cash Flows	**X**

Investing Cash Flows

Interest Received	X
Dividends Received	X
Purchase of Non-Current Assets	X
Net Investing Cash Flows	**X**

Financing Cash Flows

Debt Drawdowns	X
Debt Repayments	X
Ordinary Equity Issuance	X
Ordinary Equity Buybacks	X
Dividends Paid	X
Net Financing Cash Flows	**X**

Net Inc / (Dec) in Cash Held   X

The above is an example of what is known as a **direct** Cash Flow Statement. Pardon? What is one of those?

There are two forms to the Cash Flow Statements: direct and indirect. In many accounting jurisdictions it is stipulated that one variant must be displayed in the financial statements and the other should be the reconciliatory note to said accounts. It usually does not matter which way round this is done, as long as it is consistent from one period to the next.

Both variants affect the Net Operating Cash Flow section only of the Cash Flow Statement. They are defined as follows:

- **Direct:** This can reconcile Operating Cash Flows back to a large proportion of the bank statements. It is a summary of Cash Receipts, Cash Paid, Interest Paid and Tax Paid.

- **Indirect:** This starts with an element of the Income Statement and adds back non-cash items (deducting their cash equivalents) and adjusts for working capital movements.

A typical indirect Cash Flow Statement may compare to the direct version as follows:

		Jun 20	Jun 21	Jun 22	Jun 23	Jun 24
1. Cash Flow Statement						
Direct Cash Flow Statement						
Operating cash flow						
Cash receipts	US$'000	1,304	2,828	4,536	6,432	8,585
Direct cash payments	US$'000	(369)	(809)	(1,318)	(1,882)	(2,522)
Indirect cash payments	US$'000	(60)	(65)	(70)	(72)	(74)
Cash payments	US$'000	(429)	(874)	(1,388)	(1,954)	(2,596)
Interest paid	US$'000	(20)	(9)	(12)	(13)	(14)
Tax paid	US$'000	(40)	(191)	(582)	(955)	(1,372)
Net Operating cash flow	US$'000	815	1,754	2,554	3,509	4,604
Investing cash flows						
Interest received	US$'000	-	5	15	31	54
Purchases of Non-Current Assets	US$'000	(150)	(180)	(120)	(90)	(100)
Net Investing cash flows	US$'000	(150)	(175)	(105)	(59)	(46)
Financing cash flows						
Debt drawdowns	US$'000	20	20	-	-	-
Debt repayments	US$'000	-	-	(15)	(25)	(10)
Ordinary equity issuances	US$'000	15	25	-	10	-
Ordinary equity buybacks	US$'000	-	-	(5)	(5)	(20)
Dividends paid	US$'000	(15)	(149)	(406)	(764)	(1,250)
Net Financing cash flows	US$'000	20	(104)	(426)	(784)	(1,280)
Net increase / (decrease) in cash held	US$'000	685	1,475	2,023	2,666	3,278

As explained above, the indirect version is calculated as follows:

- Start with a line item from the Income Statement (here, Net Profit After Tax)

- Add back non-cash items (Depreciation Expense, Interest Expense and Tax Expense)

- Adjust for working capital movements (increases and decreases in Current Assets and Current Liabilities)

- Deduct the cash equivalents of the non-cash items added back:

  - Instead of Interest **Expense** deduct Interest **Paid**

  - Instead of Tax **Expense** deduct Tax **Paid**

  - Instead of Depreciation Expense *don't do anything*.

So why is Depreciation Expense excluded altogether? If you are thinking, "It's not a cash item", well, Interest Expense and Tax Expense are not cash items either. That is an insufficient reason. What is the cash equivalent of Depreciation Expense? It's the Purchase of Non-Current Assets – and that is found in Investing Activities. The reason Depreciation Expense is excluded is for two reasons: (1) yes, it is a non-cash item, but (2) it is a double count.

1. Cash Flow Statement

Indirect extract

Operating cash flow

		Jun 20	Jun 21	Jun 22	Jun 23	Jun 24
NPAT	US$'000	596	1,352	2,184	3,125	4,223
Add back:						
Depreciation	US$'000	128	173	203	225	213
Interest Expense	US$'000	4	(3)	(18)	(40)	(71)
Tax Expense	US$'000	262	576	936	1,341	1,821
Movements in working capital:						
(inc) / dec in Current Assets	US$'000	(196)	(262)	(284)	(317)	(357)
inc / (dec) in Current Liabilities	US$'000	81	118	128	143	160
Deduct:						
Interest paid	US$'000	(20)	(9)	(12)	(13)	(14)
Tax paid	US$'000	(40)	(191)	(582)	(955)	(1,372)
Net Operating cash flow	US$'000	**815**	**1,754**	**2,554**	**3,509**	**4,604**

So, which one should you model? The vast majority of modellers prefer the indirect version as it is easier to model: most will have modelled an Income Statement and (at least extracts from) the Balance Sheet, so it is easy.

Wrong. This is often what causes problems in Balance Sheet reconciliations. This facilitates the incorporation of **control accounts** and control accounts are a financial modeller's best friends. I will explain further in the next chapter. Use the direct method and calculate the indirect variant later, if required.

There is another important consideration for the Cash Flow Statement as well. Here is a sanitised version of a chart produced from a real-life model:

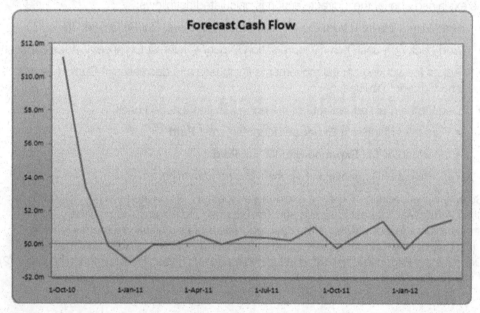

Picture yourself as the Board were back in 2010. Cash is tight and you are trying to determine precisely how much of a bank overdraft facility you require. What might you decide? About $1m? Look again.

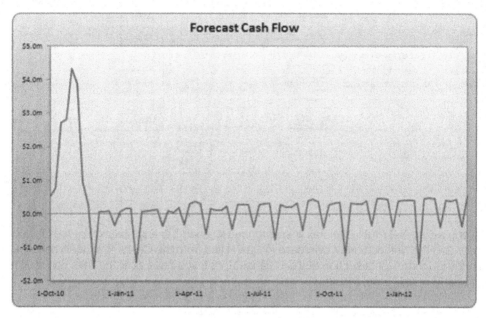

The first chart forecast cash flows on a monthly basis; the second displayed the same data weekly. Clearly, there is cyclicality in the cash flows and the troughs are deeper than the monthly output suggests. $1m would be insufficient according to the second chart. It may be even worse if modelling were undertaken on a daily basis.

The reason we prefer Income Statements to Cash Flow Statements is because the P&L frequently smooths out the inherent volatility in the latter. That is fine for understanding the trends in profitability and the overall financial performance of the business, but it may not be adequate to manage a business on a day-to-day basis. Determining the correct periodicity in a financial model is paramount in order to optimise the information available in financial forecasts.

Model Cash Flow Statements on a direct basis and use the periodicity required by the business to make effective business decisions.

Linking Financial Statements

You may have heard of the phrase "three-way integrated". It's not quite as kinky as it sounds. With regard to financial statements, "three-way" simply means incorporating all three financial statements and "integrated" means that if inputs in financial data were to change, the financials would update accordingly so that the Balance Sheet would still balance.

This requires linking up the financial statements. So how many links do you need? One? Eight? 50? The correct answer, believe it or not, is **two**:

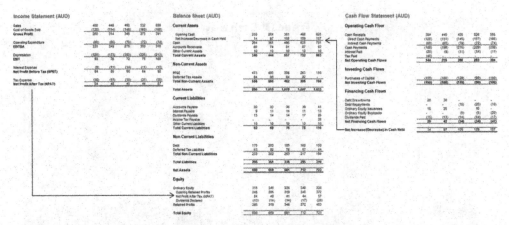

As long as the Net Profit After Tax links into the Retained Earnings section of the Balance Sheet and the Net Increase / Decrease in Cash Held from the Cash Flow Statement links into the Current Assets section of the Balance Sheet, you have all of the links you require to put a financial model together.

Appropriate Order of the Financial Statements

The three financial statements are not equal in size:

- **Income Statement:** This statement is the smallest conceptually. I am neither talking about the magnitude of the numbers nor the number of line items within the financial statements. I am considering how small or large the Income Statement is conceptually compared with the other statements.

  The Income Statement considers the Net Operating Profit after tax. The Cash Flow Statement considers Operating Cash Flows, but it also considers Investing and Financial ones too. The Balance Sheet incorporates the summary (NPAT) of the Income Statements so must also be at least as large. Therefore, the Income Statement is the smallest conceptually.

- **Cash Flow Statement:** This one is "medium" in content. As discussed above, it considers more factors than the Income Statement (albeit from a different perspective), but since it is also summarised in the Balance Sheet (Cash), it is the 'middle' statement.

- **Balance Sheet:** So, by a process of elimination, the Balance Sheet is the largest. Not only does it summarise the other two financial statements, but it also details financials not captured elsewhere, *e.g.* movements between Non-Current and Current, and transfers in Reserves.

Let me explain why this is important. Earlier, I stated that when we start to build a model, in general (after building the prerequisite construction workings in this case) we start to work our way down the Income Statement. That made sense and is commensurate with the magnitude of the concept of the financial statement. It also suggests that the Cash Flow Statement should be built second, which again makes sense, given the Balance Sheet includes a summary of the other two statements.

This gives us our conceptual order of constructing three-way integrated financial statements in a standard model:

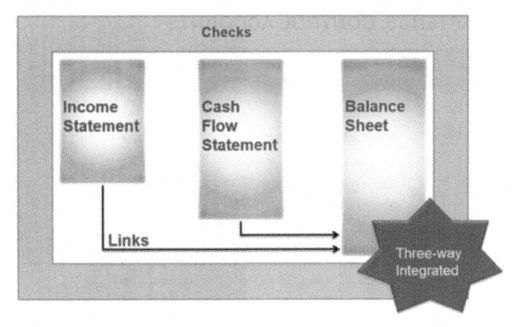

To summarise, we should:

- Build any prerequisite workings
- Develop the three financial statements, building up by line item and total
- Link the Income Statement and Cash Flow Statement into the Balance Sheet
- Add error checks to ensure no errors, that the Balance Sheet balances and is solvent (for example).

But that's not quite right here…

CHAPTER 15: CONTROL ACCOUNTS

I am going to let you in to one of the finance world's best kept secrets. Control accounts are easy to construct and even easier to understand. Consider the reconciliation of the line item Accounts Receivable (or Debtors):

	$
Accounts Receivable b/f	120,000
Sales	64,700
Cash Receipts	(82,750)
Accounts Receivable c/f	101,950

Chances are you have probably seen something similar to this before, maybe from accounting / finance studies. This reconciliation is known as a **control account**: it is a reconciliation of a Balance Sheet item from one period to the next ("b/f" means brought forward or last period and "c/f" means carried forward or current period).

Typically (although not always), the line items between the opening and closing balances come from the Income Statement and Cash Flow Statement. This is consistent with the idea that the Balance Sheet is stated at a point in time whereas the other two statements are for periods of time.

In the example above, if the opening balance of Accounts Receivable is $120,000 and we make further sales in the period of $64,700, assuming there are no bad debts (more on that later) and the cash received is $82,750, then the closing balance for Accounts Receivable has to be $101,950. In other words, assuming the opening balance was $120,000, entering:

- Sales of $64,700 in the Income Statement;
- Cash Receipts of $82,750 (as a positive number) in the Cash Flow Statement; *and*
- Closing Accounts Receivable of $101,950 in the Balance Sheet

means that the three-way integrated financial statements must balance. The end. Modelling financial statements really is that simple.

Control accounts tell you three key things:

1. **Number of calculations that need to be entered into the financial statement so that they balance:** This is always one less than the number of rows in the control account. The reason it is one less is because the opening balance is simply the closing balance calculated from the period before.

2. **The order to build the calculations into the financial statements:** This is always row 2 first, then row 3, then row 4 and so on. Think of it this way: assuming no opening balance (which there would not be in the beginning), if there were no sales, there could be no payments received. If there are no sales and no receipts, the difference between them (the amount owed, the Accounts Receivable) would also be zero. It is a logical order.

3. **It identifies the key driver:** Often you want to undertake sensitivity and scenario analysis in your models, but sometimes you may be unsure which variables should

be included in the analysis. Line 2 of the control account is always the key driver. As above, if there were no sales, there could be no payments received. If there are no sales and no receipts, the difference between them (the amount owed, the Accounts Receivable) would also be zero. To make a point, I have repeated myself deliberately. To make a point, I have repeated myself deliberately. To make a point, I have repeated myself deliberately...

Therefore, in our example, we can conclude:

- In order to make the Balance Sheet balance we need to construct three calculations which need to be incorporated into the financial statements: Sales, Cash Receipts and closing Accounts Receivable.

- The order to calculate them should be Sales, Cash Receipts and finally closing Accounts Receivable.

- The key driver of Accounts Receivable is Sales.

The last two points do not appear to be too controversial, but have you reflected on the first point?

The whole concept of double entry is you do one thing, then do another and *voila!* everything balances. Everything is performed in pairs. But I am telling you that you need to create **three** calculations. Does that go against everything you believe? Have I discussed debits and credits anywhere? (The answer is yes, in that last sentence.) Often in accounting, we talk about "reversing journals": this is code for "given we are forced into a double entry system, this is incorporated as a fiddle factor to make it work". In fact, in the example case study coming up shortly, most control accounts do not contain an even number of calculation entries. So much for double entry.

From the last two sections, I can now formulate an action plan regarding the order to construct a financial model:

Building a Financial Model

This approach remains moot on the order of calculation construction. This is how to build a hassle-free, three-way integrated financial model:

1. Create the forecast chart of accounts from either previous models, existing financials, ledgers, journals, trial balances, etc.

2. Add in the subtotals for each chart of account so that all totals flow through their respective financial statements

3. Add error and other checks to these outputs (e.g. balance checks, cash in cash flow equals cash movement on Balance Sheet) as necessary, updating the 'Error Checks' worksheet as necessary

4. Create the Opening Balance Sheet, ensuring it uses the same format as the forecast Balance Sheet

5. Ensure the Opening Balance Sheet balances, else reject

6. Add checks as necessary

7. Link the financial statements together, adding any checks as necessary

---

8. Zero the Opening Balance Sheet

9. Ensure all checks are "OK"

10. Begin with the Income Statement, take the first line item in this account (e.g. Revenue)

11. Create calculations if not already computed

12. Construct control account

13. Add checks if necessary

14. Link control account to financial statements, ensuring checks are all OK (correct if necessary)

15. Move to the next line item in the financial statement not yet calculated

16. Return to Point 10

17. Once the Income Statement is completed, consider the first line item on the Cash Flow Statement not yet linked

18. Once the Cash Flow Statement is also completed, consider the first line item on the Balance Sheet not yet linked

19. Once the Balance Sheet has been completed, return to the Opening Balance Sheet and add back the original data

20. Correct any opening balance errors if necessary.

It seems a lot, but it really isn't as bad as it sounds. There is one controversial point in here though: *zero the Opening Balance Sheet*. That sounds "interesting" but don't worry, I will be explaining why when we link the financials in the case study.

CHAPTER 16: REPEATABLE CALCULATIONS

Just ahead of the case study, I want to provide a useful technique – but with a word of warning. As you become more expert in using dynamic arrays, there is a temptation to start building really complicated calculations unnecessarily. Remember the "Rule of Thumb":

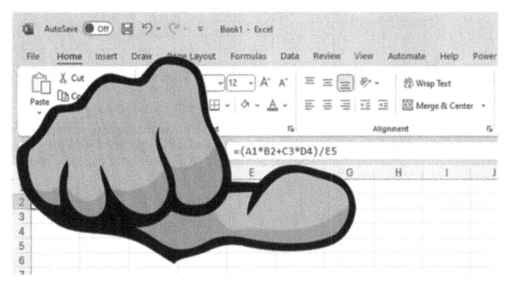

Having said that, a common requirement in building financial models is a repeatable calculation, or more accurately, a repeatable "block" or set of calculations. This might be to calculate forecast revenue for different products, depreciation for different asset classes, debt repayments for different financial instruments or tranches, and so on.

Here, I will demonstrate a technique for repeating such calculations with dynamic arrays. Brace yourselves though – it ain't pretty, but it is pretty effective.

In order to illustrate the approach as clearly as I can, I am going to make the repeatable block simple, so as not to complicate things unnecessarily. With this borne in mind, imagine I have the following collection of inputs:

Number of Periods   10
Number of Scenarios   10

	Op Bal	1	2	3	4	5	6	7	8	9	10
Scenario 1	489	996	668	206	908	519	649	626	237	860	955
Scenario 2	171	182	120	274	415	817	725	953	287	363	558
Scenario 3	516	660	574	904	648	826	725	211	385	563	457
Scenario 4	739	433	107	415	177	338	443	844	537	728	912
Scenario 5	503	693	578	377	992	427	160	639	448	675	274
Scenario 6	124	895	817	283	120	799	834	132	878	723	817
Scenario 7	574	263	251	680	586	889	748	290	952	668	261
Scenario 8	610	305	262	313	172	888	689	837	519	414	694
Scenario 9	419	548	461	840	869	270	130	608	320	277	876
Scenario 10	949	582	612	266	979	269	339	662	160	134	465

This has been set up so that the number of periods (given the range name **Periods**) and the number of scenarios (given the range name **Scenarios**) may vary between one [1] and 10, *e.g.*

	Op Bal	1	2	3	4	5	6
Number of Periods	6						
Number of Scenarios	8						

	Op Bal	1	2	3	4	5	6
Scenario 1	489	996	668	206	908	519	649
Scenario 2	171	182	120	274	415	817	725
Scenario 3	516	660	574	904	648	826	725
Scenario 4	739	433	107	415	177	338	443
Scenario 5	503	693	578	377	992	427	160
Scenario 6	124	895	817	283	120	799	834
Scenario 7	574	263	251	680	586	889	748
Scenario 8	610	305	262	313	172	888	689

I shall leave the values both set at 10 in further screenshots, but you get the idea.

To illustrate my idea, I am going to create a Control Account of this data, assuming the first column represents the opening balances, and the remaining columns state the purchases *(say)* for the particular scenario and period. Therefore, for Scenario 1, I might have a Control Account that looks like this:

Assumption

Scenario Chosen

Scenario Chosen	1

Example Output

Simple Control Account

	Op Bal	1	2	3	4	5	6	7	8	9	10
Opening Balance		489	996	668	206	908	519	649	626	237	860
Additions		996	668	206	908	519	649	626	237	860	955
Deductions		(489)	(996)	(668)	(206)	(908)	(519)	(649)	(626)	(237)	(860)
Closing Balance	489	996	668	206	908	519	649	626	237	860	955

where the Additions are simply those purchases, the Deductions are based upon the Opening Balance, and the Closing Balance is simply the sum of the above. For Scenario 2, the output might look like this:

Assumption

Scenario Chosen

Scenario Chosen	2

Example Output

Simple Control Account

	Op Bal	1	2	3	4	5	6	7	8	9	10
Opening Balance		171	182	120	274	415	817	725	953	287	363
Additions		182	120	274	415	817	725	953	287	363	558
Deductions		(171)	(182)	(120)	(274)	(415)	(817)	(725)	(953)	(287)	(363)
Closing Balance	171	182	120	274	415	817	725	953	287	363	558

and so on.

This calculation may be achieved with **OFFSET, INDEX, SUMIF** and so on, but the formula for calculation of a one-off Control Account where the scenario may be changed is not the focus here. No, what I want is to create all the relevant Control Accounts simultaneously, *e.g.*

	Op Bal	1	2	3	4	5	6	7	8	9	10
Opening Balance		489	996	668	206	908	519	649	626	237	860
Additions		996	668	206	908	519	643	626	237	860	955
Deductions		(489)	(996)	(668)	(206)	(908)	(519)	(649)	(626)	(237)	(860)
Closing Balance	489	996	668	206	908	519	649	626	237	860	955
Opening Balance		171	182	120	274	415	817	725	953	287	363
Additions		182	120	274	415	817	725	953	287	363	558
Deductions		(171)	(182)	(120)	(274)	(415)	(817)	(725)	(953)	(287)	(363)
Closing Balance	171	182	120	274	415	817	725	953	287	363	558
Opening Balance		516	660	574	904	648	826	725	211	385	563
Additions		660	574	904	648	826	725	211	385	563	457
Deductions		(516)	(660)	(574)	(304)	(648)	(826)	(725)	(211)	(385)	(563)
Closing Balance	516	660	574	904	648	826	725	211	385	563	457
Opening Balance		739	433	107	415	177	338	443	844	537	728
Additions		433	107	415	177	338	443	844	537	728	912
Deductions		(739)	(433)	(107)	(415)	(177)	(338)	(443)	(844)	(537)	(728)
Closing Balance	739	433	107	415	177	338	443	844	537	728	912
Opening Balance		503	693	578	377	992	427	160	639	448	675
Additions		693	578	377	992	427	160	639	448	675	274
Deductions		(503)	(693)	(578)	(377)	(992)	(427)	(160)	(639)	(448)	(675)
Closing Balance	503	693	578	377	992	427	160	639	448	675	274
Opening Balance		124	895	817	283	120	799	834	132	878	723
Additions		895	817	283	120	799	834	132	878	723	817
Deductions		(124)	(895)	(817)	(283)	(120)	(799)	(834)	(132)	(878)	(723)
Closing Balance	124	895	817	283	120	799	834	132	878	723	817
Opening Balance		574	263	251	680	586	889	748	290	952	668
Additions		263	251	680	586	889	748	290	952	668	261
Deductions		(574)	(263)	(251)	(680)	(586)	(889)	(748)	(290)	(952)	(668)
Closing Balance	574	263	251	680	586	889	748	290	952	668	261
Opening Balance		610	305	262	313	172	888	689	837	519	414
Additions		305	262	313	172	888	689	837	519	414	694
Deductions		(610)	(305)	(262)	(313)	(172)	(888)	(689)	(837)	(519)	(414)
Closing Balance	610	305	262	313	172	888	689	837	519	414	694
Opening Balance		419	548	461	840	869	270	130	608	320	277
Additions		548	461	840	869	270	130	608	320	277	876
Deductions		(419)	(548)	(461)	(840)	(869)	(270)	(130)	(608)	(320)	(277)
Closing Balance	419	548	461	840	869	270	130	608	320	277	876
Opening Balance		949	582	612	266	979	269	339	662	160	134
Additions		582	612	266	979	269	339	662	160	134	465
Deductions		(949)	(582)	(612)	(266)	(979)	(269)	(339)	(662)	(160)	(134)
Closing Balance	949	582	612	266	979	269	339	662	160	134	465

I understand many of you will have ideas how to create such an output already, but here, I want to construct it using ONE dynamic formula - well, two if you include the labelling! In fact, let's start with the labels as they are simpler.

I will use several key parameters:

Number of Periods	10	*Periods*
Number of Scenarios	10	*Scenarios*
Calculation Rows	4	*Calcs*
Gap Required	2	*Gap*
Calculation Block	6	*Block*

We already know **Periods** and **Scenarios**, but three others are required also:

1. **Calculation Rows:** This is the number of rows in the repeatable block. This could be an input value or you could use a function such as **COUNTA** to count the number of non-blank rows. The cell has been given the range name **Calcs**

2. **Gap Required:** This is the number of blank rows to be inserted between computational areas. This would be an input. The cell has been given the range name **Gap**

3. **Calculation Block:** This is the number of rows required in each repetition. This would be the total of **Calcs + Gap**. The cell has been given the range name **Block**.

Therefore, for 10 scenarios, we would need 10 x (4 calculation rows + 2 blank rows) = 60 rows. This would be mathematically equivalent to

=Scenarios * Block

Furthermore, for each repeated **Block**, we'd require:

- the first row to display the Opening Balance

- the second row to display the Additions

- the third row to display the Deductions

- the fourth row to display the Closing Balance

- the fifth and sixth rows to be blank

- then the cycle repeats.

Therefore, we could do with having a counter going from 1 to 60 which would highlight the range and another cycling through 1, 2, 3, 4, 5 and 6 a total of 10 times to decide what to put on each row. I feel it's time to use various functions including those used for dynamic arrays…

Labels Calculation

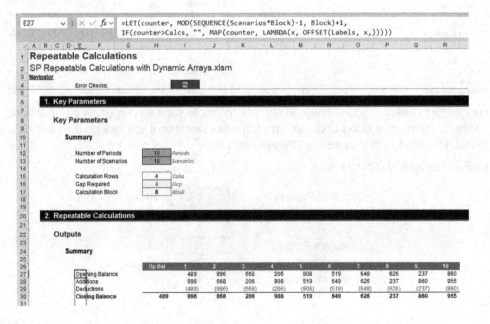

The formula for creating the labels is as follows:

=LET(counter, MOD(SEQUENCE(Scenarios * Block) - 1, Block) + 1,
IF(counter > Calcs, "", MAP(counter, LAMBDA(x, OFFSET(Labels, x,)))))

It might look horrific at first glance, but really, it isn't. Note I have used the convention that "formula level range names" defined by the **LET** function which will not be recognised outside of the **LET** function are lower-case (*e.g.* **counter**), whereas regular range names start with a capital letter (*e.g.* **Scenarios**, **Block**). This theoretically makes range names easier to follow.

We have already noted we require a counter block of **Scenarios * Block** rows (in our example, this will be 60). **SEQUENCE(Scenarios * Block)** will generate this. Then, the formula

MOD(SEQUENCE(Scenarios * Block) - 1, Block) + 1

will generate the array vector

{1, 2, 3, 4, 5, 6, 1, 2, 3, 4, 5, 6, 1, 2, 3, 4, 5, 6, 1, 2, 3, 4, 5, 6, 1, 2, 3, 4, 5, 6,

1, 2, 3, 4, 5, 6, 1, 2, 3, 4, 5, 6, 1, 2, 3, 4, 5, 6, 1, 2, 3, 4, 5, 6, 1, 2, 3, 4, 5, 6}

for a corresponding set of 60 values. **LET** simply names this sequence as **counter**. If the value selected is greater than the number of rows in the calculation block (defined as **Calcs**, with a present value of four [4]), the result will be blank (""), otherwise the formula

MAP(counter, LAMBDA(x, OFFSET(Labels, x,)))

is used. **MAP LAMBDA** is a great formula combination sequence to add to your modelling kitbag. This maps the parameter **x** in the **LAMBDA** value to the **counter**, which rotates through the integer values one [1] through six [6] a total of 10 times. For each value, **OFFSET(Labels, counter,)** is returned. This isn't going to work directly on its own (try it and see) – hence the need for this "**MAP LAMBDA**" trick.

The range name **Labels** simply refers to the cell directly above the labels for the Control Account, *viz.*

Simple Control Account

	Op Bal	1	2	3	4	5	6	7	8	9	10
Opening Balance		171	182	120	274	415	817	725	953	287	363
Additions		182	120	274	415	817	725	953	287	363	558
Deductions		(171)	(182)	(120)	(274)	(415)	(817)	(725)	(953)	(287)	(363)
Closing Balance	171	182	120	274	415	817	725	953	287	363	558

This will then generate a repeated cycle of the four descriptions with two blank rows before the next repetition.

Opening Balance
Additions
Deductions
Closing Balance

Opening Balance
Additions
Deductions
Closing Balance

Opening Balance
Additions
Deductions
Closing Balance

Opening Balance
Additions

Main Formula

So that was the easy one! The main block requires a "slightly" more sophisticated formula. You might want to sit down at this point…

```
=LET(items, Scenarios,
calcrows, Calcs,
grouprows, Block,
periods, I26#,
rowid, SEQUENCE(items * grouprows),
groupid, INT(rowid / grouprows) + 1,
calcid, MOD(rowid - 1, grouprows) + 1,
HSTACK(IF(calcid = calcrows, MAP(groupid, LAMBDA(x, OFFSET(OB_
Base, x,))),""),
DROP(REDUCE("", periods, LAMBDA(col, period, HSTACK(col,
LET(opbal, MAP(groupid, LAMBDA(x, OFFSET(OB_Base, x, period-1))),
adds, MAP(groupid, LAMBDA(x, OFFSET(Period1, x, period-1))),
IF(calcid > calcrows, "", CHOOSE(calcid,
opbal,
adds,
-opbal,
opbal + adds - opbal)))))),, 1)))
```

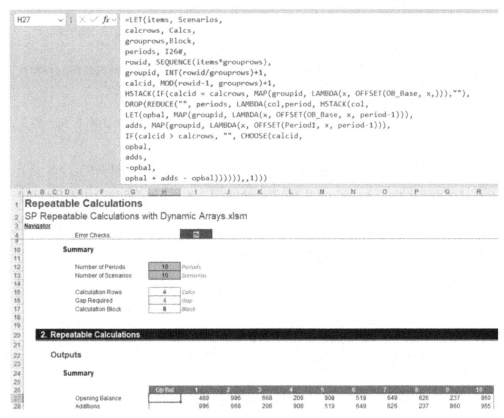

The first seven rows of this lovely formula are simply defining variables and use the same naming convention as previously, *i.e.* lower-case range names have been defined by **LET** and will therefore only be recognised by **LET**, and those starting with a capital letter are "traditional" range names, *i.e.* they will be recognised in other Excel formulae.

- **items** is defined as **Scenarios**, and has a current value of 10 in our example

- **calcrows** is defined as **Calcs**, and has a current value of four [4] in our example

- **grouprows** is defined as **Block**, and has a current value of six [6] in our example

- **periods** is equal to the dynamic array range starting in cell **I26** *(see image above)*. This is the horizontal column counter in our example:

1	2	3	4	5	6	7	8	9	10

- **rowid** is defined as **SEQUENCE(items * grouprows)**, which generates a column vector of the integer values one [1] through 60

- **groupid** is defined as **INT(rowid / grouprows) + 1**, which generates another column vector. This one essentially identifies a calculation block by generating the numbers

  {1, 1, 1, 1, 1, 1, 2, 2, 2, 2, 2, 2, 2, 3, 3, 3, 3, 3, 3, 3, 4, 4, 4, 4, 4, 4, 4, 5, 5, 5, 5, 5, 5, 6, 6, 6, 6, 6, 6, 7, 7, 7, 7, 7, 7, 8, 8, 8, 8, 8, 8, 9, 9, 9, 9, 9, 9, 9, 10, 10, 10, 10, 10, 10, 11}.

- The formula could be refined to make each cycle of six [6] the same value, but it is not necessary as there is always a blank row at the end *(see later)*. It only matters that the calculation rows show the correct calculation number

- **calcid** is defined as **MOD(rowid - 1, grouprows) + 1**, which generates the column vector

   {1, 2, 3, 4, 5, 6, 1, 2, 3, 4, 5, 6, 1, 2, 3, 4, 5, 6, 1, 2, 3, 4, 5, 6, 1, 2, 3, 4, 5, 6,
   1, 2, 3, 4, 5, 6, 1, 2, 3, 4, 5, 6, 1, 2, 3, 4, 5, 6, 1, 2, 3, 4, 5, 6, 1, 2, 3, 4, 5, 6}

- as before.

Immediately after the definition of the **calcid** variable, we have the expression

> **HSTACK(IF(calcid = calcrows, MAP(groupid, LAMBDA(x, OFFSET(OB_Base, x,))),""), Horror_Formula)**

Let's leave the **Horror_Formula** aside and concentrate on the first part. **HSTACK** effectively combines columns, and the formula

> **IF(calcid = calcrows, MAP(groupid, LAMBDA(x, OFFSET(OB_Base, x,))),"")**

defines the first column. As explained above, **calcid** in this example is cycling through the integers one [1] through six [6] a total of 10 times. This will generate a column of 60 rows. Using the **MAP LAMBDA** trick explained earlier, whenever the value of **calcid** equals the **calcrows** (**Calcs**) value of four [4], it will effectively take the corresponding result of

> **OFFSET(OB_Base, groupid,)**

Similar to **Labels** earlier, **OB_Base** has been defined as the cell containing "Op Bal" in the inputs table, *viz.*

	Op Bal	1	2	3	4	5	6	7	8	9	10
Scenario 1	489	996	668	206	908	519	649	626	237	860	955
Scenario 2	171	182	120	274	415	817	725	953	287	363	558
Scenario 3	516	660	574	904	648	826	725	211	385	563	457
Scenario 4	739	433	107	415	177	338	443	844	537	728	912
Scenario 5	503	693	578	377	992	427	160	639	448	675	274
Scenario 6	124	895	817	283	120	799	834	132	878	723	817
Scenario 7	574	263	251	680	586	889	748	290	952	668	261
Scenario 8	610	305	262	313	172	888	689	837	519	414	694
Scenario 9	419	548	461	840	869	270	130	608	320	277	876
Scenario 10	949	582	612	266	979	269	339	662	160	134	465

Therefore:

- the first computation will occur in the fourth row of the column vector, where the corresponding **groupid** value will be one [1] and the value returned will be the Opening Balance for Scenario 1 (489 in our image)

- the second computation will occur in the 10th row of the column vector, where the corresponding **groupid** value will be two [2] and the value returned will be the Opening Balance for Scenario 2 (171 in our image)

   etc.

Put simply, whenever the row represents the position of the final calculation in the block, the Opening Balance will be displayed, otherwise the cell will be empty ("").

	Op Bal
Opening Balance	
Additions	
Deductions	
Closing Balance	489

Opening Balance	
Additions	
Deductions	
Closing Balance	171

Opening Balance	
Additions	
Deductions	
Closing Balance	516

Opening Balance	
Additions	
Deductions	
Closing Balance	739

Opening Balance	
Additions	
Deductions	
Closing Balance	503

Opening Balance	
Additions	
Deductions	
Closing Balance	124

Opening Balance	
Additions	
Deductions	
Closing Balance	574

Opening Balance	
Additions	
Deductions	
Closing Balance	610

Opening Balance	
Additions	
Deductions	
Closing Balance	419

The **HSTACK** formula merely combines this with the computations for all of the periods, which is the **Horror_Formula** cited above.

The next part of the formula (viewing right through to the end) is

> **DROP(Long_Calculation,,1)**

This assumes **Long_Calculation** produces an array, and it will remove the first column of the array produced. That's not too hard to follow. Therefore, it begs the question, what is the array produced?

> **REDUCE("", periods, LAMBDA(col, period, HSTACK(col, More_Calcs...**

Ignoring the **More_Calcs** aspect of the above formula, **REDUCE** will reduce the rest of the calculations to an "accumulated value", which here, will in effect be an array of 60 rows by 11 columns – not 10 when **More_Calcs** is taken into consideration. This is because there is an initial value (**""**) – hence the need to remove this first "starter" column with the **DROP** function above.

REDUCE uses the starter value of **""** (which no doubt will cause errors in the later formulae, but it doesn't matter as it will be removed). It should be noted that we cannot leave this starter value argument empty even though it is optional. This is because **HSTACK** will not work with empty ranges / arrays and therefore will return an #*VALUE!* error.

This formula then continues for **periods** (here, 10) more times, where a **LAMBDA** will define the starter value of the empty range / accumulator (**col**) and then consider each **period** separately. Read the formula carefully: the value **periods** is the array of integer values one [1] through 10, whereas **period** considers each value separately in the following calculations. There is no typographical error in the formula. **More_Calcs** is going to return a column vector each time (one [1] column by 60 rows) and **HSTACK** will simply combine them.

It is all of above in this ***Main Formula*** section that you will replicate for other blocks of repeatable formulae. What follows now is specific to the calculations created here. You may need to use alternative **MAP LAMBDA** combinations to create your formulae, but the idea remains the same.

What now remains is

> **LET(opbal, MAP(groupid, LAMBDA(x, OFFSET(OB_Base, x, period-1))),**
> **adds, MAP(groupid, LAMBDA(x, OFFSET(Period1, x, period-1))),**
> **IF(calcid > calcrows, "", CHOOSE(calcid,**
> **opbal,**
> **adds,**
> **-opbal,**
> **opbal + adds - opbal)))**

We start with more definitions of required calculations:

- **opbal** simply cycles through **groupid**

  {1, 1, 1, 1, 1, 2, 2, 2, 2, 2, 2, 3, 3, 3, 3, 3, 3, 4, 4, 4, 4, 4, 4, 5, 5, 5, 5, 5, 5, 6, 6, 6, 6, 6, 6, 7, 7, 7, 7, 7, 7, 8, 8, 8, 8, 8, 8, 9, 9, 9, 9, 9, 9, 9, 10, 10, 10, 10, 10, 10, 11}

- and then uses the **OFFSET** function **OFFSET(OB_Base, groupid, period-1)** to return the correct value. Due to how the Control Account is defined, this is simply the values in the input table for the given scenario. We have to use **period-1** as the number of columns to move to the right (rather than **period**) as **DROP** will remove the first column, and we need to move no columns for the first **period** [1], one column for the second **period** [2], and so on

- **adds** works similarly, but has a different starting point, using **OFFSET(Period1, groupid, period-1)**. **Period1** is simply the heading cell for the first period, *viz.*

	Op Bal	1	2	3	4	5	6	7	8	9	10
Scenario 1	489	996	668	206	908	519	649	626	237	860	955
Scenario 2	171	182	120	274	415	817	725	953	287	363	558
Scenario 3	516	660	574	904	648	826	725	211	385	563	457
Scenario 4	739	433	107	415	177	338	443	844	537	728	912
Scenario 5	503	693	578	377	992	427	160	639	448	675	274
Scenario 6	124	895	817	283	120	799	834	132	878	723	817
Scenario 7	574	263	251	680	586	889	748	290	952	668	261
Scenario 8	610	305	262	313	172	888	689	837	519	414	694
Scenario 9	419	548	461	840	869	270	130	608	320	277	876
Scenario 10	949	582	612	266	979	269	339	662	160	134	465

Arguably, we could have used **OB_Base** again and changed the column movement to **period** instead.

We do not need to define the Deductions and Closing Balance as the deductions are simply the removal of the opening balance, and the Closing Balance is simply the aggregation of the other elements.

The calculations-specific formulae are now built. The first part,

IF(calcid > calcrows, "",

ensures that blank rows are entered in the cycle once the number of calculations required (**Calcs**, which is four [4]) have been performed for the **Block**. This restricts how many elements we need in our final expression, the **CHOOSE** formula:

CHOOSE(calcid, opbal, adds, -opbal, opbal + adds - opbal)

You may need more than four choices in your set of calculations. It depends on the **Calcs** figure. Here, if **calcid** (shown below)

{1, 2, 3, 4, 5, 6, 1, 2, 3, 4, 5, 6, 1, 2, 3, 4, 5, 6, 1, 2, 3, 4, 5, 6, 1, 2, 3, 4, 5, 6,

1, 2, 3, 4, 5, 6, 1, 2, 3, 4, 5, 6, 1, 2, 3, 4, 5, 6, 1, 2, 3, 4, 5, 6, 1, 2, 3, 4, 5, 6}

has a value of:

1. It will display **opbal**

2. It will display **adds**

3. It will display the negative value of **opbal**

4. It will sum the above, which is **opbal + adds - opbal** (yes, I know I could have just written **adds**, but it has been expressed this way for "clarity").

And that's it: you now have your resulting array when it is all combined, *viz.*

	Op Bal	1	2	3	4	5	6	7	8	9	10
Opening Balance		483	936	668	206	308	519	649	626	237	860
Additions		936	668	206	908	519	649	626	237	860	955
Deductions		(488)	(936)	(668)	(206)	(308)	(519)	(649)	(626)	(237)	(860)
Closing Balance	489	996	668	206	908	519	649	626	237	860	955
Opening Balance		171	182	120	274	415	817	725	953	287	363
Additions		182	120	274	415	817	725	953	287	363	558
Deductions		(171)	(182)	(120)	(274)	(415)	(817)	(725)	(953)	(287)	(363)
Closing Balance	171	182	120	274	415	817	725	953	287	363	558
Opening Balance		516	660	574	904	648	826	725	211	385	563
Additions		660	574	904	648	826	725	211	385	563	457
Deductions		(516)	(660)	(574)	(904)	(648)	(826)	(725)	(211)	(385)	(563)
Closing Balance	516	660	574	904	648	826	725	211	385	563	457
Opening Balance		739	433	107	415	177	338	443	844	537	728
Additions		433	107	415	177	338	443	844	537	728	912
Deductions		(739)	(433)	(107)	(415)	(177)	(338)	(443)	(844)	(537)	(728)
Closing Balance	739	433	107	415	177	338	443	844	537	728	912
Opening Balance		503	693	578	377	992	427	160	639	448	675
Additions		693	578	377	992	427	160	639	448	675	274
Deductions		(503)	(693)	(578)	(377)	(992)	(427)	(160)	(639)	(448)	(675)
Closing Balance	503	693	578	377	992	427	160	639	448	675	274
Opening Balance		124	895	817	283	120	799	834	132	878	723
Additions		895	817	283	120	799	834	132	878	723	817
Deductions		(124)	(895)	(817)	(283)	(120)	(799)	(834)	(132)	(878)	(723)
Closing Balance	124	895	817	283	120	799	834	132	878	723	817
Opening Balance		574	263	251	680	586	889	748	290	952	668
Additions		263	251	680	586	889	748	290	952	668	261
Deductions		(574)	(263)	(251)	(680)	(586)	(889)	(748)	(290)	(952)	(668)
Closing Balance	574	263	251	680	586	889	748	290	952	668	261
Opening Balance		610	305	262	313	172	888	689	837	519	414
Additions		305	262	313	172	888	689	837	519	414	694
Deductions		(610)	(305)	(262)	(313)	(172)	(888)	(689)	(837)	(519)	(414)
Closing Balance	610	305	262	313	172	888	689	837	519	414	694
Opening Balance		419	548	461	840	869	270	130	608	320	277
Additions		548	461	840	869	270	130	608	320	277	876
Deductions		(419)	(548)	(461)	(840)	(869)	(270)	(130)	(608)	(320)	(277)
Closing Balance	419	548	461	840	869	270	130	608	320	277	876
Opening Balance		949	582	612	266	979	269	339	662	160	134
Additions		582	612	266	979	269	339	662	160	134	465
Deductions		(949)	(582)	(612)	(266)	(979)	(269)	(339)	(662)	(160)	(134)
Closing Balance	949	582	612	266	979	269	339	662	160	134	465

You will need to add conditional formatting for borders, and emboldening, but that's not too difficult.

Next Steps

It's true this all looks pretty horrible, but much of the formula is "repeatable" (pun intended). If you use the same range names I have employed, effectively all you need to do is create the formulae for the calculation block (*i.e.* write your equivalent **opbal**, **adds**, *etc.* calculations). It is simply a calculation engine.

One other advanced point to note if you plan to use closing balances. In array (and for that matter, **DAX**) formulae, closing balances usually need to be aggregation formulae (*i.e.* summing all movements to that point). This is avoided here due to specifically using this Control Account. This was in order to highlight the approach and not include unnecessary complications.

And if you are feeling even "more advanced", perhaps you can modify the formula to turn it into its own **LAMBDA** and simplify the formula!!

I think we're ready for the case study…

CHAPTER 17: EXAMPLE MODEL BUILD

Now before we all get carried away here, let me be clear: this is a simple model build. It wouldn't matter how complicated I made this model, it would never be exactly what you, dear reader, would want. So, I am not even going to try. It's going to be complicated enough just adding in dynamic array formulae. But it's going to be *so* worth it.

It is not possible to have an example that covers everything. If I could, I'd be much richer, trust me. Therefore, you may not find exactly what you want in this example. You could argue, where are alternate inventory methodologies, provisions, foreign exchange, consolidations, indirect taxes and so on. Some cannot be covered in detail in a general book (*e.g.* indirect taxes vary from country to country and in many cases are ignored unless entities have cash flow difficulties), some are just extrapolations of what we are covering (*e.g.* inventory can be accounted for many different ways, we're just covering one here).

The intention of this case study is to demonstrate key concepts that come up time and time again, identify some of the traps and reinforce a process that should guide you each and every time through your model build, no matter how simple or complex. Don't worry about any specific formulae; ensure you get the concepts. **Concepts are key.**

The plan is simple. We are going to apply most of what we have done before in a contrived yet simple case study that will cover many of the key concepts of financial modelling; it will mirror the model created in *Introduction to Financial Modelling*, but also it will include inventory as that is particularly awkward when utilising dynamic arrays. Some readers will want to model every last detail; others may use the accompanying material to review what has been built instead. That's up to you. All I ask is you work your way through this case study in the way that most benefits you.

Ready..?

CHAPTER 17.1: INITIAL STRUCTURE

Do you really think I am going to advocate that you should build your financial model from scratch? Of course I'm not. Let's get someone else to do it instead. That's right: I'm going to get *you* to do it.

This is precisely where the template from Chapter 13 comes in. Let's use that and save it as

Financial Model with Dynamic Arrays.xlsm

I will make some "standard" assumptions about page set up, including:

- how many rows between headings in the same section (1)

- how many rows between sections (2)

- width of columns that are blank (3). Remember, worksheets should be consistent, so deleting columns in particular can cause problems within links between worksheets and hiding columns may cause confusion. These are examples of *consistency* and *transparency* respectively

- width of columns where text may be indented (3)

- the number of narrower columns at the left of the worksheet (5)

- the cell the overall error check will be in for <u>most</u> worksheets (cell **F4**). I reserve the right to move it if it will appear too wide or too narrow on certain sheets

- the column for units (column **G**)

- the columns for time series forecasting (column **J** onwards)

The details in brackets are what I have chosen. This is not mandatory. You should just be *consistent*, not just within the model you are working on, but across all models you develop. This makes it easier for regular users to understand any new model you create.

We are going to start with the template model, with the above parameters incorporated. Before we add to it, let's make sure we are all on the same page regarding time series assumptions. This means creating the following inputs on the Timing worksheet. I did warn you this would change.

Cell **H15** is <u>not</u> an assumption cell. It is a constant and if the sheet were to be protected it would not be possible to change this date. In fact, once the model build has commenced this cell should not be revised (this is why the heading in cell **C13** reads "Data (do not change once modelling has commenced)". This is because if data is entered for a particular time period and then the dates were to change, input values may become associated with the wrong period and / or duration.

Cell **H15** is so important it is even given its own range name: **Model_Start_Date**. Even if output analysis were to change (*i.e.* the dates on an output sheet started with a later date), the calculations would work using a **LOOKUP** arrangement so that on input and calculation sheets the **Model_Start_Date** would always start in the first column reserved for time series (on the above example calculation sheet, it is column **J**).

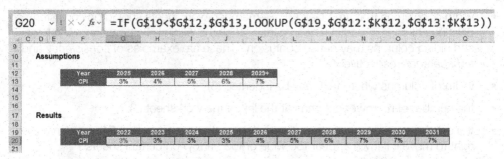

| G20 | | × ✓ fx | =IF(G$19<$G$12,$G$13,LOOKUP(G$19,$G$12:$K$12,$G$13:$K$13)) |

	C D E	F	G	H	I	J	K	L	M	N	O	P	Q
9													
10	**Assumptions**												
11													
12		Year	2025	2026	2027	2028	2029+						
13		CPI	3%	4%	5%	6%	7%						
14													
15													
16													
17	**Results**												
18													
19		Year	2022	2023	2024	2025	2026	2027	2028	2029	2030	2031	
20		CPI	3%	3%	3%	3%	4%	5%	6%	7%	7%	7%	
21													

Cell **H17** (Number of Months in a Full Period) should be 12 and the Example Reporting Month (cell **H19**) would be calculated as 6 (*i.e.* June will be the period end). With five time periods, this will give us five full years from 1 July 2024 to 30 June 2029 inclusive:

		Jun 25	Jun 26	Jun 27	Jun 28	Jun 29
Start Date		1 Jul 24	1 Jul 25	1 Jul 26	1 Jul 27	1 Jul 28
End Date		30 Jun 25	30 Jun 26	30 Jun 27	30 Jun 28	30 Jun 29
Number of Days		365	365	365	366	365
Counter		1	2	3	4	5

Models will not always be a simple as this. Quite frequently, the first period may not be of equal duration (this is known as a **stub period**). For example, imagine you were forecasting annually but the first period was only for the last nine months of the financial year. If sales were $45,000 and the year-on-year growth rate was 10%, many models would calculate the Year 2 amount to be $49,500, being $45,000 multiplied by 1 + 10%. This is wrong. The correct calculation is:

$$=\$45,000 \times 12 / 9 \times (1 + 10\%)$$

which is actually $66,000. The 12 / 9 factor scales up the stub period to an equivalent annual figure (it may need to be computed more accurately on a daily basis). Make sure you do not become a victim of this common error.

With this we have adjusted our **Timing** sheet, but there is a little more work to do to make it dynamic:

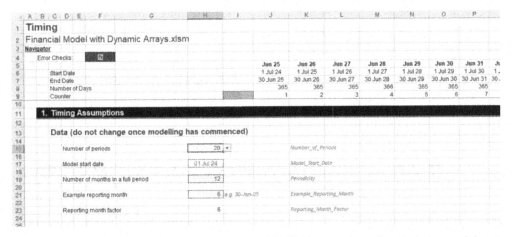

Firstly, we've added an additional input into cell **H15**, the number of periods to model, set to twenty for our example. List Data Validation is used here to limit this input to a list of numbers, integers from five [5] to 20 in this example.

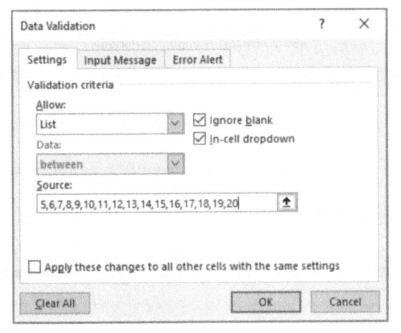

This is then considered by our adjusted formula in cell **J9**:

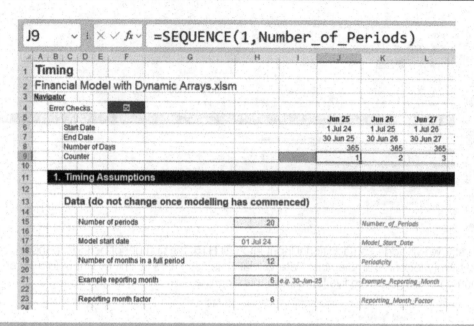

=SEQUENCE(1,Number_of_Periods)

This will ensure that our Counter in row 9 runs from one [1] to our number of periods input.

Let's now consider the end date, calculated by the formula in cell **J7**:

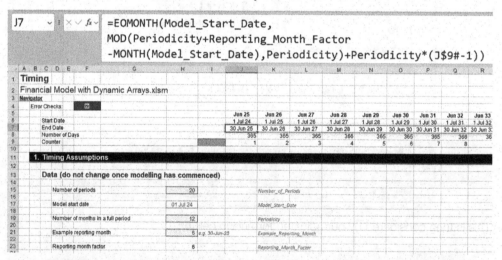

=EOMONTH(Model_Start_Date,MOD(Periodicity+Reporting_Month_Factor-MONTH(Model_Start_Date),Periodicity)+Periodicity*(J$9#-1))

This is simply the formula we covered earlier when discussing time series analysis, modified to spill in line with the rest of the formulae here.

The formula in cell **J6** considers the counter and our end dates to return the start dates:

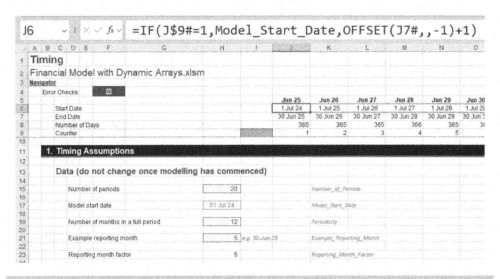

=IF(J$9#=1,Model_Start_Date,OFFSET(J7#,,-1)+1)

Note the **#** operator after our reference to **J$9** for the first argument of the **IF** statement here. This ensures that this formula will be carried out for each of our values in the array that starts in cell **J9** (generated by the **SEQUENCE** function). If the counter is equal to one [1] (*i.e.* in the first period) the start date returned will be equal to our input **Model_Start_Date**, else this formula makes use of the **OFFSET** function to return the previous period's end date and adds one [1] to this. This will (in all periods besides the first) thus return the day after the previous period's end date, which will always be the start date of the next period.

Finally, we have two very simple formulae, one in cell **J8** to calculate our number of days:

=J7#-J6#+1

this simply subtracts the start date from the end date and adds one to return the number of days in the period, and in cell **J5** the formula:

=J7#

is used to create a heading equal to the end date of the period, formatted slightly differently.

There is one more trick we've utilised, notice the black cells in row 11:

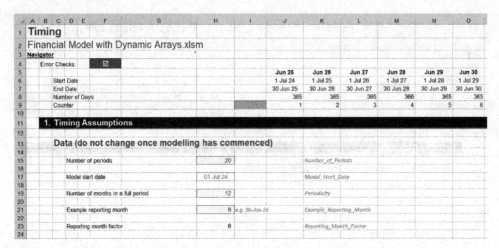

We've used Conditional Formatting to ensure that this black bar will remain the appropriate length, even when the number of periods changes but we'll look at this in more depth shortly.

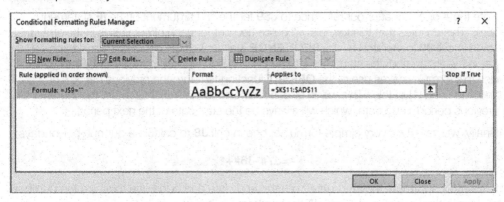

Keep the number of periods (cell **H15**) to 20 momentarily. This will make things more manageable whilst we build this model.

With that, we now have a fully dynamic Timing worksheet!

CHAPTER 17.2: ADDING SHEETS

The template is great as far as it goes, but we might need to add sheets. One way is to copy an existing worksheet, but Excel is unsure what to do with range names on the worksheet being copied. For each and every range name associated with the copied worksheet(s), you will have to decide whether to create a duplicate range name. If you have 10,000 range names, you have a fun day planned. There are no "Yes To All" or "No To All" options. Here's a tip: **don't**.

The problem with a copied range name, you may recall, is it is worksheet rather than workbook specific which can cause problems. Therefore, try not to copy a worksheet containing range names, but if you have to, always decline creating a new range name definition for that worksheet. Always refer range names back to the original worksheet.

Therefore, in this section I am not going to create a sheet copied from another: I will create one from anew. We can start by selecting the sheet tab to the left of where we want the worksheet (here, Timing) and then clicking on the "+" button at the end of the tabs section:

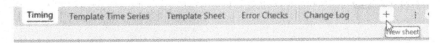

This will create a new worksheet. Let's delete the existing worksheets 'Template Time Series' and 'Change Log'. Then, let's return to the newly created sheet and right-click to rename it (we will call this one 'Calculations') and select the first five [5] columns. Right click, select column width and adjust the width to three [3].

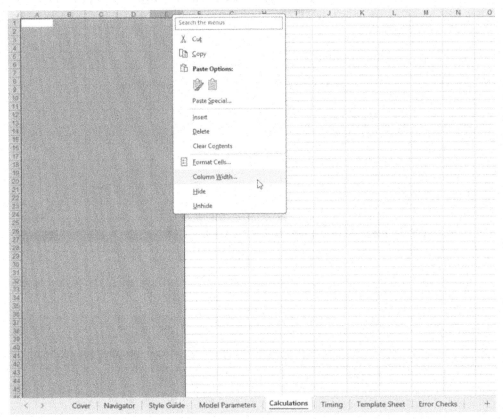

We can take the top section (cells **A1:AD13**) from our Timing sheet and just copy it over to the new sheet:

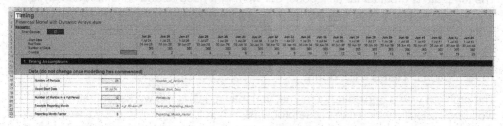

Paste this copied range into cell **A1** of the Calculations worksheet. Now, let's change the number of periods to five [5]. The Calculations sheet should look as follows:

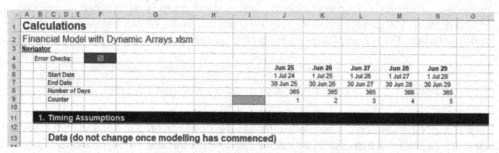

Select cell **A10** and go to **View -> Freeze Panes -> Freeze Panes** (**ALT** + **W** + **F** + **F**). Next, remove the formatting in cell **I9**. Change cell **C13** to the word "Heading" and make cell **C11** the formula

=A1

The top of the Calculations worksheet should now appear as follows:

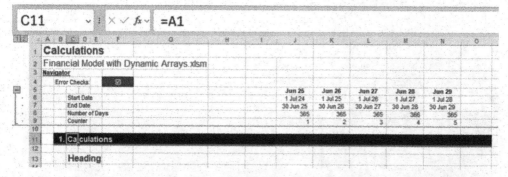

Cell **C6** should become the formula **=Timing!C6** and this formula should then be copied into cells **C7:C9**. Cell **J5** should have the formula changed to

=Timing!J5#

This formula should then be copied into cells **J6:J9**. These new formulae should then be reformatted similar to cells **K5:K9**, *viz.*

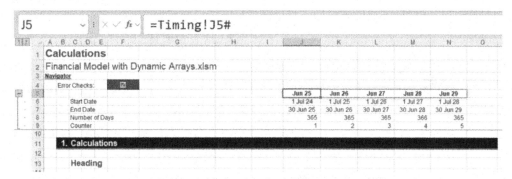

Using this new worksheet as a template, create new sheets labelled 'General Assumptions', 'Income Statement', 'Balance Sheet' and 'Cash Flow Statement', *e.g.*

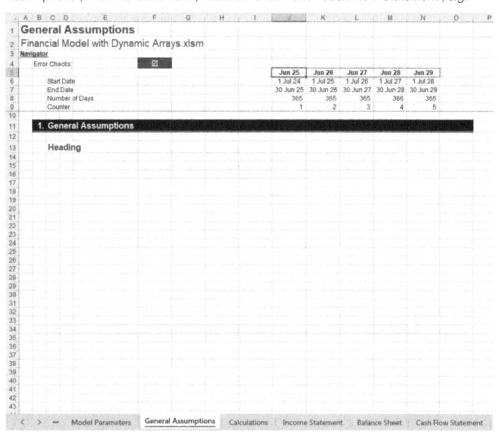

The 'Opening Balance Sheet' should be created slightly differently:

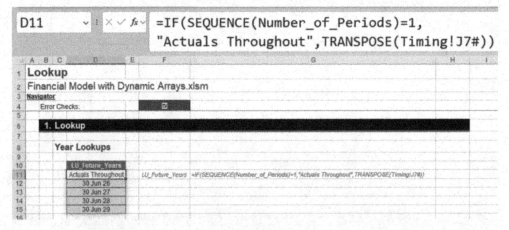

Here, no date timings are required in column **J** onwards, and only the formula

=Model_Start_Date-1

needs to be entered into cell **I5**. I shall return to this worksheet soon.

Our 'Lookup' sheet will also be a bit different as we just need it as a reference for our years. We can use the formula:

=IF(SEQUENCE(Number_of_Periods)=1,"Actuals Throughout",TRANSPOSE(Timing!J7#))

in cell **D11**. This will be used for Data Validation for our operating expenditure inputs.

An issue we run into with dynamic arrays is that as the arrays increase or decrease in size, the formatting doesn't increase or decrease with it. We can solve this issue using conditional formatting, as we did on the Timing worksheet. Conditional formatting allows us to set up formulae that dictate the formatting of a cell. This can be achieved wherever we need it by selecting the relevant cells and then selecting **Home -> Styles ->**

Conditional Formatting (**ALT** + **O** + **D**). Then, select 'New Rule', then 'Use a formula to determine which cells to format'. For the rule description our formula is

$$=J\$9=""$$

This applies the formatting when the equivalent cell in the 'Counter' row is empty. So, outside of the columns that contain our time series, the cells will be formatted to appear blank.

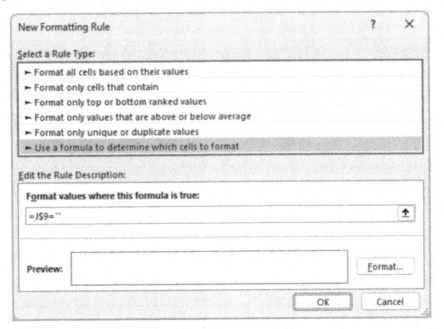

Go into format, then fill, and select 'No Color' for the background colour and set the number formatting to ";;;":

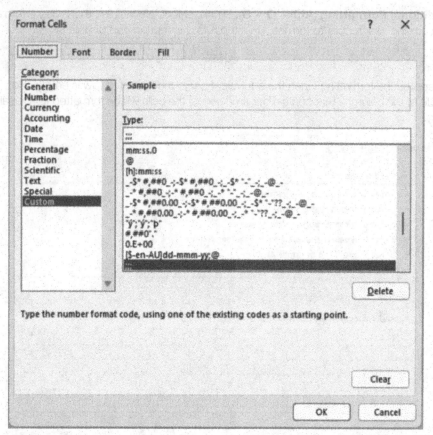

Select OK on both dialogs to return back to the sheet. This should be applied as required to any cells that may sometimes be blank, depending on the **Number_of_ Periods** assumption. In this case study this will be columns **J:AC** for most calculations. There are some exceptions however. For example, the black bars (the 'Heading 1' styled cells) are expected to extend out one column beyond the calculations and as such should have this rule applied in columns **K:AD**. The Lookup sheet is also an exception, as data goes down a column rather than across a row on this sheet, the rule should apply to the range **D12:D30**.

CHAPTER 17.3: CREATING THE FINANCIAL STATEMENT WORKSHEETS

> **Building a Financial Model**
> 1. Create the forecast chart of accounts from either previous models, existing financials, ledgers, journals, trial balances, *etc*.

Before we do this, let's add items to the 'Model Parameters' worksheet. Please add the following Section 3, including range names:

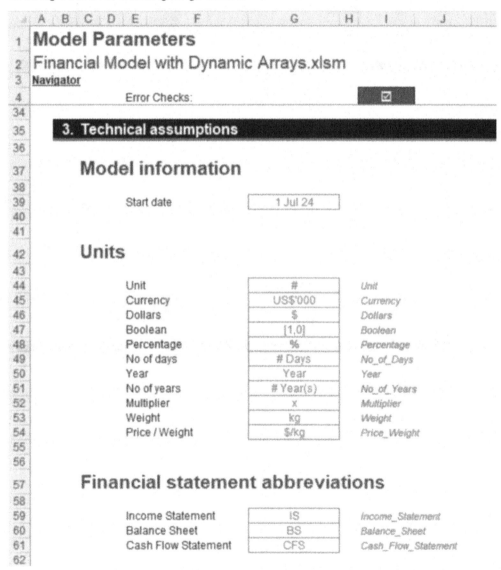

Once this is done, it's time to start setting up the financial statements. The line items will need to be agreed upon prior to creation. Obviously, this will impact the order in which you perform the calculations. We're going to create the outline for these statements, leaving the values blank for the time being.

The units in column **G** are linked to our model parameters with the formula **=Currency** to automatically update.

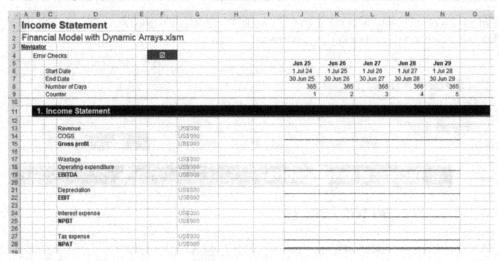

Next up is the Cash Flow Statement, prepared on a Direct basis:

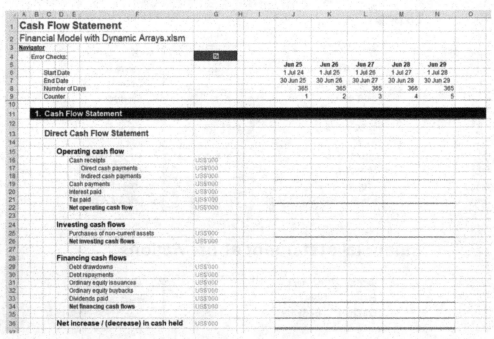

Then, the Balance Sheet:

Finally, the Opening Balance Sheet:

Opening Balance Sheet

Financial Model with Dynamic Arrays.xlsm

Navigator

Error Checks: ☑

				Jun 24
Start Date				
End Date				
Number of Days				
Counter				

1. Opening Balance Sheet

Current assets			
Cash	US$'000		2,500
Accounts receivable	US$'000		50
Inventory	US$'000		50
Other current assets	US$'000		10
Total current assets	US$'000		2,610
Non-current assets			
PP&E	US$'000		450
Deferred tax assets	US$'000		75
Total non-current assets	US$'000		525
Total assets	US$'000		3,135
Current liabilities			
Accounts payable	US$'000		30
Interest payable	US$'000		20
Dividends payable	US$'000		15
Tax payable	US$'000		40
Other current liabilities	US$'000		10
Total current liabilities	US$'000		115
Non-current liabilities			
Debt	US$'000		150
Deferred tax liabilities	US$'000		25
Total non-current liabilities	US$'000		175
Total liabilities	US$'000		290
Net assets	US$'000		2,845
Equity			
Ordinary equity	US$'000		300
Opening retained profits	US$'000		2,520
NPAT	US$'000		25
Dividends declared	US$'000		-
Retained profits	US$'000		2,545
Total equity	US$'000		2,845

Before we move on, let's take a closer look at the Opening Balance Sheet. Not only have we included totals where appropriate, compare the Opening Balance Sheet to the Balance Sheet:

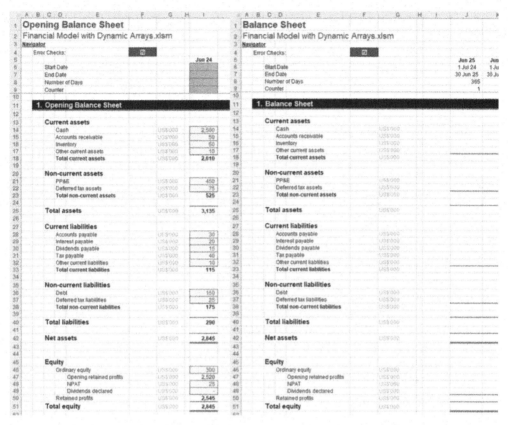

You may notice that all of the line items are in the same rows – consistency! One of the ways we've achieved this is by bringing in rows 6:9, despite them not being required. Also, notice that our opening balances are in column **I**, the column before column **J**, where our Balance Sheet starts.

There is one more thing to note, we've used a cheat to ensure the Opening Balance Sheet always balances:

=I42-SUM(I46,I48,I49)

	A B C D	E	F	G H	I	J	K	L
1	**Opening Balance Sheet**							
2	Financial Model with Dynamic Arrays.xlsm							
3	Navigator							
4	Error Checks:		☑					
5					Jun 24			
6	Start Date							
7	End Date							
8	Number of Days							
9	Counter							
41								
42	**Net assets**			US$'000	2,845			
43								
44								
45	**Equity**							
46	Ordinary equity			US$'000	300			
47	Opening retained profits			US$'000	2,520			
48	NPAT			US$'000	25			
49	Dividends declared			US$'000	-			
50	Retained profits			US$'000	2,545			
51	**Total equity**			US$'000	2,845			
52								

Cell **I47** contains a formula, ensuring that Total equity will always equal Net assets. A modeller can only be held responsible for the movement in net assets equalling the movement in net equity, so if the Opening Balance Sheet does not balance we would need to reject it – to ensure that this model will always work, we've used this cheat. You may notice a distinct lack of any dynamic arrays on this sheet, that's because we're only ever considering one period here! Making these formulae dynamic would be overkill.

CHAPTER 17.4: PREPARING THE FINANCIAL STATEMENT WORKSHEETS

With the outlines for our financial statements put together, we now need to add in the totals to ensure our figures flow through. In a normal financial modelling course, we wouldn't cover this step in detail as it is quite trivial, but there are a few subtle tweaks to be made when working with dynamic arrays.

At this stage, we will need the maximum number of periods (20 in our model) – but this is only a temporary measure. So that the model remains readable, whilst I select 20 as the **Number_of_Periods** (cell **H15** of the Timing worksheet), I shall hide Periods 5 to 19 inclusive – so take care with the next few screenshots!

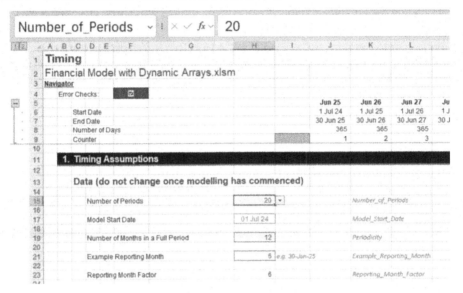

Let's begin with the Income Statement, populating the Gross Profit line on our Income Statement:

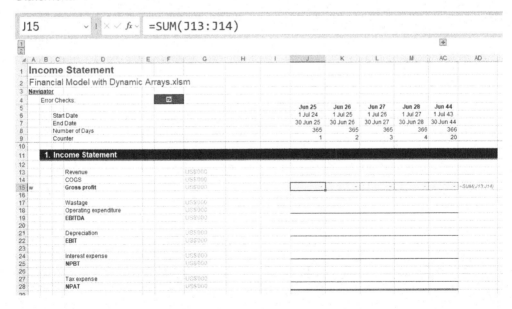

Here, I have summed the Revenue and COGS line to calculate Gross Profit, *e.g.* in cell **J15** I have

However, this is not yet quite right. This is not yet a dynamic array, so if we change the number of periods, the formula will not disappear although we may hide it with the aforementioned conditional formatting.

I will need to return to this formula later when it can be made dynamic, which will only be possible when the formulae in both rows 13 and 14 are dynamic arrays. In the meantime, I have formatted it with our WIP (Work in Progress) Style. It is gaudy so you cannot help but notice it – deliberately.

Did you also note the letter "w" placed in cell **A15**? This is to highlight the issue. You may recall from my Layout section (Chapter 10) that column **A** is used to help us notice aspects of the model that are not yet completed as they will be identified when resetting worksheets and saving the file.

This treatment is then replicated for the remaining totals on the Income Statement:

	A B C	D	E	F	G	H	I	J	K	L	M	AC	AD
1	**Income Statement**												
2	Financial Model with Dynamic Arrays.xlsm												
3	Navigator												
4	Error Checks:				☑								
5								Jun 25	Jun 26	Jun 27	Jun 28	Jun 44	
6	Start Date							1 Jul 24	1 Jul 25	1 Jul 26	1 Jul 27	1 Jul 43	
7	End Date							30 Jun 25	30 Jun 26	30 Jun 27	30 Jun 28	30 Jun 44	
8	Number of Days							365	365	365	366	366	
9	Counter							1	2	3	4	20	
10													
11	**1. Income Statement**												
12													
13	Revenue				US$'000								
14	COGS				US$'000								
15 w	**Gross profit**				US$'000			-	-	-	-	-	=SUM(J13:J14)
16													
17	Wastage				US$'000								
18	Operating expenditure				US$'000								
19 w	**EBITDA**				US$'000			-	-	-	-	-	=SUM(J15,J17:J18)
20													
21	Depreciation				US$'000								
22 w	**EBIT**				US$'000			-	-	-	-	-	=SUM(J19,J21)
23													
24	Interest expense				US$'000								
25 w	**NPBT**				US$'000			-	-	-	-	-	=SUM(J22,J24)
26													
27	Tax expense				US$'000								
28 w	**NPAT**				US$'000			-	-	-	-	-	=SUM(J25,J27)

As well as the Balance Sheet:

Balance Sheet

Financial Model with Dynamic Arrays.xlsm

Navigator

Error Checks: ☑

			Jun 25	Jun 26	Jun 27	Jun 28	Jun 44	
	Start Date		1 Jul 24	1 Jul 25	1 Jul 26	1 Jul 27	1 Jul 43	
	End Date		30 Jun 25	30 Jun 26	30 Jun 27	30 Jun 28	30 Jun 44	
	Number of Days		365	365	365	366	366	
	Counter		1	2	3	4	20	

1. Balance Sheet

Current assets								
Cash	US$'000							
Accounts receivable	US$'000							
Inventory	US$'000							
Other current assets	US$'000							
w	Total current assets	US$'000	-	-	-	-	-	=SUM(J14:J17)
Non-current assets								
PP&E	US$'000							
Deferred tax assets	US$'000							
w	Total non-current assets	US$'000	-	-	-	-	-	=SUM(J21:J22)
w	**Total assets**	US$'000	-	-	-	-	-	=SUM(J18:J23)
Current liabilities								
Accounts payable	US$'000							
Interest payable	US$'000							
Dividends payable	US$'000							
Tax payable	US$'000							
Other current liabilities	US$'000							
w	Total current liabilities	US$'000	-	-	-	-	-	=SUM(J28:J32)
Non-current liabilities								
Debt	US$'000							
Deferred tax liabilities	US$'000							
w	Total non-current liabilities	US$'000	-	-	-	-	-	=SUM(J36:J37)
w	**Total liabilities**	US$'000	-	-	-	-	-	=SUM(J33:J38)
w	**Net assets**	US$'000	-	-	-	-	-	=J25-J40
Equity								
Ordinary equity	US$'000							
Opening retained profits	US$'000							
NPAT	US$'000							
Dividends declared	US$'000							
w	Retained profits	US$'000	-	-	-	-	-	=SUM(J47:J49)
w	**Total equity**	US$'000	-	-	-	-	-	=SUM(J48:J50)

And finally, the Cash Flow Statement:

Cash Flow Statement

Financial Model with Dynamic Arrays.xlsm

Navigator

Error Checks: ☑

			Jun 25	Jun 26	Jun 27	Jun 28	Jun 44	
	Start Date		1 Jul 24	1 Jul 25	1 Jul 26	1 Jul 27	1 Jul 43	
	End Date		30 Jun 25	30 Jun 26	30 Jun 27	30 Jun 28	30 Jun 44	
	Number of Days		365	365	365	366	366	
	Counter		1	2	3	4	20	

1. Cash Flow Statement

Direct Cash Flow Statement								
Operating cash flow								
Cash receipts	US$'000							
Direct cash payments	US$'000							
Indirect cash payments	US$'000							
w	Cash payments	US$'000	-	-	-	-	-	=SUM(J17:J18)
Interest paid	US$'000							
Tax paid	US$'000							
w	Net operating cash flow	US$'000	-	-	-	-	-	=SUM(J16,J19:J21)
Investing cash flows								
Purchases of non-current assets	US$'000							
w	Net investing cash flows	US$'000	-	-	-	-	-	=SUM(J25)
Financing cash flows								
Debt drawdowns	US$'000							
Debt repayments	US$'000							
Ordinary equity issuances	US$'000							
Ordinary equity buybacks	US$'000							
Dividends paid	US$'000							
w	Net financing cash flows	US$'000	-	-	-	-	-	=SUM(J29:J33)
w	**Net increase / (decrease) in cash held**	US$'000	-	-	-	-	-	=SUM(J22,J26,J34)

CHAPTER 17.5: LINKING THE FINANCIAL STATEMENT WORKSHEETS

With our financial statements now underway, let's look at the first few steps identified in Chapter 15, Control Accounts:

> ### Building a Financial Model
>
> This approach remains moot on the order of calculation construction. This is how to build a hassle-free, three-way integrated financial model:
>
> 1. Create the forecast chart of accounts from either previous models, existing financials, ledgers, journals, trial balances, etc.
>
> 2. Add in the subtotals for each chart of account so that all totals flow through their respective financial statements
>
> 3. Add error and other checks to these outputs (e.g. balance checks, cash in cash flow equals cash movement on Balance Sheet) as necessary, updating the 'Error Checks' worksheet as necessary
>
> 4. Create the Opening Balance Sheet, ensuring it uses the same format as the forecast Balance Sheet
>
> 5. Ensure the Opening Balance Sheet balances, else reject
>
> 6. Add checks as necessary
>
> 7. Link the financial statements together, adding any checks as necessary

Let me show you what happens if you don't follow the above order. Great book, Liam, you're going to disregard your own advice! Well, let's see what happens...

Let's integrate our financial statements by linking them together, even though we haven't added checks (although we do know that the Opening Balance Sheet will always balance). Remember, there aren't 6,000 links here, just the two:

All we must do is link the net profit after tax (NPAT) into the Retained profits / earnings section of the Balance Sheet and then link the Net increase / decrease in cash held from the Cash Flow Statement into the Current assets section of the Balance Sheet. There are two common methods of doing this. In a real-life situation, I would model the two links similarly (*consistency*), but here I will show both approaches so that you can recognise them, build them and understand which is actually preferable.

Firstly, I am going to link in the net increase / decrease in cash held from the Cash Flow Statement into the Current Assets section of the Balance Sheet. We begin by linking the cash balance:

=IF(J$9=1,'Opening Balance Sheet'!$I$14,I14)+'Cash Flow Statement'!J36

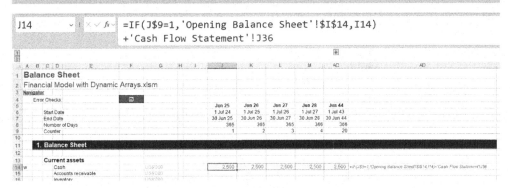

If you have linked up this calculation yourself rather than just type the formula in, you would actually have created a slightly different formula in cell **J14**:

=IF(J$9=1,'Opening Balance Sheet'!$I$14,'Balance Sheet'!I14)+'Cash Flow Statement'!J36

This formula is taking the opening cash balance from the Opening Balance Sheet (**'Opening Balance Sheet'!$I$14**), which is why this cell is anchored when it is the first period. **J$9** determines whether it is the first period and is anchored to row 9 so that if the formula is copied elsewhere it will always link to row 9, the counter. The last argument of the formula as it stands though, **'Balance Sheet'!I14**, could be perceived to be a little dangerous from a modelling viewpoint.

Note that this formula occurs on the 'Balance Sheet' worksheet. Therefore, we only require the reference **I14** – the worksheet reference **'Balance Sheet'!** is superfluous. Therefore, I have deleted it in my calculation:

=IF(J$9=1,'Opening Balance Sheet'!$I$14,I14)+'Cash Flow Statement'!J36

Not only is this easier to read, it is "safer". The worksheet reference is included whenever you point to a cell after you have previously linked to another worksheet or workbook. Up until this point Excel will refer only to the cell reference on the worksheet and not the worksheet as well, after an external reference all bets are off.

If you do not remove the worksheet reference from the formula as I have, should you copy the worksheet (depending upon how it is copied), the reference may always link to the original worksheet reference rather than the copied worksheet. This may cause inadvertent errors which are easy to miss and may lead to creating an incorrect model. To remove the possibility of this occurring, do become disciplined in removing these superfluous references as soon as they arise.

Do note I have marked row 14 as Work In Progress. This is because whilst this formula now links correctly, it is not yet a dynamic array formula, but it cannot be at this stage as the formula references are not dynamic arrays. For now, I need to move on.

Having linked the Cash Flow Statement using just one line, I am going to create a control account on the face of the Balance Sheet for NPAT in rows 47 to 50 inclusive:

J47	▾ : × ✓ fx ▾	=IF(J$9=1,'Opening Balance Sheet'!$I$50,I50)

	A B C D	E	F	G	H	I	J	K	L	M	AC		AD
1	**Balance Sheet**												
2	Financial Model with Dynamic Arrays.xlsm												
3	Navigator												
4	Error Checks:		☑										
5							Jun 25	Jun 26	Jun 27	Jun 28	Jun 44		
6	Start Date						1 Jul 24	1 Jul 25	1 Jul 26	1 Jul 27	1 Jul 43		
7	End Date						30 Jun 25	30 Jun 26	30 Jun 27	30 Jun 28	30 Jun 44		
8	Number of Days						365	365	365	366	366		
9	Counter						1	2	3	4	20		
41													
42	W	**Net assets**	US$'000				2,500	2,500	2,500	2,500	2,500	=J25-J40	
43													
44													
45		**Equity**											
46		Ordinary equity	US$'000										
47	W	Opening retained profits	US$'000				2,545	2,545	2,545	2,545	2,545	=IF(J$9=1,'Opening Balance Sheet'!$I$50,I50)	
48	W	NPAT	US$'000				-	-	-	-	-	='Income Statement'!J28	
49	W	Dividends declared	US$'000										
50	W	Retained profits	US$'000				2,545	2,545	2,545	2,545	2,545	=SUM(J47:J49)	
51	W	**Total equity**	US$'000				2,545	2,545	2,545	2,545	2,545	=SUM(J46:J50)	

The Opening retained profits (row 47) are given by

=IF(J$9=1,'Opening Balance Sheet'!$I$50,I50)

Again, I have ensured no explicit referencing of the 'Balance Sheet' (*i.e.* the worksheet the formula is actually written on). Row 48 (NPAT) is simple:

='Income Statement'!J28

For row 49, I have absolutely no idea how to calculate Dividends Declared presently, but I know these must be deducted from profits as Retained Earnings is the cumulative sum of profits retained and dividends are the profits distributed. Therefore, I leave this blank.

Since none of these rows have dynamic array formulae in them, I mark them all as Work In Progress in the usual way. It looks like I have a lot of revisiting to do!

But there is another problem. Do you see that Net assets (row 42) do not equal Total equity (row 51)? Because I have built this model out of order, I have not yet added any error checks, so the model has not automatically flagged this issue. We need to create some error checks – and fix the problem.

CHAPTER 17.6: ERROR CHECKS

Our model should warn us when there is an issue, as such there is one other thing to add at this stage: error checks. If you recall Chapter 12, I have already explained suitable initial checks for the Balance Sheet, so I am now going to add these into the Opening Balance Sheet:

The formulae I have used here are as follows:

- PF error check (**I56**): **=IF(ISERROR(I42-I51),1,0)**

- Balance check (**I57**): **=IF(I56<>0,0,(ROUND(I42-I51,Rounding_Accuracy)<>0)*1)**

- Insolvency check (**I58**): **=IF(SUM(I56:I57)<>0,0,(I42<0)*1)**

Notice that these three ranges have been given range names as well: **HL_OP_BS_Errors**, **HL_Op_BS_Balance**, and **HL_Op_BS_Insolvency**. This is so that we can create hyperlinks to these checks later. Notice, within our balance check, we've made use of our Named Range **Rounding_Accuracy**. This is a parameter found in cell **G27** of our 'Model Parameters' sheet.

We can replicate these checks on our Balance Sheet, making sure to include an overall summary of all periods for each of these checks:

A B C D	E	F	G	H I	J	K	L	M	AC	AD
1 **Balance Sheet**										
2 Financial Model with Dynamic Arrays.xlsm										
3 Navigator										
4 Error Checks:		☑								
5					Jun 25	Jun 26	Jun 27	Jun 28	Jun 44	
6 Start Date					1 Jul 24	1 Jul 25	1 Jul 26	1 Jul 27	1 Jul 43	
7 End Date					30 Jun 25	30 Jun 26	30 Jun 27	30 Jun 28	30 Jun 44	
8 Number of Days					365	365	365	366	366	
9 Counter					1	2	3	4	20	
41										
42 w **Net assets**		US$'000			2,500	2,500	2,500	2,500	2,500	=J25-J40
43										
44										
45 **Equity**										
46 Ordinary equity		US$'000								
47 w Opening retained profits		US$'000			2,545	2,545	2,545	2,545	2,545	=IF(J$9=1,'Opening Balance Sheet'!$I$30,I50)
48 w NPAT		US$'000			-	-	-	-	-	='Income Statement'!J26
49 w Dividends declared		US$'000								
50 w Retained profits		US$'000			2,545	2,545	2,545	2,545	2,545	=SUM(J47:J49)
51 w **Total equity**		US$'000			2,545	2,545	2,545	2,545	2,545	=SUM(J46:J50)
52										
53										
54 **Checks**										
55										
56 PF error check		[1,0]		☑	☑	☑	☑	☑	☑	=IF(ISERROR(J42#-J51#),1,0)
57 Balance check		[1,0]		☑	☑	☑	☑	☑	☑	=IF(J56#<>0,0,(ROUND(J42#-J51#,Rounding_Accuracy)<>0)*1)
58 Insolvency check		[1,0]		☑	☑	☑	☑	☑	☑	=IF(J56#+J57#<>0,0,(J42#<0)*1)

The formulae we've used are as follows:

- PF error check (cell **J56**): **=IF(ISERROR(J42#-J51#),1,0)**

- Balance check: (cell **J57**): **=IF(J56#<>0,0,(ROUND(J42#-J51#,Rounding_ Accuracy)<>0)*1)**

- Insolvency check (cell **J58**): **=IF(J56#+J57#<>0,0,(J42#<0)*1)**

Note that whilst these formulae all contain dynamic array references (*e.g.* **J42#, J51#**) they have been copied into each period's cell. This is because the references do not currently spill.

The overall checks in cells **I56:I58** simply make use of the **MAX** function over all period's checks to return a one [1] if there is an error in any period, else a zero [0].

Cells **I56, I57** and **I58** are then given the range names **HL_BS_Errors, HL_BS_Balance** and **HL_BS_Insolvency** respectively, as these will be the destinations of three hyperlinks.

As with our other formulae on the financial statements, these checks are not yet making use of dynamic arrays and as such should be flagged as work in progress:

A B C D	E	F	G	H I	J	K	L	M	AC
1 **Balance Sheet**									
2 Financial Model with Dynamic Arrays.xlsm									
3 Navigator									
4 Error Checks:		☑							
5					Jun 25	Jun 26	Jun 27	Jun 28	Jun 44
6 Start Date					1 Jul 24	1 Jul 25	1 Jul 26	1 Jul 27	1 Jul 43
7 End Date					30 Jun 25	30 Jun 26	30 Jun 27	30 Jun 28	30 Jun 44
8 Number of Days					365	365	365	366	366
9 Counter					1	2	3	4	20
53									
54 **Checks**									
55									
56 w PF error check		[1,0]		☑	☑	☑	☑	☑	☑
57 w Balance check		[1,0]		☑	☑	☑	☑	☑	☑
58 w Insolvency check		[1,0]		☑	☑	☑	☑	☑	☑

You may find that applying the WIP Style changes the characters displayed by the checks. This can be easily fixed by changing the font of these cells back to Wingdings (from Arial).

Notice that despite the errors flagging in row 57 of our Balance Sheet the overall error check, in cell **F4** above, is not showing any error. We still need to link these checks into our 'Error Checks' worksheet.

To do this, we first create a label for the check, in column **E** of our 'Error Checks' worksheet, and link the check into column **I**.

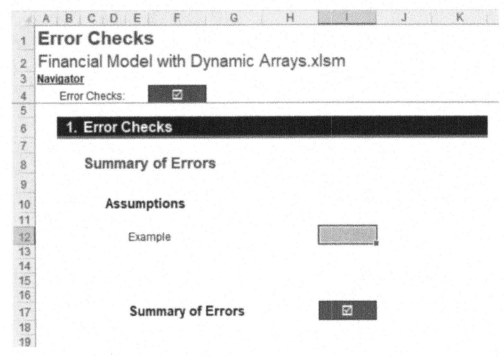

Added and formatted, these will become as follows:

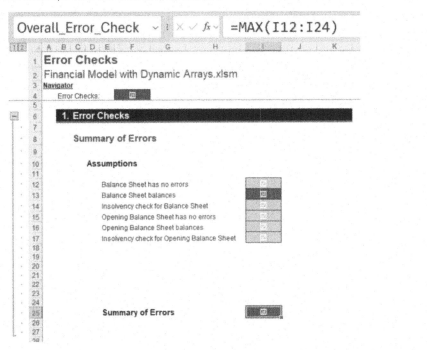

We're not done yet though, as I must also hyperlink these cells to the corresponding Named Ranges. This can be done by clicking in the cell and either pressing **CTRL + K** or navigating to the Insert tab of the Ribbon and choosing 'Link':

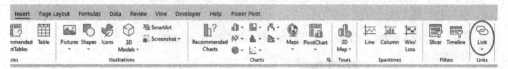

This will present us with a dialog box where we choose to link to a 'Place in This Document' and find our Named Range:

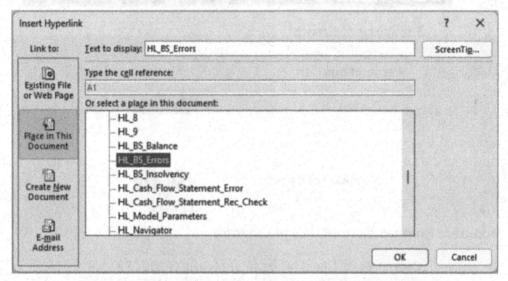

This will typically interfere with the formatting within our cell, but this can be easily remedied by making use of the Format Painter and copying the format from one of the other checks in column **I**.

Repeating this for all of our checks, I can now turn my attention to the error triggered:

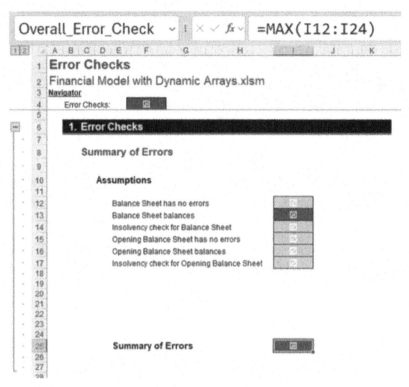

I have to return to the Balance Sheet. I can see that row 57 highlights that Net assets (row 42) no longer equals Total equity (row 51). The overall error check (cell **F4** on this worksheet) ensures you will notice this as soon as you have coded the section – which is what you want – no matter what worksheet you are on. Strike 1 for the error checks system.

Balance Sheet

Financial Model with Dynamic Arrays.xlsm

Navigator

	Error Checks:		Jun 25	Jun 26	Jun 27	Jun 28	Jun 44		
	Start Date		1 Jul 24	1 Jul 25	1 Jul 26	1 Jul 27	1 Jul 43		
	End Date		30 Jun 25	30 Jun 26	30 Jun 27	30 Jun 28	30 Jun 44		
	Number of Days		365	365	365	366	366		
	Counter		1	2	3	4	20		
42 w	**Net assets**	US$'000	2,500	2,500	2,500	2,500	2,500	=J25-J40	
43									
44									
45	**Equity**								
46	Ordinary equity	US$'000							
47 w	Opening retained profits	US$'000	2,545	2,545	2,545	2,545	2,545	=IF(J$9=1,'Opening Balance Sheet'!$I$50,I50)
48 w	NPAT	US$'000	-	-	-	-	-	='Income Statement'!J28
49 w	Dividends declared	US$'000						
50 w	Retained profits	US$'000	2,545	2,545	2,545	2,545	2,545	=SUM(J47:J49)
51 w	**Total equity**	US$'000	2,545	2,545	2,545	2,545	2,545	=SUM(J46:J50)
52									
53									
54	**Checks**								
55									
56 w	PF error check		0	0	0	0	0	0	=IF(ISERROR(J42-J51),1,0)
57 w	Balance check		0	0	0	0	0	0	=IF(J56=0,0,(ROUND(J42-J51,Rounding_Accuracy)<>0)*1)
58 w	Insolvency check		0	0	0	0	0	0	=IF(J56+J57=0,0,(J42<0)*1)

So how do I amend the issue? First of all, what is causing the issue? Net assets does not equal Total equity as we've put in two numbers from the Opening Balance Sheet, cells **I14** and **I50**, that aren't equal. I cannot carry on until I make everything balance. This causes me a little conundrum as to what I should do next. There are essentially three [3] alternatives:

1. **Add all the other opening balances to the Balance Sheet:** This will make the Balance Sheet balance as we are basically inserting the Opening Balance Sheet into the model and we know that balances. However, this causes a problem as we won't know which rows of the 'Balance Sheet' worksheet have completed formulae and which ones are work in progress. This could lead to errors of omission or even double-counting. This risk is unacceptable and therefore this option is **rejected**.

2. **Don't do anything:** We know what has caused the Balance Sheet not to balance. Let's just keep building the model and hope when we have finished the Balance Sheet balances. This is a very common approach for modellers. If you are one of those who has taken this Road to Hell, how did it work out for you? What is your record for finding the 33 Balance Sheet errors that also arose that you didn't realise? This option is also **rejected**.

3. **Cheat**: Now if I know my modellers, I think ears will have suddenly pricked up. Let's do this.

So, what does Option 3 involve? It isn't really a cheat. I know what has caused the error: I have added one opening balance number in without bringing in the others. I have already rejected the notion of bringing all of the others in so what about the contrapositive? How about I remove that opening balance instead? You may recall earlier I argued that a modeller may only be held to ensuring that changes in Net assets must equal changes in Total equity. This works for me.

How do I do this? It is easy. Head back to the Opening Balance Sheet and highlight cells **I14:I51**, then copy (**CTRL + C**) these cells. Paste these cells into the range **K14:K51** (**CTRL + V**); you only need to select cell **K14** to do this. Now, re-select cells **I14:I51** and then press the 'Delete' key on your keyboard to clear the contents of these cells. Feeling a little uncomfortable?

	A	B	C	D	E	F	G	H	I	J	K	L	M	N	O
1	**Opening Balance Sheet**														
2	Financial Model with Dynamic Arrays.xlsm														
3	**Navigator**														
4		Error Checks:				☑									
5								Jun 24							
6		Start Date													
7		End Date													
8		Number of Days													
9		Counter													
10															
11	**1. Opening Balance Sheet**														
12															
13		Current assets													
14		Cash				US$'000					2,500				
15		Accounts receivable				US$'000					50				
16		Inventory				US$'000					50				
17		Other current assets				US$'000					10				
18		**Total current assets**				US$'000					2,610				
19															
20		Non-current assets													
21		PP&E				US$'000					450				
22		Deferred tax assets				US$'000					75				
23		**Total non-current assets**				US$'000					525				
24															
25		**Total assets**				US$'000					3,135				
26															
27		Current liabilities													
28		Accounts payable				US$'000					30				
29		Interest payable				US$'000					20				
30		Dividends payable				US$'000					15				
31		Tax payable				US$'000					40				
32		Other current liabilities				US$'000					10				
33		**Total current liabilities**				US$'000					115				
34															
35		Non-current liabilities													
36		Debt				US$'000					150				
37		Deferred tax liabilities				US$'000					25				
38		**Total non-current liabilities**				US$'000					175				
39															
40		**Total liabilities**				US$'000					290				
41															
42		**Net assets**				US$'000					2,845				
43															
44															
45		Equity													
46		Ordinary equity				US$'000					300				
47		Opening retained profits				US$'000					2,520				
48		NPAT				US$'000					25				
49		Dividends declared				US$'000					-				
50		**Retained profits**				US$'000					2,545				
51		**Total equity**				US$'000					2,845				
52															
53															
54		Checks													
55															
56		PF error check				[1,0]		☑			=IF(ISERROR(K42),0,1)				
57		Balance check				[1,0]		☑			=IF(K6=0,0,IF(ROUND(K42,5),Rounding_Accuracy),0)"1)				
58		Insolvency check				[1,0]		☑			=IF(SUM(K56:K57)<>0,0,K42<0)"1)				
59															

Do you see that the error check in cell **F4** is now showing that all is well? There is no longer a misbalance in the 'Balance Sheet' worksheet:

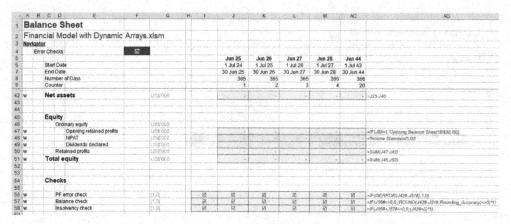

	A B C D	E	F	G	H I	J	K	L	M	AC	AD
1	**Balance Sheet**										
2	Financial Model with Dynamic Arrays.xlsm										
3	Navigator										
4	Error Checks		☑								
5						Jun 25	Jun 26	Jun 27	Jun 28	Jun 44	
6	Start Date					1 Jul 24	1 Jul 25	1 Jul 26	1 Jul 27	1 Jul 43	
7	End Date					30 Jun 25	30 Jun 26	30 Jun 27	30 Jun 28	30 Jun 44	
8	Number of Days					365	365	365	366	366	
9	Counter					1	2	3	4	20	
42 w	**Net assets**	US$'000									=J25-J40
43											
44											
45	**Equity**										
46	Ordinary equity	US$'000									
47 w	Opening retained profits	US$'000									=IF(J39<1,'Opening Balance Sheet'!$I$50,I50)
48 w	NPAT	US$'000									='Income Statement'!J28
49 w	Dividends declared	US$'000									
50 w	Retained profits	US$'000									=SUM(J47:J49)
51 w	**Total equity**	US$'000									=SUM(J46,J50)
52											
53											
54	**Checks**										
55											
56 w	PF error check	[1,0]		☑	☑	☑	☑	☑	☑		=IF(ISERROR(J42#-J51#),1,0)
57 w	Balance check	[1,0]		☑	☑	☑	☑	☑	☑		=IF(J56#<>0,0,(ROUND(J42#-J51#,Rounding_Accuracy)<>0)*1)
58 w	Insolvency check	[1,0]		☑	☑	☑	☑	☑	☑		=IF(J56#+J57#<>0,0,(J42#<0)*1)

The financial statements are now linked together. The Opening Balance Sheet has been set to zero, but it is easy to resurrect as we will just copy the data from column **K** on the Opening Balance Sheet back to column **I**. Effectively, I have just completed the following steps:

Building a Financial Model

7. Link the financial statements together, adding any checks as necessary

8. Zero the Opening Balance Sheet

9. Ensure all checks are "OK"

It's just a shame I never did it in the right order in the first place! Anyway, now that linking is completed and error checks have all been added, I now have a three-way integrated structure set up. We're good to go.

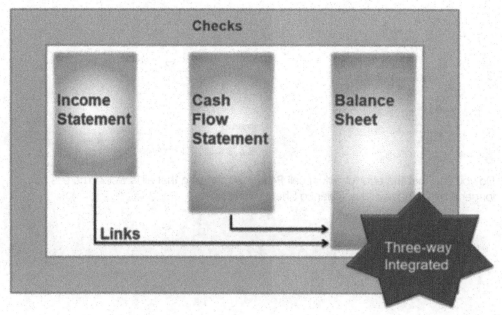

CHAPTER 17.7: REVENUE

> ### *Building a Financial Model*
>
> 10. Begin with the Income Statement, take the first line item in this account (*e.g.* Revenue)
>
> 11. Create calculations if not already computed
>
> 12. Construct control account
>
> 13. Add checks if necessary
>
> 14. Link control account to financial statements, ensuring checks are all OK (correct if necessary)

And so, we begin. To make things simpler, I will change the number of periods back to five [5]:

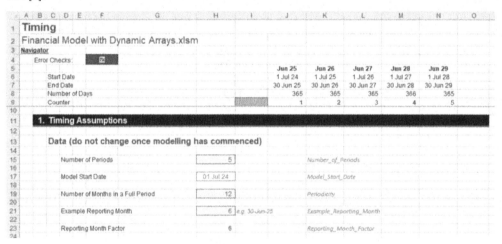

			Jun 25	Jun 26	Jun 27	Jun 28	Jun 29
Timing							
Financial Model with Dynamic Arrays.xlsm							
Navigator							
Error Checks:	☑						
			Jun 25	Jun 26	Jun 27	Jun 28	Jun 29
Start Date			1 Jul 24	1 Jul 25	1 Jul 26	1 Jul 27	1 Jul 28
End Date			30 Jun 25	30 Jun 26	30 Jun 27	30 Jun 28	30 Jun 29
Number of Days			365	365	365	366	365
Counter			1	2	3	4	5

1. Timing Assumptions

Data (do not change once modelling has commenced)

Number of Periods	5	Number_of_Periods
Model Start Date	01 Jul 24	Model_Start_Date
Number of Months in a Full Period	12	Periodicity
Example Reporting Month	6 e.g. 30-Jun-25	Example_Reporting_Month
Reporting Month Factor	6	Reporting_Month_Factor

You may recall my discussion from earlier where I said we simply work our way down the Income Statement. In this case, our Income Statement looks like this:

1. Income Statement

Revenue	US$'000
COGS	US$'000
Gross profit	US$'000
Wastage	US$'000
Operating expenditure	US$'000
EBITDA	US$'000
Depreciation	US$'000
EBIT	US$'000
Interest expense	US$'000
NPBT	US$'000
Tax expense	US$'000
NPAT	US$'000

The first line item to be modelled is therefore **Revenue**. Let's first consider the assumptions I now build in:

| J17 | | | ⌄ | ⋮ | ✕ ✓ *fx* ⌄ | =J$9#*100 |

	A	B	C	D	E	F	G	H	I	J	K	L	M	N	O
1	**General Assumptions**														
2	Financial Model with Dynamic Arrays.xlsm														
3	Navigator														
4		Error Checks:				☑									
5										Jun 25	Jun 26	Jun 27	Jun 28	Jun 29	
6		Start Date								1 Jul 24	1 Jul 25	1 Jul 26	1 Jul 27	1 Jul 28	
7		End Date								30 Jun 25	30 Jun 26	30 Jun 27	30 Jun 28	30 Jun 29	
8		Number of Days								365	365	365	366	365	
9		Counter								1	2	3	4	5	
10															
11		**1. General Assumptions**													
12															
13		**Revenue and related**													
14															
15			**Sales**												
16															
17				Projected sales		#				100	200	300	400	500	
18				Unit price		US$'000				15					
19				Inflation		%					3%	4%	5%	6%	
20															
21			**Working capital**												
22															
23				Days receivable		Year				60	60	60	60	60	

In order for our financial model to work with dynamic arrays, the majority of our inputs must be constructed as dynamic arrays too. To this end, let me consider Projected sales (row 17). The formula for this is entered into cell **J17**:

$$=J\$9\#*100$$

This gives us an assumption that is already a spilled range, with values increasing in line with the counter of the model. Of course, this may not be the case in reality – inputs may instead be hardcoded values for each period, but I will look at different input methods for different sections of the model to demonstrate the different approaches in due course.

Inflation and days receivable are also generated as spilled ranges, whereas our unit price input is just a single figure:

| J18 | | | ⌄ | ⋮ | ✕ ✓ *fx* | 15 |

	A	B	C	D	E	F	G	H	I	J	K	L
1	**General Assumptions**											
2	1. SP Case Study Starter.xlsm											
3	Navigator											
4		Error Checks:					☑					
5										Jun 25	Jun 26	Jun 27
6		Start Date								1 Jul 24	1 Jul 25	1 Jul 26
7		End Date								30 Jun 25	30 Jun 26	30 Jun 27
8		Number of Days								365	365	365
9		Counter								1	2	3
10												
11		**1. General Assumptions**										
12												
13		**Revenue and related**										
14												
15			**Sales**									
16												
17				Projected sales		#				100	200	300
18				Unit price		US$'000				15		
19				Inflation		%					3%	4%
20												
21			**Working capital**									
22												
23				Days receivable		# Days				60	60	60

The formula for Inflation is actually entered into cell **J19** even though it appears blank:

=IF(J$9#=1,,IF((J$9#+1)/100<6%,(J$9#+1)/100,6%))

Plenty of hard code here – but the point is this is an assumption, so it is acceptable. This formula simply increases the percentage up to 6% as long as it is a reporting period.

Days receivable (**J23**) is given by the very easy to follow formula

=IF(J$9#,60,)

I appreciate these assumptions are very simple. There is no point in constructing a really complex Revenue calculation since no matter how detailed I make it, I know it will neither be relevant nor appropriate as far as 99% of you will be concerned (that will be both my readers, which means only 0.02 readers will find it relevant).

I do want to comment on these input methodologies though. No matter how complex a model's calculations may become, inputs may only be entered into a model in one of four ways:

The Four Methods of Entering Inputs into a Model

There are only four ways to enter data into a financial model. The actual method may incorporate combinations of the following:

1. **Amounts:** Data is entered in as numerical (absolute) values. It may be in units, thousands, millions, GWh and so on, but ultimately it is a number. This is an ideal entry method where data is copied from elsewhere or may eventually be linked to another model (say).

2. **Percentages:** Data is typed in as a percentage or ratio of another value, be it input or calculated. This is often the approach employed for variable costs, for example.

3. **Amount and growth rates:** Data is entered in two forms, an amount in at least the first period and then a percentage thereafter. This is often the method used for sky blue forecasting and sometimes leads to what the modelling connoisseur may describe as "hockey stick projections".

4. **Combination:** Usually perceived as a more sophisticated version of the **amount and growth rates** approach, this method combines two or more input methodologies. The combination may be selected by use of a switch (manual input) or a trigger (calculation). This is often used for reforecasting or replacing forecast with actuals, *etc*. **IF** and **CHOOSE** are functions often associated with this methodology.

I have two input methodologies in this 'Revenue and Related' section:

- Revenue uses the **amount and growth rates** methodology. Do note that I put the amount (15) in one row (row 18) and the growth rate in the row below (row 19). This ensures units are not mixed up and will be treated correctly in calculations, as well as understood as intended by end users.

- The Days Receivable assumptions are **amounts**. This may be based on guesstimates or historical / trend data for the business from the past.

It is beneficial to recognise which approach is being used as developers need to be wary of the common mistakes that are associated with the different types of data input.

Returning to our model, let's visit the Calculations worksheet and begin constructing our Revenue calculations. The first step here, which surprises many when they first see this example, is replicating the relevant assumptions from the 'General Assumptions' worksheet in rows 17:29. These cells will simply link back to the 'General Assumptions' worksheet and are formatted as Internal references. This is so the calculation may be followed on a piece of paper without access to the Formula bar:

| J21 | =SCAN(J18,J19#,LAMBDA(accumulator,percentage,accumulator*(1+percentage))) |

			Jun 25	Jun 26	Jun 27	Jun 28	Jun 29	
Calculations								
Financial Model with Dynamic Arrays.xlsm								
Navigator								
Error Checks:								
Start Date			1 Jul 24	1 Jul 25	1 Jul 26	1 Jul 27	1 Jul 28	
End Date			30 Jun 25	30 Jun 26	30 Jun 27	30 Jun 28	30 Jun 29	
Number of Days			365	365	365	366	365	
Counter			1	2	3	4	5	
1. Calculations								
Revenue and related								
Sales								
Projected sales			100	200	300	400	500	='General Assumptions'.J17#
Unit price	US$'000		15					='General Assumptions'.J18
Inflation	%			3%	4%	5%	6%	=IF('General Assumptions'.J19#="","",'General Assumptions'.J19#)
Price per unit	US$'000		15	15	16	17	18	=SCAN(J18,J19#,LAMBDA(accumulator,percentage,accumulator*(1+percentage)))
Revenue	US$'000		1,500	3,090	4,820	6,749	8,942	=J17#*J21#
Working capital								
Days receivable	Year		60	60	60	60	60	='General Assumptions'.J28
Days in period	Year		365	365	366	366	365	=J8#
Closing receivables	US$'000		247	508	792	1,106	1,470	=J23#*J27#/J29#
Control account								
Opening receivables	US$'000		-	247	508	792	1,106	=OFFSET(J38#,,-1)
Revenue	US$'000		1,500	3,090	4,820	6,749	8,942	=J23#
Cash receipts	US$'000		(1,253)	(2,829)	(4,536)	(6,435)	(8,578)	=J35#-J35#-J36#
Closing receivables	US$'000		247	508	792	1,106	1,470	=J31#

I've hidden some columns here to make the explanatory formulae in column **AE** easier to read. Notice that row 17 simply links to our spilled range on the 'General Assumptions' worksheet, making use of the spilled range operator [#]. Cell **J18** then links to the input in cell **J18** of the 'General Assumptions' worksheet. Finally, note that in row 19 the formula actually starts in the seemingly blank cell (**J19**) and makes use of the **IF** function to return a blank ("") when the corresponding input cell is blank, else returning the corresponding input cell.

With these inputs brought in we can now calculate the price per unit in cell **J21**:

=SCAN(J18,J19#,LAMBDA(accumulator,percentage,accumulator*(1+percentage)))

We've made use of the **SCAN** function here. I did warn you we would be! This defines an initial value, here cell **J18**, as well as an array, here **J19#**, and finally a **LAMBDA**. This formula will apply the **LAMBDA** to the initial value, then to the result given by that, then to the result given by that and so on until the end of the array. Here, that will be 15 multiplied by 1 (as one plus the blank in cell **J19** is simply one) which gives us 15, followed by 15 multiplied by 1.03 which gives us 15.45, followed by 15.45 multiplied by 1.04 giving 16.068, and so on.

Moving on, we can now calculate revenue by simply multiplying the number of projected sales by the price per unit (cell **J23**):

=J17#*J21#

Working capital is where we consider the cash adjustment. I can begin by bringing in the days receivable assumptions from row 23 of the 'General Assumptions' worksheet in row 27 and replicating the days in period from row 8 in row 29. Next, we need to calculate closing receivables but before we do this let's take a quick aside to look at working capital.

Working Capital Adjustments

Before creating the calculations, I want to explain the working capital assumption and how it works. If money is owed, the people who owe it are **Debtors** and, assuming no write-offs of sales made, the amounts owed are known as **Accounts Receivable** or simply **Receivables**. This amount owed is viewed as an asset of the business. It isn't cash but it should convert to cash *soon*. Cynical businesses may quite rightly think if only it were that simple, but it is for the purposes of this case study.

Consider the following example:

Control Account

Opening Debtors		BS
Sales in Period	1,000	IS
Cash Receipts	(753)	CFS
Closing Debtors	247	BS

Imagine a company has just started off in business *(i.e.* has no amounts due) and generates sales of $1,000 in the period. At the end of the period, assuming no bad debts, $753 has been paid, leaving a closing debtor balance of $247. This difference is what I refer to as the **working capital adjustment**. If we had modelled the sales of $1,000 in the period, how might we generate the cash receipts forecast such that if the assumptions changed, the receipts would calculate appropriately?

Clearly, if I am given the closing debtor balances, the problem becomes trivial, so I will assume that this is not so. Therefore, I am going to consider an alternative approach and some of the associated underlying issues that need to be considered when modelling. Let me first derive an alternative method.

I will assume that the sales accrue evenly over the period of time and for the sake of this example, that period is one year (365 days). Presuming:

1. all sales are made on credit terms

2. all customers pay their invoices on the day the amounts fall due

3. no bad debts are incurred,

this can be reflected graphically as follows:

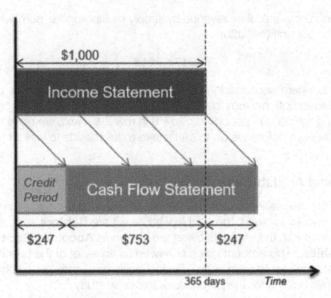

Clearly, the credit period is the "gap" at the beginning of the time period, *i.e.* 247/1000 x 365 days = 90 days. This can be represented formulaically as:

Days Receivable = (Closing Debtors x Days in Period) / Sales in Period

Rearranging, this becomes:

Closing Debtors = (Sales in Period x Days Receivable) / Days in Period,

e.g. in our example: 247 = (1000 x 90) / 365.

Therefore, in modelling, we often set the number of days receivable (and days payable) as key assumptions for cash flow forecasting. However, it is not always as simple as that. Let me explain. Consider we are planning to build a monthly model (assuming 30 days in a month) and sales for the month are again $1,000. Debtor days remain at 90 days.

Based on these calculations, we would generate the following control account:

Control Account

Opening Debtors	-	BS
Sales in Period	1,000	IS
Cash Receipts	2,000	CFS
Closing Debtors	3,000	BS

Erm, that's right: make sales of $1,000 and have $3,000 (= 90/30 x 365) owing to you by the end of the month. Also, the company pays $2,000 to customers a reclaimable $2 for each $1 spent. That's nonsense – and yet, as an experienced model auditor I have seen this erroneous calculation crop up on a regular basis. The problem is, in this current economic climate most businesses want to prepare monthly – sometimes weekly and even daily – cash flow projections. Clearly, if the days receivable or days payable assumption exceeds the number of days in each forecast period this approach is inappropriate and will lead to calculation errors. This is an example of where we ought to employ error checks to ensure that our inputs do not breach this key assumption.

There are alternatives. If payments are made exactly one month or two months or three months later (and so on), the resolution is simple: the receipts can be calculated using a simple **OFFSET** (displacement) formula.

Rather than consider that situation, let me complicate the scenario slightly. Imagine we are building a monthly forecast model, but that the days receivable are 75. For the purposes of keeping this section reasonably brief, I will simplify the problem by assuming an average number of days in a month (say, 30). Using this simplifying assumption, this will mean that payments are made on average 2.5 (2.5 = 75 / 30) months after the sale has been made.

That 2.5 months figure is important. The integer part (2) denotes how many complete months (including the current month) have sales payments outstanding. The residual (0.5 or 50%) shows the proportion of the month preceding these complete months that is also outstanding. With this borne in mind, the **OFFSET** function can now come to the rescue, *viz.*

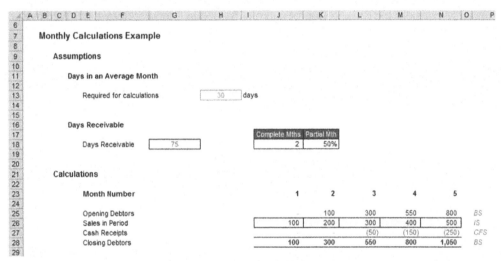

In this illustration (above), cells **J18** and **K18** break the number of days receivable (cell **G18**) into the number of whole months and residual proportion respectively, assuming that each month has 30 days (cell **H13**).

The key formula here is the calculation for Closing Debtors (Cash Receipts is simply the balancing figure). For example, the formula in cell **J28** (above) is:

```
=IF($J$18,SUM(OFFSET(J26,,,1,-MIN($J$18,J$23))),)
+IF(J$23-$J$18<=0,,OFFSET(J26,,-$J$18)*$K$18)
```

It may seem a little complex upon first inspection, but it's not as bad as it seems. Essentially, there are two parts to this formula identified by the two added **IF** statements:

1. **IF($J$18,SUM(OFFSET(J26,,,1,-MIN($J$18,J$23))),)** considers the completed number of months where sales remain outstanding and adds up the sales for these periods.

   In essence, this part of the formula checks that the number of completed months is not zero (in this case the amount is just zero), and assuming this is not the case, it sums the sales for the relevant number of completed months (*i.e.* starts with the current month and then considers the sales in previous months, working from right to left in the spreadsheet). The **MIN** formula is required to ensure that the model does not try to include periods prior to the beginning of the forecast period).

2. **IF(J$23-$J$18<=0,,OFFSET(J26,,-$J$18)*$K$18)** considers the residual (remaining) amount for the month before the earliest completed month. For example, if the credit period is 2.5 months and the current month is April, then March and April will be "whole months" where no payment has been received, with half of February's monies still outstanding too.

   The reason for the **IF** statement here is to prevent calculations considering periods before the beginning of the forecast period.

To clarify, consider the Closing Debtor figure of $1,050 in Period 5 (above, cell **N28** in the illustration). This is calculated as the sales for Periods 4 and 5 (400 + 500 respectively), plus half of the Period 3 sales (300 x 0.5 = 150), i.e. 400 + 500 + 150 = 1,050.

Working capital adjustments may become even more complicated. What if payments are not made evenly? Or that some sales are written off as payments are never made (i.e. bad debts)?

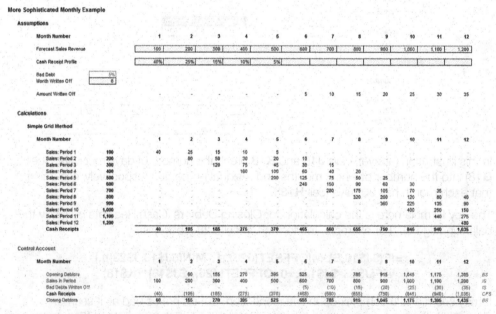

Some of you realise this looks like a depreciation grid. I shall discuss this concept more later. For the meantime, in this illustration it is worth noting that the Cash Receipt Profile percentages do not add up to 100%. This is deliberate – the missing 5% is the assumed bad debt here.

There is one other method. Large infrastructure projects may simply have cash payments input rather than calculated, triggered by certain milestone payments. This goes to show you that bigger does not always mean more complex.

Revenue Calculations

Now that I have put working capital adjustments in context, let me return to the calculations in hand, which will adopt the first approach described above:

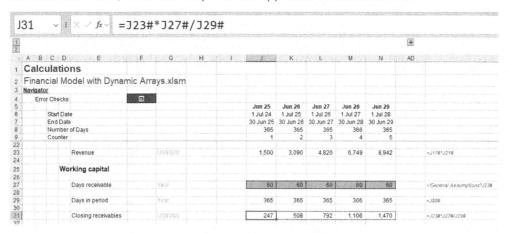

This is simply the revenue in the period, multiplied by the days receivable, divided by the number of days in the period. We just express it as dynamic ranges, *viz.*

$$=J23\#*J27\#/J29\#$$

Finally, we can begin constructing our control account. We begin by bringing in the accounts receivable from the Opening Balance Sheet, making sure we reference our now empty column **I** rather than column **K**:

| I38 | fx | ='Opening Balance Sheet'!$I$15 |

	A B C D	E	F	G	H	I	J	K	L	M	N	AD
1	**Calculations**											
2	Financial Model with Dynamic Arrays.xlsm											
3	Navigator											
4	Error Checks:			☑								
5							Jun 25	Jun 26	Jun 27	Jun 28	Jun 29	
6	Start Date						1 Jul 24	1 Jul 25	1 Jul 26	1 Jul 27	1 Jul 28	
7	End Date						30 Jun 25	30 Jun 26	30 Jun 27	30 Jun 28	30 Jun 29	
8	Number of Days						365	365	365	366	365	
9	Counter						1	2	3	4	5	
22												
23	Revenue		US$'000				1,500	3,090	4,820	6,749	8,942	=J17#*J21#
24												
25	**Working capital**											
26												
27	Days receivable		Year				60	60	60	60	60	='General Assumptions'!J23#
28												
29	Days in period		Year				365	365	365	366	365	=J$8#
30												
31	Closing receivables		US$'000				247	508	792	1,106	1,470	=J23#*J27#/J29#
32												
33	**Control account**											
34												
35	Opening receivables		US$'000				-	247	508	792	1,106	=OFFSET(J38#,,-1)
36	Revenue		US$'000				1,500	3,090	4,820	6,749	8,942	=J23#
37	Cash receipts		US$'000				(1,253)	(2,829)	(4,536)	(6,435)	(8,578)	=J38#-J35#-J36#
38	Closing receivables		US$'000				247	508	792	1,106	1,470	=J31#

Next, we'd usually calculate the opening receivables by simply linking each period's opening receivables to the previous period's closing receivables (this is known as a "corkscrew" calculation) but it's not quite this simple with dynamic arrays. This is because a dynamic array range is seen as one reference. Given the closing balance (a dynamic array) sums up items including the opening balance (another dynamic array), and the opening balance refers to the previous period's closing balance, this would create a circular argument using dynamic arrays (this would not be the case using traditional Excel formulae).

Therefore, instead, I must begin by bringing in the Revenue from row 23 into row 36 and the Closing receivables from row 31 into row 38. The **OFFSET** function can then be used to calculate the Opening receivables (row 35) by selecting the previous value in the Closing receivables:

$$\text{=OFFSET(J38\#,,-1)}$$

This will take the range **J38#**, our closing receivables, and shift this one column to the left which will effectively return the previous period's closing balance. This does not cause a circularity, as the Closing receivable did not use the Opening receivable.

Finally, we can calculate the cash receipts by taking the Closing receivables and subtracting from it the Opening receivables and the Revenue in the period:

| J37 | fx | =J38#-J35#-J36# |

	Jun 25	Jun 26	Jun 27	Jun 28	Jun 29		AD
1 **Calculations**							
2 Financial Model with Dynamic Arrays.xlsm							
3 Navigator							
4 Error Checks:	☑						
5		Jun 25	Jun 26	Jun 27	Jun 28	Jun 29	
6 Start Date		1 Jul 24	1 Jul 25	1 Jul 26	1 Jul 27	1 Jul 28	
7 End Date		30 Jun 25	30 Jun 26	30 Jun 27	30 Jun 28	30 Jun 29	
8 Number of Days		365	365	365	366	365	
9 Counter		1	2	3	4	5	
32							
33 **Control account**							
34							
35 Opening receivables	US$'000	-	247	508	792	1,106	BS =OFFSET(J38#,,-1)
36 Revenue	US$'000	1,500	3,090	4,820	6,749	8,942	IS =J23#
37 Cash receipts	US$'000	(1,253)	(2,829)	(4,536)	(6,435)	(8,578)	CFS =J38#-J35#-J36#
38 Closing receivables	US$'000	247	508	792	1,106	1,470	BS =J31#

In a typical model we could use the **SUM** function here. However, when working with dynamic arrays we've had to resort to using the addition and subtraction operators (*i.e.* **+** and **-**) as the **SUM** function would cause our arrays to coerce to a single value.

There we have it, our first control account. In column **AD**, I have stipulated which financial statement each line item is to go in (that is for the case study; in a real-life model, this may be problematic as columns may need to be extended for further forecasting analysis and cause #*SPILL!* errors).

This control account provides us with three things:

1. **Number of calculations that need to be entered into the financial statements so that they balance:** This is always one less than the number of rows in the control account. In this instance it will be four minus one, which is **three [3]**.

2. **The order to build the calculations into the financial statements:** This is always row 2 first, then row 3, then row 4 and so on. In this instance, this will be Revenue (Income Statement), Cash receipts (which will be a <u>positive</u> number in the Cash Flow Statement) and Closing receivables (Balance Sheet).

3. **It identifies the key driver:** Line 2 of the control account is always the key driver, so in this case it will be Revenue. If there was never any Revenue, there would be no Cash receipts and without either of these items, Accounts receivable would always be zero [0].

Modellers are used to doing something and then doing something else for the Balance Sheet to balance (*i.e.* double entry). Here, I have identified it will take three calculations, so I must not fret when I have included the first two calculations into the financial statements and still note that the Balance Sheet does not balance.

Firstly, we link revenue into row 13 of the Income Statement:

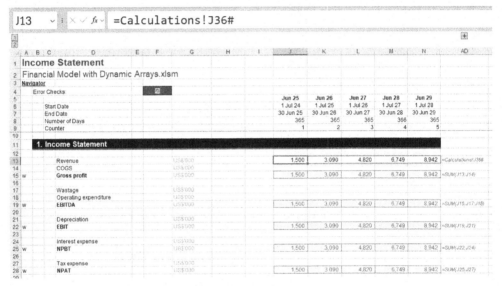

At this point our error check is flagging, *as we'd expect!* We still need to link the remaining two line items into the Balance Sheet before our model will balance.

Next, we link Cash receipts (as a negative) into row 16 of our Cash Flow Statement:

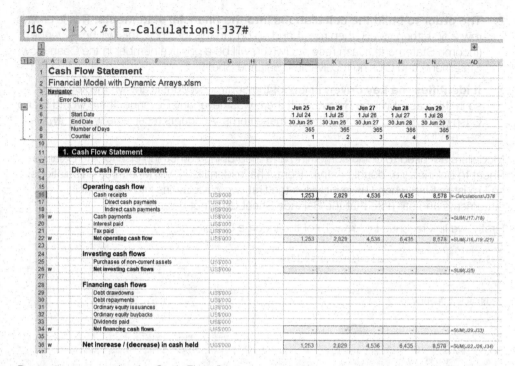

Formula bar: `J16` `=-Calculations!J37#`

Cash receipts row (J16): 1,253 | 2,829 | 4,536 | 6,435 | 8,578 =-Calculations!J37#

Cash Flow Statement
Financial Model with Dynamic Arrays.xlsm

		Jun 25	Jun 26	Jun 27	Jun 28	Jun 29	
Start Date		1 Jul 24	1 Jul 25	1 Jul 26	1 Jul 27	1 Jul 28	
End Date		30 Jun 25	30 Jun 26	30 Jun 27	30 Jun 28	30 Jun 29	
Number of Days		365	365	365	366	365	
Counter		1	2	3	4	5	

1. Cash Flow Statement

Direct Cash Flow Statement

Operating cash flow

		Jun 25	Jun 26	Jun 27	Jun 28	Jun 29	
Cash receipts	US$'000	1,253	2,829	4,536	6,435	8,578	=-Calculations!J37#
Direct cash payments	US$'000						
Indirect cash payments	US$'000						
Cash payments	US$'000	-	-	-	-	-	=SUM(J17:J18)
Interest paid	US$'000						
Tax paid	US$'000						
Net operating cash flow	US$'000	1,253	2,829	4,536	6,435	8,578	=SUM(J16:J19:J21)

Investing cash flows

Purchases of non-current assets	US$'000						
Net investing cash flows	US$'000	-	-	-	-	-	=SUM(J25)

Financing cash flows

Debt drawdowns	US$'000						
Debt repayments	US$'000						
Ordinary equity issuances	US$'000						
Ordinary equity buybacks	US$'000						
Dividends paid	US$'000						
Net financing cash flows	US$'000	-	-	-	-	-	=SUM(J29:J33)

| Net increase / (decrease) in cash held | US$'000 | 1,253 | 2,829 | 4,536 | 6,435 | 8,578 | =SUM(J22,J26,J34) |

Do you see now why the Cash Flow Statement must be prepared on the Direct basis? Using control accounts, I need to enter Cash receipts directly into the Net operating cash flow section.

Finally, I can link closing receivables into row 15 of our Balance Sheet:

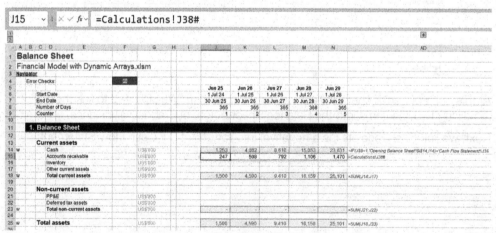

Formula bar: `J15` `=Calculations!J38#`

Balance Sheet
Financial Model with Dynamic Arrays.xlsm

		Jun 25	Jun 26	Jun 27	Jun 28	Jun 29	
Start Date		1 Jul 24	1 Jul 25	1 Jul 26	1 Jul 27	1 Jul 28	
End Date		30 Jun 25	30 Jun 26	30 Jun 27	30 Jun 28	30 Jun 29	
Number of Days		365	365	365	366	365	
Counter		1	2	3	4	5	

1. Balance Sheet

Current assets

		Jun 25	Jun 26	Jun 27	Jun 28	Jun 29	
Cash	US$'000	1,253	4,082	8,618	15,053	23,631	=IF(J\$9=1,'Opening Balance Sheet'!\$I\$14,I14)+'Cash Flow Statement'!J36
Accounts receivable	US$'000	247	508	792	1,106	1,470	=Calculations!J38#
Inventory	US$'000						
Other current assets	US$'000						
Total current assets	US$'000	1,500	4,590	9,410	16,159	25,101	=SUM(J14:J17)

Non-current assets

PP&E	US$'000						
Deferred tax assets	US$'000						
Total non-current assets	US$'000	-	-	-	-	-	=SUM(J21:J22)

| **Total assets** | US$'000 | 1,500 | 4,590 | 9,410 | 16,159 | 25,101 | =SUM(J18,J23) |

Hang on – it's <u>NOT</u> balancing! My control account method has failed. What is going on?

Let's click on the summary error hyperlink in cell **F4**. This takes me to the 'Error Checks' worksheet:

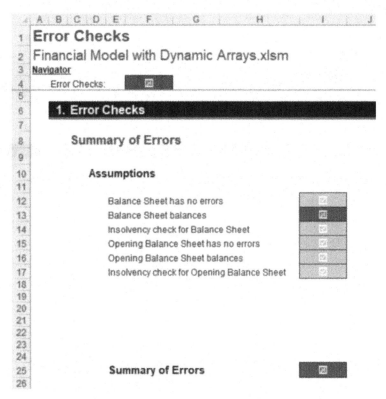

Clearly, the Balance Sheet is not balancing. Let's click on the hyperlink in cell **I13**. This sends me to the error:

What's going on? It appears to balance. Remember, we only set the number of periods to 5. Let me reset it to 20:

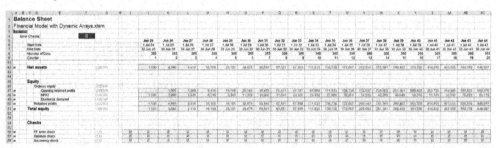

Timing

Financial Model with Dynamic Arrays.xlsm

Navigator

Error Checks: ☑

	Jun 25	Jun 26	Jun 27	Ju
Start Date	1 Jul 24	1 Jul 25	1 Jul 26	1 J
End Date	30 Jun 25	30 Jun 26	30 Jun 27	30 J
Number of Days	365	365	365	
Counter	1	2	3	

1. Timing Assumptions

Data (do not change once modelling has commenced)

Number of Periods	20 ▾	*Number_of_Periods*
Model Start Date	01 Jul 24	*Model_Start_Date*
Number of Months in a Full Period	12	*Periodicity*
Example Reporting Month	6 e.g. 30-Jun-25	*Example_Reporting_Month*
Reporting Month Factor	6	*Reporting_Month_Factor*

Returning to the Balance Sheet:

I am confused. There appears to be no error now? I shall change the number of periods back to five [5] but unhide the other columns:

404

The Balance Sheet is not balancing in the hidden columns. This is what is causing the error. It is a peculiar quirk of mixing dynamic array formulae with conventional Excel calculations. Upon closer inspection, I see that Cash is being calculated for periods where it should be blank:

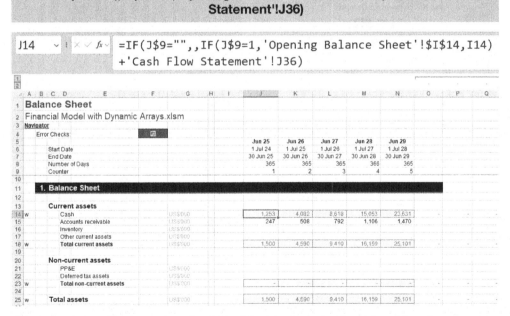

| J14 | ∨ : × ✓ ƒx ∨ | =IF(J$9=1,'Opening Balance Sheet'!$I$14,I14) |

This is causing non-blank totals throughout the Net assets section of the Balance Sheet. I need to revise the formula in cell **J14** and copy it across all periods (it will not propagate as it is not a dynamic array formula):

=IF(J$9="",,IF(J$9=1,'Opening Balance Sheet'!$I$14,I14)+'Cash Flow
Statement'!J36)

| J14 | ∨ : × ✓ ƒx ∨ | =IF(J$9="",,IF(J$9=1,'Opening Balance Sheet'!$I$14,I14)
+'Cash Flow Statement'!J36) |

This is putting zeroes into what should be blank cells, but at least the values are now zero and subsequent totals are no longer being impacted. I am not too worried about formatting here as this row is Work In Progress in any case. The misbalance is still not corrected yet though.

Row 47 is causing a similar problem:

| J47 | | × ✓ fx ∨ | =IF(J$9=1,'Opening Balance Sheet'!$I$50,I50) |

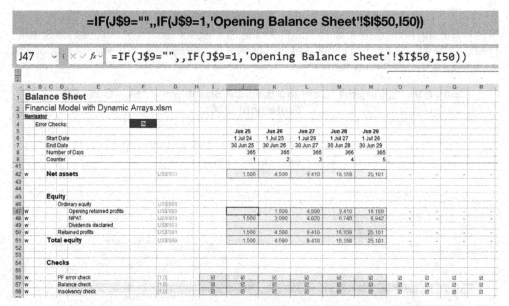

Cell **J47** should be modified and copied across:

> **=IF(J$9="",,IF(J$9=1,'Opening Balance Sheet'!$I$50,I50))**

| J47 | | × ✓ fx ∨ | =IF(J$9="",,IF(J$9=1,'Opening Balance Sheet'!$I$50,I50)) |

The problem has been caused by non-zero formulae being calculated in columns that should be zero. I have rectified this, albeit temporarily. Once all these formulae are replaced by dynamic array calculations, this issue will become redundant as calculations will not occur for other periods.

Phew! I can move on.

CHAPTER 17.8: COGS

Let's return to our Income Statement:

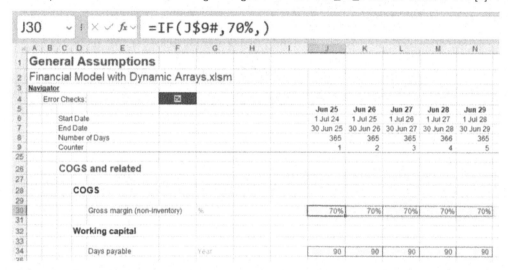

I can see that the next line item to calculate is COGS, so let's take a look at the Assumptions for this section, having changed the **Number_of_Periods** back to five [5]:

This is a pretty simple section, there are only two assumptions, the Gross margin (non-inventory) and the Days payable, both of which are already spilled ranges:

- Gross margin (non-inventory) (**J30**): **=IF(J$9#,70%,)**

- Days payable (**J34**): **=IF(J$9#,90,)**

Considering our discussion on input methodologies earlier, the first assumption uses the **percentages** method and the second the **amounts** method.

Back to the Case Study

Returning to the Calculations worksheet, we begin by bringing Revenue down from row 23 and bringing in the Gross margin (non-inventory) from row 30 of the 'General Assumptions' sheet:

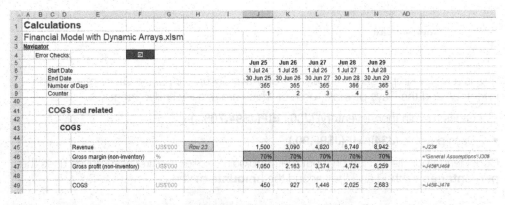

We've made use of a label here (cell **H45**) to make it clear where Revenue is coming from. This is constructed by concatenating the word "Row" with a space [" "] after it with the row from which Revenue is pulled down from, obtained by making use of the **ROW** function.

="Row "&ROW(J23)

Now, we can calculate the gross profit by simply multiplying Revenue by the Gross margin (non-inventory):

=J45#*J46#

This then allows us to calculate COGS by subtracting the Gross profit (non-inventory) from the Revenue:

=J45#-J47#

That's COGS calculated. Now I can move on to our working capital calculations. I begin by bringing in our Days payable assumption from row 34 of the 'General Assumptions' worksheet:

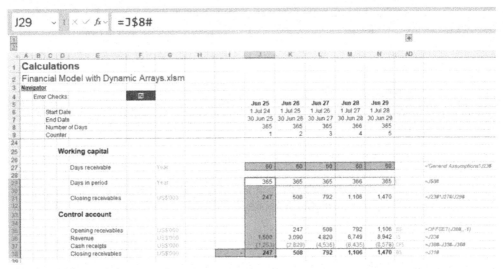

The remaining calculations for COGS are very similar to the calculations we performed for Revenue, and I can make use of this thanks to the *consistency* of our model! I will simply copy the formulae in cells **J29:J38**:

Pasting these into cell **J55** will almost complete this section:

Calculations

Financial Model with Dynamic Arrays.xlsm

Navigator

Error Checks: ☑

				Jun 25	Jun 26	Jun 27	Jun 28	Jun 29	
Start Date				1 Jul 24	1 Jul 25	1 Jul 26	1 Jul 27	1 Jul 28	
End Date				30 Jun 25	30 Jun 26	30 Jun 27	30 Jun 28	30 Jun 29	
Number of Days				365	365	365	366	365	
Counter				1	2	3	4	5	
COGS and related									
COGS									
Revenue	US$'000	Row 23		1,500	3,090	4,820	6,749	8,942	=J23#
Gross margin (non-inventory)	%			70%	70%	70%	70%	70%	='General Assumptions'!J30#
Gross profit (non-inventory)	US$'000			1,050	2,163	3,374	4,724	6,259	=J45#*J46#
COGS	US$'000			450	927	1,446	2,025	2,683	=J45#-J47#
Working capital									
Days payable	Year			90	90	90	90	90	='General Assumptions'!J34#
Days in period	Year			365	365	365	366	365	=J8#
Closing payables	US$'000			111	229	357	498	661	=J49#*J53#/J55#
Control account									
Opening payables	US$'000				111	229	357	498 BS	=OFFSET(J64#,-1)
COGS	US$'000			450	927	1,446	2,025	2,683 IS	=J49#
Cash payments	US$'000			(339)	(809)	(1,318)	(1,883)	(2,519) CFS	=J64#-J61#-J62#
Closing payables	US$'000			111	229	357	498	661 BS	=J57#

There is one more link to be made, cell **I64** must be linked to cell **I28** of the Opening Balance Sheet:

I64 ✕ ✓ *fx* ='Opening Balance Sheet'!$I$28

Calculations

Financial Model with Dynamic Arrays.xlsm

Navigator

Error Checks: ☑

				Jun 25	Jun 26	Jun 27	Jun 28	Jun 29	
Start Date				1 Jul 24	1 Jul 25	1 Jul 26	1 Jul 27	1 Jul 28	
End Date				30 Jun 25	30 Jun 26	30 Jun 27	30 Jun 28	30 Jun 29	
Number of Days				365	365	365	366	365	
Counter				1	2	3	4	5	
Control account									
Opening payables	US$'000			-	111	229	357	498 BS	=OFFSET(J64#,-1)
COGS	US$'000			450	927	1,446	2,025	2,683 IS	=J49#
Cash payments	US$'000			(339)	(809)	(1,318)	(1,883)	(2,519) CFS	=J64#-J61#-J62#
Closing payables	US$'000			111	229	357	498 BS	=J57#	

How hard was that? This is why it is so important to be *consistent* with your model layout. It makes your life easier. Further, if sections are regularly copied without error, this also suggests that the *robustness* of the model is high. It is a cheap victory for checking your model without getting a second pair of eyes; you get a second (or subsequent) section instead.

We are almost there; as before, using the control account we can identify:

1. **Number of calculations that need to be entered into the financial statements so that they balance:** This is always one less than the number of rows in the control account. In this instance it will be four minus one again, which is **three [3]**.

2. **The order to build the calculations into the financial statements:** This is always row 2 first, then row 3, then row 4 and so on. In this instance, this will be COGS (which will be a <u>negative</u> number in the Income Statement), Cash payments (Cash Flow Statement) and Closing payables (Balance Sheet).

3. **It identifies the key driver:** Line 2 of the control account is always the key driver, so in this case it will be COGS. If there were never any COGS, there would be no need to make Cash payments and without either of these items, Accounts payable would always be zero [0].

Time to insert. As with Revenue, the first financial statement for COGS is the Income Statement, but I am taking care to ensure that the link is brought in as a negative number:

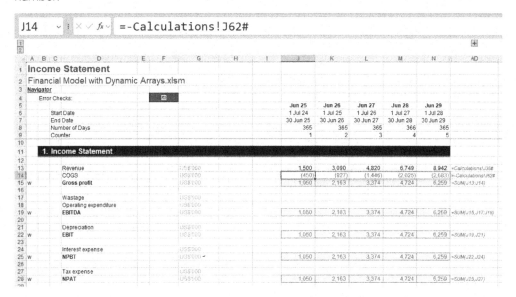

As expected, this will cause an error to flag until the other two links are created. The next link is to the Cash Flow Statement, but before that notice that both items included within the gross profit line are now dynamic arrays, so we can remove the work in progress formulae and actually create a dynamic sum of these two lines:

J15		×✓ fx✓	=J13#+J14#

Income Statement

Financial Model with Dynamic Arrays.xlsm

Navigator

							Jun 25	Jun 26	Jun 27	Jun 28	Jun 29	
Error Checks:			🔲									
							Jun 25	Jun 26	Jun 27	Jun 28	Jun 29	
Start Date							1 Jul 24	1 Jul 25	1 Jul 26	1 Jul 27	1 Jul 28	
End Date							30 Jun 25	30 Jun 26	30 Jun 27	30 Jun 28	30 Jun 29	
Number of Days							365	365	365	366	365	
Counter							1	2	3	4	5	
1. Income Statement												
Revenue			US$'000				1,500	3,090	4,820	6,749	8,942	=Calculations!J36#
COGS			US$'000				(450)	(927)	(1,446)	(2,025)	(2,683)	=-Calculations!J62#
Gross profit			US$'000				**1,050**	**2,163**	**3,374**	**4,724**	**6,259**	=J13#+J14#
Wastage			US$'000									
Operating expenditure			US$'000									
w	**EBITDA**		US$'000				1,050	2,163	3,374	4,724	6,259	=SUM(J15,J17:J18)
Depreciation			US$'000									
w	**EBIT**		US$'000				1,050	2,163	3,374	4,724	6,259	=SUM(J19,J21)
Interest expense			US$'000									
w	**NPBT**		US$'000				1,050	2,163	3,374	4,724	6,259	=SUM(J22,J24)
Tax expense			US$'000									
w	**NPAT**		US$'000				1,050	2,163	3,374	4,724	6,259	=SUM(J25,J27)

Taking care to remove the work in progress formulae and formatting from the entire row, as well as removing the 'w' in column **A**, we've successfully converted this to a dynamic array formula. Remember, we can't make use of the **SUM** function here as this would coerce our array, summing it all within one column rather than spilling:

J15		×✓ fx✓	=SUM(J13#,J14#)

Income Statement

Financial Model with Dynamic Arrays.xlsm

Navigator

							Jun 25	Jun 26	Jun 27	Jun 28	Jun 29	
Error Checks:			🔲									
							Jun 25	Jun 26	Jun 27	Jun 28	Jun 29	
Start Date							1 Jul 24	1 Jul 25	1 Jul 26	1 Jul 27	1 Jul 28	
End Date							30 Jun 25	30 Jun 26	30 Jun 27	30 Jun 28	30 Jun 29	
Number of Days							365	365	365	366	365	
Counter							1	2	3	4	5	
1. Income Statement												
Revenue			US$'000				1,500	3,090	4,820	6,749	8,942	=Calculations!J36#
COGS			US$'000				(450)	(927)	(1,446)	(2,025)	(2,683)	=-Calculations!J62#
Gross profit			US$'000				**17,671**					=SUM(J13#,J14#)
Wastage			US$'000									
Operating expenditure			US$'000									
w	**EBITDA**		US$'000				17,571	-	-	-	-	=SUM(J15,J17:J18)
Depreciation			US$'000									
w	**EBIT**		US$'000				17,571	-	-	-	-	=SUM(J19,J21)
Interest expense			US$'000									
w	**NPBT**		US$'000				17,571	-	-	-	-	=SUM(J22,J24)
Tax expense			US$'000									
w	**NPAT**		US$'000				17,571	-	-	-	-	=SUM(J25,J27)

Making use of the addition operator [**+**] avoids this issue and sums each column in our array individually:

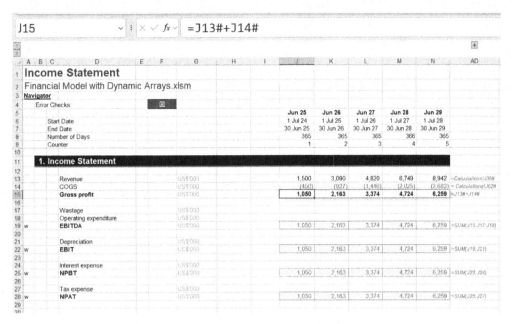

Let's now create our link to the Cash Flow Statement, bringing cash payments (from row 63 of the Calculations worksheet) into row 17 of the Cash Flow Statement:

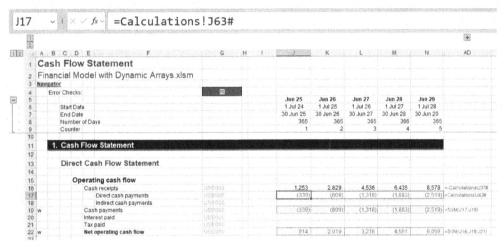

The final link to be made is linking closing payables (row 64 of the Calculations worksheet) into row 28 of the Balance Sheet and should cause the model to balance again and prevent the error from flagging:

Balance Sheet

Financial Model with Dynamic Arrays.xlsm

Navigator

			Jun 25	Jun 26	Jun 27	Jun 28	Jun 29	
Error Checks:		☑						
Start Date			1 Jul 24	1 Jul 25	1 Jul 26	1 Jul 27	1 Jul 28	
End Date			30 Jun 25	30 Jun 26	30 Jun 27	30 Jun 28	30 Jun 29	
Number of Days			365	365	365	366	365	
Counter			1	2	3	4	5	
Current liabilities								
Accounts payable		US$'000	111	229	357	498	661	=Calculations!J64#
Interest payable		US$'000						
Dividends payable		US$'000						
Tax payable		US$'000						
Other current liabilities		US$'000						
Total current liabilities	w	US$'000	111	229	357	498	661	=SUM(J28:J32)
Non-current liabilities								
Debt		US$'000						
Deferred tax liabilities		US$'000						
Total non-current liabilities	w	US$'000	-	-	-	-	-	=SUM(J36:J37)
Total liabilities	w	US$'000	111	229	357	498	661	=SUM(J33:J38)
Net assets	w	US$'000	1,050	3,213	6,587	11,311	17,571	=J25-J40
Equity								
Ordinary equity		US$'000						
Opening retained profits	w	US$'000	-	1,050	3,213	6,587	11,311	=IF(J59="",IF(J89=1,'Opening Balance Sheet'!$4$50,I50))
NPAT	w	US$'000	1,050	2,163	3,374	4,724	6,259	=Income Statement'!J28
Dividends declared	w	US$'000						
Retained profits	w	US$'000	1,050	3,213	6,587	11,311	17,571	=SUM(J47:J49)
Total equity	w	US$'000	1,050	3,213	6,587	11,311	17,571	=SUM(J46:J50)

That's it for COGS, onto the next step.

CHAPTER 17.9: INVENTORY

Returning to our Income Statement, we can see that the next line item to model is wastage:

1. Income Statement							
Revenue	US$'000		1,500	3,090	4,820	6,749	8,942
COGS	US$'000		(450)	(927)	(1,446)	(2,025)	(2,683)
Gross profit	US$'000		1,050	2,163	3,374	4,724	6,259
Wastage	US$'000						
Operating expenditure	US$'000						
EBITDA	US$'000		1,050	2,163	3,374	4,724	6,259
Depreciation	US$'000						
EBIT	US$'000		1,050	2,163	3,374	4,724	6,259
Interest expense	US$'000						
NPBT	US$'000		1,050	2,163	3,374	4,724	6,259
Tax expense	US$'000						
NPAT	US$'000		1,050	2,163	3,374	4,724	6,259

This means it's time to consider inventory, Here, I will be using an average cost of inventory approach, so I shall need both the value and the weight of the items. In order to work out our stock, I will need to consider both when we buy inventory and when it is used. In order to work this out, we will need to have two [2] control accounts. One of these is for the financial statements and as such will have to consider the monetary value of the inventory, the other is to keep track of our usage and will have to be in whatever unit we measure our consumption in, here kilograms.

Purchases and Related

As always, let's begin by considering the assumptions for this section from the 'General Assumptions' worksheet – but review them carefully:

J41		× ✓ fx	400				

Start Date	Jun 25	Jun 26	Jun 27	Jun 28	Jun 29

		Jun 25	Jun 26	Jun 27	Jun 28	Jun 29
General Assumptions						
Financial Model with Dynamic Arrays.xlsm						
Navigator						
Error Checks:	☑					
Start Date		1 Jul 24	1 Jul 25	1 Jul 26	1 Jul 27	1 Jul 28
End Date		30 Jun 25	30 Jun 26	30 Jun 27	30 Jun 28	30 Jun 29
Number of Days		365	365	365	366	365
Counter		1	2	3	4	5
Purchases and related						
Purchases						
Purchases	kg	400	775	325	550	1,000
Price	$/kg	3,990	4,750	2,800	4,160	5,000
Amount used per sale	kg	2.00	2.00	2.00	2.00	2.00
Wastage	%	3%	2%	2%	1%	1%
		Jun 24				
Opening inventory balance	kg	13				
Working capital						
Days payable	Year	30	30	30	30	30

The Purchases in row 41 have been hard coded. If you look carefully, you will see there are values in cells **J41:AC41** inclusive. The periods that are not required have been conditionally formatted to appear "invisible". During our Revenue calculations, it became clear that values for unused future periods can prove problematic. I need to ensure when referring to these on the Calculations worksheet I only take what I need.

Talking of "take", there is a dynamic array formula in cell **J42** which propagates the Price ($/kg):

> **=TAKE(IF(J$9#,{3990,4750,2800,4160,5000,4569,4712,4855,4998,5141,5284,5427, 5570,5713,5856,5999,6142,6285,6428,6571},),,Number_of_Periods)**

This is a little crafty (rather than CRaFT-y), as it generates the values

> **3990, 4750, 2800, 4160, 5000, 4569, 4712, 4855, 4998, 5141, 5284, 5427, 5570, 5713, 5856, 5999, 6142, 6285, 6428, 6571**

For each of the periods (years) one [1] to 20, depending upon whether the relevant period is a reporting period (*i.e.* less than or equal to the **Number_of_Periods**). It is a very useful method for putting specific inputs into each period, but it is opaque in that end users may not follow it, or worse, not understand how to change the inputs. You could refer to these values in assumptions cells elsewhere, but that defeats the entire purpose of this approach.

One benefit is that for cells not being reported upon (*e.g.* cell **O42** in the image below), there is no value. This avoids Balance Sheet issues later in the calculations:

O42	⌄	✕ ✓ *fx* ⌄											
A B C D	E	F	G	H	I	J	K	L	M	N	O
1 **General Assumptions**											
2 Financial Model with Dynamic Arrays.xlsm											
3 Navigator											
4 Error Checks:	☑										
5						Jun 25	Jun 26	Jun 27	Jun 28	Jun 29	
6 Start Date						1 Jul 24	1 Jul 25	1 Jul 26	1 Jul 27	1 Jul 28	
7 End Date						30 Jun 25	30 Jun 26	30 Jun 27	30 Jun 28	30 Jun 29	
8 Number of Days						365	365	365	366	365	
9 Counter						1	2	3	4	5	
36											
37 **Purchases and related**											
38											
39 **Purchases**											
40											
41 Purchases		kg				400	775	325	550	1,000	
42 Price		$/kg				3,990	4,750	2,800	4,160	5,000	
43 Amount used per sale		kg				2.00	2.00	2.00	2.00	2.00	
44 Wastage		%				3%	2%	2%	1%	1%	
45					Jun 24						
46 Opening inventory balance		kg			13						
47											
48 **Working capital**											
49											
50 Days payable		Year				30	30	30	30	30	

The Opening inventory balance, cell **I46**, is a single input (which is acceptable even in dynamic array modelling) and the heading in cell **I45** is calculated as:

> **=Model_Start_Date-1**

The remaining assumptions are similar to calculations already presented on this 'General Assumptions' worksheet:

* Amount per sale (cell **J43**): **=IF(J$9#,2,)**

* Wastage (cell **J44**): **=IF(J$9#=1,3%,IF(J$9#<4,2%,1%))**

* Days payable (cell **J50**): **=IF(J$9#,30,)**

Now I have discussed these inputs at length, let's move on to our Calculations worksheet and look at how we can bring them in dynamically:

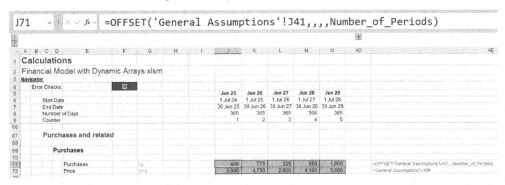

Whilst the Price assumptions may be referred to in the usual way in row 72, to ensure no values are brought in for row 71 that are not required, I have used the **OFFSET** function in cell **J71**, *viz.*

=OFFSET('General Assumptions'!J41,,,,Number_of_Periods)

The **OFFSET** function has brought in the Purchases, beginning in cell **J41** of the 'General Assumptions' worksheet and setting the width of this array equal to our named range, **Number_of_Periods**. You could use the maximum value in row 9 if you prefer, but I think citing the **Number_of_Periods** better explains the width. Thus, Price becomes another spilled range.

Next, I simply restate our referred values to convert our purchases from a weight (kg) to a currency (here, US$'000):

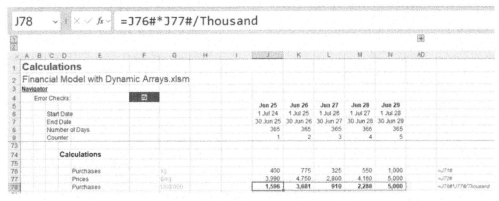

Take care when calculating this: the Purchases are in kg and the Prices are in $/kg but we want to report in $'000 so we need to remember to divide by 1,000. To avoid hardcode in the formula, we've made use of a Named Range (**Thousand**) from our 'Model Parameters' worksheet to perform this.

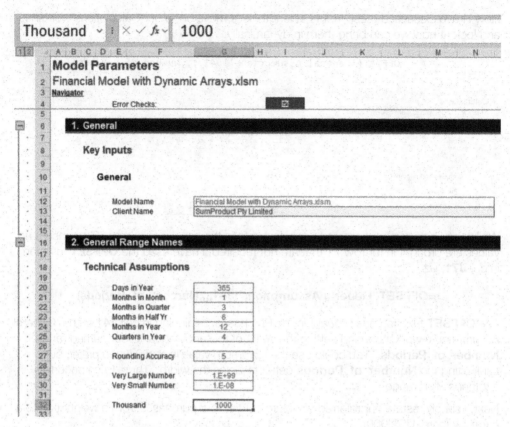

Next, I can bring in the Days payable and calculate the Closing payables. As the layout for this section is slightly different from the above sections we need to take care: we cannot simply copy and paste from above.

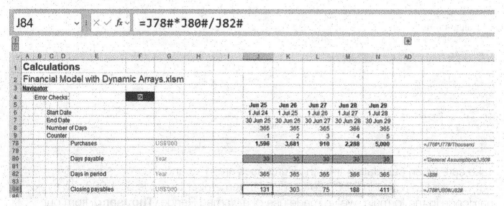

I can now construct our control account as before, linking the Closing payables from row 84 into row 91 and the purchases from row 78 into row 89. I can then use our established **OFFSET** trick in row 88 to bring in the previous period's Closing balance from row 91, and then subtracting the figures in row 88 and row 89 from the figure in row 91 produces the Cash payments in row 90:

				Jun 25	Jun 26	Jun 27	Jun 28	Jun 29		
1	Calculations									
2	Financial Model with Dynamic Arrays.xlsm									
3	Navigator									
4	Error Checks:									
5				Jun 25	Jun 26	Jun 27	Jun 28	Jun 29		
6	Start Date			1 Jul 24	1 Jul 25	1 Jul 26	1 Jul 27	1 Jul 28		
7	End Date			30 Jun 25	30 Jun 26	30 Jun 27	30 Jun 28	30 Jun 29		
8	Number of Days			365	365	365	366	365		
9	Counter			1	2	3	4	5		
85										
86	Control account									
87										
88	Opening payables	US$'000		-	131	303	75	188	85	=OFFSET(J91#,-1)
89	Purchases	US$'000		1,596	3,681	910	2,288	5,000		=J78#
90	Cash payments	US$'000		(1,465)	(3,510)	(1,138)	(2,175)	(4,777)	045	=J91#-J88#-J89#
91	Closing payables	US$'000		131	303	75	188	411	85	=J64#

Notice that the opening (brought forward) balance for Closing payables here (**I91**) is deliberately blank. This is because I have already considered this opening balance in cell **I64** for our COGS control account. Of course, in some examples this may be split out so do check notes to accounts when creating charts of accounts in the models you build.

Normally, I would link our control account to the financial statements now, but notice the deliberate blank cell **AD89**. This Purchases control account is linked to the Inventory control account and certain values are netted off, *i.e.* the purchases that are here (in row 89) will be equal and opposite to a movement in our inventory control account in due course. Therefore, they will <u>not</u> be entered into the financial statements. If I only link the other control account entries at this point, the Balance Sheet will not balance, so I need to delay this part of the process until the Inventory control account is completed.

Inventory

You might want to strap yourself in for this part: things are about to get a little more involved as we calculate inventory. It is not that the calculations or concepts are particularly complex; it is more that we have to move haphazardly through the calculations and put "holding formulae" in at certain times to accommodate calculations where some are dynamic arrays and some are not.

To start the 'Inventory and related' section, let's begin by bringing in purchases in both kg and US$'000 (remembering to construct row labels) as well as the amount used per sale and wastage inputs from our 'General Assumptions' worksheet and the projected sales from back up in row 17:

					Jun 25	Jun 26	Jun 27	Jun 28	Jun 29		
1	Calculations										
2	Financial Model with Dynamic Arrays.xlsm										
3	Navigator										
4	Error Checks:										
5					Jun 25	Jun 26	Jun 27	Jun 28	Jun 29		
6	Start Date				1 Jul 24	1 Jul 25	1 Jul 26	1 Jul 27	1 Jul 28		
7	End Date				30 Jun 25	30 Jun 26	30 Jun 27	30 Jun 28	30 Jun 29		
8	Number of Days				365	365	365	366	365		
9	Counter				1	2	3	4	5		
93											
94	Inventory and related										
95											
96	Referred values										
97											
98	Purchases	kg	Row 71		400	775	325	550	1,000		=J71#
99	Purchases	US$'000	Row 78		1,596	3,681	910	2,288	5,000		=J78#
100	Amount used per sale	kg			2.00	2.00	2.00	2.00	2.00		='General Assumptions'.J43#
101	Wastage	%			3%	2%	2%	1%	1%		='General Assumptions'.J44#
102											
103	Projected sales	=	Row 17		100	200	300	400	500		=J17#

With these brought in we can replicate our amount used per sale (in kg) and our projected sales to work out the COGS in kg:

J109	∨ : × ✓ fx ∨	=J107#*J108#

	A B C D	E	F	G	H	I	J	K	L	M	N	AD
1	Calculations											
2	Financial Model with Dynamic Arrays.xlsm											
3	Navigator											
4	Error Checks:		☑									
5							Jun 25	Jun 26	Jun 27	Jun 28	Jun 29	
6	Start Date						1 Jul 24	1 Jul 25	1 Jul 26	1 Jul 27	1 Jul 28	
7	End Date						30 Jun 25	30 Jun 26	30 Jun 27	30 Jun 28	30 Jun 29	
8	Number of Days						365	365	365	366	365	
9	Counter						1	2	3	4	5	
104												
105	Calculations											
106												
107	Amount used per sale		kg	Row 100			2.00	2.00	2.00	2.00	2.00	=J100#
108	Projected sales		#	Row 103			100	200	300	400	500	=J103#
109	COGS		kg				200	400	600	800	1,000	=J107#*J108#

Next, I will need to bring our initial Closing inventory balance (in kg) into cell **I112**. The question is, where does this come from? Since other initial opening values link straight to their corresponding control account, I shall do the same here for consistency. Unfortunately, this means that I must first move further down the sheet and construct a portion of the control accounts. Whilst this keeps to our concept of consistency, you can argue that this is to the detriment of transparency. This is why "Best Practice" is a proper noun. Sometimes, it's a judgment call.

To begin I must link cell **I136** to the assumption for the Opening inventory balance (in kg):

='General Assumptions'!$I$46

Once this value is linked to the control account in cell **I136**, it may then be referenced in cell **I112**:

=I136

A similar approach is then adopted for the dollar value of Inventory too. The initial value from

='Opening Balance Sheet'!$I$16

is linked to the initial Closing inventory balance ($) in cell **I144** and then this is referenced higher up the worksheet once more in cell **I128**:

420

I144	⌄ : × ✓ fx⌄	='Opening Balance Sheet'!$I$16

	A B C D	E	F	G	H	I	J	K	
1	**Calculations**								
2	Financial Model with Dynamic Arrays.xlsm								
3	Navigator								
4	Error Checks:		☑						
5							Jun 25	Jun 26	Jur
6	Start Date						1 Jul 24	1 Jul 25	1 Ju
7	End Date						30 Jun 25	30 Jun 26	30 Ju
8	Number of Days						365	365	
9	Counter						1	2	
104									
105	**Calculations**								
106									
107	Amount used per sale		kg	Row 100			2.00	2.00	
108	Projected sales		#	Row 103			100	200	
109	COGS		kg				200	400	
110									
111	Inventory movement pre-wastage		kg		Opening balance				
112	Closing inventory balance		kg			13			
113	Inventory balance pre-wastage		kg						
114	Wastage		%						
115	**Wastage**		kg						
116									
117	Inventory balance pre-COGS transfer		kg						
118	Inventory balance pre-COGS transfer		US$'000						
119	COGS		kg						
120	**COGS**		US$'000						
121									
122	Inventory balance pre-wastage		kg						
123	Inventory balance pre-wastage		US$'000						
124	Wastage		kg						
125	Wastage		US$'000						
126									
127	Proportion used		%		Opening balance				
128	Closing inventory		US$'000			-			
129									
130	**Inventory at hand (kg)**								
131									
132	Opening inventory		kg						
133	Purchases		kg						
134	COGS		kg						
135	Wastage		kg						
136	Closing inventory		kg			13			
137									
138	**Inventory ($)**								
139									
140	Opening inventory		US$'000						
141	Purchases		US$'000						
142	COGS		US$'000						
143	Wastage		US$'000						
144	Closing inventory		US$'000			-			
145									

Note that cells **I112** and **I128** have been formatted using the Parameter Style.

If that wasn't a little messy, don't worry, it gets worse. I need to calculate the Inventory movement pre-wastage by keeping a running total of the balances, which will require an Inventory control account in kg. However, I don't yet have the prerequisite calculations to make our Inventory control account dynamic so I will need to construct some Work In Progress formulae once more to facilitate these calculations. This will require us working through this section in an unusual order. Welcome to the wonderful world of dynamic arrays!

Let's begin by bringing the kg figures for purchases from row 98 into row 133 and COGS from row 109 into row 134 (negated):

I can't bring in wastage yet, as that is what I am endeavouring to calculate, and I cannot calculate the opening inventory as this is based on the closing inventory. Therefore, by process of elimination next up must be the Closing inventory. This will require using a **SCAN(LAMBDA)**. However, I must remember this will eventually need to include wastage as well, but we don't yet have this figure. This means that we will have to exclude wastage for the time being and return later to add wastage to this calculation:

We've used the following formula:

=SCAN(I136,J133#+J134#,LAMBDA(accumulator,value,accumulator+value))

This will begin with the opening balance, provided in cell **I136**, and add to it the figures in cells **J133** and **J134**, outputting the result in cell **J136**, and then add to that result the figures in cells **K133** and **K134**, output that result and so on. Eventually, this will also consider the figures in row 135, but we don't yet have these and as such have formatted this using the WIP Style and inserted a "w" in cell **A136**. Using a dynamic array formula, I cannot link to a range of blank cells without generating errors.

Note that as you type the formula in the variables you create, **accumulator** and **value**, they become recognised by Excel's Formula AutoComplete. You should observe that

422

these declared variables will only work inside this formula though as the **LAMBDA** has not been specified in the Name Manager (**CTRL** + **F3**).

Now I may calculate the opening balance, as usual using the **OFFSET** function:

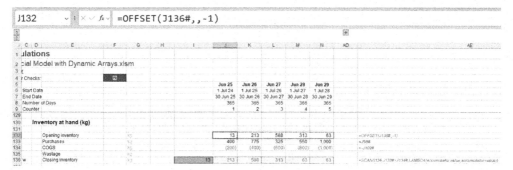

Now, I can return to our calculations above. To begin, I shall calculate our kg value for Inventory movement pre-wastage (in row 111) by summing rows 133 and 134:

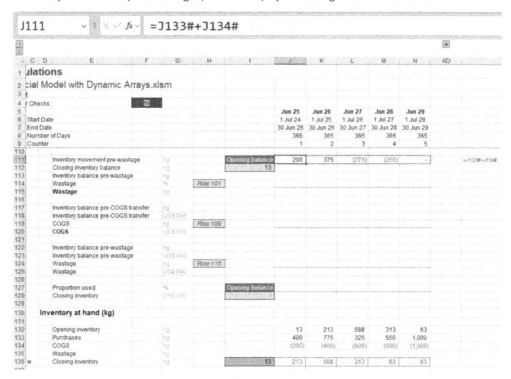

I will then use the **SCAN(LAMBDA)** technique again to calculate the Closing inventory balance:

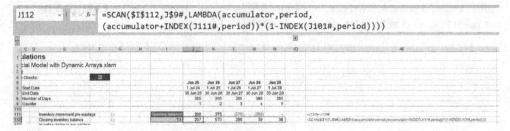

Simple, right? No? Let's work through the formula:

We begin with the initial value in **$I$112** (clearly anchored), our Inventory opening balance. The array is the counter in row 9 as I shall use this in conjunction with the **INDEX** function to return the values required. Before I consider the **LAMBDA** as a whole, let's work backwards to see what's going on here. Consider

This will reference the range **J101#**, our Wastage percentages, and select the value in this range based on its position defined by **period**. It will then subtract this from one [1] to return the percentage of inventory that does not constitute wastage. Considering the previous part:

A similar idea, this will call the reference **J111#**, our Inventory movement pre wastage, to return the relevant movement for the **period**. Now, considering the **LAMBDA** as a whole:

this will add the **accumulator** (which will always be the previous period's Closing inventory balance) to the Inventory movement in the **period** and then multiply this by one [1] less the Wastage percentage for the **period**. This will compute the amount that does not constitute wastage, which is the Closing inventory balance.

If that isn't clear (!), consider the following example:

- Opening inventory is 15kg

- Purchase in the period totals 210kg

- COGS in the period totals 125kg

- Wastage is 2%.

In this example, the Inventory balance pre-wastage would be 15 + 210 - 125, which is 100kg (an easy number to work with, that's convenient!). The Closing balance could then either be worked out by calculating wastage as 2% of 100kg and then subtracting this from the balance of 100kg to give 98kg, or (as we've done above) you could instead subtract 2% from 1 to give 98% and multiply this 98% by the 100kg to also give 98kg, *viz*:

	A	B	C	D	E	F	G
1							
2			Opening Inventory	kg	15		
3			Purchases	kg	210		
4			COGS	kg	(125)		
5			Closing Inventory (pre-wastage)	kg	100		
6							
7			Wastage	%	2%		
8							
9		**Method 1**					
10							
11			Wastage	kg	2		=E5*E7
12							
13			Closing Inventory	kg	98		=E5-E11
14							
15		**Method 2**					
16							
17			Alternate Closing Inventory	kg	98		=E5*(1-E7)
18							
19			Wastage	kg	2		=E5-E17

With that (hopefully) cleared up, let's move on.

I can now calculate the Inventory balance pre wastage by using our **OFFSET** trick on row 112 to return the Opening inventory balance and then adding to this the Inventory movement pre-wastage (from row 111):

$$=OFFSET(J112\#,,-1)+J111\#$$

Still with me? I can now bring down the Wastage percentages from row 101 and multiply this by our Inventory balance pre-wastage (row 113) to calculate the wastage in kg:

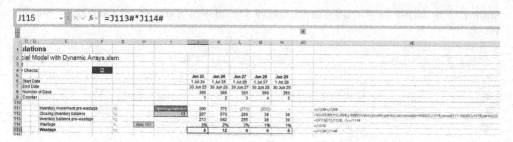

With this, I may now link wastage (as a negative) into our control account (in row 135) and amend our closing balance to include the newly completed row 135 (remembering to remove the WIP Style and the "w" in column **A**). This completes the inventory at hand (kg) control account:

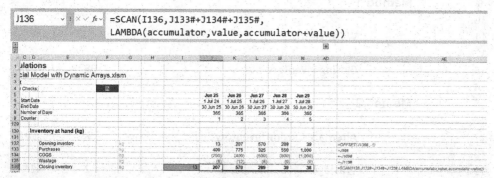

=SCAN(I136,J133#+J134#+J135#,LAMBDA(accumulator,value,accumulator+value))

We're getting there! Now I need to start considering the monetary control account. I may begin by summing rows 132 and 133 to calculate our Inventory balance pre-COGS transfer in kg (row 117):

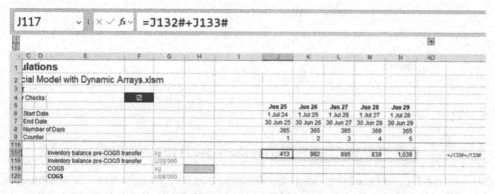

Now I need to visit the third control account, the Inventory ($) control account. I have already linked the closing balance in cell **I144** to cell **I16** of the Opening Balance Sheet. As such, I can now bring the dollar value of purchases in from row 99:

426

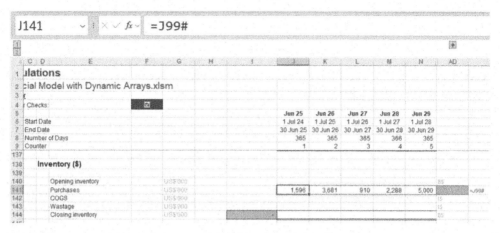

Unfortunately, I can go no further. I do not have the COGS or Wastage amounts required here yet and the Closing inventory is going to use a different formula to **SCAN(LAMBDA)**, so we'll return to this as and when we can. For now, let's return to row 118 and calculate the Inventory balance pre-COGS transfer (in $'000):

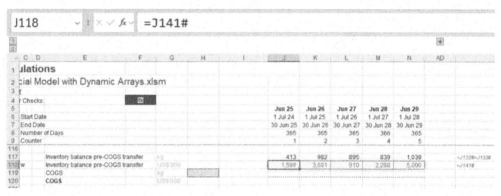

Again, this is formatted with the WIP Style for now as it will eventually need to consider the Opening balance of the inventory ($) control account – but I can't create this yet.

What I can do though is bring in the COGS value in kg (from row 109) and calculate the COGS value in US$'000 by working out the proportion (in kg) of Inventory balance pre-cogs transfer that constitutes COGS (**J119#** divided by **J117#**) and then multiplying our Inventory balance pre cogs transfer in US$'000 by this proportion:

=J118#*J119#/J117#

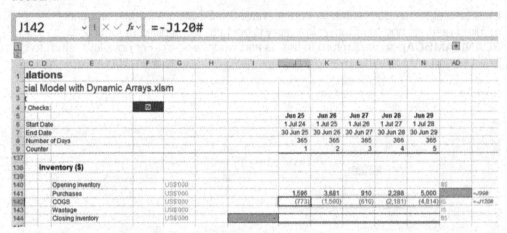

J120	$\vee$: $\times \checkmark f_x \vee$	=J118#*J119#/J117#							

C D	E	F	G	H	I	J	K	L	M	N	AD
1	ılations										
2	cial Model with Dynamic Arrays.xlsm										
3											
4	r Checks:		☑								
5						Jun 25	Jun 26	Jun 27	Jun 28	Jun 29	
6	Start Date					1 Jul 24	1 Jul 25	1 Jul 26	1 Jul 27	1 Jul 28	
7	End Date					30 Jun 25	30 Jun 26	30 Jun 27	30 Jun 28	30 Jun 29	
8	Number of Days					365	365	365	366	365	
9	Counter					1	2	3	4	5	
116											
117	Inventory balance pre-COGS transfer	kg				413	982	895	839	1,039	=J132#+J133#
118 w	Inventory balance pre-COGS transfer	US$'000				1,596	3,681	910	2,298	5,000	=J141#
119	COGS	kg	Row 109			200	400	600	800	1,000	=J109#
120	COGS	US$'000				773	1,500	610	2,181	4,814	=J118#*J119#/J117#

With our COGS figure calculated we can insert this (as a negative) into the control account:

J142	$\vee$: $\times \checkmark f_x \vee$	=-J120#							

C D	E	F	G	H	I	J	K	L	M	N	AD
1	ılations										
2	cial Model with Dynamic Arrays.xlsm										
3											
4	r Checks:		☑								
5						Jun 25	Jun 26	Jun 27	Jun 28	Jun 29	
6	Start Date					1 Jul 24	1 Jul 25	1 Jul 26	1 Jul 27	1 Jul 28	
7	End Date					30 Jun 25	30 Jun 26	30 Jun 27	30 Jun 28	30 Jun 29	
8	Number of Days					365	365	365	366	365	
9	Counter					1	2	3	4	5	
137											
138	Inventory ($)										
139											
140	Opening inventory	US$'000								85	
141	Purchases	US$'000				1,596	3,681	910	2,298	5,000	=J99#
142	COGS	US$'000				(773)	(1,500)	(610)	(2,181)	(4,814)	=J120#
143	Wastage	US$'000								15	
144	Closing inventory	US$'000								85	

Let's now return to row 122 and begin calculating our wastage in US$000. First, I will calculate our Inventory balance pre-wastage in kg by subtracting the COGS in kg (row 119) from the Inventory balance pre-COGS transfer in kg (row 117). I may then repeat this calculation using COGS in US$'000 (row 120) and the Inventory balance pre-COGS transfer in US$'000 (row 118) to calculate our Inventory balance pre-wastage in US$'000. After bringing our wastage figure in kg from row 115 into row 124, I may then perform the weighting calculation that we used to calculate COGS in US$'000 to calculate similarly Wastage in US$'000:

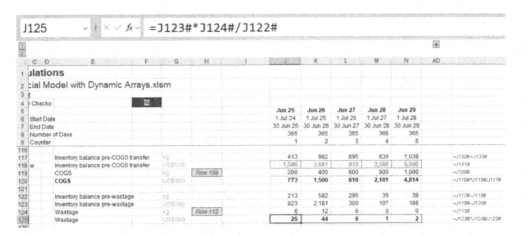

We can now link Wastage back to the final control account:

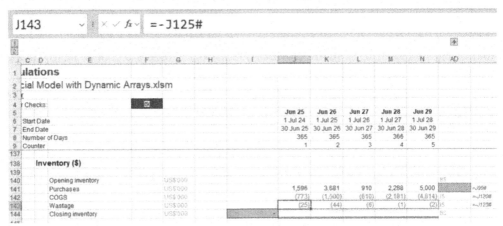

You might think I may now calculate our Closing inventory and Opening inventory as normal, and then link this into our work in progress calculation in row 118. Unfortunately, this is not the case. Due to the way dynamic arrays work, Excel would identify this as a circular calculation so instead we're going to employ a trick to calculate the Closing balance for this account.

I begin by returning to row 127 and calculating the proportion of inventory used in the kg control account. This is calculated by negating the sum of COGS and the Wastage, then dividing this by the sum of the Opening inventory and the Purchases, *viz.*

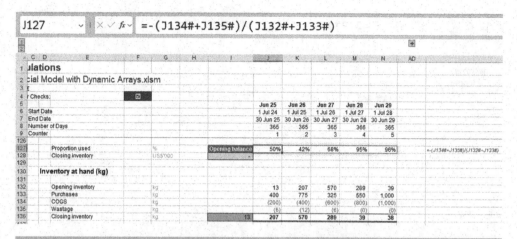

				Jun 25	Jun 26	Jun 27	Jun 28	Jun 29
Start Date				1 Jul 24	1 Jul 25	1 Jul 26	1 Jul 27	1 Jul 28
End Date				30 Jun 25	30 Jun 26	30 Jun 27	30 Jun 28	30 Jun 29
Number of Days				365	365	365	366	365
Counter				1	2	3	4	5
Proportion used	%	Opening balance		50%	42%	68%	95%	96%
Closing inventory	US$'000							
Inventory at hand (kg)								
Opening inventory	kg			13	207	570	269	39
Purchases	kg			400	775	325	550	1,000
COGS	kg			(200)	(400)	(600)	(800)	(1,000)
Wastage	kg			(6)	(12)	(6)	(0)	(0)
Closing inventory	kg		13	207	570	289	39	38

=-(J134#+J135#)/(J132#+J133#)

Note that this figure will be the same for both control accounts, so I may use this value to calculate the Closing inventory in US$'000, as long as I have an opening balance to start with. Therefore, I employ a **SCAN(LAMBDA)** function that uses the counter (in row 9) as the array, similar to previously:

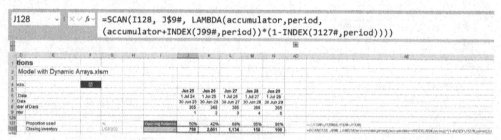

The formula I have used is as follows:

=SCAN(I128, J$9#, LAMBDA(accumulator,period,
(accumulator+INDEX(J99#,period))*(1-INDEX(J127#,period))))

This will take the range **J99#**, the Purchases (US$'000), by the **period** to return the purchases for the **period** and then add this to the **accumulator**, the previous **period**'s Closing balance. This will then reference the range **J127#**, the Proportion used, to return the relevant figure for the **period** and then subtract this from one [1] to provide the proportion remaining. The previous **period**'s Closing balance plus the Purchases for the **period** are then multiplied by the proportion remaining to return the Closing balance.

Now this is completed, I may link row 144 to row 128 to calculate the closing balance for this control account, and then (in row 140) use the **OFFSET** trick once more on row 144 to calculate the Opening balance:

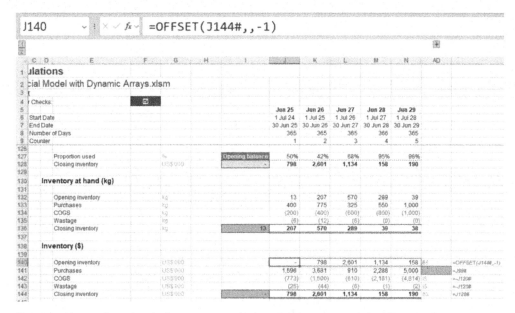

Finally, with our Opening balance now calculated, I may amend the Work In Progress formula in **J118** to include the Opening balance (row 140) (remembering to remove the WIP Style and the "w" in column **A**):

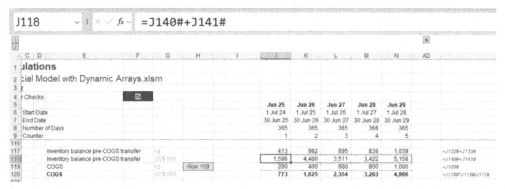

Hopefully, you now see the value of this book concerning financial modelling with dynamic arrays, because some sections are a little technical and require you to work through the calculations in an unexpected order.

Completing the Control Accounts

Still, we're not yet finished. We now have two control accounts completed and five links to be made to our financial statements, ignoring the netted off Purchases.

Beginning with the Purchases control account:

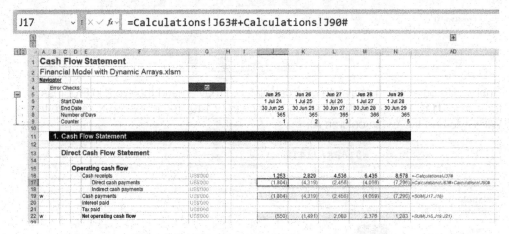

The first link to be made is to the Cash Flow Statement, linking cash payments from row 90 of the Calculations sheet into row 17 of the Cash Flow Statement, note that there is already a value in row 17 of the Cash Flow Statement, so we add **J90** to this:

| J17 | =Calculations!J63#+Calculations!J90# |

	A B C D E	F	G H I	J	K	L	M	N	AD
1	Cash Flow Statement								
2	Financial Model with Dynamic Arrays.xlsm								
3	Navigator								
4	Error Checks:								
5				Jun 25	Jun 26	Jun 27	Jun 28	Jun 29	
6	Start Date			1 Jul 24	1 Jul 25	1 Jul 26	1 Jul 27	1 Jul 28	
7	End Date			30 Jun 25	30 Jun 26	30 Jun 27	30 Jun 28	30 Jun 29	
8	Number of Days			365	365	365	366	365	
9	Counter			1	2	3	4	5	
10									
11	1. Cash Flow Statement								
12									
13	Direct Cash Flow Statement								
14									
15	Operating cash flow								
16	Cash receipts	US$000		1,253	2,829	4,536	6,435	8,578	=Calculations!J37#
17	Direct cash payments	US$000		(1,804)	(4,319)	(2,456)	(4,059)	(7,296)	=Calculations!J63#+Calculations!J90#
18	Indirect cash payments	US$000							
19 w	Cash payments	US$000		(1,804)	(4,319)	(2,456)	(4,059)	(7,296)	=SUM(J17:J18)
20	Interest paid	US$000							
21	Tax paid	US$000							
22 w	Net operating cash flow	US$000		(550)	(1,491)	2,080	2,376	1,283	=SUM(J16,J19:J21)

As soon as I do this, the model will no longer balance, which is what we would expect. I still have four [4] more links to make.

The next link is linking closing payables from row 91 of the Calculations sheet into row 28 of the Balance Sheet. Again, note that there is already a value here and we will be adding the two values together:

| J28 | =Calculations!J64#+Calculations!J91# |

	A B C D	E	F	G H I	J	K	L	M	N	AD
1	Balance Sheet									
2	Financial Model with Dynamic Arrays.xlsm									
3	Navigator									
4	Error Checks:									
5					Jun 25	Jun 26	Jun 27	Jun 28	Jun 29	
6	Start Date				1 Jul 24	1 Jul 25	1 Jul 26	1 Jul 27	1 Jul 28	
7	End Date				30 Jun 25	30 Jun 26	30 Jun 27	30 Jun 28	30 Jun 29	
8	Number of Days				365	365	365	366	365	
9	Counter				1	2	3	4	5	
26										
27	Current liabilities									
28	Accounts payable		US$000		242	531	431	685	1,072	=Calculations!J64#+Calculations!J91#
29	Interest payable		US$000							
30	Dividends payable		US$000							
31	Tax payable		US$000							
32	Other current liabilities		US$000							
33 w	Total current liabilities		US$000		242	531	431	685	1,072	=SUM(J28:J32)

Moving on to our Inventory control account:

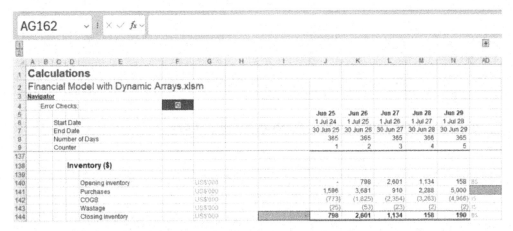

The first link to be made is linking COGS to the Income Statement:

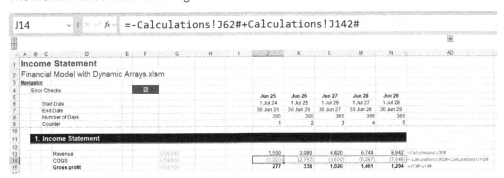

Next, I bring Wastage into the Income Statement:

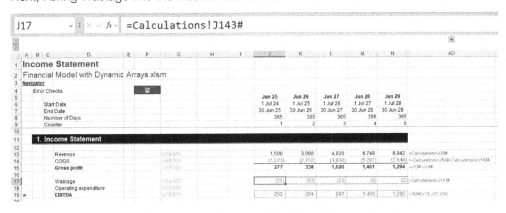

Finally, we can bring closing inventory into row 16 of the Balance Sheet:

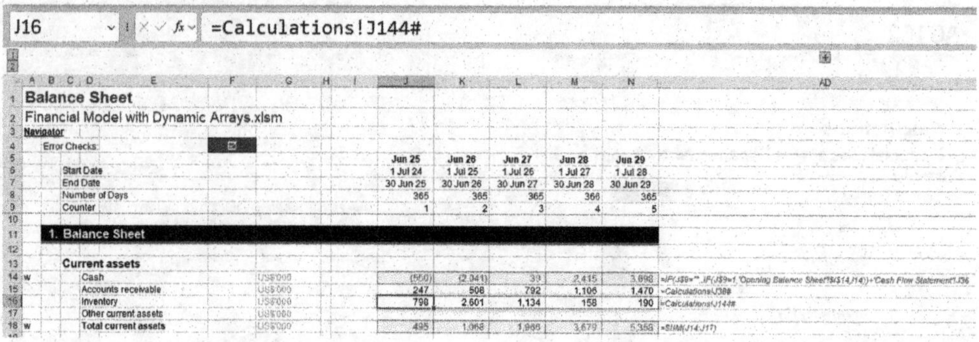

Balance Sheet

Financial Model with Dynamic Arrays.xlsm

Navigator

			Jun 25	Jun 26	Jun 27	Jun 28	Jun 29	
	Error Checks:	☑						
	Start Date		1 Jul 24	1 Jul 25	1 Jul 26	1 Jul 27	1 Jul 28	
	End Date		30 Jun 25	30 Jun 26	30 Jun 27	30 Jun 28	30 Jun 29	
	Number of Days		365	365	365	366	365	
	Counter		1	2	3	4	5	

1. Balance Sheet

Current assets

w	Cash	US$'000	(560)	(2,341)	39	2,415	3,898	=IF(J9=",",IF(J9=1,'Opening Balance Sheet'!\$J\$14,J14)+'Cash Flow Statement'!J36
	Accounts receivable	US$'000	247	508	792	1,105	1,470	=Calculations!J38#
	Inventory	US$'000	790	2,601	1,134	158	190	=Calculations!J144#
	Other current assets	US$'000						
w	Total current assets	US$'000	495	1,068	1,965	3,679	5,358	=SUM(J14:J17)

And it balances! Inventory was a bit of a tough one, but I hope you've taken *stock* of the situation. *[It's very cruel to make people suffer through your terrible jokes straight after they've suffered through the inventory calculations – Editor.]* We've completed our inventory calculations, what's next?

CHAPTER 17.10: OPERATING EXPENDITURE

Returning to the Income Statement, we can see the next line item to consider is Operating expenditure:

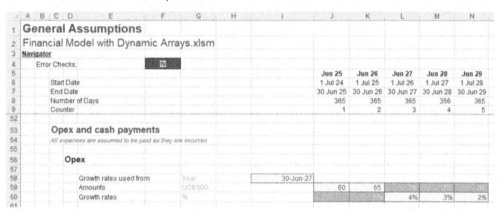

1. Income Statement

Revenue	US$'000	1,500	3,090	4,820	6,749	8,942
COGS	US$'000	(1,223)	(2,752)	(3,800)	(5,287)	(7,648)
Gross profit	US$'000	277	338	1,020	1,461	1,294
Wastage	US$'000	(25)	(53)	(23)	(2)	(2)
Operating expenditure	US$'000					
EBITDA	US$'000	252	284	997	1,460	1,292
Depreciation	US$'000					
EBIT	US$'000	252	284	997	1,460	1,292
Interest expense	US$'000					
NPBT	US$'000	252	284	997	1,460	1,292
Tax expense	US$'000					
NPAT	US$'000	252	284	997	1,460	1,292

Let's first consider the assumptions:

	A B C D	E	F	G	H	I	J	K	L	M	N
1	**General Assumptions**										
2	Financial Model with Dynamic Arrays.xlsm										
3	**Navigator**										
4	Error Checks:										
5							Jun 25	Jun 26	Jun 27	Jun 28	Jun 29
6	Start Date						1 Jul 24	1 Jul 25	1 Jul 26	1 Jul 27	1 Jul 28
7	End Date						30 Jun 25	30 Jun 26	30 Jun 27	30 Jun 28	30 Jun 29
8	Number of Days						365	365	365	366	365
9	Counter						1	2	3	4	5
52											
53	**Opex and cash payments**										
54	All expenses are assumed to be paid as they are incurred										
55											
56	**Opex**										
57											
58	Growth rates used from	Year		30-Jun-27							
59	Amounts	US$'000					60	65			
60	Growth rates	%							4%	3%	2%
61											

This uses a slightly more complex version of the amount and growth rates input methodology, which again, I shall briefly remind you about.

And Again: The Four Methods of Entering Inputs into a Model

There are only four ways to enter data into a financial model. The actual method may incorporate combinations of the following:

1. **Amounts:** Data is entered in as numerical (absolute) values. It may be in units, thousands, millions, GWh and so on, but ultimately it is a number. This is an ideal entry method where data is copied from elsewhere or may eventually be linked to another model (say).

2. **Percentages:** Data is typed in as a percentage or ratio of another value, be it input or calculated. This is often the approach employed for variable costs, for example.

---

3. **Amount and growth rates:** Data is entered in two forms, an amount in at least the first period and then a percentage thereafter. This is often the method used for sky blue forecasting and sometimes leads to what the modelling connoisseur may describe as "hockey stick projections".

4. **Combination:** Usually perceived as a more sophisticated version of the **amount and growth rates** approach, this method combines two or more input methodologies. The combination may be selected by use of a switch (manual input) or a trigger (calculation). This is often used for reforecasting or replacing forecast with actuals, *etc.* **IF** and **CHOOSE** are functions often associated with this methodology.

Here, I have made use of a Data Validation dropdown list (**ALT** + **D** + **L**) to allow users to select a date to begin using growth rates from, prior to this the input amounts will be used and after this growth rates will be applied to prior figures instead.

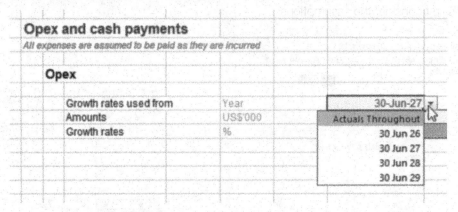

It is worth noting how to construct lists using dynamic arrays. If I select the data validated cell (**I58**) and use the keyboard shortcut **ALT** + **D** + **L**, I get the 'Data Validation' dialog, *viz.*

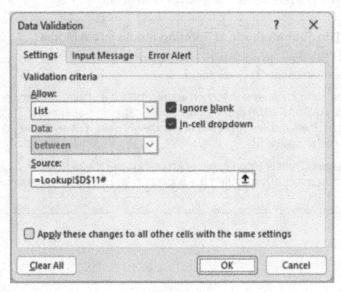

Notice the reference in the 'Source:' input:

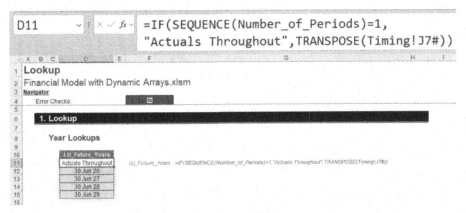

It is the range **LU_Future_Years**. This is a dynamic array we created earlier. The key issue is that the actual number of rows in the range may vary. At the time of writing, referencing the range name in the dialog will not cause the range to contract or extend. You have to reference the head cell of the spilled array (cell **D11** on the Lookup worksheet) and add the "**#**" symbol manually:

=Lookup!$D$11#

Then it will work as intended. It's a useful trick to add to your toolbox when building financial models using dynamic arrays.

The remaining inputs here are already dynamic arrays, so bringing these into the Calculations worksheet will be easy:

- Amounts (cell **J59**): **=IF(J$9#,55+J$9#*5,)**

- Growth rates (cell **J60**, formatted as a percentage): **=IF(J$9#=1,,IF((7-J$9#)
/100>1%,(7-J$9#)/100,1%))**

It should be noted that the formula for Growth rates starts in column **J**, not column **K**. Don't be fooled by the empty cell formatting. That is only to aid understanding for end users.

To begin, let's bring in the 'Growth rates used from' date and construct a flag to identify if the growth rate should be used:

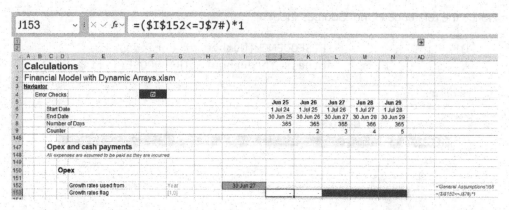

The flag uses the following formula:

=($I$152<=J$7#)*1

This will check if **$I$152** is less than or equal to each value in the array **J$7#** and return a value of either TRUE or FALSE for each one. This is then multiplied by one [1] to convert these TRUE and FALSE values to ones [1] and zeros [0] respectively.

The amount and growth rate assumptions are then brought in from the 'General Assumptions' worksheet. Note that the formula to bring in Growth rates begins in the seemingly blank cell **J156**:

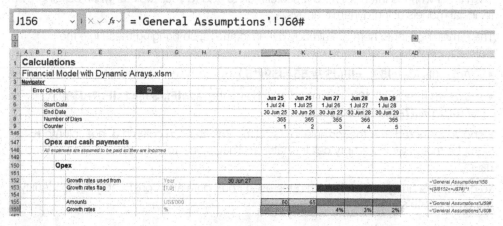

Note that I've made use of Conditional Formatting in row 153 to highlight when Growth rates are in use:

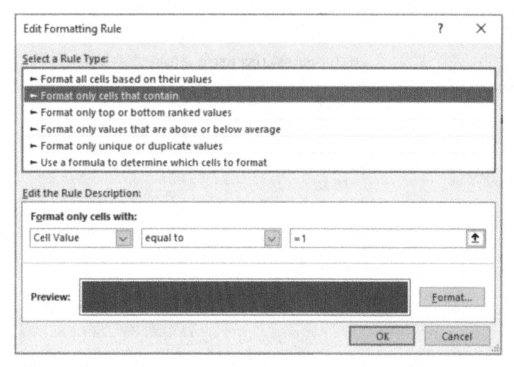

When not working with dynamic arrays, I may use a pretty simple formula to facilitate this calculation:

$$=IF(J153=0,J155,I158*(1+J156))$$

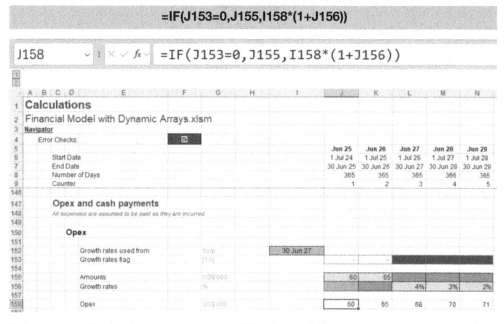

This formula will take the values from row 155 when the flag in row 153 equals zero [0], else it will take the previous period's operating expenditure and multiply this by one [1] plus the growth rate in row 156.

Another way of creating the same logic is by using flags rather than the **IF** function instead:

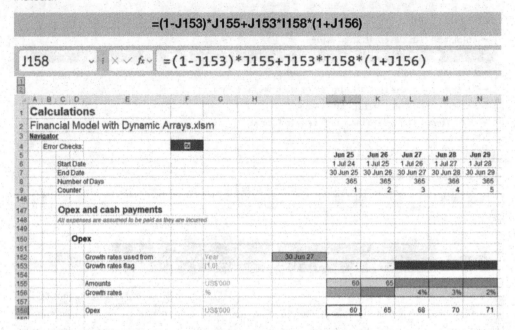

The first part of this formula:

(1-J153)*J155

takes the **value_if_true** from the **IF** function (**J155**) and multiplies it by one [1] minus the flag (**J153**) meaning that this will resolve to the value in **J155** when the flag is equal to zero [1] and zero [0] when the flag is equal to one [1].

The second part of this formula:

+J153*I158*(1+J156)

adds on the flag (**J153**) multiplied by our earlier **value_if_false** argument (**I158*(1+J156)**). This will result in **I158*(1+J156)** when the flag is equal to one [1] and zero [0] when the flag is equal to zero [0].

This means that the overall formula will either resolve to:

=J155+0

when the flag is equal to zero [0] or:

=0 + I158*(1+J156)

when the flag is equal to one [1].

As you can see, this formula will return only amounts from row 155 when the flag is equal to zero [0] and only apply growth rates to prior period's Operating expenditure when the flag is equal to one [1], achieving the same as our earlier **IF** statement. This still isn't a dynamic array formula though. We need an equivalent **SCAN(LAMBDA)** formula to calculate operating expenditure here.

The initial value for the **SCAN** function here is simply one [1], and the array will be the counter as we will need to choose the **n**th value in a list. The **LAMBDA** will then need to make use of the **INDEX** function to identify the correct flag, amount and growth rate to use in order to facilitate the calculation we just discussed, giving us the following formula:

> **=SCAN(1,J$9#,LAMBDA(accumulator,period,**
> **(1-INDEX(J153#,period))*INDEX(J155#,period) +**
> **INDEX(J153#,period)*accumulator*(1+INDEX(J156#,period))))**

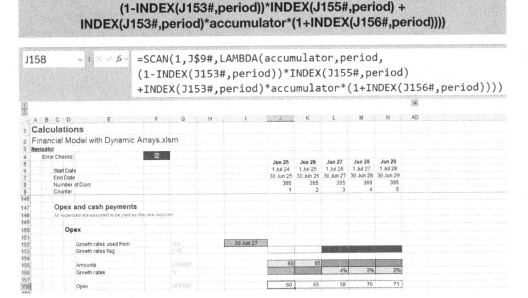

I appreciate that this is quite a lengthy formula, so let's walk through the **LAMBDA** one more time. The first part,

> **(1-INDEX(J153#,period))*INDEX(J155#,period)**

will identify the flag for the period, subtract this from one [1] (effectively converting a one [1] to a zero [0] and a zero [0] to a one [1]). It will then multiply this by the amount for the **period**, returning the amount when the flag is equal to zero [0] and a zero [0] when the flag is equal to one [1].

The second part,

> **+ INDEX(J153#,period)*accumulator*(1+INDEX(J156#,period))**

will add on to the first part, the flag multiplied by the **accumulator** (the previous **period**'s Operating expenditure), multiplied by one [1] plus the growth rate for the period. Remember that one of these parts will always resolve to zero [0] resulting in either just the amount (from row 155) or just the previous period's operating expenditure grown by the rate specified in row 156.

Moving on, I may now construct the Operating expenditure control account:

A B C D	E	F	G	H	I	J	K	L	M	N	AD
Calculations											
Financial Model with Dynamic Arrays.xlsm											
Navigator											
Error Checks:		☑									
						Jun 25	Jun 26	Jun 27	Jun 28	Jun 29	
Start Date						1 Jul 24	1 Jul 25	1 Jul 26	1 Jul 27	1 Jul 28	
End Date						30 Jun 25	30 Jun 26	30 Jun 27	30 Jun 28	30 Jun 29	
Number of Days						365	365	365	366	365	
Counter						1	2	3	4	5	
Opex		US$'000				60	65	68	70	71	
Working capital											
Days payable		Year									
Days in period		Year									
Closing payables		US$'000									
Control account											
Opening payables		US$'000									BS
Opex		US$'000									IS
Cash payments		US$'000									CFS
Closing payables		US$'000									BS

Note that despite there being no days payable assumption here, I still have left space for it, albeit formatted as a deliberately blank cell. This keeps the layout consistent whilst allowing us to easily adjust the calculations if assumptions do change and there is suddenly a Days payable set of assumptions to consider here.

You may notice that the layout here is consistent with both our COGS and Revenue Working capital sections. It seems I can simply copy the formulae from one of these:

A B C D	E	F	G	H	I	J	K	L	M	N	AD
Calculations											
Financial Model with Dynamic Arrays.xlsm											
Navigator											
Error Checks:		☑									
						Jun 25	Jun 26	Jun 27	Jun 28	Jun 29	
Start Date						1 Jul 24	1 Jul 25	1 Jul 26	1 Jul 27	1 Jul 28	
End Date						30 Jun 25	30 Jun 26	30 Jun 27	30 Jun 28	30 Jun 29	
Number of Days						365	365	365	366	365	
Counter						1	2	3	4	5	
Revenue and related											
Sales											
Projected sales		#				100	200	300	400	500	
Unit price		US$'000				15					
Inflation		%					3%	4%	5%	6%	
Price per unit		US$'000				15	15	16	17	18	
Revenue		US$'000				1,500	3,090	4,820	6,749	8,942	
Working capital											
Days receivable		Year				60	60	60	60	60	
Days in period		Year				365	365	365	366	365	=J8#
Closing receivables		US$'000				247	508	792	1,106	1,470	=J23#*J27#/J29#
Control account											
Opening receivables		US$'000					247	508	792	1,106 BS	=OFFSET(J36#,-1)
Revenue		US$'000				1,500	3,090	4,820	6,749	8,942 IS	=J23#
Cash receipts		US$'000				(1,253)	(2,829)	(4,536)	(6,435)	(8,578) CFS	=J38#-J35#-J36#
Closing receivables		US$'000			-	247	508	792	1,106	1,470 BS	=J31#

and then paste this into cell **J164**:

	Jun 25	Jun 26	Jun 27	Jun 28	Jun 29	
Calculations						
Financial Model with Dynamic Arrays.xlsm						
Navigator						
Error Checks:						
Start Date	1 Jul 24	1 Jul 25	1 Jul 26	1 Jul 27	1 Jul 28	
End Date	30 Jun 25	30 Jun 26	30 Jun 27	30 Jun 28	30 Jun 29	
Number of Days	365	365	365	366	365	
Counter	1	2	3	4	5	
Working capital						
Days payable	Year					
Days in period	Year	365	365	365	366	365	=J$8#
Closing payables	US$'000	#REF!	#REF!	#REF!	#REF!	#REF!	=J158#*J162#/J164#
Control account						
Opening payables	US$'000		#REF!	#REF!	#REF!	#REF!	BS =OFFSET(J173#,-1)
Opex	US$'000	60	65	68	70	71	IS =J158#
Cash payments	US$'000	#REF!	#REF!	#REF!	#REF!	#REF!	CFS =J173#-J170#-J171#
Closing payables	US$'000	#REF!	#REF!	#REF!	#REF!	#REF!	BS =J166#

but that would be wrong. Here, **J166** refers to the range **J162#**. As **J162** is blank, it does not currently spill in line with the rest of these references and so, the formula does not calculate as intended. Don't fret though, it's easy to fix! I simply need to enter the following formula into cell **J162** so that it spills in line with the rest of these ranges, albeit only ever filling the range with zeros [0]:

=IF(J$9#,,)

J162   =IF(J$9#,,)

	Jun 25	Jun 26	Jun 27	Jun 28	Jun 29	
Calculations						
Financial Model with Dynamic Arrays.xlsm						
Navigator						
Error Checks:						
Start Date	1 Jul 24	1 Jul 25	1 Jul 26	1 Jul 27	1 Jul 28	
End Date	30 Jun 25	30 Jun 26	30 Jun 27	30 Jun 28	30 Jun 29	
Number of Days	365	385	365	366	365	
Counter	1	2	3	4	5	
Working capital						
Days payable	Year					=IF(J$9#,,)
Days in period	Year	365	365	365	366	365	=J$8#
Closing payables	US$'000	-	-	-	-	-	=J158#*J162#/J164#
Control account						
Opening payables	US$'000	-	-	-	-	-	BS =OFFSET(J173#,-1)
Opex	US$'000	60	65	68	70	71	IS =J158#
Cash payments	US$'000	(60)	(65)	(68)	(70)	(71)	CFS =J173#-J170#-J171#
Closing payables	US$'000	-	-	-	-	-	BS =J166#

Notice again that the Closing payables in cell **I173** is left deliberately blank as I have already considered this figure within our COGS control account.

With that, our Operating expenditure control account is complete and there are three (yes, three!) links to be made to the financial statements. Despite the fact that the Operating expenditure and Cash payments currently balance one another, I must still put Closing payables into the Balance Sheet just in case assumptions change at a later date.

Our first link, Opex, will be a negative number within the Income Statement:

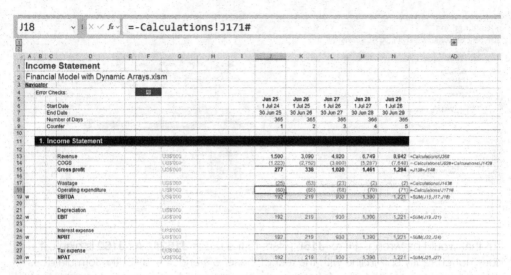

The model still doesn't balance, as we'd expect. With that, we can now remove the WIP formula and style from row 19 and replace this with a dynamic array:

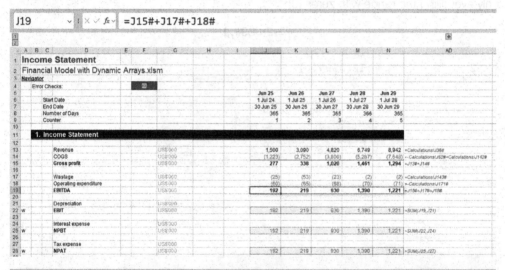

=J15#+J17#+J18#

Take care to remove the old formula (and formatting) from all of the columns, else you may run into an #*SPILL!* error.

Next, I can link Cash payments into the Indirect cash payments line of the (Direct) Cash Flow Statement:

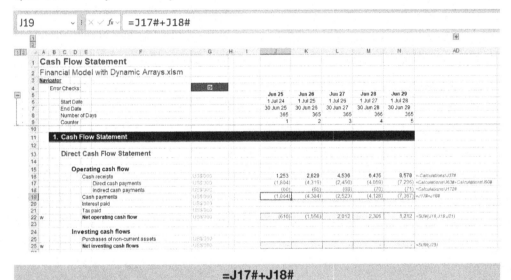

The model does now balance, but we mustn't forget there is one more link to make. But before that, I have another Work In Progress formula to replace: row 19 may now be updated with a dynamic array formula:

=J17#+J18#

Finally, I can add the Closing payables into the Accounts payable line on the Balance Sheet:

	A B C D	E	F	G	H	I	J	K	L	M	N		AD
1	**Balance Sheet**												
2	Financial Model with Dynamic Arrays.xlsm												
3	Navigator												
4	Error Checks		☑										
5							Jun 25	Jun 26	Jun 27	Jun 28	Jun 29		
6	Start Date						1 Jul 24	1 Jul 25	1 Jul 26	1 Jul 27	1 Jul 28		
7	End Date						30 Jun 25	30 Jun 26	30 Jun 27	30 Jun 28	30 Jun 29		
8	Number of Days						365	365	365	366	365		
9	Counter						1	2	3	4	5		
26													
27	**Current liabilities**												
28	Accounts payable		US$'000				242	531	431	685	1,072	=Calculations!J64#+Calculations!J91#+Calculations!J173#	
29	Interest payable		US$'000										
30	Dividends payable		US$'000										
31	Tax payable		US$'000										
32	Other current liabilities		US$'000										
33	w	**Total current liabilities**	US$'000				242	531	431	685	1,072	=SUM(J28:J32)	
34													

=Calculations!J64#+Calculations!J91#+Calculations!J173#

We've completed up to EBITDA in our Income Statement. What's next? Bring it on!

CHAPTER 17.11: CAPITAL EXPENDITURE

Returning to our Income Statement, it's clear that Depreciation is next, which means it's time to consider Capital expenditure.

1. Income Statement						
Revenue	US$'000	1,500	3,090	4,820	6,749	8,942
COGS	US$'000	(1,223)	(2,752)	(3,800)	(5,287)	(7,648)
Gross profit	US$'000	277	338	1,020	1,461	1,294
Wastage	US$'000	(25)	(53)	(23)	(2)	(2)
Operating expenditure	US$'000	(60)	(65)	(68)	(70)	(71)
EBITDA	US$'000	192	219	930	1,390	1,221
Depreciation	US$'000					
EBIT	US$'000	192	219	930	1,390	1,221
Interest expense	US$'000					
NPBT	US$'000	192	219	930	1,390	1,221
Tax expense	US$'000					
NPAT	US$'000	192	219	930	1,390	1,221

Theory

The next line item required is Depreciation, but to calculate this we need to understand the concept of capital expenditure first. **Capital expenditure** is the cost to procure any asset that meets the following criteria:

- the asset must have an economic life of greater than one year when purchased

- it is held for continuing use in the business

- the asset must generate an accounting profit / economic return

- the value of the asset when purchased must exceed a *de minimis* limit which varies from geographic region / accounting jurisdiction.

The idea is that capital expenditure tends to be expensive (*e.g.* acquiring a building, purchasing a fleet of cars) and expensing all of these costs in any one period would lead to an horrific loss and go against the accruals concept. The intention is to match the costs over the life of the profits they generate (hence the test for profitability).

There are four common methods of depreciation. They are based on the **depreciable amount**, which is defined as the original price of the asset less its estimated resale price (**residual** or **salvage value**):

1. **Straight Line:** By far the most common method, this approach linearly apportions the depreciable amount evenly over the remaining number of periods. Favoured by accountants and statutory reporting, for many industries and sectors it is the simplest and least contentious approach. This gets its name as plotting time against an asset's remaining value (known as **Net Book Value**) will generate a straight line on a chart.

447

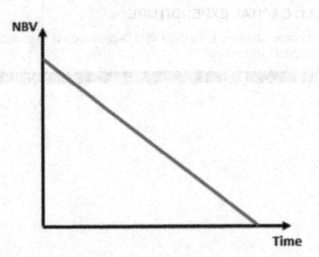

2. **Diminishing Value or Declining Balance:** This approach calculates a proportion of the remaining value to depreciate each year, based on the initial purchase price, not the depreciable amount. The rate is usually a function of the economic life and a multiplier.

   For example, consider an asset purchased for $1,000 that has a depreciable amount of $1,000 also. The asset has a four year life and a multiplier of 2.0x (this is known as **Double Declining Balance**). This would give a depreciation rate of 2.0 / 4 = 50% on the remaining balance:

	$
	1,000.00
Depn: P1	(500.00)
	500.00
Depn: P2	(250.00)
	250.00
Depn: P3	(125.00)
	125.00
Depn: P4	(62.50)
	62.50

   It should be noted that the depreciation rate can never be above 100%, that only the depreciable amount can be depreciated and that in some jurisdictions, the remainder of the depreciable amount is written off in the final economic period.

   This method is frequently used in many jurisdictions / territories for tax computations.

3. **Sum Of Digits (SOD):** This method considers the economic life but apportions on an increasing or decreasing proportion each year. For example, a four year economic life might depreciate the depreciable amount by 1/10 in Year 1, 2/10 in Year 2, 3/10 in Year 3 and 4/10 in Year 4, where the common denominator 10 =

1 + 2 + 3 + 4. (This can be decreasing as well as increasing.) This approach is becoming less and less common.

4. **Usage Basis:** This amortises the depreciable amount based on what proportion of the asset is estimated to have been used in a particular year. This is quite common in the mining and resources industries.

Typically, 21st century modelling tends to assume no residual value so that generally the depreciable amount is the initial purchase price.

Excel has several functions that calculate depreciation:

- **SLN(cost, residual_value, economic_life)** calculates the depreciable amount each year. This is simply **=(cost - residual_value) / economic_life**

- **DB(cost, residual_value, economic_life, year_number, [months_left_in_1ˢᵗ_ year])** calculates the depreciation on a declining balance basis. The fixed rate is calculated as **1 - ((residual_value / cost) ^ (1 / economic_life))**. This is good for finding the depreciation in later years quickly. Note that **months_left_in_1ˢᵗ_year** allows you to calculate depreciation for part-year acquisitions; left blank, it assumes the first year is a full year

- **DDB(cost, residual_value, economic_life, year_number, [factor])** calculates the Double Declining Balance, *i.e.* **2 / economic_life** for a particular **year_number**. If **factor** is specified, the formula uses the **factor** rather than 2, *e.g.* a **factor** of 3 would effectively be "triple declining balance"

- **VDB(cost, residual_value, economic_life, starting_year_number, ending_ year_number, [factor], [no_switch])** calculates the Variable Declining Balance, similar in operation to the **DDB** function. It ensures that the **residual_value** is achieved at the end of the **economic_life** by switching to straight line depreciation when this becomes higher than the declining balance amount. If you do not want this switch to occur set **no_switch** to FALSE (the default value if unspecified is TRUE). The **factor** works similarly to the same argument in the **DDB** function

- **SYD(cost, residual_value, economic_life, year_number)** calculates the depreciation on a Sum Of Years Digits basis on a declining basis (*i.e.* depreciation is front-loaded).

Got it? Me neither. Do you know I have *never* used any of these functions in a model? That is why I don't provide copious examples for each and the fact they were not described earlier as I talked through various key functions in Excel. If you use any of these functions you are trusting Microsoft has got its sums right and is performing the calculation *exactly* as you want. It is opaque and end users do not tend to be very trusting of numbers that appear to come out of thin air. Besides, these functions only consider the capital expenditure for a particular period. What happens when you have to work it out for multiple periods? First principles work well.

In fact, it is worth starting with first principles because depreciation is by far the area of financial modelling most frequently modelled incorrectly. Let me show you. Consider the following example:

A	B	C	D	E	F	G	H	I	J	K	L	M	N	O
2	Capex:		1,000											
3	Economic Life:		10											
5	Period No.		1	2	3	4	5	6	7	8	9	10		
6	Opening NBV		1,000	1,000	1,000	1,000	1,000	1,000	1,000	1,000	1,000	1,000		=IF(D$5=1,$D$2,C8)
7	Depreciation													
8	Closing NBV		1,000	1,000	1,000	1,000	1,000	1,000	1,000	1,000	1,000	1,000		=SUM(D6:D7)

Have a go at this. Create the above spreadsheet. Imagine depreciation is to be calculated on a straight line basis with an initial amount of $1,000 (cell **D2**) and an economic life of 10 years (cell **D3**). Just put one formula in cell **D7** to be copied across so that the depreciation is calculated correctly. Don't worry about making it a dynamic array yet. This is not as easy as you may think.

Once you think you have a solution, change the Capex to $2,000 in cell **D2**:

A	B	C	D	E	F	G	H	I	J	K	L	M	N	O
2	Capex:		2,000											
3	Economic Life:		10											
5	Period No.		1	2	3	4	5	6	7	8	9	10		
6	Opening NBV		2,000	1,800	1,600	1,400	1,200	1,000	800	600	400	200		=IF(D$5=1,$D$2,C8)
7	Depreciation		(200)	(200)	(200)	(200)	(200)	(200)	(200)	(200)	(200)	(200)		
8	Closing NBV		1,800	1,600	1,400	1,200	1,000	800	600	400	200	-		=SUM(D6:D7)

So far so good? Now try changing the economic life to 20 years in cell **D3**:

A	B	C	D	E	F	G	H	I	J	K	L	M	N	O
2	Capex:		2,000											
3	Economic Life:		20											
5	Period No.		1	2	3	4	5	6	7	8	9	10		
6	Opening NBV		2,000	1,900	1,800	1,700	1,600	1,500	1,400	1,300	1,200	1,100		=IF(D$5=1,$D$2,C8)
7	Depreciation		(100)	(100)	(100)	(100)	(100)	(100)	(100)	(100)	(100)	(100)		
8	Closing NBV		1,900	1,800	1,700	1,600	1,500	1,400	1,300	1,200	1,100	1,000		=SUM(D6:D7)

Still a walk in a park? Don't get too confident just yet. Now change the economic life to eight [8] years:

A	B	C	D	E	F	G	H	I	J	K	L	M	N	O
2	Capex:		2,000											
3	Economic Life:		8											
5	Period No.		1	2	3	4	5	6	7	8	9	10		
6	Opening NBV		2,000	1,750	1,500	1,250	1,000	750	500	250	-	-		=IF(D$5=1,$D$2,C8)
7	Depreciation		(250)	(250)	(250)	(250)	(250)	(250)	(250)	(250)	-	-		
8	Closing NBV		1,750	1,500	1,250	1,000	750	500	250	-	-	-		=SUM(D6:D7)

Have you over-depreciated? I reckon some of you will have. If you have negative numbers in row 8 that is **wrong,** and I will have to send the auditors round.

This is a common mistake that is not always as easy as this to spot. Here, we have no additional capital expenditure, all we are doing is depreciating the opening amount. If capital expenditure keeps going up, it may be very easy not to notice that over-depreciation is occurring.

For those still with me and thinking, "Try harder Liam", okay, I shall. I am going to change the economic life to 6.8 years:

	A	B	C	D	E	F	G	H	I	J	K	L	M	N	O
1															
2		Capex:		2,000											
3		Economic Life:		6.8											
4															
5		Period No.		1	2	3	4	5	6	7	8	9	10		
6		Opening NBV		2,000	1,706	1,412	1,118	824	529	235	-	-	-		=IF(D$5=1,$D$2,C8)
7		Depreciation		(294)	(294)	(294)	(294)	(294)	(294)	(235)	-	-	-		
8		**Closing NBV**		**1,706**	**1,412**	**1,118**	**824**	**529**	**235**	**-**	**-**	**-**	**-**		=SUM(D6:D7)
9															

If you are still with me, you are doing very well, but I am not finished yet. Try changing the economic life to 0.8 years:

	A	B	C	D	E	F	G	H	I	J	K	L	M	N	O
1															
2		Capex:		2,000											
3		Economic Life:		0.8											
4															
5		Period No.		1	2	3	4	5	6	7	8	9	10		
6		Opening NBV		2,000	-	-	-	-	-	-	-	-	-		=IF(D$5=1,$D$2,C8)
7		Depreciation		(2,000)	-	-	-	-	-	-	-	-	-		
8		**Closing NBV**		**-**	**-**	**-**	**-**	**-**	**-**	**-**	**-**	**-**	**-**		=SUM(D6:D7)
9															

Technically, this isn't capital expenditure as the economic life is less than one year, so it should be fully expensed. However, to get it out of the Closing NBV I have fully amortised the amount.

Still with me? Last one: make Capex $(1,000) and the Economic Life two [2] years:

	A	B	C	D	E	F	G	H	I	J	K	L	M	N	O
1															
2		Capex:		(1,000)											
3		Economic Life:		2.0											
4															
5		Period No.		1	2	3	4	5	6	7	8	9	10		
6		Opening NBV		(1,000)	(1,000)	(1,000)	(1,000)	(1,000)	(1,000)	(1,000)	(1,000)	(1,000)	(1,000)		=IF(D$5=1,$D$2,C8)
7		Depreciation		-	-	-	-	-	-	-	-	-	-		
8		**Closing NBV**		**(1,000)**	**(1,000)**	**(1,000)**	**(1,000)**	**(1,000)**	**(1,000)**	**(1,000)**	**(1,000)**	**(1,000)**	**(1,000)**		=SUM(D6:D7)
9															

Again, this shouldn't be capital expenditure, but there is absolutely no way I am adding depreciation back.

Did you make it to the end? If you did, I suggest you are a brilliant modeller or you may have peeked ahead. Here is the formula I used:

Formula bar — cell **D7**: `=-IF(OR($D$2<0,$D$3<=1),MAX(D6,0),MIN(D6,($D$2/$D$3)))`

	A	B	C	D	E	F	G	H	I	J	K	L	M	N	O
2	Capex:			1,000											
3	Economic Life:			10											
5	Period No.			1	2	3	4	5	6	7	8	9	10		
6	Opening NBV			1,000	900	800	700	600	500	400	300	200	100		=IF(D$5=1,$D$2,C8)
7	Depreciation			(100)	(100)	(100)	(100)	(100)	(100)	(100)	(100)	(100)	(100)		=-IF(OR($D$2<0,$D$3<=1),MAX(D6,0),MIN(D6,($D$2/$D$3)))
8	Closing NBV			900	800	700	600	500	400	300	200	100	-		=SUM(D6:D7)

I have no real plans to go through the formula in cell **D7**,

=-IF(OR($D$2<0,$D$3<=1),MAX(D6,0),MIN(D6,($D$2/$D$3)))

because it is <u>wrong</u> also. It may allow for negative Capex, Economic Life of less than or equal to one year and ensure no over-depreciation, but it will not cope with part-period acquisitions / disposals, revaluations, changes in economic life, *etc.*

If you had tried to use the **SLN** function how did you do? That wouldn't have been a great deal of use either. This is what I mean about going back to first principles. Depreciation is awkward, no matter what method you choose.

But it gets worse. What happens if you have multiple periods of capital expenditure? Let me create another example.

Formula bar — cell **E7**: `=IF(E$4<$B7,,MIN($C7-SUM($D7:D7),$C7/$C$2))`

	A	B	C	D	E	F	G	H	I	J
1										
2		Economic Life:	4							
3										
4		Period Number:			1	2	3	4	5	6
5		Capex:			1,000	2,000	3,000	4,000	5,000	6,000
6										
7		Depn - Yr 1	1,000		250	250	250	250	-	-
8		Depn - Yr 2	2,000		-	500	500	500	500	-
9		Depn - Yr 3	3,000		-	-	750	750	750	750
10		Depn - Yr 4	4,000		-	-	-	1,000	1,000	1,000
11		Depn - Yr 5	5,000		-	-	-	-	1,250	1,250
12		Depn - Yr 6	6,000		-	-	-	-	-	1,500
13		Total Depn			250	750	1,500	2,500	3,500	4,500

The above is known as a **depreciation grid**. Cells **C7:C12** transpose the values in cells **E5:J5** using the **OFFSET** function (*e.g.* the formula in cell **C7** is **=OFFSET($D$5,,$B7)**, given the contents of cells **B7:B12** are simply numbers made to look like text using number formatting). The formula in the grid (*e.g.* cell **E7**) is:

=IF(E$4<$B7,,MIN($C7-SUM($D7:D7),$C7/$C$2))

This calculates the depreciation amount assuming the period is a period where depreciation should be calculated. The grid is great for explaining how depreciation works. Users understand the logic without looking at the formula – which is probably just as well given what lurks beneath. There is a major disadvantage with this method though. A few years back, I had to construct several hundred depreciation calculations

452

where users required monthly calculations for a 20-year period. That means each grid had 240 columns and 240 rows, *i.e.* 57,600 calculations per grid. Yuck!

There is a shorter method, using a **SUM(OFFSET)** method. Look at the following alternative calculation:

E20			f_x	=SUM(OFFSET(E19,,,,-E17))							

⏴A	B	C	D	E	F	G	H	I	J	K	L
1											
2	Economic Life:		4								
3											
4	Period Number:			1	2	3	4	5	6		
5	Capex:			1,000	2,000	3,000	4,000	5,000	6,000		
6											
7	Depn - Yr 1	1,000		250	250	250	250	-	-		
8	Depn - Yr 2	2,000		-	500	500	500	500	-		
9	Depn - Yr 3	3,000		-	-	750	750	750	750		
10	Depn - Yr 4	4,000		-	-	-	1,000	1,000	1,000		
11	Depn - Yr 5	5,000		-	-	-	-	1,250	1,250		
12	Depn - Yr 6	6,000		-	-	-	-	-	1,500		
13	Total Depn			250	750	1,500	2,500	3,500	4,500		
14											
15											
16	Period Number:			1	2	3	4	5	6		
17	Depreciation Width:			1	2	3	4	4	4		=MIN(E$16,$C$2)
18	Capex:			1,000	2,000	3,000	4,000	5,000	6,000		=E5
19	Depreciation:			250	500	750	1,000	1,250	1,500		=E18/$C$2
20	Total Depn			250	750	1,500	2,500	3,500	4,500		=SUM(OFFSET(E19,,,,-E17))

It may not look intuitive to begin with but allow me to talk you through it.

- Row 17 takes the minimum of the period counter and the economic life. This formula is used to determine how many periods need to be considered. The maximum number of periods is 4 here, so that no year's capital expenditure may be over-depreciated.

- Row 18 simply restates the capital expenditure from row 5.

- Row 19 is another simple formula: it simply takes the capital expenditure figure and divides it by the economic life (I have simplified the formula in this example, in a real model we would need to ensure that the economic life is a positive integer).

- Row 20 simply uses the **SUM(OFFSET)** approach to add up amounts. The formula in cell **E20**,

=SUM(OFFSET(E19,,,,-E17))

starts with the Depreciation in cell **E19** and does not move any rows or columns. Given the **height** parameter is unspecified it is assumed to be 1 (*i.e.* just row 19) but the **width** parameter is -1. A **width** of 1 or -1 simply means the column you are in so for the first period, the amount is simply **=SUM(250)** which equals 250.

For **F20**, the **OFFSET** function starts in cell **F19**, does not move anywhere, has a **height** of 1 and a width of -2, which is column **F** and the column to the immediate left (**E**). The formula evaluates to **=SUM(500+250)** which equals 750.

Moving on, cell **I20** (Period 5) takes the sum of the value in cell **I19** and the three cells to the left. This formula evaluates to **=SUM(1250+ 1000+750+500)** which equals 3,500.

This method is shorter, but perhaps not quite so transparent. This is where judgment is required. Sometimes with Best Practice Modelling you need to make a call when two or more of the four qualities conflict. Here, I am having to decide which I require more: *transparency* (so use the grid) versus *robustness* (using the **SUM(OFFSET)** method). In our case study – that's right, I haven't completely forgotten about it – I have chosen the **SUM(OFFSET)** approach, albeit modified to use dynamic arrays.

Before I wrap this section up, I need to extend the **SUM(OFFSET)** idea for depreciation. This works fine if the rate remains constant, but what happens if it can change each period (*i.e.* you are using just about any other depreciation method)?

Reverse Depreciation Rates Method

This is the "universal" formula but is conceptually even more complex than **SUM(OFFSET)**. This uses **SUMPRODUCT(OFFSET,OFFSET)**. Consider the following example:

	A	B	C	D	E	F	G	H	I	J	K	L
E17					fx	=SUMPRODUCT(OFFSET($E3,,,,E$16),OFFSET($J5,,,,-E$16))					
1												
2		Period Number:			1	2	3	4	5	6		
3		Capex:			1,000	2,000	3,000	4,000	5,000	6,000		
4		Depreciation			15.0%	22.4%	43.8%	18.8%				Cell J4: =1-SUM(E4:I4)
5		Reverse Depreciation:					18.8%	43.8%	22.4%	15.0%		=OFFSET($D4,,MAX($2:$2)-E$2+1)
6												
7		Depn - Yr 1	1,000		150	224	438	188	-	-		=IF(E$2<$B7,,$C7*OFFSET($D$4,,E$2-$B7+1))
8		Depn - Yr 2	2,000		-	300	448	876	376	-		=IF(E$2<$B8,,$C8*OFFSET($D$4,,E$2-$B8+1))
9		Depn - Yr 3	3,000		-	-	450	672	1,314	564		=IF(E$2<$B9,,$C9*OFFSET($D$4,,E$2-$B9+1))
10		Depn - Yr 4	4,000		-	-	-	600	896	1,752		=IF(E$2<$B10,,$C10*OFFSET($D$4,,E$2-$B10+1))
11		Depn - Yr 5	5,000		-	-	-	-	750	1,120		=IF(E$2<$B11,,$C11*OFFSET($D$4,,E$2-$B11+1))
12		Depn - Yr 6	6,000		-	-	-	-	-	900		=IF(E$2<$B12,,$C12*OFFSET($D$4,,E$2-$B12+1))
13		Total Depn			150	524	1,336	2,336	3,336	4,336		=SUM(E7:E12)
14												
15												
16		Period Number:			1	2	3	4	5	6		=E2
17		Total Depn			150	524	1,336	2,336	3,336	4,336		=SUMPRODUCT(OFFSET($E3,,,,E$16),OFFSET($J5,,,,-E$16))

In this example, I have made the depreciation methodology the "Liam Random Method" where I have put arbitrary percentages in cells **E4:I4**, with **J4** the balancing figure. Ignoring row 5 for a moment, the depreciation grid in rows 7:13 calculates the depreciation on a period-by-period basis using the formula:

=IF(E$2<$B7,,$C7*OFFSET($D$4,,E$2-$B7+1))

in cell **E7** for instance. This formula may look terrible, but the first argument determines whether depreciation should be calculated as in my previous example and the **OFFSET** calculation simply ensures the right percentage is used in each period as the percentages 'move' depending upon which row you are in. You will admit though it is not the world's simplest calculation even though it is still fairly easy to understand if the calculation were simply printed out.

We can get a lot smarter though.

- Consider the Total Depreciation in cell **E13**. This is simply 1,000 x 15%, which is **=E3*E4** or **=SUMPRODUCT(E3,J5)** (even if this does look like over the top).

- Now examine the Total Depreciation in cell **F13**. This is (1,000 x 22.4%) + (2,000 x 15%) or **=SUMPRODUCT(E3:F3,I5:J5)**.

- I shall keep going. Look at the Total Depreciation in cell **G13**. This is (1,000 x 43.8%) + (2,000 x 22.4%) + (3,000 x 15%) or **=SUMPRODUCT(E3:G3,H5:J5)**.

Do you see where I am going? By reversing the depreciation rates in row 4 using the formula

=OFFSET($D4,,MAX($2:$2)-E$2+1)

in cell **E5** for instance, I have a row vector that I can cross-multiply with the Capex in row 3 using the **SUMPRODUCT** function. The final argument in the formula above merely moves the reference **MAX($2:$2)-E$2+1** columns to the right. This effectively moves Period 1 to Period 6, Period 2 to Period 5 and so on.

I may get more and more product formulae depending upon the number of periods, but the **SUMPRODUCT** formula remains fairly simple, once someone has explained it. The formula in cell **E17** is actually not that bad:

=SUMPRODUCT(OFFSET($E3,,,,E$16),OFFSET($J5,,,,-E$16))

It may look horrible to start off with, but it's not that bad when considered systematically. The two **OFFSET** functions simply keep expanding the two row vectors, the first further right and the second further left. It won't actually be long before this formula is simpler than its long hand equivalent which will not even be a consistent formula period to period.

Back to the Case Study

Still with us? Let me get back to the model by taking a look at the assumptions for this section on the 'General Assumptions' worksheet:

I72		f_x	=IF(I71=0,,1/I71)									
	A B C D	E	F	G	H	I	J	K	L	M	N	
1	**General Assumptions**											
2	Financial Model with Dynamic Arrays.xlsm											
3	Navigator											
4	Error Checks:		☑									
5							Jun 25	Jun 26	Jun 27	Jun 28	Jun 29	
6	Start Date						1 Jul 24	1 Jul 25	1 Jul 26	1 Jul 27	1 Jul 28	
7	End Date						30 Jun 25	30 Jun 26	30 Jun 27	30 Jun 28	30 Jun 29	
8	Number of Days						365	365	365	366	365	
9	Counter						1	2	3	4	5	
62												
63	**Capex and related**											
64												
65	**Capital expenditure**											
66												
67	Capital expenditure	US$'000					150	180	120	90	100	
68												
69	**Accounting depreciation - straight line**											
70												
71	Remaining life of existing assets	# Year(s)		5 years								
72	Annual rate	%		20%								
73												
74	Economic life of new capex	# Year(s)		4 years								
75	Annual rate	%		25%								

There is only one asset class specified here. Obviously, a real model may have multiple categories but the treatment we use here may simply be expanded for however many classes you need. The Capital expenditure here is not a spilled array, so we'll again have to use the **OFFSET** function to reference the required inputs when bringing these into the Calculations worksheet.

There is also the Remaining life of the existing assets and Economic life of new capex here which are simply numbers making use of number formatting to display " years" after. You will see the annual rates have been calculated as

$$=IF(I71=0,,1/I71)$$

and

$$=IF(I74=0,,1/I74)$$

respectively. By calculating the reciprocal whilst checking for zero [0] to prevent an #DIV/0! error occurring, subsequent formulae will not require similar checks. Having these percentages will allow us to multiply by these rates, rather than divide by the asset lives and having to create #DIV/0! error traps for each period.

Let's move on to the Calculation sheet. We begin by bringing in existing assets from cell **I21** of the Opening Balance Sheet and using the **OFFSET** function to bring in Capital expenditure from the 'General Assumptions' worksheet:

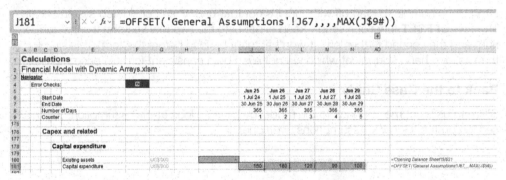

Next, I bring in the asset lives and annual rates assumptions too:

Next, I wish to calculate the depreciation on existing assets. This will be hard to follow at present as the Opening Balance Sheet is presently zero, and as such the opening value here is zero [0] too. To make this easier to follow I'm going to temporarily hardcode a value of 100 into cell **I180**, applying the WIP Style to ensure I do not forget to amend this:

456

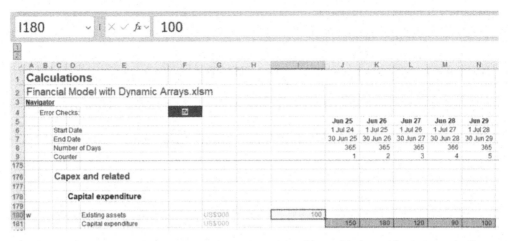

I may then calculate depreciation for existing assets. Since this is not for any particular period, I will enter this calculation in column **I** (cell **I91**) and this is simply the existing asset value, cell **I180**, multiplied by the annual rate, cell **I186**:

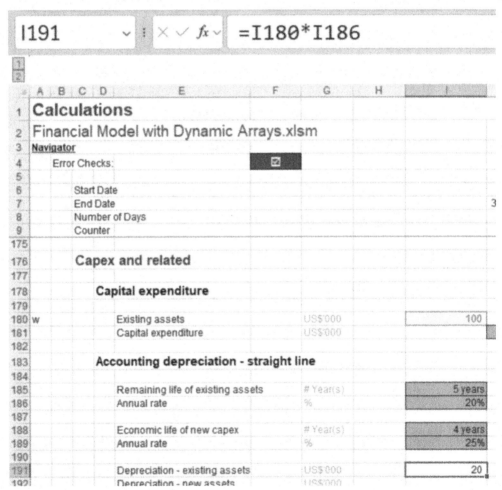

This isn't a dynamic array formula – and doesn't need to be. It will only ever be performed in this one column.

The depreciation for new assets is then calculated as the capital expenditure array (**J181#**) multiplied by the rate for new capex (**$I$189**):

=J181#*$I$189

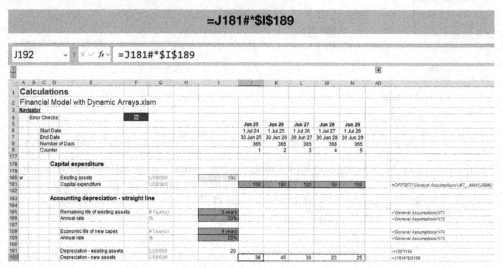

I can then calculate the Aggregate depreciation - existing assets (row 193) using the following formula:

=IF(J$9#>$I$185,,$I$191)

This will apply the depreciation calculated in cell **I191** in periods where the counter is not greater than the asset life. I've temporarily unhidden the columns and increased the **Number_of_Periods** (cell **H15** of the Timing sheet) to 7 in the next screenshot to make the profile more easily visible:

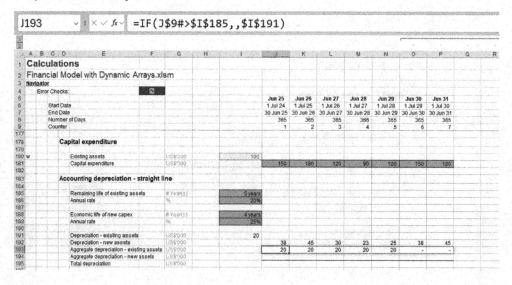

As you can see, this will return the depreciation for the remaining five [5] years of the assets life and then return zero [0].

With the **Number_of_Periods** restored to 5, I can move on.

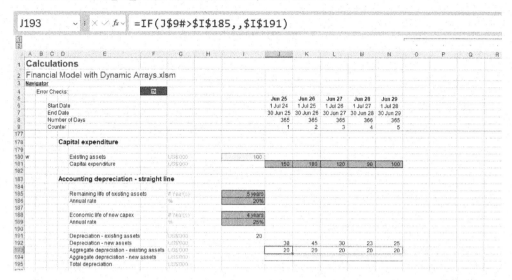

To calculate the Aggregate depreciation - new assets (row 194), I will need to exploit the **MAP** function with **LAMBDA**. I know I discussed this earlier in the book (see Chapter 7), but arguably, the next formula is sufficiently sophisticated to warrant a second, perhaps more relevant, glance.

The MAP Function Revisited

Calculation of the aggregate depreciation on new assets will require the use of the **MAP** function. Before I do this, let's take a look at a quick example to reiterate how this function works.

Here, we've generated a list of numbers from one [1] to five [5] through the use of the **SEQUENCE** function (column **C**) and hardcoded the first five [5] letters of the alphabet next to this in column **D**:

I want to make use of the **OFFSET** function in cell **F5** to return a list of our letters (I appreciate that there are easier ways to do this without the use of the **OFFSET** function, but those ways wouldn't work for our depreciation calculation!). Simply using the formula:

=OFFSET(D4,C5#,)

does not give us the desired result.

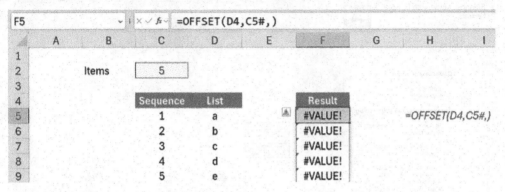

OFFSET and dynamic arrays simply do not work like that, we will have to use a **MAP(LAMBDA)** function.

The formula we must use is:

=MAP(C5#,LAMBDA(x,OFFSET(D4,x,)))

This will perform the **LAMBDA** function for each value in the array **C5#**, first offsetting cell **D4** by one [1] row and returning "a", then by two [2] rows and returning "b", and so on for each value in **C5#**.

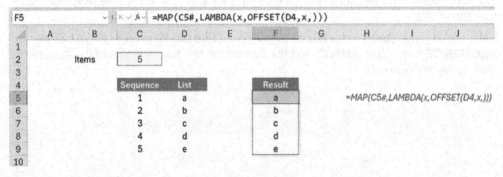

This is the way we will have to make **OFFSET** work for our depreciation calculations.

Back to the Case Study Again

Returning to row 194 of our calculations sheet, I can construct a **MAP(LAMBDA)** function to calculate the aggregate depreciation for new assets.

The formula I will use is as follows:

> **=MAP(J9#,LAMBDA(period,SUM(OFFSET(INDEX(J192#,period),,,,-MIN(period,$I$188)))))**

Let's work through this. The first argument of this **MAP** function is the array **J9#**. This is the counter and will be used to lookup the correct starting point for our **OFFSET** as well as help define the width of it. Next comes the **LAMBDA**. This will sum the results of the **OFFSET** function for each **period**. But what exactly does the **OFFSET** function do here? The first argument of our **OFFSET** function is as follows:

> **INDEX(J192#,period)**

This will look up the depreciation for new assets (row 192) acquired in this **period** and is the starting point for our **OFFSET**. The next three [3] arguments of the **OFFSET** function are left blank, as I do not wish to move any rows down or columns across and I want to keep the default height of one [1]. The final argument, **width**, is as follows:

> **-MIN(period,$I$188)**

It's easier to first think of this as simply -**$I$188**. I want the **OFFSET** function to extend a number of columns to the left equal to the economic life of new assets, **I188**. This will ensure that all assets that have not yet been fully depreciated have their depreciation included within the **SUM**. The **MIN** function here simply takes the minimum of the current period (row 9) and the asset life, ensuring that the **OFFSET** function does not expand too far to the left and include any values prior to column **J**.

To recap, this formula will identify a range beginning in the corresponding column of row 192 (the depreciation for new assets) for each **period**. This range will expand to the left to look back to the earliest period for which assets still need depreciation, and then sum this range to add up all of the required depreciation figures.

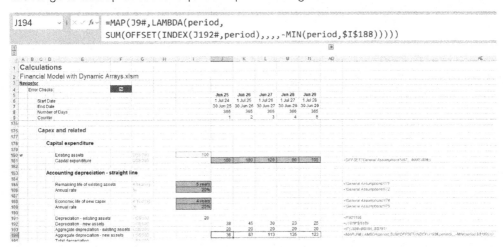

I may then simply add together the two aggregate depreciation lines (for both existing and new assets) to calculate the total depreciation:

					Jun 25	Jun 26	Jun 27	Jun 28	Jun 29
	Calculations								
	Financial Model with Dynamic Arrays.xlsm								
	Navigator								
	Error Checks:	☑							
					1 Jul 24	1 Jul 25	1 Jul 26	1 Jul 27	1 Jul 28
	Start Date				30 Jun 25	30 Jun 26	30 Jun 27	30 Jun 28	30 Jun 29
	End Date				365	365	365	366	365
	Number of Days				1	2	3	4	5
	Counter								
	Depreciation - existing assets	US$'000		20					
	Depreciation - new assets	US$'000			38	45	30	23	25
	Aggregate depreciation - existing assets	US$'000			20	20	20	20	20
	Aggregate depreciation - new assets	US$'000			38	83	113	135	123
	Total depreciation	US$'000			58	103	133	155	143

With these calculations complete, I will now amend cell **I180** by linking it back to cell **I21** of the Opening Balance Sheet:

					Jun 25	Jun 26	Jun 27	Jun 28	Jun 29
	Calculations								
	Financial Model with Dynamic Arrays.xlsm								
	Navigator								
	Error Checks:	☑							
					1 Jul 24	1 Jul 25	1 Jul 26	1 Jul 27	1 Jul 28
	Start Date				30 Jun 25	30 Jun 26	30 Jun 27	30 Jun 28	30 Jun 29
	End Date				365	365	365	366	365
	Number of Days				1	2	3	4	5
	Counter								
	Capex and related								
	Capital expenditure								
	Existing assets	US$'000							
	Capital expenditure	US$'000			150	180	120	90	100

I am now in a position to construct the control account for depreciation / capital expenditure. Cell **I202** will also link to cell **I21** on the Opening Balance Sheet. The Capital expenditure (in row 200) simply links to row 181, the Depreciation (row 201) simply negates the value in row 195, the Closing net book value (row 202) uses our **SCAN(LAMBDA)** approach to aggregate all movements in the control account, starting with the opening balance in cell **I202**, and finally the opening net book value (row 199) uses our **OFFSET** trick on row 202:

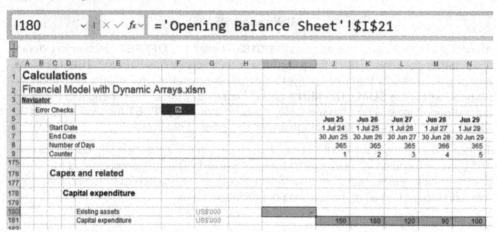

=SCAN(I202,J200#+J201#,LAMBDA(accumulator,depreciation,accumulator+ depreciation))

Hopefully, this expression is starting to become as familiar as stick standard Excel techniques like **INDEX MATCH**.

With this control account complete, we now have three [3] links to be made to our financial statements. First, I link Capital expenditure (as a negative) into row 25 of the Cash Flow Statement:

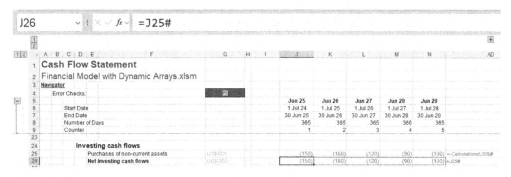

As expected, an error is flagging within our model as the Balance Sheet no longer balances.

With the addition of this line to our Cash Flow Statement, I may now amend the Work In Progress formula in row 26 of our Cash Flow Statement:

| J26 | ✓ × ✓ fx | =J25# |

	A B C D E	F	G H I	J	K	L	M	N	AD
1	**Cash Flow Statement**								
2	Financial Model with Dynamic Arrays.xlsm								
3	Navigator								
4	Error Checks								
5				Jun 25	Jun 26	Jun 27	Jun 28	Jun 29	
6	Start Date			1 Jul 24	1 Jul 25	1 Jul 26	1 Jul 27	1 Jul 28	
7	End Date			30 Jun 25	30 Jun 26	30 Jun 27	30 Jun 28	30 Jun 29	
8	Number of Days			365	365	365	366	365	
9	Counter			1	2	3	4	5	
23									
24	**Investing cash flows**								
25	Purchases of non-current assets	US$'000		(150)	(180)	(120)	(90)	(100)	=-Calculations!J200#
26	**Net investing cash flows**	US$'000		(150)	(180)	(120)	(90)	(100)	=J25#

The next link to be made is to our Income Statement, linking Depreciation into row 21:

J21 | × ✓ fx | =Calculations!J201#

Income Statement

Financial Model with Dynamic Arrays.xlsm

					Jun 25	Jun 26	Jun 27	Jun 28	Jun 29	
	Start Date				1 Jul 24	1 Jul 25	1 Jul 26	1 Jul 27	1 Jul 28	
	End Date				30 Jun 25	30 Jun 26	30 Jun 27	30 Jun 28	30 Jun 29	
	Number of Days				365	365	365	365	365	
	Counter				1	2	3	4	5	
	1. Income Statement									
	Revenue	US$'000			1,500	3,090	4,820	6,749	8,942	=Calculations!J36#
	COGS	US$'000			(1,223)	(2,752)	(3,800)	(5,287)	(7,648)	=Calculations!J62#+Calculations!J142#
	Gross profit	US$'000			277	338	1,020	1,461	1,294	=J13#+J14#
	Wastage	US$'000			(25)	(53)	(23)	(2)	(2)	=Calculations!J143#
	Operating expenditure	US$'000			(60)	(65)	(68)	(70)	(71)	=Calculations!J171#
	EBITDA	US$'000			192	219	930	1,390	1,221	=J15#+J17#+J18#
	Depreciation	US$'000			(38)	(83)	(113)	(135)	(123)	=Calculations!J201#
w	**EBIT**	US$'000			155	137	817	1,255	1,098	=SUM(J19:J21)
	Interest expense	US$'000								
w	**NPBT**	US$'000			155	137	817	1,255	1,098	=SUM(J22:J24)
	Tax expense	US$'000								
w	**NPAT**	US$'000			155	137	817	1,255	1,098	=SUM(J25:J27)

This allows us to remove another work in progress formula, in row 22 here:

J22 | × ✓ fx | =J19#+J21#

Income Statement

Financial Model with Dynamic Arrays.xlsm

					Jun 25	Jun 26	Jun 27	Jun 28	Jun 29	
	Start Date				1 Jul 24	1 Jul 25	1 Jul 26	1 Jul 27	1 Jul 28	
	End Date				30 Jun 25	30 Jun 26	30 Jun 27	30 Jun 28	30 Jun 29	
	Number of Days				365	365	365	365	365	
	Counter				1	2	3	4	5	
	1. Income Statement									
	Revenue	US$'000			1,500	3,090	4,820	6,749	8,942	=Calculations!J36#
	COGS	US$'000			(1,223)	(2,752)	(3,800)	(5,287)	(7,648)	=Calculations!J62#+Calculations!J142#
	Gross profit	US$'000			277	338	1,020	1,461	1,294	=J13#+J14#
	Wastage	US$'000			(25)	(53)	(23)	(2)	(2)	=Calculations!J143#
	Operating expenditure	US$'000			(60)	(65)	(68)	(70)	(71)	=Calculations!J171#
	EBITDA	US$'000			192	219	930	1,390	1,221	=J15#+J17#+J18#
	Depreciation	US$'000			(38)	(83)	(113)	(135)	(123)	=Calculations!J201#
	EBIT	US$'000			155	137	817	1,255	1,098	=J19#+J21#

Of course, the model still doesn't balance as we have one more link to be made, linking the Closing net book value into row 21 (PP&E, Property, Plant & Equipment) of the Balance Sheet:

J21 | × ✓ fx | =Calculations!J202#

Balance Sheet

Financial Model with Dynamic Arrays.xlsm

					Jun 25	Jun 26	Jun 27	Jun 28	Jun 29	
	Start Date				1 Jul 24	1 Jul 25	1 Jul 26	1 Jul 27	1 Jul 28	
	End Date				30 Jun 25	30 Jun 26	30 Jun 27	30 Jun 28	30 Jun 29	
	Number of Days				365	365	365	365	365	
	Counter				1	2	3	4	5	
	Non-current assets									
	PP&E	US$'000			113	210	218	173	150	=Calculations!J202#
	Deferred tax assets	US$'000								
w	**Total non-current assets**	US$'000			113	210	218	173	150	=SUM(J21:J22)
w	**Total assets**	US$'000			397	823	1,540	3,049	4,535	=SUM(J19:J23)

The model now balances again. I have completed our Capital expenditure and Depreciation calculations.

CHAPTER 17.12: DEBT

As I'm sure you're expecting by now, we're going to return to our Income Statement to see what comes next:

1. Income Statement						
Revenue	US$'000	1,500	3,090	4,820	6,749	8,942
COGS	US$'000	(1,223)	(2,752)	(3,800)	(5,287)	(7,648)
Gross profit	US$'000	277	338	1,020	1,461	1,294
Wastage	US$'000	(25)	(53)	(23)	(2)	(2)
Operating expenditure	US$'000	(60)	(66)	(68)	(70)	(71)
EBITDA	US$'000	192	219	930	1,390	1,221
Depreciation	US$'000	(38)	(83)	(113)	(135)	(123)
EBIT	US$'000	155	137	817	1,255	1,098
Interest expense	US$'000					
NPBT	US$'000	155	137	817	1,255	1,098
Tax expense	US$'000					
NPAT	US$'000	155	137	817	1,255	1,098

Interest expense is our next line item. However, I cannot calculate this until I consider debt in general.

Over the years, I have seen various forms of business and project financing, including equity, shareholder loans, senior debt, mezzanine finance, hire purchase, bonds, convertibles, warrants and so on. *Prima facie*, this myriad of financial instruments can obfuscate the uninitiated, but like this last phrase, the jargon can be simplified.

No matter what the financial instrument, the mechanics essentially boil down to two key elements:

- **Return on finance:** the yield to investors or the costs of capital to the recipient of capital (e.g. interest, dividends); *and*

- **Return of finance:** repayments (or conversion) of original capital issued / drawn down.

And it really is as simple as that. The logic behind how the calculations may vary, such as when capital and returns are paid or rolled up, what order it is paid in and so on, but the computations may be summarised by two control accounts (*i.e.* summaries that show / reconcile how the Balance Sheet varies from one period to the next):

Returns of Finance

Opening Balance (*e.g.* Debt / Equity) b/f	XX	*Previous period Balance Sheet item*
Additions (*e.g.* drawdowns / issuances / conversions)	X	*Typically in Cash Flow Statement*
Returns on finance rolled up (*e.g.* "interest capitalised")	X	*Usually a Balance Sheet movement*
Deductions (*e.g.* repayments / buybacks / conversions)	(X)	*Typically in Cash Flow Statement*
Closing Balance (*e.g.* Debt / Equity) c/f	XX	*Current period Balance Sheet item*

Opening Return Payable (*e.g.* Interest Payable) b/f	XX	*Previous period Balance Sheet item*
Return Accrued (*e.g.* Interest Expense)	X	*Income Statement or Balance Sheet movement*
Return Paid (*e.g.* Interest Paid)	(X)	*Cash Flow Statement*
Closing Return Payable (*e.g.* Interest Payable) c/f	XX	*Current period Balance Sheet item*

The 3 R's of Debt Modelling

When both businesses and lenders consider debt they look at two key aspects: **risk** and **return**. These are important for credit risk modelling / portfolio analysis, etc. However, when undertaking financial modelling, it is the third 'R' that is often the most important.

In a financial model, risk and return are usually modelled via simple inputs and occasional what-if analysis. **Ranking**, on the other hand, affects the entire financial structure of the model:

1. Debt Cascade

	Date 1	Date 2	Date 3	Date 4	Date 5	Date 6	Date 7	Date 8	Date 9	Date 10	Date 11	Date 12
Cashflow Before Funding	(16.0)	(0.2)	(0.5)	(0.5)	(0.5)	4.3	6.7	6.8	6.8	7.1	7.3	7.4
Funding	16.0	-	-	-	-	-	-	-	-	-	-	-
Cashflow After Funding	-	(0.2)	(0.5)	(0.5)	(0.5)	4.3	6.7	6.8	6.8	7.1	7.3	7.4
Tax	-	-	-	-	-	-	-	-	-	-	-	-
Cashflow Available before WC Funding	-	(0.2)	(0.5)	(0.5)	(0.5)	4.3	6.7	6.8	6.8	7.1	7.3	7.4
Working Capital Facility Funding	-	0.2	0.5	0.5	0.5	-	-	-	-	-	-	-
Cash Flow Available for Debt Service (CFADS)	-	-	-	-	-	4.3	6.7	6.8	6.8	7.1	7.3	7.4
Senior Debt Service	-	(0.4)	(0.4)	(0.4)	(0.4)	(1.7)	(1.7)	(1.7)	(1.7)	(1.7)	(1.7)	(1.7)
Cashflow Available for Debt Service Reserve Account	-	(0.4)	(0.4)	(0.4)	(0.4)	2.6	5.0	5.1	5.1	5.4	5.6	5.7
Debt Service Reserve Account	-	4.0	0.0	-	-	(2.6)	(0.8)	0.0	0.0	(0.0)	(0.0)	0.0
Cashflow Available for Mezzanine	-	3.6	(0.4)	(0.4)	(0.4)	-	4.2	5.1	5.1	5.4	5.6	5.7
Mezzanine Debt Service	-	(2.7)	-	-	-	-	(3.1)	(3.8)	(3.8)	(4.1)	(4.2)	(4.3)
Cashflow Available for WC Facility	-	0.9	(0.4)	(0.4)	(0.4)	-	1.0	1.3	1.3	1.4	1.4	1.4
Working Capital Facility	-	(0.2)	(0.0)	(0.0)	(0.0)	-	(1.0)	(0.5)	-	-	-	-
Cashflow Available for Equity	-	0.7	(0.4)	(0.4)	(0.5)	-	-	0.7	1.3	1.4	1.4	1.4
Dividends	-	5.3	5.2	5.2	5.3	(2.0)	(2.0)	(2.2)	(2.3)	(3.0)	(3.1)	(3.4)
Net Cashflow	-	5.9	4.7	4.8	4.8	(2.0)	(2.0)	(1.4)	(1.0)	(1.6)	(1.7)	(1.9)
Cash Balance B/f	-	-	5.9	10.7	15.4	20.2	18.3	16.2	14.8	13.8	12.1	10.4
Cash Balance C/f	-	5.9	10.7	15.4	20.2	18.3	16.2	14.8	13.8	12.1	10.4	8.4

As the above graphic shows, if the order of service repaying capital changes, the entire logic will change. This may affect interest / debt service cover ratios (see below). It is important in scoping any such model that the order is understood and how it will be affected by such factors as:

- Conversion of financial instruments

- Breach of covenants or other ratios

- Liquidation / insolvency.

It is not correct to assume that the order of financing will never change.

Capitalised vs. Rolled Up

There is confusion between the jargon used by the banking industry and accountants when considering debt mechanics:

Scenario	Banking term	Accounting term
Interest is not paid (either by agreement or due to insufficient funds) and is added to the outstanding principal for future interest calculations	Interest capitalised	Interest rolled-up
Interest is not added to the balance but is paid (although there may be a slight timing issue)	Interest amortised (principal is amortised similarly)	When accrued: interest expense When paid: interest paid
Regardless of whether paid or not in reality, interest meets the criteria specified in the relevant accounting standards to be held in the Balance Sheet	n/a	Interest capitalised
When capitalised under accounting rules, the interest charge is released to the P&L over the life of a project on some agreed equitable basis	n/a	Interest amortised

When holding conversations with financiers, be sure you are on the same page before building interest into a financial model. Debt term sheets can be difficult enough to understand without unnecessarily adding to the complexity.

Return of Finance

Let's return to the 'General Assumptions' worksheet:

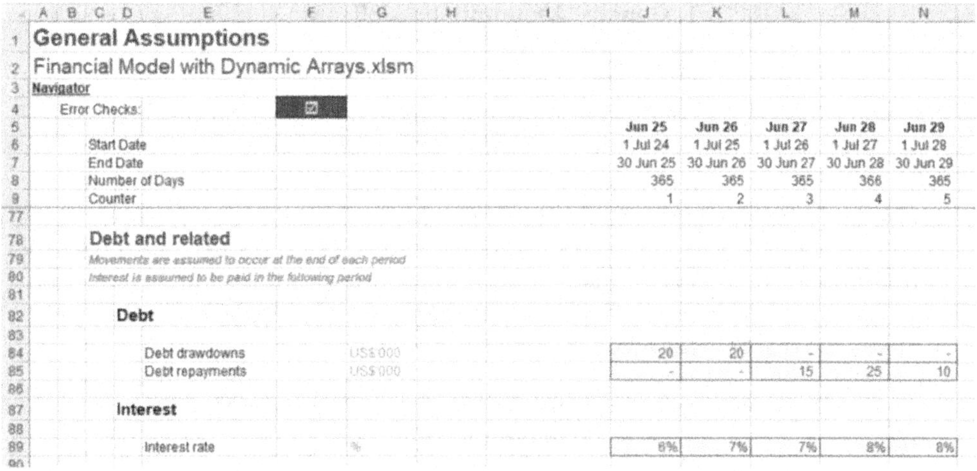

The first thing to note here is the text in cells **C79** and **C80**. Firstly, it says that "Movements are assumed to occur at the end of each period". This means that the average debt balance will be solely based upon the opening balance, thus avoiding any circular calculations and making interest calculations much easier. Next, we have

"Interest is assumed to be paid in the following period" meaning that there will be a one [1] period delay on paying interest, pretty straightforward.

We have three [3] assumptions to consider here, the Debt drawdowns (**J84**) which are a spilled range:

=IF(J$9#<3,20,)

However, the Debt repayments (row 85) and Interest rates (row 89) are just hardcoded figures for each period, no formulae here! This means that I will need to make use of the **OFFSET** function to bring these into the Calculations sheet. With this all borne in mind, navigating to the Calculations worksheet we begin by bringing in the drawdown and repayment assumptions:

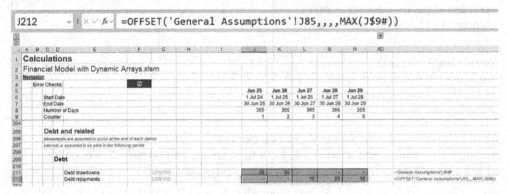

Row 211 (Debt drawdowns) is simply a link back to the assumptions. However, cell **J212** (Debt repayments) contains the formula

=OFFSET('General Assumptions'!J85,,,,MAX(J$9#))

Note here I have used **MAX(J$9#)** as a viable alternative to **Number_of_Periods**.

Do remember that debt movements may be much more complex in reality. You may have various financial instruments, with various tranches, and that the amounts may depend upon past and / or projected future cashflows. Here, I have dynamic array formulae to contend with so I'm keeping it simple.

With this, we can already construct our return *of* finance control account. Cell **I219** links to cell **$I$36** of the Opening Balance Sheet (Debt), Debt drawdowns (row 217) links to row 211, Debt repayments (row 218) negates the figures in row 212, Closing debt (row 219) makes use of a **SCAN(LAMBDA)** formula,

=SCAN(I219,J217#+J218#,LAMBDA(accumulator,movement, accumulator+movement))

and our opening debt (row 216) simply makes use of the **OFFSET** trick.

=OFFSET(J219#,,-1)

By now, you should be expecting these formulae:

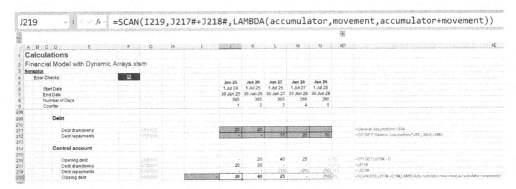

We now have three [3] line items to link into the financial statements, although you may notice that despite us working down the Income Statement none of the items within this control account link to the Income Statement. The Income Statement is just the route planner here.

The first link to be made is Debt drawdowns into row 29 of the Cash Flow Statement:

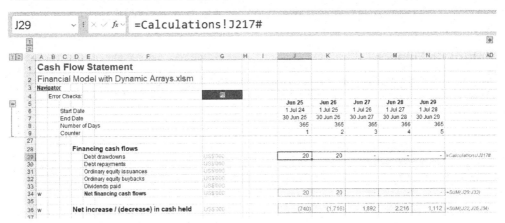

Unsurprisingly an error is now flagging as the Balance Sheet no longer balances.

Debt repayments comes just below this, linking into row 30 of the Cash Flow Statement:

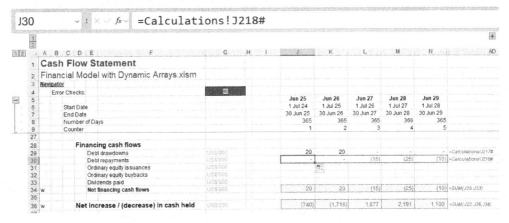

Finally, Closing debt links into row 36 of the Balance Sheet and will satisfy the outstanding error check:

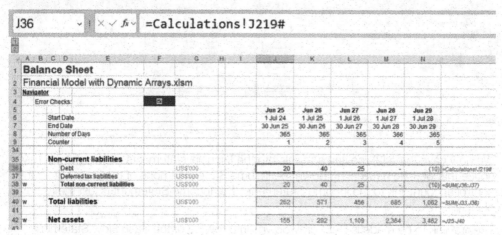

We've got our return *of* finance calculated but it's time to consider our return *on* finance, the interest.

Return on Finance

Returning to our Calculations sheet, I begin by using the **OFFSET** function to bring the interest rate assumptions in to row 223:

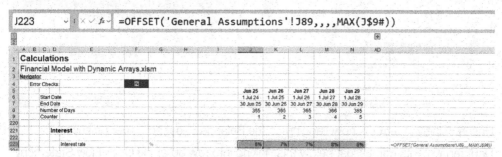

Next, I want to bring our Opening debt balance down from row 216 and the Days in the period down from row 8:

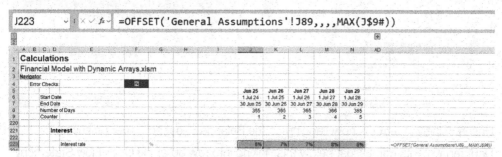

Then, I want to bring in the days in a standard year. We'll use the **IF** trick from earlier to ensure our named range, **Days_in_Year**, propagates across as required:

=IF(J9#,Days_in_Year,)

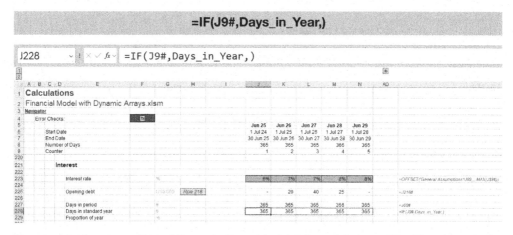

To calculate the proportion of the year, I want to take the minimum of the Days in period divided by days in a standard year and one [1]:

=MIN(J227#/J228#,1)

However, the **MIN** function coerces our arrays and as such, doesn't work here. Instead, I shall use an **IF** statement to check if the Days in the period is less than the days in a standard year to define the numerator to use here:

=IF(J227#<J228#,J227#,J228#)/J228#

This will divide the number of Days in the period by the number of days in a standard year if the days in the period is less than the number of days in a standard year, else it will divide the number of days in a standard year by itself, resulting in one [1] or 100%.

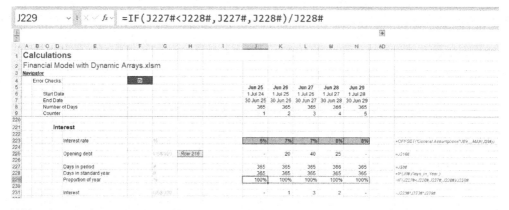

With this calculation in place, I may now calculate the Interest as the Opening debt balance multiplied by the Interest rate multiplied by the Proportion of the year:

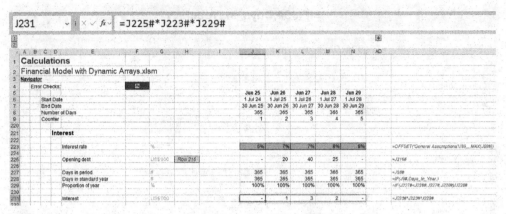

This is assuming interest is calculated on a simple (*i.e.* non-compounding) basis. If not, the formula will need to be modified using a **SCAN(LAMBDA)** type technique.

All that's left now is the control account. Cell **I238** (Interest payable) links to cell **$I$29** of the Opening Balance Sheet. The Interest expense simply equals row 231.

There is a nice trick to calculate the Closing interest payable. This can simply equal row 236. If that doesn't make sense to you then remember that "Interest is assumed to be paid in the following period", meaning that the only outstanding interest payable will be that which is incurred in the period. I may then calculate our opening interest payable using the **OFFSET** trick and finally, Interest paid can simply negate the opening interest payable (row 235) as "Interest is assumed to be paid in the following period". Easy.

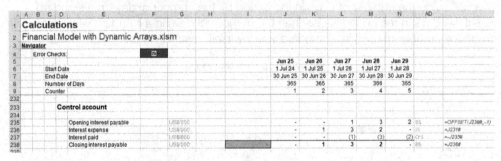

I now have three [3] links to make to the financial statements. The first is Interest expense, which links into row 24 of the Income Statement as a negative reference:

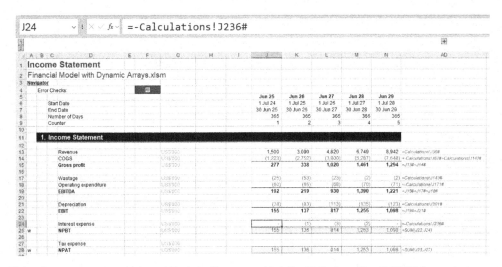

This allows us to amend our Work In Progress Net Profit Before Tax (NPBT) formula in row 25:

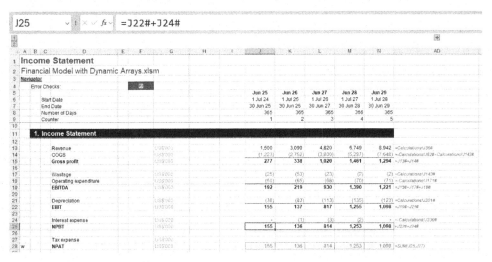

Next, I can link interest paid into row 20 (Interest paid) of the Cash Flow Statement:

Finally, Closing interest payable links into row 29 of the Balance Sheet:

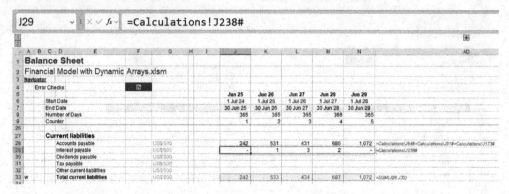

The model now balances, and I have completed our debt calculations for this model.

CHAPTER 17.13: TAXATION

The Income Statement is nearly complete:

1. Income Statement							
Revenue	US$'000		1,500	3,090	4,820	6,749	8,942
COGS	US$'000		(1,223)	(2,752)	(3,800)	(5,287)	(7,648)
Gross profit	US$'000		277	338	1,020	1,461	1,294
Wastage	US$'000		(25)	(53)	(23)	(2)	(2)
Operating expenditure	US$'000		(60)	(55)	(68)	(70)	(71)
EBITDA	US$'000		192	219	930	1,390	1,221
Depreciation	US$'000		(38)	(83)	(113)	(135)	(123)
EBIT	US$'000		155	137	817	1,255	1,098
Interest expense	US$'000		-	(1)	(3)	(2)	-
NPBT	US$'000		155	136	814	1,253	1,098
Tax expense	US$'000						
NPAT	US$'000		155	136	814	1,253	1,098

They say there's only two things certain in life: death and taxes. I can't help but wonder, what happens if the taxman dies..?

This book is only going to cover company (income) tax. Indirect taxes such as Goods and Services Tax (GST) or Value Added Tax (VAT) vary too much from territory to territory and are not usually included in a model as essentially the company is collecting taxes on behalf of the State. Similarly, state and federal taxes, capital gains taxes, mining resources tax, "need a new tax" tax *etc.* are to be ignored as the rules for how they are calculated varies under different circumstances. For the purposes of simplification, I am going to assume a very simple income tax with a flat tax rate of 30%.

Now this tax may be a simple or a complex calculation. Consider the following Interest Expense control account:

Opening Interest Payable	10
Interest Expense	20
Interest Paid	(10)
Closing Interest Payable	20

This all makes sense, now let me change it to Tax:

Opening Tax Payable	10
Tax Expense	20
Tax Paid	(10)
Closing Tax Payable	97

Pardon? What happened there? Welcome to the wonderful world of **Accounting v. Taxation**. Accounting is all about producing a true and fair view of the world (although the terms "true" and "fair" are never actually defined anywhere), whereas you could say that the Tax authorities do not give two figs for true and fair. *You* could say that. I won't. I might get taxed.

To be "fair", there are many more accounting auditors than their tax counterparts. It is important for shareholders and stakeholders to have a true and fair view of a company's accounts in order to form a view for the basis of making future decisions. Tax authorities, by and large, tend to look for a simple prescriptive rule book, *e.g.* if companies A and B both make the same profit from the same sources with similar cost and financing structures, they should pay a similar level of tax. Therefore, there tend to be simplifying rules.

Accounting works on an accruals basis, dealing with revenue and cost recognition which may differ from tax. This will give rise to **timing differences**, often referred to as **temporary differences**. But there are other types of difference too. If I choose not to pay tax, get taken to court and I am fined, that would be a legitimate expense to me and would have to be shown in my Income Statement. However, I can't claim this as a tax deduction – how cool would that be..?

This would be an example of a **permanent difference**, that is, an amount that will never reconcile between accounting and taxation. Any income or expenditure derived from breaking the law is usually excluded from a tax calculation. Other examples may be costs or income assessable to a different type of tax, and so on.

It is not always bad news. It usually is though. You might wish to consider **Liam's Law of Tax**:

> **Liam's Law of Tax**
>
> Often in tax legislation, rules may be ambiguous. If this occurs, calculate the tax to be paid under the different possibilities. Whichever is the worst for you is the one that was meant.

I have yet to find an exception to this rule and remember:

> All rules have exceptions, except this one.

It's best not to think about that too much.

Most of the time, expenses are disallowed, but sometimes revenue is non-assessable. For example, if you are creating a forecast of worldwide revenues for all subsidiaries of a group of companies, all external income must be included for accounting purposes. That may not be the case for tax: Tax treaties, double taxation relief and other rulings may be in place that permanently exclude some income from the tax calculation.

Permanent differences need to be recognised in a model as these must be adjusted for in calculating the Tax Expense. For example,

	$	$
Net Profit Before Tax		1,000
Adjustments:		
Deduct: Non-Assessable Revenue	(100)	
Add Back: Disallowable Expenses	200	
Accounting Taxable Profit	1,100	
Tax Expense (@ 30%)		(330)
Net Profit After Tax		670

The permanent differences are adjusted for to derive an **Accounting Taxable Profit** of $1,100. The tax rate of 30% is applied to this to generate a Tax Expense of $330, leaving a Net Profit After Tax (NPAT) of $670. The effective tax rate here is 33%, being 330 / 1,000.

Timing differences on the other hand lead to **deferred tax** issues instead as these differences will eventually reconcile. The most common cause of a timing difference is depreciation, *e.g.*

Assumptions

Economic Life	4 years
Tax Life	4 years

	Accounting	Tax	Difference	Tax Effect
Multiplier	n/a	2.0x		
Depreciation Rate	25%	50%		
	$	$	$	$
Capex	1,000	1,000		
Depn: Yr 1	(250)	(500)	250	75
	750	500		
Depn: Yr 2	(250)	(250)	-	-
	500	250		
Depn: Yr 3	(250)	(125)	(125)	(38)
	250	125		
Depn: Yr 4	(250)	(125)	(125)	(38)
	-	-	-	-

In this example, the $1,000 non-current asset in question has both an economic life and a tax life of four years. There is absolutely no reason why these values should coincide, but I am keeping it simple for this example.

No residual value is assumed. For accounting purposes, depreciation is calculated on a straight line basis of 25% p.a. For tax purposes, I am assuming a double declining balance method, which would be 50% of the remaining balance. Assuming the asset is disposed of at the end of four years, the final year's tax balance is written down to zero.

Let me compare the differences (the first of the two shaded columns in the figure above). In the first year, more depreciation may be claimed for the tax calculation than under the comparable accounting calculation. This will lead to a lower taxable profit, meaning less tax to pay. This is usually what happens in the early years of tax depreciation: companies benefit from these **accelerated capital allowances**, sometimes referred to as **ACAs**.

In our example, the profit in the first period would be $250 higher. With a tax rate of 30%, this would mean the tax to pay would be $75 less. This is real money. Whilst it all balances out in the end (*i.e.* the total differences for the actual amount and the tax effected amounts sum to zero), taking into account the time value of money, this would be of benefit to a company.

Why would a Tax authority do this? Remember, Tax authorities work for the government of the territory to which they pertain, and they want to encourage economic investment. By providing beneficial capital allowances, companies may be encouraged to spend more in a territory, providing more jobs, economic growth and ultimately more taxable income.

The tax effect shows what the benefit is worth – measurements of worth are shown in the Balance Sheet at their tax effected (*i.e.* after tax) amounts. If we receive a benefit of $75 now and the differences eventually sum to zero, in the future we will have to pay $75 more than accounting forecasts will show. Since it is in the future, this will be a **tax deferred liability**.

This all ties up with the patented *Liam Theory of Smiley Faces*:

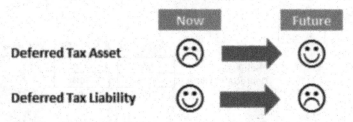

Who would have equated tax with smiley faces? Only a madman, I suspect. A deferred tax liability provides a benefit now, but will cause a greater cost later. Deferred tax assets create bad news now, but good news later.

The most common cause of a deferred tax asset occurs when losses are made. If I make a $1m loss this year, will the Tax authority send me flowers, provide counselling and kiss it all better? Will they reimburse me 30%? Careful, these are trick questions. Depending upon how you answer, you may be sectioned in your nearest Mental Health facility.

No. In most jurisdictions (if not all), the Tax authority will not provide any sort of "refund". However, most territories will allow you to memorialise the loss to use against future profits. Some countries may allow you to use the loss to offset profits in earlier periods. Some may restrict their use (so they may only be carried forward several years and / or against similar activities that caused the loss and / or assume the majority of owners remain the same). This is not a book on the intricacies of taxation. I will be keeping it very simple.

If you make a loss of $1m, the Tax Credit for the period (assuming a 30% tax rate) would be 30%. That is correct as it is associated with the period. However, you will not receive any cash back. Assume you make $3m profit the following year. Normally, you would have to pay $900,000 tax on this. However, in many territories you can offset the loss against this profit and pay tax on only $2m, *i.e.* $600,000. The loss is worth $300,000 as this is the amount it has saved. This could have been calculated in the first instance as $1m x 30%, which is the tax effected amount. Even though there is pain now, you could recognise this as a **deferred tax asset** on the Balance Sheet – as long as it may be assumed you will make a profit in future years / before the tax credit expires, if applicable.

Accounting regulations suggest you discount this amount to take into account the time value of money, but nowhere can you find guidance on how this might be calculated. It doesn't really matter though. For financial modelling and management accounts, deferred tax assets are calculated, but you will seldom see one in statutory accounts.

The reason for this is that auditors have to sign off on statutory accounts. If they acknowledge a deferred tax asset on the face of the Balance Sheet, they are signing off that the company that has just made a loss will make a profit again in the future. Would you be prepared to bet everything you own that this would be the case? No? Neither would auditors. There have been case law precedents where investors have successfully sued auditors for displaying deferred tax assets on a company that subsequently went into liquidation. The investors argued that they could infer auditors were signing off that the company would be profitable again in the future and relied upon this inference in making their investment decisions. Courts have agreed. Hence deferred tax assets are as likely to be seen on the face of statutory accounts as white is likely to be the new black (if that happens, be extra careful on zebra crossings).

Deferred tax is a definite Friday afternoon accounting rule. I say this because:

- Deferred tax assets and deferred tax liabilities are always non-current even if they will crystallise three nanoseconds from now.

- They should be netted off in the accounts (why would you net depreciation differences against tax losses?).

There are other causes of deferred tax, such as revaluations, but that is for another book. I think we have more than enough to go on with. I can now revisit the tax control account from earlier:

Opening Tax Payable	10
Tax Expense	20
Tax Paid	(10)
Movement in Deferred Tax Assets	(15)
Movement in Deferred Tax Liabilities	92
Closing Tax Payable	97

The reason the control account didn't balance was because we hadn't completed it. There were line items missing, namely the **Movement** in Deferred Tax Assets and the **Movement** in Deferred Tax Liabilities. I have stressed **Movement** because Deferred Tax Assets and Deferred Tax Liabilities are to be found in the Balance Sheet and amounts in this financial statement must be shown cumulatively. We will need to keep a running total (*i.e.* more control accounts) of these balances.

I think we are good to go!

Back to the Case Study: Tax Expense

I think it is time to consider the inputs on the 'General Assumptions' worksheet:

									Jun 25	Jun 26	Jun 27	Jun 28	Jun 29
1	**General Assumptions**												
2	Financial Model with Dynamic Arrays.xlsm												
3	Navigator												
4	Error Checks:				☑								
5										Jun 25	Jun 26	Jun 27	Jun 28	Jun 29
6	Start Date									1 Jul 24	1 Jul 25	1 Jul 26	1 Jul 27	1 Jul 28
7	End Date									30 Jun 25	30 Jun 26	30 Jun 27	30 Jun 28	30 Jun 29
8	Number of Days									365	365	365	366	365
9	Counter									1	2	3	4	5
91														
92	**Taxation**												
93														
94	Tax rate												
95														
96	Tax rate		%		30%								
97														
98	Permanent differences												
99														
100	Non-assessable revenue		US$'000						25	25	25	25	25
101	Disallowable expenses		US$'000						40	16	25	30	50
102														
103	Tax depreciation (declining balance)												
104														
105	Declining balance multiplier		x		2.00x								
106														
107	Remaining life of tax assets		# Year(s)		5 years								
108	Annual rate		%		40%	=IF(I107=0,,$I$105/I107)							
109														
110	Tax asset life of new capex		# Year(s)		4 years								
111	Annual rate		%		50%	=IF(I110=0,,$I$105/I110)							
112														
113	**DTA**												
114	DTAs are assumed to arise through losses carried forward												
115														
116	DTA		US$'000										
117														
118	**DTL**												
119	DTLs are assumed to arise through depreciation timing differences												
120														
121	DTL		US$'000										
122														
123	Tax payable and paid												
124														
125	Payment delay		# Year(s)		1 year								

That's a lot of assumptions, and it serves as a warning – this is perhaps the most complicated section of this model.

However, there is nothing particularly controversial with regard to these assumptions, now I have put them in context. In reality, Non-Assessable Revenue and Disallowable Expenses (rows 100 and 101) may need to be provided by a tax expert and may need the construction of a linked or separate financial model.

As always, I have made these two assumptions inconsistent. The Non-assessable revenue (cell **J100**) implements a dynamic array formula

=IF(J$9#,25,)

However, the Disallowable expenses (row 101) have hard coded inputs once more, again hidden in later periods by conditional formatting.

Do note also that the Deferred Tax Assets and Deferred Tax Liabilities (cells **I116** and **I121** respectively) are not inputs. These are linked from the figures supplied in the Opening Balance Sheet.

Finally, the Payment delay (cell **I125**) is simply a hardcoded value of one [1].

Enough putting it off, let's move on to the Calculations sheet and begin by bringing in our non-assessable revenue and disallowable expenses:

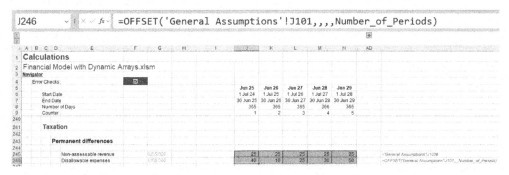

Non-assessable revenue is easily referenced in cell **J245**:

='General Assumptions'!J100#

But, as mentioned above, the Disallowable expenses require the **OFFSET** referencing method in cell **J246**:

=OFFSET('General Assumptions'!J101,,,,Number_of_Periods)

We will also need to bring in the Net Profit Before Tax (NPBT) from row 25 of the Income Statement:

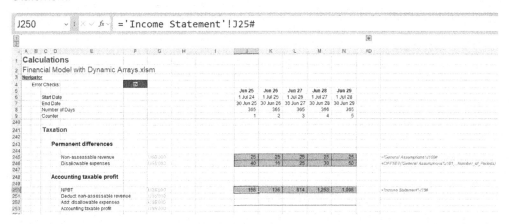

We can then negate the Non-assessable revenue and reference the Disallowable expenses and add these two figures to our NPBT to calculate the Accounting taxable profit:

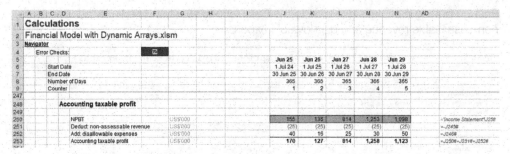

I then bring in the Tax rate, ensuring it spills using the **IF** trick for dynamic arrays:

> **=IF(J$9#,'General Assumptions'!$I$96,)**

and then multiply this by the Accounting taxable profit to calculate the Tax expense / (credit):

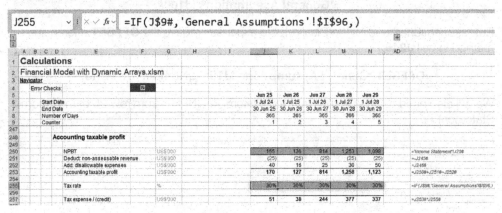

Do note that the Tax expense / (credit) can be positive, zero or negative. This is because it is accruals based and merely displays the tax attributable to the Accounting taxable profit.

Tax Depreciation

Pretty straightforward so far, right? Sadly, it won't be for long. Continuing our journey down the Calculations worksheet it's time to consider Tax depreciation. I will begin by bringing the existing assets from cell **I180** into cell **I262**, the Capital expenditure from row 181 into row 263 and the Tax depreciation assumptions from the 'General Assumptions' worksheet as follows:

You might want to get a coffee, a comfortable chair and some headache tablets at this point. Next, let's consider the formula to calculate depreciation for existing assets:

```
=LET(depreciate,LAMBDA(period,REDUCE(0,SEQUENCE(,period),
  LAMBDA(accumulator,period,accumulator+($I$262-accumulator)*IF
  (period=$I$267,1,$I$268)))),MAP(J9#,LAMBDA(period,
  IF(period=1,depreciate(period),depreciate(period)- depreciate(period-1)))))
```

I did try and warn you. Let's now try and explain this formula.

To begin with, I'm going to temporarily hardcode a value of 100 into cell **I262** and you might wish to unhide some of the columns so that the formula is easier to follow:

Calculations

Financial Model with Dynamic Arrays.xlsm

Navigator

					Jun 25	Jun 26	Jun 27	Jun 28	Jun 29
Error Checks	☑								
					1 Jul 24	1 Jul 25	1 Jul 26	1 Jul 27	1 Jul 28
Start Date					30 Jun 25	30 Jun 26	30 Jun 27	30 Jun 28	30 Jun 29
End Date					365	365	365	366	365
Number of Days					1	2	3	4	5
Counter									

Tax depreciation (declining balance)									
Capital expenditure									
Existing assets	US$'000	Row 180	100						
Capital expenditure	US$'000	Row 181			150	180	120	90	100
Declining balance multiplier	x		2.00x						
Remaining life of tax assets			5 Year(s)						
Annual rate	%		40%						
Tax asset life of new capex			4 Year(s)						
Annual rate	%		50%						
Depreciation - existing assets	US$'000				40	24	14	9	13
Depreciation - new assets	US$'000								
Total depreciation	US$'000								

As you can see the calculation is taking 40% (the annual rate in cell **I268**) of 100 (the value of our existing assets in **I262**) in the first year, resulting in 40. In the second year it is taking 40% of the outstanding value of the asset, 60 (100 minus 40), to give 24. In the third year it is taking 40% of the outstanding value of the asset, 36 (100 minus 40 minus 24) , to give 14.4 and so on until the final year. In the final year the depreciation is equal to the full outstanding value of the asset, 12.96 (100 minus 40 minus 24 minus 14.4 minus 8.64), *viz*.

	A	B	C	D	E	F	G	H	I	J	K
1											
2						Period 1	Period 2	Period 3	Period 4	Period 5	Period 6
3		Existing assets	US$'000	100							
4											
5		Annual rate	%	40%							
6											
7		Depreciation	US$'000			40.00	24.00	14.40	8.64	12.96	-
8											
9		Outstanding asset value	US$'000			60.00	36.00	21.60	12.96	-	-
10											

Let's revisit the formula:

```
=LET(depreciate,LAMBDA(period,REDUCE(0,SEQUENCE(,period),LAMBDA
(accumulator,period,accumulator+($I$262-accumulator)*IF(period=$I$267,1,
$I$268)))),MAP(J9#,LAMBDA(period, IF(period=1,depreciate(period),
depreciate(period)- depreciate(period-1)))))
```

I need to break this down *[you're telling me! – Ed.]*. The first **LAMBDA**, defined as **depreciate** by the **LET** function is as follows:

```
LAMBDA(period,REDUCE(0,SEQUENCE(,period),LAMBDA(accumulator,period,
accumulator+($I$262-accumulator)*IF(period=$I$267,1,$I$268))))
```

484

This effectively builds a custom function within this formula, called **depreciate**, that we can call later on. This custom function tracks the cumulative depreciation of the asset. To understand how, we must first look at the final argument of this custom function:

> **LAMBDA(accumulator,period,accumulator+($I$262-accumulator)*IF (period=$I$267,1,$I$268))**

Working backwards, this will calculate the current asset value by subtracting the **accumulator** (the cumulative depreciation at the beginning of the period) from **$I$262** (the initial asset value) here:

> **($I$262-accumulator)**

This is then multiplied by either **$I$267** (the annual rate) or, if the asset is in its final year of life one [1] (for full write-off) to give the depreciation for the **period** here:

> **($I$262-accumulator)*IF(period=$I$267,1,$I$268))**

The resulting depreciation for the period is then added to the **accumulator** (the cumulative depreciation at the beginning of the period) to result in the cumulative depreciation at the end of the period.

The remaining parts of this custom function:

> **LAMBDA(period,REDUCE(0,SEQUENCE(,period)**

are much more straight forward:

- **period** is simply the name given to the argument of the custom function

- the first argument of the **REDUCE** function, zero [0], is simply the initial cumulative depreciation, which will always be zero [0]

- and the second argument of the **REDUCE** function, **SEQUENCE(,period)**, simply creates a columnar array such that this function will carry itself out a number of times equal to the **period** argument (once in period 1 to calculate the cumulative depreciation at the end of period 1, twice in period 2 to calculate the cumulative depreciation at the end of period 2, and so on.

Now all that's left is the final argument of the **LET** function, the **MAP** function:

> **MAP(J9#,LAMBDA(period,**
> **IF(period=1,depreciate(period),depreciate(period)- depreciate(period-1))))**

This **MAP** function here will carry out its final argument for each value in **J9#**. Let's take a closer look at this final argument:

> **LAMBDA(period,IF(period=1,depreciate(period),depreciate(period)-**
> **depreciate(period-1)))**

In period 1 this is straightforward. It carries out the **depreciate** function for period 1. As the **depreciate** function tracks cumulative depreciation, in subsequent periods we must instead carry out the **depreciate** function for the period and then subtract from this the result of the **depreciate** function for the prior period. This calculates the difference in cumulative depreciation between the two **period**s, which is the depreciation for the **period**.

With that cleared up (hopefully!), let's amend cell **I262** so that it references **I180** once again before we consider the depreciation on new assets:

						Jun 25	Jun 26	Jun 27	Jun 28	Jun 29
Calculations										
Financial Model with Dynamic Arrays.xlsm										
Navigator										
Error Checks:			☑							
	Start Date					1 Jul 24	1 Jul 25	1 Jul 26	1 Jul 27	1 Jul 28
	End Date					30 Jun 25	30 Jun 26	30 Jun 27	30 Jun 28	30 Jun 29
	Number of Days					365	365	365	366	365
	Counter					1	2	3	4	5
	Tax depreciation (declining balance)									
		Capital expenditure								
		Existing assets	US$'000		Row 180					
		Capital expenditure	US$'000		Row 181	150	180	120	90	100
		Declining balance multiplier	x			2.00x				
		Remaining life of tax assets				5 Year(s)				
		Annual rate	%			40%				
		Tax asset life of new capex				4 Year(s)				
		Annual rate	%			50%				
		Depreciation - existing assets	US$'000			-	-	-	-	-
		Depreciation - new assets	US$'000							
		Total depreciation	US$'000							

Let's now put in the formula for Depreciation - new assets. It's another beauty:

$$
\begin{aligned}
&\texttt{=BYCOL(DROP(REDUCE(0,J9\#,LAMBDA(accumulator,currentperiod,}\\
&\texttt{LET(depreciate,LAMBDA(period,REDUCE(0,SEQUENCE(,period),}\\
&\texttt{LAMBDA(accumulator,counter,accumulator+IF(counter<currentperiod,,}\\
&\texttt{(INDEX(J263\#,1,currentperiod)-accumulator)*IF(counter=I270+currentperiod-}\\
&\texttt{1,1,\$I\$271))))),}\\
&\texttt{VSTACK(accumulator,MAP(J9\#,LAMBDA(period,IF(period=1,depreciate(period),}\\
&\texttt{depreciate(period)-depreciate(period-1)))))))),1),LAMBDA(column,SUM(column)))}
\end{aligned}
$$

```
J274        × ✓ fx   =BYCOL(DROP(REDUCE(0,J9#,LAMBDA(accumulator,currentperiod,
                     LET(depreciate,LAMBDA(period,REDUCE(0,SEQUENCE(,period),
                     LAMBDA(accumulator,counter,accumulator
                     +IF(counter<currentperiod,,(INDEX(J263#,1,currentperiod)-accumulator)
                     *IF(counter=I270+currentperiod-1,1,$I$271))))),
                     VSTACK(accumulator,MAP(J9#,
                     LAMBDA(period,
                     IF(period=1,depreciate(period),depreciate(period)-depreciate(period-1)))))))),1),
                     LAMBDA(column,SUM(column)))
```

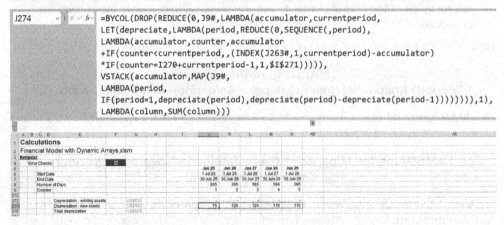

I'm sure that's crystal clear; there is no need to explain. What do you mean you don't quite follow it!? OK, here goes nothing.

Let's begin by explaining the big picture first. This is tax. When we build a tax model, we have tax sections we use in every model, we put the numbers in and it just works! This is the template, if you don't quite get it you shouldn't let that put you off of using this as dynamic arrays are very powerful. Therefore, it isn't the end of the world if this seems a little difficult to follow.

A reminder of the monstrous formula:

> **=BYCOL(DROP(REDUCE(0,J9#,LAMBDA(accumulator,currentperiod,**
> **LET(depreciate,LAMBDA(period,REDUCE(0,SEQUENCE(,period),**
> **LAMBDA(accumulator,counter,accumulator+IF(counter<currentperiod,,**
> **(INDEX(J263#,1,currentperiod)-accumulator)*IF(counter=I270+currentperiod-**
> **1,1,$I$271))))),**
> **VSTACK(accumulator,MAP(J9#,LAMBDA(period,IF(period=1,depreciate(period),**
> **depreciate(period)-depreciate(period-1)))))))),1),LAMBDA(column,SUM(column)))**

Upon close inspection, you will see this uses a similar approach to the previous formula. I define a **depreciate** function to calculate the cumulative depreciation:

> **LET(depreciate,LAMBDA(period,REDUCE(0,SEQUENCE(,period),**
> **LAMBDA(accumulator,counter,accumulator+IF(counter<currentperiod,,**
> **(INDEX(J263#,1,currentperiod)-accumulator)*IF(counter=I270+currentperiod-**
> **1,1,$I$271)))))**

and we call this for each value in **J9#** using the **MAP** function:

> **MAP(J9#,**
> **LAMBDA(period,IF(period=1,depreciate(period),depreciate(period)-**
> **depreciate(period-1))))**

The difference here is that we employ **VSTACK** to carry this out for each Capital expenditure entry in row 263 (effectively creating a depreciation grid). The **DROP** function is used to remove any superfluous rows, and the **BYCOL** function is added to sum the resulting grid, column by column.

Let's break this formula down and consider one part at a time:

| J274 | | | ⌄ | ⠇ | ✕ ✓ *fx* ⌄ | =REDUCE(0,$J9#,LAMBDA(accumulator,currentperiod, |

```
=REDUCE(0,$J9#,LAMBDA(accumulator,currentperiod,
LET(depreciate,LAMBDA(period,REDUCE(0,SEQUENCE(,period),
LAMBDA(accumulator,counter,accumulator+
IF(counter<currentperiod,,
(INDEX($J263#,1,currentperiod)-accumulator)*
IF(counter=$I$270+currentperiod-1,1,$I$271))))),
depreciate(J9))))
```

	A B C D	E	F	G	H	I	J	K	L	M	N
1	**Calculations**										
2	Financial Model with Dynamic Arrays.xlsm										
3	Navigator										
4	Error Checks:		☑								
5							Jun 25	Jun 26	Jun 27	Jun 28	Jun 29
6	Start Date						1 Jul 24	1 Jul 25	1 Jul 26	1 Jul 27	1 Jul 28
7	End Date						30 Jun 25	30 Jun 26	30 Jun 27	30 Jun 28	30 Jun 29
8	Number of Days						365	365	365	366	365
9	Counter						1	2	3	4	5
260											
261	**Capital expenditure**										
262	Existing assets		US$'000	Row 180		-					
263	Capital expenditure		US$'000	Row 181			150	180	120	90	100
264											
265	Declining balance multiplier		x		2.00x						
266											
267	Remaining life of tax assets				5 Year(s)						
268	Annual rate		%		40%						
269											
270	Tax asset life of new capex				4 Year(s)						
271	Annual rate		%		50%						
272											
273	Depreciation - existing assets		US$'000				-	-	-	-	-
274	No VSTACK, MAP, DROP or BYCOL		US$'000				-	-	-	-	50

The formula I have employed here is similar, although I have removed the **VSTACK**, **MAP**, **DROP** and **BYCOL** portions:

=REDUCE(0,$J9#,LAMBDA(accumulator,currentperiod,LET(depreciate,LAMBDA (period,REDUCE(0,SEQUENCE(,period),LAMBDA(accumulator,counter,accumulator+ IF(counter<currentperiod,,(INDEX($J263#,1,currentperiod)-accumulator)* IF(counter=$I$270+currentperiod-1,1,$I$271))))),depreciate(J9))))

You may notice that this isn't a dynamic array (as I have removed the **MAP** function) and that it has been copied across the columns manually. As such some of the references have been anchored here, I will remove this superfluous anchoring once I reintroduce the **MAP** function. You may also notice that this is also only outputting depreciation for the capital expenditure in the final period (as I have removed the **VSTACK** function) but this isn't what's important right now.

Let's begin by inspecting the **depreciate** function defined within this formula:

LAMBDA(period,REDUCE(0,SEQUENCE(,period),LAMBDA(accumulator,counter, accumulator+ IF(counter<currentperiod,,(INDEX($J263#,1,currentperiod)-accumulator)* IF(counter=$I$270+currentperiod-1,1,$I$271)))))

This checks if the **counter (J9#)** is less than or equal to the **currentperiod** (a columnar array of one [1] to our **period**, *i.e.* the year the asset currently being considered will be acquired). If it is then zero [0], it is added to the **accumulator** (the cumulative depreciation) as we are constructing a depreciation grid and if the **counter** is less than the **currentperiod** then the asset has not yet been procured and is not ready to be depreciated. This may be clearer when I reintroduce the **VSTACK** function shortly.

Continuing with the **depreciate** function:

> **LAMBDA(period,REDUCE(0,SEQUENCE(,period),LAMBDA(accumulator,counter, accumulator+**
> **IF(counter<currentperiod,,(INDEX($J263#,1,currentperiod)-accumulator)***
> **IF(counter=$I$270+currentperiod-1,1,$I$271)))))**

If the **counter** is not less than the **currentperiod** then the asset is ready to be depreciated, and as such I may use **INDEX** to reference the capital expenditure profile (**J263#**) by the **currentperiod** to return the asset's original purchase price. The **accumulator** (cumulative depreciation) is subtracted from this to give the asset's current value. This is then multiplied by either **$I$271** (the annual rate), or one [1] if the **counter** (**J9#**) is equal to **$I$270** (the asset life) plus the **currentperiod** (the period in which the asset I'm currently considering was acquired) minus 1, *i.e.* the asset is in its final year of life.

To reiterate more simply, in each period, for each instance of capital expenditure, the asset's original purchase price is looked up. This then has the cumulative depreciation subtracted from it. This is then multiplied by the annual rate (unless it is the final period, then it is multiplied by one [1]) to calculate the depreciation in the period.

However, in its current form this returns cumulative depreciation for items brought in period 5. This is because this is the final period for which amounts are calculated and the formula is not subtracting the prior results of the **depreciate** function. First, I can force the formula to return all interim values by making use of the **VSTACK** function to stack the **accumulator** alongside the results of the **depreciate** function:

J274	f_x	=REDUCE(0,$J9#,LAMBDA(accumulator,currentperiod,
		LET(depreciate,LAMBDA(period,REDUCE(0,SEQUENCE(,period),
		LAMBDA(accumulator,counter,accumulator+
		IF(counter<currentperiod,,
		(INDEX($J263#,1,currentperiod)-accumulator)*
		IF(counter=$I$270+currentperiod-1,1,$I$271))))),
		VSTACK(accumulator,depreciate(J9)))))

	A	B	C	D	E	F	G	H	I	J	K	L	M	N
1	**Calculations**													
2	Financial Model with Dynamic Arrays.xlsm													
3	Navigator													
4		Error Checks:					☑							
5										Jun 25	Jun 26	Jun 27	Jun 28	Jun 29
6		Start Date								1 Jul 24	1 Jul 25	1 Jul 26	1 Jul 27	1 Jul 28
7		End Date								30 Jun 25	30 Jun 26	30 Jun 27	30 Jun 28	30 Jun 29
8		Number of Days								365	365	365	366	365
9		Counter								1	2	3	4	5
259			**Tax depreciation (declining balance)**											
260														
261				Capital expenditure										
262				Existing assets		US$'000	Row 180		-					
263				Capital expenditure		US$'000	Row 181			150	180	120	90	100
264														
265				Declining balance multiplier		x			2.00x					
266														
267				Remaining life of tax assets					5 Year(s)					
268				Annual rate		%			40%					
269														
270				Tax asset life of new capex					4 Year(s)					
271				Annual rate		%			50%					
272														
273				Depreciation - existing assets		US$'000				-	-	-	-	-
274				No MAP, DROP or BYCOL		US$'000				-	-	-	-	-
275						US$'000				75	113	131	150	150
276						US$'000				-	90	135	158	180
277						US$'000				-	-	60	90	105
278						US$'000				-	-	-	45	68
279						US$'000				-	-	-	-	50

With all interim values now being returned, I can reintroduce the **MAP** function. This will make the formula dynamic, which will allow me to remove the superfluous anchoring. This also ensures that, for all periods besides the first, the prior period's cumulative depreciation is subtracted from the current period's cumulative depreciation:

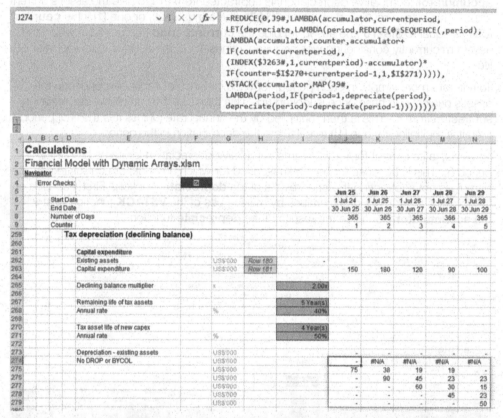

Next, I must employ the **DROP** function to get rid of the erroneous row at the top:

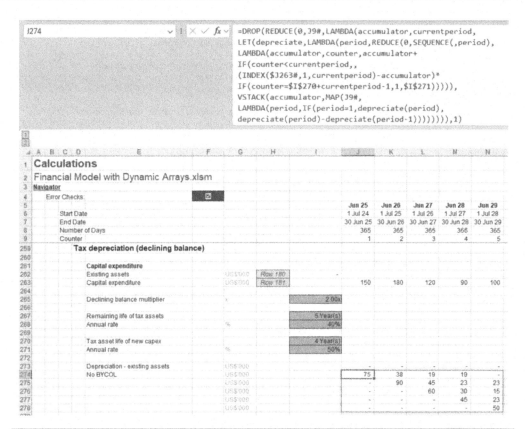

```
=DROP(REDUCE(0,J9#,LAMBDA(accumulator,currentperiod,LET(depreciate,LAMBDA
(period,REDUCE(0,SEQUENCE(,period),LAMBDA(accumulator,counter,accumulator+
    IF(counter<currentperiod,,(INDEX(J263#,1,currentperiod)-accumulator)*
                IF(counter=I270+currentperiod-1,1,$I$271))))),
                    VSTACK(accumulator,MAP(J9#,
        LAMBDA(period,IF(period=1,depreciate(period),depreciate(period)-
                    depreciate(period-1)))))))),1)
```

Finally, I can employ the **BYCOL** function to sum each column:

```
=BYCOL(DROP(REDUCE(0,J9#,LAMBDA(accumulator,currentperiod,LET(depreciate,
    LAMBDA(period,REDUCE(0,SEQUENCE(,period),LAMBDA(accumulator,counter,
                        accumulator+
    IF(counter<currentperiod,,(INDEX(J263#,1,currentperiod)-accumulator)*
                IF(counter=I270+currentperiod-1,1,$I$271))))),
                    VSTACK(accumulator,MAP(J9#,
        LAMBDA(period,IF(period=1,depreciate(period),depreciate(period)-
                    depreciate(period-1)))))))),1),
                LAMBDA(column,SUM(column)))
```

I now have the formula for row 274 to calculate the Tax depreciation on new assets:

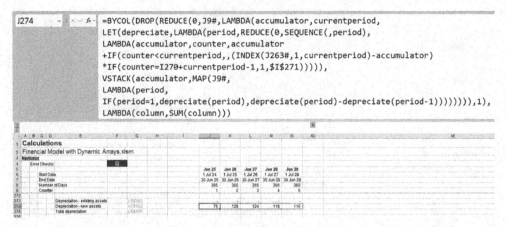

```
J274          =BYCOL(DROP(REDUCE(0,J9#,LAMBDA(accumulator,currentperiod,
              LET(depreciate,LAMBDA(period,REDUCE(0,SEQUENCE(,period),
              LAMBDA(accumulator,counter,accumulator
              +IF(counter<currentperiod,,(INDEX(J263#,1,currentperiod)-accumulator)
              *IF(counter=I270+currentperiod-1,1,$I$271)))))),
              VSTACK(accumulator,MAP(J9#,
              LAMBDA(period,
              IF(period=1,depreciate(period),depreciate(period)-depreciate(period-1))))))))),1),
              LAMBDA(column,SUM(column)))
```

Let's end the Tax depreciation section with a nice easy calculation: the Total depreciation in row 275 which is *very* simple:

=J273#+J274#

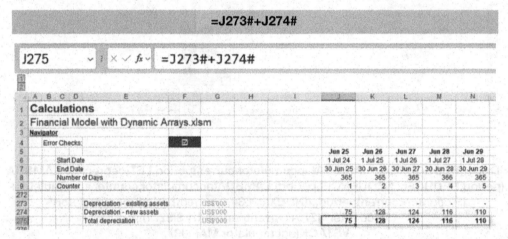

Accounting Depreciation

You're probably planning to run a mile at this point, aren't you? Relax. This one's easy.

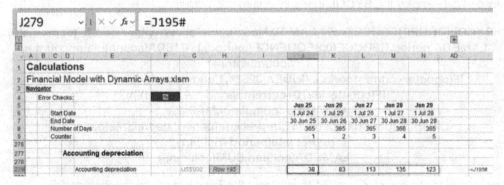

This formula merely references the Accounting depreciation calculated back in Section 17.11.

=J195#

That was no fun. No PhDs for understanding this sub-section.

Depreciation Timing Difference

To calculate tax, as explained in the *Theory* section earlier, we need to add back the Accounting depreciation and deduct the Tax depreciation from the Accounting taxable profit. This requires the Depreciation timing difference being computed:

Multiplying this Depreciation timing difference (row 285) by the prevailing Tax rate will calculate our Movement in Deferred Tax Liabilities (DTLs), *viz.*

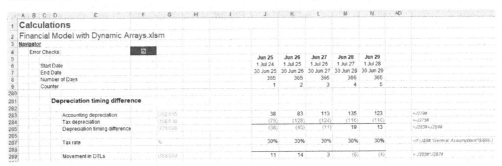

Again, the Tax rate (cell **J287**) is calculated using **IF**:

=IF(J$9#,'General Assumptions'!$I$96,)

The Movement in DTLs (**J289**)

=-J285#*J287#

is negated here so that it may be viewed as a positive number. This is because it is a liability, and liabilities are shown as positive numbers in our Balance Sheet.

Moreover, the Movement in DTLs will be in our final Tax control account, but it will not be the movement that is referenced in the financial statements. This is because this is a Balance Sheet entry, and Balance Sheet items are cumulative by their very nature. Therefore, we need to keep a running total using a "mini" control account:

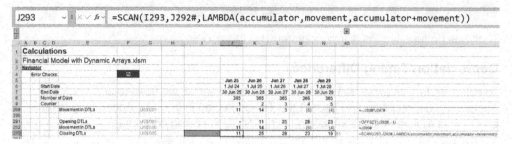

| J293 | | ▾ | × ✓ fx ▾ | =SCAN(I293,J292#,LAMBDA(accumulator,movement,accumulator+movement)) |

A B C D	E	F	G	H	I	J	K	L	M	N	AD
1 Calculations											
2 Financial Model with Dynamic Arrays.xlsm											
3 Navigator											
4 Error Checks		☑									
5						Jun 25	Jun 26	Jun 27	Jun 28	Jun 29	
6 Start Date						1 Jul 24	1 Jul 25	1 Jul 26	1 Jul 27	1 Jul 28	
7 End Date						30 Jun 25	30 Jun 26	30 Jun 27	30 Jun 28	30 Jun 29	
8 Number of Days						365	365	365	366	365	
9 Counter						1	2	3	4	5	
289 Movement in DTLs	US$'000					11	14	3	(6)	(4)	=J289#/J97#
290											
291 Opening DTLs	US$'000					-	11	25	28	23	=OFFSET(J293#,,-1)
292 Movement in DTLs	US$'000					11	14	3	(6)	(4)	=J289#
293 Closing DTLs	US$'000					11	25	28	23	19	=SCAN(I293,J292#,LAMBDA(accumulator,movement,accumulator+movement))

J292, the Movement in DTLs is simply a dynamic array reference to row 289. Cell **I293** links to the corresponding assumption in cell **I21** of the 'General Assumptions' worksheet

='General Assumptions'!I121

which in turn came from cell **I37** of the Opening Balance Sheet.

The Closing DTLs (cell **J293**) uses the usual **SCAN(LAMBDA)** syntax

=SCAN(I293,J292#,LAMBDA(accumulator,movement,accumulator+movement))

and the Opening DTLs (cell **J291**) uses the "now standard" **OFFSET** approach:

=OFFSET(J293#,,-1)

I will use the Closing DTLs for the Balance Sheet reference later, but for now, I can see I am in a position to start the calculations for Tax payable and Tax paid.

Tax Payable and Paid, Part 1

The discussion on Tax payable and Tax paid needs to be separated into two parts. That is because there is a challenging area of modelling that must be performed in the midst of those calculations, but more on that in a moment. First, I can calculate the Taxable profit / (loss) before losses, which is simply the aggregation of the Accounting taxable profit (row 253) and the Depreciation timing difference just calculated recently (row 285).

| J299 | | ▾ | × ✓ fx ▾ | =J297#+J298# |

A B C D	E	F	G	H	I	J	K	L	M	N	AD
1 Calculations											
2 Financial Model with Dynamic Arrays.xlsm											
3 Navigator											
4 Error Checks		☑									
5						Jun 25	Jun 26	Jun 27	Jun 28	Jun 29	
6 Start Date						1 Jul 24	1 Jul 25	1 Jul 26	1 Jul 27	1 Jul 28	
7 End Date						30 Jun 25	30 Jun 26	30 Jun 27	30 Jun 28	30 Jun 29	
8 Number of Days						365	365	365	366	365	
9 Counter						1	2	3	4	5	
294											
295 Tax payable and paid											
296											
297 Accounting taxable profit	US$'000					170	127	814	1,258	1,123	=J253#
298 Depreciation timing difference	US$'000					(38)	(45)	(11)	19	13	=J285#
299 Taxable profit / (loss) before losses	US$'000					132	82	803	1,277	1,136	=J297#+J298#

Row 299's Taxable profit / (loss) before losses does not generate exactly the correct numbers that may be used to calculate Tax payable. This is because the amount may be reduced by any existing Tax loss. Further, if the Taxable profit / (loss) before losses is a negative number, this will be added to the losses and may be used to offset future profits.

Therefore, at this juncture, I need to consider keeping a running total of tax losses created and used. This is achieved by constructing what is known as a **Tax losses memorandum**.

Tax Losses Memorandum

As past losses may offset future taxable profits in many jurisdictions of the world (which is what this model is assuming here), I need to record all losses generated and how they are then utilised. Since tax rates may vary period on period (even though they do not in this simple case study), I have to keep track of the losses themselves. I do this rather than track any taxable benefits associated with them (*i.e.* calculating the "tax effected" amounts by multiplying the tax losses used by the prevailing tax rate for the period in which they were used). This is because it is much simpler to do.

In *Introduction to Financial Modelling*, the calculation of such a Tax losses memorandum was reasonably straightforward. However, this is not the case when considering dynamic arrays. This is because not only are the tax losses generated from the Taxable profit / (loss) before losses figures, but they are also used based upon these same figures albeit in different periods.

In legacy (non-dynamic array) modelling, this is fine as no circularity ensues as calculations are based upon past figures. Unfortunately, with dynamic arrays, each range (Tax losses and Taxable profit / (loss) before losses) is treated as one object, so this is considered circular logic. Therefore, I need to avoid the circularity and get inventive.

Similarly to the *Tax depreciation* subsection, I am going to construct a simpler example first before considering our case study. Please review the following image:

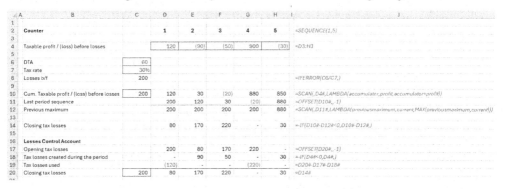

Row 4 of the above image contains a dynamic array input of Taxable profit / (loss) before losses figures, similar to row 299 of the Calculations sheet in our case study. Cell **C6** contains an assumption for the opening Deferred Tax Asset (60), which is assumed to be entirely attributable to past losses. Cell **C7** contains a global Tax rate assumption of 30%.

Since all amounts on the Balance Sheet are tax effected (*i.e.* after the effects of corporate taxation), I assume that the DTA is calculated as the aggregate tax losses unused multiplied by the tax rate. Therefore, if I divide the DTA by the Tax rate,

=IFERROR(C6/C7,)

this will give me the opening tax losses brought forward – just what I require for my Tax losses memorandum. This value (200) in cell **C8** is then linked to cells **C10** and **C20**.

In cell **D10**, the Cumulative Taxable profit / (loss) before losses is calculated using our usual **SCAN(LAMBDA)** approach, *i.e.* in cell **D10**, I have the formula

=SCAN(,D4#,LAMBDA(accumulator,profit,accumulator+profit))

This is keeping a running total of the Taxable profit / (loss) before losses. Don't worry about the losses brought forward being in cell **C10**: this is so it may form part of the array in the next row.

Cell **D11** calculates what I call the Last period sequence using the formula

=OFFSET(D10#,,-1)

Like opening balances for a control account, it references the last period figure, this time for Taxable profit / (loss) before losses, except in the first period it calls the loss brought forward as a positive number (not exactly an intuitive idea, but please bear with me).

To avoid the circularity, I need to construct the following algorithm:

1. Calculate the cumulative Taxable profit / (loss) before losses to evaluate to the cumulative amount up to that period

2. Create a previous maximum which determines the previous maximum amount of the taxable profit / losses before losses

3. Subtract the cumulative Taxable profit / (loss) before losses from the previous maximum

4. If this value is negative, record it as a positive number

5. This is effectively the Closing tax losses figure.

This will effectively return the Closing tax losses for the control account. Some of you think, why not reverse the calculation in Step 3 *(above)* as there will then be no need to negate a positive value. I prefer to do it this way to make it clear it is part of a Tax loss calculation.

To calculate the Previous maximum, in cell **D12** of my simple example I have the formula

=SCAN(,D11#,LAMBDA(previousmaximum,current,MAX(previousmaximum,current)))

which calculates the required previous maximum.

The Closing tax losses are then calculated in cell **D14**:

=-IF(D10#-D12#<0,D10#-D12#,)

This is clearly following Steps 3, 4 and 5 of the above algorithm. Then, it is simple to calculate the Tax losses control account:

*   Tax losses created during the period (cell **D18**) uses the formula **=-IF(D4#<0,D4#,)**

*   Closing tax losses (cell **D20**) uses the formula **=D14#**, *i.e.* it references the value just calculated

- Opening tax losses (cell **D17**) uses the usual **OFFSET** technique,
  =OFFSET(D20#,,-1)

- Tax losses used (cell **D19**) is then the balancing figure, **=D20#-D17#-D18#**

Now that I have explained this away from the "noise" of the actual case study, let's look at the same calculations in the dynamic array model we are building.

The DTA (cell **I314**) is linked to cell **I116** on the 'General Assumptions' worksheet and the Tax rate (cell **I315**) is linked to cell **I96** on the same 'General Assumptions' sheet. Given the Opening Balance Sheet is presently all zero, it is difficult to see what the calculations are doing, so I will hard code a value into cell **I314**:

Cell **I316** has grossed up the DTA to calculate the Opening tax losses:

=IF(I315=0,,I314/I315)

This value has then been linked into cell **I318** (the value retained to the left of the Cumulative taxable profit / (loss) before losses) and also **I328**, the initial value for the Losses control account.

Rows 318 to 322 have similar calculations to those I walked through in my simplified example:

- Cumulative taxable profit / (loss) before losses (cell **J318**):
  =SCAN(,J299#,LAMBDA(accumulator,profit,accumulator+profit))

- Last period sequence (cell **J319**):
  =OFFSET(J318#,,-1)

- Previous maximum (cell **J320**):
  =SCAN(,J319#,LAMBDA(previousmaximum,current,MAX(previousmaximum,current)))

- Closing tax losses (cell **J322**):
  =-IF(J318#-J320#<0,J318#-J320#,)

The Tax losses control account is also similar to before:

- Tax losses created during the period (cell **J326**) uses the formula
  =-IF(J299#<0,J299#,0)

- Closing tax losses (cell **J328**) uses the formula **=J322#**

- Opening tax losses (cell **J325**) uses the usual **OFFSET** technique,
  =OFFSET(J328#,,-1)

- Tax losses used (cell **J327**) is then the balancing figure, **=J328#-J325#-J326#**

The movement in this control account represents the Movement in DTAs, which is one of the items we need to calculate for the financial statements as it is the cumulative total that is required. Therefore, I need to complete this section:

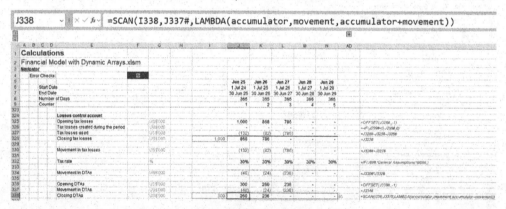

The Movement in tax losses (cell **J330**) is given by

$$=J326\#+J327\#$$

Using the Tax rate with the **IF** trick once more in cell **J332**,

$$=IF(J\$9\#,'General\ Assumptions'!\$I\$96,)$$

I can calculate the Movement in DTAs (Deferred Tax Assets) in cell **J334**, *viz.*

$$=J330\#*J332\#$$

This Movement in DTAs will be in our final Tax control account, but it will not be the movement that is referenced in the financial statements. Again, because this a Balance Sheet entry, we need to keep a running total using a "mini" control account:

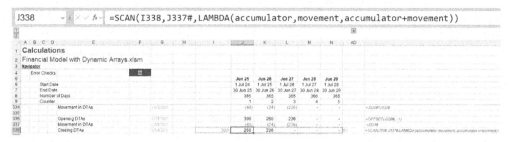

Cell **J337**, the Movement in DTAs is simply a dynamic array reference to row 334. Cell **I338** brings in the Opening DTA from **I314**. The Closing DTAs (cell **J338**) uses another **SCAN(LAMBDA)** calculation

=SCAN(I338,J337#,LAMBDA(accumulator,movement,accumulator+movement))

and the Opening DTLs (cell **J336**) uses the **OFFSET** technique:

=OFFSET(J338#,,-1)

Like the Closing DTLs, I will use the Closing DTAs for the Balance Sheet soon, but now, Let's reset the formula in cell **I314** of the Calculations sheet (DTA):

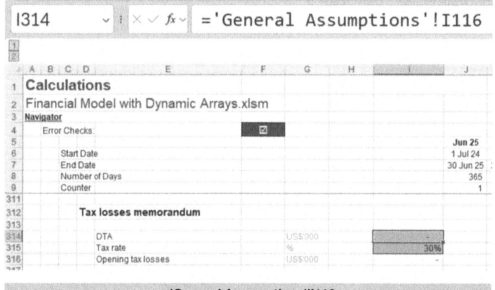

='General Assumptions'!I116

This makes the whole of the Tax losses memorandum section a lot less interesting:

Calculations

Financial Model with Dynamic Arrays.xlsm

Navigator

						Jun 25	Jun 26	Jun 27	Jun 28	Jun 29
Error Checks:		☑								
						1 Jul 24	1 Jul 25	1 Jul 26	1 Jul 27	1 Jul 28
Start Date						30 Jun 25	30 Jun 26	30 Jun 27	30 Jun 28	30 Jun 29
End Date						365	365	365	366	365
Number of Days						1	2	3	4	5
Counter										

Tax losses memorandum										
DTA	US$'000									
Tax rate	%		30%							
Opening tax losses	US$'000				-					
Cumulative taxable profit / (loss) before losses	US$'000				132	214	1,017	2,294	3,430
Last period sequence	US$'000				-	132	214	1,017	2,294
Previous maximum	US$'000				-	132	214	1,017	2,294
Closing tax losses	US$'000				-	-	-	-	-
Losses control account										
Opening tax losses	US$'000				-	-	-	-	-
Tax losses created during the period	US$'000				-	-	-	-	-
Tax losses used	US$'000				-	-	-	-	-
Closing tax losses	US$'000				-	-	-	-	-
Movement in tax losses	US$'000				-	-	-	-	-
Tax rate	%				30%	30%	30%	30%	30%
Movement in DTAs	US$'000				-	-	-	-	-
Opening DTAs	US$'000				-	-	-	-	-
Movement in DTAs	US$'000				-	-	-	-	-
Closing DTAs	US$'000				-	-	-	-	-

Time to return to the calculations for Tax payable and Tax paid.

Tax Payable and Paid, Part 2

I am now in a position to complete these calculations.

Calculations

Financial Model with Dynamic Arrays.xlsm

Navigator

						Jun 25	Jun 26	Jun 27	Jun 28	Jun 29	
Error Checks:		☐									
						1 Jul 24	1 Jul 25	1 Jul 26	1 Jul 27	1 Jul 28	
Start Date						30 Jun 25	30 Jun 26	30 Jun 27	30 Jun 28	30 Jun 29	
End Date						365	365	365	366	365	
Number of Days						1	2	3	4	5	
Counter											
Tax payable and paid											
Accounting taxable profit	US$'000				170	127	814	1,258	1,123	=J253#
Depreciation timing difference	US$'000				(38)	(45)	(11)	19	13	=J265#
Taxable profit / (loss) before losses	US$'000				132	82	803	1,277	1,136	=J297#+J298#
Tax losses used	US$'000				-	-	-	-	-	=J327#
Taxable profit / (loss) after losses	US$'000				132	82	803	1,277	1,136	=J299#+J300#
Tax rate	%				30%	30%	30%	30%	30%	=IF(J299#,'General Assumptions'!$J$96,)
Tax payable for period	US$'000				40	24	241	383	341	=IF(J301#>0,J301#*J302#,)

You may recall (what seems like a lifetime ago now) that I calculated the Taxable profit / (loss) before losses in cell **J299**:

> **=J297#+J298#**

The Tax losses used (cell **J300**) come straight from the Tax losses control account:

> **=J327#**

Therefore, the Taxable profit / (loss) after losses (cell **J301**) is simply the sum of the last two rows:

> **=J299#+J300#**

I need to bring in the Tax rate again now (cell **J302**)

> **=IF(J$9#,'General Assumptions'!$I$96,)**

in order to calculate the Tax payable for the period (cell **J303**):

> **=IF(J301#>0,J301#*J302#,)**

Because this forms the basis of a cash payment, this value, unlike its Tax expense counterpart (cell **J257**) must be restricted to a non-negative value. I cannot think of anywhere in the world where tax authorities will pay you if you make a loss!

Almost there. Now, I need to reference the Payment delay:

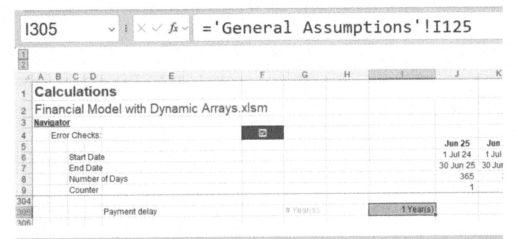

> **='General Assumptions'!I125**

The next interim control account identifies the Tax paid:

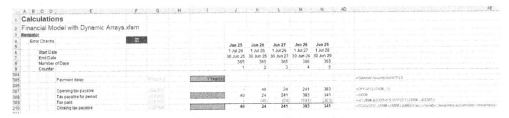

The initial value for the Closing tax payable (cell **I310**) references the Tax payable on the Opening Balance Sheet:

> **='Opening Balance Sheet'!$I$31**

Note the apparently empty cell **I308**. This is <u>not</u> blank. Instead, it references the value in cell **I310**. This is so it can be picked up in the **OFFSET** formula used to calculate Tax paid.

Just before Tax paid, the Tax payable for period (a kind of tax proxy for Tax expense rather than a Balance Sheet item) (cell **J308**) references row 303:

> **=J303#**

Now we get to Tax paid (cell **J309**). This contains the following formula:

> =-IF(J$9#-$I$305<0,0,OFFSET(J308#,,-$I$305))

The **logical_test** at the start of the **IF** statement determines whether the calculation should be made. It prevents cells being referenced before column **I** in case the Payment delay (cell **I305**) is greater than one [1] year. Otherwise, the formula considers the Payment delay when negating the Tax payable reference.

The Closing tax payable (cell **J310**) sums up the movements in the usual way:

> =SCAN(I310,J308#+J309#,LAMBDA(accumulator,movement,accumulator+movement))

Finally, the Opening tax payable uses the **OFFSET** function to select the last period's Closing tax payable:

> =OFFSET(J310#,,-1)

I am now in a position to put all the calculations together for the final Tax control account.

Tax Control Account

Finally!

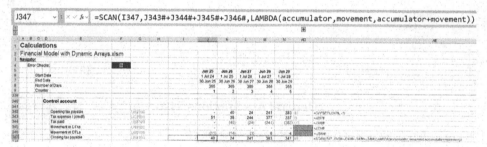

There are six [6] line items for this account, the majority of which are simple dynamic array range references.

- Tax expense / (credit) (cell **J343**): =J257#

- Tax paid (cell **J344**): =J309#

- Movement in DTAs (cell **J345**): =J334#

- Movement in DTLs (cell **J346**): =-J289#

- Initial Closing tax payable (cell **I347**): =I310

- Closing tax payable (cell **J347**):
  =SCAN(I347,J343#+J344#+J345#+J346#,
  LAMBDA(accumulator,movement,accumulator+movement))

- Opening tax payable (cell **J342**): =OFFSET(J347#,,-1).

This control account provides us with the usual three [3] things:

1. **Number of calculations that need to be entered into the financial statements so that they balance:** This is always one less than the number of rows in the control account. In this instance it will be six minus one, which is **five [5]**.

2. **The order to build the calculations into the financial statements:** This is always row 2 first, then row 3, then row 4 and so on. In this instance, this will be Tax expense / (credit) (Income Statement) (which will be negated), Tax paid (Cash Flow Statement) and Closing tax payable (Balance Sheet). The "mini" control accounts will have to be referenced for the Closing DTAs and Closing DTLs (both Balance Sheet).

3. **It identifies the key driver:** Line 2 of the control account is always the key driver, so in this case it will be Tax expense / (credit). If there was never any Tax expense, there would be no Tax paid, *etc.*

Let's begin. First, I need to link the Tax expense (row 343) to the Income Statement (cell **J27**). I remember that this reference should be negated:

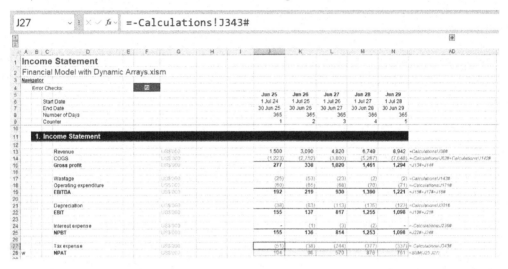

The formula and formatting in row 28 may now be finalised:

503

The Income Statement is now finished. However, the Balance Sheet does not balance (which is expected at this stage). Talking of the Balance Sheet, now that the Income Statement is completed, there is formatting and a formula elsewhere that needs adjustment:

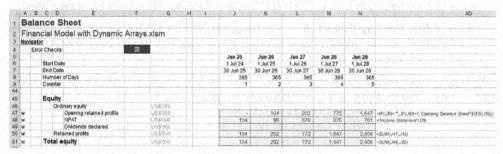

Row 48 (NPAT) can be modified:

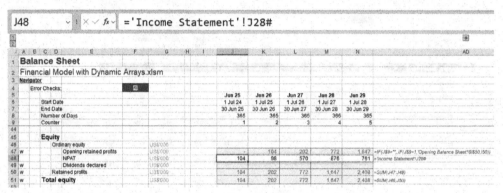

Let's move on to the second item from the control account. Tax paid (row 344). This needs to be linked to cell **J21** in the Cash Flow Statement, *viz.*

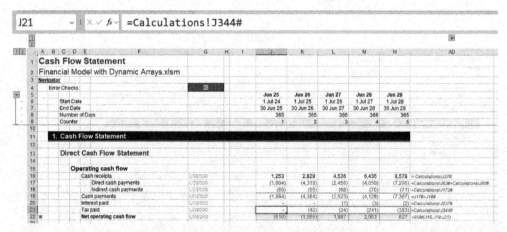

Again, the total for this section, 'Net operating cash flow' can be reformatted and the formula may now be a dynamic array formula:

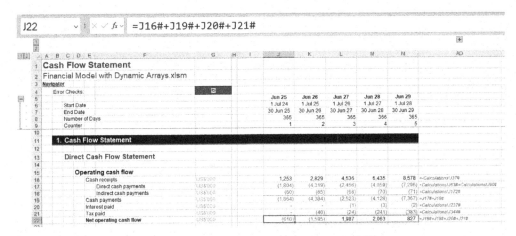

The next entry on the Tax control account is the Movement in DTAs:

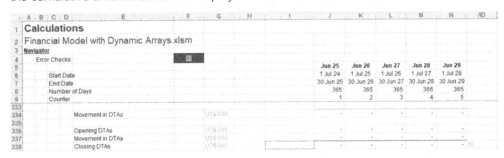

This is – as the name suggests – a *movement*. However, this is a Balance Sheet item, so the cumulative amount should be displayed. This was calculated in row 338:

This links to row 22 (Deferred tax assets) of the Balance Sheet:

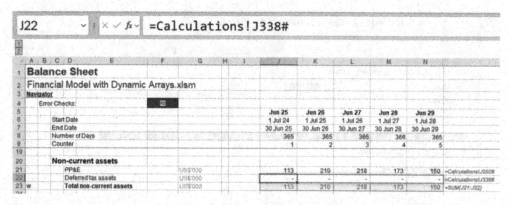

You can tell we are getting towards the end of the model development. I can modify row 23 to turn it into a dynamic array and reformat it:

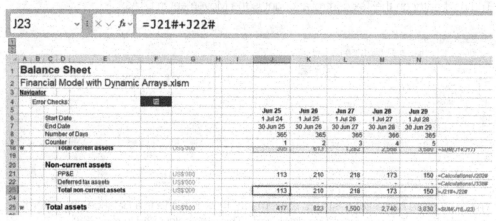

The next entry on the Tax control account is the Movement in DTLs:

A B C D	E	F G H	I	J	K	L	M	N	AD
1 Calculations									
2 Financial Model with Dynamic Arrays.xlsm									
3 Navigator									
4 Error Checks:									
5				Jun 25	Jun 26	Jun 27	Jun 28	Jun 29	
6	Start Date			1 Jul 24	1 Jul 25	1 Jul 26	1 Jul 27	1 Jul 28	
7	End Date			30 Jun 25	30 Jun 26	30 Jun 27	30 Jun 28	30 Jun 29	
8	Number of Days			365	365	365	366	365	
9	Counter			1	2	3	4	5	
339									
340	**Control account**								
341									
342	Opening tax payable	US$'000		-	40	24	241	383	BS
343	Tax expense / (credit)	US$'000		51	38	244	377	337	IS
344	Tax paid	US$'000		-	(40)	(24)	(241)	(383)	CFS
345	Movement in DTAs	US$'000		-	-	-	-	-	
346	Movement in DTLs	US$'000		(11)	(14)	(3)	6	4	
347	Closing tax payable	US$'000		-	40	24	241	383	BS

Similar to the Movement in DTAs, this item is also a Balance Sheet element, and therefore, the cumulative amount should be displayed. This was calculated in row 293:

This links to row 37 (Deferred tax liabilities) of the Balance Sheet:

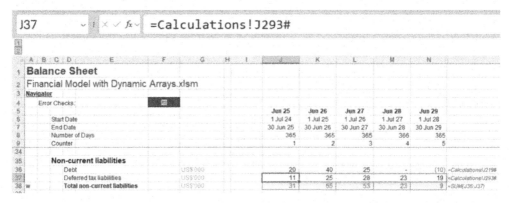

Again, I can modify row 38 to turn it into a dynamic array and reformat it:

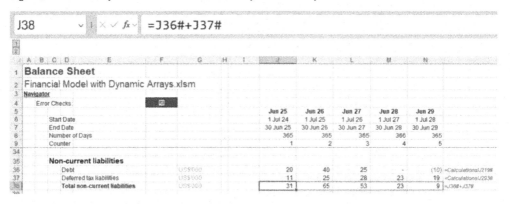

We finally get to the end of the control account:

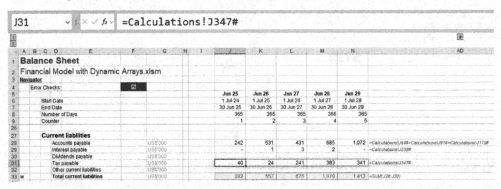

				Jun 25	Jun 26	Jun 27	Jun 28	Jun 29	
1	**Calculations**								
2	Financial Model with Dynamic Arrays.xlsm								
3	Navigator								
4	Error Checks:								
5					Jun 25	Jun 26	Jun 27	Jun 28	Jun 29	
6	Start Date				1 Jul 24	1 Jul 25	1 Jul 26	1 Jul 27	1 Jul 28	
7	End Date				30 Jun 25	30 Jun 26	30 Jun 27	30 Jun 28	30 Jun 29	
8	Number of Days				365	365	365	366	365	
9	Counter				1	2	3	4	5	
339										
340	**Control account**								
341										
342	Opening tax payable	US$'000			-	40	24	241	383	BS
343	Tax expense / (credit)	US$'000			51	38	244	377	337	IS
344	Tax paid	US$'000			-	(40)	(24)	(241)	(383)	CFS
345	Movement in DTAs	US$'000			-	-	-	-	-	
346	Movement in DTLs	US$'000			(11)	(14)	(3)	6	4	
347	Closing tax payable	US$'000			40	24	241	383	341	BS

The Closing tax payable (row 347) links to Tax payable (cell **J31**) of the Balance Sheet:

J31		× ✓ fx	=Calculations!J347#

				Jun 25	Jun 26	Jun 27	Jun 28	Jun 29	AD
1	**Balance Sheet**								
2	Financial Model with Dynamic Arrays.xlsm								
3	Navigator								
4	Error Checks:								
5					Jun 25	Jun 26	Jun 27	Jun 28	Jun 29	
6	Start Date				1 Jul 24	1 Jul 25	1 Jul 26	1 Jul 27	1 Jul 28	
7	End Date				30 Jun 25	30 Jun 26	30 Jun 27	30 Jun 28	30 Jun 29	
8	Number of Days				365	365	365	366	365	
9	Counter				1	2	3	4	5	
26										
27	**Current liabilities**								
28	Accounts payable	US$'000			242	531	431	685	1,072	=Calculations!J64#+Calculations!J91#+Calculations!J173#
29	Interest payable	US$'000			-	1	3	2	-	=Calculations!J238#
30	Dividends payable	US$'000								
31	Tax payable	US$'000			40	24	241	383	341	=Calculations!J347#
32	Other current liabilities	US$'000								
33	w Total current liabilities	US$'000			282	557	675	1,070	1,413	=SUM(J26:J32)

The Balance Sheet balances once more. Tax has now been accounted for. With the Income Statement completed, what's next..?

CHAPTER 17.14: EQUITY

> ### Building a Financial Model
>
> 17. Once the Income Statement is completed, consider the first line item on the Cash Flow Statement not yet linked.

I have just shown that the Income Statement is complete.

1. Income Statement

Revenue	US$'000	1,500	3,090	4,820	6,749	8,942
COGS	US$'000	(1,223)	(2,752)	(3,800)	(5,287)	(7,648)
Gross profit	US$'000	277	338	1,020	1,461	1,294
Wastage	US$'000	(25)	(53)	(23)	(2)	(2)
Operating expenditure	US$'000	(60)	(65)	(68)	(70)	(71)
EBITDA	US$'000	192	219	930	1,390	1,221
Depreciation	US$'000	(38)	(83)	(113)	(135)	(123)
EBIT	US$'000	155	137	817	1,255	1,098
Interest expense	US$'000	-	(1)	(3)	(2)	-
NPBT	US$'000	155	136	814	1,253	1,098
Tax expense	US$'000	(51)	(38)	(244)	(377)	(337)
NPAT	US$'000	104	98	570	876	761

With corresponding line items already entered on other financial statements, I need only fill in the blanks. It's time to move on to the second of our three financial statements, the Cash Flow Statement:

1. Cash Flow Statement

Direct Cash Flow Statement

Operating cash flow						
Cash receipts	US$'000	1,253	2,829	4,536	6,435	8,578
Direct cash payments	US$'000	(1,804)	(4,319)	(2,458)	(4,059)	(7,296)
Indirect cash payments	US$'000	(60)	(65)	(68)	(70)	(71)
Cash payments	US$'000	(1,864)	(4,384)	(2,523)	(4,128)	(7,367)
Interest paid	US$'000	-	-	(1)	(3)	(2)
Tax paid	US$'000	-	(40)	(24)	(241)	(383)
Net operating cash flow	US$'000	(610)	(1,595)	1,987	2,063	827
Investing cash flows						
Purchases of non-current assets	US$'000	(150)	(180)	(120)	(90)	(100)
Net investing cash flows	US$'000	(150)	(180)	(120)	(90)	(100)
Financing cash flows						
Debt drawdowns	US$'000	20	20	-	-	-
Debt repayments	US$'000	-	-	(15)	(25)	(10)
Ordinary equity issuances	US$'000					
Ordinary equity buybacks	US$'000					
Dividends paid	US$'000					
Net financing cash flows	US$'000	20	20	(15)	(25)	(10)
Net increase / (decrease) in cash held	US$'000	(740)	(1,755)	1,852	1,948	717

The Cash Flow Statement is almost complete. There are only three lines left and they all relate to Equity, *i.e.* owner's funds.

When discussing financing in general earlier, you may recall I stated that no matter what the financial instrument, the mechanics essentially boil down to two key elements:

- **Return on finance:** the yield to investors or the costs of capital to the recipient of capital (e.g. interest, dividends); *and*

- **Return of finance:** repayments (or conversion) of original capital issued / drawn down.

The aim is to create the two appropriate control accounts:

Returns of Finance

Opening Balance (*e.g.* Debt / Equity) b/f	XX	*Previous period Balance Sheet item*
Additions (*e.g.* drawdowns / issuances / conversions)	X	*Typically in Cash Flow Statement*
Returns on finance rolled up (*e.g.* "interest capitalised")	X	*Usually a Balance Sheet movement*
Deductions (*e.g.* repayments / buybacks / conversions)	(X)	*Typically in Cash Flow Statement*
Closing Balance (*e.g.* Debt / Equity) c/f	XX	*Current period Balance Sheet item*

Returns on Finance

Opening Return Payable (*e.g.* Dividend Payable) b/f	XX	*Previous period Balance Sheet item*
Return Accrued (*e.g.* Dividend Declared)	X	*Income Statement or Balance Sheet movement*
Return Paid (*e.g.* Dividend Paid)	(X)	*Cash Flow Statement*
Closing Return Payable (*e.g.* Dividend Payable) c/f	XX	*Current period Balance Sheet item*

For Equity, the Return **of** Equity is Equity Buybacks (the drawdown is Equity Issuance); the Return **on** Equity is the Dividends Received and, where quoted the gain on the price of any shares (Share Capital). Equity is the most basic form of capital. At the end of the day, somebody must own the company.

Equity Inputs

For the purposes of our case study, the final inputs on the 'General Assumptions' worksheet are as follows:

J138		× ✓ *fx*	=IF(J$9#*5/100+20%<50%,J$9#*5/100+20%,50%)

	A B C D	E	F	G	H	I	J	K	L	M	N	O
1	**General Assumptions**											
2	Financial Model with Dynamic Arrays.xlsm											
3	Navigator											
4	Error Checks:		☑									
5							Jun 25	Jun 26	Jun 27	Jun 28	Jun 29	
6	Start Date						1 Jul 24	1 Jul 25	1 Jul 26	1 Jul 27	1 Jul 28	
7	End Date						30 Jun 25	30 Jun 26	30 Jun 27	30 Jun 28	30 Jun 29	
8	Number of Days						365	365	365	366	365	
9	Counter						1	2	3	4	5	
127												
128	**Ordinary equity and related**											
129												
130	**Ordinary equity**											
131												
132	Equity issuances		US$'000				15	25	-	10	-	
133	Equity buybacks		US$'000				-	-	5	5	20	
134												
135	**Dividends**											
136	Dividends are assumed to be paid in the period after they are declared											
137												
138	Dividend payout ratio		%				25%	30%	35%	40%	45%	

Equity issuances and Equity buybacks are always likely to be entered inputs as it takes time to arrange shareholder stakes (whether it is via a prospectus or a private sale). Therefore, having rows 132 and 133 contain hardcode is not surprising. I will need to use the **OFFSET** approach to reference these values on the Calculations worksheet.

The other input, Dividend payout ratio is my final dynamic array formula on the 'General Assumptions' worksheet:

> **=IF(J$9#*5/100+20%<50%,J$9#*5/100+20%,50%)**

That will be easier to reference – something you have probably realised now you are this far into the book.

Return of Equity

There are two control accounts to formulate here. The first is the Closing Equity control account. Let's bring in the linked cells first:

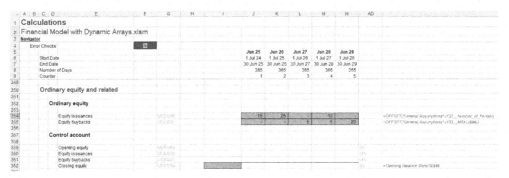

The Ordinary equity assumptions, Equity issuances (cell **J354**) and Equity buybacks (cell **J355**) use the usual **OFFSET** referencing approach:

> **=OFFSET('General Assumptions'!J132,,,,Number_of_Periods)**

and

> **=OFFSET('General Assumptions'!J133,,,,MAX(J$9#))**

For old time's sake, I use **Number_of_Periods** and **MAX(J$9#)** to determine the **width**. This is <u>not</u> Best Practice, but I wanted to leave you with one final reminder that both approaches work.

The initial Closing Equity balance (cell **I362**) contains the following link:

> **='Opening Balance Sheet'!$I$46**

Now, the control account becomes easy. Do you see that this section is very similar to the Debt control account created earlier in Section 17.12?

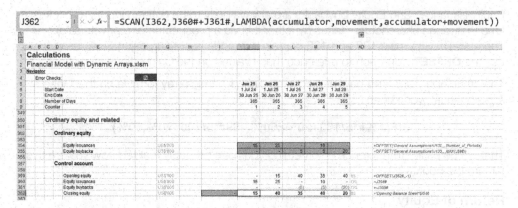

I am already in a position to construct our return *of* finance control account. Equity issuances (cell **J354**) links to row 360, Equity buybacks (cell **J355**) is negated in row 361, Closing equity (cell **J362**) makes use of a **SCAN(LAMBDA)** formula,

> **=SCAN(I362,J360#+J361#,LAMBDA(accumulator,movement,accumulator+movement))**

and our Opening equity (cell **J359**) simply makes use of the **OFFSET** trick.

> **=OFFSET(J362#,,-1)**

We now have three [3] line items to link into the financial statements, none of which are the Income Statement given this is not anything to do with income and expenditure, plus the Income Statement has now been completed.

It took seconds: yet another advantage of *consistency*. At this point, I can confirm:

1. **Number of calculations that need to be entered into the financial statement so that they balance:** It is back to three [3].

2. **The order to build the calculations into the financial statements:** This is always row 2 first, then row 3, then row 4 and so on. In this instance, this will be Ordinary equity Issuances (Cash Flow Statement), Ordinary equity Buybacks (also Cash Flow Statement) and Ordinary Equity (Total Equity section of the Balance Sheet).

3. **It identifies the key driver:** Line 2 of the control account is always the key driver, so in this case it will be Equity Issuances. If there were never any equity, there would be no buybacks, no closing equity and in fact no company.

The first link to be made is Ordinary equity issuances into row 31 of the Cash Flow Statement:

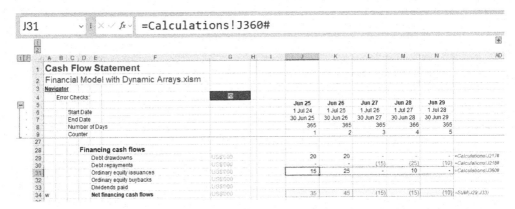

The error check is once more triggered as the Balance Sheet no longer balances, as expected. Ordinary equity buybacks are next. linking into row 32 of the Cash Flow Statement:

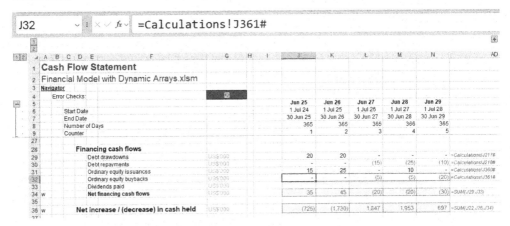

Finally, Closing equity links into row 46 of the Balance Sheet (Ordinary equity) and will satisfy the outstanding error check:

Balance Sheet

Financial Model with Dynamic Arrays.xlsm

Navigator

Error Checks:

		Jun 25	Jun 26	Jun 27	Jun 28	Jun 29	
Net assets	US$'000	119	242	807	1,687	2,428	=J25-J40
Equity							
Ordinary equity	US$'000	15	40	35	40	20	=Calculations!J352#
Opening retained profits	US$'000		104	202	772	1,647	=IF(J50="",IF(J$9=1,'Opening Balance Sheet'!$J$30,J50))
NPAT	US$'000	104	98	570	876	761	='Income Statement'!J26#
Dividends declared	US$'000						
Retained profits	US$'000	104	202	772	1,647	2,408	=SUM(J47:J49)
Total equity	US$'000	119	242	807	1,687	2,428	=SUM(J46:J50)

We've got our return *of* finance calculated but it's time to consider our return *on* finance, the interest.

Return on Equity

This leaves us with the dividends calculation. I have already discussed this in Section 1.15 when explaining **MAX** and **MIN**, but I know that was a *long* time ago now. To save you flicking backwards and forwards through this book, let me discuss dividends again – now in the context of the case study.

Dividends may only be paid out of what are known as distributable reserves (this is a bit of an oxymoron as dividends are also known as **distributions**). Revaluation reserves, share premium accounts, capital redemption reserves are all non-distributable. Essentially, dividends may only be paid out of the current year's Net Profit After Tax (NPAT) and the aggregation of all previous years' profits after past distributions, Retained Earnings. Dividends may not make the Balance Sheet's Total Equity become negative. This shows insolvency and this sort of distribution is illegal in most territories. Given non-distributable reserves may not become negative and that I already have a Balance Sheet check in place for this, I will be concentrating on NPAT and Retained Earnings here.

In this case study, the dividends are going to be a proportion of NPAT. This method is known as the **dividend payout ratio method**. However, I need to check what the maximum dividend is I can use before I calculate this relatively straightforward metric.

To derive the maximum dividend, let me consider some scenarios. Let's imagine the following scenario:

Retained Earnings	100
NPAT	40
Maximum Dividend	**140**

It isn't rocket science that if Retained Earnings and NPAT are both positive, then the maximum dividend allowed is the sum of the two.

Retained Earnings	100
NPAT	(40)
Maximum Dividend	60

If NPAT is negative, but Retained Earnings are positive and exceed the NPAT figure, then the maximum dividend allowed is the net of the two figures. Should the net be negative, no dividend is allowed.

Retained Earnings	(100)
NPAT	40
Maximum Dividend	40

Here is the one that surprises people. If Retained Earnings is negative but NPAT is positive, regardless of whether the net is positive or negative, the maximum dividend allowed is the NPAT amount. This may seem incomprehensible upon first thought, but it is dependent upon two conditions:

- The company's auditors must sign off on it. This is to ensure the company is still seen to be a going concern (*i.e.* it can still continue to operate and trade its way out of any short-term difficulties).

- The shareholders must vote for it. Almost as hilarious as when Members of Parliament solemnly vote for their 50% pay rise each year.

If you think about it some more, this makes sense. Remember, dividends cannot be paid if the company is insolvent. The auditors check to see whether the company can "afford" it for other reasons. But if you don't allow this scenario how would anyone ever attract share capital for a start-up company? A new company may have to provide for certain factors which may never come to fruition. A large non-current asset may have to be written off as not fit for purpose if a company's strategy changes without any cash consequence. Is it acceptable that shareholders have to wait 10 years for the Retained Earnings losses to be covered even if the business is hugely profitable in the meantime? No, and this is precisely why this is the rule.

The next scenario is more obvious:

Retained Earnings	(100)
NPAT	(40)
Maximum Dividend	-

With both a negative NPAT and Retained Earnings, there is no leeway now. These scenarios seem to suggest the following formula:

=MAX(NPAT + Retained Earnings, NPAT, 0)

This allows for the above scenarios. The check to ensure that the value is non-negative (*i.e.* the inclusion of zero in the **MAX** formula) is so that shareholders do not get asked to pay a dividend to the company. I can't imagine that would go down too well.

We are not done yet though. Let's go back to the penultimate scenario but now consider the cash position as well:

Retained Earnings	(100)
NPAT	40
Cash Available	30
Maximum Dividend	30

Here, the Cash Available is the total amount of cash available to pay the dividend. Technically, this includes any cash reserves built up over time, but many companies only consider the cash position for the period the dividend relates to (this is the scenario I shall be modelling in the case study shortly). This is so management feels comfortable they aren't eroding profits.

This seems to suggest the formula:

=MIN(MAX(NPAT + Retained Earnings, NPAT, 0), Cash Available)

Let me just check with slightly revised numbers:

Retained Earnings	(100)
NPAT	40
Cash Available	(30)
Maximum Dividend	(30)

In this scenario, the company is overdrawn. Oops. Here, this company is going to be asking for money again from its shareholders. Not a good idea. This leads to the slightly revised – and finally correct – formula:

Maximum Dividend = MAX(MIN(MAX(NPAT + Retained Earnings, NPAT), Cash Available), 0)

Ah yes, the wonderful **MAX(MIN(MAX))** formula. It may not be the prettiest formula in the world, but the point is, it gives the right number. And that's where I would leave this discussion if this book were *Introduction to Financial Modelling*. But it isn't.

We have already noted that **MAX** and **MIN** will not spill on their own. But it's worse than that. I need to consider three calculated financial statement items:

1. Retained Earnings
2. NPAT
3. Cash available for dividends

in order to calculate the dividends. These dividends will then have an impact on future

1. Retained Earnings

2. NPAT

3. Cash available for dividends

Dynamic arrays treat this as a circularity. I see a big problem needing to be solved with a horror formula. Standby, dear reader, standby.

There is no need to stall for time. Where metaphysical angels fear to tread, let's kick down that metaphorical door! I never "meta" problem I wasn't prepared to tackle... *[Please stop – Ed.]*

Let's return to the Calculations worksheet for the Dividends control account derivation. It's going to be a very bumpy ride. The first stop is straightforward:

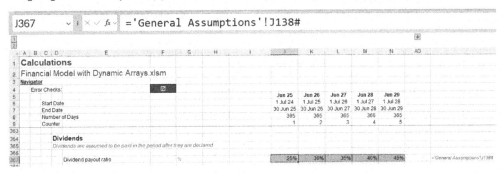

The Dividend payout ratio (cell **J367**) is simply

='General Assumptions'!J138#

But now we hit our first problem:

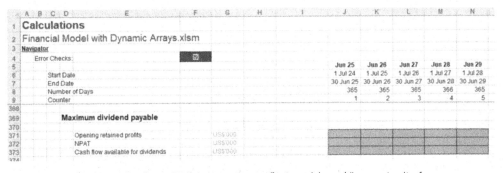

Opening retained profits (row 371) presents our first problem / "opportunity for improvement". Let's inspect the intended source:

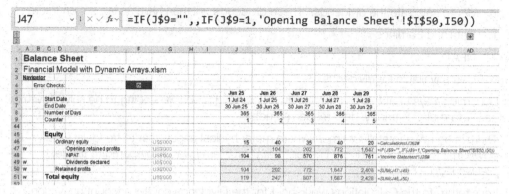

The formula in cell **J47** of the 'Balance Sheet' worksheet is clearly a Work In Progress:

> ## =IF(J$9="",,IF(J$9=1,'Opening Balance Sheet'!$I$50,I50))

Unless I am using something like the **OFFSET** approach to reference these numbers, my calculation on the Calculations sheet will not be a dynamic array and hence another Work In Progress formula. I am very reluctant to introduce much more Work In Progress at this late stage. I am trying to *reduce* it now. I think that's what I should do here.

I need row 47 on the Balance Sheet to become a dynamic array formula. This means I need to convert Retained profits (row 50) to a dynamic array formula – albeit an interim one. Retained profits needs to consider the NPAT (row 48) and Dividends declared (row 49) movements. Unfortunately, Dividends declared have not yet been calculated so row 49 is blank. Therefore, I will write an interim formula for row 50:

```
J50        =SCAN('Opening Balance Sheet'!$I$50,J48#,
             LAMBDA(accumulator,profits,accumulator+profits))
```

I have entered the following formula into cell **J50**:

> ## =SCAN('Opening Balance
> ## Sheet'!$I$50,J48#,LAMBDA(accumulator,profits,accumulator+profits))

This formula remains Work In Progress as the second argument of **SCAN** should also be referencing row 49, which is not yet possible. However, the formula is a dynamic array now (and will cause #*SPILL!* errors unless formulae in subsequent cells across the row are cleared).

This means I can finalise the formula in row 47:

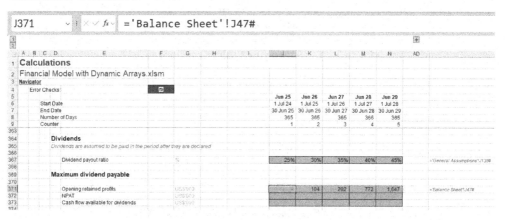

Cell **J47** (Opening retained profits) now contains the equation

=IF(J9#=1,'Opening Balance Sheet'!$I$50,OFFSET(J50#,,-1))

i.e. in the first period, this formula will link back to the Opening Balance Sheet, otherwise it will take the previous period's Retained profits.

Now this formula is a dynamic array calculation, I can reference it back on the Calculations worksheet:

The NPAT reference (cell **J372**) is also straightforward:

The Cash flow available for dividends seems more complicated but in truth, it isn't:

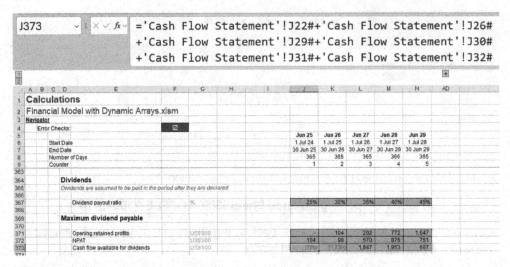

J373 fx ='Cash Flow Statement'!J22#+'Cash Flow Statement'!J26#
+'Cash Flow Statement'!J29#+'Cash Flow Statement'!J30#
+'Cash Flow Statement'!J31#+'Cash Flow Statement'!J32#

	E	F	G	H	I	J	K	L	M	N	AD
1	**Calculations**										
2	Financial Model with Dynamic Arrays.xlsm										
3	Navigator										
4	Error Checks:		☑								
5						Jun 25	Jun 26	Jun 27	Jun 28	Jun 29	
6	Start Date					1 Jul 24	1 Jul 25	1 Jul 26	1 Jul 27	1 Jul 28	
7	End Date					30 Jun 25	30 Jun 26	30 Jun 27	30 Jun 28	30 Jun 29	
8	Number of Days					365	365	365	366	365	
9	Counter					1	2	3	4	5	
363											
364	**Dividends**										
365	Dividends are assumed to be paid in the period after they are declared										
366											
367	Dividend payout ratio	%				25%	30%	35%	40%	45%	
368											
369	**Maximum dividend payable**										
370											
371	Opening retained profits	US$'000				-	104	202	772	1,647	
372	NPAT	US$'000				104	98	570	876	781	
373	Cash flow available for dividends	US$'000				(725)	(1,730)	1,847	1,953	697	
374											

The formula is given by

> ='Cash Flow Statement'!J22#+'Cash Flow Statement'!J26#+'Cash Flow
> Statement'!J29#
> +'Cash Flow Statement'!J30#+'Cash Flow Statement'!J31#+'Cash Flow
> Statement'!J32#

When you inspect the Cash Flow Statement, it is easy to understand:

	E	F	G	H	I	J	K	L	M	N
1	**Cash Flow Statement**									
2	Financial Model with Dynamic Arrays.xlsm									
3	Navigator									
4	Error Checks:			☑						
5						Jun 25	Jun 26	Jun 27	Jun 28	Jun 29
6	Start Date					1 Jul 24	1 Jul 25	1 Jul 26	1 Jul 27	1 Jul 28
7	End Date					30 Jun 25	30 Jun 26	30 Jun 27	30 Jun 28	30 Jun 29
8	Number of Days					365	365	365	366	365
9	Counter					1	2	3	4	5
10										
11	**1. Cash Flow Statement**									
12										
13	**Direct Cash Flow Statement**									
14										
15	**Operating cash flow**									
16	Cash receipts	US$'000				1,253	2,829	4,536	6,435	8,578
17	Direct cash payments	US$'000				(1,804)	(4,319)	(2,456)	(4,059)	(7,296)
18	Indirect cash payments	US$'000				(60)	(65)	(68)	(70)	(71)
19	Cash payments	US$'000				(1,864)	(4,384)	(2,523)	(4,128)	(7,367)
20	Interest paid	US$'000				-	-	(1)	(3)	(2)
21	Tax paid	US$'000				-	(40)	(24)	(241)	(383)
22	Net operating cash flow	US$'000				(610)	(1,595)	1,987	2,063	827
23										
24	**Investing cash flows**									
25	Purchases of non-current assets	US$'000				(150)	(180)	(120)	(90)	(100)
26	Net investing cash flows	US$'000				(150)	(180)	(120)	(90)	(100)
27										
28	**Financing cash flows**									
29	Debt drawdowns	US$'000				20	20	-	-	-
30	Debt repayments	US$'000				-	-	(15)	(25)	(10)
31	Ordinary equity issuances	US$'000				15	25	-	10	-
32	Ordinary equity buybacks	US$'000				-	-	(5)	(5)	(20)
33	Dividends paid	US$'000				-	-	-	-	-
34 w	Net financing cash flows	US$'000				35	45	(20)	(20)	(30)
35										
36 w	Net increase / (decrease) in cash held	US$'000				(725)	(1,730)	1,847	1,953	697

This formula takes all the cash generated for the year, which is the Net operating cash flow (row 22), Net investing cash flows (row 26) and all of the Net financing cash flows (row 34) except for Dividends paid (row 33) – which is what I am trying to calculate.

I cannot refer to row 34 as this will cause a circularity in *any* version of Excel. Therefore, I must link to all the other items in this section, *i.e.* rows 29 to 32 inclusive.

I am going to skip a calculation now and calculate the Dividend based on ratio. Be careful with this in practice. This is a common approach in financial modelling but can lead to volatile dividend payments – something shareholders do **not** want. This can lead to discounted share price valuations – but that's a topic for another time.

The formula is relatively simple:

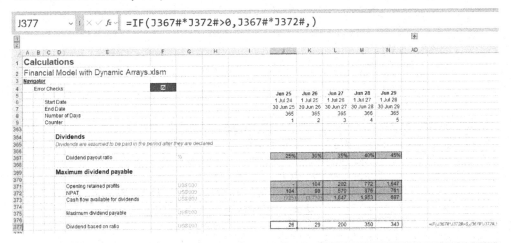

$$\text{=IF(J367\#*J372\#>0,J367\#*J372\#,)}$$

Effectively this is multiplying the Dividend payout ratio (row 367) by NPAT (row 372) and ensuring the value is non-negative.

Arguably, I could have had this positioned on the Calculations worksheet before the Maximum dividend payable (wouldn't that have been a good idea?), but these things happen. The next formula deserves its own subsection...

Maximum Dividend Payable

And so, the fun begins. I have left the best to last.

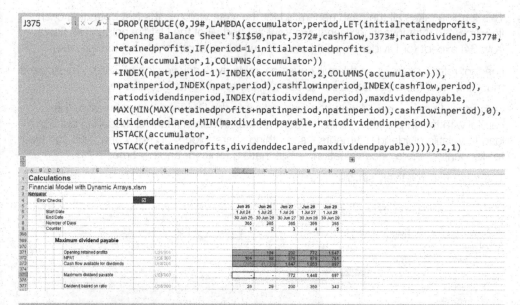

```
J375    ✓ ⅰ × ✓ fx   =DROP(REDUCE(0,J9#,LAMBDA(accumulator,period,LET(initialretainedprofits,
                     'Opening Balance Sheet'!$I$50,npat,J372#,cashflow,J373#,ratiodividend,J377#,
                     retainedprofits,IF(period=1,initialretainedprofits,
                     INDEX(accumulator,1,COLUMNS(accumulator))
                     +INDEX(npat,period-1)-INDEX(accumulator,2,COLUMNS(accumulator))),
                     npatinperiod,INDEX(npat,period),cashflowinperiod,INDEX(cashflow,period),
                     ratiodividendinperiod,INDEX(ratiodividend,period),maxdividendpayable,
                     MAX(MIN(MAX(retainedprofits+npatinperiod,npatinperiod),cashflowinperiod),0),
                     dividenddeclared,MIN(maxdividendpayable,ratiodividendinperiod),
                     HSTACK(accumulator,
                     VSTACK(retainedprofits,dividenddeclared,maxdividendpayable)))),2,1)
```

**=DROP(REDUCE(0,J9#,LAMBDA(accumulator,period,
LET(initialretainedprofits,'Opening Balance
Sheet'!$I$50,npat,J372#,cashflow,J373#,
ratiodividend,J377#,retainedprofits,
IF(period=1,initialretainedprofits,INDEX(accumulator,1,COLUMNS(accumulator))
+INDEX(npat,period-1)-INDEX(accumulator,2,COLUMNS(accumulator))),
npatinperiod,INDEX(npat,period),
cashflowinperiod,INDEX(cashflow,period),
ratiodividendinperiod,INDEX(ratiodividend,period),
maxdividendpayable,
MAX(MIN(MAX(retainedprofits+npatinperiod,npatinperiod),cashflowinperiod),0),
dividenddeclared,
MIN(maxdividendpayable,ratiodividendinperiod),
HSTACK(accumulator,
VSTACK(retainedprofits,dividenddeclared,maxdividendpayable)))),2,1)**

Any questions..?

This formula makes more sense if I drop **DROP**:

Maximum dividend payable EXPLAINED	US$'000		-	-	104	202	572	1,097
			#N/A	-	-	200	350	343
			#N/A	-	-	772	1,448	697

**=REDUCE(0,J9#,LAMBDA(accumulator,period,
LET(initialretainedprofits,'Opening Balance
Sheet'!$I$50,npat,J372#,cashflow,J373#,
ratiodividend,J377#,retainedprofits,
IF(period=1,initialretainedprofits,INDEX(accumulator,1,COLUMNS(accumulator))
+INDEX(npat,period-1)-INDEX(accumulator,2,COLUMNS(accumulator))),
npatinperiod,INDEX(npat,period),
cashflowinperiod,INDEX(cashflow,period),**

```
    ratiodividendinperiod,INDEX(ratiodividend,period),
    maxdividendpayable,
    MAX(MIN(MAX(retainedprofits+npatinperiod,npatinperiod),cashflowinperiod),0),
    dividenddeclared,
    MIN(maxdividendpayable,ratiodividendinperiod),
    HSTACK(accumulator,
    VSTACK(retainedprofits,dividenddeclared,maxdividendpayable)))))
```

Our output here is the **accumulator**. This is an unlabelled matrix, where the first row is Retained profits, the second row is the Dividend declared and the final row is the Maximum dividend payable – which I am trying to compute. The **DROP** function merely removes the rows and columns I don't need. However, they are necessary to the computation unless I plan to build a separate model for each **period**.

For the first row of this array, Retained profits, for **period** 1, this will be the initial Retained profits, given the variable **initialretainedprofits** in the second line of the equation. It is the first item defined by the **LET** function as is equal to

'Opening Balance Sheet'!$I$50

I50	⌄ : ✕ ✓ *fx* ⌄				

	A B C D	E	F	G H I	J	K
1	**Opening Balance Sheet**					
2	Financial Model with Dynamic Arrays.xlsm					
3	**Navigator**					
4	Error Checks:		☑			
5				Jun 24		
6	Start Date					
7	End Date					
8	Number of Days					
9	Counter					
44						
45	**Equity**					
46	Ordinary equity		US$'000			300
47	Opening retained profits		US$'000			2,520
48	NPAT		US$'000			25
49	Dividends declared		US$'000			-
50	Retained profits		US$'000			2,545
51	Total equity		US$'000			2,845

In subsequent **period**s, the calculation will take the last period's Retained profits, achieved by taking the value in the final column of the first row of our **accumulator** at present

INDEX(accumulator,1,COLUMNS(accumulator))

then adding on the previous **period**'s NPAT,

+INDEX(npat,period-1)

where **npat** has been previously defined as

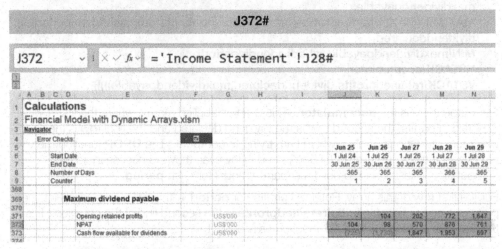

and subtracting any Dividends declared in the prior period. This is achieved by taking the value in the final column of the second row of our **accumulator**:

-INDEX(accumulator,2,COLUMNS(accumulator)))

This is all represented by the highlighted section of our monster formula:

```
=DROP(REDUCE(0,J9#,LAMBDA(accumulator,period,
LET(initialretainedprofits,'Opening Balance
Sheet'!$I$50,npat,J372#,cashflow,J373#,
ratiodividend,J377#,retainedprofits,
IF(period=1,initialretainedprofits,INDEX(accumulator,1,COLUMNS(accumulator))
+INDEX(npat,period-1)-INDEX(accumulator,2,COLUMNS(accumulator))),
npatinperiod,INDEX(npat,period),
cashflowinperiod,INDEX(cashflow,period),
ratiodividendinperiod,INDEX(ratiodividend,period),
maxdividendpayable,
MAX(MIN(MAX(retainedprofits+npatinperiod,npatinperiod),cashflowinperiod),0),
dividenddeclared,
MIN(maxdividendpayable,ratiodividendinperiod),
HSTACK(accumulator,
VSTACK(retainedprofits,dividenddeclared,maxdividendpayable))))),2,1)
```

Next, let's consider the NPAT in the period (**npatinperiod**), which is simply

INDEX(npat,period)

The variable **cashflow** is defined as **J373#**

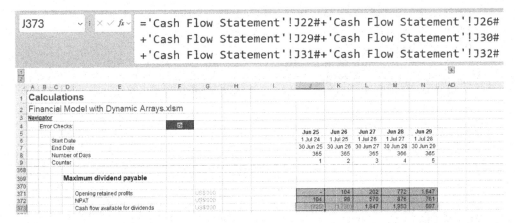

The **cashflowinperiod** is therefore defined as

> ### INDEX(cashflow,period)

The Dividend based on ratio, **ratiodividend**, is defined as **J377#**.

| J377 | ⌄ | ✕ ✓ *fx* ⌄ | =IF(J367#*J372#>0,J367#*J372#,) |

	Jun 25	Jun 26	Jun 27	Jun 28	Jun 29
Start Date	1 Jul 24	1 Jul 25	1 Jul 26	1 Jul 27	1 Jul 28
End Date	30 Jun 25	30 Jun 26	30 Jun 27	30 Jun 28	30 Jun 29
Number of Days	365	365	365	366	365
Counter	1	2	3	4	5

Maximum dividend payable

	US$'000				
Opening retained profits		-	104	202	772	1,647
NPAT		104	98	570	876	761
Cash flow available for dividends		(725)	(1,730)	1,847	1,953	697
Maximum dividend payable		-	-	772	1,448	697
Dividend based on ratio		26	29	200	350	343

This is why this needed defining before the Maximum dividend payable. The **ratiodividendinperiod** is thus given by

> ### INDEX(ratiodividend,period)

Hopefully, pattern recognition is starting to set in now. The next two definitions in the **LET** function should be easy to follow given my preamble. The Maximum dividend payable, **maxdividendpayable**, is given by

> ### MAX(MIN(MAX(retainedprofits+npatinperiod,npatinperiod),cashflowinperiod),0)

whilst the Dividend declared, **dividenddeclared**, is formulated as

> ### MIN(maxdividendpayable,ratiodividendinperiod)

This has defined the following parts of the monster formula:

```
=DROP(REDUCE(0,J9#,LAMBDA(accumulator,period,
LET(initialretainedprofits,'Opening Balance
Sheet'!$I$50,npat,J372#,cashflow,J373#,
ratiodividend,J377#,retainedprofits,
IF(period=1,initialretainedprofits,INDEX(accumulator,1,COLUMNS(accumulator))
+INDEX(npat,period-1)-INDEX(accumulator,2,COLUMNS(accumulator))),
npatinperiod,INDEX(npat,period),
cashflowinperiod,INDEX(cashflow,period),
ratiodividendinperiod,INDEX(ratiodividend,period),
maxdividendpayable,
MAX(MIN(MAX(retainedprofits+npatinperiod,npatinperiod),cashflowinperiod),0),
dividenddeclared,
MIN(maxdividendpayable,ratiodividendinperiod),
HSTACK(accumulator,
VSTACK(retainedprofits,dividenddeclared,maxdividendpayable))))),2,1)
```

With all of our outputs prepared, I may now **HSTACK** the **accumulator**, to force
this formula to evaluate for all periods, with the **VSTACK** of **retainedprofits**,
dividenddeclared and **maxdividendpayable**.

As explained earlier, this gives us an array with **retainedprofits** in row 1,
dividenddeclared in row 2 and **maxdividendpayable** in row 3. I use the **DROP**
function to drop the first two [2] rows to leave the Maximum dividend payable row. I also
DROP the first column as this is where the **accumulator** was **HSTACK**ed (good word
that!). It only contains the initial value of **REDUCE** before being stacked with the first
period results (*i.e.* zero [0] the first argument of the **REDUCE** function in this case. The
VSTACK and **HSTACK** functions cannot deal with empty entries).

In essence, **VSTACK** is used to stack three [3] separate calculations of Retained profits,
Dividends declared and the Maximum dividend payable into a three-row array. **HSTACK**
then stores these results of these three calculations for each period so that I may recall
them later with **INDEX** for the next period.

The idea behind this formula is to avoid the circularity among the calculations of previous
closing and current Opening retained profits and Dividends declared when using dynamic
arrays. Hence, I need to incorporate the whole Retained profits' control account into this
formula.

If this giant formula is a little too hard-on-the-eyes for you, later I shall demonstrate a way
to make this more succinct through the use of a custom **LAMBDA** function. Check out
Chapter 19 for more details (or else wait until you get there!).

Congratulations! You made it to the end of this section.

(That's a message for myself...)

Let's return to the task in hand.

Return of Return on Equity

Sorry, I couldn't resist that title. I think I have earned a light-hearted moment after that
last topic, don't you think?

Allow me to recap where I am in the modelling:

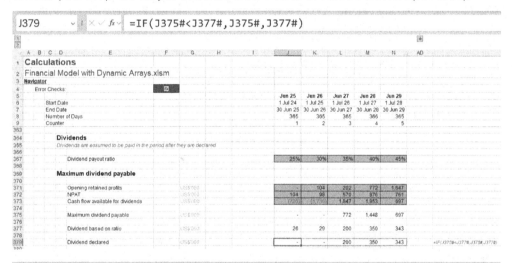

I have now calculated the Maximum dividend payable (row 375) and the Dividend based on ratio (row 377). It's easy to calculate the Dividend declared from here (cell **J379**):

J379	✓ × ✓ fx ✓	=IF(J375#<J377#,J375#,J377#)

=IF(J375#<J377#,J375#,J377#)

This formula calculates the minimum of the Maximum dividend payable, and the Dividend declared without using a **MIN** formula, which would not work with dynamic arrays. No test for negativity is required as neither of the two references may produce negative values.

I can now create the control account. I note in cell **D365** it states that

Dividends

Dividends are assumed to be paid in the period after they are declared

This means dividends are paid one period later; the control account will be straightforward.

	E	F	J Jun 25	K Jun 26	L Jun 27	M Jun 28	N Jun 29	AD
Calculations								
Financial Model with Dynamic Arrays.xlsm								
Navigator								
Error Checks:								
			1 Jul 24	1 Jul 25	1 Jul 26	1 Jul 27	1 Jul 28	
Start Date			30 Jun 25	30 Jun 26	30 Jun 27	30 Jun 28	30 Jun 29	
End Date			365	365	365	366	365	
Number of Days			1	2	3	4	5	
Counter								
Dividend declared	US$'000		-	-	200	350	343	=IF(J375#<J377#,J375#,J377#)
Control account								
Opening dividend payable	US$'000		-	-	-	200	350	=OFFSET(J386#,,-1)
Dividend declared	US$'000		-	-	200	350	343	=J379#
Dividends paid	US$'000		-	-	-	(200)	(350)	=-J383#
Closing dividend payable	US$'000		-	-	200	350	343	=J384#

The first calculation is for the initial Closing dividend payable in cell **I386**. This equals

='Opening Balance Sheet'!$I$30

The next calculation is for the second line of the control account, namely Dividends declared (cell **J384**). This equals the value calculated in row 379:

=J379#

The next calculation reverts to row 386, cell **J386** to be precise (Closing dividend payable). Since we know that dividends are assumed to be paid in the period after they are declared, we may deduce that the closing balance must equal the Dividend declared for the current period, *i.e.*

=J384#

The Opening dividend payable refers to the previous period's closing balance, so cell **J383** calls the **OFFSET** function once more:

=OFFSET(J386#,,-1)

Finally, the Dividends paid must equal the negated value of the Opening dividend payable, *i.e.* in cell **J385**:

=-J383#

This is the fun with dynamic arrays: you have to think through the order of calculations very carefully.

That leads us to analysing our control account as always:

1. **Number of calculations that need to be entered into the financial statement so that they balance:** Surprise, surprise, it's three [3].

2. **The order to build the calculations into the financial statements:** This is always row 2 first, then row 3, then row 4 and so on. In this instance, this will be Dividends Declared (Balance Sheet as a <u>negative</u> number), Dividends Paid (Cash Flow Statement) and Dividends Payable (Balance Sheet).

3. **It identifies the key driver:** Line 2 of the control account is always the key driver, so in this case it will be Dividends Declared. If there is nothing to declare, there cannot be any amounts paid or owed.

This control account differs from the Tax control account in how it deals with the movement in a Balance Sheet item. The key driver here is Dividends declared, which resides on the Balance Sheet. Since this relates to a period of time, normally I would have to calculate the cumulative sum before it could be referenced on the Balance Sheet, but this is not the case here. This is because Dividends Declared has a special place on the Balance Sheet: it is part of the Income Statement link and forms part of the internal working of the Retained profits control account:

			Jun 25	Jun 26	Jun 27	Jun 28	Jun 29
1	**Balance Sheet**						
2	Financial Model with Dynamic Arrays.xlsm						
3	Navigator						
4	Error Checks:	☑					
5			Jun 25	Jun 26	Jun 27	Jun 28	Jun 29
6	Start Date		1 Jul 24	1 Jul 25	1 Jul 26	1 Jul 27	1 Jul 28
7	End Date		30 Jun 25	30 Jun 26	30 Jun 27	30 Jun 28	30 Jun 29
8	Number of Days		365	365	365	366	365
9	Counter		1	2	3	4	5
44							
45	**Equity**						
46	Ordinary equity	US$'000	15	40	35	40	20
47	Opening retained profits	US$'000		104	202	772	1,647
48	NPAT	US$'000	104	98	570	876	761
49 w	Dividends declared	US$'000					
50 w	Retained profits	US$'000	104	202	772	1,647	2,408
51 w	**Total equity**	US$'000	119	242	807	1,687	2,428

I start linking the financial statements. Dividends declared is a negative value in row 49 of the Balance Sheet:

J49 =-Calculations!J384#

			Jun 25	Jun 26	Jun 27	Jun 28	Jun 29	
1	Balance Sheet							
2	Financial Model with Dynamic Arrays.xlsm							
3	Navigator							
4	Error Checks:	☑						
5			Jun 25	Jun 26	Jun 27	Jun 28	Jun 29	
6	Start Date		1 Jul 24	1 Jul 25	1 Jul 26	1 Jul 27	1 Jul 28	
7	End Date		30 Jun 25	30 Jun 26	30 Jun 27	30 Jun 28	30 Jun 29	
8	Number of Days		365	365	365	366	365	
9	Counter		1	2	3	4	5	
44								
45	Equity							
46	Ordinary equity	US$'00	15	40	35	40	20	=Calculations!J36#
47	Opening retained profits	US$'000		104	202	772	1,647	=IF(J38=1,"",'Opening Balance Sheet'!$I$50,OFFSET(J30,-1))
48	NPAT	US$'000	104	98	570	876	761	='Income Statement'!J94
49	Dividends declared	US$'000	-	-	(200)	(350)	(143)	=-Calculations!J384#
50 w	Retained profits	US$'000	104	202	772	1,647	2,408	=SCAN('Opening Balance Sheet'!$I$50,J48,LAMBDA(accumulator,profit,accumulator+profit))
51 w	**Total equity**	US$'000	119	242	807	1,687	2,428	=SUM(J46:J50)

Adding this entry in has not caused the Balance Sheet to misbalance. This is because Dividends declared are not presently included in the Retained profits subtotal (row 50). This was necessary for the dividends calculation earlier in this section.

However, I can now remove the remaining Work In Progress formats and modify the formulae in the Equity section of the Balance Sheet, as all other entries are now dynamic arrays. This will cause the expected error in the model, *viz.*

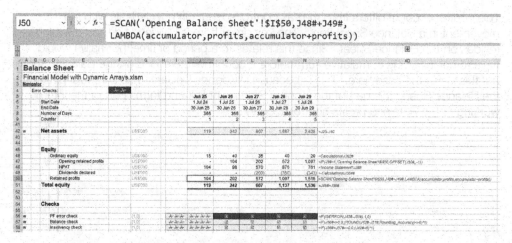

Retained profits (cell **J50**) has been redefined as

> **=SCAN('Opening Balance Sheet'!$I$50,J48#+J49#,**
> **LAMBDA(accumulator,profits,accumulator+profits))**

The Dividends declared (**J49#**) have now been added in.

Total equity (cell **J51**) has been modified to create a total using dynamic arrays:

> **=J46#+J50#**

Take note of the error checks. They are different to the usual errors:

This is because of how the three error checks in cells **J56**, **J57** and **J58** have been defined:

- PF error check (cell **J56**): **=IF(ISERROR(J42#-J51#),1,0)**

- Balance check: (cell **J57**): **=IF(J56#<>0,0,(ROUND(J42#-J51#, Rounding_Accuracy)<>0)*1)**

- Insolvency check (cell **J58**): **=IF(J56#+J57#<>0,0,(J42#<0)*1)**

These formulae all contained dynamic array references (*e.g.* **J42#**, **J51#**) but were copied into each period's cell. This was because the references did not spill – but now, with Total Equity (cell **J51**) having been redefined, *#SPILL!* errors have been produced. The symbol in the check is how *#SPILL!* looks in Wingdings font. I shall fix these shortly – but not yet!

Let's move on.

The second calculation is to link row 385 (Dividends paid) to row 33 of the Cash Flow Statement:

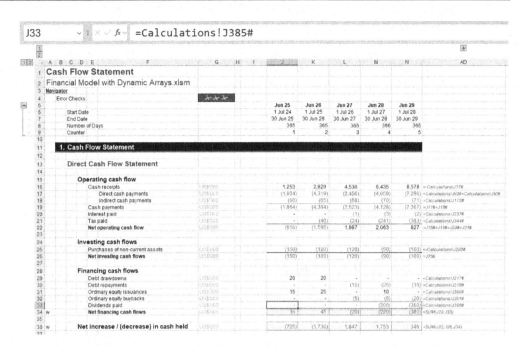

The Cash Flow Statement is now completed – once I have revised rows 34 and 36:

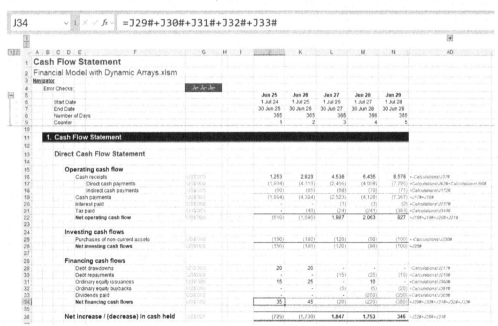

Net financing cash flows (cell **J34**) now contains the dynamic array summation

=J29#+J30#+J31#+J32#+J33#

Similarly, the Net increase / (decrease) in cash held (cell **J36**) has been changed to

=J22#+J26#+J34#

The Cash Flow Statement now contains dynamic array formulae only. This means row 14 of the 'Balance Sheet' worksheet should be changed too:

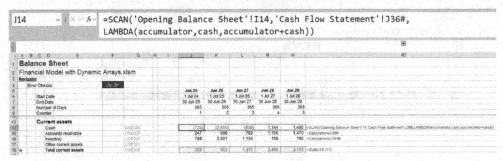

The Cash balance in cell **J14** has now been changed to

> ## =SCAN('Opening Balance Sheet'!I14,'Cash Flow Statement'!J36#,
> ## LAMBDA(accumulator,cash,accumulator+cash))

I am not too concerned (yet!) about some of the large negative balances as I realise the Opening Balance Sheet values are presently all zero.

I shouldn't stop there though. I might as well review row 18. Whilst it is true row 17 has not yet been populated, I can create a Work In Progress dynamic array formula that sums this section excluding Other current assets (row 17):

| J18 | $\times \checkmark f_x$ | =J14#+J15#+J16# |

Balance Sheet
Financial Model with Dynamic Arrays.xlsm
Navigator
Error Checks

				Jun 25	Jun 26	Jun 27	Jun 28	Jun 29
	Start Date			1 Jul 24	1 Jul 25	1 Jul 26	1 Jul 27	1 Jul 28
	End Date			30 Jun 25	30 Jun 26	30 Jun 27	30 Jun 28	30 Jun 29
	Number of Days			365	365	365	366	365
	Counter			1	2	3	4	5
	Current assets							
	Cash	US$'000		(725)	(2,456)	(609)	1,144	1,490
	Accounts receivable	US$'000		247	508	792	1,106	1,470
	Inventory	US$'000		798	2,801	1,134	158	190
	Other current assets	US$'000						
w	**Total current assets**	US$'000		320	853	1,317	2,408	3,151	=J14#+J15#+J16#

Whilst Total current assets (cell **J18**) remains Work In Progress, at least it is now a dynamic array summation:

> ## =J14#+J15#+J16#

This allows me to complete the Total assets (cell **J25**) though:

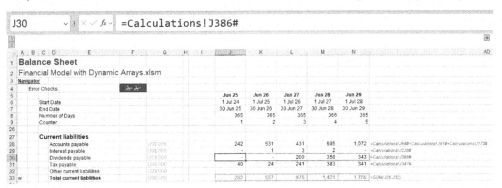

J25	✓	↓	× ✓ *fx* ✓	=J18#+J23#

	A B C D	E	F	G	H	I	J	K	L	M	N
1	**Balance Sheet**										
2	Financial Model with Dynamic Arrays.xlsm										
3	Navigator										
4	Error Checks:										
5							Jun 25	Jun 26	Jun 27	Jun 28	Jun 29
6	Start Date						1 Jul 24	1 Jul 25	1 Jul 26	1 Jul 27	1 Jul 28
7	End Date						30 Jun 25	30 Jun 26	30 Jun 27	30 Jun 28	30 Jun 29
8	Number of Days						365	365	365	366	365
9	Counter						1	2	3	4	5
17	Other current assets	US$'000									
18 w	Total current assets	US$'000					320	653	1,317	2,408	3,151	=J14#+J15#+J16#
19											
20	**Non-current assets**										
21	PP&E	US$'000					113	210	218	173	150	=Calculations!J202#
22	Deferred tax assets	US$'000					-	-	-	-	-	=Calculations!J338#
23	Total non-current assets	US$'000					113	210	218	173	150	=J21#+J22#
24											
25	**Total assets**	US$'000					432	863	1,535	2,581	3,301	=J18#+J23#
26											

=J18#+J23#

I can now add my final item in from the control account, Closing dividend payable (row 386). This should be entered into cell **J30** of the Balance Sheet (Dividends payable):

J30	✓	↓	× ✓ *fx* ✓	=Calculations!J386#

	A B C D	E	F	G	H	I	J	K	L	M	N		AD
1	**Balance Sheet**												
2	Financial Model with Dynamic Arrays.xlsm												
3	Navigator												
4	Error Checks												
5							Jun 25	Jun 26	Jun 27	Jun 28	Jun 29		
6	Start Date						1 Jul 24	1 Jul 25	1 Jul 26	1 Jul 27	1 Jul 28		
7	End Date						30 Jun 25	30 Jun 26	30 Jun 27	30 Jun 28	30 Jun 29		
8	Number of Days						365	365	365	366	365		
9	Counter						1	2	3	4	5		
26													
27	**Current liabilities**												
28	Accounts payable	US$'000					242	531	431	685	1,072	=Calculations!J54#+Calculations!J91#+Calculations!J173#
29	Interest payable	US$'000					-	1	3	2	-	=Calculations!J238#
30	Dividends payable	US$'000					-	-	200	350	343	=Calculations!J386#
31	Tax payable	US$'000					40	24	241	383	341	=Calculations!J347#
32	Other current liabilities	US$'000											
33 w	Total current liabilities	US$'000					282	557	875	1,421	1,756	=SUM(J28:J32)

The error check is still not satisfied due to the #*SPILL!* errors. Before I return to the checks at the foot of the Balance Sheet which may be providing all sorts of false information (do ignore them presently), let's just adjust three more total formulae on this worksheet.

Let's look at row 33. Again, I note row 32 (Other current liabilities) has not yet been populated, but I can create a Work In Progress dynamic array formula that sums this section excluding Other current liabilities (row 32):

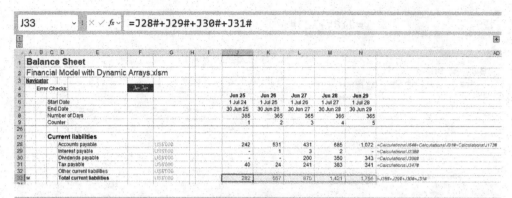

The formula bar shows: J33 | =J28#+J29#+J30#+J31#

	A B C D	E	F	G	H	I	J	K	L	M	N		AD
1	**Balance Sheet**												
2	Financial Model with Dynamic Arrays.xlsm												
3	Navigator												
4	Error Checks:												
5							Jun 25	Jun 26	Jun 27	Jun 28	Jun 29		
6	Start Date						1 Jul 24	1 Jul 25	1 Jul 26	1 Jul 27	1 Jul 28		
7	End Date						30 Jun 25	30 Jun 26	30 Jun 27	30 Jun 28	30 Jun 29		
8	Number of Days						365	365	365	366	365		
9	Counter						1	2	3	4	5		
26													
27	**Current liabilities**												
28	Accounts payable	US$'000					242	531	431	685	1,072	=Calculations!J54#+Calculations!J91#+Calculations!J173#
29	Interest payable	US$'000					-	1	3	2	-	=Calculations!J238#
30	Dividends payable	US$'000					-	-	200	350	343	=Calculations!J300#
31	Tax payable	US$'000					40	24	241	383	341	=Calculations!J347#
32	Other current liabilities	US$'000										
33	w	Total current liabilities	US$'000				282	557	875	1,421	1,756	=J28#+J29#+J30#+J31#

=J28#+J29#+J30#+J31#

This formula remains Work In Progress due to Other current liabilities being omitted.

Next, I will modify Total liabilities (row 40):

The formula bar shows: J40 | =J33#+J38#

	A B C D	E	F	G	H	I	J	K	L	M	N
1	**Balance Sheet**										
2	Financial Model with Dynamic Arrays.xlsm										
3	Navigator										
4	Error Checks:										
5							Jun 25	Jun 26	Jun 27	Jun 28	Jun 29
6	Start Date						1 Jul 24	1 Jul 25	1 Jul 26	1 Jul 27	1 Jul 28
7	End Date						30 Jun 25	30 Jun 26	30 Jun 27	30 Jun 28	30 Jun 29
8	Number of Days						365	365	365	366	365
9	Counter						1	2	3	4	5
32	Other current liabilities	US$'000									
33	w	Total current liabilities	US$'000				282	557	875	1,421	1,756	=J28#+J29#+J30#+J31#
34											
35	**Non-current liabilities**										
36	Debt	US$'000					20	40	25	-	(10)	=Calculations!J219#
37	Deferred tax liabilities	US$'000					11	25	28	23	19	=Calculations!J283#
38	Total non-current liabilities	US$'000					31	65	53	23	9	=J36#+J37#
39											
40	**Total liabilities**	US$'000					313	622	928	1,443	1,764	=J33#+J38#
41											
42	w	**Net assets**	US$'000				119	242	607	1,137	1,536	=J25-J40

The Work In Progress markers may be removed at this point, as this formula is now a complete and correct dynamic array computation, summing up the Total current liabilities (row 33) and the Total non-current liabilities (row 38), *viz.*

=J33#+J38#

The last amendment to totals is for Net assets (cell **J42**):

534

J42		▾	:	× ✓	*fx* ▾	=J25#-J40#				

Balance Sheet

Financial Model with Dynamic Arrays.xlsm

Navigator

Error Checks:

	A B C D	E	F	G H I	J	K	L	M	N	AD
					Jun 25	Jun 26	Jun 27	Jun 28	Jun 29	
	Start Date				1 Jul 24	1 Jul 25	1 Jul 26	1 Jul 27	1 Jul 28	
	End Date				30 Jun 25	30 Jun 26	30 Jun 27	30 Jun 28	30 Jun 29	
	Number of Days				365	365	365	366	365	
	Counter				1	2	3	4	5	
	Total assets	US$'000			432	863	1,535	2,581	3,301	=J18#-J23#
	Current liabilities									
	Accounts payable	US$'000			242	531	431	685	1,072	=Calculations!J64#+Calculations!J91#+Calculations!J173#
	Interest payable	US$'000			-	1	3	2	-	=Calculations!J238#
	Dividends payable	US$'000			-	-	200	350	343	=Calculations!J386#
	Tax payable	US$'000			40	24	241	383	341	=Calculations!J347#
	Other current liabilities	US$'000								
w	**Total current liabilities**	US$'000			282	557	875	1,421	1,756	=J28#+J29#+J30#+J31#
	Non-current liabilities									
	Debt	US$'000			20	40	25	-	(10)	=Calculations!J219#
	Deferred tax liabilities	US$'000			11	25	28	23	19	=Calculations!J293#
	Total non-current liabilities	US$'000			31	65	53	23	9	=J36#+J37#
	Total liabilities	US$'000			313	622	928	1,443	1,764	=J33#+J38#
	Net assets	US$'000			119	242	607	1,137	1,536	=J25#-J40#

Net assets still equals Total assets (row 25) less Total liabilities (row 40), but it is now expressed as a dynamic array formula:

=J25#-J40#

I have been busy. I have incorporated the three entries from the Dividends control account and made numerous changes to row totals throughout the Cash Flow Statement and the Balance Sheet. And what thanks do I get? Very little, if the error checks are anything to go by:

Balance Sheet

Financial Model with Dynamic Arrays.xlsm

Navigator

Error Checks:

	A B C D	E	F	G H I	J	K	L	M	N
					Jun 25	Jun 26	Jun 27	Jun 28	Jun 29
	Start Date				1 Jul 24	1 Jul 25	1 Jul 26	1 Jul 27	1 Jul 28
	End Date				30 Jun 25	30 Jun 26	30 Jun 27	30 Jun 28	30 Jun 29
	Number of Days				365	365	365	366	365
	Counter				1	2	3	4	5
	Net assets	US$'000			119	242	607	1,137	1,536
	Equity								
	Ordinary equity	US$'000			15	40	35	40	20
	Opening retained profits	US$'000			-	104	202	572	1,097
	NPAT	US$'000			104	98	570	876	761
	Dividends declared	US$'000			-	-	(200)	(350)	(343)
	Retained profits	US$'000			104	202	572	1,097	1,516
	Total equity	US$'000			119	242	607	1,137	1,536
	Checks								
w	PF error check	[1,0]							
w	Balance check	[1,0]							
w	Insolvency check	[1,0]							

It is possible your error checks may look slightly different at this point, albeit they will still be wrong. The three formulae in rows 56, 57 and 58 are correct. All the row totals are now spilled dynamic arrays. What's gone wrong?

The issue is that the three [3] error check formulae are all dynamic array formulae – and yet they have been entered into all periods' cells. This has caused #SPILL! errors. All I need to do is delete the contents of cells **K56:AC58**:

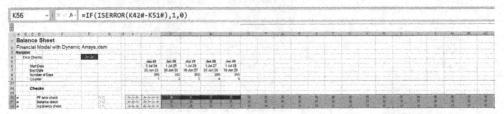

Once I have done this:

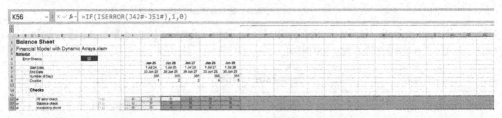

Success!

All I need to do now is alter the formulae in cells **I56:I58** so that they too are dynamic and remove the Work In Progress formatting:

				Jun 25	Jun 26	Jun 27	Jun 28	Jun 29
Balance Sheet								
Financial Model with Dynamic Arrays.xlsm								
Navigator								
Error Checks:	☑							
				Jun 25	Jun 26	Jun 27	Jun 28	Jun 29
Start Date				1 Jul 24	1 Jul 25	1 Jul 26	1 Jul 27	1 Jul 28
End Date				30 Jun 25	30 Jun 26	30 Jun 27	30 Jun 28	30 Jun 29
Number of Days				365	365	365	366	365
Counter				1	2	3	4	5
1. Balance Sheet								
Current assets								
Cash	US$'000			(725)	(2,456)	(609)	1,144	1,490
Accounts receivable	US$'000			247	508	792	1,106	1,470
Inventory	US$'000			798	2,601	1,134	158	190
Other current assets	US$'000							
Total current assets	US$'000			320	653	1,317	2,408	3,151
Non-current assets								
PP&E	US$'000			113	210	218	173	150
Deferred tax assets	US$'000			-	-	-	-	-
Total non-current assets	US$'000			113	210	218	173	150
Total assets	US$'000			432	863	1,535	2,581	3,301
Current liabilities								
Accounts payable	US$'000			242	531	431	685	1,072
Interest payable	US$'000			-	1	3	2	-
Dividends payable	US$'000			-	-	200	350	343
Tax payable	US$'000			40	24	241	383	341
Other current liabilities	US$'000							
Total current liabilities	US$'000			282	557	875	1,421	1,756
Non-current liabilities								
Debt	US$'000			20	40	25	-	(10)
Deferred tax liabilities	US$'000			11	25	28	23	19
Total non-current liabilities	US$'000			31	65	53	23	9
Total liabilities	US$'000			313	622	928	1,443	1,764
Net assets	US$'000			119	242	607	1,137	1,536
Equity								
Ordinary equity	US$'000			15	40	35	40	20
Opening retained profits	US$'000			-	104	202	572	1,097
NPAT	US$'000			104	98	570	876	761
Dividends declared	US$'000			-	-	(200)	(350)	(343)
Retained profits	US$'000			104	202	572	1,097	1,516
Total equity	US$'000			119	242	607	1,137	1,536
Checks								
PF error check	[1,0]			☑	☑	☑	☑	☑	☑
Balance check	[1,0]			☑	☑	☑	☑	☑	☑
Insolvency check	[1,0]			☑	☑	☑	☑	☑	☑

I've used the following formula in cell **I56**:

=MAX(J56#)

This formula can then be copied down to cells **I57:I58**.

Finally, we can move on.

CHAPTER 17.15: SINGLE ENTRY ACCOUNTING

Building a Financial Model

18. Once the Cash Flow Statement is also completed, consider the first line item on the Balance Sheet not yet linked.

Having just completed the Cash Flow Statement,

1. Cash Flow Statement

Direct Cash Flow Statement

Operating cash flow						
Cash receipts	US$'000	1,253	2,829	4,536	6,435	8,578
Direct cash payments	US$'000	(1,804)	(4,319)	(2,456)	(4,059)	(7,296)
Indirect cash payments	US$'000	(60)	(65)	(66)	(70)	(71)
Cash payments	US$'000	(1,864)	(4,384)	(2,523)	(4,128)	(7,367)
Interest paid	US$'000	-	-	(1)	(3)	(2)
Tax paid	US$'000	-	(40)	(24)	(241)	(383)
Net operating cash flow	US$'000	(610)	(1,595)	1,987	2,063	827
Investing cash flows						
Purchases of non-current assets	US$'000	(150)	(180)	(120)	(90)	(100)
Net investing cash flows	US$'000	(150)	(180)	(120)	(90)	(100)
Financing cash flows						
Debt drawdowns	US$'000	20	20	-	-	-
Debt repayments	US$'000	-	-	(15)	(25)	(10)
Ordinary equity issuances	US$'000	15	25	-	10	-
Ordinary equity buybacks	US$'000	-	-	(5)	(5)	(20)
Dividends paid	US$'000	-	-	-	(200)	(350)
Net financing cash flows	US$'000	35	45	(20)	(220)	(380)
Net increase / (decrease) in cash held	US$'000	(725)	(1,730)	1,847	1,753	346

my attention now turns to the two links outstanding for the Balance Sheet:

1. Balance Sheet

Current assets						
Cash	US$'000	(725)	(2,456)	(609)	1,144	1,490
Accounts receivable	US$'000	247	508	792	1,106	1,470
Inventory	US$'000	798	2,601	1,134	158	190
Other current assets	US$'000					
Total current assets	US$'000	320	653	1,317	2,408	3,151
Non-current assets						
PP&E	US$'000	113	210	218	173	150
Deferred tax assets	US$'000	-	-	-	-	-
Total non-current assets	US$'000	113	210	218	173	150
Total assets	US$'000	432	863	1,535	2,581	3,301
Current liabilities						
Accounts payable	US$'000	242	531	431	685	1,072
Interest payable	US$'000	-	1	3	2	-
Dividends payable	US$'000	-	-	200	350	343
Tax payable	US$'000	40	24	241	383	341
Other current liabilities	US$'000					
Total current liabilities	US$'000	282	557	875	1,421	1,756
Non-current liabilities						
Debt	US$'000	20	40	25	-	(10)
Deferred tax liabilities	US$'000	11	25	28	23	19
Total non-current liabilities	US$'000	31	65	53	23	9
Total liabilities	US$'000	313	622	928	1,443	1,764
Net assets	US$'000	119	242	607	1,137	1,536
Equity						
Ordinary equity	US$'000	15	40	35	40	20
Opening retained profits	US$'000	-	104	202	572	1,097
NPAT	US$'000	104	98	570	876	761
Dividends declared	US$'000	-	-	(200)	(350)	(343)
Retained profits	US$'000	104	202	572	1,097	1,516
Total equity	US$'000	119	242	607	1,137	1,536

There are just two [2] line items left: Other current assets and Other current liabilities. There are no more assumptions for the Assumptions worksheet, so I conclude there are no movements to model for these line items.

Alright, so if there are no movements to model, this poses a conundrum, what are the balancing items *without exception*?

The answer is surprising: *nothing*. Welcome to the dark world of single-entry accounting.

I could just link these two line items directly from the Opening Balance Sheet, but I advise against this on the grounds of *consistency*. Therefore, I am going to add the two most boring control accounts of all time to the Calculations sheet:

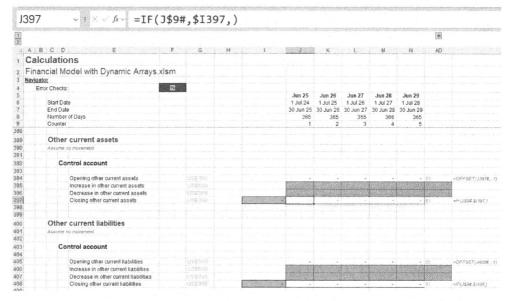

Wow. That was exciting. To make financial modelling (and in particular getting the financial statements to work) easily – just leave your brain at the door.

Here, for Other current assets, I have linked the initial Closing other current assets (cell **I397**) to its counterpart on the Opening Balance Sheet:

='Opening Balance Sheet'!$I$17

The Closing other current assets (cell **J397**) then propagates this value:

=IF(J$9#,$I397,)

and the Opening other current assets (cell **J394**) then uses the usual **OFFSET** formula:

=OFFSET(J397#,,-1).

Very similarly, for Other current liabilities, I have linked the initial Closing other current liabilities (cell **I408**) to its counterpart on the Opening Balance Sheet:

='Opening Balance Sheet'!$I$32

The Closing other current liabilities (cell **J408**) then copies this value across the relevant cells:

> =IF(J$9#,$I408,)

and the Opening other current liabilities (cell **J405**) then uses another **OFFSET** formula:

> =OFFSET(J408#,,-1).

All I have to do is link these closing balances into the Balance Sheet. This is because there are only two lines in each of these control accounts – so only <u>one</u> link to the financial statements (*i.e.* the Balance Sheet) is required.

Other current assets (row 17):

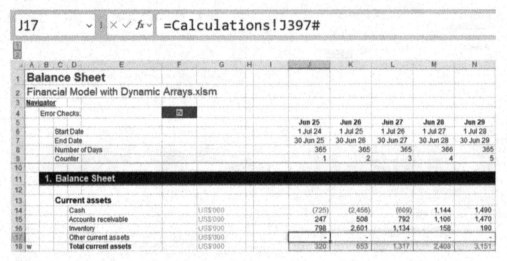

This amount is not yet included in the subtotal, so the error check cannot currently be relied upon. The Total current assets formula may now include row 17, thus removing the Work In Progress formatting:

=J14#+J15#+J16#+J17#

Now, the error check can be trusted.

Next, I consider Other current liabilities (row 32):

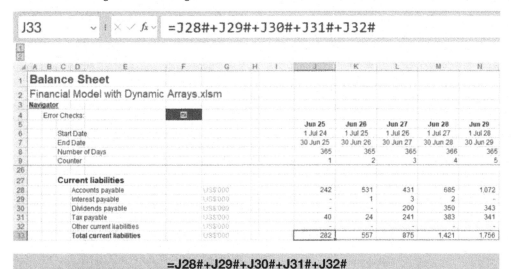

Again, this amount is not yet included in the subtotal, so the error check is not yet reliable. The Total current liabilities formula may now include row 32, thus removing the final Work In Progress formatting from the Balance Sheet:

J32	fx	=Calculations!J408#

Balance Sheet
Financial Model with Dynamic Arrays.xlsm

		Jun 25	Jun 26	Jun 27	Jun 28	Jun 29
Start Date		1 Jul 24	1 Jul 25	1 Jul 26	1 Jul 27	1 Jul 28
End Date		30 Jun 25	30 Jun 26	30 Jun 27	30 Jun 28	30 Jun 29
Number of Days		365	365	365	366	365
Counter		1	2	3	4	5

J33	fx	=J28#+J29#+J30#+J31#+J32#

=J28#+J29#+J30#+J31#+J32#

The error check is still satisfied, and I *appear* to have completed the financial statements. That's not quite true though. There are still two [2] things left outstanding.

> **Building a Financial Model**
>
> 19. Once the Balance Sheet has been completed, return to the Opening Balance Sheet and add back the original data.
>
> 20. Correct any opening balances if necessary.

Now the three main financial statements have been completed and all checks are satisfied, it is time to turn my attention back to the 'Opening Balance Sheet' worksheet.

	A B C D	E	F	G H	I	J	K
1	**Opening Balance Sheet**						
2	Financial Model with Dynamic Arrays.xlsm						
3	Navigator						
4	Error Checks:		☑				
5					Jun 24		
6	Start Date						
7	End Date						
8	Number of Days						
9	Counter						
10							
11	**1. Opening Balance Sheet**						
12							
13	**Current assets**						
14	Cash	US$'000					2,500
15	Accounts receivable	US$'000					50
16	Inventory	US$'000					50
17	Other current assets	US$'000					10
18	Total current assets	US$'000					2,610
19							
20	**Non-current assets**						
21	PP&E	US$'000					450
22	Deferred tax assets	US$'000					75
23	Total non-current assets	US$'000					525
24							
25	**Total assets**	US$'000					3,135
26							
27	**Current liabilities**						
28	Accounts payable	US$'000					30
29	Interest payable	US$'000					20
30	Dividends payable	US$'000					15
31	Tax payable	US$'000					40
32	Other current liabilities	US$'000					10
33	Total current liabilities	US$'000					115
34							
35	**Non-current liabilities**						
36	Debt	US$'000					150
37	Deferred tax liabilities	US$'000					25
38	Total non-current liabilities	US$'000					175
39							
40	**Total liabilities**	US$'000					290
41							
42	**Net assets**	US$'000					2,845
43							
44							
45	**Equity**						
46	Ordinary equity	US$'000					300
47	Opening retained profits	US$'000					2,520
48	NPAT	US$'000					25
49	Dividends declared	US$'000					-
50	Retained profits	US$'000					2,545
51	Total equity	US$'000					2,845
52							

You may recall earlier that I removed all of the data from the Opening Balance Sheet (column I) in order to have the checks work as I wanted. Yes, it was a bit of a cheat, but as I have stated several times modellers are only responsible for the movements in Total Equity and Net Assets, not the cumulative amounts. Therefore, if I made the base position zero, it would have only one impact on my modelling – it would make it easier.

All I have to do is remember to put it back at the end of the exercise. Let's do that now. I am going to copy (**CTRL + C**) cells **K14:K51** and paste them back into cells **I14:I51**. They must neither be dragged back using the mouse nor cut and paste back into position (the latter can give rise to some rather lovely #*REF!* errors). Assuming there is no error upon pasting, I can then delete column **K**:

									Jun 24
1	**Opening Balance Sheet**								
2	Financial Model with Dynamic Arrays.xlsm								
3	Navigator								
4	Error Checks:				☑				
5									
6	Start Date								
7	End Date								
8	Number of Days								
9	Counter								
10									
11	**1. Opening Balance Sheet**								
12									
13	**Current assets**								
14	Cash				US$000				2,500
15	Accounts receivable				US$000				50
16	Inventory				US$000				50
17	Other current assets				US$000				10
18	Total current assets				US$000				2,610
19									
20	**Non-current assets**								
21	PP&E				US$000				450
22	Deferred tax assets				US$000				75
23	Total non-current assets				US$000				525
24									
25	**Total assets**				US$000				3,135
26									
27	**Current liabilities**								
28	Accounts payable				US$000				30
29	Interest payable				US$000				20
30	Dividends payable				US$000				15
31	Tax payable				US$000				40
32	Other current liabilities				US$000				10
33	Total current liabilities				US$000				115
34									
35	**Non-current liabilities**								
36	Debt				US$000				150
37	Deferred tax liabilities				US$000				25
38	Total non-current liabilities				US$000				175
39									
40	**Total liabilities**				US$000				290
41									
42	**Net assets**				US$000				2,845
43									
44									
45	**Equity**								
46	Ordinary equity				US$000				300
47	Opening retained profits				US$000				2,520
48	NPAT				US$000				25
49	Dividends declared				US$000				-
50	Retained profits				US$000				2,545
51	**Total equity**				US$000				2,845

All is well and the exercise is complete – *sort of*. The final Income Statement:

Income Statement

Financial Model with Dynamic Arrays.xlsm

Navigator

									Jun 25	Jun 26	Jun 27	Jun 28	Jun 29
Error Checks:			☑										
Start Date									1 Jul 24	1 Jul 25	1 Jul 26	1 Jul 27	1 Jul 28
End Date									30 Jun 25	30 Jun 26	30 Jun 27	30 Jun 28	30 Jun 29
Number of Days									365	365	365	366	365
Counter									1	2	3	4	5
1. Income Statement													
Revenue			US$'000						1,500	3,090	4,820	6,749	8,942
COGS			US$'000						(1,247)	(2,783)	(3,810)	(5,292)	(7,648)
Gross profit			US$'000						253	327	1,011	1,457	1,293
Wastage			US$'000						(25)	(53)	(23)	(2)	(2)
Operating expenditure			US$'000						(60)	(65)	(68)	(70)	(71)
EBITDA			US$'000						167	209	920	1,386	1,220
Depreciation			US$'000						(128)	(173)	(203)	(225)	(213)
EBIT			US$'000						40	36	717	1,161	1,008
Interest expense			US$'000						(9)	(12)	(13)	(14)	(12)
NPBT			US$'000						31	25	704	1,147	996
Tax expense			US$'000						(14)	(5)	(211)	(345)	(306)
NPAT			US$'000						17	20	493	801	690

The final Cash Flow Statement:

Cash Flow Statement

Financial Model with Dynamic Arrays.xlsm

Navigator

									Jun 25	Jun 26	Jun 27	Jun 28	Jun 29
Error Checks:					☑								
Start Date									1 Jul 24	1 Jul 25	1 Jul 26	1 Jul 27	1 Jul 28
End Date									30 Jun 25	30 Jun 26	30 Jun 27	30 Jun 28	30 Jun 29
Number of Days									365	365	365	366	365
Counter									1	2	3	4	5
1. Cash Flow Statement													
Direct Cash Flow Statement													
Operating cash flow													
Cash receipts					US$'000				1,303	2,829	4,536	6,435	8,578
Direct cash payments					US$'000				(1,834)	(4,319)	(2,456)	(4,059)	(7,296)
Indirect cash payments					US$'000				(60)	(65)	(68)	(70)	(71)
Cash payments					US$'000				(1,894)	(4,384)	(2,523)	(4,128)	(7,367)
Interest paid					US$'000				(20)	(9)	(12)	(13)	(14)
Tax paid					US$'000				(40)	-	-	(102)	(366)
Net operating cash flow					US$'000				(650)	(1,565)	2,001	2,191	831
Investing cash flows													
Purchases of non-current assets					US$'000				(150)	(180)	(120)	(90)	(100)
Net investing cash flows					US$'000				(150)	(180)	(120)	(90)	(100)
Financing cash flows													
Debt drawdowns					US$'000				20	20	-	-	-
Debt repayments					US$'000				-	-	(15)	(25)	(10)
Ordinary equity issuances					US$'000				15	25	-	10	-
Ordinary equity buybacks					US$'000				-	-	(5)	(5)	(20)
Dividends paid					US$'000				(15)	-	-	(172)	(320)
Net financing cash flows					US$'000				20	45	(20)	(192)	(350)
Net increase / (decrease) in cash held					US$'000				(780)	(1,700)	1,861	1,909	381

The final Balance Sheet:

Balance Sheet

Financial Model with Dynamic Arrays.xlsm

Navigator

				Jun 25	Jun 26	Jun 27	Jun 28	Jun 29
Error Checks:		☑						
Start Date				1 Jul 24	1 Jul 25	1 Jul 26	1 Jul 27	1 Jul 28
End Date				30 Jun 25	30 Jun 26	30 Jun 27	30 Jun 28	30 Jun 29
Number of Days				365	365	365	366	365
Counter				1	2	3	4	5

1. Balance Sheet

			Jun 25	Jun 26	Jun 27	Jun 28	Jun 29
Current assets							
Cash	US$'000		1,720	20	1,881	3,789	4,170
Accounts receivable	US$'000		247	508	792	1,106	1,470
Inventory	US$'000		823	2,616	1,139	158	190
Other current assets	US$'000		10	10	10	10	10
Total current assets	US$'000		2,800	3,154	3,822	5,064	5,840
Non-current assets							
PP&E	US$'000		473	480	398	263	150
Deferred tax assets	US$'000		99	114	-	-	-
Total non-current assets	US$'000		572	594	398	263	150
Total assets	US$'000		3,372	3,747	4,219	5,326	5,990
Current liabilities							
Accounts payable	US$'000		242	531	431	685	1,072
Interest payable	US$'000		9	12	13	14	12
Dividends payable	US$'000		-	-	172	320	310
Tax payable	US$'000		-	-	102	366	320
Other current liabilities	US$'000		10	10	10	10	10
Total current liabilities	US$'000		261	553	729	1,396	1,724
Non-current liabilities							
Debt	US$'000		170	190	175	150	140
Deferred tax liabilities	US$'000		63	82	78	57	44
Total non-current liabilities	US$'000		233	272	253	207	184
Total liabilities	US$'000		494	825	982	1,603	1,908
Net assets	US$'000		2,877	2,922	3,237	3,723	4,082
Equity							
Ordinary equity	US$'000		315	340	335	340	320
Opening retained profits	US$'000		2,545	2,562	2,582	2,902	3,383
NPAT	US$'000		17	20	493	801	690
Dividends declared	US$'000		-	-	(172)	(320)	(310)
Retained profits	US$'000		2,562	2,582	2,902	3,383	3,762
Total equity	US$'000		2,877	2,922	3,237	3,723	4,082

There you go. All finished. Except we're not…

CHAPTER 17.17: INDIRECT CASH FLOW EXTRACT

There is one more addition to make to the Financial Statements. As I explained earlier, there are two forms to the Cash Flow Statements: **direct** and **indirect**. These show two presentations of the Net Operating cash flow:

- **Direct:** This can reconcile Operating Cash Flows back to a large proportion of the bank statements. It is a summary of Cash Receipts, Cash Paid, Interest Paid and Tax Paid

- **Indirect:** This starts with an element of the Income Statement and adds back non-cash items (deducting their cash equivalents) and adjusts for working capital movements.

A typical indirect Cash Flow Statement may compare to the direct version as follows:

1. Cash Flow Statement

Direct Cash Flow Statement

Operating cash flow

Cash receipts	US$'000	1,303	2,829	4,536	6,435	8,578
Direct cash payments	US$'000	(1,834)	(4,319)	(2,456)	(4,059)	(7,296)
Indirect cash payments	US$'000	(60)	(65)	(68)	(70)	(71)
Cash payments	US$'000	(1,894)	(4,384)	(2,523)	(4,128)	(7,367)
Interest paid	US$'000	(20)	(9)	(12)	(13)	(14)
Tax paid	US$'000	(40)	-	-	(176)	(376)
Net Operating cash flow	US$'000	(650)	(1,565)	2,001	2,117	822

Indirect extract

Operating cash flow

NPAT	US$'000	17	10	484	803	694
Add back:						
Depreciation	US$'000	128	173	203	225	213
Interest Expense	US$'000	9	23	29	11	(4)
Tax Expense	US$'000	14	1	207	346	308
Movements in working capital:						
(inc) / dec in Current Assets	US$'000	(971)	(2,051)	1,189	667	(386)
inc / (dec) in Current Liabilities	US$'000	212	289	(100)	254	387
Deduct:						
Interest paid	US$'000	(20)	(9)	(12)	(13)	(14)
Tax paid	US$'000	(40)	-	-	(176)	(376)
Net Operating cash flow	US$'000	(650)	(1,565)	2,001	2,117	822

As explained above, the indirect version is calculated as follows:

- Start with a line item from the Income Statement (here, Net Profit After Tax)

- Add back non-cash items (Depreciation Expense, Interest Expense and Tax Expense)

- Adjust for working capital movements (increases and decreases in Current Assets and Current Liabilities)

- Deduct the cash equivalents of the non-cash items added back:

  - Instead of Interest **Expense** deduct Interest **Paid**

  - Instead of Tax **Expense** deduct Tax **Paid**

  - Instead of Depreciation Expense *don't do anything*. It's a double count.

Most will have modelled an Income Statement and therefore used the Income Statement to work back to the Cash Flow Statement. We have made *transparent* assumptions instead using control accounts and that has necessitated using the direct method.

Control accounts are a financial modeller's best friends. Now, should it be required, the Indirect Extract is easy to compute:

		F	G	H	I	J	K	L	M	N		AD
1	**Cash Flow Statement**											
2	Financial Model with Dynamic Arrays.xlsm											
3	Navigator											
4	Error Checks:											
5						Jun 25	Jun 26	Jun 27	Jun 28	Jun 29		
6	Start Date					1 Jul 24	1 Jul 25	1 Jul 26	1 Jul 27	1 Jul 28		
7	End Date					30 Jun 25	30 Jun 26	30 Jun 27	30 Jun 28	30 Jun 29		
8	Number of Days					365	365	365	365	365		
9	Counter					1	2	3	4	5		
38												
39	**Indirect extract**											
40												
41	Operating cash flow											
42												
43	NPAT					17	20	493	801	690	='Income Statement'!J28#	
44	Add back:											
45	Depreciation					128	173	203	225	213	='Income Statement'!J21#	
46	Interest expense					9	12	13	14	12	='Income Statement'!J24#	
47	Tax expense					14	5	211	345	306	='Income Statement'!J27#	
48	Movements in working capital											
49	(inc) / dec in current assets					(970)	(2,054)	1,192	667	(396)	=-(Calculations!J36#+Calculations!J37#+Calculations!J141#+Calculations!J142#+Calculations!J143#)	
50	inc / (dec) in current liabilities					212	289	(100)	254	387	=Calculations!J62#+Calculations!J63#+Calculations!J89#+Calculations!J90#+Calculations!J171#+Calculations!J172#	
51	Deduct:											
52	Interest paid					(20)	(0)	(12)	(15)	(14)	=J20#	
53	Tax paid					(40)	-	-	(102)	(368)	=J21#	
54												
55	**Net operating cash flow**					(650)	(1,565)	2,001	2,191	831	=J43#+J45#+J46#+J47#+J49#+J50#+J52#+J53#	

NPAT, Depreciation, Interest Expense and Tax Expense are all linked in from the Income Statement (negating all of the costs as they are added back).

- NPAT (cell **J43**): **='Income Statement'!J28#**

- Depreciation (cell **J45**): **=-'Income Statement'!J21#**

- Interest expense (cell **J46**): **=-'Income Statement'!J24#**

- Tax expense (cell **J47**): **=-'Income Statement'!J27#**

The movements in working capital do not require me to have to create convoluted formulae using Balance Sheet movements. I can simply link to the movements in the various control accounts calculated – but unlike in legacy Excel, I cannot include the blank rows of Other current assets and Other current liabilities in dynamic array formulae. Remember:

- an increase in a non-cash Current Asset is a bad thing from a cash perspective as it is tying up the cash; decreases release cash.

- an increase in Current Liabilities means payments are piling up. This may be good from a cash flow perspective, but it is a questionable tactic for supplier relations and the ongoing credibility of the firm.

Therefore, the formula for (increase) / decrease in current assets (cell **J49**) is given by

**=-(Calculations!J36#+Calculations!J37#
+Calculations!J141#+Calculations!J142#+Calculations!J143#)**

The formula for increase / (decrease) in current liabilities (cell **J50**) is given by

**=Calculations!J62#+Calculations!J63#+Calculations!J89#
+Calculations!J90#+Calculations!J171#+Calculations!J172#**

Interest paid and Tax paid just link to rows 20 and 21 of the Operating cash flow (direct method) in the same worksheet. Finally, each of these rows are summed (using the addition operator [+]) to calculate the Net operating cash flow,

=J43#+J45#+J46#+J47#+J49#+J50#+J52#+J53#

Once this has been completed, checks may be put in place to ensure model integrity is assured:

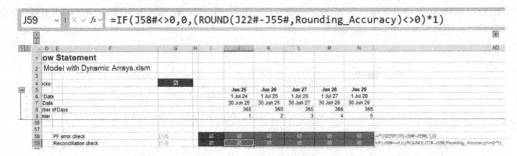

The first check here checks for *prima facie* errors (similar to the checks in the Balance Sheet), whereas the second check then confirms that the two methods of constructing the Net Operating cash flow coincide.

These are very similar to the *prima facie* and balance checks used for the Balance Sheet earlier:

- PF Error Check (cell **J58**): **=IF(ISERROR(J36#+J55#),1,0)**

- Reconciliation Check (cell **J59**):
  =IF(J58#<>0,0,(ROUND(J22#-J55#,Rounding_Accuracy)<>0)*1)

Cells **I58** and **I59** (the summary checks) are then named **HL_Cash_Flow_Statement_Error** and **HL_Cash_Flow_Statement_Rec_Check** respectively. The following formula is used in cell **I58**:

> **=MIN(SUM(J58#),1)**

This is then copied down to cell **I59**.

These checks may then be added to the 'Error Checks' worksheet:

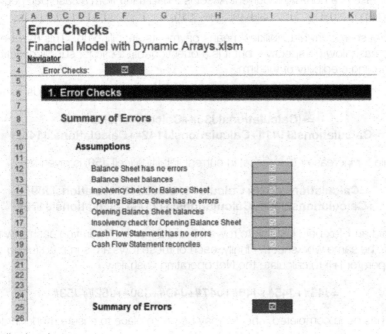

We're finally done!

CHAPTER 17.18: CASE STUDY WRAP-UP

This isn't intended to be a long section, I just wanted to conclude as this is the B-I-G dynamic array case study in the book. Model development can be very daunting for the uninitiated and the inexperienced, but it is something that can be learnt. You need a methodology. That is what I have spent a long time developing.

- You need to be acquainted with the key functions in model construction. Several come up time and time again and I discussed these earlier.

- Be comfortable with the functionalities of Excel. Number formatting is useful. Use Styles. Consider hyperlinks, conditional formatting and data validation amongst other functionalities.

- Create a good template and *use it*.

- Make your models **C**onsistent, **R**obust, **F**lexible and **T**ransparent – **CRaFT**.

- Use control accounts. They are your friends and make your life easy.

- Learn from your mistakes. Don't be afraid to make them as long as they are different each time. I am a firm believer that you only learn from what comes back to bite you.

- Don't be scared of dynamic arrays, **LET**, **LAMBDA** and eta lambdas.

- Use the modelling process explained earlier, *viz.*

Building a Financial Model

This approach remains moot on the order of calculation construction. This is how to build a hassle-free, three-way integrated financial model:

1. Create the forecast chart of accounts from either previous models, existing financials, ledgers, journals, trial balances, *etc.*

2. Add in the subtotals for each chart of account so that all totals flow through their respective financial statements

3. Add error and other checks to these outputs (*e.g.* balance checks, cash in cash flow equals cash movement on Balance Sheet) as necessary, updating the 'Error Checks' worksheet as necessary

4. Create the Opening Balance Sheet, ensuring it uses the same format as the forecast Balance Sheet

5. Ensure the Opening Balance Sheet balances, else reject

6. Add checks as necessary

7. Link the financial statements together, adding any checks as necessary

8. Zero the Opening Balance Sheet

9. Ensure all checks are "OK"

10. Begin with the Income Statement, take the first line item in this account (*e.g.* Revenue)

11. Create calculations if not already computed

---

12. Construct control account

13. Add checks if necessary

14. Link control account to financial statements, ensuring checks are all OK (correct if necessary)

15. Move to the next line item in the financial statement not yet calculated

16. Return to Point 10

17. Once the Income Statement is completed, consider the first line item on the Cash Flow Statement not yet linked

18. Once the Cash Flow Statement is also completed, consider the first line item on the Balance Sheet not yet linked

19. Once the Balance Sheet has been completed, return to the Opening Balance Sheet and add back the original data

20. Correct any opening balance errors if necessary.

Hopefully, this process has made sense, hangs together and provides you with the confidence to go and build much more complex models with dynamic arrays. This case study has concentrated solely on the mechanics, discussing key concepts as we went. Real life models are larger and more complex, but the principles remain the same.

Good luck and enjoy it!

CHAPTER 18: RATIO ANALYSIS

To finish, I want to discuss **ratio analysis**. This is typically used to review published statutory accounts after taking into account certain details, typically found in the Notes to the Accounts. However, it is just as pertinent to the world of financial model development. I would strongly recommend reviewing draft models to see if things look odd or inconsistent with previous assumptions or historical data. Seldom do model developers perform this review. I highly recommend it.

Not only is the data required readily available in most models, using ratios rather than absolute calculations allows comparison between previous years, previous models and with peers in a similar industry at a similar stage in their business lifecycle. Errors may be identified and once corrected, trends can be derived to identify improvements / deficiencies and assess the underlying story of the business evaluated.

There are limitations to ratio analysis. Most ratios are derived from accounting data and these line items are dependent upon the accounting policies of the firm and the accounting standards of the jurisdiction. As more companies convert to report by International Financial Reporting Standards (IFRS), comparisons between companies in similar sectors but different geographical locales will become easier. However, due to the accounting policies adopted, ratios should always be considered over the longer term in conjunction with other methods of financial analysis (*e.g.* discounted cash flow).

Ratios are often separated into various categories, *e.g.* profitability, liquidity, asset management, debt (gearing), equity and market value. However, there is no universal agreement as to either how these ratios should be calculated or categorised. It is possible to discover that different texts use slightly different formulae for the computation of many ratios. Therefore, when comparing a calculated ratio with a published ratio or an industry average, make sure that the formula used in the calculation is consistent with the published ratio.

I have already included DSCR within the model, but additional ratio analysis can be useful, which is why I left space in the model between row 332 and 344:

		Jun 24	Jun 25	Jun 26	Jun 27	Jun 28	Jun 29	Jun 30	Jun 31	Jun 32	Jun 33	
1	**Operations**											
2	Project Finance - Financial Modelling Exercise.xlsm											
3	Navigator											
4	Error Checks											
5												
6	Start Date	1 Jul 23	1 Jul 24	1 Jul 25	1 Jul 26	1 Jul 27	1 Jul 28	1 Jul 29	1 Jul 30	1 Jul 31	1 Jul 32	
7	End Date	30 Jun 24	30 Jun 25	30 Jun 26	30 Jun 27	30 Jun 28	30 Jun 29	30 Jun 30	30 Jun 31	30 Jun 32	30 Jun 33	
8	Number of Days	366	365	365	365	365	365	365	365	366	365	
9	Construction period	1	2	3	-	-	-	-	-	-	-	
10	Operations period	-	-	-	1	2	3	4	5	6	7	
11	Counter	1	2	3	4	5	6	7	8	9	10	
317	**Ratios**											
319	Debt service	-	-	-	3.003	3.024	3.049	3.066	3.071	3.071	-	=305
321	CFADS	-	-	5.500	3.442	3.662	3.903	3.945	4.106	4.032	3.816	=Cash Flow Waterfall!L16
323	Closing Debt Balance	-	-	16.000	13.557	11.042	8.445	5.751	2.938	-	-	=250
325	Debt flag	-	-	1	1	1	1	1	1	1	-	=254
327	Interest rate	3.20%	3.15%	3.30%	3.50%	3.75%	4.10%	4.40%	4.50%	4.50%	4.50%	=296
329	**DSCR**											
330	DSCR	0.00x	0.00x	0.00x	1.15x	1.28x	1.28x	1.20x	1.34x	1.31x	0.00x	=IFERROR(J321=0,J319=0,J321/J319)
332	**LLCR**											
333	CFADS Applied	-	-	3.442	3.662	3.903	3.945	4.106	4.032	-		=321*J325
336	PV CFADS	19.074	19.674	20.324	17.593	14.391	11.078	7.621	3.858	-	-	=(J333+J010)/(1+K327)
337	LLCR	0.00x	0.00x	1.27x	1.30x	1.30x	1.31x	1.33x	1.31x	0.00x	0.00x	=J323/J336
339	**PLCR**											
340	CFADS Applied	-	-	5.500	3.442	3.662	3.903	3.945	4.106	4.032	3.816	=321
342	PV CFADS	26.925	27.773	23.189	20.550	17.468	14.282	10.965	7.353	3.652	-	=K340+(K342/(1+K327))
344	PLCR	0.00x	0.00x	1.45x	1.52x	1.58x	1.66x	1.91x	2.50x	0.00x	0.00x	=J323/J342

We've chosen to include the Loan Life Coverage Ratio (LLCR) and the Project Life Coverage Ratio (PLCR).

Let's first explain the PLCR, one of the criticisms aimed at the DSCR method is that it does not take into account the time value of money. PLCR rectifies this as it takes the present value of all future cash available and compares it to the current debt balance, viz.

PLCR = NPV of Future CFADS / Closing Debt Balance

NPV, or Net Present Value, is a measure of what future cash flows are worth now. If interest rates are 10% p.a., then $110 in a year's time would be worth $100 now, $121 in two years' time would be worth $100 and $133.10 would be worth $100 now. This is because $100 \times (1 + 10\%) = \$110$, $100 \times (1 + 10\%)^2 = \$110$ and $100 \times (1 + 10\%)^3 = \$133.10$. Dividing by $(1 + \text{discount factor})^{\text{number of years}}$ brings a future value back to its present value. Adding up present values is known as the Net Present Value. You can read more about this in Chapter 15.

As for the LLCR, this is essentially a restricted form of the PLCR method. The sole difference is that instead of considering all future periods' CFADS only available cash flows during the debt period are permissible for the NPV calculation.

LLCR = NPV of Future CFADS Restricted to Debt Period / Closing Debt Balance

Our model example uses the interest rate as the discount factor.

Considering the Project Life Coverage Ratio (PLCR) first, row 340 references CFADS as cited in row 321. The Present Value of CFADS (row 342) is calculated as follows in cell **J342**:

=(K340+K342)/(1+K327)

It takes the CFADS for the next year and this formula's counterpart for the next period and divides by (1 + interest rate). This has the effect of calculating the Net Present Value of all future CFADS.

Row 344, PLCR,

=IF(J323=0,,J342/J323)

takes this value and divides it by the Closing debt balance in row 323, *i.e.* it calculates the PLCR.

The Loan Life Coverage Ratio (LLCR) computations in rows 332 to 337 perform a similar computation but only calculate the ratio over the life of the loan using the Debt flag in row 325.

CFADS Applied (row 333) multiplies CFADS (row 321) by the Debt flag (row 325) as this ratio should only consider CFADS over the life of the loan. The Present Value of CFADS (row 335) is then calculated as it was for PLCR, albeit now using the CFADS Applied for LLCR (row 333):

$$=(K333+K335)/(1+K327)$$

The ratio can then be calculated in row 337 as the Present Value of CFADS (row 335) divided by the Closing Debt Balance (row 323), as long as the Closing Debt Balance is not zero [0]:

$$=IF(J323=0,,J335/J323)$$

Whilst we have chosen these three ratios (which are all Debt ratios), there are plenty that could be considered. Let's take a look.

Profitability Ratios

Profitability ratios measure a company's operating efficiency, including its ability to generate income and cash flow. Cash flow affects the company's ability to obtain debt and equity financing and therefore ensure the company's long-term viability and ultimately profitability.

$$\text{Gross Profit Margin} = \frac{\text{Gross Profit}}{\text{Sales}}$$

This is the calculation that shows the ratio of contribution divided by sales. This ratio considers the profit of direct costs. In essence, the gross profit ratio is essentially the percentage mark-up on merchandise from its cost. This ratio is essential in understanding break-even analysis.

It is best used when the splits of direct costs and sales revenue by category can be determined.

$$\text{Net Profit Margin} = \frac{\text{Net Profit}}{\text{Sales}}$$

Sometimes known as the EBITDA margin, this ratio differs from the Gross Profit Margin in that it includes the indirect costs in the calculation also.

This demonstrates company profitability before capital expenditure requirements, financing and taxation and is often seen as an operating cashflow ratio proxy.

$$\text{EBIT Margin} = \frac{\text{Earnings Before Interest and Taxation}}{\text{Sales}}$$

Similar to Net Profit (EBITDA) Margin, this considers profitability including capital expenditure but excluding financing and taxation considerations.

$$\text{Net Income Margin} = \frac{\text{Net Income}}{\text{Sales}}$$

This provides the ultimate profitability as a proportion of sales allowing for easy comparison to other companies.

It can be argued this ratio is too high level as it is unclear how the profitability is derived between direct costs, indirect costs, capital expenditure attribution (i.e. depreciation), financing and taxation.

$$\text{Return on Assets} = \frac{\text{Net Income}}{\text{Average Total Assets}}$$

The return on assets ratio, often called the return on total assets, is a profitability ratio that measures the net income produced by total assets during a period by comparing net income to the average total assets, i.e. it measures how efficiently a company can manage its assets to produce profits during a period.

That is, this ratio measures how profitable a company's assets are.

$$\text{Return on Net Assets} = \frac{\text{Net Income}}{\text{Average Net Assets}}$$

The return on net assets depicts how much the Balance Sheet "sweats" profitability.

Net Assets equals Total Assets less Total Liabilities and is therefore equal to Total Equity. Therefore, depending upon how equity is defined, this ratio is often the equivalent of Return On Equity.

$$\text{Return on Capital Employed} = \frac{\text{Earnings Before Interest and Taxation}}{\text{Average Total Assets -}\atop\text{Average Current Liabilities}}$$

Capital Employed is defined as Total Assets less Current Liabilities, which is effectively Total Debt + Total Equity.

This is effectively an accounting return proxy for the return on weighted capital.

ROCE is a long-term profitability ratio because it shows how effectively assets are performing while taking into consideration long-term financing. This is why ROCE is considered a more useful ratio than Return On Equity to evaluate the longevity of a company.

$$\text{Return on Equity} = \frac{\text{Net Income}}{\text{Average Total Owners' Equity}}$$

The return on equity ratio or ROE is a profitability ratio that measures the ability of a firm to generate profits from its shareholders' investments in the company.

554

ROE is also an indicator of how effective management is at using equity financing to fund operations and grow the company.

$$\text{Return on Shareholders' Equity} = \frac{\text{Net Income}}{\text{Average Common Stock}}$$

Similar to Return On Equity, this specifically looks at the return on the average Common Stock (Share Capital).

Liquidity Ratios

These ratios analyse the ability of a company to pay off both its current liabilities as they become due as well as their long-term liabilities as they become current. These ratios frequently consider the ability to turn other assets into cash to pay off liabilities and other current obligations.

It should be emphasised that liquidity is not only a measure of how much cash a business has. It is also a measure of how easy it will be for the company to raise enough cash or convert assets into cash.

$$\text{Current Ratio} = \frac{\text{Current Assets}}{\text{Current Liabilities}}$$

The current ratio is a liquidity ratio that measures a firm's ability to pay off its short-term liabilities with its current assets.

This means that a company has a limited amount of time in order to raise the funds to pay for these liabilities, due within one year. Current assets like cash, cash equivalents, and marketable securities can easily be converted into cash in the short term.

Companies with larger amounts of current assets will find it easier to pay off current liabilities when they become due without having to sell off key long-term, revenue generating assets.

$$\text{Quick Ratio} = \frac{\text{Current Assets - Inventory}}{\text{Current Liabilities}}$$

The quick ratio (alternatively known as the acid test ratio) is a liquidity ratio that measures the ability of a company to pay its current liabilities when they come due with only quick assets.

Quick assets are current assets that can be converted to cash within the short-term (typically 90 days).

Cash, cash equivalents, short-term investments or marketable securities, and current accounts receivable are considered quick assets.

Short-term investments or marketable securities include trading securities and available for sale securities that can easily be converted into cash within the next 90 days.

Marketable securities are traded on an open market with a known price and readily available buyers. Inventory is specifically excluded.

$$\text{Cash Ratio} = \frac{\text{Cash and Cash Equivalents}}{\text{Current Liabilities}}$$

This is the ratio of a company's total cash and cash equivalents to its current liabilities.

A highly restrictive liquidity ratio, the cash ratio is most commonly used as a measure of company liquidity. It can therefore determine if, and how quickly, the company can repay its short-term debt. A strong cash ratio is useful to creditors when deciding how much debt, if any, they would be willing to extend to the asking party.

$$\text{Net Working Capital Ratio} = \frac{\text{Current Assets - Current Liabilities}}{\text{Total Assets}}$$

Not to be confused with the Working Capital Ratio (another name for the Current Ratio), this ratio notes the level of surplus / deficit in working capital as a proportion of total assets.

This can provide a reader of the proportion of capital used in operations as a proportion of the total assets utilised.

Asset Management Ratios

Profitability ratios measure a company's operating efficiency, including its ability to generate income and cash flow. Cash flow affects the company's ability to obtain debt and equity financing and therefore ensure the company's long-term viability and ultimately profitability.

Many of these ratios in particular are based on using year-end balances (either in averages or in closing balances). Reporting companies are aware of this and this can lead to Balance Sheet manipulation. Auditors cannot remedy this situation: their role is merely to report that amounts are true and fair as at the reporting date.

$$\text{Receivables Turnover} = \frac{\text{Net Credit Sales}}{\text{Average Accounts Receivable}}$$

This ratio should actually be net credit sales, but this figure is not always readily available and sales are often used as a proxy in practice, even if this is technically incorrect.

This measures the level of turnover within one year: the lower this figure, the more it demonstrates the inefficiency of the Accounts Receivable team to collect owed monies.

$$\text{Days Receivable} = \frac{\text{Average Accounts Receivable}}{\text{Net Credit Sales}} \times 365$$

This alternative ratio is easier to understand for many: essentially, this divides the last ratio into 365 (the number of days in a year) to derive how long it takes to recover credit sales.

$$\text{Inventory Turnover} = \frac{\text{Cost of Goods Sold}}{\text{Average Inventory}}$$

This ratio measures the level of inventory turnover within one year: this figure needs to be compared against previous years and industry averages to have any real meaning.

$$\text{Days Inventory} = \frac{\text{Average Inventory}}{\text{Cost of Goods Sold}} \times 365$$

This alternative ratio is easier to understand for many: essentially, this divides the last ratio into 365 (the number of days in a year) to derive how long cash is tied up in inventory.

$$\text{Payables Turnover} = \frac{\text{Cost of Goods Sold + Operating Expenditure}}{\text{Average Accounts Payable}}$$

This ratio measures the level of turnover within one year: the lower this figure, the longer it takes the company to make its payments to creditors which may suggest cash flow difficulties, for example.

$$\text{Days Payable} = \frac{\text{Average Accounts Payable}}{\text{Cost of Goods Sold + Operating Expenditure}} \times 365$$

This alternative ratio is easier to understand for many: essentially, this divides the last ratiointo 365 (the number of days in a year) to derive how long is taken on average before creditors are paid.

Working Capital Cycle = Days Receivable + Days Inventory - Days Payable

Not strictly a ratio, this calculation computes how long working capital is tied up in the company's business. If this extends over time or is greater than the industry average this may suggest a company may soon suffer cash flow problems (if not already).

$$\text{Working Capital Turnover} = \frac{365}{\text{Working Capital Cycle}}$$

This alternative ratio is perhaps not as easy to understand. Essentially, this divides the last ratio into 365 (the number of days in a year) to derive how frequently the working capital is turned over in one year.

$$\text{Fixed Assets Turnover} = \frac{\text{Sales}}{\text{Average Fixed Assets}}$$

This measures the level of fixed assets turnover within one year. This ratio is an efficiency measure to see how productive its fixed assets are in generating sales.

$$\text{Total Assets Turnover} = \frac{\text{Sales}}{\text{Average Total Assets}}$$

Similar to the previous ratio, the asset turnover ratio is an efficiency ratio that measures a company's ability to generate sales from its assets by comparing net sales with average total assets.

Debt (Gearing) Ratios

Sometimes referred to as solvency ratios, this looks at longer-term concerns affected by debt rather than shorter-term issues derived from operations. These ratios consider the level of debt carried by the business, how this financial leverage affects the business and its ability to service its financing obligations.

$$\text{(Total) Debt Ratio} = \frac{\text{Current and Long-Term Liabilities}}{\text{Total Liabilities and Owners' Equity}}$$

This ratio measures the level of total liabilities as a proportion of the total liabilities and equity added together.

The idea behind this ratio is that all forms of liability are financing the business in some shape or form (e.g. not paying a tax creditor means that the cash may be used elsewhere in the short term).

$$\text{(Total) Debt to (Total) Equity Ratio} = \frac{\text{Current and Long-Term Liabilities}}{\text{Owners' Equity}}$$

Similar to the above ratio, this ratio measures the level of total liabilities as a proportion – this time of just owners' equity.

This can be useful as an accounting proxy for determining ungearing and re-gearing betas for valuation purposes.

$$\text{Total Equity Multiplier} = \frac{\text{Total Liabilities and Owners' Equity}}{\text{Owners' Equity}}$$

This financial leverage ratio measures the amount of a firm's assets that are financed by its shareholders by comparing total assets with total shareholder's equity.

Like all liquidity ratios and financial leverage ratios, the equity multiplier is an indication of company risk to creditors. Companies that rely too heavily on debt financing will have high debt service costs and will have to raise more cash flows in order to pay for their operations and obligations.

$$\text{Long Term Debt Ratio} = \frac{\text{Long-Term Debt}}{\text{Total Liabilities and Owners' Equity}}$$

Similar to the Total Debt ratio, this measures more specific debt as a proportion of the total liabilities and equity added together.

$$\text{Long Term Debt to Shareholders' Equity} = \frac{\text{Long-Term Debt}}{\text{Common Stock}}$$

This ratio tightens the focus even more, specifically looking at Debt to Equity.

$$\text{Times Interest Earned} = \frac{\text{Earnings before Interest and Taxation}}{\text{Interest Expense}}$$

The times interest earned ratio, sometimes called the P&L interest coverage ratio, is a coverage ratio that measures the proportionate amount of income that can be used to cover interest expenses in the future.

In some respects the times interest ratio is considered a solvency ratio because it measures a firm's ability to make interest and debt service payments. Since these interest payments are usually made on a long-term basis, they are often treated as an ongoing, fixed expense. As with most fixed expenses, if the company can't make the payments, it could go bankrupt and cease to exist. Thus, this ratio could be considered a solvency ratio.

In practice, the cash versions of this metric are more commonplace as accounting figures may be manipulated.

$$\text{Debt Service Coverage Ratio} = \frac{\text{Cash Flow available for Debt Servicing}}{\text{Principal and Interest Paid}}$$

This is an extremely important ratio for financing. Cash Flow Available for Debt Servicing (CFADS) is defined as operating and investing income excluding interest paid and (usually) debt drawdowns and equity issuances. More often than not this only considers the cash generated in the period and excludes any opening cash balance.

This measures the company's ability to meet all of its debt obligations (i.e. principal and interest).

Financiers prefer this value to be between 1.20 and 1.50 (too low can trigger a default, too high may trigger a cash sweep).

$$\text{Interest Coverage Ratio} \ = \ \frac{\text{Cash Flow available for Debt Servicing}}{\text{Interest Paid}}$$

Similar to the DSCR, this ratio is used to confirm interest obligations may be met (often used when principal is not yet due).

Equity Ratios

Equity ratios are measures shareholders will pay particular interest in. They need to understand how the market values the business compared to book values and what the price / performance equates to on a per share basis.

$$\text{Earnings per Share} \ = \ \frac{\text{Net Income}}{\text{Average Number of Shares}}$$

Earnings per share (EPS), also called net income per share, is a market prospect ratio that measures the amount of net income earned per share of average stock outstanding for the period in question.

Earnings per share is also a calculation that shows how profitable a company is on a shareholder basis. Therefore, a larger company's profits per share can be compared to smaller company's profits per share, but this will mean they need to make more profit. Size is sometimes "normalised" in this metric.

This is still meaningful if negative.

$$\text{Dividend per Share} \ = \ \frac{\text{Dividend Declared}}{\text{Average Number of Shares}}$$

Similar to EPS, this measure is useful for minority shareholders who cannot necessarily access the earnings attributed to them.

This cannot be negative.

$$\text{Book Value per Share} \ = \ \frac{\text{Owners' Equity}}{\text{Closing Number of Shares}}$$

This measures the Owners' Equity (or Net Assets) ascribed to each share. Note that this should be undertaken on a closing balance, rather than an average balance, basis.

$$\text{Dividend Payout Ratio} \ = \ \frac{\text{Dividends Paid}}{\text{Net Income}}$$

This reports how much of the current period's profit is paid out. Depending upon the law where the company resides and its retained earnings, this figure can be greater than 100%.

$$\text{Retention Ratio} = \frac{\text{Net Income - Dividends Paid}}{\text{Net Income}}$$

This ratio reports how much of the current period's profit is retained and hence reinvested. Dividend Payout Ratio plus Retention Ratio should equal 100%.

$$\text{Financial Leverage Ratio} = \frac{\text{Total Liabilities and Owners' Equity}}{\text{Total Owners' Equity}}$$

Some may consider this metric better positioned in another category, but the financial leverage ratio measures the value of equity in a company by analysing its overall debt picture.

These ratios either compare debt or equity to assets as well as shares outstanding to measure the true value of the equity in a business.

When shareholders own a majority of the assets, the company is said to be less leveraged. When creditors own a majority of the assets, the company is considered highly leveraged. All of these measurements are important for investors to understand how risky the capital structure of a company and if it is worth investing in.

$$\text{Return on Equity} = \frac{\text{Net Income}}{\text{Average Total Owners' Equity}}$$

Also situated in profitability, the return on equity ratio or ROE is a profitability ratio that measures the ability of a firm to generate profits from its shareholders' investments in the company.

ROE is also an indicator of how effective management is at using equity financing to fund operations and grow the company.

Sometimes this is calculated on the Du Pont basis, where it is calculated as the Net Income Margin multiplied by Total Assets Turnover multiplied by the Financial Leverage Ratio. Whichever method is adopted, the results should equate (the Du Pont method provides more information).

Market Value Ratios

A subset of equity ratios, these measures specifically address market value. These ratios pre-suppose the company is marketable and a valuation is readily available.

$$\text{Price Earnings Ratio} = \frac{\text{Price per Share}}{\text{Earnings per Share}}$$

The price earnings ratio, often called the P/E ratio, is a market prospect ratio that calculates the market value of a stock relative to its earnings by comparing the market price per share by the earnings per share.

Investors often use this ratio to evaluate what a stock's fair market value should be by predicting future earnings per share.

The P/E ratio helps investors analyse how much they should pay for a stock based on its current earnings. This is why the price to earnings ratio is often called a price multiple or earnings multiple.

This ratio is not calculated when EPS is negative.

$$\text{Market to Book Ratio} = \frac{\text{Price per Share}}{\text{Book Value per Share}}$$

Similar to the P/E ratio, this measure shows the market uplift to show whether investors have valued the company's performance at a premium or a discount.

Example

Ratios Example

Income Statement

	2024
Sales	1,200
Cost of Goods Sold	900
Administrative Expenses	300
Depreciation	129
Earnings Before Interest and Taxes	(129)
Interest Expense	20
Taxable Income	(149)
Taxes	(34)
Net Income	(115)
Dividends	50
Addition to Retained Earnings	(165)

Other Information

No. of Shares Outstanding (Millions)	400
Price Per Share	4.83

Cash Flow Statement

	2024
Operating Cash Flows	
Cash Receipts	1,200
Cash Payments	(1,200)
Interest Paid	(20)
Tax Paid	34
Net Operating Cash Flows	14
Investing Cash Flows	
Net Capex (Payments) / Proceeds	-
Interest Received	-
Net Investing Cash Flows	-
Financing Cashflows	
Debt Drawdowns	-
Debt Repayments	-
Equity Issuances	-
Equity Buybacks	-
Dividends Paid	(50)
Net Financing Cashflows	(50)
Cash Movement for 2024	(36)

Balance Sheet

ASSETS	2024	2023
Current Assets		
Cash	564	600
Accounts Receivable	600	600
Inventory	1,100	1,100
Total Current Assets	2,264	2,300
Fixed Assets		
Non-Current Assets	1,000	1,000
less: Accumulated Depreciation	(1,029)	(900)
Total Fixed Assets	(29)	100
TOTAL ASSETS	2,235	2,400

LIABILITIES AND OWNERS' EQUITY	2024	2023
Current Liabilities		
Bank Overdraft	-	-
Accounts Payable	800	800
Interest Payable	-	-
Dividends Payable	-	-
Tax Payable	-	-
Total Current Liabilities	800	800
Long-Term Liabilities		
Long-Term Debt	200	200
Other Long-Term Liabilities	-	-
Total Long-Term Liabilities	200	200
Owners' Equity		
Common Stock	400	400
Capital Surplus	500	500
Retained Earnings	335	500
Total Owners' Equity	1,235	1,400
TOTAL LIABILITIES AND OWNERS' EQUITY	2,235	2,400

Ratios

Profitability		Liquidity	
Gross Profit Margin	25.00%	Current Ratio	2.83x
Net Profit Margin		Quick Ratio	1.46x
EBIT Margin	(16.75%)	Cash Ratio	0.75x
Net Income Margin	(9.50%)	Net Working Capital Ratio	0.68x
Return On Assets	(4.96%)		
Return On Net Assets	(8.75%)	**Debt / Gearing**	
Return On Capital Employed	(8.50%)		
Return On Equity	(8.73%)	Total Debt Ratio	0.45x
Return On Shareholders' Equity	(28.75%)	Total Debt to Total Equity Ratio	0.81x
		Total Equity Multiplier	1.81x
Asset Management		Long-Term Debt Ratio	0.09x
		Long-Term Debt to Shareholders' Equity	0.50x
Receivables Turnover	2.00		
Days Receivable	182.50	Times Interest Earned	(6.45x)
Inventory Turnover	0.82x	Debt Service Coverage Ratio	1.70x
Days Inventory	446.11	Interest Coverage Ratio	1.70x
Payables Turnover	1.50		
Days Payable	243.33	**Equity**	
Working Capital Turnover	0.95x	Earnings Per Share	(0.29)
Working Capital Cycle (Days)	385.28	Dividend Per Share	0.13
		Book Value Per Share	3.09
Fixed Assets Turnover	33.80x		
		Dividend Payout Ratio	(43.48%)
Total Assets Turnover	0.52x	Retention Ratio	143.48%
		Dividend Yield	2.70%
Market Value Ratios		Financial Leverage Ratio	1.76x
		Return On Equity (Du Pont Method)	(8.73%)
Price / Earnings Ratio			
Market to Book Ratio	1.50		

CHAPTER 19: GOING OUT AS A LAMBDA

You might still be having nightmares about the Maximum dividend payable formula from earlier:

```
J375    =DROP(REDUCE(0,J9#,LAMBDA(accumulator,period,LET(initialretainedprofits,
        'Opening Balance Sheet'!$I$50,npat,J372#,cashflow,J373#,ratiodividend,J377#,
        retainedprofits,IF(period=1,initialretainedprofits,
        INDEX(accumulator,1,COLUMNS(accumulator))
        +INDEX(npat,period-1)-INDEX(accumulator,2,COLUMNS(accumulator))),
        npatinperiod,INDEX(npat,period),cashflowinperiod,INDEX(cashflow,period),
        ratiodividendinperiod,INDEX(ratiodividend,period),maxdividendpayable,
        MAX(MIN(MAX(retainedprofits+npatinperiod,npatinperiod),cashflowinperiod),0),
        dividenddeclared,MIN(maxdividendpayable,ratiodividendinperiod),
        HSTACK(accumulator,
        VSTACK(retainedprofits,dividenddeclared,maxdividendpayable))))),2,1)
```

Calculations — Financial Model with Dynamic Arrays.xlsm

			Jun 25	Jun 26	Jun 27	Jun 28	Jun 29
Start Date			1 Jul 24	1 Jul 25	1 Jul 26	1 Jul 27	1 Jul 28
End Date			30 Jun 25	30 Jun 26	30 Jun 27	30 Jun 28	30 Jun 29
Number of Days			365	365	365	366	365
Counter			1	2	3	4	5
Maximum dividend payable							
Opening retained profits			-	104	202	772	1,847
NPAT			104	98	570	876	761
Cash flow available for dividends			(700)	(1,730)	1,847	1,953	697
Maximum dividend payable			-	-	772	1,448	697
Dividend based on ratio			26	29	200	350	343

```
=DROP(REDUCE(0,J9#,LAMBDA(accumulator,period,
LET(initialretainedprofits,'Opening Balance
Sheet'!$I$50,npat,J372#,cashflow,J373#,
ratiodividend,J377#,retainedprofits,
IF(period=1,initialretainedprofits,INDEX(accumulator,1,COLUMNS(accumulator))
+INDEX(npat,period-1)-INDEX(accumulator,2,COLUMNS(accumulator))),
npatinperiod,INDEX(npat,period),
cashflowinperiod,INDEX(cashflow,period),
ratiodividendinperiod,INDEX(ratiodividend,period),
maxdividendpayable,
MAX(MIN(MAX(retainedprofits+npatinperiod,npatinperiod),cashflowinperiod),0),
dividenddeclared,
MIN(maxdividendpayable,ratiodividendinperiod),
HSTACK(accumulator,
VSTACK(retainedprofits,dividenddeclared,maxdividendpayable))))),2,1)
```

Don't panic, I'm not going to explain it again! Whilst the goal of this book was to build a financial model with dynamic arrays, in the case study I wanted to concentrate on achieving precisely that.   However, now that I have completed that task in hand, I will leave you with an alternative way of presenting this calculation so that you don't have such an eyesore in the Formula bar.

You can convert the giant formula for Maximum dividend payable into a short **LAMBDA** function so that users can apply it without having to remember the complex calculations behind it. The following image shows the alternative calculation below the dynamic array version:

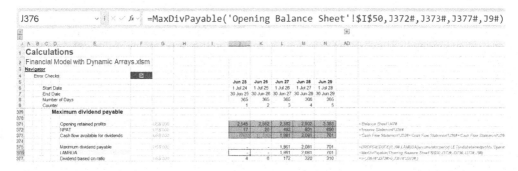

=MaxDivPayable('Opening Balance Sheet'!$I$50,J372#,J373#,J377#,J9#)

Better, yes? This looks much simpler because most of the complexity has been hidden away in the Name Manager, out of sight of the Formula bar.

To make the **MaxDivPayable** function above work, I need to create a named range called **MaxDivPayable** with the following formula:

```
=LAMBDA(initialretainedprofits,npat,cashflow,ratiodividend,periodcounter,
DROP(REDUCE(0,periodcounter,LAMBDA(accumulator,period,
LET(retainedprofits,IF(period=1,initialretainedprofits,INDEX
(accumulator,1,COLUMNS(accumulator))+INDEX(npat,period-1)-INDEX
(accumulator,2,COLUMNS(accumulator))),
npatinperiod,INDEX(npat,period),
cashflowinperiod,INDEX(cashflow,period),
ratiodividendinperiod,INDEX(ratiodividend,period),
maxdividendpayable,
MAX(MIN(MAX(retainedprofits+npatinperiod,npatinperiod),cashflowinperiod),0),
dividenddeclared,
MIN(maxdividendpayable,ratiodividendinperiod),
HSTACK(accumulator,
VSTACK(retainedprofits,dividenddeclared,maxdividendpayable)))))),2,1))
```

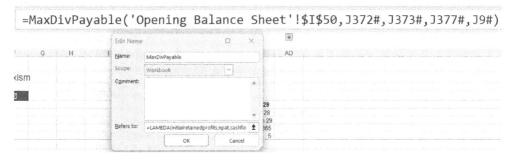

The difference between the horror formula and this one is that I have created a custom **LAMBDA** function to perform the *same* steps as the old formula. The cell references in the old formula have been replaced with parameter **LAMBDA** arguments, listed before the calculation of the **LAMBDA** function (the section beginning with the **DROP** function). These parameters are **initialretainedprofits**, **npat**, **cashflow**, **ratiodividend** and **periodcounter**.

Then, whenever a user needs to calculate the Maximum Dividend Payable, they can simply call the function in a cell by typing **=MaxDivPayable(** – the same way you'd call any other function! Then, users may simply reference the appropriate range for each of the five [5] arguments. There is even a ToolTip for the function that will show what to input for each argument.

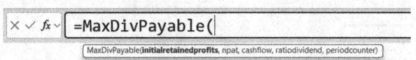

I could use a similar approach for any other formula too; I have chosen this one as it is an excellent example of how you may utilise a named **LAMBDA** to make your end model more user friendly.

CHAPTER 20: AND FINALLY...

We got there!

This book has attempted to show you financial modelling using dynamic arrays is nothing to be scared of apart from one or two Tolstoy-esque formulae. The model built has been relatively simple overall, but as I say in all of these books, understanding concept is *everything*.

Dynamic arrays cause you to have to model out of order. It tests your logic, but once you crack it, you realise it's not that difficult and it is all about pattern recognition.

I've been lucky enough to have the number of Microsoft Most Valuable Professional (MVP) awards now in double digits. I have worked in this industry for over 30 years, led three modelling teams, written over 4,000 articles, 10+ books, been a runner-up for the Excel Lifetime Achievement Award in 2023 and won the inaugural Lifetime Achievement Award for Financial Modelling by the Financial Modeling Institute (shame they can't spell that properly) back in 2021. I think a lot of people expected me to hang up my modelling boots at that stage. Sorry no; I'm only just getting started!

Here's to your dynamic array modelling journey.

Liam

Dec 2023

INDEX

Symbols

$ (dollar sign), in absolute referencing, 81-90
1-D Data Tables, 130-133
2-D Data Tables, 133-135
#CALC! errors, 191-193
@ operator, 177-180
# (spilled range operator), 176-177
#SPILL! errors, 170-174

A

absolute referencing, 81-90
accelerated capital allowances (ACAs), 477
accounting depreciation, 492-493
accrual basis, 329-330
acid test ratio, 555
adding worksheets to workbooks, 365-370
add-ins
  accessing, 72
advanced options, 158-159
aggregation functions, 263
aggregator checks, 313
alert checks, 284, 306, 312
amortised (debt modeling), 466-467
Analysis ToolPak, loading, 72
apostrophe ('), formulas as text, 86-87
applying range names, 116
arrays, 162-167. See also dynamic arrays
  definition of, 32, 42, 163
  entering formulas in, 165-167
  legacy formulas versus dynamic array
     formulas, 180-181
  LOOKUP with, 32-35, 43
  SUMPRODUCT with, 25-26
  types of, 162-163
ARRAYTOTEXT function, 263
asset management ratios, 556-558
automatic calculation, 155
autosave option, 157

B

balance sheets, 332-334
  creating, 372-373
  error checks, 383-390
  final in example model build, 544-545

linking, 381-382
preparing, 378-379
single entry accounting, 538-541
size of, 340
best practices, 281-287
  consistency, 98, 281-283
  flexibility, 284-285
  robustness, 283-284
  Rule of Thumb, 5, 345
  transparency, 98, 285-287
beta channel functions, 279
binary searches, 40
BODMAS principle, 308
book value per share, 560
BYCOL function, 231-235, 487-492
BYROW function, 231-235

C

#CALC! errors, 191-193
calculation options, 155
calculation order, 212-213
calling LAMBDA function, 220-221
capital employed, 554
capital expenditure, 447-464
  depreciation, 447-454
  MAP function, 459-460
  reverse depreciation, 454-455
capitalised (debt modeling), 466-467
case study. See example model build
cash flow statements, 334-339
  capital expenditure, 463
  creating, 372
  equity, 509-537
  final in example model build, 544
  indirect cash flow extract, 546-548
  linking, 381-382
  preparing, 379
  size of, 340
cash ratio, 556
cell contents, hiding, 95-96
CELL function, 290-293
cells
  as arrays, 162
  definition of, 163
  empty / blank, 326-327

RAISING ARRAYS FOR MODELLING

This book tries hard to raze a laugh (yes, that's what was meant…). Instead, through numerous examples and case studies, it details the impact of the ecosystem introduced by dynamic arrays in Excel, injecting life into the jaded, stale world of financial modelling.

From comparing the old methodologies to the new frontiers, this book considers how dynamic arrays have reshaped Excel and made it Turing complete, with its liberal use of LET, LAMBDA, eta lambdas et al. LET invites complexity but reduces memory requirements, LAMBDA allows you to build anything, and dynamic arrays make it easy to quite literally extend your ideas and your way of thinking. See for yourself.

Through a dynamic array of Best Practice tips, tricks, functions and features, Financial Modelling using Dynamic Arrays shows you how to revamp and reinvent your financial models with Excel 365. Recreate your development kit in this brave new world. Erase the old and embrace the arrays!